The Laws of the Internet

Fourth edition

Dedication

To Kian, Reece and Leo

The Laws of the Internet

Fourth edition

Dr Paul Lambert BA, LLB, LLM, CTMA
Adjunct Lecturer, Lawyer, Consultant

Edition Contributors

Intellectual Property
Philip Johnson, Professor of Commercial Law, University of Cardiff

Data Protection
Dr Paul Lambert, BA, LLB, LLM, CTMA, Adjunct Lecturer, Lawyer,
Consultant

Contract
Rick Canavan, Nottingham Trent University

Tort
Timothy Press, University of Cardiff

Crime
Laura Scaife, Addleshaw Goddard

Tax
Laura Edgar, Queen Mary University of London

Competition
Charlie Markillie and Ash Sheppard, Competition, EU & Regulatory,
Eversheds

Regulation
Michael Ryan, Arnold & Porter

Bloomsbury Professional

Bloomsbury Professional Ltd, Maxwelton House, 41–43 Boltro Road, Haywards Heath, West Sussex, RH16 1BJ

© Bloomsbury Professional Ltd 2015

Bloomsbury Professional is an imprint of Bloomsbury Publishing plc

A CIP Catalogue record for this book is available from the British Library.

ISBN: 978 1 84766 894 3

Typeset by Phoenix Photosetting, Chatham, Kent
Printed and bound by CPI Group (UK) Ltd, Croydon, CR0 4YY

Foreword to the First Edition

Judging by some of the stuff one reads – particularly from journalists – the Internet will throw laws, or many of them, into chaos. The suggestion seems to be the law cannot cope with the breakdown of national barriers, the cross-border implications of the interlinking of computers world-wide. The scenario painted is that the Internet will be a lawless dimension, with lawyers and clients having no idea what to do or how to control the activities of others. Clive Gringras is to be congratulated on not only debunking this myth but by doing so in a constructive (and readable) way. What he has done here is to consider, subject by subject, what rules the courts will develop and apply. As always what the law will do is develop appropriate rules by analogy. Contract, tort (including special variants of old torts, eg negligently allowing a virus to spread and new ways of defaming people), intellectual property (particularly trade marks and copyright), questions of jurisdiction, crime, data protection, and so on all have passed under his intelligent consideration. Of course there are, as yet, few actual cases on most points. So he has used his imagination to create problems and indicate how the law is likely to answer them. Because he understands the Internet and how it works well, his imaginary problems are realistic. Moreover he has up-to-date intelligence of case law from other countries (particularly the US) which supplement his fictional examples. Anyone with an Internet problem will find this book a first port of call – and in many cases may well find an answer, or a reasonable prediction of the answer. In one area where he obviously does not feel entirely at home, namely tax (who would blame him?), he has sought assistance from Conrad McDonnell of Gray's Inn Chambers.

There is something of a spate of books which carry the names of firms of solicitors. Many (but not all) are rather slight works, rushed out after some new piece of legislation and not telling you much that is not in the Act. This is far from such a work. Nabarro Nathanson are to be congratulated on allowing Mr Gringras to put in what must have been a vast amount of work.

Hon Sir Robin Jacob
January 1997

Preface to the Fourth Edition

As indicated in the first edition, this book is a first port of call and also in many instances furnishes an answer to pressing internet related legal problems. The various chapters address a whole host of separate internet related activities from personal data, intellectual property, tax, contract, tort, crime and many others. Each chapter has been updated to encompass changes since the last edition as well as many contemporary pressing internet legal problems. It aims to provide a context and description of applicable relevant laws and regulations centred on internet activities and internet commercial activities. The cross border nature of the chain of internet activities is also considered. Related technologies are also considered and referred to. Continuing the tradition of the text, many practical issues and suggestions are included.

To some extent many of the original queries which arose in the first edition with the rise of the commercial internet are to a large extent reasonably answered, whether in terms of extending laws and case law, or in terms of the creation of new laws. However, as the contemporary internet develops, there is an escalation in new business models, activities, processes, an increasing volume of online trade, massive involvement in internet and social activities, and issues with an ever increasing amount of data being created from internet activities. More nuanced issues, and in some instances new issues, arise.

However, some of the issues we had thought of as being solved have arisen afresh. As we write, the reader will be no doubt aware of increasing volume of, and media interest in, current internet legal problems. These range from vast data breaches, hacking, to whether personal data can be transferred from Europe to the US for commercial purposes, issues relating to forgetting, to multinational taxation issues – already an issue of political controversy in parliament.

So even today, there remains a continuing need for this iconic legal text. One can speculate that depending on how some of the current issues might be resolved, there may be a need in future editions to encompass some of the legal-policy and political traditions in a nuanced understanding of the pressures competing to shape aspects of contemporary internet laws. For example, the proposed Data Protection Regulation is understood to be the most lobbied piece of EU legislation to date. That was even before the *Google Spain* Right to be Forgotten case and the *Schrems Prism* case striking out the EU-US Safe Harbour data transfer agreement.

I would like to thank all of the contributors without whom the present volume could not have been possible. Great appreciation must also go to all of those in Bloomsbury Professional and particularly Jane Bradford.

However, perhaps the greatest appreciation, of both current and past readers as well as the contributors, goes to the foresight of Clive Gringras and Elle

Todd for the great task of writing earlier editions and in particular to Clive for the first edition at a very important time in relation to a newly developing and important legal area. The foresight of the first edition is reflected in the vast array of current IT and internet legal issues facing organisations, lawyers and policy makers.

Paul Lambert
October 2015

Contents

Table of Cases

PARA

PARA

Q

R

PARA

Y

Z

Table of Statutes

References to paragraphs in **bold** indicate that the text is reproduced in part or in full

Table of Statutory Instruments

References to paragraphs in **bold** indicate that the text is reproduced in part or in full

CHAPTER ONE

Introduction

'The Lord came down to look at the city and tower that man had built, and the Lord said: "If, as one people with one language for all, this is how they have begun to act, then nothing that they propose to do will be out of their reach." … That is why it was called Babel, because there the Lord confounded the language of all the earth …'

Genesis 11: 6–7

1.1   Few people now living have not heard of or used the internet. Some may even wonder how they coped before it existed or, indeed, do not even recall such a time. To determine how laws may apply to the internet one needs to have more than merely an observer's appreciation; a working knowledge is required. Fortunately, the internet can be easily described. (The variety of content, models and activities contained thereon might take somewhat longer – if indeed that is actually possible.)

The importance of the internet is not limited to feline expression (apologies to the IP Kat) and entertainment. Serious legal, policy and societal issues also arise. These range from extensions of existing legal concepts such as intellectual property (eg copyright, trade marks and branding online), defamation and other torts, online abuse (eg threats, trolling, defamation, sextortion, revenge porn, image scraping for illicit use, shaming, etc), to issues such as the real net/dark net, VAT and taxation, competition and arguments in relation to anti-competitive behaviour, internet freedom/net neutrality, internet access, human right internet access, adults and children online, new disruptive products and services online or using the internet, privacy, data protection, security, breaches, Big Data, the online Cloud, the rapidly evolving Internet of Things, crime, crowd activities, internet freedom, protest and 'Springs' (eg Arab Spring), internet currencies. This list is by no means exhaustive, nor could any list in relation to the internet be. Fundamentally, it is about new products, services, activities and better ways of doing things and interacting with others, here and on the other side of the globe. It is social, educational and commercial. It brings (and permits) wholly new activities as well as bringing new ways of undertaking existing activities.

To begin with, the internet is a global network of computers all speaking the same language. To understand the internet, therefore, it is useful first to appreciate computers. Computers are simple machines: they understand only the numbers zero and one. The reason that computers are able to show colours on a screen, play sounds and process data is that they are very accurate and quick translators. With incredible speed they are able to convert a full-length movie into a long stream of zeros and ones. And with the same speed they can convert a similar stream of zeros and ones into a sound, or a document, or a program. Everything passing into and out of a computer will, at some point, be reduced to binary: two numbers, zero and one.

It is not difficult to connect two computers, say by a wire, and send a stream of these binary numbers from one computer to the other. Each number one in the stream is represented by an 'on' electrical pulse; each zero by an 'off' pulse. These pulses last for a fraction of a second allowing the numbers describing a picture to be transmitted in minutes. A difficulty arises in ensuring that the computer receiving such a stream translates the zeros and ones correctly. As a simple example, the receiving computer may be ready to receive a binary description of a picture, but is instead sent a binary translation of a document. The receiving computer will attempt to translate the zeros and ones, actually a document, into a picture; there will be confusion. It is evidently crucial that to connect computers successfully they both must speak the same language. This 'digital Esperanto' is the key to the internet.

LANGUAGE AND NETWORKS

1.2   The many variations of this digital Esperanto are called 'protocols'. As long as the sending and receiving computers are using the same protocols, they will be able to share information, in a raw binary form, with absolute accuracy.

A 'network' is a group of computers connected together using the same protocols; they are using the same phrase book. Information stored on one computer on the network can be readily sent, or accessed, by any other computer on the network. In a company this allows one individual to access a file that has been created on somebody else's machine across a network, or 'intranet'. The connection between these computers on a network is not always a simple copper wire. A set of wireless radio devices can be used as a link; they convey information using pulses across the radio spectrum rather than electricity. Links between computers do not even have to be in the same building. 'Wide area networks', or WANs, can stretch across many hundreds of miles.

The key is to ensure that each of the computers connected to the network uses the same protocols. If they do, it will not matter greatly whether a stream of ones and zeros has come from across the corridor or from across the Atlantic Ocean. The receiving computer will be able to translate them appropriately, no matter the length of their journey. The internet builds on this technology.

INTERNETWORKING

1.3   In 1969 the US Department of Defense commissioned the construction of a super-network, called ARPANET: the Advanced Research Projects Agency Network. This military network was intended to connect computers across the

American continent, with one special feature. If one part of this great network was destroyed, the communications system would remain operative. The information passing through the system was required to detour around the damaged part and arrive at its destination by another route.

The ARPANET was demonstrated in 1972. The network consisted of 40 computers connected by a web of links and lines. The detouring feature was accomplished by allowing a stream of binary information from one computer to pass through other computers on the network, rather than always having to flow directly from A to B.

One example will illustrate this: three computers, A, B and C, are connected in a triangle. A can communicate directly with both B and C. Similarly, B has a line of communication with A and C. If A has to send information to B it has a direct route. However, if this route is damaged, or blocked, it can send the information to C with an instruction to pass it on to B: A to B through C. On a larger scale, this allows every computer connected to a network to send information to any other computer on the network. The information simply has to be passed from one computer to another, gradually nearing its destination.

One further advance was made to secure the information being sent from A to B. Instead of sending the information as one long stream, the sending computer splits the data into discrete packets. Each packet, like an envelope, contains the information being sent and has an address of where it must arrive. The packet also has a number that denotes its place in the whole data stream. If any packets are lost, or blocked, they can be re-sent. When all the packets have arrived, the receiver assembles the chunks of digital data into the continuous data stream. This so-called 'packet-switched' network allows many computers to use the same communication lines and allows one data stream to travel by different routes to speed delivery over congested lines.

The demonstration of packet-switched networks and routing in 1972 was such a success that the InterNetworking Working Group was created. The internet was born. *The New York Times* wrote on 15 April 1972: '[the] experimental network … may help bring to realization a new era in scientific computation'.

THE INTERNET

1.4   The 40 or so computers on the late 1970s ARPANET, each using the same protocols, were added to: by 1981, over 200 computers were connected, from all around the world. When the first edition of this book was published, in May 1997, this number of hosts had reached about 20 million. Now, worldwide usage figures are in the billions and connections are increasing. This vast collection of computers is the internet, the largest network of computers in the world.

The majority of the links and connections between computers are permanent and allow digital streams to be sent back and forth extremely quickly. In addition, each host computer connected to the internet has a unique numeric address or internet protocol address. This means that a digital stream can be directed from any computer connected to the internet to any other computer connected to the internet, anywhere in the world. The impact of this is great when one appreciates that almost the whole of modern culture can now be reduced to a digital form. Digital information includes colour pictures, animations and movies, high-quality music and sound, text with typefaces and layout, even three-dimensional images.

The real power of today's internet is that it is available not only to anyone with a computer and a telephone line, but now through various different devices (phones and PDAs) and access mediums (mobile, wireless, cable, satellite).

By connecting a piece of hardware called a modem to a personal computer, any information can be converted into a digital stream of ones and zeros. The modem can then send this translation down a telephone or cable line to one of the computers already connected to the internet. The two computers can then pass information between themselves, using a common protocol. Alternatively, some devices now already come wi-fi enabled, allowing connection to the internet via radio waves in special wi-fi 'hotspots'.

Since a device connected to the internet can connect with any other device on the internet, a personal computer or even a pocket-sized device can now connect with any of the millions of computers on the internet.

Like human languages, computer protocols work in both directions. They allow information to be easily sent from a home or office computer, or even a mobile phone, to any other such device on, or with access to, the internet. What is more important is that they allow any computer to gain access to information from any other computer on the internet: libraries are now literally at our fingertips; a shop simply needs to connect to the internet to advertise to the world. One language allows the world of computers to share a world of information. The law, in contrast with this transnational system, often operates within defined jurisdictional boundaries. The practical resolution of these opposites forms a common thread through each of the following chapters.

THE COST

1.5   Sharing a world of information sounds expensive, but it is not. To connect to the internet, one needs only to connect to a computer already connected. The first cost is therefore the price of the connection, often a telephone call or subscription to allow connection to that connected computer, or credit payment made via a web browser log-in for intermittent wi-fi usage. The user is not charged for the cost of sending or receiving information beyond that first computer unless a particularly quick or secure route is chosen. What is levied, however, is a price to connect to this computer.

The companies controlling these first-port-of-call computers are known as internet service providers (ISPs). Their computers are called 'servers', as is any computer permanently connected to the internet. The computers that pay for the connection charges, the users' computers, are called 'clients'.

Some ISPs provide more than purely a connection to the internet through their server: they provide materials and services on their own servers. This has the advantage of being quicker to view, safer to access and more focused on the needs of the users. These companies provide more than simply an email address and a ramp to the internet: they commission, license and provide their own services tailored for their members. And they are paid for these value-added services either directly through a subscription, a share of the connection charges paid by their users, or indirectly through selling advertising or 'space' on their pages. On top of connection charges, some websites may charge for membership or other access to their services – whether that be a forum, community or chatroom. Others provide their services for free and rely on advertising revenue to fund their activities.

These companies are often the targets for litigation. They are blamed for the copyright infringing material that other people leave on their computers; some say that they should be culpable for facilitating the transmission of obscene images and movies; there are even suggestions that they should be responsible for publishing others' defamatory statements. Each chapter raises the question of how the law treats these piggies-in-the-middle, as well as the individual primarily responsible.

Increasingly many services, such as social media and social networking are provided 'free' in the sense of remuneration. These services are often possible on a free model on the basis that the operator is remunerated from advertising on the service. More recently, some have suggested that some of these services may not in fact be free at all, as the users knowingly or unknowingly trade their personal data, which can be utilised in honing and targeting advertising. However, there is a counter argument that many services and internet activities would not be possible with these types of advertising models, and that some or all of these require (certain) personal data.

INTERNET CONCEPTS

1.6   Using several different protocols, the internet has been able to provide various services to its connected computers. In the similar way that the word 'chat' has a different meaning in French from its meaning in English, so can two protocols used across the internet allow servers to pass different information to clients. Different uses of protocols give the internet its utility. What follows is a tour of some of the different features of the internet. To appreciate the tour it may help to remember that the information being shunted around the network is still that digital stream of ones and zeros. The various features are produced by simply applying a different protocol to this stream before and after it is sent between computers. The method of conversing is largely the same; what changes is the language being used.

IP addresses and domain names

1.7   Every server permanently connected to the internet has a unique identification number, or internet protocol address. To make it easier for humans to remember, these numbers have a unique literary equivalent called a domain name that is allocated by one of the internet registries. Commercial entities tend to use .com (pronounced Dot Com) or their national domain name suffix, such as .co.uk (pronounced Dot Co Dot UK). Academic institutions use the suffix 'ac'. Often the suffix includes information relating to where the domain has been registered. For example, the University of Oxford has the domain, 'oxford.ac.uk'. Often government bodies may use the .gov domain. Scuffles arise because there are a limited number of domain names and they are usually allocated on a first-come first-served basis. The chapter on intellectual property considers the legal implications of this.

Email

1.8 'Email' is short for electronic mail. The word 'mail' should be understood at its widest: the electronic mail system over the internet can carry more than simple messages and letters. A picture, a sound, in fact anything that can be created and stored on a computer can be sent as electronic mail to any other computer connected to the internet.

First, the item is digitally packed into an appropriate parcel. Like physical items sent by the post, items require suitable packaging. The equivalent of a vase sent through the conventional post is a picture, or a sound or a movie sent over the internet. These require a digital 'padded envelope'; the common one is called Multipurpose Internet Mailing Extensions (MIME). MIME, and its more secure sister S/MIME have special ways of treating every eight, fragile one or zero that make up multimedia objects. Plain old text does not need each eight, one or zero so does not need to be parcelled up in any special way: the standard internet protocols are adequate to cope with this simple text. Most email programs automatically choose the correct type of encoding to ensure that the object survives the electronic transmission to its recipient.

It is vital to realise that standard electronic mail copies the contents of the digital envelope; it does not actually send the material from the creator's machine. So, electronic mail, unlike its terrestrial equivalent, does not touch the original created by the sender; instead it provides an identical copy to each recipient. This has its advantages: copies are automatically retained of all outgoing mail. However, it also has some disadvantages: malicious code that piggy-backs electronic messages may also be copied onto the recipient's computer. And, of course, in the eyes of copyright law, a copy is being made of a copyright work.

Once the text or multimedia object is appropriately encoded, the sender simply needs to tack on an address for the email. All email addresses are in the format: username@domain. To receive electronic mail, one needs to have an agreement with the controller of the domain. Some domains are controlled by employers, and they provide email addresses to their staff like direct telephone numbers. Members of staff will have their name, or other reference, before the '@' symbol.

Controllers of other domains, like ISPs, rent out user names on their domains and also provide access to the internet or other services.

Pseudo-anonymity

1.9 Sending a postcard anonymously is easy: simply do not sign it. Sending an email anonymously is more difficult: it is 'signed' by it being sent from you.

The way that internet users have attempted to remain anonymous include lying about who they are when they establish their own email address, or to send their emails via an 'anonymous remailer'. This is a computer on the internet which runs a special program. This program strips any incoming emails of their headers: this removes the identification of from where the email originated. The program then sends this stripped email to the intended recipient, purporting to be from someone else. If the anonymous remailer keeps a log of who is the actual author of a message, they may be ordered by a court to reveal who is the actual sender of the message. If the remailer automatically deletes a log, or never even kept one, of course no court order can then restore the identification of the email sender.

A stronger method of remaining anonymous is to send an email via more than one anonymous remailer and to scramble or 'encrypt' all but the next email in the chain. In this way, even if a court were to order a remailer to reveal the sender's identity they would only have access to the details of the remailer who sent them the message and to the next in the chain. To reveal the identity, therefore, all the remailers would have to co-operate with the court order, and all the remailers would have had to maintain logs. This said, problems of identifying defendants over the internet should not be exaggerated; it is far easier to send a truly anonymous postcard than a truly anonymous email.

Instant messaging (IM)

1.10   Instant messaging is just that. Email is a 'store and forward' system for exchanging information. When the email is sent from your computer, its first destination is your internet service provider or email provider. From there it is hurried across the internet to an inbound mail server and finally into the recipient's mailbox. If the recipient is not connected to the internet at the moment of receipt in their mailbox, they may not know it has arrived. Worse still, it is difficult for you to know that they were not there.

Instant messaging addresses these two deficiencies of the email system: it is instant and you can tell whether someone is connected or not. Like email, messages can consist of more than mere text: pictures, documents and even, because of its instantaneous nature, video and audio can be sent using instant messaging.

Bulletin boards

1.11   Digital bulletin boards are similar to their physical counterparts. Anyone with access to the board can pin up a message or question, and any other person can leave a reply on the board. Also like a physical bulletin board, someone is ultimately responsible for it. Someone must remove old messages; perhaps even remove rude or defamatory messages. On the internet that person is often called a moderator, or is simply the provider 'hosting' the bulletin board. This means that the provider stores the messages on equipment under their control; it is a moot point whether the messages left by their users are also under their control. This will be considered later in the book, but particularly in relation to defamation and copyright.

When a message is posted onto a digital bulletin board, what is technically occurring is that the person is sending an email to the board. This is reproduced in a readable format for any user of the board to see. If a reader wishes to reply to the message, they have a choice. They may either send an email directly and privately to the person who left the message, or they can send a reply that will be stored on the bulletin board itself. It will be listed just below the first message for all to see. This process of replying to a message can occur many times, thus creating a 'conversation thread'.

As explained earlier, an email does not need to be a written note; it may be a digitised picture, a digitised sound recording or even a digital movie. These families of emails can also be left on bulletin boards not for people to reply to, but for people to download, to view or hear. Obscene and indecent pictures and copyright infringement are rife on unmoderated bulletin boards. The issue of when the operator of the board becomes liable for such illegal postings is a vital point that is considered in this book.

Forums

1.12 Many service providers run bulletin boards only for access by their members. These are called 'forums'. Each forum has a title that indicates the sorts of conversation threads and files that can be found on the board. An ISP may host a legal forum. Within the forum there may be many different sections, eg some dealing with family law, others with recent cases. Occasionally these forums will be unmanned, or 'unmoderated'; anything posted on the board will remain for a certain time. It is more usual to find that forums have a moderator who vets and deletes offensive messages. This book considers the vexed question of whether by doing this the ISP becomes legally responsible for the messages left on the system.

User-generated content

1.13 The last few years have witnessed an astonishing increase in websites relying on content produced and uploaded by users themselves. Forums and bulletin boards based on text are now surpassed by services, allowing users to view other users' photos, films, videos and hear their sound recordings. YouTube is a prime example. This clearly presents challenges for the service provider, as the risk of unlawful content being posted increases, and judgments must be made as to when to intervene, when and if to monitor, what to restrict and how to act in the event of a complaint. A wrong decision can have far-reaching legal ramifications, even though the content may not be the website owner's.

File transfer protocol

1.14 File transfer protocol, or 'ftp' for short, is what it purports to be: a language that allows files to be transferred from one computer to another. For ftp there are usually two significant computers: the ftp server and the client. The ftp server is simply a computer connected to the internet that stores the files to be transferred. The client is the computer that receives the files stored, and transferred by, the server. To access an ftp site, unlike a website, one is usually required to enter a password. This should not indicate that an ftp site is particularly secure: the majority of ftp sites are termed 'anonymous ftp' meaning that anyone may gain access simply by using the word 'anonymous' or 'guest' as a password.

When a client has gained access to a site it is rather like seeing the contents of a computer's hard disk. There are directories or folders and within those directories there are files. Each of the files may be retrieved, usually by double-clicking on the file name or icon. In addition to retrieving files though, rather like a bulletin board, it is possible to upload a file from one's computer to the ftp server. This lack of control over the content of a site can cause legal problems for the owner of the ftp site. If copyright materials are uploaded by an anonymous depositor, the owner may be a secondary infringer of the copyright in the works. And because the primary defendant may be difficult to trace, the ftp site owner is an obvious alternative choice.

World Wide Web

1.15 When most people refer to the 'internet', they are really talking about a large aspect of it called the World Wide Web. The World Wide Web, or 'the web', is the most user-friendly use for the internet. Yet, it is not the internet, and the internet is not the World Wide Web.

The web, like all the technologies described so far, is merely a common language that allows one computer to understand another when they communicate across telecommunications lines and links information and documents on the internet. The web was invented by the British scientist Tim Berners-Lee working in CERN.

Accessing a computer on the web allows a user, or viewer, to do many things. Viewers can see colourful images and graphics, hear sounds and music, see animations and short movies. They can also interact with the accessed computer, or server, in such a way as to allow the viewer to download any material in digital form to his own computer. They can share files across peer-to-peer networks. However, these superficial aspects of the web do not explain where it got its name. This explanation reveals the most powerful aspect of the web and the source of the main legal issues involved in its use.

Links

1.16 Computers connected to the World Wide Web mainly store their information in a special form; it is called Hypertext Markup Language, or HTML. This common language is primarily a language of layout and design. It allows the owner of a computer to format some information, say a table, and store it on their website or 'home page'. Anyone who accesses that site will see the table as intended. The same goes for graphics, animations and so on. The web therefore offers, for the first time, an opportunity for the owner of a server computer to control exactly what is seen by a person accessing that computer. HTML also offers hypertext.

Hypertext is a way of designing a document with links to other documents. It is most easily understood with an example. Some of the footnotes in this book refer the interested reader to other materials, often a case. But if that interested reader wanted actually to read the referred case, they would have to go to their law library, pick the book from the shelf and turn to the appropriate page. A hypertext version of this book would work as follows. A reader who was interested in the case would merely position an on-screen arrow over the footnote, where the case was mentioned, and press a button on their mouse. The case would then appear on the screen replacing or neighbouring the page of the digitised book. So hypertext is a way of connecting one document to another by means of a link. Links on web pages are usually shown by the word denoting the link being underlined and coloured blue. Pictures, animations, in fact anything you can 'click' on, can also serve as links.

The real power of a link on a website can be understood when one appreciates that the link may be to a document held on any other computer anywhere else on the World Wide Web. So, an internet version of this book could just as easily link a reader to a US case stored on a web server in the United States as to an English case stored on a web server somewhere in England. Also having followed a link to another web page, one can just as easily follow a link from that page to another page on the web. These vast numbers of links, criss-crossing between digital pages across the planet, warrant the title 'World Wide Web'.

Browsers

1.17   Like other aspects of the internet, the web only works while all the computers that use it understand a common language. The web's main language is HTML. To allow a viewer's computer to interpret this language into a collection of text, pictures and sound, the computer must use a 'browser'. This is a program that not only shows the web page on the viewer's screen as was intended but also it helps the viewer navigate around the World Wide Web. All browsers have a core of common features. They all allow a user to visit a particular site on the web by typing in the site's address. All browsers also have a set of navigation buttons. These are vital if one is to get back to where one came from. In a sense, the browser lays down digital string through the maze of the web so allowing one to click the 'back' icon to the last turning. As a final aid to navigation, browsers will store a collection of the addresses of favourite pages or sites, so that one can return to a favourite place without having to retrace one's steps each time.

Navigation aids

1.18   Of course, having millions of pages of information at one's fingertips is useful only if it is easy to find the information needed. However well-stocked a library, there will be few visitors if the books are in an uncatalogued random order. Portals and search engines bring order to the chaotic layout of the web.

Portals are, at their most basic, simply a collection of links under a particular topic. For example, a law firm may wish to advertise its clients. To do this it could have a page on its website that features a list of links to its clients' web pages. An academic may use a website to collect a series of links to useful websites for research purposes. Link lists bring to the internet what the Dewey decimal system brings to our randomly stocked library.

Search engines are websites that find every site on the web that mentions a particular term (eg Google, Bing, Yahoo!). Google can trawl its record of *billions of* documents for one word in under a second. For example, in 0.19 seconds the Google search engine found over 1,360,000 instances of the phrase 'needle in a haystack' on the web.

THIS BOOK

1.19   This book tackles the legal issues arising from the internet under chapter headings appropriate to a law textbook. This does not mean that the book is for lawyers only. Where possible, the law is explained in plain English; it is envisaged that someone in an e-commerce business or from the internet industry (and even an internet user) will be able to use this book as a first port of call. To help these clients and their advisers, the text is highlighted with hundreds of fictional scenarios and their legal effect. For some basic questions, a glance at one of these may be all that is needed to appreciate the law on a point. This said, readers should always seek specific legal advice, rather than rely entirely on the text and scenarios in this book. It should be noted that these scenarios, and the names used, are fictitious, and any resemblance to real persons or companies, alive or operating, now or in the past, is purely coincidental.

The author appreciates that even legal readers who use the internet regularly will be unfamiliar with its use of technical internet terms. For this reason two policies have been adopted. The first policy is never to assume technical knowledge; whenever required, this book explains the technology. The second policy adopted is never to use a technical term where a simplified one will suffice. It is more important that lawyers who advise about the internet truly understand it, rather than simply repeat the latest internet jargon.

There are many excellent general texts on contract, tort, crime and the topics of the other chapters of this book. This book is not intended to replace these works; the intention is that it will supplement them. This book, therefore, only refers to laws when it is apparent that the internet raises unique issues about the legal area that may not be covered in existing general literature. One of the many interesting aspects of practising in this area is that so many unique and new issues are constantly raised. The internet and the laws that define it are always changing, and inevitably at different speeds. Case law in many areas considered in this chapter remains in surprisingly short supply; this fact necessitates the formation of opinions and beliefs based in part on conjecture, on assumptions about how past and new laws may be interpreted, and always with an eye to future developments at home and abroad. As before, I have not shied from offering interpretations and opinions, while recognising these may be open to change and challenge.

Importantly, a disclaimer. This book examines the English laws that apply to the internet. The internet is a transnational beast, however. It will therefore often be prudent to consult the laws of other jurisdictions to check what they have to say on any particular issue. Similarly it is hoped that this book will serve those from abroad who wish to know English law's approach to an internet issue.

Chapter outlines

Chapter 2: Contract

1.20

- Fully revised and updated.

- More detailed analysis of the interaction between classical contract law and internet-based contracting.

- Consideration of recent case developments such as *Pretty Pictures v Quixote Films* and *Immingham Storage Co Ltd v Clear plc*.

Chapter 3: Tort

1.21

- Fully revised and updated.

- Full analysis of the impact of the Defamation Act 2013 and regulations.

- The requirement for serious harm.

- The single publication rule.

- The defences of truth, honest opinion and publication in the public interest.

- The defences for secondary publishers, website operators and peer-reviewed statements in scientific or academic journals.

- The provisions restricting actions against non-domiciled persons.

- The impact of important recent defamation cases pre-dating the 2013 Act such as *Tamiz v Google Inc.* and *Jameel v Dow Jones & Co.*

- The potential impact of the new press regulation regime for website operators and bloggers.

- An analysis of the risk of internet-related activities giving rise to patent infringement claims and threats by patent trolls;

- An overview of the potential for tortious liability arising from claims in negligence, the wrongful interference with property, malicious falsehood and other economic torts.

Chapter 4: Intellectual property

1.22

- Fully revised and updated;

- Examines the developments relating to Adwords and Keyword advertising;

- Considers the role of trade mark functions, as developed before the Court of Justice;

- Looks at the reputation aspects of trade marks and websites;

- Exhaustions and last sale;

- Communication to the public;

- Licensing;

- Airline screen-scraping;

- Blocking;

- Photographs;

- Search engines;

- Copyright and economic policy;

- The test and standard for copyright and the cases of *Infopaq*, *SAS* and *Dataco*;

- Framing, deep linking etc and current ECJ decisions;

- Caching, hosting and conduit defences and other defences.

Chapter 5: Crime

1.23

- Fully revised and updated.

- For the most part, social network site operators adopt responsible positions on illegal, inappropriate, and offensive content hosted on their sites in the terms and conditions they require for use of their services. Internet service providers and social media also already have a legal obligation to co-operate with the police during investigations of allegations of harassment, stalking, etc.

- In relation to users' understanding of what may constitute criminal activity, it has been a consistent theme that although the posters who have been prosecuted may have few friends on Facebook or followers on Twitter, their posts in many cases were returned on search result engines and thereby brought to the attention of a much wider audience than they might have intended.

- A key game changer presented by social media is that once the message is posted, the original recipients of the message may copy, re-post, re-tweet or save a copy, thereby bringing the message to a much wider audience even if the author subsequently decided to delete their own post.

- Prosecuting cases with a social media element.

- In 2013, the DPP issued final Guidelines on Prosecuting Cases Involving Communications Sent via Social Media (the Guidelines). The Guidelines are designed to give clear advice to prosecutors who have been asked either for a charging decision or for early advice to the police, as well as in reviewing those cases which have been charged by the police. The Guidelines are primarily concerned with offences that may be committed by reason of the nature or content of a communication sent via social media. However, the Guidance states that where social media is simply used to facilitate some other substantive offence, prosecutors should proceed under the legislation governing the substantive offence in question (eg contempt of court, harassment, public disorder).

- Contempt.

- Enormous volumes of material can now be stored, communicated, and redistributed to a mass audience which is now causing real issues in relation to the law of contempt. Historically, newspapers would fade from memory to become 'tomorrow's chip paper'. Now, information on the internet is potentially available forever once it has been posted, and can be found by anyone using a simple search. Social media in particular, which has a viral quality, means that individuals can communicate information to very large numbers of people in a short space of time. The law relating to contempt has struggled to keep abreast of issues raised which are peculiar to microsites, as individuals posting content may simply view their behaviour as expressing their opinion on topical matters or issues that have affected them privately rather than an attempt to prejudice legal proceedings.

Ch 6: Data protection

1.24

- Fully revised and updated;
- Increasing pressure on personal data, profiling, new data collections, business models;
- New EU data protection regime;
- Key changes;
- Enhanced rights, obligations and penalties;
- Security and data breach;
- Increasing fines and prosecutions;
- RIPA, DRI case, DRIPA and DRIPA case;

- Leveson;

- New data protection cases;

- Damages issues;

- Right to be forgotten;

- Privacy by design/data protection by design;

- Revenge porn;

- Hacking;

- Piracy and end user identity;

- Big data;

- Internet of Things (IoT);

- Vidal-Hall, JK Rowling, Cheryl Cole, DRI, Max Schrems, Safe Harbour, Google Spain.

Chapter 7: Tax

1.25

- Fully revised and updated;

- Update on OECD/G20 BEPs action plan on base erosion and profit shifting;

- New UK diverted profits tax;

- Implementation of place of supply rules for services;

- New VAT rules for intra EU B2C supplies of electronic services.

Chapter 8: Competition

1.26

- Fully revised and updated.

- The Enterprise and Regulatory Reform Act 2013 established a new UK competition regulator – The Competition and Markets Authority ('CMA') which took over the functions of the OFT and CC from 1 April 2014.

- Council Regulation (EC) No 1/2003 of 16 December 2002, the Treaty on the Functioning of the European Union ('TFEU') replaced arts 81 and 82 of the Treaty establishing the European Community ('EC Treaty').

- The CMA is now responsible for both phase 1 and phase 2 merger investigations as a single entity.

- The EU Commission cleared the Google/Doubleclick transaction under the EU Merger Regulation after an in-depth phase 2 investigation. The Commission concluded that the transaction would be unlikely to have harmful effects on consumers, either in ad-serving or in intermediation on online advertising markets.

- The European Commission has begun an investigation into the E-Commerce sector.

Chapter 9: Regulation

1.27

- Fully revised and updated.

- The addition of a section describing the application of Ofcom's 'General Conditions of Entitlement' to ISPs.

- The addition of a section on 'net neutrality' (open internet) discussing Ofcom's policy and proposed EU legislation concerning practices such as traffic blocking, throttling and paid prioritisation.

- A discussion of the Consumer Contract Regulations 2013 and the rules applicable to 'distance contracts' concluded over the internet. (These rules replace the Consumer Protection (Distance Selling) Regulations 2000 discussed in the third edition.)

- A discussion of the UK legislation implementing the EU's Audio-Visual Media Services Directive and the role of Ofcom, ATVOD and ASA in regulation of content provided over the internet.

- An updated discussion of the rules regulating the provision of financial products and services over the internet taking into account the recent changes to the FCA's guidance on communication of financial promotions over the internet and the FCA's March 2015 guidance on Social Media and Customer Communications.

- An updated discussion of the rules regulating the provision of online gambling services, which have been significantly affected by the adoption of the Gambling (Licensing and Advertising) Act 2014.

New and evolving issues

1.28   As highlighted above there is a constant stream of legal issues arising from the internet.

Some of these are the natural extension of existing law to the internet arena. Examples include intellectual property online, such as copyright, trade marks and branding. Other examples include defamation (on websites, chatrooms, bulletin boards, review sites, rate sites, social media, search engines, etc) and other torts.

Other issues are new and in some instances still evolving. These include, for example:

- online abuse (eg revenge porn);
- the real net/dark net;

- VAT and taxation;

- competition and arguments in relation to anti-competitive behaviour;

- internet freedom and net neutrality;

- internet access and arguments for a human right to internet access;

- adults online, children online;

- new disruptive products and services online or using the internet;

- privacy, data protection, security, breaches;

- Big Data, the online Cloud;

- the Internet of Things;

- crime;

- crowd activities;

- internet freedom, protest and 'Springs' (eg Arab Spring);

- Bitcoin and internet currencies;

- EU–US personal data transfers and Safe Harbour/Post Safe Harbour (eg Schrems CJEU case, Umbrella Agreement, US Bills aiming to provide US protection for European personal data and related actions);

- facial recognition;

- deletion, right to be forgotten, expanding and other take down issues;

- cloud password storage services;

- privacy as a commercial selling point (eg Apple), differentiator and competitive advantage;

- Privacy by Design, data protection by design and security by design; and

- increasing uses and sources of electronic evidence.

These lists are by no means exhaustive, nor could any list in relation to the internet be.

The internet is about new products, services, activities and better ways of doing things and interacting with others, here and on the other side of the globe. It brings (and permits) wholly new activities as well as bringing new ways of undertaking existing activities. It is social, educational and commercial. Serious legal, policy and societal issues also arise.

Ultimately, the issues surrounding the internet, technology, software, technology and intellectual property are constantly changing and evolving. So in addition to a volume such as this, it can be useful to look out for annual reviews and annual predictions of these issues, such as for example the Society of Computer and Law's annual predictions.

At the time of writing, the Advocate General and Court of Justice in the *Schrems v Commissioner* case, has put the nail in the EU–US Safe Harbour personal data transfer agreement. Lawyers, policymakers as well as an international technology sector are keenly considering what happens now after the Court of Justice decision.[1] The agreement is invalid. This invalidates the transfer of personal data from the EU to the US. This has major implications.

---

1   *Schrems v Commissoner*, Case C-362/14, AG Bot, 23 September 2015, available at http://eur-lex. europa.eu/legal-content/EN/TXT/?qid=1395932669976&uri=CELEX:62014CC0362.

CHAPTER TWO

Contract

> 'The customer pays his money and gets a ticket. He cannot refuse it. He cannot get his money back. He may protest to the machine, even swear at it. But it will remain unmoved. He is committed beyond recall. He was committed at the very moment when he put his money into the machine.'
>
> Lord Denning, *Thornton v Shoe Lane Parking*[1]

2.1   That Lord Denning's comment should have perhaps more resonance to the average person today than it did in 1970 is largely attributable to electronic commerce – or 'e-commerce'. In 2014 British consumers spent £104 billion buying goods and services online. Disregarding business-to-business e-commerce dealings, proof, if it were needed, that in comfortably under two decades, through rapid development and refinement, e-commerce is now a fact of our everyday lives and still ignoring the vast sums spent online in business to business dealings.

Whatever financial or societal reasons are given for this, whatever 'paradigm shifts' are held responsible, one fact is certain: if consumers and businesses did not believe that the transactions into which they entered were legally enforceable, they would simply eschew the vast marketplace provided by the internet. This chapter will consider how English contract law applies to consumer and business contracts entered into using the internet.

The internet gives businesses access to a vast number of consumers, gives businesses access to each other and, increasingly, opportunities for individuals to meet each other and even to create, publicise and share their own content. The first large-scale consumer and business use that was made of the web was the erection of websites for marketing and advertising purposes. These sites acted primarily as a shop window, informing potential customers of the *existence* of companies and their products or services but not offering the possibility of selling them. Sales were concluded in parallel through more traditional means of communication. As websites have become more sophisticated and high-quality graphical and interactive content has become the norm, commercial websites have morphed into particular online environments providing not only space for near limitless 'window' shopping but also crucially, embedding the means

---

1   [1971] 2 QB 163 at 169.

to select products, conclude contracts for them and securely make payment. Websites not only offer convenience and immediacy for consumers (and in the case of software, for example, immediacy of delivery) and a wider audience for sellers, they have also transformed the way that businesses transact with each other, providing specialised platforms for procurement and payment and the management of purchasing.

These commercial benefits create novel issues for contract law.

FORMATION OF CONTRACT

2.2   In the main this chapter does not consider the terms of a contract made over the internet; the main concern is to analyse the validity of contracts made over the internet. This is an important distinction. Under English common law, an agreement becomes legally binding when four elements of formation are in place: offer, acceptance, consideration and an intention to create legal relations. In some circumstance these can be clearly identified, discrete elements that fall into a broadly chronological and linear sequence, which may be preceded by an invitation to treat, although the four elements may be found without necessarily going through each of these.

For contracts entered into over the internet (or other 'information society service', therefore including mobile services as well as interactive television offerings), the UK's Electronic Commerce (EC Directive) Regulations 2002 ('Electronic Commerce Regulations')[2] and Consumer Protection (Distance Selling) Regulations 2000 ('Distance Selling Regulations'),[3] together with certain other content-specific regulations, introduce new pre-contract formalities, in particular for consumers and, in the case of the Electronic Commerce Regulations, businesses which do not agree otherwise. Along with these formal requirements, law, statute and a body of regulatory and self-regulatory codes and guidance prescribe the content of a contract. For example, an e-commerce contract may be validly formed, but one of its terms may be ineffective under other rules. This section focuses on the formation of a contract, examining each of the four elements and key stages in turn, and highlights those additional features specific to the internet of which businesses and their advisers should be aware.

Contracting via the internet

2.3   There will usually be no reason why a contract may not be formed over the internet, whether via a website, email or other form or electronic communication, such as a live online 'chat', provided that each of the four elements required to

---

2   These Regulations implement Directive 2000/31/EC of the European Parliament and of the Council of 8 June 2000 on Certain Legal Aspects of Information Society Services, in particular electronic commerce, in the Internal Market, OJ L179/1 ('Electronic Commerce Directive').

3   This Regulation implements Directive 97/7/EC on the protection of consumers in respect of distance contracts. See Chapter 9 for analysis.

form a valid contract is satisfied. Indeed, the Electronic Commerce Directive requires all member states to ensure that their legal systems allow contracts to be concluded by electronic means and that any legal obstacles to the process are removed.[4] Steps have been taken by the UK government to provide for this, as considered below.

There are, however, exceptions to this principle that contracts may equally be made using digital means as with more traditional (tangible) mediums. These exceptions are: (i) where the parties have agreed that a contract (or amendments to it) must be formed otherwise (in which case there will not be requisite intention to be bound if this is not followed); and (ii) where there is a statutory requirement that a document or agreement must be in a specific format. Each is considered below.

Stipulation by the parties

2.4   There may be various reasons, public policy or otherwise, why parties may choose to contract or amend contracts in a format other than via the internet. In most situations this will be because parties desire evidence and a physical record of the contract. In others, it will simply be because this is the way they 'have always done things'. Although the use of technical means (such as a pdf to seek to prevent a document from being amended, and digital signatures – see **2.52**)), and the fact that email communications are now commonplace in disclosure, have gone a long way towards assuring parties that they will have robust evidence in the event of a dispute, some still prefer to seek reliance on paper contracts and records.[5]

Whatever the parties' choice, it is essential that this be made clear. Those who draft and review contracts are urged to consider references to 'writing' carefully, to ensure that email correspondence is included or removed as required, and clearly exclude electronic contracting or amendments if this is intended. The decision in *Hall v Cognos*[6] provides a useful warning on this point. In this case, Mr Hall failed to submit an expenses claim within the stipulated time limit. In response to an email requesting an extension, Mr Hall was told 'okay' by his manager. The company subsequently refused to grant the extension and Mr Hall brought a claim against them. The court held that the claims policy, which formed a part of Mr Hall's contract of employment, (which stated that any variations had to be 'in writing and signed by the parties') had been varied by the email. The email constituted writing and the printed name of the sender at the top of the email was judged a signature. This case sends out a further warning to parties on the use of email for making binding contractual statements since, in this case, the manager who emailed back the confirmation did not even have authority to agree the variation. However, he was held to have ostensible authority sufficient to bind the company.

---

4   Recitals 34 to 38 and art 9.
5   Indeed this may be a stipulation of some companies' insurance policies.
6   *Hall v Cognos Ltd* (unreported, 1997).

In *Pretty Pictures v Quixote Films*,[7] email communications were held not to bind the parties to a contract, since the emailed statement said that 'I hope we now have a deal. I look forward to your confirmation and receiving a deal memo by fax.' Although the other party said that the 'deal is now approved' and that he would send the contract by email, the judge held that there was no binding contract. This was because the common intention of the parties was that the contract would only become binding when each signed some form of memorandum or other paper copies to be given or exchanged, or if the contract were amended to provide for electronic signing, communication or delivery (see **2.52** below for further details in relation to digital signatures).

By contrast, in *Immingham Storage Co Ltd v Clear plc*[8] the Court of Appeal held that a contract was formed by an exchange of emails notwithstanding that the signed quotation returned by email to the offeror, which was held to have been accepted and formed a binding agreement with the offeree stated that a 'formal contract will follow in due course'.

The problem illustrated in these cases is a failure to clearly identify not just the means by which a contract is made but the documents that will form that contract, a problem illustrated in *Von Hatzfeldt Windenburg v Alexander*[9] and implicitly noted by Lord Wright in *Hillas v Arcos*.[10] It is not therefore a novel one, or one directly related to the use of electronic communications. Notwithstanding the differing outcomes in these cases, they are all evidence of the need for parties to be clear in identifying the 'medium' by which their contract is to be made to avoid both uncertainty and potentially costly litigation.

Statutory requirement

2.5 The Electronic Communications Act 2000 gives Parliament the right to amend old statutes which specifically require the use of ink and paper, in order to facilitate electronic commerce. Some statutes have already been changed through regulation in this way. An example is the Consumer Credit Act 1994 (Electronic Communications) Order 2004, amending the Consumer Credit Act 1974, to enable consumer credit agreements to be concluded and most notices and documents[11] to be provided by electronic means. This removes the prior requirement that they must be in paper form.

However, the Electronic Communications Act still requires that each statute be amended in turn. With this piecemeal approach, some statutes still remain unamended. It remains important that parties consider whether there may be

---

7 *Pretty Pictures v Quixote Films Ltd* [2003] EWHC 311 (QB).
8 *Immingham Storage Co Ltd v Clear plc* [2011] EWCA Civ 89.
9 *Von Halzfeldt Wildenburg v Alexander* [1912] 1 Ch 284.
10 *W N Hillas & Co Ltd v Arcos Ltd* [1932] UKHL 2 at [10] per Lord Wright.
11 Note that default, enforcement and termination notices have been singled out (by way of the Consumer Credit (Enforcement, Default and Termination notices) (Amendment) Regulations 2004) as a special case and still retain a requirement that they be provided in paper format since such notices are deemed to have significant impact on the rights of debtor and hired. The assumption is that default is likely to be due to financial hardship which in turn means that the individual may no longer have access to electronic communications.

any statutes that apply to the subject matter of such contract and its form which would require that specific requirements be followed.

It should be noted that, where legislation simply refers to a requirement that something be 'in writing', without any other requirement (ie the statutory context is neutral as to the medium and does not, for example, refer to the need for paper copies), the Interpretation Act 1978 states that:

> 'Writing includes typing, printing, lithography, photography and other modes of representing or reproducing works in a visible form, and expressions referring to writing are construed accordingly.'[12]

The Law Commission's interpretation of this is that:

> 'Writing includes its natural meaning as well as the specific forms referred to. The natural meaning will include any updating of its construction; for example, to reflect technological developments.'[13]

With this in mind and considering the extent to which electronic 'writing' is now pervasive, it is difficult to foresee that electronic communications such as emails or website order processes could fail to constitute 'writing'.

Of course, in the majority of contracts, particularly in the electronic commerce arena, there will be no statutory requirement providing for specific forms, whether in writing or otherwise. To this extent, general common law principles will apply and it is clear from a number of cases, that there is no reason why a contract may not be concluded via electronic means, provided that the requisite elements are met.[14]

Pre-contract information

2.6   The Electronic Commerce Directive and its implementing legislation oblige almost every owner of a website established in the European Economic Area (EEA) to provide certain information to its visitors, whether the website permits transactions or not, and regardless of whether users of the website are acting in a consumer or business capacity. These requirements fall outside the established elements of contract formation in requiring an additional layer of information to be provided for internet services.

In the UK, further information requirements apply pursuant to the Companies Act 1985 (as amended pursuant to the Companies Act 2006[15]), and the Business Names Act 1985. These require that a company (and in respect of the Business Names Act 1985, also a partnership or other trading entity) registered in England

---

12   Interpretation Act 1978, Sch 1.
13   Para 3.7, 'Electronic Commerce: Formal Requirements in Commercial Transactions, advice from the Law Commission, December 2001'.
14   See, for example, *Hall v Cognos Ltd* (unreported, 1997) and *NBTY Europe Ltd (Formerly Holland & Barrett Europe Ltd) v Nutricia International BV* [2005] All ER (D) 415 (Apr).
15   Amendments were made to ss 349 and 351 of the Companies Act 1985 pursuant to the Companies Act 2006 and the Companies (Registrar, Languages and Trading Disclosures) Regulations 2006.

and Wales place certain key contact and other particulars regarding the company on all of its websites and in official business correspondence. Companies are generally advised to include it in all email correspondence by default to avoid the need to determine whether it is actually a business email or not.

We examine the Electronic Commerce Directive requirements in this chapter by first assessing where a website owner is 'established'. We then consider the manner of provision and nature of the information which EEA-established entities must make available to all visitors to a website. Finally we analyse the nature of the additional 'transactional' information that may need to be provided prior to orders being taken.

Establishment of providers

2.7   The Electronic Commerce Directive does not have extraterritorial reach; it binds only member states, meaning here, those established within the EEA (EU Member States with Iceland, Liechtenstein and Norway). The concept of establishment, however, in relation to websites, is problematic. Large websites are often hosted simultaneously on multiple servers which may be situated anywhere on the planet and may be used interchangeably. Consequently, they may be many thousands of miles from where those who control them are physically established.

Location of servers not conclusive

2.8   The Electronic Commerce Regulations, which implement the Directive, however, take a pragmatic view of establishment:

> '"established service provider" means a service provider who is a national of a Member State or a company or firm as mentioned in Article 48 of the Treaty and who effectively pursues an economic activity using a fixed establishment for an indefinite period, but the presence and use of the technical means and technologies required to provide the service do not, in themselves, constitute an establishment of the provider …'[16]

In effect, therefore, the location of one's servers does not change where one is established. The question of establishment is first one of from where the economy activity of a fixed establishment is being pursued. Having determined this, one must then determine whether or not the use of the fixed establishment is for an indefinite period or not. Employees working in a leased building are the sort of situation envisaged here. One cannot conclude anything from the mere fact that servers are, or are not, inside the building.

Multiple establishments

2.9   Complications arise where more sophisticated companies have multiple locations providing support to a particular website. For example, a company with a website could be headquartered in Japan but technical control and maintenance

---

16   Reg 2(1), part definition.

of the site is undertaken by a team based in California, while, all the content on the website is created by a group of freelance Irish web designers which posts finished articles to an editor in an office in Dublin, and customer support is handled from the UK. The site's credit card processing is conducted in Germany and all goods are shipped from local distribution centres around the world. In this scenario, determining where the company is established is not straightforward.

The Electronic Commerce Regulations and Electronic Commerce Directive clearly envisage such a scenario. We are told, 'in cases where it cannot be determined from which of a number of places of establishment a given service is provided, that service is to be regarded as provided from the place of establishment where the provider has the centre of his activities relating to that service'.[17]

In the scenario above, therefore, the place of establishment on this basis may well be considered to be Japan because this is where the main base is. However, there is a concern associated with this definition being used to interpret where a multiple-state-located service provider is established for the purposes of the Electronic Commerce Directive and Electronic Commerce Regulations. The recital and definition would seem to suggest that different services may have different centres of activities relating to them. What follows from this is the possibility that the service of, say, ordering a product from a website is centred within the UK but the service of delivering it is centred in the US. In other words, one service is EU-centred; the other, from the same website, may not be. In such circumstances, the service provider may be unsure whether the legislation applies. In the first scenario, therefore, the management services undertaken in Japan may be viewed as separate to the Irish editorial service and UK customer support. As will be explained, the contractual sanctions for not complying with the Electronic Commerce Regulations are potentially severe enough that any UK service provider is advised to assume that they are established in the EEA, for the purposes of the Electronic Commerce Regulations.

General information to all

2.10 If a service provider is established in the EEA, they must make available certain general information about themselves. This information must be made available to the recipients of their service (ie a website) 'in a form and manner which is easily, directly and permanently accessible'. If a service provider fails to do this, they may be liable in damages by their visitors for breach of statutory duty.[18]

Alongside this, the information requirements contained in the Companies Act 1985 (as amended) and the Business Names Act 1985 in relation to websites and emails duplicate the requirements previously required in respect of business stationery and other documents. Such information must be legible. Failure to comply with these non-Electronic Commerce Regulations requirements is a criminal offence carrying a fine of up to £1,000.

---

17 Reg 2(1). Recital 19 is similar.
18 The Electronic Commerce (EC Directive) Regulations 2002, reg 13.

Information to be made available

2.11 The scope of the information to be made available pursuant to the Companies Act 1985 consists of the company name, place of registration (ie England and Wales), registered number and registered address. The Business Names Act 1985 requires that, in the case of a partnership, the name of each partner, in the case of an individual, his name and, in the case of a company, the corporate name, is given clearly and legibly.

The information required under the Electronic Commerce Regulations (discussed below) is as follows:[19]

1. the name of the service provider;

2. the geographic address at which the service provider is established;

3. the details of the service provider, including his electronic mail address, which make it possible to contact him rapidly and communicate with him in a direct and effective manner;

4. where the service provider is registered in a trade or similar register available to the public, the register in which the service provider is entered and his registration number, or equivalent means of identification in that register;

5. where the provision of the service is subject to an authorisation scheme, the particulars of the relevant supervisory authority;

6. where the service provider exercises a regulated profession:

    (i)   the details of any professional body or similar institution with which the service provider is registered;

    (ii) his professional title and the member state where that title has been granted;

    (iii) a reference to the professional rules applicable to the service provider in the member state of establishment and the means to access them;

7. where the service provider undertakes an activity that is subject to value added tax, the VAT number; and

8. where prices are referred to, these shall be indicated clearly and unambiguously and, in particular, shall indicate whether they are inclusive of tax and delivery costs.

Again it should be stressed that this information must be provided regardless of whether the website in question is transactional or not.

Form and manner of information

2.12 The above information must be 'made available to the recipient of the service ... in a form and manner which is easily, directly and permanently

---

19 The Electronic Commerce (EC Directive) Regulations 2002, regs 6(1)(a)–(g) and 6(2).

accessible'.[20] Unlike specific transactional information mentioned below, the above information may be made available at any time during the encounter with the website visitor. This said, one should note that this information must be 'easily' accessible. Burying the information after numerous other pages on a website is unlikely to satisfy this requirement. A link from the homepage to a list of this information is probably the most obvious way to make the information available. Some website operators may choose to include this information within their standard 'Terms and Conditions'. This too is likely to be acceptable but with one caveat. This information must be made available 'permanently'. Consequently, websites must not be designed so that the information is, say, only available while one is conducting a particular activity or about to finish placing an order. The information must be able to be accessed even after a visitor has enjoyed the site. Another common place to position this information on non-transactional sites is in an 'About Us' or 'Contact and Legal Details' section.

Example 2.1

An online news service has a subscription service: individuals pay £15 each month to access the service's database of past news articles. The Electronic Commerce Regulations' 'General Information' is made available through a link to the right of the search area on the site. The link is called 'About Us', but the page on which it is housed is only accessible during the course of a paid month and not afterwards. It is therefore arguable that the information is not 'permanently' accessible and so is non-compliant.

Transactional information prior to order

2.13   If a service provider is established in the EEA and is soliciting orders from visitors to its website, it must provide specific information about its transactions to potential consumers and businesses (additional requirements specific to consumer-only transactions are considered separately in this chapter) who do not agree otherwise. This information must be provided to the recipients of their service 'in a clear, comprehensible and unambiguous manner'.

If a service provider fails to do this, they may be held liable by their visitors for damages in breach of statutory duty.[21] In addition, they must allow a consumer to identify and correct input errors prior to placing their order. If the service provider does not make this facility available, the consumer may rescind the contract.[22] Should the customer so cancel, the service provider may apply to the court to order that the consumer may not rescind the contract.'[23]

Website owners and their advisors are therefore strongly advised to pay particular attention to the following section. An owner of a website may well choose to ignore the requirement to make available the general information. If they do so, they are taking the low-cost risk of an action for damages for breach

---

20   Reg 6(1).
21   Reg 13.
22   Reg 15.
23   Reg 15.

of statutory duty. Few website owners, in contrast, can afford to run the risk that any of their contracts could simply be rescinded by the customer at any time.

Provision of information in clear, comprehensible and unambiguous manner

2.14   The scope of the information to be provided in a 'clear, comprehensive and unambiguous manner' prior to the order being placed is simple to understand.[24] It nevertheless may be complex to implement and include on certain websites. The six headings below detail the information required and special concerns of each requirement.

Technical steps to conclude contract

2.15   Regulation 9(1)(a) provides that a website must provide for the user of the website the steps which will result in the conclusion of a contract. The most clear and comprehensive way for this to be achieved is by the use of a 'crumb trail' at the top of the ordering section of the site. A 'crumb trail' is a line of text showing all the steps needed to enter the contract with the current step highlighted. Having, say, 'Choose – Provide Credit Card – Confirm' at the top of the screen certainly does go some way to be clear and comprehensive. What is needed in addition, however, is some explanation of the meaning of each of these steps. A link from each with a short description would ensure that the 'crumb trail' is not ambiguous as to, for example, when the order is complete.

Filing of concluded contract

2.16   Website owners are obliged by reg 9(1)(b) to provide information before the order is placed as to whether or not the concluded contract will be filed and, if so, whether it will be accessible. Although it is obviously trivial to state this in such a way as to comply with the Electronic Commerce Regulations, it may be more difficult to comply with the actual statement itself.

Many websites allow a user to access their previous orders. This, however, is only one aspect of the concluded contract. The other aspect is the text of the contract itself incorporating the prevailing Terms and Conditions from the website. The difficulty here is that these terms and conditions are subject to frequent changes and the current terms to which a user may now have access may not be the same terms on which they contracted. To comply with the filing requirement, therefore, customers must be able to continue access the historical Terms and Conditions used to conclude each order. This may be onerous and as such, most websites will generally elect to state that the contract will not be filed.

How to identify and correct input errors

2.17   Regulation 9(1)(c) obliges websites to provide in a clear, comprehensible and unambiguous manner information about how customers may identify and correct input errors before they place an order. In addition, the website is obliged

---

24   Reg 11.

to make available 'appropriate, effective and accessible' technical means to identify and correct input errors.

The easiest way to comply with this is to require a user either to confirm an order and ideally to allow them adjust it. There is unlikely to be a problem so long as the customer is left in no doubt that the order details on the confirmation page of the ordering procedure may be rejected, and then altered, or accepted. Many websites go further to allow confirmed orders to be modified before goods are dispatched.

Example 2.2

CD410.co.uk is a website which sells music CDs for no more than £10 each. Its designers omit to alter their ordering pages to allow individuals to correct input errors. Instead, by the 'Confirm' button, they state: 'Don't worry if you've made a mistake and have ordered the wrong thing, simply pop it back unsealed in the post to us with 30 days and we'll credit the money back to you!' In this scenario, CD410.co.uk will not have complied with the requirement to allow individuals to correct errors before they place their order; each customer will be able to rescind the contract at any time not only within their stipulated 30 days.

Languages offered for contract

2.18   Finally, reg 9(1)(d) requires that websites must provide details of the languages that are offered for conclusion of the contract. There is no stipulation that a website must contract in a range of languages merely that where alternatives are available this is drawn to the attention of users.

Relevant codes of conduct

2.19   Many website operators are members of voluntary or mandatory codes of conduct. Where this is the case, a list of these must be provided prior to the order being placed, together with information about how to consult the codes electronically.[25]

Terms and conditions for storage and reproduction

2.20   It is sensible for most websites to allow each customer to see the site's terms and conditions before they can place an order. If they cannot see the terms and conditions, there is a risk that a court will deem that the terms and conditions (or at least some of them) have not been 'incorporated' into the contract with the customer. This is discussed below.

Where terms and conditions are provided, the Directive and Regulations impose a further obligation that the website operator must make the contract available to the recipient in such a way that allows him to 'store and reproduce' it.[26] Historically, simply allowing the user to print the terms would suffice but as desktop printing becomes less common and crucially as websites are accessed

---

25   Reg 9(2).
26   Reg 9(3).

through mobile devices, tablets, etc, this requirement is perhaps not properly met by allowing users to save a copy of the terms and conditions or have the option of having the terms emailed to them. Providing for all options would seem to unambiguously satisfy reg 9(3).

Offers and invitations to treat

2.21 Having provided visitors with the requisite information set out above, websites can then proceed with the formalities required to conclude contracts with their visitors.

It is discussed below that an offer, met with suitable acceptance, consideration and an intention to create legal relations can form a contract binding on both parties. An owner of a website may not want to contract with every party who gains access to their site. For example, the owner may want to contract with parties exclusively from their own, rather than from any country.[27] They may also want to provide protection against becoming automatically bound to a contract where there is an error (such as in pricing) in the website or otherwise until they have had an opportunity to approve or confirm the order. Owners of websites should therefore ensure that the advertising aspect of the site is construed as an 'invitation to treat', not as an offer and consequently, that the customer will usually be the party making the offer in submitting an order, which can then be accepted, or not, at website discretion.

Webvertisements

2.22 One fundamental of e-commerce is that suppliers use websites to conduct business. Like a billboard, a website advertises products and services, but unlike a billboard it can also assist the supplier to complete the sale. In doing so, a website can be designed to advertise the features of a product or services; it can even allow a viewer to examine the product in a restricted form.[28] After examining the product or the advertising, a viewer may then select the part of the website or follow other prompts to enter a contract to acquire the product or services. The internet in effect fuses the advertising and the shop. The law, in contrast, has distinguished between advertising and shop displays.[29] This unique commercial situation has legal ramifications.

27 This is happening increasingly where a supplier wishes to create geographical price differentials or where the supplier wishes to avoid the laws (often mandatory consumer protection in nature) of a particular jurisdiction.
28 Software can be downloaded from a website in a 'crippled' form. For example, a word processor may be downloaded but may be prevented from printing or saving: it provides a 'test drive'. If the user is content with the product he may then re-access the website to form a contract to receive the uncrippling key.
29 *Pharmaceutical Society of Great Britain v Boots Cash Chemists Ltd* [1953] 1 QB 401; see *Carlill v Carbolic Smoke Ball Co* [1893] 1 QB 256.

Shops and adverts

Shop invitations

2.23   There is well-established authority for the proposition that the display of goods and their prices in a shop window or shelf are not offers to sell those goods; they are merely invitations to any customer to make an offer to purchase them.[30] On intimating that they wish to purchase the goods, the customer makes an offer to the retailer, which the retailer may choose to accept or reject. Website owners should desire the same legal mechanics, whether they are supplying to businesses or, in particular, to consumers. Indeed, by doing so, those website owners contracting with consumers will be more easily able to comply with the 'placing of the order' rules of the Electronic Commerce Directive.[31]

Advertisement offers

2.24   For the purposes of offers, the law distinguishes shop displays from certain advertisements. It is therefore essential that those who wish to contract over the internet understand this difference. The law assesses advertisements in two categories: those which promote unilateral contracts and those promoting bilateral contracts. A unilateral contract is one in which money, generally, is offered to another party to perform some act without that person promising anything in return. A person accepting the offer does not need to communicate this fact to the offeror or to complete the contract; he simply needs to do what is required of him.

This legal notion was most recently re-confirmed by the Court of Appeal in *Bowerman v ABTA*[32] A travel agent's physical premises displayed the standard ABTA scheme of protection notice. This included the statement: 'ABTA [a travel agent association] arranges for you to be reimbursed the money that you have paid for your holiday [if there are financial difficulties with the agent]'. The travel agent became insolvent and the claimant sought to recover the cost of the holiday from ABTA. The Court of Appeal held that this published statement would constitute an offer and, as such, was accepted and formed a contract with the claimant and any customer doing business with the travel agent.

Example 2.3

A website that offers advertising space to vendors runs a promotion. Its site advertises, 'If you visit our pages three times this month and don't buy anything from our advertisers, we'll credit £10 to your bank account!' This site risks creating a unilateral contract, which the entire internet community may accept.

---

30   See *Warlow v Harrison* (1859) 1 E & E 309 and its more modern equivalent, *Pharmaceutical Society of Great Britain v Boots Cash Chemists Ltd* [1953] 1 QB 401.
31   Art 11.
32   *Bowerman v Association of Travel Agents Ltd* [1995] NLJR 1815.

A bilateral contract, in contrast, has both parties making a promise. Each offer is usually accepted by a communication of the other's promise.

Web invitations

2.25   The owner of a website has little reason to prefer a unilateral contract to a bilateral contract, and where possible should seek to be viewed by the courts as a shopkeeper. The main point to make is that the law looks not simply at the words used for a contract, but the objective intention behind them. This means that if a website would induce a reasonable person into viewing statements on the pages as offers, so will a court. In *Bowerman*, Hobhouse LJ states this succinctly:

> 'The document as reasonably read by a member of the public would be taken to be an offer of a legally enforceable promise … It suffices that ABTA intentionally published a document which had that effect. A contracting party cannot escape liability by saying that he had his fingers crossed behind his back.'

An owner of a website therefore must err on the side of caution in creating a web invitation.

One method is for the owner of the website to state that it will not be bound by any communication or 'order' from a user, but the site owner will inform that party if it accepts the communication or order. This creates three factors in favour of the site owner. First, it goes some way to preventing the reasonable person from thinking the owner has made an offer which can be accepted automatically. The second point relates to the first: it provides evidence to a court that the site owner did not intend to make an offer. Simply using indicative words above a link such as 'make an offer' may not be enough.[33] Third, by explaining the stages to conclude the contract, the website will comply with art 10 of the Electronic Commerce Directive and reg 9 of the Electronic Commerce Regulations as discussed above. This legislation states that, prior to an order being placed by a consumer or a business not having agreed otherwise, the service provider must 'clearly, comprehensively and unambiguously' provide:[34]

> '(a) the different technical steps to follow to conclude the contract;
>
> (b)   whether or not the concluded contract will be filed by the service provider and whether it will be accessible;
>
> (c)   the technical means for identifying and correcting input errors prior to the placing of the order;
>
> (d)   the languages offered for the conclusion of the contract.'

In addition, the following information must also be made available:

> '[an indication of] any relevant codes of conduct to which [the website owner] subscribes and information on how these codes can be consulted electronically.'

---

33   Eg *Harvela Investments Ltd v Royal Trust Co of Canada (CI) Ltd* [1986] AC 207.
34   Art 9(1).

These pre-contractual consumer formalities may not be contracted out of by a supplier's contract. And, as described above, the sanctions for ignoring these requirements include not only damages but rescission of the contract.[35]

If such an option is taken by the website owner, then it is of course necessary that (not least to comply with the requirements listed above), particularly with consumers, the contractual process and the point at which a binding contract is made, is clear. This will involve not only ensuring that the statements made pre-order are transparent at this point, but also those made to confirm it (as considered below).

Example 2.4

A retailer advertises its products on a website. To process an order, the consumer must provide certain information and then click the button labelled 'Submit'. Before the consumer submits this information the website clearly states that their information is to allow the site owner to decide whether to accept their offer. This allows the site owner to check the product type and cost entered and reject, for example, any offer for a television less than £30 as a minimum price for any television. This application of 'backstop logic' reduces the cost of mistakes. It will be important however that the site owner is clear in subsequent communications or confirmations of this order, as to at what point in time acceptance occurs.

It is mentioned above that the courts view a shop's shelves as invitations to treat and not offers. A website owner may therefore attempt to argue that the site is more like a shop's shelves than anything else, and that it should be viewed accordingly. While this analogy appears reasonably accurate, it may not withstand the strain of a court's detailed scrutiny, especially in respect of digital goods/content.

A justification for not holding shops as making offers to sell goods displayed in their stores is to ensure that, if the shop's stock is depleted, a prospective buyer cannot sue the shopkeeper for damages.[36] Where a website is offering not physical but digital goods for 'sale',[37] it is difficult to assert that supplies can be exhausted. One of the features of digital products distributed over the internet is that they are, in effect, in infinite supply. The primary justification for the rule therefore, is based in part on a commercial factor that is absent from a digitally distributing website.[38] Whatever the common law justification, the Electronic Commerce Directive is concerned with a consumer (or business that has not agreed otherwise) 'placing the order'. It follows, therefore, that to have known of the possibility of being able to place an order, the website displayed an invitation to treat.[39]

---

35 See 'Transactional information prior to order' at **2.13**.
36 See *Esso Petroleum v Customs and Excise Comrs* [1976] 1 WLR 1 at 11.
37 See 'Type of contract', at **2.64**.
38 Of course, a limited licence may have been imposed on the supplier restricting the number of digital products he can supply.
39 Art 11(1).

Misrepresentations

2.26   The distinction between an invitation to treat and an offer is that an offer, met with acceptance, may form a contract. An invitation to treat does not serve as an offer: the courts construe that taking up the invitation is an offer (or possibly 'order' in the language of the Electronic Commerce Directive). The distinction does not entitle a website to induce a consumer to enter a contract by using misleading statements. If a factual statement made prior to a contract being formed is classified as misleading, the induced party may be entitled to claim damages, rescind the contract, or even both. If an individual is concerned that an invitation to treat or statement on a website may constitute such a misrepresentation, he should take proper legal advice. It is worth noting that the established law and statute on misrepresentation are equally and fully applicable to a contract formed over the internet as to one formed in other ways. Website owners who simply use their sites as a 'billboard' for contracts that are formed in other ways must therefore consider that the content of their site may induce someone to enter a contract.[40] It makes no legal difference to the law of misrepresentation that the misrepresentation is on a website but that the contract is not formed over the internet. They must also ensure that they provide the general information as described in **2.6** above.

Timing and location of offers

2.27   Once it has been determined that an offer was made two further useful pieces of information can be gleaned: precisely when the offer was made and where it was made. When a court deems an offer is made is often vital. At any moment up to acceptance, an offer can be retracted. Where an offer was made has some relevance to the applicable law for a contract, in the absence of choice, and the relevant section of this chapter will consider this in greater depth.[41]

When an offer is made

2.28   It is often relevant for the purposes of a contract dispute to determine when an offer is made. Under the Electronic Commerce Directive (for consumers) or otherwise (not for consumers), any offer can be revoked before acceptance. Therefore, the first question to answer is when was an offer made. The need for discussion arises because electronic communications are often delayed in transmission and a court will have to decide whether a revocation of the communication will be deemed to take effect before the conclusion of the contract. In short, the court has a choice: offers may be deemed to be made at the time of sending or at some time later.

---

40   There may also be a misrepresentation by the viewer, say, as to the means of payment or the country of his residence.
41   See 'The Rome Convention', at **2.97**.

Consumer's offers

2.29   The Electronic Commerce Directive appears, at first glance, to simplify greatly when a consumer's internet offer is deemed received: 'the [offer] … [is] deemed to be received when the part[y] to whom [it is] addressed [is] able to receive [it]'.[42]

The wording used by the Directive, however, does not resolve the difficulties posed by offers that are delayed or are incoherent on arrival.

Delayed offers

2.30   *Adams v Lindsell*[43] is well-established authority as to when an offer is deemed to take effect. In *Adams*, wool was offered for sale by a letter sent to the claimants. Because of a mistake made by the offerors the letter arrived two days late, at which time it was promptly accepted. The court held that the contract was formed on acceptance, despite the offer being delayed. The court indicated, more than once, that its decision was partially founded on the reason for delay being the offeror's mistake. If the offeror had included a time limit on the efficacy of the offer, however, a late acceptance would not have bound them. There are many parallels between the way in which website offers and emails are communicated and the postal service and delays can be suffered for very broadly similar reasons. These are not instantaneous means of communication in the way that telephone and fax are and must be analysed discretely.

Post, fax, email and instant messaging

2.31   An email or instant messages can be seen as akin to a posted letter being delivered to a pigeon-hole ready for collection. For the purposes of this chapter they will be treated as being synonymous with one another as the mode of transmission is broadly the same. Emails and instant messages (eg those sent via iMessage or Whatsapp – two of the most popular) are not instantaneous, unlike faxes and telephone calls, although the time between sending and receiving may be so short as to give the appearance of them being so.

An email is sent to an internet service provider (ISP) who, like the Royal Mail, attempts to deliver it as quickly and accurately as possible. But as with the Royal Mail, mistakes can occur and emails can arrive garbled, late or even not arrive at all. The similarities with the Royal Mail go further: the Royal Mail does not usually deliver post abroad; that is left to the local postal system of the foreign country. The Royal Mail delivers the mail to only the 'first stop' outside England. The same applies to emails: they are passed between many different carriers to arrive at their final destination. The only distinction for the purposes of this chapter between email and instant messages are that instant messages are sent via a common, third-party platform to which both parties connect rather than being transmitted to across potentially a number of servers or networks to reach the recipient.

---

42   Art 11(1) and reg 11(2).
43   (1818) 1 B & Ald 681.

Unlike a telephone call and fax, some emails are delivered not to the recipient's desk, but to an electronic pigeon-hole for collection. This pigeon-hole is the 'inbox'. Many users of email must log into their ISP account to check on the arrival of an email; often users must collect their email, it is not 'delivered' to them. This technical framework serves as a useful backdrop for the discussion which now follows on when an offer is deemed to have been made. It will also be useful when acceptances are considered later.[44]

Emails can be misaddressed, delayed by any server or router on the way, and worse than ordinary mail, they may not be 'collected' for some time after delivery. This is a situation comparable to sending an offer to a pigeon-hole abroad. Many parties are involved in the transmission of the message, and even on arrival the recipient must act to retrieve it.

Before dealing with the English and European legal resolutions to this situation, a technical point must be made. Certain email systems permit a 'read' and a 'receive' receipt to be automatically returned to a sender of an email. The 'receive' receipt usually informs the sender that the email has not been received by the individual, but by his ISP; if analogies are useful, the receipt informs senders when the mail arrives in the inbox. The 'read' receipt informs when the individual retrieves the email from the ISP. Even there, like a letter in an unopened envelope, the email may not be read for some time.

Deemed receipt of emails

2.32   A sent and received email offer will be deemed received because it is able to be accessed but this will not necessarily apply in the case of businesses, who may agree otherwise (eg an agreement that the un-accessed offer is not deemed as being received).[45]

Consequently (assuming no other agreement has been made in the case of non-consumers), if a sender improperly addresses the email and it does not arrive, no order has been placed, no offer made. If the sender properly addresses the email, or properly uses the website, but the supplier is unable to access the order, the order is not deemed received. This will be the situation if it is the sender's ISP that is at fault. It is even the conclusion if it is the supplier's website that is at fault. In short, a problem in transmission outside the sender's control will affect the sender's legal position in making an offer before a particular date.

Practically, where it is possible to agree otherwise in business relationships, the best practice is to make any electronic offer subject to a date on which the offer will lapse. Specifying this date in relative terms, for instance, five days after receipt, poses problems unless the offeror provides a definition of exactly what

---

44   See 'Timing of acceptances', at **2.42**.
45   The Electronic Commerce Directive, art 11(1), second indent; Electronic Commerce (EC Directive) Regulations 2002, reg 11(2).

is 'receipt'. A simpler and more certain method is to specify an objective date and time.[46]

Example 2.5

A consumer places an order for a wine box from the 'Swig It' website which is delayed by two days owing to the 'site's internet Service Provider having a computer fault. Unlike *Adams v Lindsell* the delay was out of the control of the offeror; a court will deem the order as being deemed received when it is accessible to the website owner – ie, not until the two days have passed.

Acceptance

2.33   There is little special about the terms of an acceptance made over the internet, as opposed to one made in any other way. The acceptance must unequivocally express assent to all the terms of the offer. Much has been written about what constitutes such an acceptance. It is useful here to draw out the special methods of accepting over the internet and so this section is divided into consideration of acceptances via websites and via email. The section then goes on to consider timing of acceptances, authentication and mistake.

It has been mentioned that an email can have a 'read' and a 'receive' receipt.[47] Receiving one of these will not constitute an acceptance of an emailed offer. An automatically generated receipt of an offer (or order) is not an acceptance of the terms of an offer. Even an email sent in reply that states the recipient's intention to reply in due course will not be an acceptance.[48]

Means of acceptance

Websites

2.34   An acceptance needs to assent to an offer. It does not, in general, need to be in any particular form (although see **2.3** above for a more detailed discussion on formats and internet contracting generally). For this reason, where a website is established to make or complete contracts, its owner should be aware of what conduct may bind him. This is of paramount importance. Contracts made over the web are rarely completed by two humans: a website operates automatically according to a set of instructions, often called a script. In this respect, it is crucial

---

46   If no mention is made of the lifespan of the offer, the courts will imply a lapse after a reasonable time. See *Chemco Leasing SpA v Rediffusion Ltd* [1987] 1 FTLR 201. To assess what is reasonable the courts will take into account many factors including the subject matter of the contract and the method of communicating the offer. Clearly with an email offer, the expiration will be implied sooner than an offer made by post. See *Quenerduaine v Cole* (1883) 32 WR 185.
47   See 'Delayed offers', at **2.30**.
48   See *OTM Ltd v Hydranautics* [1981] 2 Lloyd's Rep 211.

that the owner of a website understands how a contract can be completed because, generally, a website operates without supervision. This section examines two scenarios: first where, as advised, a website accepts an offer and second, where it makes one.

(A) Website acceptance and acknowledgement

2.35   Having discussed when and how offers can be made it is now relevant to determine how and when acceptances are made. The general rule is that an acceptance must be communicated to the person making the offer. The Electronic Commerce Directive also obliges offerees to acknowledge the receipt of an offer (order) 'without undue delay and by electronic means' unless agreed otherwise in the case of non-consumers.[49] An acknowledgement of receipt may well also be the acceptance of the offer. Fortunately, the two may be dealt with separately. Otherwise this would then bind the supplier into accepting the offer 'without undue delay and by electronic means'. The supplier is entitled first to acknowledge receipt of the offer, and then (potentially later) to accept the offer. If a supplier does not acknowledge receipt of the order, they may be sued for damages for breach of statutory duty.[50]

Suppliers should take care over the language used in any acknowledgement. They should ensure that it does not act as an acceptance and so, inadvertently, form a contract earlier than intended.

Example 2.6

A young school child orders a birthday present from a website to arrive for her father the next day. The website, on receiving the order, immediately sends an email to the child stating: 'Thank you for your order. This is now being processed.' Such ambiguous language could be deemed as being an acceptance and not a mere acknowledgement. The website may now be unable to refute the order.

Any person making any offer may waive the general rule that acceptance must be communicated and can instead permit acceptance by conduct. This general rule is examined in the light of e-commerce transactions.

Communication of acceptance

2.36   The acknowledged rule is that acceptance of an offer must be communicated to the offeror.[51] This must not be confused with the Electronic Commerce Directive's rule that acknowledgement of a consumer's offer must also be communicated. In addition, as the Court of Appeal has stated:[52]

---

49   Electronic Commerce Directive, art 11(1), first indent; Electronic Commerce Regulations, reg 11(1)(a).
50   Reg 13.
51   [1974] 1 WLR 155 at 157.
52   *Allied Marine Transport Ltd v Vale do Rio Doce Navegacao SA* [1985] 1 WLR 925 at 927.

'We have all been brought up to believe it to be axiomatic that acceptance of an offer cannot be inferred from silence, save in the most exceptional circumstances ...'

The question is, what are the 'most exceptional circumstances' when it is appropriate for an acceptance to be silent? These exceptional circumstances stem from the reasons for the rule: to protect both offeror and offeree.

The rule protects the offeror from being bound by a contract without knowing that the offer is accepted. An exception to this may be, therefore, where the offeror expressly or impliedly waives the requirement of communication. For example, an offer to sell goods may be made by sending goods to an offeree who can accept the offer by using them.[53] Here there is not mere silence or inactivity; there is conduct indicating acceptance.

Conversely before the Electronic Commerce Directive, offerees were also protected by this rule. If they did not wish to accept an offer, it was not felt undesirable that offerors could put them to the trouble of communicating a refusal.[54] Indeed, authority from an established precedent, *Felthouse v Bindley*,[55] indicates that the offeror can waive communication of acceptance, but not waive an unequivocal external manifestation of acceptance so as to bind the offeree. Communication of acceptance may also be deemed 'waived' by the 'custom and practice' of the area of commerce.[56] The Electronic Commerce Directive alters these common law rules for consumers and businesses who do not agree otherwise. Service providers must acknowledge offers/orders, whether they intend to accept them or not.

That the above is good law is not doubted; its bearing on standard practice for electronic commerce, is. For the most part it is suppliers who draft the offers being made over the internet, particularly on the web. In this situation it is difficult to see any unfairness in holding an acceptor, (ie the supplier), bound despite making no contact to that effect: it would appear that the onus is on the owner of a website to state categorically what will constitute acceptance.[57] For transactions unless otherwise agreed in the case of non-consumers, this is stipulated by art 10(1)(a), but for all business transactions, it is surely best practice. Contracting over the internet may therefore reverse the court's assumptions in *Felthouse v Bindley* because the offeree generally drafts the offer. If that party does not specify the method of acceptance, and also does not reply to a submitted offer it risks the serious possibility of being bound by numerous contracts without having made explicit approval. Even if a stipulation as to the method of acceptance is made in the email or on the website, if the offeree drafted these terms and accepts by another method, the offeree can be viewed as having waived that specified

53 *Weatherby v Banham* (1832) 5 C & P 228. Interestingly, the Electronic Commerce Directive, recital 34 and the Electronic Commerce Regulations, reg 11(2)(b), clearly envisage that acknowledgement of the order may only be by the provision of the service ordered.

54 *Chitty on Contracts* vol 1 at §2-063 (twenty-ninth edition) Sweet & Maxwell, 2004. Also see *Chitty on Contracts* (thirty-second edition) Sweet & Maxwell, 2015.

55 (1862) 11 CBNS 869.

56 *Minories Finance Ltd v Afribank Nigeria Ltd* [1995] 1 Lloyd's Rep 134 at 140.

57 See *Jonathan Wren & Co Ltd v Microdec plc* 65 Con LR 157, QBD Technology and Construction Court.

method. A court will look to whether the offeror has been prejudiced by the changed method of acceptance.[58] Of course, readers will recall that consumer-focused transactions are required to state the steps necessary to follow to conclude the contract.[59]

Acceptance by conduct

2.37 The website can accept an offer, 'on behalf' of its owner, by certain conduct. For example, a viewer can click a button on a web page to send a request for some software and the software may then begin to download to the viewer's computer. This positive action can be viewed as an acceptance of the offer made by the viewer without the owner (or offeree) having expressly assented to the offer itself.[60] But, our courts commonly apply an 'objective' test to interpret the actions of the offeree. Conduct will therefore be regarded only as acceptance if the reasonable person would be induced into believing that the offeree has unequivocally accepted the offer.

Completing an order by downloading a file to the consumer is likely to be construed as acceptance by the reasonable person.[61] Owners must therefore carefully construct their websites. The owner must ensure that the website is able to validate the terms of the offer from the viewer. Generally this is achieved by the website having a contract or order page that the viewer is encouraged to complete, submit, or offer, by clicking a link or button. On receiving this notification the website will automatically start the downloading of digital material to the viewer. But the automation of this acknowledgement of receipt and acceptance places a burden on the site owner: he must ensure that the terms of the offer submitted are the terms of the offer expected. It is essential that a viewer cannot submit an offer with an adjustment to the terms, say lowering the price. This would be a counter-offer which may, unwittingly, be accepted by downloading the requested material to the viewer.

There is a technical method to achieve this certainty. The web page should clearly state the terms of the order. Included within these terms should be a clause to the effect that an acceptance will only be valid where an offer is received through the website.[62] This, to some extent, prevents an adjusted offer being sent by email and automatically accepted.

Controllers of sites should pay much attention to their automatic checking programs: an error may result in the owner being bound to a contract that would have been unacceptable (see also **2.51** on mistakes).

---

58 See generally *Robophone Facilities v Blank* [1966] 1 WLR 1428.
59 Electronic Commerce Directive, art 10(1)(a).
60 See *Brogden v Metropolitan Rly* (1877) 2 App Cas 666.
61 See *Northern Foods plc v Focal Foods Ltd* [2001] EWCA Civ 1262, [2001] All ER (D) 306 (Jul), in which Focal supplied goods to Northern and later disputed that such supply deemed their acceptance of the loss-making price for the goods. The Court of Appeal held that a letter sent by Focal to Northern was accepted by the conduct of supplying the goods. See also Electronic Commerce Regulations, reg 11(2)(b) in relation to 'acknowledgement by providing services'.
62 See *Frank v Wright* (1937) OQPD 113 where acceptance was specified to be received in writing, but was not valid where made orally.

Example 2.7

A website provides the terms of an offer to download software from the site at a cost of £60. The site is structured so that the viewer must type the words, 'I Agree' in a box, at which point the website acknowledges and accepts the offer by downloading to the viewer the requested software. One viewer types 'I agree to pay £30'. Because the automatic checking program looks simply for the words 'I Agree', but not exclusively, the software is downloaded to the viewer in error. A contract may have been formed at the lower price.

(B) Consumer acceptance

2.38   This chapter advises against websites making offers. Nevertheless, for the sake of completeness, rather than recommendation, this section examines this method of contracting.[63] Many of the same legal considerations are applicable here as for when the website accepts an offer.

Acceptance by conduct

2.39   It has been explained that conduct can constitute acceptance.[64] In the scenario where a website makes an offer, it will be the conduct of the consumer, or viewer, which the courts will examine to check for acceptance. It is in the interests of the website to ensure that the conduct by the consumer is therefore as unequivocal and unambiguous as possible.

Example 2.8

A web page has a scrollable window headed 'Licence'. Below this window is a button labelled 'download software'. A viewer clicks on this button to download the software and is later accused of breaching the licence provisions. The viewer may have an arguable case that his conduct was not in relation to the terms of the licence, but in relation, simply, to gaining access to the software. A more thoughtful page design may have removed this problem.

Conduct is regarded as acceptance, and, for services, acknowledgement of receipt of the order, only if the reasonable person would be induced into believing the offeree has accepted. This 'objective' test can create difficulties for the operator and designer of a web page. Many digital consumers using the web for commerce view it like a shop, only a 'virtual' one. They may therefore be surprised, and not aware, that to acquire a product they must not only provide payment but also then consent to a licence. Their more usual tangible purchases involve simply paying in exchange for receiving the product. On this basis it is difficult to fathom how a court could objectively construe as acceptance the clicking of a button that denotes downloading the product rather than accepting the licence. Under Scottish law, a case concerning 'shrink-wrapped' computer software showed the court's readiness to construct two contracts out of the

---

63   See 'Shop invitations', at **2.23**.
64   See 'Acceptance by conduct', at **2.37**.

supply of computer software transaction.[65] First, the retail sale of the physical box of software containing the product. This contract is between the retailer and consumer. The second is purported by the software publisher to be between them and the consumer; the so-called 'shrink-wrap licence'. In this case, the consumer did not break the 'shrink-wrapping' and so was decreed not to have a contract with the software publisher. Bearing in mind this case, owners of websites should not shy from explaining that clicking a button will bind that person to obligations regarding the material that they will acquire. This provides the background for the final issue pertaining to the acceptance by the conduct of a consumer – ignorance of offer.

Ignorance of offer: lack of intention

2.40   It can be appreciated that, even with provision of the information required by the Electronic Commerce Directive, consumers could click on a button labelled 'download' without envisaging that they may be entering an explicit, rather than implied, contract: consider the eagerness to acquire some new software or material and consider the typical ignorance that the acquisition is subject to an explicit licence. It is also possible to press the wrong button. In such a situation, Electronic Commerce Directive or not, the courts may be reluctant to bind unwitting offerees simply because they have performed an action[66] that purportedly indicates acceptance. A further reason that the courts may not hold consumers bound by their action is that, in not knowing of the offer, the consumers have no intention to be legally bound by their actions.

The solution to these possible problems is for any website that seeks to bind users to be explicit, avoid uncertainty and 'go further' than merely 'make available' the 'Terms and Conditions'. One method is to prevent the viewer being able to perform the conduct before they have scrolled, or paged, through the entire contract. True, an individual may simply click on a 'next page' link without actually reading the text of the contract; but, at least they then have a weaker argument that their conduct does not objectively indicate acceptance and that they were ignorant of the offer.

Conduct also becomes relevant in terms of amendments to terms and conditions. Increasingly, websites seek to provide that updates to the terms and conditions are deemed accepted by a website user by conduct if they use the website after the amended terms and conditions have been uploaded to the site. Even some offline providers have sought to direct customers to check their website regularly for amendments to their terms to which they are bound. Any provider who uses such techniques should be alert to the problems this presents, particularly when dealing with consumers. The key issue is that this of course places the entire burden on the user to proactively check the site terms, plough through them for changes and then take the decision whether to continue to use the services or exercise any cancellation rights on this basis. Not even the fanatical, alert to this requirement, in the first place would do so! It is unlikely

---

65 *Beta Computers (Europe) v Adobe Systems Europe* 1996 SLT 604.
66 For example, clicked on a link or icon. See *Specht v Netscape Communications Corpn and America Online Inc US District Court of Southern District of New York*, 3 July 2001.

that a unilateral amendment in this way, particularly where it relates to changes which impose new obligations on the consumer or reduce the comfort they have, will be enforceable (being unfair under the Unfair Terms in Consumer Contracts Regulations 1999), unless something more is done to bring it to the consumer's attention to indicate their acceptance to it. In the case of registered users, sending an email with updated changes is one option, another would be drawing the new terms or changes to their attention when they next log onto the site. For non-registered users where no contact details or log-in are available, this will not be possible. With such user terms, there may already be problems with proving that they are enforceable contractually (although as considered in Chapter 3, the main point of such terms is usually to provide a disclosure for tortious purposes and an intellectual property notice). A prominent notice placed on the home page (particularly where major changes have been made) may assist.[67]

Example 2.9

The home page of a website features only one line of legal text to avoid looking too ominous. It states, 'By proceeding you agree to be bound by our terms.' The word 'terms' is underlined on the site to indicate a link to the terms of the website. This may not bind the viewer, but if it does, there is a likelihood that onerous exclusions of liability will not operate against the viewer. The website owner should find other ways of ensuring that those onerous terms are definitely read by the viewer, for example, by inclusion of a tick box confirming acceptance and which must be 'ticked' if the viewer wishes to continue.

Email acceptance

2.41   Email is increasingly being used by parties to enter into contracts to ensure speed of communication and agreement and avoid the need for acquiring physical signatures. Identifying the point of 'acceptance' is often more difficult with emails than with a website order process however since there is less likely to be a clearly identifiable 'act' that occurs equivalent to the clicking of an 'I accept' or the sending of an order confirmation. It is more likely with email communications that the medium will have been used alongside other offline communications, for negotiations and therefore isolating the final point at which the parties are bound will more frequently come down to an interpretation of the words used.

Issues may easily arise where parties are seeking to reach agreement as to a variation of an existing arrangement or to settle a dispute with each party taking a different interpretation of the other's position or their own proposals.

---

67   The US Court of Appeals case for the Ninth Circuit in the case of *Douglas v USDC Central District* (DC number CV-06-03809-GAF) provides some guidance on this topic, albeit from the US. In that case, the court held that a telecommunications company could not enforce updated terms and conditions placed on its website against a user. However, in this case, the user never used the website, paying via credit card separately. The initial terms also failed to draw attention to how such changes would be notified – both aspects which clearly worked against the provider.

In some cases a party may try to seek reliance on the principle set out in *Chitty on Contracts*, General Principles that 'where parties are genuinely at cross-purposes as to the subject matter of the contract and the terms of the offer and acceptance are so ambiguous that it is not possible to point to one or the other of the interpretations as the more probable, the court must necessarily hold that no contract exists.'[68] However, as recent cases such as that of *NBTY Europe Ltd (Formerly Holland & Barrett Europe Ltd)*[69] indicate, a finding of 'impossibility' is a high threshold. Again, parties are therefore here urged to treat email communications with as much certainty and precision and with such clarity as to whether something is agreed and accepted, as they would with more traditional paper correspondence. As considered above in **2.4**, it is also essential that such caution is passed down to employees and managers to guard against the risk of a party becoming bound through their more lax correspondence.

One further point to note is that, as mentioned earlier, an email can have a 'read' and a 'receive' receipt. Receiving one of these will not constitute an acceptance of an emailed offer. An automatically generated receipt of an offer (or order) is not an acceptance of the terms of an offer. Even an email sent in reply that states the recipient's intention to reply in due course will not be an acceptance. Issues of acceptance with email contracting is therefore heavily bound up with intention (see **2.57**). The problems of timing and non-receipt are considered in further detail in the next section.

Timing of acceptances

2.42   Because an offer may normally be revoked at any point until acceptance, it is obviously vital to appreciate when acceptance is deemed to have taken place over the internet. Unlike for offers, the Electronic Commerce Directive and Electronic Commerce Regulations do not specify when acceptance is deemed to be received.

Example 2.10

Onepotatotwo.com sells seeds to consumers through its website. During July, a consumer selects some seeds through the site and confirms his order by clicking an icon labelled 'I accept'. The moment he does this he receives an email from onepotatotwo.com thanking him for the order and confirming the seeds are on their way. Before reading the email, he sees the seeds being sold at seedyseedsmart.com at a reduced price. Even though he has not read the email, as he was able to, the contract was concluded. (However, as a consumer, he may be able to take advantage of the cooling-off period under the Distance Selling Regulations in order to cancel the contract and obtain a refund (for which, see **Chapter 9**)).

One person may make an offer which is acknowledged as being received and is accepted immediately by the other person. But if that offer is withdrawn before

---

68   *Chitty on Contracts*, General Principles vol I at 5-060 (29th edition) Sweet & Maxwell, 2004. Also see *Chitty on Contracts* (32nd edition) Sweet & Maxwell, 2015.
69   *NBTY Europe Ltd (Formerly Holland & Barrett Europe Ltd) v Nutricia International BV* [2005] All ER (D) 415 (Apr).

the acceptance is received by them there may be a conflict. The possible legal outcomes are that the contract was made when the acceptance was sent; or when, and if, it arrives at the recipient.

English law does not resolve or offer guidance on this critical timing issue, nor does the Electronic Commerce Directive (although it is interesting to note that early drafts did contemplate the inclusion of sections clarifying the moment at which the contract is concluded). In this respect, English and European law (unlike that of the US) has not equivocally followed in statute the approach set down in the UNCITRAL Model Law approach.[70] This states that, unless otherwise agreed between the originator and the addressee, the time of receipt of a data message is the time at which it enters the designated information system or, if a designated information system has not been selected, the time at which the data message is retrieved by the addressee.[71]

Nor does English case law to date cover this timing point in relation to email or website acceptances. It is therefore necessary to extrapolate from the law relating to acceptance by post, telephone and telex.

When a viewer reads or views a website, packets of digital information pass between the site and the client. An acceptance by either party will, generally, be immediately received by the other. The more difficult questions of timing of acceptances are therefore seldom pertinent for web communication or for 'instant' messages. For emails the issues are more complex.

This discussion is therefore in halves: the first considers acceptance by email where it is reasoned that the 'postal rule' will usually apply; the second considers acceptance over a website where it is submitted the more general rule will apply that the contract is formed when the acceptance is received. Again, readers should note that the Electronic Commerce Directive addresses only timing of 'orders' and not acceptances.

Acceptance by post, telephone and telex

2.43   Where acceptances are sent by post there is a generally applicable rule that the English courts have used to determine the deemed time of acceptance.[72] Acceptance takes place when that letter is posted. Where acceptances are made by an instantaneous form of communication, such as telephone or telex, another rule has been generally applied.[73] Acceptance is deemed to take place when the acceptance is communicated to the offeror.

It is a moot point whether these rules should be mechanically applied, or whether they are, as is more likely, a starting point to assess what is fair between the parties. Certainly the courts have stated that the posting rules should not be applied where it would lead to 'manifest inconvenience or absurdity'.[74] And there are occasions where this would be the case: it would be absurd for an

---

70   UNCITRAL Model Law on Electronic Commerce (1996) with additional art 5 *bis* as adopted in 1998 Guide to Enactment.
71   Ibid, art 15(2).
72   See *Adams v Lindsell* (1818) 1 B & Ald 681.
73   See *Entores Ltd v Miles Far East Corpn* [1955] 2 QB 327, and *Brinkibon Ltd v Stahag Stahl und Stahlwarenhandelgesellschaft mbH* [1983] 2 AC 34.
74   *Holwell Securities Ltd v Hughes* [1974] 1 WLR 155 at 161.

acceptance to be deemed accepted at the time of posting if it is delayed in the post because the offeree wrongly addressed it. It is perhaps as much as can be hoped, therefore, that this chapter explains what would not be manifestly inconvenient or absurd for email acceptances. It is essential that those who would seek to rely on the following section for email acceptances are aware that it is simply guidance. Even after almost 200 years of examination of the postal rule, there is no universally applicable rule; there are merely pointers for the parties and the court.[75]

Acceptances by email

2.44   As mentioned earlier, email is not quite like the post and it is certainly not like instantaneous communication by the telephone.[76] It is sometimes slower than the post, and the arrival of the acceptance by email is far more reliant on the recipient than the sender. It is not like a fax or telephone for two reasons. First, there is no direct line of communication between sender and receiver. Instead, the email is broken into chunks and sent as a collection of packets, each with an 'address' for the recipient. The arrival of an email is therefore far more fragmented than a telephone call. The second, and central, difference between the two is that with a telephone call it is possible to check that the intended recipient has heard the acceptance. With email this is near to impossible but is often quite necessary. Emails are sent using protocols, precise languages, which allow one computer to pass on information accurately to another. But sometimes these protocols are used incorrectly and an email may arrive entirely garbled or missing a few important characters such as zeros and pound signs. This problem must be combined with the issue that an email requires its recipient to collect it, rather like collecting mail from a pigeon-hole. It is therefore difficult, unlike a phone call, to check that the offeror has received the acceptance and to check that it is unequivocal.

Reasonableness of email acceptance

2.45   Like the posting rules, the first issue to consider in relation to an acceptance is whether it is reasonable to use email to accept. A rule of thumb applied in postal cases has been that if an offer is made by post, it is reasonable to accept by post. This, at first blush, appears applicable to email; it may not be. Some email users are permanently connected to their internet service provider: as soon as an email arrives for them, they are notified and can immediately view the message. What is more common, however, is that a user's email arrives to a server which the user must contact by modem to access any messages: the

75 This is not to say that organisations have not lobbied to clarify and harmonise the position: the UN Convention on Contracts for the International Sales of Goods (adopted in Vienna, 1980) contains provisions dealing with acceptance, offer and withdrawal of an offer (arts 14–24); see also, the EC Communication from the Commission to the Council and the European Parliament on European Contract Law, Com (2001) Final, 11 July 2001.
76 Readers should note that since the first edition of this text *Chitty* has now altered its view on this issue to confirm this point. See *Chitty on Contracts* (Sweet & Maxwell, 29th edition, 2004) Volume 1 at §2-046; cf § 2-031 (27th edition). Also see *Chitty on Contracts* (32nd edition) Sweet & Maxwell, 2015.

connection is not permanent. These users are not always notified that an email awaits them. They must simply log-on on the off-chance that an email is ready for them. For these remote email users, a period of days may elapse before they check for any email. It may therefore be less reasonable that an important acceptance is emailed to one of these remote users, than for an offer to be sent from one of these users. That said, it is submitted that the senders have at least some responsibility to inform their recipients not to reply by email if they collect their email infrequently.

Priority over subsequent communications

2.46   Because an email is not instantaneous, if it is reasonable to use email to accept,[77] it is not absurd to deem the time of making the contract as the time of sending the email where otherwise a later acceptance sent would act prejudicially. A later posting or email should not 'beat' the earlier acceptance sent by email. Of course, convenience and policy have a role to play in balancing the interests of the two competing offerees.[78] It would not be reasonable to prefer the earlier sent email if it was addressed incorrectly, or was sent in full knowledge that the offeror's email server had crashed.[79]

Accepted but not received

2.47   Emails can be delayed in their transmission, sometimes through no fault of the offeree. As one early example (there are many more), on 13 April 1998, software flaws crippled an AT&T data network for about 24 hours. This affected millions of consumers who tried to send, and hoped to receive, emails during the period.[80] Less often an email will not be received at all. There are three possible reasons for this. First, the sender sends the acceptance to an incorrect email address: it is extremely unlikely that a court will grant such carelessness with the benefit of the doubt; the email will not be acceptance. A second reason that the email may not be received is owing to a fault at some point in the transmission process. As another example, on 17 July 1997 hundreds of thousands of email messages sent to known addresses simply 'bounced back' as though the addresses did not exist. The cause of this was an employee of Network Solutions Inc (who at the time maintained the 'master' address list) who was working the night shift and failed to react to an alarm.[81] Like a loss in the Royal Mail, a court must weigh the fairness to the offeree against the unfairness to the offeror, who may have already contracted with another party. Even so, it is still likely that the contract will have been formed at the time of sending the email.[82] The third, and most common, reason that an email acceptance will not be received is that its recipient does not retrieve it. This may be because the person no longer checks their email

---

77   See 'Reasonableness of email acceptance', at **2.45**.
78   *Brinkibon Ltd v Stahag Stahl und Stahlwarenhandelgesellschaft mbH* [1983] 2 AC 34 at 41.
79   See *Bal v Van Staden* [1902] TS 128 in which it was held unreasonable to insist that an acceptance be deemed accepted where the sender knew of postal delays.
80   *USA Today*, 23 April 1998.
81   *The Times*, 19 July 1997.
82   See *Household, Fire and Carriage Accident Insurance Co Ltd v Grant* (1879) 4 Ex D 216.

inbox, or because the person sees who the message is from and deletes it without reading it. In both of these situations, the email would constitute acceptance; an offeror's recklessness will not prevent the formation of a contract.

It follows from the above that an email acceptance sent, but not yet received, cannot be 'beaten' by a later sent revocation of the offer. This rule is well established under rules of postal acceptance and there seems little justification to adjust it for acceptances over the internet.[83]

Inaccurate transmission

2.48   It has been mentioned that an email may arrive missing, or including, certain characters and it may even be entirely illegible. The legal significance of a flawed email is that its sender may never know. In this way email differs to a large extent from a telephone acceptance, and to a smaller extent to a fax acceptance. During a telephone call one can check that an acceptance has been heard; fax machines will report an error if a fax cannot be sent with sufficient quality, or there is no paper at the receiver's end. In contrast, if an email is garbled, it is impossible for the offeree to know before it is too late. For this reason, it would be both inconvenient and absurd for any other rule to apply other than making the offeror bound by a garbled email. The offeror, having not specified an alternative method of acceptance, is not at liberty to presume it is a counter-offer.

This rule is not purely based on technical realities and policy; it is also based on evidential matters. As with a fax, the sender retains a copy of that which is sent. On the other hand, it is often possible, using digital translators, to unscramble the received email to establish whether it was an unequivocal acceptance.[84]

Example 2.11

An insurance firm establishes a website and allows potential customers to submit details of their works of art for insurance. All valuations and contracts are formed over the internet. The firm sends by email to a customer an offer of insurance for a painting; this customer types his acceptance by email but, unfortunately, this is not sent across the internet as the customer has not paid his monthly fee to his internet Service Provider. The painting is then stolen. The customer will not be able to benefit from the delay in the post, as the delay was attributable to his fault.

Acceptances over the web

2.49   Unlike email communications, on the web the client and server are in simultaneous communication for most purposes. The communication between the two has the quality of a telephone conversation between computers rather than humans. Either party will be immediately aware if the other party 'goes

---

83   Offerors over the internet must not forget that to revoke an offer the withdrawal must actually reach the offeree. A reversal of the postal rule will not apply. See *Re London and Northern Bank* [1900] 1 Ch 220.

84   A binary document, say a word processing document, which is emailed as text, may be irreversibly scrambled. Other types of modification, however, such as a '£' becoming a '#', can be reversed to indicate to the court the true nature of the acceptance.

offline'. This is because when one party sends digital data to the other, these data are sent together with a checksum which allows the receiving computer to check that the correct information has been received. A checksum is almost the equivalent of someone saying 'Okay?' after asking a question over the telephone; it is a way of checking that the silence is due to acquiescence rather than absence.

If the client loses contact with the server, the server will 'know' of this situation within seconds, as its checksums and 'received data' will not arrive; if the server loses contact from the client very often a message will appear to the effect of 'server not responding'. In law this 'knowledge' of non-transmission makes a crucial difference. In *Entores Ltd v Miles Far East Corpn* Lord Denning considered for the first time when an acceptance sent by telex should be considered as making a contract.[85] It is instructive to follow closely Denning LJ's reasoning in this case: this will demonstrate that a website acceptance greatly differs from an email acceptance and should be treated like a telephone, or telex, acceptance.

First, Denning LJ considered the hypothetical case where one person, in the earshot of another, shouts an offer to the other person.[86] The person hears the offer and replies, but his reply is drowned by noise from an aircraft flying overhead. Denning LJ was clear that there is no contract at the moment of the reply. The accepting person must wait until the noise has gone and repeat the acceptance so the other can hear it. Next, Lord Denning took the case of a contract attempted to be made over the telephone. An offer is made but in the middle of the reply of acceptance the line goes 'dead'. Denning LJ was again clear that there is no contract at this point because the acceptor will know that the conversation has abruptly been broken off. Finally, Lord Denning considered use of telex to form a contract. Again, if the line goes dead in the middle of the sentence of acceptance, the teleprinter motor will stop. If the line does not go dead, but, say, the ink dries up, the clerk at the receiving end will send back a message 'not receiving'. In all of Lord Denning's examples the person sending the acceptance knows that it has not been received or has reason to know it.

Parallels with acceptance over a website are now obvious: if a communication of acceptance is sent from or to a website, it will become immediately obvious if a problem has occurred which blocks the communication. Like a telephone acceptance, a server will always 'know' whether a message has been received by its intended recipient; it is waiting for received data to signify that the message has been received. And like a telex acceptance, if a client sends a message to the server but there is some problem preventing transmission, the client will receive, not unlike the telex clerk's message, a 'server not responding' message. It is therefore submitted that communications over the web differ from those by email. The contract is complete when the acceptance is received by the offeror.

85 [1955] 2 QB 327. Applied by the House of Lords in *Brinkibon Ltd v Stahag Stahl GmbH* [1983] 2 AC 34.
86 [1955] 2 QB 327 at 332.

Example 2.12

A company which sells ties establishes a website that allows viewers to select a pattern and length for a tie. After selecting the tie, the viewer is asked to click the 'I want to buy' icon. The company's web server then sends an automatic receipt of offer and acceptance of offer. The server is notified that this acceptance does not reach the viewer. No contract is formed because the non-delivery of the acceptance was known to the company before the viewer left its site. It should have retransmitted the acceptance, maybe by email.

Battle of the forms

2.50   The rapidity of email and automatic confirmations of receipt lend the internet to contractual negotiations where previously faxes had been used. This may allow a 'battle of the forms' to commence. This is where two standard-form email contracts are exchanged, each differing slightly from the other but claiming to govern the legal relationship entirely. The situation may be resolved by no contract being formed; there is no agreement. What can be more problematic is that a contract is formed on one party's terms when that was not expected. Except for the issues of location and timing already mentioned, there is little that the internet will add to established methods of judging the result of a battle of the forms.[87]

Mistake

2.51   Given the tendency for websites to provide automatic acceptances of orders placed, there is a risk that mistakes will arise which could lead to the formation of a contract on terms that the website owner does not anticipate. We have discussed above some of the safeguards that website owners may put in place, including ensuring that there is a space between acknowledgement and acceptance and that the terms of any offer made by a user are checked. It is worth considering here, however, the circumstances in which a party may have redress due to a mistake, and how such risks may be further mitigated with some examples.

A common scenario for mistakes is where a pricing error on a website leads to goods being advertised at a lower price than the website owner is willing to accept.

The risk of website pricing errors was first brought to public attention in September 1999, when a Sony television was offered for £2.99 on the Argos website. The correct price was in fact £299. Argos initially refused to honour the orders; proceedings against them were later abandoned due to costs. In 2002, another well-known retail name, Kodak, advertised a 'special deal' package comprising camera, docking station, memory card and paper for just £100. The true figure was over £329. Customers placing orders received automated email

---

87   *British Road Services Ltd v Arthur V Crutchley Ltd* [1967] 2 All ER 785 and *Butler Machine Tool Co Ltd v Ex-Cell-O Corpn (England) Ltd* [1979] 1 WLR 401.

confirmations, but on spotting the mistake, Kodak wrote to these customers, withdrawing the offer. County court proceedings were initiated by several customers, and under increasing media scrutiny Kodak agreed to fulfil the confirmed orders.

In *Hartog v Colin and Shields*[88] the court held that a buyer should have known that a price per pound rather than per item offer was a mistake, and that the seller did not mean to sell at that price. The buyer's acceptance of the offer did not form a binding contract. Although it was not in the end tested before the courts, Kodak may have had a difficult time in seeking to rely on this case, given the labelling of the package as a 'special deal' and given that the low price was advertised during sale time. This contrasts with the Argos situation where the £2.99 was more obviously a mistake more akin to *Hartog*.

A later incident, again involving Argos, demonstrates how simple changes made to a website ordering process can greatly assist. In this later case, Argos advertised a television valued at £349 on its website for just 49p. However, in the interim since the previous pricing mistake, Argos had amended its terms and conditions (accepted and incorporated when orders were placed). These now stated that, if errors in the price of goods were identified, customers would be informed and given an opportunity to reconfirm the order at the correct price or to cancel it or, where the customer could not be contacted, the order would be cancelled by Argos. Steps were also taken to ensure that it was clear to customers that an email acknowledgement of an order was not the same as a confirmation that it would be fulfilled without condition.

Authentication and digital signatures

2.52 The signature is a familiar way of an individual making apparent on paper that they are who they say they are and that, often, they agree to be bound by whatever they are signing below. The signature, therefore, generally provides 'authentication' of the signatory. It is also an indication of 'acceptance' or 'consent' to a legally binding commitment. Sometimes, legislation and statute demands that a signature is provided, for example, in assignments of copyright.[89] Sometimes individuals decide that, for a particular contract, a signature will be their agreed sign of acceptance.

In both examples, the use of a computer, software and the internet to provide, generate and deliver these signatures is an important issue. As outlined in **2.3** above, if legislation insists on ink and paper (as opposed to just any type of signature) for certain transactions, then e-commerce's benefits will not be felt in areas of commerce simply because of this bureaucracy. Similarly, if individuals do not feel comfortable in relying upon digital signatures, they too may not derive benefits from electronic commerce's speed and geographical reach. The European Union and the UK have implemented legislation to facilitate digital signatures being usable and relied upon in commerce.

88   *Hartog v Colin and Shields* [1939] 3 All ER 566.
89   Copyright, Designs and Patents Act 1988, s 90.

The EC Directive on a Community Framework for Electronic Signatures[90] attempts, among other issues, to create a common understanding across Europe as to what constitutes an 'electronic signature'. Clearly, electronic commerce across Europe would be hampered if member states differed on what an acceptable 'technical' standard is for an electronic signature. Further, the Directive requires that member states ensure that an electronic signature is not denied legal effectiveness in legal proceedings merely because it is in an electronic form and has not been created by a secure electronic device or by a particular third party.[91] In short, basic electronic signatures (as opposed to advanced ones, considered below), like paper ones, need not be generated in any particular way nor need they be created (read 'witnessed') by any particular person. As with paper signatures, it is open to a court to call into question the reliability, and possible forgery, of an electronic signature. Even so-called 'advanced signatures' are not beyond the rules applicable to proper signatures.[92]

The UK's Electronic Communications Act 2000 and Electronic Signatures Regulations 2002 introduce the key element of the Electronic Signatures Directive, being that, merely because a signature is electronic does not prevent a court from relying upon its veracity in a dispute.[93] The UK statutory framework for electronic communications does however contain some important departures from the Directive as considered below in the context of basic and advanced signatures.

Basic electronic signatures

2.53   A basic electronic signature would cover all manner of sign or signature.

However, unlike the Directive, for the purpose of evidencing such electronic signature in legal proceedings, the Electronic Communications Act states that both this signature and 'the certification by any person of such signature, shall each be admissible in evidence in relation to any question as to the authenticity of the communication or data or as to the integrity of the communication or data'. This means that, although in many cases just having some kind of electronic signature (such as an 'I accept' or 'I confirm' button, or the typing in of a user's name) will be sufficient to form the contract, if there is a question over the validity or authenticity, certain additional certification criteria will be relevant when put before the court. 'Certification' to this extent, means that a person should have made a statement (whether before or after making the communication) that:[94]

'(a)   the signature;

(b)   a means of producing, communicating or verifying the signature; or

(c)   a procedure applied to the signature;

---

90   OJ No L13, 19 January 2000, at 12.
91   Art 5.
92   Arts 2 and 5 and recital 20.
93   Section 7(1).
94   Section 7(3).

52

is (either alone or in combination with other factors) a valid means of establishing the authenticity of the communication or data, the integrity of the communication or data, or both.'

What this means is that if one wishes to utilise a basic electronic signature to conclude a contract, one might also be required to produce a statement, technical in nature, which is a valid means of proving the signature and document are not forged and are reliable.

There is no prescribed form for any such statement, and in most cases, whether or not a signature is in fact authentic will come down to a matter of evidence gleaned after the event.

It is interesting that, in relation to the few English cases that we have had on electronic signatures, the courts have not considered the issues of certification, or indeed the ECA at all. This is presumably because, in the few cases we have had, the focus has been on what constitutes a signature in the context of an email communication, rather than on whether or not the signatures in question were genuine or not. In the cases of both *Hall v Cognos*[95] and *Nilesh Metha v Fernandes*,[96] the question arose as to whether the sending of an email constituted a signed document. Different judgments emerged. In *Hall v Cognos*, as considered earlier in this chapter, variations to a company policy could only be made where they were signed in writing. The Industrial Tribunal held that the presence of the name of the sender at the top of the email was a sufficient signature. In *Nilesh Metha v Fernandes*, the question arose as to whether an email relating to a guarantee constituted a sufficient signature for the purposes of s 4 of the Statute of Frauds. This statute refers to the need for documents to be 'in writing and signed by the party charged therewith'. The email in question contained only the name of the sender in the header and the judge held that, given that this had been inserted automatically and not deliberately, on an objective basis, the email or document had not been signed. He went on to state (again without consideration of the ECA) that a party could have signed the email for the purposes of the statute in question had they typed in their name or last name prefixed by some or all of his initials or using his initials and possibly by using a pseudonym or a combination of letters and numbers. However, the fact that the document in question was an email, as opposed to being in paper form, was immaterial.

The outcome of these cases demonstrates that the approach of the courts to the use of emails and signatures is still unclear, although a signature is more likely to be found where the person 'signing' has had to actively do something to affirm their consent or agreement (as opposed to just sending an email). However, in each of these cases, no arguments were made that the 'signatures' were forgeries or otherwise inauthentic. Rather the basis for contesting them was that the marks were not signatures at all. In this respect, key legal issues associated with the Electronic Communications Act and Regulations and basic signatures did not arise. On this basis, readers should be aware that, although a signature may be found in email communications, website owners and contracting parties may still

---

95 *Hall v Cognos Ltd* (unreported, 1997).
96 *Nilesh Metha v J Pereira Fernandes SA* [2006] 1 All ER (Comm) 885.

wish to consider the insertion of statements fulfilling the criteria of the Electronic Communications Act and Regulations or to use an advanced electronic signature in order to provide evidence in the event that it is contested.

Advanced electronic signatures

2.54   The Electronic Signature Regulations also provide for a regulated regime for the development of advanced or qualified electronic signatures. The advantage of such signatures is that they do not need accompanying statements to be admitted for evidence purposes, since they are already deemed to incorporate such tests.[97] These super-strength electronic signatures would satisfy any legal requirement for a signature in respect of the signed data. However, one must consider that UK legislation usually twins the word 'signature' with another, 'writing'. Every piece of legislation that refers to both these words remains impervious to digitalisation: the legislation itself will need amending to bring it into the binary age.

A further crucial issue about the electronic signatures legislation is it does not 'fast-forward' existing legislation into the electronic world in this respect. It does not 'search and replace' the word 'signature' in legislation with the words 'signature, digital or otherwise'. If old legislation states currently that 'writing' and 'signatures' are required for a particular legal instrument, the grand-sounding Electronic Communications Act 2000 does nothing to change this requirement.

Advisors should therefore ensure that their clients, while eager to embrace electronic commerce, do not misread the European Directive and the Electronic Communications Act 2000 and Electronic Signatures Regulations 2002. Old legislation may still insist upon paper signatories, or the parties may themselves choose this too, as explained in more detail in **2.3**, and all too frequently references are made by parties to using a 'digital signature' without proper understanding or clarification as to whether this is basic (with or without statement) or advanced.

Consideration

2.55   As an oversimplification, perhaps, it can be stated that the English law of contract distinguishes breakable promises from enforceable contracts.[98] Consideration given in return for a promise is the main ingredient that turns promises into contracts. Consideration has been variously defined as 'something of value in the eye of the law';[99] '[d]etriment to the promisee';[100] 'the price for which the promise is bought';[101] and there is much academic debate as to its exact ambit.

---

97 Technically, these must meet the hurdles of Annexes I, II and III of the Directive.
98 Although, a promise made in a deed may be enforceable. This is considered out of the scope of this chapter, but it may be noted that there appears little preventing a deed being made using electronic methods.
99 *Thomas v Thomas* (1842) 2 QB 851 at 859.
100 Holdsworth W, *History of English Law*, Vol 8, at 11.
101 *Dunlop Pneumatic Tyre Co Ltd v Selfridge Ltd* [1915] AC 847 at 855.

English law has always recognised that mutual promises may be adequate consideration for each other, thus forming a contract. If a builder promises to repair a roof and the unfortunate homeowner promises to pay on completion of the repair, a binding contract is formed. No services have been provided yet and no money has been given.[102] Similarly, promises to pay over the internet are enough to form the consideration to create a contract.

Example 2.13

A video shop with a website offers DVDs for sale. A viewer selects a DVD for £15 from the website and types 'I Agree' in the requisite box together with a credit card number. The DVD is shipped immediately at which point the shop discovers that the credit card number is fictitious. That the agreement has been completed over the internet is of no legal consequence: the viewer's promise to provide the £15 will be 'valuable' (ie of value) consideration for the shop to enforce the contract.

It is only important for this chapter to assess whether the factual reality of contracting using the internet affects the doctrine of consideration. For general statements, readers are advised to look to specialist texts. One contractual situation is particular to the internet: the consideration needed to cement a web-wrap contract.[103] These are agreements at the 'front' of a website which purport to bind their viewers to a contract should they proceed to view the rest of the site.

Web-wrap consideration

2.56   It is now common that to enter a website one must click a link labelled, 'I Agree to the terms above'. These terms are generally divided into two sections: the top section expresses the intellectual property rights that the site owner licenses to viewers; the bottom section attempts to exclude liability for any damage caused by the site. This section will not address the terms of these contracts, but merely whether there is consideration for the licence.

If a web-wrap contract is properly constructed it seems likely that there is consideration to form a binding contract with the viewer. What the developer of the website must attempt to create is a set of mutual promises that will form the consideration for the contract. One method of achieving this is to actually prevent a viewer who does not click the 'I Agree' link or icon from entering the site itself. Promising the viewer access to the site if the 'I Agree' link is selected then forms one of the promises to bind the contract. The other promise must come from the viewer. This, of course, is to promise to abide by the terms of licence. This prevention can then be classed as a promise to allow the viewer into the website if he agrees to the terms on the screen. Such a legally robust

---

102 If this was not the law, there could never be an action in contract for non-payment. The defendant would argue that, having not paid, no consideration has been provided; no contract therefore subsists.
103 The use of 'digital cash' in exchange for goods or services raises issues not of consideration but of performance of a contract. For this reason the legal issues involved with digital cash are examined under 'Performance: Payment' at **2.59**.

suggestion would have no commercial support unless the site was very worried about exposing itself to liability.

Website designers and legal advisers should work together to ensure that the contract is formed at the correct time. The contract will not work retroactively; if a website owner is concerned to exclude liability for material on his home page a contract should appear before the home page. From a designer's perspective, foisting a legal document on a new viewer may not be appropriate.[104] Ultimately the disciplines of law, design and IT must meet in the middle: the greater the risk of liability and infringement (outside an implied licence) the greater the need for a lawyer to ensure the site binds visitors to a contract. Many sites may well decide it is better to run the risk of there being no valid contract than to risk losing an annoyed visitor to a competing site.

Intention

2.57   The fourth and final ingredient to create a binding contract is an intention to create legal relations. The reason that this is a factor in resolving a contractual issue over the internet is that often only one human is involved. When a person makes an agreement with a website, the site accepts or rejects the communication by the person according to a computer program being run at the time. A human does not sit on the server side of the website. This raises the issue of how the contract can be formed without this direct intention. It is not complicated, nor unique to the internet, but is a factor which advisers should not overlook: bugs in these programs will not negative the owner's intention.

Programmed intention

2.58   In *Thornton v Shoe Lane Parking*[105] Mr Thornton accepted a contract by driving a car into a car park. In that case, Lord Denning stated that the automatic reaction of the car park turning a light from red to green and thrusting a ticket was enough to create a contract.[106] All the ingredients were present. It is of no legal consequence that the contract was physically completed by a machine. The court looks objectively to whether a contract can be said to have been made: has the user been induced reasonably to believe that a contract was being made or offered? In comparison, it is of no legal consequence that a computer program completes the contract over the internet; many contracts are 'made' with machines. That a computer program is being relied upon, however, can be of commercial significance to its owner.

Usually web-wrap contracts and automated email contracts use an express agreement. If, as a result of a bug in the contracting program, the viewer's offer is accepted in error, the court will presume that there was the requisite intention. The offeror has the heavy burden to prove that there was no intention to have

---

104 A contract in a frame and a simple home page can be an acceptable compromise.
105 [1971] 2 QB 163.
106 [1971] 2 QB 163 at 169.

a legal consequence.[107] The subjective opinion of, say, the owner of the website is of little consequence to the court,[108] unless the viewer knew of the lack of intention.

Example 2.14

For the payment of £10 a website allows its viewers to download pictures of a certain quality. An additional payment of £2 allows viewers to download the pictures at a higher resolution, which are more appropriate for professional use in brochures and magazines. An error in the Java script permits viewers to download any of the pictures for £10. The website owner will be hard pressed to claim the extra £2: the viewers are unlikely to know of the private intention.

Owners of websites who seek to use them for forming contracts should be aware that an error in their automated program may be of great financial consequence, as can be taken from the Kodak and Argos examples given in **2.51** above. Such validation programs should be carefully checked and, where possible, the owner should seek to obtain an indemnity from the programmer against such loss or, if not, insurance.

PERFORMANCE: PAYMENT

Internet payment

2.59   It has been discussed that the internet can be used to make an offer and accept that offer. What has not been explained is how the internet can be used to pay for the goods or services that may be the subject of the offer.

The introduction to this book explains in detail that everything passing through the internet consists of digital ones and zeros. What varies is the way that digital stream is translated into an item at the end of its journey. The same can be said for methods of payment: unless the payment is made outside the confines of the internet, the payment must be converted into zeros and ones.[109] There are two problems with this that do not concern us, but which are mentioned for completeness. The first problem is associated with the way the internet moves digital streams between computers: they do not move directly; they can pass through many different computers on their way to a destination. Passing money through unknown computers is clearly unsafe. The second problem is that if digital money consists of only ones and zeros in a long string, it may be easy to duplicate the money. Any computer could potentially become a forgery for digital bank notes.

The technical solutions to both these problems are being addressed by many companies across the world. There are many companies using sophisticated encryption methods to secure the payment technically. Internet browsers and

---

107   *Edwards v Skyways Ltd* [1964] 1 WLR 349 at 355.
108   See *Smith v Hughes* (1871) LR 6 QB 597.
109   A contract could be made over the internet and a cheque sent by conventional mail.

website servers allow credit card details to be sent over the internet securely; some companies issue what is, in effect, a digital travellers' cheque that can also be sent securely across the internet. To the banking industry, the European Central Bank, the Bank of England and banking lawyers this issue of cash is obviously both interesting and important. Indeed, it has prompted the Electronic Money Directive and requisite UK legislation.[110] For the seller, buyer and their lawyers these new 'forms' of payment do not have any dramatic impact on contract law. Regulators, policy makers and, eventually, courts will also have to grapple with electronic 'currencies' such as Bitcoin.

Credit card non-payment

2.60   That there is a contract must be distinguished from who should pay for the goods or services, and what happens if that payment does not arrive. With a charge or credit card, the customer, by presenting a valid card, or by issuing a valid set of numbers, honours his obligations under the contract. Of course, at this point, a further contract comes into existence between the card company and the user to pay to the card company the full sum under the vendor's contract. If the card company does not pay the vendor, and the card was valid, the vendor's right of action is against the card company, not the individual.[111] One justification for this is that if the vendor was entitled to pursue the customer for payment in cash, the customer would lose the benefit of the payment by credit and, often, the insurance over the goods.[112] This would therefore increase the burden on the customer.

The commercially safest way of trading over the internet is for vendors to insist on receiving and then validating payment before providing their side of the bargain. Terms to this effect should be incorporated into any standard form electronic commerce contract.

Digital cash non-payment

2.61   Digital cash has two species. The first, more primitive, is like a charge card. The issuing bank provides the payment to the vendor on presentation of appropriate authority. The sum is then withdrawn from the user's account and transferred to the vendor's. Over the internet this appropriate authority will be no more than the card number and, perhaps, its expiry date. This species can be called 'third party digital cash'. The second species of digital money is close to actual cash and will be called 'pure digital cash'. A customer has an agreement with

---

110 Directive 2000/46/EC on the taking up, pursuit of and prudential supervision of the business of electronic money institutions (and to a lesser extent, Directive (2000/28/EC)); The Financial Services and Markets Act 2000 (Regulated Activities) (Amendment) Order 2002; The Electronic Money (Miscellaneous Amendments) Regulations 2002.

111 *Re Charge Card Services Ltd* [1989] Ch 497, generally approved by the Court of Appeal in *Re Bank of Credit and Commerce International SA* (No 8) [1996] 2 All ER 121 at 133.

112 See, for example, the Consumer Credit Act 1974, s 75 which makes the credit card company liable for the vendor's misrepresentations and breaches of contract.

a digital cash provider[113] who allows the customer to send encrypted messages which represent sums of money. Once a customer sends one of these encrypted messages to a vendor, it can then be subsequently used by the vendor without having to go to the issuing bank for exchange into cash. The only time when the message will be exchanged into more regular currency is when someone seeks to deposit it in their bank. This new form of payment does not greatly strain existing contractual principles of payment.

Third-party digital cash

2.62   As with a credit card, it is likely that a court will find that the issuing company is liable for the payment, rather than the user.[114] This view is carefully stated as being 'likely'. Both vendor and user should consider that the Court of Appeal has concluded that, merely because a third party has agreed to make payment to a vendor does not automatically mean that the risk of non-payment is removed from the user.[115]

Pure digital cash

2.63   Paying by the second species of digital money can be thought of as sending cash for most legal purposes. If the encrypted sum is lost on the internet, or perhaps intercepted, the intended receiver will, no doubt, claim that payment has not been made. To some extent this is the general rule: sending a banknote in the post, which is lost, will not constitute payment.[116] However, this appears inequitable where the intended receiver expressly permits payment to be made by such a method. Indeed, there is followed authority that if the intended receiver impliedly, or as will be the situation over the internet, expressly, authorises transmission of payment in a particular way, the sender is discharged of liability if he follows the guidelines of transmission.[117]

Example 2.15

A website offers two methods for its viewers to pay to gain access to its materials: by credit card and by digital cash. A viewer sends by email the digital cash, accesses the materials, but the cash is never received. The viewer may not be liable to pay again. The site impliedly authorises its customers to pay using the internet as the conduit: the owner may not be able to transfer this risk to its customers having so authorised them.

If a website seeks to allow payment to be made using digital cash, in either species, it must face the reality that the sum may not arrive. It should therefore incorporate into its contracts a term stipulating that its performance under the

---

113 Or so-called Electronic Money Issuer pursuant to the Financial Services and Markets Act 2000 (Regulated Activities) (Amendment) Order 2002 and as discussed further in Chapter 9.
114 See 'Credit card non-payment', at **2.60**.
115 See *Re Charge Card Services Ltd* [1988] 3 All ER 702 at 707.
116 See *Luttges v Sherwood* (1895) 11 TLR 233.
117 *Norman v Ricketts* (1886) 3 TLR 182.

contract will be honoured only after receipt of the digital cash. Customers, in anticipation of this, should be wary of sending uninsured digital cash over the internet. If the contract is suitably worded and held enforceable, the customer may lose the money and not benefit from the contract.

TYPE OF CONTRACT

2.64 Many owners of websites do not only make contracts over the internet, but also try to perform them over the internet. Software companies distribute software from websites; information and picture libraries provide digital copies of their information. Movies and music are sent (and streamed) across the internet for payment. The various intellectual property rights that may vest in these items are discussed in the chapter on intellectual property. What is important here is to examine what should be the nature of the contract with the receiver of the digital information. The answer is a licence, and certainly not a sale, but justification for this is provided below. The first justification is to attempt to sidestep the principle of exhaustion of rights; the second, peculiar to digitised material, is to grant a licence to the user of the material.

Exhaustion of rights

2.65 If digitised copyright goods are sold, rather than licensed, within the EU there is a risk that the exhaustion of rights principle will apply. This principle is broadly that once goods protected by intellectual property rights are sold in any member state with the consent of the owner, national intellectual property laws cannot be used to block the goods' entry into another member state. The Copyright, Designs and Patents Act 1988 states this explicitly at s 27(5).

Retention of title

2.66 Partially as an attempt to avoid the application of this principle, many producers of digital material do not sell it; they license it. To avoid being viewed as selling the material many manufacturers include a 'shrink-wrap' licence, which explicitly retains title in the goods being passed to the consumer and states words to the effect, often in emboldened capitals, 'This software is not sold to you; we are licensing it to you'.

Using is copying

2.67 The material downloaded over the internet is likely to be given legal recognition and protection as a copyright work under the Copyright, Designs and

Patents Act 1988. It is this intellectual property right that forms the foundation for any transaction.

For digital material to be used, it may first be transferred into a computer's memory.[118] This transfer exactly reproduces in the memory of the computer the words and characters of the material sent from the server. The material on the server remains unchanged and intact; two copies of the material now exist. An obvious comparison is that when one views a painting, the painting remains on the canvas and there is no need to copy the work. A digital version of the same painting can only be viewed by being copied.

The Copyright, Designs and Patents Act 1988 grants certain rights to the owner of a copyright work. In particular, s 16(1)(a) states that the owner has the exclusive right to copy the work. Thus, without a licence from the owner, under s 16(2), copying the work can constitute infringement of the copyright in the work. Copying any copyright work is defined widely as reproducing the work as a whole, or any substantial part, in any material form. This includes storing the work in a medium by electronic means.[119]

The viewer of the actual painting, like the viewer of the digitised version, is able to enjoy viewing an artistic work which attracts copyright protection. However, the viewing of the canvas does not involve a reproduction of the work in a material form. It can be seen, therefore, that normal use of a painting does not copy the copyright work. Conversely, an accurate application of the Copyright, Designs and Patents Act 1988 suggests that normal usage of any downloaded material will be regarded as a copy of the copyright work. This is because the digitised material is necessarily reproduced by downloading it from the server into the computer's memory.

Implied licence

2.68   The above analysis may appear to indicate that if the owner of a website does not give an express licence to each viewer of the site, each viewer is an infringer. This is not the case: copying a copyright work is not infringement if there is a licence permitting that copying. In the situation of the internet there is undoubtedly a licence for authorised viewers and downloaders of material to copy the work.

First, the law is likely to imply a licence into the actions of the website owner for reasons of business necessity. Second, a court could apply the so-called 'rule of non-derogation from grant' to prevent the publisher, having supplied the material, then alleging infringement.[120] Third, but specifically for computer programs, the Directive on the Legal Protection of Computer Programs at art 5.1 specifies that the 'lawful acquirer' of a computer program shall not require authorisation by the copyright owner to run a computer program in the absence

---

118 This transfer is called 'loading'. This should not be confused with 'running' a program when a computer carries out the instructions specified by a program that has already been loaded.
119 Copyright, Designs and Patents Act 1988, ss 16(3)(a) and 17(2).
120 See *British Leyland v Armstrong* [1986] RPC 279.

of specific contractual provisions. Fourth, temporary copies of works other than new programs or databases will be permitted for lawful use of the work.[121]

Express licence

2.69   For programs, therefore, the Copyright, Designs and Patents Act 1988 expressly provides that a user has a right to copy the program into memory for its use. Until the implementation of the Copyright Directive, art 5.1, viewers of graphics and sound, movies and music, must rely on implications by the common law to legitimise their activities. Even after the implementation of art 5.1, non-temporary use will rely on common law. And for programs, graphics and sound alike, the supplier of those materials may have to accept a court's wide understanding of what type of licence is implied. For example, a designer of a graphic image used as a backdrop for a website frame may not want its viewers to copy the image onto their own publications. To expressly prevent these unwanted uses, owners of copyright material used on the internet are advised to use on-screen licences that leave no non-temporary uses of the material to doubt or disagreement.

In providing a licence over the copyright material some publishers go further to attempt to exclude liability for certain damage caused by the material. The efficacy of these exclusion clauses is examined in the chapter on tort, but one point is worth noting here. The English courts will not uphold every exclusion clause. This is particularly true where the clause excludes liability to a consumer.

The conclusion from this section is simple: publishers should include express licences over their digital work to avoid exhaustion of rights and disagreements over acceptable use of the work.

Auctions

2.70   There is no comprehensive definition of 'auction' in English statute, and yet determining whether or not a transaction has been conducted by one remains important in terms of contract law and certain consumer protection regulations.

The significance stems from the Sale of Goods Act 1979, which states that:

> 'A sale by auction is complete when the auctioneer announces its completion by the fall of the hammer, or in other customary manner; and until the announcement is made any bidder may retract his bid.'[122]

In effect, this sets when acceptance takes place and a binding contract formed, and the point up to which the bid or offer may be retracted.

---

121 See the Copyright, Designs and Patents Act 1988, ss 50A, 50B, 50C, inserted by the Copyright (Computer Programs) Regulations 1992, SI 1992/3233, reg 8. Also, art 5.1 of the EC Copyright Directive 2001.
122 Sale of Goods Act 1979, s 57(2).

This presents obvious problems for internet auction processes. Not only is a virtual hammer hard to pinpoint, but there is a real risk that individuals have to be given an opportunity to retract bids at any stage, requiring fast re-adjustments to current highest bid prices which simply may not be possible. Further, the running of traditional auctions involves consideration of various restrictions and obligations on the auctioneer which have been developed through case law, the establishment of a fiduciary duty to the vendor, and certain information and potential licence conditions that certain London boroughs impose on auctions conducted in their locale.

It is little wonder then that the 'auctions' we see in the internet arena, have sought to deviate from the traditional auction model, for example through the removal of an identifiable auctioneer, replacing this with a model that introduces vendors to potential buyers directly.

However, not being an auction presents its own problems. Auctions (again undefined) with business buyers are currently excluded from the implied terms requirements of the Unfair Contract Terms Act 1977 as to description, quality and fitness (provided there is a notice put up to this purpose and exclusions satisfy the reasonableness test).[123] The Consumer Protection (Distance Selling) Regulations 2000 also currently exempt auctions entirely and therefore the consequent prior and post-contract information requirements and the need to provide a cooling-off period to buyers (see **Chapter 9** for more details), do not apply.

Not only is there no statutory definition of an auction, but there has also been no case law on what constitutes an 'auction' for the purposes of references to them in English statutes (such as those listed above) to date. This leaves the position of such remodelled internet auctions somewhat unclear. In Germany, some clarity has been given in a judgment of the German Federal Court of Justice which held that a consumer buying from a business through eBay is granted a right to revocation of such contract,[124] even though the exemption for auctions has also been incorporated into Germany's implementing legislation of the Distance Selling Directive. In this judgment eBay was deemed not to be an auction.

It is becoming increasingly evident that further consideration of the status of such trading models is needed and this is, at the time of writing, a subject of discussion in the European Commission. It is reasonable that online auction models involving competitive bidding but following very different contractual structures to traditional auctions should be treated differently from their offline, physical counterparts however. Providing a right to renege on a deal made through an online auction at will potentially renders the outcome and indeed the involvement of genuine bid-placers in it, a farce.

---

123 Note that the Sale and Supply of Goods to Consumers Regulations 2002 amended the Unfair Contract Terms Act 1977 to apply protections to consumer buyers in respect of new goods and second-hand goods auctioned over the internet or by phone where the consumer cannot attend in purpose. See reg 14 of these Regulations amending s 12 of the Act.
124 *BGH Utreil* 3 November 2004 – VIII ZR 375/03.

JURISDICTION

2.71   Every contract may form the basis of a dispute. Because the internet allows an owner of a website to conduct transactions with consumers and businesses from anywhere on the planet it is convenient for that owner to know where he can rightfully sue and be sued. The question over where a contract should be litigated is a question of private international law, or the conflict of laws. It should also be remembered of course that the question as to where proceedings may be brought must be considered separately from questions of enforcement and the law which will govern such proceedings (issues covered in subsequent sections).

For the purpose of jurisdiction, it is important to consider first whether or not the parties to the contract made express provision as to which courts will hear a dispute and to establish the geographical elements relevant to the dispute in question in order to determine which rules need to be looked at and will determine the jurisdiction where no such binding choice was made. The Brussels Regulation on Jurisdiction and the Enforcement of Judgments in Civil and Commercial Matters is the appropriate starting place for any contract formed over the internet involving other European member states (Denmark signing up in 2007).[125] For European Free Trade Association (EFTA) countries, Switzerland, Iceland and Norway (with the exception of Liechtenstein), similar rules under the Lugano Convention regulate jurisdiction and enforcement issues. If outside of these, then English common law rules will apply.

First, therefore, one must assess whether the Brussels Regulation or Lugano Convention apply or whether it 'transfers' jurisdiction to the English common law and then to assess, accordingly what rules apply which will largely depend on whether the parties made an express choice and on the nature of the contract itself.

Brussels Regulation and Lugano Convention

Civil and commercial matter

2.72   Most contracts made over the internet will fall within art 1, that is, the resulting dispute is a civil and commercial matter. Before deciding that the Regulation applies, litigants are advised to consider specialist texts and cases from the European Court which highlight the broad scope of art 1 under the previous 1968 Brussels Convention.

Domicile of defendant

2.73   Subject to articles outside the scope of this chapter, the fundamental issue for the purposes of the Regulations and Lugano Convention is where the defendant is domiciled. Article 2 establishes that persons domiciled in a member

---

125 This entered into force, replacing the Brussels Convention, on 1 March 2002 (2001 OJ L012, 16.01.2001).

state[126] can be sued in the courts of that state, sometimes with the claimant having a choice of another forum. Articles 59 and 60 direct the English courts to consider the domicile of the defendant with reference to the UK's 'internal law'.[127] Even for e-commerce contracts, jurisdiction hinges on 'domicile', an essentially static concept which is mostly unrelated to the complex factors such as where a server is based.[128]

For Regulation purposes, a defendant can be domiciled in one of two types of state: a member state or a non-member state. If the defendant is domiciled within a member state, the Regulation rules apply; if outside, the common law rules or the rules of the Lugano Convention will apply. These two outcomes are decided, currently, with reference to the Civil Jurisdiction and Judgments Act 1982, as amended.

Individual's domicile

UK domicile

2.74 An individual is domiciled within the UK only if he is resident in the UK and the nature and circumstances of his residence indicate that he has a substantial connection with the UK.[129] It is presumed, unless proved otherwise, that being resident for the last three months or more will constitute the requisite substantial connection.[130] The ownership, control or access to a website anywhere in the world is wholly irrelevant for the purposes of jurisdiction over an individual under the Regulation. If an individual is a UK resident nothing will be gained for jurisdiction purposes by locating a web server 'offshore'.

Member state or EFTA state domicile

2.75 If an individual is not domiciled in the UK for the purposes of the Regulation, one must decide whether the individual is domiciled within another member state. If he is not domiciled in a member state, the Regulation will not apply to the dispute.

An individual is domiciled in a state other than the UK if that other state would view him as domiciled in that state. Therefore, to determine whether a defendant in an internet contract dispute is domiciled within a member state that person's domicile must be assessed from that state's legal perspective.[131] Failing this, the Civil Jurisdiction and Judgments Act 1982 (as amended), s 41(7) establishes the test to determine whether a defendant is domiciled outside member states.

---

126 Ie any member state and excluding Switzerland, Iceland and Norway which (as EFTA countries) apply the rules of the 1988 Lugano Convention.
127 The Civil Jurisdiction and Judgments Act 1982 (as amended by both the Civil Jurisdiction and Judgments Act 1991 and the Civil Jurisdiction and Judgments Order 2001), ss 4 and 42.
128 Prescribed as being relevant tests by the Civil Procedure Rules 1998, rr 6.18(g) and 6.19(1).
129 Civil Jurisdiction and Judgments Act 1982 (as amended by both the Civil Jurisdiction and Judgments Act 1991 and the Civil Jurisdiction and Judgments Order 2001), s 41(2).
130 Civil Jurisdiction and Judgments Act 1982 (as amended by both the Civil Jurisdiction and Judgments Act 1991 and the Civil Jurisdiction and Judgments Order 2001), s 41(6).
131 Brussels Regulation, art 59(2).

For those domiciled in EFTA countries (other than Liechtenstein), the Lugano Convention applies similar rules.

Non-member state or EFTA state domicile

2.76   An individual is domiciled outside all the EFTA and EU member states if none of those states would deem him to be domiciled within their jurisdiction and if a further two-part test is satisfied. First, the individual must be resident in the non-member state, and second, the nature and circumstances of his residence indicate that he has a substantial connection with that state.[132] One is not required to consult the non-member state's law on domicile.

Example 2.16

An English programmer who lives in England allows downloads of his shareware programs to be made from an American web server. Another programmer, also from England, appropriately transfers his digital cash payment for the software but does not receive a working copy of the software and so litigates. Without a jurisdiction clause in the contract, the English courts will have jurisdiction over the dispute as the defendant is domiciled in England. The location of the server is of no relevance for jurisdiction over the programmer in the English courts.

If the result of the domicile tests is that an individual defendant is domiciled within a member state, the Regulation will apply to any other questions of jurisdiction. If the result is that the defendant is domiciled outside the member states, the English common law rules on jurisdiction will apply.[133] These are described after the Regulation regime.[134]

Company's or other legal person's domicile

2.77   A company or other legal person has its domicile in the state where it has its statutory seat, or central administration, or principal place of business.[135] A sole trader or partner in a business being sued on his own can be sued where his principal residence is (see the rules for individuals above).

UK domicile

2.78   A company or other legal person is domiciled within the UK if it was incorporated or formed under a law of a part of the UK, and its registered office or other official address is in the UK; or if its central administration or principal place of business is in the UK.[136] Again, the ownership, control or access to a website anywhere in the world is mostly irrelevant for the purposes of jurisdiction

---

132 Civil Jurisdiction and Judgments Act 1982 (as amended by both the Civil Jurisdiction and Judgments Act 1991 and the Civil Jurisdiction and Judgments Order 2001), s 41(7).
133 Art 4.
134 See 'Common law jurisdiction over contracts', at **2.88**.
135 Art 60(1).
136 Civil Jurisdiction and Judgments Act 1982 (as amended by both the Civil Jurisdiction and Judgments Act 1991 and the Civil Jurisdiction and Judgments Order 2001), s 42(2).

under the Regulation. A corporation which is, in effect, based in the UK will not be able to avoid the jurisdiction of the English courts simply by using an offshore server.

Member state or EFTA state domicile

2.79   If a company or other legal person is not domiciled in the UK for the purposes of the Regulation, one must decide whether it is domiciled within another member state or EFTA state. If it is not, the Regulation or Lugano Convention will not apply to the dispute; questions of jurisdiction are decided with recourse to the common law. A company or other legal person is domiciled in a state other than the UK if it satisfies two tests.

First, the English courts must be satisfied that the company or other legal person was incorporated or formed under the law of that other member state, or, its central management and control is exercised in that state.[137]

The second test that must also be affirmatively answered, is that the entity shall not have been incorporated or formed under the law of a part of the UK, or, shown not to be regarded by the courts of the other member state or EFTA state to have its seat within that member state.[138] If either test is not satisfied, the common law rules on jurisdiction will apply;[139] these are discussed after the Regulation rules.

Example 2.17

A health-food company is incorporated and operates from England. It sells edible flowers across the world. Its server is physically based in New Zealand and the domain name has a suffix indicating a New Zealand firm. A French supplier of health food enters into a contract, over the internet, for a large shipment of particular sweet edible flowers. The contract does not have a jurisdiction clause. The flowers do not arrive and the health-food company claims it is not at fault. The French supplier tries to sue the company in the English courts. The use of an offshore server will have no bearing on the court's jurisdiction over the company. The English courts will have jurisdiction over the company at least for the reason that it would consider the company as having its seat within England.

Non-member state or EFTA state domicile

2.80   If both of the previous tests fail to establish the defendant as domiciled in the UK or another member state or EFTA state, the common law rules on jurisdiction will apply.

---

137 Civil Jurisdiction and Judgments Act 1982 (as amended by both the Civil Jurisdiction and Judgments Act 1991 and the Civil Jurisdiction and Judgments Order 2001), s 43(3).
138 Civil Jurisdiction and Judgments Act 1982 (as amended by both the Civil Jurisdiction and Judgments Act 1991 and the Civil Jurisdiction and Judgments Order 2001), s 43(4).
139 Art 4.

Regulation jurisdiction over contract

2.81   Having decided that the Regulation or Lugano Convention applies (all involving 'contracting states'), unless the contract is classed as a consumer, insurance or employment contract or unless the contract has a jurisdiction clause, the defendant may be sued in the courts of his domicile[140] or 'in the courts for the place of performance of the obligation in question'.[141]

Place of performance for sale of goods or supply of services

2.82   For sales of goods and supplies of services unless agreed otherwise, there are two presumptions as to the place of their performance. Where goods are sold (or should have been sold) under contract, the relevant court is in the place in a contracting state where the goods were delivered or should have been delivered. In the case of services, a similar approach must be followed. The relevant court is the one in the contracting state where the services were provided or should have been provided.[142] If neither presumption applies, one must look to resolve the more general question of where was the 'place of performance of the obligation in question'.[143]

Example 2.18

A website called StockTaken.de operates from and is based in Germany. It allows business users to specify what industrial equipment they need and at what price. Once sufficient numbers of buyers have pledged an interest in particular equipment, an invoice is issued to the buyers and the equipment shipped to them. There is no jurisdiction clause in the agreements between StockTaken.de and its buyers. A business in England receives the equipment it ordered, faulty. Despite StockTaken.de being based in Germany, it may be sued in the English courts as its principal obligation, breached, must have been to deliver non-defective equipment in England.[144]

Example 2.19

OurFastParts.com operates an EU business-to-business website allowing its members to barter parts for vehicles. No money changes hands. One member, the Seller, lists the parts he wants to 'sell' and other members, the Buyers, will bid for those parts using their own parts which they want to sell. After a certain period, the Seller may conclude his barter with a Buyer. To avoid disputes about which is the relevant court for this bilateral delivery of goods, the member agreement states that 'the Parties irrevocably agree that for the purposes of the Brussels Regulation, Article 5, the place of performance of the obligation to trade the Parts shall be the place in the Member State where the Seller delivered or should have delivered his Parts'.

---

140 Art 2(1).
141 Art 5(1)(a).
142 Art 5(1)(b).
143 Art 5(1)(c).
144 See *MBM Fabri Clad Ltd v EisenUnd Huntle werke Thale AG* (3 November 1999, unreported), CA.

Other obligations

2.83   Where the contract does not relate to sales of goods or supplies of services, one must concentrate on the 'obligation in question'. Lord Goff puts this as 'regard must be had to the contractual obligation under consideration and not to the contract as a whole'.[145] This may result in a court which does not have the closest connection with the dispute being seized of the action. It should therefore be obvious that the pleading of the contractual claim, or rather, the principal contractual obligation, is critical to any question of jurisdiction. Further, advisers should note that to determine what is the principal obligation, they might rely on what law would apply to the obligation.[146]

Europe-based owners of websites who are concerned about being sued outside their home state should therefore be concerned to have jurisdiction clauses in their contracts if their principal obligations must be performed outside their home state[147] or if their e-commerce agreements are with consumers. As will be discussed, consumers can sue and can only be sued in their home state.[148] As many of the users of the internet are consumers but the majority of website owners are suppliers or professionals, this application of jurisdiction will frequently occur. Those who own websites, therefore, may find themselves having to litigate and be sued away from home.

Consumer contracts

2.84   At first glance it may appear there is a straightforward answer to the question of which is the correct forum for a dispute over a contract made with a consumer. The Brussels Regulation contains rules to protect consumers in relation to consumer contracts, from being sued, or having to sue, otherwise than in the member state of their domicile.[149] What is important is that art 15 of the Brussels Regulation defines a 'consumer contract', *inter alia*, as one concluded

---

145 *Union Transport plc v Continental Lines SA* [1992] 1 WLR 15 at 19H, referring to *Etablissements A de Bloos SPRL v Societes en Commandité par Actions Bayer* (Case 14/76) [1976] ECR 1497. Also see *Custom Made Commercial Ltd v Stawa Metallban GmbH* (C– 288/92) [1994] ECR I–2913, paras 14–23 and *Barry v Bradshaw and Co (a firm)* [2000] CLC 455, CA. Note the reluctance of Lord Justice Pitt to accept that: 'When a professional man is instructed to perform services in one jurisdiction he becomes liable to another Brussels Convention jurisdiction if the services include dealing with a public authority in that other jurisdiction'.

146 *Industrie Tessili Italiana Corp v Dunlop* (Case 12/76) [1976] ECR 1473, para 13; *Custom Made Commercial Ltd v Stawa Metallban GmbH* (C–288/92) [1994] ECR I–2913, para 26; *GIE Groupe Concorde v Master of Vessel Suhadiwarno Panjan* (C–440/97) [1999] ECR I–6307, para 32; *Leathertex Divisione Sinitetici SpA v Bodetex BVBA* (C–420/97) [1999] 2 All ER (Comm) 769.

147 See *MBM Fabri Clad Ltd v Eisen Und Huntle werke Thale AG* (3 November 1999, unreported), CA.

148 Arts 15, 16 and 17.

149 Brussels Convention, arts 13 and 14, and the Brussels Regulation, arts 15 and 16. The Civil Jurisdiction and Judgments Act 1982, s 8(1) and (2) (as amended by the Civil Jurisdiction and Judgments Order 2001) specifies that, in the UK, the courts where a consumer must be sued and can sue are those in the 'part' of the UK where they are domiciled. At the time of writing the three parts are: England and Wales, Scotland and Northern Ireland.

which can be regarded as being outside the consumer's trade or profession[150] where the contract is:

(a)   for the sale of goods on instalment credit terms; or[151]

(b)   for a loan repayable by instalments, or for any other form[152] of credit, made to finance the sale of goods; or

(c)   in all other cases, the contract has been concluded with a person who pursues commercial or professional activities in the member state of the consumer's domicile, or, by any means, directs such activities to that state or the several states including that state, and the contract falls within the scope of such activities.[153]

Article 15(1)(c) was introduced into the Brussels Regulation. It broadened the definition of a consumer contract which existed under art 13 of the Brussels Convention and which still exists in the Lugano Convention. These refer to the conclusion of the contract being preceded by a specific invitation addressed to the consumer or by advertising and where the consumer took steps necessary for the conclusion of that contract. The reason for the new concept of 'consumer contract' was to ensure that consumers who transact, for example, over the internet are protected by the special rules on jurisdiction.[154]

Articles 15(1)(a) and (b) are self-explanatory and not 'internet' specific. The same is not true for art 15(1)(c). This new addition to the Brussels rules of jurisdiction was meant to provide certainty to consumer and to businesses. As the following discussion will illustrate, it does not. Fortunately there are steps that businesses can take to minimise the risk of being sued in a member state other than their own or one acceptable to them.

The express right of a consumer to bring an action in their home jurisdiction under art 15(1)(c) of the Brussels Regulation can apply in two situations. First, where the supplier 'pursues commercial or professional activities in the member state of the consumer's domicile and the contract falls within the scope of such activities'. The second situation is where the supplier 'by any means directs commercial or professional activities to the member state of the consumer's domicile or to several States including that member state and the contract falls within the scope of such activities'. These two situations will be examined separately.

Pursuing activities in consumer's member state

2.85   A key aspect to this situation is that the contract being litigated must fall within the scope of the activities being pursued in the member state

---

150 Brussels Regulation, art 15(1).
151 Brussels Regulation, art 15(1)(a).
152 Brussels Regulation, art 15(1)(b).
153 Brussels Regulation, art 15(1)(c).
154 See, for example, the various speakers reported in the Department of Trade and Industry's Consumer Affairs Report on the Revision of the Brussels Convention and the Proposals for a Community Regulation (2 November 1999).

of the consumer's domicile. This is important. Many businesses conduct a great number of commercial and professional activities abroad. A website may promote employment opportunities for individuals living in the member state. Glossy advertisements in financial newspapers within that member state may also promote the business in a wider sense. On paper, the business may appeal to current and potential shareholders and stakeholders in the business. The business may also regularly attend trade fairs and exhibitions in the member state to illustrate the business's success, almost as a way to ward off competitors. And all these activities may be actively pursued within the consumer's member state.

What art 15(1)(c) requires, however, is something more. The pursuit of the activities within the consumer's member state must relate to the consumer's contract under dispute.[155]

Example 2.20

Ionise is an Italian company that operates a website selling its biochemical, free-standing, air-conditioning unit. The unit is expensive but is very popular in small offices in London. Ionise regularly attend trade shows in the UK where it communicates with its local distributors. Without any other activity in the UK, consumers who order a unit for their home will not benefit from the additional protection afforded by the Brussels Regulation.

Many European businesses will wish to be selective as to which member states' jurisdictions they are subject. These businesses must examine all of their activities within each particular contracting member state of concern. They will need to ensure that any contracts entered into with consumers in that contracting member state are not related to any other commercial or professional activities pursued in those member states.

By any means directs activities to several member states

2.86   This second leg of art 15(1)(c) begs the obvious question: when is a website 'directed' to several member states? This question is partially settled by the decision of the CJEU in *Lokman Emrek v Vlado Sabranovic*,[156] although this decision is not without controversy (and at odds with previous guidance published by the Commission) and it would seem that many such cases will turn on their own facts. What is apparent from *Lokman* is that there need be no causative link between the fact that a website is accessible in a particular location and the consumer ultimately transacting through the website. In *Lokman*, a French car dealer located near the German border made various modifications to his practices, such as having a German mobile phone, to

---

155 The European Council and Commission's Joint Statement on arts 15 and 68 states that 'for Article 15.1(c) to be applicable it is not sufficient for an undertaking to target it's [sic] activities at the member state of the consumer's residence, or at a number of member states including that member state; a contract must also be concluded within the framework of it's [sic] activities'.
156 [2013] EUECJ C-218/12.

encourage German clients to buy from him. The buyer however, had never visited the website having been directed to the seller by recommendations from friends.

The CJEU held that no causative link was required, merely that the website should be directed to several member states per se. The decision is explained on the grounds that to come to any other conclusion would run counter to the consumer protection impetus contained in art 15(1)(c) and that to read it otherwise would be to needlessly read into it an 'unwritten condition'.

The decision in *Lokman*, however, still does not fully address the question of when a website is directing activities to several member states. As noted above, this question is likely only to be answered based on the evidence available in each individual case, however, some guidance may be derived from the Joint Statement issued by the European Council and Commission which states:

> 'the mere fact that an internet site is accessible is not sufficient for Article 15 to be applicable, although a factor will be that this internet site solicits the conclusion of distance contracts and that a contract has actually been concluded at a distance, by whatever means. In this respect, the language or currency which a website uses does not constitute a relevant factor.'

One takes from this that it is the conduct of commerce in the member state that determines whether or not activities are directed to that member state. If those from the UK, for instance, cannot transact with the site (but can still view it) it would seem that the Council and Commission deem this not to be 'directed' at the UK. And this is even the case if the site is written in English and uses pounds sterling and not euros. This can be contrasted with the view taken by the UK government who offer a more e-commerce-friendly interpretation:

> 'We believe that [to determine whether a website falls within Article 15(1)(c)]:
>
> • it would be necessary to look at the nature of any given website;
>
> • websites giving information in different Community languages and currencies and offering to deliver to EU countries might well be covered by Article 15;
>
> • some websites (eg a site in English with prices in pounds and confining orders to UK customers) might be hard to describe as directed anywhere but the UK.'

The UK government here appears to be taking a narrower view than the European Council and Commission. It is essentially concluding that the mere fact that a transaction takes place on a site does not mean that the site has been directed at any particular member state. It is the 'nature' of the website that determines where, if anywhere, it is directed.

These are very different approaches. The Council and Commission explain that one must avoid transacting with consumers in a particular member state; the UK government explains that one must avoid appealing to consumers in a particular member state. Given the very wide reading given to the article recently by the CJEU in *Lokman*, it would seem that the Commission's interpretation may well prevail.

On this basis, how does one structure a website to avoid the bite of art 15(1)(c)? It is not trivial. Nevertheless, steps can be taken to reduce a business's chance of transacting over the internet with consumers within a particular member state. First, the business can operate a website which requests the user's jurisdiction from a 'drop-down' menu or a series of flags. This allows the business to shield out a consumer from a particular country. More sophisticated still, a business can make technical checks of the user's computer and connecting server. For example, the business can check for the server time zone and the language setting of the user's browser. In addition, the business can conduct a 'reverse DNS lookup' where the domain name of the user's service provider is used to locate the server. Not one of these steps is foolproof. Combined, however, these checks can provide a reasonable approximation of whether the user is based in a 'friendly' member state. If they are not based in the 'friendly' member states, make sure not to transact with them after they access the site.

Example 2.21

'NotWeeMen' is a company arranging adventure activities in the Scottish Highlands. The company has two main types of clientele: businesses conducting 'away days' in the UK and men arranging stag nights in Glasgow city centre. It ensures that all of its advertising outside the UK is about 'corporate bonding' and is contained in business journals. Its website, in contrast, solely describes the stag activities, is written only in English and features a price list of 'stag activities' in pounds sterling. It also details the various trains and planes that fly from around the UK to Glasgow. The company does not pursue the 'stag' activities in the EU by virtue of its advertising.

Jurisdiction clauses: express choice

2.87   Parties to a contract are generally free to choose which court(s) will consider any disputes arising under the contract. An English court will usually regard a court in a member state or an EFTA state as having exclusive jurisdiction over a dispute where the parties to a contract have prescribed it in the contract.[157] However, there are a few twists and exceptions to parties' right to choose.

Contracts involving consumers, or even employees or in rare cases, where a local court is deemed to have special expertise for the matter in question, may have a different outcome regardless of what the parties have agreed. The position in relation to consumer contracts where a jurisdiction clause can only add to but not derogate from the protection afforded to consumers[158] is set out below.

In addition, two European Court of Justice cases have cast a significant shadow on the comfort that exclusive jurisdiction clauses may previously have given, even where the exceptions set out above do not apply. Both cases concerned the application of art 27 of the Brussels Regulation, which provides that, where proceedings regarding the same cause of action are brought in the courts of different contracting states, any court other that the court first seized of the action

---

157 Brussels Regulation, art 23(1).
158 Brussels Regulation, art 17. Also see *Benincasa v Dentalkit Srl* [1998] All ER (EC) 135.

should stay proceedings until the first court has established jurisdiction, following which the other court must decline it. In the case of *Erich Gasser GmbH v MISAT SRL*,[159] MISAT brought proceedings in the Italian courts against Erich Gasser despite the inclusion of an exclusive jurisdiction clause in the contract between them in respect of the Austrian courts. Gasser brought proceedings seven months later in the Austrian courts claiming exclusive jurisdiction pursuant to art 23 of the Brussels Regulation. The ECJ held that the Austrian courts had to stay proceedings whilst the Italian courts decided whether or not they had jurisdiction, despite the parties' previous express choice.

This decision was endorsed in the case of *Turner v Grovit*,[160] in which the ECJ held that anti-suit injunctions (interim orders preventing another party from pursuing parallel proceedings in a foreign court) were incompatible with the Brussels Convention as relates to contracting states.

The conclusion from these two cases is that parties may now bring proceedings quickly in a foreign court for tactical reasons, despite being bound to a contractual agreement only to bring an action in another court in order to frustrate actions being brought there. Even though the initial proceedings may ultimately fail, this requires the other party to contest it and will, at the very least, lead to increased cost and wasted time.

Example 2.22

A UK consumer downloads some software from a French website after selecting an icon labelled 'I Agree' at the bottom of a set of terms and conditions. The contract makes clear that no goods are being sent to the consumer and that, anyway, no title passes to the consumer; the consumer is gaining only a licence to use the software. The final clause of the contract, in capitals, is 'By clicking "I Agree", you submit to the French courts to resolve any dispute arising under or related to this licence'. The consumer at a later date seeks to sue in an English court the owner of the website for breach of contract as the software is defective. The French website owner may have some success in preventing the English courts from accepting jurisdiction because the contract was a licence of software not a contract for a sale of goods or supply of services. As a result the jurisdiction clause may apply despite the contract being with a consumer.

Common law jurisdiction over contracts

2.88   If the defendant to an internet contract is not domiciled within a contracting state,[161] the court must apply its domestic laws to determine jurisdiction.[162] The main method is considered below: service out of the jurisdiction with permission. The aspect of this is jurisdiction to serve out the next, the application of the courts' discretion.[163] Service by presence in England is not considered in any

---

159   *Erich Gasser GmbH v MISAT SRL* [2005] QB 1.
160   *Turner v Grovit* [2004] All ER (EC) 485.
161   See 'Domicile of defendant', at **2.73**.
162   Art 4.
163   See 'Discretion under service out' at **2.94**.

detail;[164] readers are advised to consult more general texts on private international law.

Service out

2.89   There are two separate and distinct aspects to serving out of the jurisdiction.[165] The first aspect is jurisdiction: does the claimant's claim fall within one of the sub-rules of CPR r 6.20(5) and (6). Although not yet deeply analysed by the courts, it is likely that this test does not need to be satisfied to any high degree of proof: a good arguable case that the claim is covered by one of the sub-rules is probably sufficient.[166] The second aspect, which will not be covered here in great detail, is one of discretion: no permission to serve a claim out of the jurisdiction will be given unless the court is satisfied that England and Wales is the proper place in which to bring the claim. This is specified by CPR r 6.21(2A).

Jurisdiction under a contract sub-rule

2.90   The most common sub-rules that will apply in certain cases for e-commerce contracts entered over the internet is CPR r 6.20(5). This is where:[167]

'a claim is made in respect of a contract where the contract ...'

The rule then goes on to describe a number of contracts which will fall for consideration under this rule. These include: a contract made within the jurisdiction; a contract made by or through an agent trading or residing within the jurisdiction; a contract containing a term that the court shall have jurisdiction to determine any claim made in respect of a breach of contract within the jurisdiction. For the purposes of internet contracts, however, the most contentious rule is where the contract was made within the jurisdiction.

Where a contract is made

2.91   The earlier part of this chapter focuses on when a contract is deemed to have been made when formed by email or over the web. It is now appropriate to consider where such a contract is formed. The implications of where a contract is formed are great. For example, if contracts made over the web are made at the place of the server it will be simple for an organisation always to ensure that their contracts are formed outside Europe, or any other jurisdiction they wish to avoid. A server can be physically located anywhere in the world despite its owner and clients being elsewhere. Conversely, if a contract is deemed to be formed wherever a consumer is situated at the time of making a contract the owner of a website may find himself making contracts throughout the world.

---

164 See CPR, r 6.2.
165 See *Seaconsar v Bank Merkazi Jomhouri Islami Iran* [1994] 1 AC 438, which applied, and it is suggested remains applicable, under the old Rules of the Supreme Court, Ord 11.
166 See *Attock Cement Co Ltd v Romanian Bank for Foreign Trade* [1989] 1 All ER 1189, which applied, and it is suggested remains still applicable, under the old Rules of the Supreme Court, Ord 11.
167 Of course, CPR r 6.20(1) and r 6.20(8) may be more appropriate in some circumstances.

There is no case law on this area although by analogy it is submitted that contracts made using email will be viewed as being made where the acceptance (not acknowledgement) email is sent and contracts made over the web will be viewed as being made where the client is located.

Email contracts

2.92   It has been suggested that an emailed acceptance is very like a posted acceptance in the eyes of the law: it can go astray and it depends on the actions of a third party for proper delivery without the sender necessarily knowing of its arrival.[168] In such circumstances this chapter has suggested that the exception should apply to the general rule of 'communication of acceptance': the so-called 'postal rule' should apply deeming the time of making the contract the time of its posting, not its receipt. It follows that the contract is completed when the letter is posted, or for our purposes, when the email is sent. This author's view is that the Electronic Commerce Regulations add little to the private international law question of where a contract is formed.[169]

The 'postal rule' also applies if an acceptance is not simply delayed in the post but if the acceptance never reaches the offeror.[170] It must therefore be true that the contract is also made at that place of posting; if this were not the case, a letter which becomes lost in the post may be deemed to form a contract at a place where it was meant to arrive at a time before it could have arrived and, in fact, at a place where it never arrives. To avoid such fictions, the rule applied by the English courts has been that 'acceptance is complete as soon as the letter is put into the letter box, and that is the place where the contract is made'.[171]

For a contract made purely using email, it is submitted that the place where the contract is made is the place from where the acceptor sent the email; it is not from where the server which sends the email is located. Just as a postal contract is made from the place at which the acceptor no longer has control over the letter (ie the letterbox), so the place where an email contract is made is at the acceptor's computer.

Website contracts

2.93   Contracts made over the web, as previously examined, differ considerably from email contracts.[172] On the assumption made earlier that the general rule applies, and that there is no binding contract until notice of acceptance is able

---

168 See 'Acceptances by email', at **2.44**.
169 See Electronic Commerce Regulations 2002, reg 5 and Electronic Commerce Directive, art 1(4).
170 See *Household Fire and Carriage Accident, Insurance v Grant* (1879) 4 Ex D 216.
171 *Entores Ltd v Miles Far East Corpn* [1955] 2 QB 327 at 332, per Denning LJ. See also *Benaim v Debono* [1924] AC 514. This common law rule should be contrasted with the Electronic Commerce (EC Directive) Regulations 2002, reg 11(2) which specifies when an order (which may be the acceptance) is deemed to be received.
172 See 'Acceptances over the Web', at **2.49**.

to be accessed by the offeror, the contract is made at the place where the offeror could receive notification of the acceptance; where the offeror is.[173]

Example 2.23

An American, who uses a German Internet Service Provider, sends an email to an English property developer. The email contains a certain offer to buy the individual's holiday home in Florida. The English property developer firmly accepts the offer by sending an email from his London offices. Technically, this email acceptance is sent from London, to a French server and then on to the American's inbox located in Germany. The American reads the email using a laptop computer and a mobile phone while in Mexico. If the contract is deemed to be formed when the English email was sent, it will be formed at the place where it was sent: London.

Example 2.24

A bookseller based in Chicago establishes a website within a portal which is based in New York. The portal uses a standardised online order form which ensures users make offers which are then accepted, if appropriate, by the individual stores. A teacher in England orders two books by American authors and the website responds with an acceptance notice that the books would be delivered to the teacher's address. This contract is made in England because the notification of acceptance, to the teacher, is received in England.

The conclusion that a website 'makes' contracts wherever its customers are, assuming the website accepts and properly acknowledges acceptance, accords with the case law and also accords with the business reality of the web. The web, more than any other medium, allows vendors from around the world to sell easily to English consumers. For a vendor, it is akin to having an agent in every town in the world who can visit every customer at home. A user only needs to make a local phone call to and receive acceptances from foreign vendors at home. The contracts being formed have every indication that they are being made in England.

The reason for discussing where a contract is made, it will be recalled, was to demonstrate that an English consumer could serve a claim form out of England to a foreign website owner in respect of a contract. However, even if a dispute falls within one of the sub-rules under CPR r 6.20 a court has discretion whether to permit the service out.

Discretion under service out

2.94   It is not sufficient simply to satisfy a court of a good arguable case under one of the sub-rules under CPR r 6.20. The claim must also be a proper case for service out under CPR r 6.21(1). The discretion to serve out includes

---

173 See *Entores v Miles Far East Corpn* [1955] 2 QB 327 at 336 per Parker LJ; also *Brinkibon Ltd v Stahag Stahl GmbH* [1983] 2 AC 34 at 41 and 43 respectively, per Lord Wilberforce and Lord Fraser.

as a main factor, an assessment, perhaps not overtly, of whether England is the *forum conveniens*, the most suitable forum in which to hear the dispute. This will be considered briefly in the following section on staying actions.[174] This discretionary factor should not be overlooked by legal advisers: for a contract made over the internet it may be difficult to persuade a court to serve out. If the defendant, in contrast, is domiciled in Europe, the court has far less discretion over jurisdiction.[175]

Staying actions

2.95　It is always open to a putative defendant to apply to stay the common law jurisdiction of the English courts by pleading that it is not the most suitable forum in which to resolve the dispute.[176] Whether a court stays an action is decided with recourse to the principle of *forum non conveniens*. This principle is impressively explained and stated in the House of Lords decision in *Spiliada Maritime Corpn v Cansulex Ltd*.[177] In a later case Lord Goff explains *forum non conveniens* as 'a self-denying ordinance under which the court will stay (or dismiss) proceedings in favour of another clearly more appropriate forum'.[178] A full discussion of this case is beyond the scope of this chapter, but an appreciation of its implications is worthwhile. Until courts approach electronic commerce and internet disputes with the familiarity and understanding that they approach, say the telephone and telex, litigators must be prepared to argue that despite the transnational nature of the internet, some forums are more suitable than others.

Lord Goff provided the leading judgment given in *Spiliada*. He set out a number of guidelines[179] that may guide a court as to whether England is a suitable and appropriate forum: the court must, in effect, balance the suitability of England against that of another forum. This forum must be clearly and distinctly more appropriate: one 'with which the action [has] the most real and substantial connection'.[180] At this point, 'the court may nevertheless decline to grant a stay if persuaded by the claimant, on whom the burden of proof then lies, that justice requires that a stay should not be granted'.[181]

This discretion, unlikely to be disturbed on appeal,[182] may be of paramount importance in an internet dispute. In contrast to most other means of communication, the internet can make it appear that a defendant has little connection with any country. A server may be in a country far away from the

---

174　The court's assessment is the same, although for service out, the claimant must ask the court to exercise discretion; for staying service as of right, the defendant must persuade the court to stay the action.

175　See the Court of Appeal's interpretation of the Civil Jurisdiction and Judgments Act 1982, s 49 in *Re Harrods (Buenos Aires) Ltd* [1992] Ch 72.

176　CPR, Pt 11 provides the necessary procedure.

177　[1987] AC 460.

178　*Airbus Industrie GIE v Patel* [1999] 1 AC 119 at 132C.

179　The necessary details of these guidelines can be found in specialist texts but readers are also directed to the very full judgments in *Lubbe v Cape plc* [2001] 1 Lloyd's Rep 139, CA.

180　*The Abidin Daver* [1984] 1 All ER 470, at 478 per Lord Keith.

181　*Connelly v RTZ Corpn plc* [1998] AC 854 at 872A, per Lord Goff for the House of Lords restating the second stage of the *Spiliada* test.

182　[1986] 3 All ER 843 at 846–847 per Lord Templeman.

defendant's domicile. Worse than this, a defendant may be using a hosting company situated on the other side of the world. The contract and possibly digital product that is the root of the dispute may have passed through as many as one hundred countries. Worse still, it is a question of technical semantics to resolve whether the digital product moved from the server to the claimant, whether the claimant 'collected' the digital product from the server, or even streamed.

These issues, and many more like them, may be used to cloud the answer to which is the *forum conveniens* for the dispute. The pivotal question before the courts should be: which is the suitable forum in the interests of all the parties and the ends of justice?

The answering of this question involves examining the mechanics of hearing the dispute as well as its geographical basis. In illustration, often it is important to know where the relevant evidence is held and where the relevant witnesses live.[183] For many internet disputes, however, such factors may not be weighty enough to disturb the jurisdiction of the court. Computer files will often be the main evidence and often the party in England will be the sole human witness to the contract itself. So, for an internet dispute, the jurisdiction of the English court may be less easily upset. As a further illustration, the issue of convenience, often a factor for the court, may be less convincing when all of the actual evidence is in a digital format. Such evidence can be sent to England, over the internet, cheaply, quickly and accurately. Again, the actual nature of the internet may lead to the conclusion that little is lost by hearing the dispute in England.

The court must consider all the relevant factors, such as where the defendant and claimant are and which law will apply to this dispute. It is discussed in the next section that, without a choice of law clause, English law will generally apply to contracts made over the web with English consumers. Even with a choice of law clause, protection for English consumers will apply in addition to the stated law. And Lord Goff in *Spiliada* notes that the law of the dispute will often be a relevant factor.[184] What can be concluded from all this is that presence of the internet in a contract dispute will never create the situation where no court is appropriate to hear the case.

CHOICE OF LAW

2.96 Even as long ago as 1980, debates were commencing around the problems of examining the choice of law over computer networks such as the internet:[185]

183 See [1986] 3 All ER 843 at 855.
184 With reference to *Crédit Chimique v James Scott Engineering Group Ltd* 1982 SLT 131. In this Scottish case, Lord Jauncey goes further and asks that a court look not simply at the fact that foreign law will be applied, but to look deeper at the nature of the foreign law. It may be that it is trivial for an English court to turn its mind to the foreign law, but it also may be that the law is so alien that the most appropriate court to consider the legal issues is a court which regularly deals with them.
185 Organisation for Economic Co-operation and Development, Explanatory Memorandum, Guidelines on the Protection of Privacy and Transborder Flows of Personal Data, 13, 36 (1980).

'[T]he question of choice of law ... is particularly difficult in the case of international computer networks where, because of dispersed location and rapid movement of data, and geographically dispersed processing activities, several connecting factors could occur in a complex manner involving elements of legal novelty.'

The following section is included because the internet makes the questions of choice of laws more prevalent. As e-commerce expands, more contracts will be formed between parties in different jurisdictions.[186] It is essential that the law which applies to a contract is established before applying the reasoning in this chapter. Readers must not be confused into concluding that the Electronic Commerce Directive, and its implementing Electronic Commerce (EC Directive) Regulations 2002, address these questions of private international law. First, they may only apply to those Information Service Providers which are established within the EEA. Second, the statutes certainly do not determine which country's law will apply in a given situation. They merely prevent an Information Service Provider established in a member state outside the UK being restricted from conducting activities inside the UK which would have been legal in their member state.[187] This section therefore describes nothing wider than the application of English law to a contract.

The Rome Convention

2.97   Where the litigation over a dispute takes place in England, and its substance is a contractual obligation made over the internet, the Rome Convention[188] will generally apply.[189] This section is concerned mainly with those contracts where one party contracts using a website. Before considering the Convention in greater detail one must address the obvious, and logically,

---

186 It is, of course, correct to state that the telephone, telex and fax also allow transnational contracts to be made. The significant difference between the internet and these other means of communication is that there are no temporal, financial or logistical problems with contacting a website abroad. The site is permanently switched on, time differences are not a relevant factor; the cost may be no more than that of a local phone call, and there is no increase in marginal cost, unlike fax, telex and telephone.

187 Reg 4.

188 The Rome Convention is incorporated into the Contracts (Applicable Law) Act 1990. References to articles within the Convention can be located in the Schedules to the domestic statute. The Convention can be interpreted by recourse to the Giuliano and Lagarde report (OJ 1980, C282/10), see the Contracts (Applicable Law) Act 1990, s 3(3)(a).

189 The justification for this bold statement is that the Convention applies to contracts made after 1 April 1991 (art 17). In view of the youth of widespread electronic commerce it is presumed that contracts made using the internet were made after this date. Attention is drawn to art 1(2) which lists the exceptions of its application. These include, among others, contractual obligations relating to wills and succession (art 1(2)(b)) obligations arising under negotiable instruments to the extent that the obligations arise out of their negotiable character (art 1(2) (c)) questions governed by the law of companies such as creation, legal capacity, and personal liability of officers and members (art 1(2)(e)) and questions as to whether an agent is able to bind a principal (art 1(2)(f)). To give definitive advice, therefore, advisers should consult a specialist text.

first question: what is a contract? The answer is not merely that which English law considers to be a contract. The laws of some other Convention countries do not demand 'consideration' or 'privity'. As a consequence, courts (and litigants before them) 'must clearly strive to take a single, international or "autonomous" view of the concept of contractual obligations …'[190] and not merely rely on an English-law view of a contract.

For the purposes of the Rome Convention, and therefore English law, there are two possible types of contract that can be made over the internet: one in which the law that will govern the contract is agreed, and one in which it is not. These two possibilities will be dealt with, but it is worthwhile noting here that there is little justification for not including an applicable law in a contract. It provides more certainty, and some insurance policies will only protect claims under contracts governed by English law.

Express choice of law

2.98   The first issue to understand is that although an e-commerce contract may contain an agreed choice of law, other laws may be applicable in addition. It will be seen below that certain mandatory laws of England will be applied despite choice, and that consumers benefit from certain other protections.

It is significant that no special words are required to choose a law for a contract. The Convention states that a choice can be express, or demonstrated with reasonable certainty by the terms of the contract or the circumstances of the case.[191] Both parties should be aware, therefore, that an express choice may be deemed to have been made even where a contract does not express 'The Law governing this contract will be the laws of England'. Where a contract entered into over the internet does express the choice in such unambiguous terms, that law will apply to the contract. In certain circumstances a chosen law will be modified by English mandatory laws and consumer protective measures.[192]

Demonstration of choice

2.99   The Giuliano and Lagarde report provides some guidance of what is a demonstration with reasonable certainty that a contract is governed by a particular law.[193] Where a standard form is used, such as Lloyd's policy of marine insurance, it can be taken that a choice of English law has been made. However, this does not suggest that a standard form of a lesser known company can suffice as a reasonably certain demonstration. This is especially the case when contracting over the internet where it is possible, for example, unknowingly, to enter a contract to buy a US piece of software but from a French distributor. In

190 *Raiffeisen Zentralbank Österreich AG v Five Star General Trading LLC* [2001] 3 All ER 257, at 26, para 33.
191 Art 3(1).
192 See 'Modifications to express or demonstrated law', at **2.100**.
193 OJ 1980, C282/10 at C282/17.

this scenario there will not be sufficient certainty to demonstrate any choice of law for the contract.

Other indicators within the terms of the contract may demonstrate this certainty. For example, references to the courts of England. In a shipping dispute, an arbitration clause in favour of England provided a 'strong indication of the parties' intention to choose English Law as the applicable law'.[194] References to English statutes are also indicative. References to the Copyright, Designs and Patents Act 1988 or the Consumer Credit Act 1974, may leave a court in no doubt that English law was always intended to apply despite the lack of its expression.

Example 2.25

A web-wrap contract expresses that the jurisdiction of California shall apply for all disputes but that this will not exclude the application of any consumer protection laws applicable in the consumer's place of residence. No express choice of law is made. This confusion over jurisdiction and choice of law, and the lack of other indicators, will be unlikely to demonstrate the reasonable certainty required that a particular law was deliberately chosen.

Modifications to express or demonstrated law

Mandatory rules

2.100 Even though an e-commerce contract may expressly state that the law of France should apply, if all the other relevant factors to the situation at the time of choice are connected with one country only, the mandatory rules of that country will remain applicable.[195] A mandatory rule is one that cannot be derogated from by contract.[196] Examples from English law include the Employment Rights Act 1996. The most relevant example for contracting over the internet is the Unfair Terms in Consumer Contracts Regulations 1999 and the Unfair Contract Terms Act 1977 (UCTA), s 27(2).[197] This particular Act is discussed below.

A mandatory law will apply in the limited circumstances that all relevant factors are connected with one country. This is a high burden and one which will be difficult to satisfy where the parties reside in different countries. In such a situation, clearly not all the relevant factors are connected with solely one country. And where downloading, or shipment, occurs from a country other than that of the purchaser's residence the mandatory rules will be unlikely to operate.

One more point must be made about mandatory rules. The mandatory rules that may apply need not be those from England. The first test is to establish a country with which all the elements of the situation are connected. This country may be somewhere other than England. And if the second aspect of the test

---

194 *Egon Oldendorff v Libera Corpn* [1996] 1 Lloyd's Rep 380, QBD, per Clark J.
195 Rome Convention, art 3(3).
196 A statute may state that it applies only to contracts governed by English law. If it does not, it is a matter of statutory construction to establish whether the statute is a mandatory law.
197 Unfair Contract Terms Act 1977, s 27(2)(a) states that the Act will apply also if a term in a contract appears to have been included 'wholly or mainly' to avoid the operation of the Act.

is satisfied, that the laws are mandatory, the English court must apply them in addition to the chosen or demonstrated law of the contract.

Example 2.26

A website, based in England and controlled by an English company, uses the same contract for all those who wish to download its software. The contract specifies that the law of New York will apply. If an American contracts with the website and is then sued in England, it is unlikely that English mandatory rules will apply. In contrast, if an English consumer contracts with the site, it may appear that all the relevant elements relate to England so that the mandatory rules will apply.

This difference in application depending on who makes a contract with a website can pose certain difficulties: the main one is that, if the same contract is used for all jurisdictions, its effect will differ for different consumers (as opposed to businesses). Web owners should be conscious that using one standard form contract, and allowing a person from any jurisdiction to complete that contract, may result in an unforeseen situation. Where possible a website should use a contract that is, at the least, predictable for each of the possible locations from where a consumer may contract. Some website owners have a home page where their viewers must select their residence from a list before a contract is presented for their acceptance.

Modifications by the Electronic Commerce Directive?

2.101 Some readers may be confused by the paragraph above: do the Electronic Commerce Directive and Regulations not do away with this issue? The Electronic Commerce Directive does introduce, within the EU, a so-called 'country of origin rule'. This can be summed up as: 'what is legal at home should be legal abroad'.[198] The Directive does, however, specifically avoid 'trumping' the Rome Convention. Article 4 states that 'this Directive does not establish additional rules on private international law nor does it deal with the jurisdiction of the courts'. And for consumer contracts, the 'country of origin' rule or 'internal market' is weakened further. Indeed, the Directive clearly avoids suggesting that any member state's law could trump the law that would otherwise apply to a consumer contract. For example, 'contractual obligations concerning consumer cont[r]acts'.[199] The Electronic Commerce Directive does not, therefore, eliminate the need to look first to the law governing the contract under the Rome Convention and then to any mandatory laws that may be 'layered' on top of the applicable law.

Application of UCTA

2.102 Where a court deems that the mandatory laws of England do apply to a contract it is necessary to check whether UCTA applies. The Act will apply to certain contracts governed by non-English law, where either or both:

---

198 Art 3(1) and 3(2).
199 Art 3(3), Annex, sixth indent.

'the [choice of law] term appears to the court ... to have been imposed wholly or mainly for the purpose of enabling a party imposing it to evade the operation of this Act; or in the making of the contract one of the parties dealt as consumer, and he was then habitually resident in the United Kingdom, and the essential steps necessary for the making of the contract were taken there, whether by him or by others on his behalf.'

It is important to realise that the operation of this does not strike down the choice of foreign law; it merely makes the operation of that law subject to the effect of UCTA.

Despite the above, not all the protection that UCTA provides to consumers and businesses will be applicable to certain contracts made over the internet. This is because, if the contract is an 'international supply contract', UCTA's rules on 'excluding or restricting' liability[200] will not apply. There is no such similar exclusion in the Unfair Terms in Consumer Contracts Regulations.

An international supply contract has three features.[201] First, it must be either a contract for the sale of goods or one under or in pursuance of which the possession or ownership of goods passes. Second, it must be made between parties whose places of business or residences are in territories of different states. The third feature is that there must be an international aspect to the contract: the goods must be carried from one territory to another; or, the acts constituting offer and acceptance must have been done in different states; or, the contract must provide for the goods to be delivered to a place other than where these acts are done.

So, although an English court may decide that UCTA applies to regulate a foreign contract, a foreign seller of goods who forms contracts over the internet will not be bound by UCTA's restraints on exclusion of liability clauses. Applying the same reasoning, the operation of UCTA can prevent a foreign supplier of services from unreasonably excluding liability.

Example 2.27

An American wine seller sets up a website with its standard form contract expressing no jurisdiction clause but an express choice that the law of New York shall apply to any disputes. A UK consumer is made ill by some corked wine delivered and understands that under the Unfair Contract Terms Act 1977 the supplier's contract could not exclude its liability. This Act will not apply to prevent this exclusion of liability because the contract is for the international supply of goods.

This contrast between the application of the Act to goods and services may be crucial to the supply of digital information over the internet. The supply of software over the internet is likely not to be classified as a sale of goods, indeed no title passes and there is no physical possession. Certainly, if the *obiter dictum* of Sir Iain Glidewell is followed,[202] supplies of software made over the internet

---

200 Unfair Contract Terms Act 1977, s 26(1).
201 Unfair Contract Terms Act 1977, s 26(3) and (4).
202 See *St Alban's City and District Council v International Computers Ltd* [1996] 4 All ER 481 at 492–494.

will not be international supply contracts for the purposes of UCTA. As a result these contracts will be subject to UCTA's rules on the exclusions and restrictions of liability.

It is worth noting that the Law Commission and the Scottish Law Commission have advocated in the course of their report and proposals on UCTA that s 26 should not be replicated in any reform of the legislation and that express provisions in new legislation are needed to prevent attempts to evade the consumer protections offered by art 5 of the Rome Convention by means of a choice of foreign law. The Commissions had specific concerns that art 5 would not in and of itself necessarily protect consumers only temporarily resident in a member state with which the contract is most closely connected.[203]

Example 2.28

Two American software suppliers set up websites to provide software to English consumers. Both suppliers utilise an on-screen contract which excludes all liability and choose the contract to be governed by 'the Laws of the State of New York to the extent that all non-American consumer protection provisions will be inapplicable'. One supplier provides the software by shipping it on a CD to the English consumer. UCTA will not operate to restrict the application of the exclusion clause because this is an international supply contract. The other supplier decides to download the software to consumers using the internet. UCTA will operate to restrict the application of the exclusion clause because the contract is not an international supply contract as no goods are passed.

Consumer contracts

2.103   Far more common than the application of a mandatory rule to a contract is the application of a particular mandatory rule, consumer protection laws. Article 5(2) expresses that in certain circumstances a choice of law made by the parties shall not deprive the consumer of the protection afforded by the mandatory rules from the law of his country of habitual residence. It was once thought that this provision will have very limited effect because English consumers generally buy from English suppliers under contracts governed by English law. This certainly was the case even for goods manufactured abroad. The internet alters this though; the digital landscape is covered with foreign suppliers contracting directly with local consumers, missing out the domestic supplier. It is now relevant for these manufacturers to appreciate the effect of art 5. It will affect their decision whether to sell over the internet and what legal advice they should take.[204] It should be repeated here that the Electronic Commerce Directive expressly does not reduce the applicability of the Rome Convention. It also does not reduce the mandatory protection afforded to consumers by the laws of their domicile.

---

203 The Law Commission and the Scottish Law Commission Unfair Terms in Contracts, Report on a reference under s 3(1)(e) of the Law Commissions Act 1965, February 2005.
204 It may not be enough simply to seek the advice of a domestic lawyer; to understand fully the possible effect of a web contract, legal advice should be solicited from other jurisdictions where potential contracting parties may reside.

Before considering these circumstances, which are usually satisfied over the web, one must address what is a consumer contract. The courts may not consider a licence over copyright material to be a consumer contract as it is neither for the supply of goods or supply of services. The German Bundesgerichtshof held that a timeshare contract was neither a contract for the supply of goods nor services within the meaning of art 5.[205] On the basis that such a licence is classified as a consumer contract, parties contracting over the internet should appreciate the conditions that must prevail for the consumer protection to apply.

Websites and consumers

2.104   Article 5(2) specifies that there are three ways in which the mandatory consumer protective laws will apply to a contract where a choice of law has been made or demonstrated appropriately. One of these ways directly concerns a contract made over the internet:

> 'if in that country the conclusion of the contract was preceded by a specific invitation addressed to him or by advertising, and he had taken in that country all the steps necessary on his part for the conclusion of the contract ...'

This chapter has explained that a court may view a website as a form of advertising. This is very likely where the website does not even attempt to block viewers from specified countries, either technically or by consent. It has also been explained that clicking a download button, or simply agreeing to a contract, will be sufficient to show that the consumer has taken all the necessary steps[206] in the country of his habitual residence. This provision will therefore often act to introduce consumer protective laws into a contract that a website owner never envisaged.

The fact that the similar provisions of the Brussels Convention have been amended in the Brussels Regulation begs one simple question: Does the current Rome Convention have a more narrow application than the Brussels Regulation? The answer to this question is found below at 2.105 below.

Avoiding certain consumers

2.105   Avoiding the ambit of art 5 is difficult both technically and legally because it remains impossible to 'block' totally all access to a website from one particular jurisdiction. The website owner must make a decision: is he happy to contract with a consumer from every country in the world? If there is a jurisdiction that the owner seeks to avoid there are two methods to employ. First, technical solutions. Ensure that the web pages that precede the contract stress

---

205 VIII ZR 316/96, RIW 1997, 875, 19 March 1997.
206 This careful drafting avoids the older problem of deciding where a contract was concluded. All that must be determined is where the consumer carried out all the steps necessary on his part to complete the contact. It will therefore make no difference whether the website is so constructed as to accept offers or make them. It is also submitted that the effect of the Electronic Commerce Directive's 'acknowledgement' is also irrelevant here. The relevant country will be identical.

that the site is not intended for those consumers from the unwanted jurisdiction. This may be effective. The Giuliano and Lagarde report advises that:[207]

> '[i]f… the German replies to an advertisement in American publications, even if they are sold in Germany, the [art 5(2)] rule does not apply unless the advertisement appeared in special editions of the publication intended for European countries.'

One can also ensure that a web server establishes what language is 'set' for the consumer's internet browser. This will allow the filtering of some jurisdictions by the unique languages spoken there. A further refinement of those filtered can be achieved by running a 'reverse DNS look-up'. This resolves the domain name of the Internet Service Provider being used by the consumer. A domain name ending in '.com' may indeed give little indication of the jurisdiction of the consumer. In contrast, an Internet Service Provider with a domain name ending in '.co.uk' gives a fair indication that the consumer using it is from the UK. Then the actual server being used to access the internet can be located on the planet with a high degree of accuracy. Of course, the server may not be local to the consumer for a number of reasons. Although also not precise, one further check can be made of the consumer's time zone. Collectively these solutions can weed out consumers from unsought territories.

The second method is to ensure, as is suggested, that the contract is not accepted by the consumer, but rather offered; the website should accept. With this mechanism in place it becomes easy to ask consumers to complete details of where they are habitually resident or to where they want the goods, if relevant, shipped. The site can reject the offers from the unwanted jurisdiction. It can be seen that if the website made offers, even with conditional drafting as to habitual residence, it could be in breach of contract by refusing to supply to certain locations.

Example 2.29

A website sells 'self-help' manuals. The website allows any consumer to fill in his details, including address and payment details. The contract chooses Swiss law. On clicking a button labelled 'Let me help myself' (an acceptance button), the manuals are sent to the consumer by mail. By fulfilling each order without checking the habitual residence of the consumer, the website may be leaving itself open to litigation or unexpected defences. It may be that the site should refuse to contract with consumers from certain jurisdictions.

These steps are also relevant, as explained above, to avoid the bite of art 15 of the Brussels Regulation. It remains relevant, therefore, to consider whether drafting differences between the Rome Convention, art 5 and Brussels Regulation, art 15, are commercially relevant. This author has always expressed the view that both the Brussels Convention, art 13 and Rome Convention, art 13 apply to protect most consumers accessing websites.[208] This author's view is therefore that the changes introduced by the Brussels Regulation were introduced not to

---

207 OJ 1980, C282/10 at C282/24.
208 Gringras *The Laws of the Internet* (1st edition, 1997), at 38 and 50.

change the law but to clarify it. The majority of the delegates of the contracting states certainly had the view that changes to the Brussels Convention were not needed.[209] Website operators should not, therefore, assume that the current Rome Convention is now exposed as not protecting consumers. The Rome Convention, but more so, the Brussels Regulation, protects consumers who contract using websites that make no attempt to exclude them.

Absence of choice

2.106 Although it has been advised that a contract should always have a statement as to the law that will apply, there will be situations where a contract has no such statement. To cover these situations, rather than endorse them, the following section considers how a court will establish the applicable law. As above for an express choice, the section later goes on to address the radical difference made by contracting with a consumer without an express choice of law.

Without a choice under art 3, the general rule is that the applicable law shall be that of the country with which the contract is most closely connected.[210] There is a presumption, however, which is of direct relevance to website contracts. Article 4(2) makes the presumption that the contract is most closely connected with the country in which the person is located who effects the characteristic performance. The following section breaks down this article into two discrete elements: characteristic performance and location.

Characteristic performance

2.107 For a unilateral contract made over the internet, the performance which is characteristic will always be straightforward. For a bilateral contract, as is recommended for the internet, the answer may be more involved.[211] The Giuliano and Lagarde report illustrates the complexity over what is performance in a bilateral contract.[212]

> 'It is the performance for which the payment is due, ie depending on the type of contract, the delivery of goods, the granting of the right to make use of an item of property, the provision of a service ... which usually constitutes the centre of gravity and the socio-economic function of the contractual transaction.'

Where a viewer enters a website to download material or order its supply, the website owner will be the person effecting the characteristic performance.

209 European Commission Proposal, (1999) OJ C376/1.
210 Rome Convention, art 4(1).
211 Art 4(5) explains that if the characteristic performance cannot be determined (not that where it is effected cannot be determined) the presumptions of arts 2, 3 and 4 will not apply and the court may choose the country with which the contract as a whole is more closely connected as the basis for the applicable law. This must be shown to the court by the party seeking to establish a country other than that determined by art 4(2) (*Definitely Maybe (Touring) Ltd v Marek Lieberberg Kanzertagentur GmBH* [2001] 4 All ER 283).
212 OJ 1980, C282/10 at C282/20.

Providing money or digital cash is not, as seen, characteristic performance.[213] Where a business logs on to a business-to-business website to conduct electronic procurement or other corporate activity, again, it will be the website owner who effects the characteristic performance. For example, in a bidding contract, the provision of the bidder's professional services was considered to be the characteristic performance.[214] In a contract between a client and lawyer, the French court determined that the lawyer's provision of legal advice was the characteristic performance.[215] A distribution agreement, however, has a characteristic performance of supply to the distributor, not the supply to third parties by the distributor.[216] It can be said with some conviction that a website owner will usually be the contracting party making the characteristic performance.

Location

2.108   Once the characteristic performance of the contract is established, art 4(2) provides a separate test to determine the law that will apply to that internet contract. It is vital not to make the wrong assumption that having determined the characteristic performance of a contract one has also found the law that will apply. The correct approach is to assess which party makes the characteristic performance and then to determine which law reflects this transaction. There are two possibilities: first, the contract has been entered into in the course of that party's trade or profession; second, the contract has been entered into otherwise.

Course of trade or profession

2.109   It is likely that those parties who own a website to make contracts will be considered to be acting within their trade or profession. In this situation, art 4(2) states that the law that shall apply is that of the country where the principal place of business is situated, with a proviso. If the terms of the contract specify that the performance is to be effected through a different place of business, the law of that place shall apply.

Example 2.30

A Parisian clothes manufacturer sets up a website in Paris and allows retailers to place their orders over the web. There is no choice of law made on the online order form. The clothes being shipped will constitute the characteristic performance of the contract. The manufacturer effects this performance, so the law of the principal place of business, France, will apply to the contract. If the contract specifies that the clothes shall be shipped from a German warehouse, the law of Germany shall apply being a place of business other than the principal one.

---

213 More involved transactions such as a contract for the provision of digital cash can create strange results with this reasoning. It would appear that the location of the account determines the law of the contract rather than the bank's location (*Sierra Leone Telecommunications Co Ltd v Barclays Bank plc* [1998] 2 All ER 821 at 827).
214 *HIB Ltd v Guardian Insurance Co* [1997] 1 Lloyd's Rep 412 QB.
215 *S v K D* 1983, J146, Tribunal de Grande Instance de Paris.
216 *Print Concept GmBH v GEW (EC) Ltd* [2001] ECC 36, CA.

Website's place of business

2.110   Contracts made over the internet grant freedoms to both parties: neither needs to be located in the same country as the website that takes and completes an order. It is possible that an order to acquire a digitised picture is made from England, and that the order is placed with a German company, trading out of Germany, but that the server which digitally effects the performance is located in the US. It would be equally easy if the server is located in Vietnam, or anywhere else in the world with a telephone network. The obvious question is therefore, does a server that can effect performance constitute a place of business? It is submitted, in the absence of any direct authority, that a server per se cannot constitute a place of business. This conclusion is drawn from a number of factors.

The wording of art 4(2) indicates that effecting the characteristic performance through a place does not necessarily constitute a place of business. This can be reasoned from the wording of the article that performance must be effected through a place of business other than the principal place of business. It does not merely state that performance through another place will trump the principal place of business.[217]

The Giuliano and Lagarde report complements this point. It states that:[218]

> '[t]he law appropriate to the characteristic performance defines the connecting factor of the contract from the inside, and not from the outside by elements unrelated to the essence of the obligation such as the nationality of the contracting parties or the place where the contract was concluded.'

This interpretation suggests that it is naïve to look solely at where a server is plugged in. What the Convention requires is to look to the reality of the transaction; the characteristic performance must be linked to 'the social and economic environment of which it will form a part'.[219] Indeed, the Giuliano and Lagarde report endorses this holistic approach by later stating: '[t]he place where the act was done becomes unimportant ... Seeking the place of performance or the different places of performance and classifying them becomes superfluous.'[220] A company needs to do far more than simply connect a server abroad to have established a place of business there.

What and where is 'a place of business' is a vexed question for the purposes of choice of law and there are differing definitions concerning taxation and the service of proceedings. But there is little doubt that the policy considerations when establishing jurisdiction over a defendant differ from those to establish from where performance was effected. It is inappropriate and an over-simplification of the relevant factors to attempt to utilise a court's views on 'place of business' from one area of the law, say jurisdiction, to another, choice of law.

---

217 It is admitted that such a literal analysis of a European Convention is, perhaps, inappropriate, and that a more purposive approach should be used. This follows.
218 OJ 1980, C282/10 at C282/20.
219 OJ 1980, C282/10 at C282/20.
220 OJ 1980, C282/10 at C282/21.

> *Example 2.31*
>
> An Italian publisher charges viewers to read its newspaper which it uploads daily on to its two websites, one in Italy and one based in New York for speed purposes. Its contract with viewers has no choice of law clause, but does stipulate that, when demand is high, the American server may supply the information. When a viewer accesses the newspaper, and unbeknown to him, receives this information through the American server, the law of the contract will not be that of New York. A server simply based in New York is an insufficient link to constitute a place of business. The law that will apply is that of the place of the principal place of business: Italy.

Outside trade or profession

2.111 Where a party is not acting within his trade or profession but uses a website to make a contract, a slightly different, but more certain, rule applies. In this situation, art 4(2) states that the law that shall apply is that of the country where, for an individual, he habitually resides at the time. For a corporate or unincorporated entity, the law that applies is that of the place of its central administration.

The commercial reaction to this academic debate is short: where possible specify a law for any e-commerce contract made over the internet. There is some truth in the statement that not providing a choice of law gives slightly more opportunity for argument at an interim stage as to which law will apply to a contract. This opportunity comes at the cost of distinctive uncertainty.

Modifications to applicable law

Consumer contracts

2.112 What constitutes a consumer contract under art 5(2) has already been addressed in some detail.[221] It was found that a contract made over the web with a consumer will generally benefit from the protection afforded under the Convention.[222] Where the contract does not provide a choice of law, the effect of the transaction being a consumer contract is far more critical.

If no choice of law is made and art 5(2) is applicable, art 5(3) specifies that the law which governs the contract is that of the consumer's habitual residence.[223] This is in stark contrast to where a consumer contract does include a choice of law. In that situation, art 5(2) does not deprive the consumer of the protection afforded by the mandatory rules from his habitual residence.

---

221 See 'Consumer contracts', at **2.84**.
222 See 'Websites and consumers', at **2.104**.
223 Subject to the two exceptions that the rule does not apply to a contract of carriage or a contract where the services are to be supplied to the consumer exclusively in a country other than that in which he has his habitual residence. See the Rome Convention, art 5(4).

Example 2.32

A website sells 'self-help' manuals. The website allows any consumer to fill in his details, including address and payment details. On clicking a button labelled, 'Let me help myself' (an acceptance button), the manuals are sent to the consumer by mail. By fulfilling each order without checking the habitual residence of the consumer, the website will be forming contracts under many different laws all around the world. Its contracts may be unenforceable, or worse, they may be illegal. To avoid leaving itself open to these risks it must include a choice of law and refuse to contract with consumers from certain jurisdictions.

There is an elementary solution to the problem that any law could apply to a contract if any consumer is allowed to contract: choose a law for the contract. Then, to ameliorate the effect from the consumer's mandatory rules, apply the technical and legal precautions already described to 'block' certain jurisdictions.[224]

---

224 See 'Avoiding certain consumers', at **2.105**.

CHAPTER THREE

Tort

INTRODUCTION

3.1   Given the ability of computers to be controlled via a network and in turn to control many aspects of our lives (including the operation of our domestic appliances), the commission of almost any tort could involve the internet as part of the chain of events. There is not enough space here for the compendious account of the law of non-contractual obligations that might require. Instead, the topics in this chapter are chosen and approached on the basis of their relevance to activities that depend on the internet and any particular issues or difficulties that might arise from the involvement of the internet in them. Where the involvement of the internet does not affect the application of the basic legal principles of a topic, relatively little weight is given to it. Another area where the boundaries of this chapter are limited is in the overlap with contract law: other chapters in this book address some issues of contract law.

There are not so many legal principles that run unchanged across the diverse range of legal actions and remedies dealt with in this chapter, but there are a few over-arching issues. Though tort (leaving aside the infringement of intellectual property rights) is not an area that has seen much intervention from the EU, there is one aspect of EU law that is relevant across the board – the protections given to certain information services by the Electronic Commerce Directive. The propensity of the internet to facilitate activities across national boundaries means that some analysis of the international dimension is necessary; the combination of forensic and procedural techniques whereby the identity of internet users can be determined (so they can be contacted and, if necessary, sued) needs explanation; and the principles of joint tortfeasorship apply generally.

Accordingly, this chapter starts with a brief technical and commercial description of the internet in order to introduce the different players who will feature in the subsequent sections and the terminology used to describe them. It then looks at the over-arching issues; and finally it addresses the substantive tort topics.

THE INTERNET AND THOSE INVOLVED IN IT

3.2   The internet is generally defined as the infrastructure of data connections that joins private networks and computers on a global basis. The logical glue that joins these hardware elements together is the use of the TCP/IP protocol for sending and receiving packets of data between devices. TCP/IP stands for 'Transmission Control Protocol/Internet Protocol'. The TCP part defines a logical standard for putting digital data into packets for transmission and receipt, the IP part is a numerical system for addressing computers. A computer IP address on a local network would look like 192.168.1.99 (for version 4 of the IP protocol) or fd00:ac98:2917 for version 6. The TCP protocol defines a space in each packet for the IP addresses of the sending and receiving computers. Each computer attached to the internet needs a unique IP address and the allocation of IP addresses to internet operators is controlled by the Internet Assigned Numbers Authority.[1]

The internet is not the world wide web, though the web lives on the internet. Other systems of information exchange also inhabit the internet – the text-based and bulletin-board like Usenet system, email and the ftp system for exchanging files all pre-date the web. The World Wide Web Consortium defines the web as 'an information space in which the items of interest, referred to as resources, are identified by global identifiers called Uniform Resource Identifiers (URI)'.[2] A URI is the type of web address we are used to, for example www.libelreform. org/latest-news (a page of the Libel Reform Campaign's website). The word 'resource' is used as resources include web pages but also sound or video resources and so on that may be linked to from web pages and which have their own URIs. To implement the web, Sir Tim Berners-Lee (its inventor) developed three standards: the domain-name system which translates web addresses to IP addresses; http (the Hyper-text Transfer Protocol) which enables communication between web resources via hyperlinks; and html (hyper-text markup language) which is a text-based way of defining the content and some aspects of the layout of web pages, including hyperlinks. He also had to write the first web-browser and server software. To be on the web therefore, something has to be accessible via a URI. All the standards mentioned here are open standards, so software implementing them can be written and sold (or distributed as free and open-source software) by anyone. Typically TCP/IP is implemented by a computer's operating system whereas the programs implementing the world-wide web protocols will be distributed along with web server and web browser software that may come from a different supplier.

The technical distinctions introduced here may be relevant to various tortious scenarios. A resource can be on the web in the sense of being accessible via a URI, but if there are no links to that URI from other public web pages, and the owner of the resource does not tell anyone else where to find it, then it cannot be said to be published (communicated to another person) for the purposes of defamation or malicious falsehood. Normally, of course, anyone who places a resource on a web server will do so with the intention of making it public so will make sure it is linked to via the home page of a website they control. But it is possible to

1 Or IANA, see www.iana.org for details of the organisation's constitution and scope of operation.
2 See www.w3.org/Help/#webinternet and the w3.org website more generally.

configure a web server to limit access to users from certain IP addresses[3] or to logged-on users of the host website. Alternatively, publication could occur by email, by placing on a publicly accessible ftp server or by posting to a Usenet group. For some legal purposes the distinction between communicating to one or more defined people and the world at large is important, as will be apparent from the following sections of this chapter.[4]

Relatively mature industry sectors have evolved to provide and assist in the use of the internet and web and an understanding of the different roles typically involved is necessary to understand the likely parties to any scenario. The physical network infrastructure (which is separate from the telephone network) is owned and controlled by a mixture of private companies and state-owned organisations. Larger internet users will pay for a direct connection to one of these infrastructure companies. Smaller users and private individuals will gain access via their telecommunications provider (who will either be an infrastructure provider or have a connection to the internet via one). In this chapter the term 'internet service provider' (ISP) is used, unless the contrary is indicated, to mean this type of provider. It is possible to host a website or email server on computers which are connected to the internet via a typical domestic connection, but not normally practical. So smaller and private users who wish to have a website or dedicated email server will typically contract with a hosting company to host the site on their computers. Hosting companies do have direct access to the internet and many ISPs provide hosting services in addition to internet access (they will almost always provide a sub-domain for each user, an email address and at least rudimentary web-page hosting under that sub-domain).

Users will contact their host to configure their web or email servers, upload content and so on using their internet connection via their ISP. The level of control the hosting client has over their site depends on the nature of their hosting package. At the large end of the scale, the client may have access to a dedicated server computer which they can configure remotely right down to the bare bones of the operating system. In practice these days, that computer may be a virtual computer created by virtualisation software running on the host's farm of connected server computers. At the economy end of the scale, the host will provide shared hosting, where specific software running on a server shares its resources between clients and allows the clients to control their site content and access some configuration options via a web-based interface. With shared hosting, the software running on the server is the host's responsibility, the client's responsibility is restricted to some configuration options and the design and content of their site, though the latter can include scripts that run on the server and control the operation of the website. In all cases, the client's access to their server or website will be via the internet and protected by a username and password.

In this chapter the person who is responsible for the creation and content of a site (whether on their own servers or through a hosting company) is referred to as a 'site operator' (following the language of the Defamation Act 2013). The

---

3   This can be used to limit access to certain geographical areas, as IP addresses are assigned on a geographical basis, but the limitations are easily overcome by the use of proxies.
4   Copyright law has its own concept of 'communication to the public' dealt with in **Chapter 4**.

site may contain user-generated content, but the operator will have the ultimate power over that content. If there is a separate hosting company, that company may also have power over the content of their customers' sites, and their contract with clients will provide for when they can intervene, but they will not exercise any day-to-day control over or supervision of their clients' sites. The same goes for the content of email services the host provides.

A web page itself consists of plain text written in html. In an old-fashioned static website, each page was contained in a separate file located on the server and written by an author, either directly in html or using editing software similar to a word processor. Html allows for pictures, video, etc to be included on web pages by special types of link to separate files containing the material concerned. When an internet user browses to a web page the host's server responds to the http/https request sent by the browser by sending the html file back, which renders the web page on the screen. The browser will also have to fetch any picture or other resources referred to by the page. Those resources could be located on the same server as the web page, or could be located on another server which could be controlled by someone else.

A modern 'dynamic' web page ends up as the same thing – html sent by a web server to a browser programme in response to an http/https request, but it gets there by a completely different route. A dynamic website consists of a database containing or referring to resources on the server and software which generates web pages 'on the fly' in response to requests for web pages. The combination of the software and database is often referred to as a 'content management system', CMS for short. The host's web server software forwards requests to the CMS and gets the generated html back. Content management systems can include a sophisticated web-based 'front-end' by which the client can design their website, upload content to it, control which parts are made public and so on. Web hosts which offer shared hosting will typically offer a choice of a few content management systems for their clients to use to generate their sites with. Perhaps the best-known CMS is Wordpress,[5] which focuses mainly on enabling the creation of blogs, but can also be used to generate other types of website. Third parties can provide templates for use with content management systems to help users generate whatever type of website they want to create – an online shop or discussion forum for example.

The point of a dynamic website is that the content delivered to the browsing visitor can be tailored to them. The most recent blogs appear at the top of the page automatically once they are uploaded via the CMS; the current time and weather for the visitor's location will appear and so on. Websites that contain user-generated content can be generated relatively easily with a minimum of coding expertise; for example Wordpress blogs can be configured to allow comments by visitors, which can be either let through automatically or stored to await moderation by the site operator. Web forums can be created that require users to log in and agree to terms and conditions. Large social networking sites will use specially written software to generate the user experience, but they

---

5   See http://wordpress.org. Wordpress is the most popular CMS by number of websites using it according to Web Technology Surveys (w3techs.com) on 20/08/2015.

operate on a broadly similar model. The key to the dynamic nature of such sites is the use of programmes (called 'scripts') on the server to generate the final web page in response to any particular request. Scripts can present sophisticated functionality to the site visitor such as text or picture editing. Scripts are also how the CMS provides the site operator with the tools to create the site.

Thus, the end product, a website, is the result of the operation of all these layers of software, and negligence or malice can result in any one of those layers malfunctioning in a damaging and potentially tortious way. Bugs that can be exploited or which result in error may appear in the operating system, the web server software, the CMS, scripts provided in a third-party template or in the material specifically created or modified by the site operator. The question of liability and the level of care expected by the various players will depend on their precise role: a client of a shared hosting company will have to rely on the host to keep the web server software up to date and resistant to attack, whereas the operator of a dedicated server will have that responsibility themselves.

Cloud computing represents a development of this approach. Rather than using software located on a local machine, a cloud client accesses data and software resources located on a server to carry out IT functions such as programming, data storage, word processing and so on.

Email is simpler to describe. Email communication takes place between email servers which are located on the internet. Email users send and receive emails by downloading them from and uploading them to their email provider's server using email client software or a web interface provided by the mail server software and accessed by web browser software. An email sent to a separate server from the sender's is generally sent irretrievably: the recipient may never read it and may delete it without reading it, but the sender will have lost control of it. Some email systems allow emails sent to a recipient on the same server (eg internal emails within an organisation) to be recalled before they are read.

In all these situations (operation of websites, access to email and cloud services) the user will typically access their system or service with a simple username and password login. Clearly, if a login can be hacked into, all manner of unfortunate results might occur, including loss of or damage to user data and the publication of objectionable material ostensibly by the user. This raises the possibility of liability for those consequences on the part of whoever caused the login to be compromised.

OVER-ARCHING LEGAL TOPICS

EU Law – the Electronic Commerce (EC Directive) Regulations 2002

3.3   These implement the Electronic Commerce Directive, 2000/31. These provide general defences to any civil liability for damages or criminal liability that might otherwise arise for various categories of internet intermediary. They do not prevent a claimant obtaining a civil injunction.

Regulation 17, the 'mere conduit' defence, provides a complete defence for network intermediaries and ISPs who either transmit content or provide access to content, provided they do not initiate the transmission, alter the content they transmit or select the recipient. In a case where an ISP or intermediary is tortiously liable in some way (generally they are not liable at all other than for example copyright infringement, as will be seen) and so may be injuncted (as the defence does not cover that), art 15 of the Directive is important. This requires that no general obligation 'to monitor the information which they transmit or store, nor a general obligation actively to seek facts or circumstances indicating illegal activity' shall be imposed. This has been held, in the context of copyright infringement, to preclude a requirement for ISPs to install technology that monitors traffic (even if this would be effective).[6] It would not prevent a requirement to remove specific stored material drawn to the attention of the ISP (if they did store anything) or the blocking of access to specific websites or parts of websites.[7]

Regulation 18, the 'caching' defence, protects ISPs and others who make temporary copies of material that are not strictly necessary for communication, but speed it up. Typically, an ISP will cache copies of web pages that are popular with its customers on its servers, which will have the effect of reducing the access times for that material. By providing those pages from its cache rather than simply passing on the request for the page and then forwarding the page, as received from its original source, to the customer, an ISP is taking itself outside the mere conduit defence and acting in the nature of a host, so may possibly be a publisher for the purposes of defamation. For the defence to apply the cached copy must be updated and the policy of caching must comply with industry norms.

Regulation 19, the 'hosting' defence is one of most relevance to those who provide storage facilities:

> 'Where an information society service is provided which consists of the storage of information provided by a recipient of the service, the service provider (if he otherwise would) shall not be liable for damages or for any other pecuniary remedy or for any criminal sanction as a result of that storage where –
>
> '(a) the service provider –
>
> > (i) does not have actual knowledge of unlawful activity or information and, where a claim for damages is made, is not aware of facts or circumstances from which it would have been apparent to the service provider that the activity or information was unlawful; or
> >
> > (ii) upon obtaining such knowledge or awareness, acts expeditiously to remove or to disable access to the information; and
>
> (b) the recipient of the service was not acting under the authority or the control of the service provider.'

---

6   *Scarlet Extended SA v Société belge des auteurs, compositeurs et éditeurs SCRL (SABAM)*, Case c-70/10, [2012] ECDR 4.

7   There will be problems in justifying a remedy that blocks both innocent content and content that gives rise to a tort, and in any event blocking is a blunt and ineffective instrument given that material can be copied and moved between URIs so easily.

Information society service is defined in art 2.2 of Directive 98/48/EC (amending Directive 98/34) on information in the field of technical standards and regulations as follows:

- Any service normally provided for remuneration, at a distance, by electronic means and at the individual request of a recipient of services.

- For the purposes of this definition:

  - 'at a distance' means that the service is provided without the parties being simultaneously present;

  - 'by electronic means' means that the service is sent initially and received at its destination by means of electronic equipment for the processing (including digital compression) and storage of data, and entirely transmitted, conveyed and received by wire, by radio, by optical means or by other electromagnetic means;

  - 'at the individual request of a recipient of services' means that the service is provided through the transmission of data on individual request.

This defence thus potentially covers web hosting companies and also website owners who allow user-generated content which they do not vet in advance, but there are issues with its application to the latter category and to free services. The 'individual request' requirement could be met by social networking sites that require a login, but may be difficult to stretch to sites that allow comments to be posted without any requirement for signing up. Allowing comments could be argued to amount to providing a service consisting of the storage of information, but that can be debated since typically the commenter loses control over the comments once made. Social networking services and the ability to comment on things are mostly not provided as services for remuneration – though they are often offered as ancillary to another service such as an online shop or music streaming service.

In *Metropolitan International Schools Ltd v Designtechnica Corpn and Others*, Eady J noted this difficulty and decided that a broad interpretation of Directive 98/48 should be favoured so that the search engine Google (which does not charge for searching) should be regarded as a provider of Information Society Services.[8] In *Papasavvas*[9] the Court of Justice confirmed that websites that generate remuneration from advertising will be included in the definition of 'for remuneration'. It also held that a newspaper site that contained articles posted by the newspaper was not covered by the defence 'since it had knowledge of the information posted and exercised control over that information'.

---

8   *Metropolitan International Schools Ltd (trading as Skillstrain and/or Train2Game) v Designtechnica Corpn (trading as Digital Trends) and Others* [2009] EWHC 1765 (QB), [2011] 1 WLR 1743.
9   *Papasavvas v O Fileleftheros Dimosia Etairia Ltd and Others* Case C-291/13, [2015] 1 CMLR 24.

In *McGrath v Dawkins*[10] HHJ Moloney QC held that Amazon.com had the benefit of this defence in relation to reviews and comments posted to their book-selling site, but he did not consider the definition of 'Information Society Services' contained in Directive 98/48, considering only the wording of art 19 of the Regulations. *Papasavvas* was not concerned with a mixed content situation, that is where there is both edited and user-generated content, but a purposive interpretation of the Directive ought to permit the defence to apply to part of the content of a site, as was held in *McGrath*. However it appears from the European Court of Human Rights case *Delfi*[11] that the Estonian Court of Appeal has interpreted equivalent legislation implementing Directive 2000/31 as not providing a defence for comments on a news site. According to the Grand Chamber, the Estonian Court of Appeal:

> 'deemed the Information Society Services Act [which applied the e-Commerce Directive] inapplicable. It observed that the applicant company had placed a note on its Internet site to the effect that comments were not edited, that the posting of comments that were contrary to good practice was prohibited, and that the applicant company reserved the right to remove such comments. A system was put in place whereby users could notify the applicant company of any inappropriate comments. However, the County Court considered that this was insufficient and did not allow adequate protection for the personality rights of others. The court found that the applicant company itself was to be considered the publisher of the comments, and it could not avoid responsibility by publishing a disclaimer stating that it was not liable for the content of the comments.'

It does not appear that the Estonian Court referred the matter to the Court of Justice, so pending a ruling from the Court of Justice on this issue the applicability of this defence to comments on sites which also carry edited content (which will include blogs) remains a little uncertain, though it is submitted that the *McGrath* view is the correct one.

If the defence does apply to an operator, only once they have been notified of the presence of defamatory material on the site do they have to take action. The provisions of regulation 19(a)(ii) are commonly known as the 'notice and take down' procedure.

If the defence does not apply, defences of similar overall intent are available for defamation (see **3.12** below) and copyright infringement (**Chapter 4**).

Identifying internet users – law and technology

3.4   Identifying the presence of a civil wrong may be no use unless the potential defendant can be identified (they may be overseas, in which case the next section is relevant). It is possible that it will be difficult to identify the

---

10   *Christopher Anthony Mcgrath, MCG Productions Limited v Professor Richard Dawkins*, The Richard Dawkins Foundation for Reason and Science, Amazon EU SARL (trading as Amazon. co.uk), Vaughan John Jones, [2012] Info TLR 72.
11   See 'Freedom of expression and other fundamental rights' at **3.36** below

real-world person corresponding to an online identity: a website may not reveal who its operator is or who hosts it. However, the technology of the internet (see above) means that it will be possible to find out about who operates a domain. For example, the proprietor of a domain name can be identified from the registrar for that domain. Their records will reveal the IP address from which a particular post on a forum was sent. That IP address might be part of a block of addresses assigned to a particular ISP. That ISP's records will reveal which of their customers that IP address was assigned to at the relevant time, possibly including a physical address and payment details.

English and Welsh law provides a variety of methods for obtaining information from people about actual or potential claims. The one most relevant to identifying internet users is the rule in *Norwich Pharmacal*.

The rule in *Norwich Pharmacal*

3.5   Under this rule the court may order someone who is not a potential party to a claim to disclose information to a potential claimant where they are likely to possess evidence that is relevant to the claim.[12]

Such orders have been made in order to identify wrongdoers and to find and preserve evidence. The applicant must first show they have a bona fide claim, so such orders cannot be used for 'fishing expeditions'. The applicant must also show that it is likely that the respondent does have relevant material that cannot practicably obtained by other means. They are normally obtained by *ex-parte* application to the court, though the victim of the order (who may not be a defendant or possible defendant) has the right to contest the order on a subsequent *inter partes* hearing. The applicant must undertake to pay the costs of the respondent, who will not incur any cost liability themselves unless they contest the order.

It has become established that respondents (at least if they are innocent of any wrongdoing themselves) are entitled to force an applicant to obtain a court order and only then disclose the information without incurring a costs liability. Most site operators will choose to do this in order not to be seen to be acting against the interests of their users and also to protect themselves from legal liability to their users in contract, confidentiality/privacy or pursuant to data protection legislation.[13]

The granting of the order is discretionary, and the courts have to balance the legitimate right to a remedy of the applicant with the rights of privacy, confidentiality and to the protection of data of the respondent and the site users whose data is sought to be disclosed. Thus the court has refused to grant orders in the case of an application that would have required a journalist to reveal his source, as this would have been a disproportionate infringement of the right to

12   *Norwich Pharmacal Co v Customs and Excise Commissioners* [1974] AC 133, [1973] 3 WLR 164, HL.
13   See *G v Wikimedia Foundation Inc* [2009] EWHC 3148 (QB), [2010] EMLR 14.

freedom of expression.[14] Orders are typically granted against web hosts and site operators. The rationale given for this in one of the first such cases concerning identities of website users, *Totalise plc v The Motley Fool Ltd,*[15] was that journalists take editorial responsibility for what they publish whereas typically websites do not, and indeed often publish disclaimers reminding visitors of this. Similarly, in balancing the right to privacy and confidentiality of the site's users with the right of the applicant, the balance may fall in favour of the applicant,[16] but may not. In *Totalise* Aldous LJ in the Court of Appeal commented:

> '25 In a case such as the present, and particularly since the coming into force on 2 October 2000 of the Human Rights Act 1998, the court must be careful not to make an order which unjustifiably invades the right of an individual to respect for his private life, especially when that individual is in the nature of things not before the court: see the Human Rights Act 1998, section 6, and the European Convention for the Protection of Human Rights and Fundamental Freedoms, articles 10 and (arguably at least) 6(1).'

These principles were applied in *Sheffield Wednesday Football Club Ltd v Hargreaves,*[17] a defamation case, where the court ordered the disclosure of details of posters on a website whose posts were clearly defamatory, but refused to order disclosure in relation to posts that were arguably defamatory, but more in the nature of insults so unlikely to cause great damage. The severity of the wrong suffered by the applicant was balanced against the site users' rights to privacy and data protection. (Contrast the different situation in *Totalise* which the judge characterised as a 'concerted campaign' presenting a 'very considerable threat'.)

In practice most sites will promise to keep user details secret in their terms and conditions, but a court order can override this and well-drafted terms will state that the obligation is subject to any requirement of the law or a court order. The applicant does not have to undertake to take proceedings against people identified as a result of the order being complied with.

Joint liability

3.6   The law of tort recognises that two or more people can be liable for the same tort where:

- one of them caused or procured the other to commit a tort; or

- where the tort is committed as part of a common design between them.

---

14   Following *Goodwin v United Kingdom*, Application No 17488/90, (1996) 22 EHRR 123 where the ECtHR held that requiring a journalist to reveal his sources was an infringement of his art 10 right to freedom of expression.

15   [2001] EMLR 29, QBD, overturned on appeal only as to the costs order; [2001] EWCA Civ 1897; [2002] 1 WLR 1233, where the Court of Appeal discussed the exercise of the court's discretion.

16   In accordance with the general rule where documents are disclosed as a result of litigation, the applicant will undertake only to use the information for the purposes for which it is asked, or with further permission of the court, so a measure of confidentiality will be preserved.

17   [2007] EWHC 2375 (QB), 2007 WL 3001772 (transcript).

In internet scenarios, much of the case law has developed as a result of cases on copyright infringement: websites which knowingly encourage and enable their users to infringe have been held jointly liable themselves.[18] By contrast, simply providing the tools with which to infringe does not result in liability.[19] The law is reluctant to undermine separate corporate identity by holding an individual who owns or runs a company to be jointly liable for its actions in tort unless, for example, they set the company up to pursue a wrongful purpose.[20]

JURISDICTION AND CHOICE OF LAW IN TORT CASES

3.7   Jurisdiction (the question of whether or not the courts of a particular jurisdiction must, may or may not hear a particular case) and choice of law (the question of what system or systems of law that court should apply to a case or a discrete legal issue that arises in it) are aspects of private international law. The 'international' in that phrase is somewhat misleading: it is not the law that is international; it is the subject matter the law deals with. The courts of each jurisdiction will apply that jurisdiction's private international law rules in determining these and similar questions. True, in some respects UK[21] private international law is influenced by international treaties to which the UK is a party, or is EU law, but the same can be said for many aspects of substantive law. If it is necessary to consider the approach that would be taken by the courts of an overseas jurisdiction to these matters, local advice should be sought, though where that country is part of the European scheme it will be possible for an English and Welsh lawyer to come to a view because of the harmonisation of the law in this area.

A good practical approach to dealing with these issues is to consider jurisdiction first (as to which choice of law *may* be a relevant factor) and then to consider what system of law the UK courts will apply if they should or may accept jurisdiction.

Jurisdiction

3.8   One of two codes apply; which one depends on the domicile of the defendant:

- For defendants domiciled within the EU or a state that is a party to the Brussels or Lugano Conventions, the European scheme applies.

- For defendants domiciled elsewhere, the common law applies.

---

18   For example websites which facilitate file-sharing or up/downloading: *Twentieth Century Fox Film Corp v Newzbin Ltd* [2010] EWHC 608 (Ch), [2010] FSR 21.

19   *CBS Songs Ltd v Amstrad Consumer Electronics plc* [1988] AC 1013, [1988] RPC 567.

20   *Canon Kabushiki Kaisha v Green Cartridge Co (Hong Kong) Ltd* [1997] AC 728, [1997] FSR 817 Privy Council (Hong Kong).

21   The rules relating to jurisdiction which apply between the three jurisdictions of the UK are contained in Civil Jurisdiction and Judgments Act 1982, Sch 4, which broadly follows the European scheme. The outward-facing private international law rules of Scotland and Northern Ireland follow the English and Welsh rules.

The European Scheme

3.9   So far as the EU states (apart from Denmark) are concerned, the law is in EU Regulation 1215/2012 on Jurisdiction and the Recognition and Enforcement of Judgments in Civil and Commercial Matters.[22] As between the other EU states and Denmark, the Brussels Convention (which pre-dated the Regulation) applies as Denmark opted out of the Regulation.[23] As between EU states and the EFTA states Iceland, Norway and Switzerland, the Lugano Convention applies, as it applies between those states. Collectively these will be referred to as 'Convention States'. Though there are minor differences, for present purposes the schemes implemented by these instruments can be considered identical and they are all subject to the jurisdiction of the European Court of Justice to hear preliminary references. All Convention States mentioned are bound by the scheme, so it applies to allocate jurisdiction between them. Should a case be brought before a court in a state outside the scheme, it will of course not be bound by the scheme and will apply its own rules. Regulation article numbering is used in the discussion that follows.

The scheme applies to disputes in civil and commercial matters, and this includes the law of obligations. The basic rule for determining jurisdiction is:

- defendants must be sued in the courts of their place of domicile (art 2); but

- they can alternatively be sued in tort matters, in 'the place where the harmful event occurred', which has been interpreted by the ECJ as:

    – the courts of the place of the event giving rise to the damage; or

    – the courts of the place where the damage occurred – but if jurisdiction is founded under this limb, the claim must be limited to damages relating to that jurisdiction.[24]

There are other rules that might result in other states being permitted to accept jurisdiction, or a state that can accept jurisdiction having to decline it or stay proceedings:

- Acceptance of jurisdiction: if a defendant has taken a step in a claim (other than to challenge jurisdiction) then they are deemed to have accepted jurisdiction and the court may continue with the case (art 24).

- Jurisdiction agreements: if there is a related contract, jurisdiction may have been agreed in advance, and it can be agreed between the parties after the event (art 23).

---

22   This is a re-cast version of Regulation 44/2001, which was itself substantially in the form of the Brussels and Lugano Conventions.
23   Though in 2005 Denmark entered into an agreement with the EU to apply Regulation 44//2001 and any amendments made to it, so from 2005 Regulation 44/2001 effectively applied to Denmark. Denmark has similarly agreed to abide by the terms of Regulation 1215/2012, but it is the Danish implementing law that applies, not the Regulation.
24   *Shevill v Presse Alliance SA* [1995] 2 AC 18.

- Multiple defendants, etc: where a court has jurisdiction in relation to one defendant, other defendants (provided the claims are connected) and third parties, etc may be included in the case (art 6).

- Same cause of action: where the same cause of action has already started in another jurisdiction to which the scheme applies, the second court must stay proceedings and then decline jurisdiction when the first court's jurisdiction is confirmed (art 27).

- Related cause of action: where a related cause of action is being carried on in another court within the scheme, the second court may stay proceedings pending an outcome in the first case.

- Protected jurisdictions: people dealing as consumers, insured parties and employees in employment matters can sue in their home courts in addition to any other place that would have jurisdiction under the Regulation (arts 8–21).

- Exclusive jurisdiction: where the claim involves title to real property, validity of registered IP rights, or the constitution, etc, of corporations, the courts of the place where the property is or where the corporation is registered have exclusive jurisdiction (art 24).

Domicile is defined as the place where an individual resides or a company has its seat. In cases where activity is conducted over a network that spans national boundaries, the question of where a harmful event occurs will depend on a close analysis of the elements of the tort alleged and the technology used, and is discussed in relation to the individual torts below.

It is now clear that the 'defendants must be sued where they are domiciled' rule is a hard one. In particular, it applies even where the case has no connection whatever with any other Convention State but does have a connection with another jurisdiction, and even where there is no connection with the UK apart from the defendant's domicile.[25] This also applies where the claim involves an asset or right outside Europe but is not covered by any of the areas of exclusive jurisdiction.[26] The effect of this is that the applicable law will almost certainly be a foreign law (see below). Prior to the cases mentioned, the approach of the UK courts to such cases was that they had a discretion to refuse jurisdiction following common law principles.

The common law scheme

3.10   This scheme applies where the European scheme does not; that is, where the defendant is not domiciled in a Convention State. The basic rule is that of

---

25   Ibid and *Owusu v Jackson and Others* (Case C-281/02), where an accident occurred on a holiday in Jamaica. Only one defendant was in the UK and there was no other connection with the UK and no connection with any other Convention state, but the defendant could still be sued here.

26   *Lucasfilm v Ainsworth* [2011] UKSC 39; [2012] 1 AC 208, so the UK courts had to apply US copyright law to acts of infringement in the US where the defendant was UK domiciled.

forum non conveniens and the modern statement of that is in the *Spiliada* case.[27] This states that the UK courts should accept jurisdiction over a case unless the case can be more conveniently tried in another jurisdiction. The court will ask the basic question 'Could this case be more conveniently litigated elsewhere?' Note that this question requires another jurisdiction to be more convenient, not just as convenient if the UK court is to decline jurisdiction. In deciding the issue, the court looks at all factors, including:

• location of parties;

• location of documents and witnesses;

• applicable law (see below under 'choice of law');

• location of subject matter; and

• availability of legal aid.

The court will not generally look into arguments about which system has a better procedure or one more favourable to a particular party in a particular case (eg the UK and US procedures provide for wide-ranging disclosure of documents, other jurisdictions do not; the US has procedures for pre-trial cross-examination of witnesses as part of the discovery process, the UK does not).

UK courts will generally accept jurisdiction over a claim where the defendant has 'submitted to the jurisdiction'. This can be done by:

• agreeing that the courts in England and Wales will deal with any disputes before the claim has arisen, for example by signing a contract with a jurisdiction clause in it which covers the dispute in question;

• agreeing that the courts in England and Wales should deal with the dispute (eg in a letter) after the dispute has arisen; or

• taking a step in the proceedings other than to challenge jurisdiction (eg filing an acknowledgment of service indicating an intention to defend, or a defence). It is possible to acknowledge service of a claim form indicating an intention to challenge jurisdiction, which will not amount to submission.

However, that is not the end of the matter because English and Welsh law enforces compliance with jurisdictional rules partly by means of rules of procedure found in Civil Procedure Rule 6.36. This restricts the ability of claim forms to be served in cases where the address given for the defendant as its address for service is outside the jurisdiction: unless the provisions of Rule 6.36 can be complied with, the claim form cannot be served outside the jurisdiction and will be marked as such. The rule is easily complied with where the defendant is domiciled in a Convention State by the claimant certifying that the English and Welsh courts have jurisdiction. To comply with the rule for defendants with addresses for service elsewhere the claim must fall within one of the categories set out in para 3.1 of Practice Direction 6B.

27   *Spiliada Maritime Corp v Cansulex Ltd* [1987] AC 460, HL.

'(9) A claim is made in tort where:

    (a) damage was sustained within the jurisdiction; or

    (b) the damage sustained resulted from an act committed within the jurisdiction.'

There are also categories covering related claims, co-defendants, where the defendant has submitted to the jurisdiction and where there is a jurisdiction agreement. If the claim falls within one of the categories the court has a discretion to accept jurisdiction. The claimant must apply *ex parte* to the court for permission to serve the claim form out of the jurisdiction with supporting evidence. In exercising its discretion, the court will apply *Spiliada* principles.

Once the courts have got hold of a case, whether after giving permission to serve out or because the defendant has been served within the jurisdiction, jurisdiction can still be challenged:

- by the defendant, who can argue that the case did not fall within the rules and/or that the court should exercise its discretion to decline jurisdiction; or

- by the court of its own motion (this might apply where permission to serve out was not needed but the UK jurisdiction is inappropriate).

It is considered an abuse of the process to serve defendants who are temporarily within the jurisdiction where there are no other arguments for UK jurisdiction.

Applicable law (or choice of law)

3.11   Here also there are two schemes, but the division is by the type of action rather than the location of the parties.

For claims in defamation and malicious falsehood, the common law choice of law rules apply.[28] This is dealt with further in the section on defamation below.

For all other tort claims, the law is now contained in the Rome II Regulation.[29] This has the basic rule that the applicable law is the law of the place where the damage occurred. As we have seen that is not necessarily the same place as the place where the harmful event occurred. Exceptions to this basic rule are:

- Where claimant and defendant 'both have their habitual residence in the same country at the time when the damage occurs, the law of that country shall apply'.[30]

- Where the case is 'manifestly more closely connected' to a different country, the law of that country shall apply. The Regulation gives an

---

28   The Private International Law (Miscellaneous Provisions) Act 1995 excludes defamation and malicious falsehood from its scope (s 13).

29   Regulation 864/2007 on the law applicable to non-contractual obligations. This does not apply to 'non-contractual obligations arising out of violations of privacy and rights relating to personality, including defamation' (art 1.2(g)).

30   Above art 4.2.

example where there is a contract or pre-existing relationship that provides such a connection.[31]

DEFAMATION

3.12   The UK has traditionally been regarded as one of the most claimant-friendly places to bring a claim. The advent of the internet, which has the effect that publication anywhere is (at least arguably) publication everywhere, certainly highlighted this and has given rise to the concept of 'libel tourism', where claimants sue in London even though they, the defendant and the publication complained of are based overseas. This and other perceived defects in the law referred to below gave rise to calls for reform that resulted in the Defamation Act 2013. In places the Act introduced major change to the law; in other respects it was more a case of codification of the common law with some tweaking and with a view to simplification where the common law was perceived to be too complex. Many of its key provisions have yet to be tested in court,[32] so it remains to be seen how effectively the Act achieved its objectives.

Overview of the law

3.13   According to the leading practitioner work on the subject,[33] 'Defamation is committed when the defendant publishes to a third person words or matter containing an untrue imputation against the reputation of the claimant.' All of the words used there have their own meaning, specific to the law of defamation, but that statement provides a useful set of headings under which to organise any discussion. The key features are as follows:

- The burden of proof is on the defendant to show that the statement is true, as a defence, not for the claimant to show it is untrue. The claimant simply has to prove that a defamatory statement was published.

- Publication in the law of defamation means communicated to a person other than the claimant.

- Imputation is a term of defamation law. It incorporates the law's appreciation of the need for all statements to be interpreted in context, thus apparently unobjectionable words may be in fact defamatory. The word 'meaning' could be used instead, provided it is understood not to result from an a contextual or literal interpretation of the words, and that defamation law has

---

31 Above art 4.3.
32 For a discussion of the effects of the Act and the legislative history (which will inform its interpretation) see James RK Price and Felicity McMahon (eds), *Blackstone's Guide to the Defamation Act 2013* (Oxford University Press, 2013).
33 *Gatley on Libel and Slander* (10th edn, Sweet & Maxwell, 2004).

its own particular approach to divining the meaning of a communication from its context.

- A defamatory statement may be in any form: spoken or written words, moving or static images or multimedia communications can carry a defamatory meaning. And, of particular relevance to this work, the manner of communication is not prescribed, so communications via networks, including the internet, can be defamatory.

- It has been held that to be defamatory the imputation should tend to 'lower the claimant in the estimation of right-thinking people', or tend to cause others to shun or avoid the claimant, or tend to expose the claimant to 'hatred, ridicule or contempt'.

- An important introduction in the 2013 Act was the requirement that the defamatory statement must cause 'serious harm' to the claimant: although case law will have to develop that concept, it can be assumed that a genuinely minor slight will not give rise to a cause of action.

- While the harm must be serious, it does not, except in certain circumstances, have to be quantified. The circumstances where it must be (ie where 'special damage' must be proved) are where the claimant is a corporation trading for profit, not an individual; and where the communication was made orally not in writing (in which case it is slander, not libel).

- Finally, there are several full and partial defences to the action which serve to protect free speech and give some shelter from the law to innocent intermediaries.

Distinction between libel and slander

3.14   Put simply, any defamatory statement put in writing is libel, and no special damage need be proved in order successfully to sue in defamation for it. If the statement was not in writing, special damage must be shown.

One might propose that the reason behind such a rule is that written statements have a permanence which means they can be re-visited again and again, so the impact of the defamatory meaning is greater. Unfortunately such an interpretation cannot be reconciled with the way in which the law has developed.

The absence of a convincing underlying principle makes the extension of this rule to the networked digital world tricky. It is established that electronic documents should be treated in the same way as those written on paper for these purposes, so most common forms of internet-based communication will undoubtedly amount to libel: emails, internet text applications, posts and comments on social networking sites and internet fora, blog posts and comments thereon all have a permanence that places on the libel side of the line.

And as noted in the introduction, defamatory meanings can be conveyed in images, animations, sound recordings and videos, so applications that focus more on these types of media will also be caught.

Parliament has intervened to make statements in plays put on at theatres[34] and broadcasts[35] treated as libel not slander. The definition of broadcast requires multiple recipients, so would not include one-to-one live internet communications.

Thus a problem area is that of real-time communications made via digital networked systems where there is no obviously accessible permanent record. Network communication hardware and software tends to operate in a way that requires copies of communications to be kept, even if only temporarily. There may well be temporary copies of the underlying documents and images, or of sections of video or audio streams, in a local cache or buffer even if they are not kept permanently for future reference. In systems that operate on a client-server rather than a peer-to-peer model, there may be copies stored on the server, and there will also be temporary copies stored on the network hardware for caching and buffering purposes. The precise nature of the technology being used is relevant to the question of whether copies are kept and how permanent or accessible they are.

The defences afforded by the Information Society Directive will deal with many of these copies in the sense of preventing liability on the part of the network services provider. But that fact does not deal fully with the problem.

The end result is that the question of whether or not any particular networked communication is potentially libel or slander is not clear, but probably:

- telephony and network communications closely analogous to it will be categorised as slander; and

- email, chat and similar communications where there is a permanent record will be categorised as libel.

Who may sue and be sued – individuals, corporations and public bodies

3.15   The general rule is that any natural or legal person can sue, unless there is a specific rule that they cannot, subject to special rules that apply to particular classes of claimant.

Thus in addition to individuals, corporations, firms and unincorporated associations can all be claimants, though it must be borne in mind that the individuals forming those bodies, or acting on their behalf, might also be defamed and would be able to bring a personal action if that was the case.

The situation of claimants or defendants in overseas countries is dealt with in 'the international element' (see **3.44**) below.

Once a person is deceased, their estate cannot bring any action for defamation in respect of statements made after their death, and any cause of action in

34   Theatres Act 1968, s 4(1).
35   Broadcasting Act 1990, s 166, which uses the definition of a programme service from the Communications Act 2003, which includes both analogue and digital broadcasts (s 405).

defamation that may have existed at the time of death ceases, even if a claim had been commenced (this is different from the normal rule for torts). Similarly, once a defendant dies all claims against them cease, though claims against others in respect of the same publication can continue.

Prior to the 2013 Act, the position of trading companies and corporations was that they can sue, but they can only be damaged by injury to their trading or business reputation. Thus although the damage caused had to be of a financial nature, special damage (eg actual loss of income) did not need to be proved.

Section 1(2) of the 2013 Act requires claimants which are 'bodies that trade for profit' to demonstrate that the defamation has caused or is likely to cause 'serious financial loss' to them. This rule reflects the combination of the pre-existing requirement for financial loss to be proved in such cases with the serious harm requirement.

Statements against the goods or services of a company might be actionable if they also reflect on the business as a whole (as distinct from simply being an example of a defective product or an occasion of poor service). Allegations about the internal operations of a company (how it treats staff or manages its finances) can also result in damage to the company's trading reputation, for example making it difficult to hire staff or raise finance, or putting off customers who adopt an ethical approach to purchasing.

Allegations against a company officer will be actionable by the company if they reflect on the company itself, for example where the individual controls the company and can be regarded as its *alter ego*.

Not all corporate claimants will be trading for profit; for example charitable organisations, and such corporations will not have to show serious financial loss, but will have to show serious harm to their reputation.

Local government corporations and the Crown may not sue in defamation.[36] This rule will extend to local and national governmental bodies and agencies, though the precise scope of body that falls within this rule is unclear. However, this rule does not prevent officers from bringing an action if they can make out the elements of the cause of action, nor does it extend to actions for malicious falsehood (dealt with under the next main heading in this chapter).

Special damage and financial loss

3.16   As we have seen above, in cases of slander special damage must be proved and corporations who trade for profit must prove 'serious financial loss'.

Special damage means identifiable loss, and has the same meaning in defamation as it does in other area of the law (ie the loss must be pecuniary in nature or capable of being estimated in money). 'Financial loss' clearly means the same thing. The question of seriousness of loss is discussed below at **3.19**.

36   *Derbyshire County Council v Times Newspapers* [1993] AC 534.

Defamatory statements

3.17   As already noted, a statement, for the purposes of defamation, can be in any form and need not consist solely of words. Images accompanied by words, or on their own, can be defamatory. This exposes clearly the first problem facing a court deciding if a statement is defamatory – what does the statement actually say? The second question can then be considered – is that defamatory of the claimant?

The defamatory meaning (or imputation) of the statement

3.18   The law in this area needs to be considered alongside the procedure by which defamation claims are tried. Currently, Practice Direction 53.2.3 requires claimants to state in their 'statement of case' (a document prepared during the early stages of litigation) what they allege the defamatory meaning of the matter complained of to be. Alternatives may be claimed, as long as they are not factually inconsistent. For example, the claimant may assert a very clearly defamatory meaning (if that was held to be the meaning, they would have the defendant on toast and a defence of truth or fair comment would be impossible to sustain) and a milder meaning in the alternative (which might only arguably be defamatory and would be easier to defend against).

A quirk of the law of defamation, the 'single meaning rule', must be borne in mind here. The finder of fact must determine a single meaning for the statement.[37] This applies even where several meanings are possible, and would be appreciated as alternatives by the ordinary person, and this imposes some artificiality on the situation.[38] The single meaning rule is difficult to justify on any rational basis but the courts have accepted that only Parliament can change it (and the 2013 Act does not do so). It is largely a defendant-friendly provision – if a defamatory meaning would be taken by a significant number of people, but a non-defamatory one is predominant, then the dominant meaning will be taken. Of course, a statement may convey several separate imputations.

In judge-only cases, the judge will separate their final decision into the two questions 'what is the meaning' and 'is it defamatory' (even before the 2013 Act, which abolished any presumption in favour of jury trials in defamation cases, judge-only trials were becoming more common). In such cases, it also became common for the judge to find what the meaning of the words complained of was as a preliminary issue, before going on to consider at trial if that meaning was defamatory and if any defence was made out.[39]

The law considers the ordinary 'right-thinking member of society' as providing the standpoint from which the questions of meaning and defamatory nature are considered. This person (who is hypothetical, so the courts will not consider evidence from ordinary people to determine meaning) will make inferences from

---

37   *Slim v Daily Telegraph* [1968] 2 QB 157.
38   This is quite unlike the evidence-based approach in the tort of passing-off, for example, where if a substantial number of recipients of a marketing message interpret in a way that means the cause of action is made out, then the case will succeed.
39   See eg *BCA v Singh* [2010] EWCA Civ 350.

the statement, and the nature of those inferences will depend on the context in which the statement is made.

The whole published material must be considered, so where specific words are in issue, what is said elsewhere may render an apparently defamatory statement not so, or give a defamatory meaning to an apparently innocent statement. Where a published work or article is part of a series, preceding issues in the series may be taken into account. And where other publications (whoever published them) are referred to, they may be taken into account. This is likely to be important to bloggers and contributors to web-based discussions, where debates (or arguments or 'flame wars') may extend over a period of time and a number of articles, posts, or tweets which may link extensively to further material. The question of what other material should be taken into account in such situations is one for the judge who will consider what the ordinary person would take into account. In *Jane Clift v Martin Clarke*,[40] on the hearing of an application for a *Norwich Pharmacal* order, the judge held that comments posted to an article that was itself not complained of had to be read in the context of that article and that:

> '32 In my view, the postings are clearly one or two-liners, in effect posted anonymously by random members of the public who do not purport, either by their identity or in what they say, to have any actual knowledge of the matters in issue. It is difficult to see in the context, and having regard to their content, how any reasonable, sensible reader could take either of them seriously, or indeed how they could conceivably have caused any damage to the Claimant's reputation.
>
> 33 It is wholly unreal in my view, for example, to suppose that anyone will have read the postings, or gained access to them, detached from the very favourable and positive descriptions, including by the Claimant herself, in the substantive articles of what happened, and in particular of her vindication in the court proceedings. I note that the Claimant herself in correspondence described the Defendant's coverage of her case as excellent, careful and supportive.
>
> …
>
> 36 The postings are in reality, it seems to me, no more than "pub talk", as it has sometimes been described, and I consider it fanciful to suggest any reasonable sensible reader would construe them in any other way. ….'

The judge refused an order on the basis that the material was not defamatory, not that it was not defamatory enough to warrant an order. Each case will have to be considered on its own facts, but it does appear that the law recognises a distinction between comments on substantive articles and the articles themselves when it comes to their interpretation. This principle might also be extended to tweets commenting on issues raised in more lengthy and permanent media formats.

The ordinary member of society is not a member of a small group, so when considering what might be inferred from a statement, the court will not consider special knowledge, which the ordinary person will not have, as part

---

40 [2011] EWHC 1164 (QB), 2011 WL 441883 (transcript).

of the factual background against which meaning is judged. This is subject to the rather technical concept of an 'innuendo' that is part of the law of defamation. Where it can be shown by the claimant that the statement was published to a person or persons who possessed particular knowledge which affected the meaning they might get from a statement, then those 'extraneous facts' can be taken into account when deciding the meaning of the statement.[41] These extraneous facts might be specialist knowledge possessed by certain recipients, or facts (such as gestures, tone of voice and so on) that would have been apparent to those witnessing the statement live. Where a statement is published to the whole world, it is enough for the claimant to show that some recipients knew of the extraneous facts. Claimants must set out in their statement of case when they are relying on an innuendo and the facts relied on. Practice Direction 53.2 gives a definition of innuendo as 'a meaning alleged to be conveyed to some person by reason of knowing facts extraneous to the words complained of'.

The meaning to be given to repetitions and quotations of what other people have said raises complications. The rule is that the meaning is that of the statement quoted, even when accompanied by a statement that the defendant does not believe the statement to be true.[42] The pre-2013 Act reason for this is that the repetition of gossip will have the effect of increasing the damage to the claimant's reputation however it is expressed. To put it another way, the defence of truth must apply to what was said, not to the fact that someone else said it. Even accompanying the repetition with the quotation of a denial from the claimant will not necessarily cure the publication of defamatory content. Since the 2013 Act, the effect of any accompanying statement or subsequent correction or apology may have an effect on the presence of serious harm, dealt with below.

More indirect references to statements made elsewhere can also amount to repetition of defamatory imputations. In *The Lord McAlpine of West Green v Sally Bercow*, the defendant noted that the claimant was trending on twitter and asked why, followed by 'innocent face'.[43] At the time reports were circulating widely that a well-known figure had been accused (not by the police) of very serious conduct and speculation was rife as to their identity (the accusations were later published). The accusations were completely false, though the claimant was the subject of them. The judge held that the tweet carried the meaning of associating the claimant with those accusations (as their natural meaning inferred from all the facts, not by way of innuendo) and applied the repetition rule to find that the tweet was defamatory.

41 The classic example is *Tolley v Fry* [1931] AC 333 HL, where the imputation to the world was that a golfer had taken sponsorship money, but the innuendo to those who knew Tolley was an amateur golfer was that he had compromised his amateur status (at a time when that was a serious matter).
42 This is known as the 'repetition rule', and has been upheld (and held to be compliant with human rights considerations) in *Mark v Associated Newspapers Ltd* [2002] EWCA Civ 772, [2002] EMLR 38.
43 [2013] EWHC 1342 (QB) 2013 WL 2110791.

The need for serious harm

3.19   Defamatory statements are those which affect the reputation of the claimant. (Precisely how they must do that is addressed shortly.) The law has always recognised that there is a minimum threshold to be overcome before a statement that might do *some* damage to reputation is considered defamatory. This was summarised in the case of *Thornton*[44] and required the publication complained of to result in a tendency or likelihood of substantial adverse consequences for the claimant. The consequences might be insubstantial because of the limited level of publication, or because the claimant had no reputation capable of being damaged, and the same rule applied to corporate claimants as to individual claimants. Section 1 of the Defamation Act 2013 set out to codify such a requirement and arguably raise that threshold[45] and states:

'1.   Serious harm

  (1)   A statement is not defamatory unless its publication has caused or is likely to cause serious harm to the reputation of the claimant.

  (2)   For the purposes of this section, harm to the reputation of a body that trades for profit is not "serious harm" unless it has caused or is likely to cause the body serious financial loss.'

This wording introduced two main differences from the common law: the harm must be serious, and instead of a tendency to cause it, there must be a likelihood of causing it.

The need for serious harm thus may represent an additional test cases must pass even where the presence of a defamatory statement is found. The Act is worded to set a threshold that must be overcome; it does not appear itself to change the definition of what is defamatory (as to which see below). Accordingly, the test remains the same, but it is possible that for some defamatory effects, for example ridicule on its own, meeting the 'serious harm' threshold might be very difficult in practice.

Serious harm was considered in *Cooke v MGN Ltd.*[46] That concerned a corporate claimant, so serious financial harm had to be shown. The judge decided the defamatory meaning of the statements as a preliminary issue and held that:

•   Serious harm meant more than substantial (in the sense of 'not insubstantial') harm.

•   Seriousness should be viewed from the date of the hearing, bearing in mind what had happened and what might happen as a result of the statement.

•   In some cases it would be clear from the words complained of that the harm would be serious, but in other cases (such as the one before him) evidence that the harm was serious was needed.

---

44   *Thornton v Telegraph Media Group Ltd* [2010] EWHC 1414, also in *Jameel (Yousef) v Dow Jones & Co Inc* [2005] EWCA Civ 75. Both cases concerned claimants based overseas where the presence of a reputation in the UK to be damaged was slight.
45   The desire to discourage trivial claims is clear from the legislative history.
46   [2014] EWHC 2831 (QB); [2015] 1 WLR 895.

- In deciding seriousness of harm, the court could take into account corrections and apologies that had already been published. This could have an effect on the impact of the repetition rule referred to above.

- (*Obiter*) that where the issue was 'likely' harm, a claimant would need to demonstrate that it was more probable than not that harm would occur in the future.

In *Ames and Another v Spamhaus Project Ltd and Another*[47] the judge noted that the serious harm test was a higher test than the one in *Thornton* and *Jameel* and held that accusing claimants based primarily in California of being spammers was likely to cause serious harm to their reputation in the UK.

So, subject to the caveat that the serious harm requirement must be met, the following principles from the pre-2013 Act case law appear to remain valid.

What makes a statement defamatory – general principles

3.20   When considering the defamatory nature of the statement, as interpreted in the light of the above, again the ordinary person is considered, but they are assumed to know the meaning even if they would need to have it explained to them (eg if it was written in a foreign language or contained technical jargon).

The following three statements are recognised as ways a statement can be defamatory:

- The statement would tend to 'lower the claimant in the estimation of right-thinking people'.[48]

- The statement would tend to cause others to shun or avoid the claimant.[49]

- The statement would tend to expose the claimant to 'hatred, ridicule or contempt'.[50]

The law starts from the presumption that the claimant is of unblemished character, so it is up to the defendant to show otherwise and possibly make out a defence of truth or honest opinion (see 'defences' below).

Again it is the 'ordinary right-thinking member of society' that matters. Thus, a person who cultivates an edgy image would not be able to sue for being portrayed as wholesome and conventional, even if that was not true and would be considered defamatory to a class of people who would not be regarded as 'right-thinking'.[51] This might be thought to pose a problem in the case of allegations of conduct that would only be considered defamatory by a small group (eg a

---

47 [2015] EWHC 127 (QB), [2015] 1 WLR 3409.
48 *Sim v Stretch* [1936] 2 All ER 1237.
49 *Youssoupoff v MGM Pictures Ltd* (1934) 50 TLR 581.
50 *Parmiter v Coupland* (1840) 6 M & W 105, 108.
51 In *Byrne v Dean* [1937] 1 KB 818, the allegation was that the member of a club had shopped them to the authorities over the presence of unregulated gambling machines on the premises. This would clearly have damaged Mr Byrne's reputation with club members, but was not defamatory.

minority religious following whose customs the ordinary person would be unaware of). Such problems can often be overcome by casting the imputation of the allegedly defamatory statement in general terms, for example as one of hypocrisy.

However, the question must be answered for the particular claimant in the particular circumstances of the defamatory statement. So a statement that a professional footballer stayed up late drinking before an important game might be considered defamatory, whereas the same allegation against a Sunday league player would not be.

The question must be answered in the context of the attitudes and morals of the time when the statement was made. In many areas, these have changed markedly over the past few decades (consider attitudes to sexual matters and discriminatory views), so past cases must be viewed cautiously. Older cases may set out principles that are still relevant, but it cannot be assumed that the outcome of a case on similar facts would be the same.

Particular examples of defamatory statements

3.21   Notwithstanding the warning about older cases given above, and the effect of the 2013 Act and the serious harm test considered above that, here are some examples of statements that have been held to be defamatory.

Allegations of criminal activity (except perhaps in the case of some strict liability offences such as some motoring offences) are defamatory. Thus references to criminal prosecutions or investigations are liable to be interpreted as containing a defamatory allegation that someone is guilty of an offence, or other questionable activity that might cause a criminal investigation. The law has developed a rather detailed approach to this, referred to as *Chase* levels 1, 2 and 3.[52] The levels of meaning (which are not exhaustive but are the main possibilities) are: that the claimant was guilty of misconduct, that there were reasonable grounds to suspect that, and that there were grounds to investigate whether they were guilty of the misconduct. Clearly the fact of a police investigation against someone may mean that the lowest level is true (though it may not) but nothing higher. This explains the reluctance of the mainstream media to report on criminal investigations until there is a charge or summons (when defences are available). The identity of a person who is under investigation or whose conduct is being discussed in some way, but whose identity has not been revealed, is a popular subject of gossip in both face to face and online conversations. Such speculation may well involve a *Chase* level 1 or 2 meaning which may be untrue, thus the defence of truth will not be available.

Similar comments to those in the above paragraph would apply to non-criminal investigations, for example investigations into misconduct by a professional body or doping against a sportsperson.

Statements that someone is a liar will have to be interpreted in context. Some forms of lying (eg to avoid embarrassment in social situations) would not be considered a blot on anyone's character. But if in context the implication is that

52   *Chase v News Group Newspapers Ltd* [2002] EWCA Civ 1772, [2003] EMLR 11.

the claimant is the type of person who will lie in order to obtain an advantage or influence others, that will be defamatory and could clearly cause serious harm to a reputation.

While exposing someone to hatred or contempt is clearly defamatory, ridicule, without more, has always been a difficult area, and the prospects of serious harm flowing from mere ridicule seem unlikely. Even under the previous law, insults which do not contain specific statements of defamatory fact often fell on the non-defamatory side of the line.[53]

Where someone carries on a trade or profession, an allegation that they are incompetent at it will be defamatory.[54] This needs to be contrasted with an allegation of making a mistake on a particular occasion, which will not be unless the circumstances give rise to the imputation that the claimant does so persistently or because of some underlying incompetence.

As for shunning and avoiding, statements which have been held to cause a person to be shunned or avoided have included allegations of having a mental illness or communicable disease. The ordinary person would have sympathy for such a person, but might still tend to avoid them in some situations. The extent of the shunning or avoiding would need to be considerable for the 'serious harm' test to be met, and in addition s 14 of the 2013 Act requires special damage to be proved in cases of slander where the statement complained of is that the claimant has an infectious disease.

Allegations that someone is insolvent or cannot pay their debts will lower them in the estimation of others, though this needs to be distinguished from an allegation of poverty, which might not have the same effect.

A distinction has to be made between hurt feelings and damage to reputation. Making false statements about people is highly likely to damage their feelings, but will not necessarily damage their reputation. In the case of business claimants, damage to the business is not the same thing as damage to reputation (though there may be separate actions available in passing-off or malicious falsehood).

But it must also be noted that false statements can easily give rise to a defamatory imputation that might be actionable. The most common example is perhaps that the claimant is a hypocrite, or has lied in the past, or inhabits a personal fantasy world, which might arise where the published statement is at odds with what the claimant has said about themselves in the past. This is particularly likely to arise in the case of public figure claimants whose history, status and views are likely to be well known to many. In modern times, allegations of a sexual nature are far less likely to be defamatory than would have been the case even 20 years ago (homosexuality and infidelity being cases where views have changed, for example), but imputations of hypocrisy are likely to arise in relation to imputations of a sexual or moral nature.

It should also be noted that asserting true facts about someone might give rise to an action for breach of confidence or of the right to a private and family life

---

53 *Berkoff v Burchill* [1996] 4 All ER 1008, CA, is a case which was defamatory – an actor was referred to as 'hideously ugly' in a review.

54 Whereas to say of a lawyer that they are a hopeless cook (whatever the true situation) would not be, unless there are other facts giving rise to a defamatory imputation.

(allegations of sexual conduct being an example) or, if taken out of context, give rise to a false imputation or innuendo.

No requirement for malice or intention

3.22   Although older statements of the law required malice, this was assumed simply from the fact that a defamatory statement was made. In modern times, there is no requirement for malice and the tort of defamation does not have a mental element (although a mental element is part of some of the defences).

Following this principle of strict liability, it is no defence to a defamation claim that the defendant did not know that the words were defamatory, or honestly believed the statement was true (though the statutory procedure of amends deals with this situation).

The statement must be about the claimant

3.23   This is a particular aspect of the question of the meaning of the statement, as it also is decided by reference to the ordinary person – who would they think the statement is about? As with other aspects of meaning noted above, who the defendant thought they were talking about is irrelevant.

Thus the claimant does not have to be named, so long as their identity would be apparent in context. For this purpose, the special knowledge of those who know the claimant is relevant (they are after all where the claimant's reputation resides). So newspapers have been held liable to claimants who happened to share a name or appearance with a person reported on or photographed, such that the ordinary person would recognise them.[55]

This is undoubtedly a draconian rule and it can be envisaged that a viral internet video that depicts a person in a defamatory way could well cause people who happen to look like that person to think of taking action. Similarly, where someone is referred to by name on web page etc, a search for that name will reveal the item and it might appear, to their friends, to be about a different person of that name. The results of the search may display the original comment short of its context.[56] In such situations the true person referred to might become apparent by investigating the context of the post, but it is not clear how much of that context can be taken into account in determining meaning – see the discussion above. If the wrong identity is held to be the correct one for the purposes of defamation, as the defamation is unintentional a defence will be available if there is an apology and an offer to pay some compensation.

---

55   *Hulton & Co v Jones* [1910] AC 20, *Newtstead v London Express Newspaper Ltd* [1940] 1 KB 377.

56   Internet and website search engines often show items or extracts from the site's database of posts, comments, etc. The visitor has to click through to see the item within the discussion of which it formed part. Someone visiting the site via its front page and clicking through the structure would be much more aware of the context by the time they got to the item than someone who comes across the item as a result of a search.

In *O'Shea v MGN Ltd*[57] it was suggested that the operation of this rule could result in the defendant's art 10 ECHR right being infringed in a way that was not proportionate to the need to defend the claimant's reputation, but it is not clear that this approach will be followed.[58]

It is possible for members of a group to sue individually in certain circumstances where the group is referred to:

- the class is so small or so ascertainable that what is said of the class is necessarily said of every member of it; or

- the words, although they purport to refer to a class, yet in the circumstances of the particular case in fact refer to an individual.[59]

The requirement for publication

3.24   First, it is important to note that there are two distinct meanings for the concept of publication in the law of defamation. There is publication as a necessary element of the tort (only publishers of defamatory statements can be liable for defamation); and there is the partial defence afforded by s 1 of the Defamation Act 1996, which is only available to those who are not authors, editors or publishers of statements. These meanings are different. The first meaning is discussed next, the second below under 'defences for publishers, broadcasters etc'. Following the terminology used by the courts, the first type of publication is called, where confusion might otherwise arise, 'common law publication'. Electronic communication and making available on the internet are publications, as the cases on defamatory meaning noted above illustrate.

Publication at common law means communication to at least one person other than the claimant.[60] The fact that the recipient is under a duty of confidence in respect of the communication does not prevent it being a publication for this purpose. The concepts of 'the public' and 'to publish' are thus very different in the law of defamation compared to their meaning for the laws of copyright, confidence and patents. Of course, the circumstances of the publication can have an effect on the amount of damages that might be recoverable and in some situations the circumstances of the communication mean that a defence of qualified or absolute privilege might apply. The act of publication is receipt of a message (or browsing to a website) – see 'The international element ...' at **3.44** below, but note also the limitation provisions in 'The one-year limitation period and the "single publication rule"' at **3.27** below.

The only limit on this principle is that the defendant must have intended to publish the statement, so where someone composes and records a statement and another person, without the knowledge or consent of the first, then publishes it,

---

57   *O'Shea v MGN Ltd* [2001] EMLR 40 (QB).
58   It was doubted by the Court of Appeal in *Baturina v Times Newspapers Ltd* [2011] EWCA Civ 308 para 29.
59   *Knuppfer v London Express Newspapers, Limited* [1943] KB 80.
60   *Riddick v Thames Board Mills* [1977] QB 881.

the second person is a publisher but the first is not. However, if publication was a foreseeable consequence of the acts of the first person then both are liable, and there may be joint liability where there is a common design. The effect of this is that in the context of a newspaper, the proprietor, editor and journalist are all jointly liable for publication of material written by the journalist and published in the paper. Distributors and vendors are liable as separate publishers but will have the defence under s 1 of the 1996 Act (below), as long as they are unaware of the defamatory content.

Internet communications and publication

3.25   As explained at **3.2** above, all of the people mentioned there are involved in some way in the chain of communication that results in defamation, but not all of them can be regarded as publishers of anything. For those that are or might be publishers, defences (see later) may be available.

Website operators will have control over the structure and content of their site. They may create content themselves or decide what outside content to put on. In this respect they are clearly publishers by analogy with newspaper editors. But where there is user-generated content, the situation is more complex. With such content, the operator may decide to vet all submissions in advance and only allow approved content to be seen on the site, or may decide to allow the content straight through. In the latter case, the operator may decide to keep the site content under review and intervene if it appears that users are violating the site rules or doing something that might expose the operator to legal liability, such as uploading unlawful material or defaming others. This process of review after the event is generally known as 'moderation'. 'Moderation' is also used to describe the prior vetting of comments etc posted by users. More extensive control over content in the nature of exercising editorial control is not generally referred to as moderation.

With non-commercial sites, the operator may enlist the help of site users to act as moderators, giving them some site administration privileges so they can do so (ordinary users will not have power over other users' material, and may only have limited power to edit or remove their own material). Operators of more commercial sites will use employees or contractors for this. Moderators' actions may be to remove or hide posts or material, to edit or redact it or to ban users. The role of moderators is essentially reactive, to close discussion threads that get out of hand, ban users who breach the rules and, possibly, take down material that might expose the site owner to legal risk.

The law is a little unclear as to the position of hosts and 'hands off' operators of sites with user-generated content. In *Tamiz v Google Inc*,[61] Google provided a blogging platform upon which a blog was set up to which the material complained of was posted. The Court of Appeal was clear that once Google had notice that the content was allegedly defamatory, they were publishers of it, but suggested

---

61   [2013] EWCA Civ 68.

(*obiter*) that until that point they were not.[62] In the earlier case of *Godfrey v Demon*, an ISP (which provided internet access but also hosted the material complained of) was held to be a publisher of the material they hosted, akin to a bookseller, irrespective of their state of knowledge.[63]

By contrast, site operators who vet material prior to making it public are exercising editorial control and are publishers. In *McGrath v Dawkins*[64] the site in question required posts initiating discussions (starting forum threads) to receive prior moderation, but allowed further posts on the topic to be made without prior approval. The judge accepted that the moderator approving an initiating post would be personally liable as a publisher, but observed that if at trial the facts remained that it could only be shown that the defendant was one of four people who might have approved the post, then on the balance of probabilities the case against the defendant would have to fail.

The position of sites where there is moderation after the event is more difficult. Of course, the site user who posted the content is and will remain a publisher of it; they are in the position of the journalist in the newspaper scenario. It is submitted following *Tamiz* that the site operator will not be a publisher of user-generated content that is published automatically, and so long as the material concerned is not scrutinised then that situation will continue. However, knowledge of the defamatory nature of the content on a site will render the operator liable for it. Thus if a moderator were to consider a post and remove, edit or redact it, or decide to leave it as it is, they will have exercised editorial control and made the operator a publisher of the edited or redacted statement. By analogy with the newspaper situation and following *McGrath*, the moderator themselves would also be a publisher. This issue is discussed further in relation to the defence under s 1 of the Defamation Act 1996 below.

In *McGrath* the position of Amazon.com, on whose online bookselling website reviews were posted was considered. Amazon allowed reviews to be posted without prior moderation but had a policy for dealing with complaints about material. But it appears that Amazon did not argue that they were not, or not until a certain stage, publishers at all, simply arguing that they had the benefit of a defence under s 1 of the Defamation Act 1966 and also under the Distance Selling Directive.[65]

The law is clearer in regard to network intermediaries. In *Bunt v Tilley and Others*[66] it was held that the defendant's ISP (which provided the internet access whereby the defendant was able to post material to websites not controlled by the ISP) was not a publisher of the material by analogy with post and telephony service providers, who are not considered publishers. In any event, the defence available

---

62 From a technical perspective, Google took no active step to publish the material. They gave sufficient control over their hardware to enable the blogger to publish it, so their situation is a little different from that of a newspaper proprietor whose employees cause publication by laying out the pages and causing printing and distribution.

63 *Godfrey v Demon Internet Ltd* [2001] QB 201, though this finding was strictly *obiter* as the claim was restricted to the time after notice had been given of the defamatory nature of the material hosted.

64 See n 10 above.

65 See below.

66 [2006] EWHC 407 (QB); [2007] 1 WLR 1243.

under the Electronic Commerce Directive will be available to pure intermediaries such as ISPs and the operators of network hardware. In *Metropolitan International Schools Ltd v Designtechnica Corpn and Others*, one of the defendants was Google Inc but in its capacity of search engine operator rather than blog host (different from its capacity in *Tamiz*). Some searches submitted to them returned links to defamatory web pages, but also placed those links in the context of a 'snippet' of text from the page, of which complaint was also made. Eady J held that an internet search engine was not a publisher of material that was thrown up by searches submitted to it, including the content of the snippet, on the basis of the lack of any human control or intervention in publishing the material:[67]

> '64 Against this background, including the steps so far taken by the third defendant to block the identified URLs, I believe it is unrealistic to attribute responsibility for publication to the third defendant, whether on the basis of authorship or acquiescence. There is no doubt room for debate as to what further blocking steps it would be open for it to take, or how effective they might be, but that does not seem to me to affect my overall conclusion on liability. This decision is quite independent of any defence provided by section 1(1) of the 1996 Act, since if a person is not properly to be categorised as the publisher at common law, there is no need of a defence: see eg *Bunt v Tilley* [2007] 1 WLR 1243, para 37.'

(The s 1 defence is dealt with below.)

Thus search engines *can* become publishers of material on sites they have indexed for searching, but only after they have been notified of the offending material and had the opportunity to take whatever steps are practical to limit the material they return in response to searches. The judge distinguished the *Godfrey* situation, as it is easier to remove content from a static site than it is to control what is returned by an internet search. The judge also considered the balance between freedom of expression and defamation in deciding that further action by Google would be disproportionate.

A different situation is where content is automatically 'scraped' from elsewhere on the internet and reproduced or embedded on a site (as happens with price-comparison sites and so on). If the basis for finding and scraping content is determined by the site operator, it is submitted that such operators are not in the same position as Google, where the user decides on the search terms, and therefore may be publishers at common law.

Publication by linking

3.26   The question of whether linking to a website or web page that is not controlled by the linker but which contains defamatory content amounts to publication of that content is closely related to the *Metropolitan International Schools* situation noted above, but that case is complicated by the fact that Google supplied snippets from the linked site (originating from its own database

---

67   See n 8 above.

generated by the operation of its web-crawling software) as well as providing links.[68] The question of simple web links has been considered by the Supreme Court of Canada in *Crookes v Newton*.[69] The links complained of included links to a site on which ten articles were available, three of which were allegedly defamatory, and some direct links to allegedly defamatory articles. The Supreme Court upheld the finding that none of these links amounted to publication. However, the comments of some of the justices, that linking *on its own* does not amount to publication, raise the question of what has to be added to or around a link to cause it to do so. The majority held that unless the page carrying the link actually repeats the defamatory material linked to, that material is not published (so links which embed content would amount to publication). They equated links to references in paper publications. Two minority judges felt that the context in which the link is made could be publication if it adopted the linked-to content without it being repeated, and one justice felt that in some circumstances merely linking to a specific item could amount to publication of that item, though not in the particular case.

It is not clear that the UK courts will adopt the 'linking without repetition cannot amount to publication' approach. The Canadian Supreme Court in *Crookes* considered broad public policy as well as the detail of the concept of publication (which the minority tended to focus more on). It is highly arguable that a link to specific material which conveys the message 'hey go read this!' amounts to publishing that material at common law, even if it is not reproduced. If the linking page goes on to discuss the issues in such a way that a visitor would need to follow the link in order to follow the argument, so that the following of the link was an inevitable consequence of the link being provided, then the basic test for publication (see above) is met and the argument for linking amounting to publication becomes even stronger. The fact that the link was provided in response to a search is also part of the context, and that was referred to in *Metropolitan International Schools* – see the discussion under the heading above.

In the UK case *McGrath v Dawkins*[70] a first website hyperlinked to the discussion forum of a second. The judge left the question of whether the first site was a publisher of material on the forum to be decided as a question of fact at trial.

The question of whether someone is a publisher at all may well not be of great importance to them as a result of the various defences available to physical and network intermediaries and website owners. These are dealt with below.

It should also be noted that in some situations content from another site can be displayed on a web page. This (embedding) is not the same as linking and would clearly amount to publication (the site visitor would not know the source(s) of the content unless they examined the html source of the page). (Consider also image search results.)

---

68 The judgment does not give prominence to the question of the source (the Google database or the site linked to) of the content of the snippet, so it is difficult to disentangle the issues.
69 [2011] SCC 47.
70 See n 10 above.

The one-year limitation period and the 'single publication rule'

3.27   It can be seen from the above that each repetition or re-publication of a defamatory statement is a further actionable defamatory statement. Given the short limitation period of one year, described in the next paragraph, the implications of this are substantial. In this respect, English and Welsh law was at odds with the US, where there is a 'single publication rule' which prevents further publications from being treated as separate causes of action where they flow from a single initial publication. In *Loutchansky v Times Newspapers Ltd*[71] the Court of Appeal declined to introduce such a rule and held that in relation to website content, for so long as material remains on the web, each reading of it by a visitor is a separate libel which starts a fresh period of limitation running. However, in *Jameel*[72] it did note that a long delay in bringing an action could result in the claim being struck out as an abuse of the process.

The limitation period for defamation claims is one year by virtue of s 4A of the Limitation Act 1980. By virtue of s 32A of that Act, the court has a discretion not to apply that period having regard to all the circumstances of the case. In particular, the court can have regard to the length of and reasons for the claimant's delay and, where the delay was caused by ignorance of relevant facts, the time those facts became known to the claimant and the claimant's promptness and reasonableness once they became aware of facts giving rise to a claim.

The 2013 Act introduced a single publication rule into English and Welsh law – which was definitely an example of reform rather than codification-with-tweaking. Section 8 is as follows:

'8. Single publication rule

(1)   This section applies if a person –

(a)   publishes a statement to the public ("the first publication"), and

(b)   subsequently publishes (whether or not to the public) that statement or a statement which is substantially the same.

(2)   In subsection (1) "publication to the public" includes publication to a section of the public.

(3)   For the purposes of section 4A of the Limitation Act 1980 (time limit for actions for defamation etc) any cause of action against the person for defamation in respect of the subsequent publication is to be treated as having accrued on the date of the first publication.

(4)   This section does not apply in relation to the subsequent publication if the manner of that publication is materially different from the manner of the first publication.

---

71   (*Nos 2–5*) [2002] QB 783 (CA) at para 73; the case concerned the newspaper defendant's insistence to maintain on the web an archived copy of a newspaper article that was defamatory.
72   *Jameel (Yousef) v Dow Jones & Co Inc* [2007] 1 AC 359 (HL), which again preserved the existing rules on publication.

(5) In determining whether the manner of a subsequent publication is materially different from the manner of the first publication, the matters to which the court may have regard include (among other matters) –

    (a) the level of prominence that a statement is given;

    (b) the extent of the subsequent publication.

(6) Where this section applies –

    (a) it does not affect the court's discretion under section 32A of the Limitation Act 1980 (discretionary exclusion of time limit for actions for defamation etc), and

    (b) the reference in subsection (1)(a) of that section to the operation of section 4A of that Act is a reference to the operation of section 4A together with this section.'

The phrase 'publication to the public', even with the 'part of the public' qualification, would mean that the rule does not apply to communications to single or closed groups of individuals that would amount to actionable publications at common law. What is not clear is how limited the publication can be before the section does not apply. Is the theoretical scope of publication relevant, or the practical scope? A blog may have only a few followers, yet be available to the whole world; by contrast technical means may be used to limit the availability of something to a defined group that is extensive. Would an invitation-only Facebook group be the public? A relevant fact may be that in an email to a list of recipients, once it is sent the recipients are defined, whereas the members of the access-limited group can change without the need to take any specific steps in relation to particular items available to the group.[73]

If the initial publication is 'to the public' then, for the rule to apply to subsequent publications (ie to have the effect that those subsequent publications do not count for limitation purposes) the subsequent publications must satisfy two requirements: their content must be 'substantially the same' (s 8(1)(b)); and the manner of publication must not be substantially different (s 8(4)). The Explanatory Notes to the Bill[74] contain an example set in the online world: where an article that was once deep in a site such that several links needed to be followed to get to it is linked to directly from the front page. Another example would be re-publishing online content in print or vice versa.

Finally it can be noted that when s 32A of the 1980 Act is combined with sub-s 8(6) of the 2013 Act the court has ample discretion to waive the limitation period where injustice would otherwise be done, so publishers should be wary of relying on this rule in situations where the facts change and the status or relevance of the content changes with them.

---

73 In technical terms, if permissions on the server are set to allow access to member of named group, changing the membership of the group changes who can see all items for which access to that group is permitted.

74 Dated 10 May 2012 and available at www.publications.parliament.uk/pa/bills/cbill/2012-2013/0005/en/13005en.htm.

All the issues discussed under this heading will require a detailed examination by the courts and it is possible that the end result will not be such a great change from the position prior to the 2013 Act.

Joint and vicarious liability for publication

3.28   See generally **3.3** above. The long-standing principle that the journalist, editor and proprietor of a newspaper are jointly liable for publication is easily applied to similar internet scenarios, but the underlying principle of a common design must be borne in mind. A host or operator of a social networking site is not in the same position as a publisher as no conscious decision to print and distribute is needed, so no common design automatically arises with those who do take editorial decisions over site content.[75] In *McGrath* two websites were controlled by different companies which were under the overall control of the same person. The judge left the question of that person's liability for the acts of the companies to be decided at trial.[76] Employers are, however, vicariously liable for the publications of their employees.

General defences

The defence that the statement was true

3.29   The Defamation Act 2013, in s 2, sets out a statutory defence of truth that replaced and abolished the previous common law defence of justification. The explanatory notes to the Bill state that s 2 was intended 'broadly to reflect the current law while simplifying and clarifying certain elements'. The statutory modification to the defence contained in s 5 of the Defamation Act 1952 is also abolished, but replaced by similar words in s 2(2) and (3), with a similar intent.

The burden of proving truth remains on the defendant;[77] this was not changed by the 2013 Act and has been held to be consistent with the European Convention on Human Rights.[78] The defendant must prove that the precise words or imputation are true.

The 2013 Act in s 2(1) states that:

'(1) It is a defence to an action for defamation for the defendant to show that the imputation conveyed by the statement complained of is substantially true.'

Although this is expressed in slightly different words from the classic statements of the defence of justification contained in the case law, the basic requirement for 'substantial truth' reflects the cases on justification precisely.[79]

---

75   The copyright cases involving file-sharing support the view that more than mere site operation is needed for a common design, see *Newzbin* n 18 above.
76   Note 10 above.
77   *Bell v Lawes* (1882) 51 LJQB.
78   *McVicar v UK* (2002) 35 EHRR 22.
79   See eg *Chase* n 52 above.

By s 2(2) and (3) of the Act:

'(2) Subsection (3) applies in an action for defamation if the statement complained of conveys two or more distinct imputations.

(3) If one or more of the imputations is not shown to be substantially true, the defence under this section does not fail if, having regard to the imputations which are shown to be substantially true, the imputations which are not shown to be substantially true do not seriously harm the claimant's reputation.'

This differs from the defence contained in s 5 of the Defamation Act 1996 (which is repealed) by the inclusion of 'serious harm' rather than 'substantial harm'. The explanatory note to the Bill links this change to the 'serious harm' requirement introduced by s 1 of the Act. An example of the operation of this rule is where there are imputations that the claimant lied in a number of respects. If one of these imputations turns out to be false, that may have little effect on the claimant's reputation in the light of the proven lies.

The procedure the parties must follow has already been referred to. Just as a claimant must set out what the alleged defamatory imputation of the matter complained of is, so a defendant, when claiming justification, had to set out what it is that they sought to justify at trial. This requirement has been preserved, Practice Direction 35.2.5 having been amended to refer to the defence of truth, and requiring the defendant to:

'(1) specify the defamatory meanings he seeks to justify; and

(2) give details of the matters on which he relies in support of that allegation'.

The defamatory meanings asserted by the defendant may be different from those asserted by the claimant, it may be that the defendant contends for a lesser, but still defamatory meaning, and asserts that it is true.

The rather complex set of rules developed in case law prior to the 2013 Act concerning what meanings a defendant could and could not put forward as being justified was influenced by the fact that most defamation claims proceeded to a jury trial. The current status of many of these rules is in doubt as now jury trials have been abolished, the basis for the rules will have changed, and in any event the 2013 Act has abolished the defence of justification. So, for example, any defamatory meaning that the statement was capable of carrying (in the sense that a properly directed jury might find that to be the meaning) would have had to be put to the jury and, if the jury found that to be the meaning, the defence of justification might succeed. Now, the ordinary rule of civil procedure that a defence can be struck out if it has no real prospect of success would presumably be applied to speculative truth claims. Furthermore, the status of many of these rules (were they part of the substantive law relating to the defence, so now abolished, or rules of procedure that might survive) is not always clear. Sorting out how many (and how much) of the previous common law rules survive will be a difficult task for the courts.

Honest belief

3.30   Section 3 of the Defamation Act 2013 introduced a defence of 'honest belief' and at the same time, in s 3(8), abolished the defence of fair comment. The s 3 defence requires the defendant to show the following elements in relation to the defamatory statement:

- It must be an expression of opinion (as distinct from a statement of fact).

- It must indicate its factual basis (ie the facts on which it is based), and the defendant must prove those facts to be true.

- It must be one that could be held by an honest person on the basis of any fact that existed at the time.

The defence will not be available if the claimant proves that the defendant did not hold the opinion.

This defence certainly changes some aspects of the previous fair comment defence: the opinion no longer needs to be on a matter of public interest; and the honest person test applies to any fact that existed at the time of the statement, not (as previously) the facts expressly or impliedly referenced as supporting the opinion. Other aspects of it mirror the previous law: the fact/opinion distinction; the other aspects of the honest person test; and the need for supporting facts to be indicated. However, the abolition of the fair comment defence means that the courts will not be obliged to follow their previous case law on these issues if they determine that Parliament intended otherwise. As to the intention of Parliament, the explanatory note to the Bill indicated that the distinction between fact and opinion was intended to be broadly the same as previously, but it did express the hope that the new law would be simpler and avoid the complexities of the old.[80] With this in mind, the case law under the old 'fair comment' defence is summarised below.

The statement must be of opinion not fact. What is fact and what is opinion is decided with reference to the ordinary person, but this has not prevented the question from becoming fraught with technicalities. An important distinction is between statements that are unsupported by facts, and statements that are supported with reference to fact. An unsupported statement that someone is a crook will be taken as a statement of fact that they are a criminal. Such a statement made with a discussion of evidence of that person's conduct may be regarded as a statement of the opinion that the person is dishonest. Of course, the facts referred to may be defamatory and the statement of or reference to them may give rise to an action, so it is important, if this defence is to be useful, that the facts relied on are checked.[81]

An illustration of the difficulty can be found in *British Chiropractic Association v Singh*.[82] Eady J at first instance held that statements made by science journalist Simon Singh that the BCA promoted chiropractic treatments 'even though there

---

80   See 'Defamation Act 2013' n 32 above for a full discussion of the legislative history.
81   The approach to distinguishing fact from opinion are summarised in *Yeo v Times Newspapers Ltd* [2014] EWHC 2853 at paragraphs [84]–[98].
82   See n 39 above.

is not a jot of evidence' for their efficacy and that it 'happily promotes bogus treatments' involved the statements of fact that there was no evidence, and that the BCA were aware of this. The Court of Appeal overturned this aspect of the judgment, holding that in context the 'no evidence' statement was one of opinion not fact. More generally, it held that on matters of scientific controversy, the different views on the issue were likely to be opinion not fact. Given that much of the debate on scientific controversies takes place on the world wide web, this case represents a significant development. The Court of Appeal also commented, *obiter* that the 'fair comment' defence would better be called 'honest opinion'.

The facts on which the statement is based must be expressly or implicitly indicated in the statement. A problem area is where the supporting facts are not in the defamatory statement but referred to in it. References to other published documents have been held to incorporate the facts in those other documents, and such references may be implied where it would be clear that the opinion is based on those facts. In the context of statements in hypertext format, links to the material upon which the facts are based would no doubt suffice.

The facts on which the opinion was based must be true. They may also be contained in a privileged communication (such as evidence given in court – see privilege below). A defendant has to prove the truth of the facts on which the opinion was founded.

The opinion must have been one that could have been made by an honest person. This part of the test is difficult to nail down, in *Joseph v Spiller*[83] the Supreme Court held that an honest person might be prejudiced, or exaggerated or obstinate in his views. The opinion for this purpose is the defamatory meaning of the words used as determined by the court – the 'single meaning'. This may not, of course, be the meaning the maker of the statement wanted to convey, but where this rule operates to limit freedom of expression the court has applied human rights principles to hold that the defendant is not liable for expressing (without malice) themselves in a way that carries an additional imputation.[84] The new, more relaxed requirement that the opinion of the honest person can be based on any fact that existed at the time of the defamatory statement would presumably require the fact to be also true at that time, and require the defendant to set out any such facts relied on it its defence and prove their truth.[85]

Statements having absolute privilege

3.31   Privilege applies to acts of communication rather than the content of communications, in other words it is the occasion that is privileged. Privileged occasions at common law are:

- statements made in Parliament (but not reports of them);

- reports, papers, etc ordered to be published by either House of Parliament;

---

83   [2009] EWCA Civ 1075.
84   *Lait v Evening Standard Ltd* [2011] EWCA Civ 859.
85   The amended Civil Procedure Rule and its Practice Direction are silent on this, but in general parties must set out the facts upon which they rely in their statement of case.

- judicial proceedings, which includes the privilege over communications between a lawyer and their client for the purpose of obtaining or giving legal advice or preparing for legal proceedings;

- reports of UK court proceedings; and

- communications between certain officers of state.

Section 14 of the Defamation Act 1996, as amended by the Defamation Act 2013, provides that 'A fair and accurate report of proceedings in public before a court to which this section applies, if published contemporaneously with the proceedings, is absolutely privileged'. The Act goes on to list the courts to which the privilege applies:

'(3) This section applies to –

(a) any court in the United Kingdom;

(b) any court established under the law of a country or territory outside the United Kingdom;

(c) any international court or tribunal established by the Security Council of the United Nations or by an international agreement;

and in paragraphs (a) and (b) "court" includes any tribunal or body exercising the judicial power of the State.'

(The international element was added by the 2013 Act.)

The detail of the law on absolute privilege is not discussed here; it can be found in practitioner works on defamation and civil procedure and, in the case of court reporting, press and media law.

Qualified privilege

3.32   This is a privilege recognised by the common law, but extended by statute. As with absolute privilege, qualified privilege applies to occasions on which statements might be made. The qualification in these cases is that the privilege only applies if the maker of the statement was not motivated by malice. The occasions of qualified privilege can be put under the following headings:

- The statement was made in performance of a duty (not necessarily a legal duty, it could be a moral or social duty) and the recipient was a person to whom the statement should be made in order to comply with that duty.[86]

- The defendant had an interest in the matter which is the subject of the communication and the recipient had the same interest, or an interest in receiving the information. This would apply to communications between individuals within an organisation, provided the communication was to do with the organisation's operation.[87]

---

86   *Adam v Ward* [1917] AC 309 per Lord Atkinson at 334.
87   *Bryanston Finance Ltd v de Vries* [1975] QB 703.

Thus these two categories of privilege do not generally apply to statement that are published widely, but only to specific communications to defined people or groups. The occasions of qualified privilege are not a closed list, in each case it is a question of fact for the court.

The defence was extended by s 15 of the Defamation Act 1996 to include the publication of reports in certain categories provided the matter in the report was of public concern, or the publication of it was in the public interest. That section was extensively amended by s 7 of the 2013 Act to replace 'public concern' with 'public interest' and to add to the lists of categories of reports covered by the defence, particularly to give them an international dimension.

The list of categories is extensive and set out in Sch 1 to the Act. For those in Part II of the Schedule, the privilege may be lost following s 15(2):

'(2) In defamation proceedings in respect of the publication of a report or other statement mentioned in Part II of that Schedule, there is no defence under this section if the plaintiff shows that the defendant –

(a) was requested by him to publish in a suitable manner a reasonable letter or statement by way of explanation or contradiction, and

(b) refused or neglected to do so.'

For this purpose 'in a suitable manner' means in the same manner as the publication complained of or in a manner that is adequate and reasonable in the circumstances.

Meaning of 'malice' for the purposes of qualified privilege

3.33   The meaning of malice is set out in *Horrocks v Lowe*.[88] Lord Diplock held that for malice an improper motive had to be dominant. Even if the defendant's dominant motive was to injure the claimant, generally something more was required to show malice, which would normally require the defendant to either not believe the truth of their statement or be reckless as to its truth or falsity. The knowledge or recklessness test does not apply to people who are under a duty to pass information on.

Publication on a matter of public interest – Defamation Act 2013, s 4

3.34   Prior to the Act, the courts had developed a defence that was thought of as a further category of qualified privilege in *Reynolds v Times Newspapers*.[89] This was that the statement was made 'to the world at large' on a matter of public concern, and in this context the absence of malice was interpreted to mean 'responsible journalism'.

In *Flood*[90] it was held that 'A responsible journalist would have appreciated that some readers might have read the article as indicating that there were strong grounds for suspecting that Det Sgt Flood was guilty of corruptly selling

88 [1975] AC 135 at 149–150.
89 [2001] 2 AC 127.
90 *Flood v Times Newspapers Ltd* [2012] UKSC 11; [2012] 2 AC 273.

sensitive information, while others might read it as alleging no more than that there were grounds to investigate whether he had done so, and the claim to *Reynolds* privilege had to be assessed having regard to this range of meanings.'

Thus the 'single meaning rule' is not used in determining which meanings a responsible journalist should bear in mind when deciding whether to publish; a responsible journalist would consider the different meanings that might be read into the piece.

Section 4(6) of the 2013 Act states 'The common law defence known as the *Reynolds* defence is abolished', but s 4(1)–(5) set out a defence with many similar features, so as with the other replacement defences in the Act, while earlier case law no longer has the force of precedent, some of the principles developed in it may be carried into the new law. While s 4 is of great relevance to the press, it applies to all publishers including bloggers, posters of comments and tweeters.

The s 4 defence:

'(1) It is a defence to an action for defamation for the defendant to show that –

    (a) the statement complained of was, or formed part of, a statement on a matter of public interest; and

    (b) the defendant reasonably believed that publishing the statement complained of was in the public interest.

(2) Subject to subsections (3) and (4), in determining whether the defendant has shown the matters mentioned in subsection (1), the court must have regard to all the circumstances of the case.

(3) If the statement complained of was, or formed part of, an accurate and impartial account of a dispute to which the claimant was a party, the court must in determining whether it was reasonable for the defendant to believe that publishing the statement was in the public interest disregard any omission of the defendant to take steps to verify the truth of the imputation conveyed by it.

(4) In determining whether it was reasonable for the defendant to believe that publishing the statement complained of was in the public interest, the court must make such allowance for editorial judgement as it considers appropriate.

(5) For the avoidance of doubt, the defence under this section may be relied upon irrespective of whether the statement complained of is a statement of fact or a statement of opinion.'

Subsection (3) is a statutory version of the extension to the *Reynolds* defence contained in *Jameel (Mohammed) v Wall Street Journal*.[91] This has the effect that allegations publicly made by parties to a dispute may be reported, even if untrue and defamatory (as is likely if there is a substantial dispute of fact), that is a softening of the repetition rule. However, note that the account must be accurate and impartial – this would limit the ability to comment freely on the parties and the likely outcome.

---

91   [2007] 1 AC 359.

The public interest in s 4(1)(a) and (b) refers to different aspects of the matter: the subject matter of the statement or publication which is being reported on must be in the public interest (s 4(1)(a)); and the publication of that material must be in the public interest (s 4(1)(b)). As to the public interest generally, this is not defined in the Act and the Explanatory Note indicates that the existing law is to be preserved. In *Reynolds*, Lord Bingham stated that:

> 'By [the public interest] we mean matters relating to the public life of the community and those who take part in it, including within the expression '"public life"' activities such as the conduct of government and political life, elections (subject to section 10 of the Act of 1952, so long as it remains in force) and public administration, but we use the expression more widely than that, to embrace matters such as (for instance) the governance of public bodies, institutions and companies which give rise to a public interest in disclosure, but excluding matters which are personal and private, such that there is no public interest in their disclosure.' [92]

Thus there can be a public interest in the affairs of non-public bodies such as companies and charities, particularly large ones. In considering whether publication is in the public interest, the reference to personal and private matters indicates the more general concept that a balance needs to be struck where publication might infringe other rights. Case law in this area, as in others, has held that there is a public interest in the right of freedom of expression.

Reasonable belief that publication is in the public interest is not at first sight the same as the 'responsible journalism' part of the *Reynolds* rule. However, the Explanatory Notes to the Act indicate an intention to preserve the case law in this area, so in effect a requirement for responsible journalism remains. The Act has not sought to define the public interest in any way.

The broad requirement to take into account all the circumstances of the case in s 4(2) is intended to direct the court away from the development of detailed lists of factors to take into account, which might become effectively a series of hurdles to overcome. In *Reynolds* Lord Nicholls had proposed ten non-exhaustive factors which had been criticised in this way, but a balance between complexity and certainty needs to be struck. Lord Nicholls said (re-formatted for clarity):

> 'Depending on the circumstances, the matters to be taken into account include the following. The comments are illustrative only.
>
> 1.   The seriousness of the allegation. The more serious the charge, the more the public is misinformed and the individual harmed, if the allegation is not true.
>
> 2.   The nature of the information, and the extent to which the subject matter is a matter of public concern.
>
> 3.   The source of the information. Some informants have no direct knowledge of the events. Some have their own axes to grind, or are being paid for their stories.
>
> 4.   The steps taken to verify the information.

92   See n 89 above.

5. The status of the information. The allegation may have already been the subject of an investigation which commands respect.

6. The urgency of the matter. News is often a perishable commodity.

7. Whether comment was sought from the plaintiff. He may have information others do not possess or have not disclosed. An approach to the plaintiff will not always be necessary.

8. Whether the article contained the gist of the plaintiff's side of the story.

9. The tone of the article. A newspaper can raise queries or call for an investigation. It need not adopt allegations as statements of fact.

10. The circumstances of the publication, including the timing.

This list is not exhaustive.'[93]

These are a thoughtful run-through of the most obvious 'circumstances of the case' likely to be relevant, so in practice the courts will probably continue to use the ten factors, while being aware of the possibility that in any particular case not all of them will be relevant and there may be factors not on the list that are. One further factor that might be relevant is the resources available to the publisher – an individual blogger will not have a team of fact-checkers available, whereas the editor of a newspaper would. Nevertheless, some editorial judgment is required and so this defence will not be available to bloggers, commenters and tweeters who simply repeat matter that interests them, even if they accompany that with a statement of opinion. Some journalistic effort must be exerted.

The 'editorial judgment' of s 4(4) also reflects the previous common law position as set out above.

Statements in peer-reviewed academic or scientific journals – Defamation Act 2013, s 6

3.35   A number of notorious cases[94] against scientists and science journalists prior to the Act gave rise to concern that defamation law might chill scientific debate – as in the *Singh* case, probably the action would have failed, but there was a concern at the chilling effect of the threat of litigation by a well-funded organisation against a lone academic. The defence provides that publications in peer-reviewed journals are privileged unless 'shown to be made with malice', and if the review itself is published, that is also covered. 'Peer review' means independent review by the editor of the journal and one or more persons with expertise in the scientific or academic area concerned.

---

93   See n 89 above.
94   See *BCA v Singh* n 39 above and also the work of Dr Peter Wilmshurst, whose criticism of the scientific basis for medicines and medical products led to his being threatened and sued for defamation in the UK courts, although no cases proceeded as far as a substantive hearing, see for example 'British cardiologist sued by American company for a Canadian article', Sense About Science, www.senseaboutscience.org/pages/british-cardiologist-sued-by-american-company-for-a-canadian-article.html retreived retrieved 22/07/ July 2015.

Apart from confirming that a journal can be in electronic form, there is no definition of a journal: presumably a one-off publication would not count. There are no definitions of malice or of what science or academia are, presumably the definition of malice used for qualified privilege will be applied to the situation.

Freedom of expression and other fundamental rights

3.36   It has become clear in the years since the Human Rights Act 1997 was passed that the rights in the Convention will always take precedence over common law or statutory provisions, and that the UK courts will interpret the law in order to ensure that it is Convention compliant. A detailed discussion of the precise way in which that has arisen and the approach of the courts generally, and a detailed discussion of the precise scope of the Convention is beyond the scope of this Chapter. The impact of Convention rights will be discussed where they arise, the underlying legal approach is dealt with here.

The internet is an ideal place for human rights to clash with each other and with other rights. Freedom of expression is likely to clash with the right to a private and family life, the right of people to protect their personal or professional reputation and so on.

Even without the 2013 Act, recent developments in the law have shifted the balance towards defendants. The courts have paid consideration to fundamental rights although not expressed to be dictated by the HRA.[95] As will be seen from the cases referred to in this chapter, judges commonly call on human rights principles not only to provide a defence, but also to inform thinking on what does and does not amount to defamation in the first place.

There is a specific statutory provision in s 12(4) of the Human Rights Act 1998:

'(4) The court must have particular regard to the importance of the Convention right to freedom of expression and, where the proceedings relate to material which the respondent claims, or which appears to the court, to be journalistic, literary or artistic material (or to conduct connected with such material), to –

(a) the extent to which –

(i) the material has, or is about to, become available to the public; or

(ii) it is, or would be, in the public interest for the material to be published;

(b) any relevant privacy code.'

This was applied by Tugendhat J in *Ajinomoto Sweeteners Europe SAS v Asda Stores Ltd*,[96] to justify finding the non-false one of two possible meanings the

---

95   See for example *Derbyshire v Times Newspapers* [1993] AC 534 and *John v MGN Ltd* [1997] QB 586, CA.
96   [2010] EWCA Civ 609, [2011] QB 497, see 'Malicious falsehood' **3.50** below.

single meaning for the purposes of the tort of malicious falsehood. This was approved by the Court of Appeal, but they held that the single meaning rule did not apply to malicious falsehood cases. In relation to the single meaning rule and human rights, it appeared to approve counsel's disapproval:

> 'So far I have deliberately said nothing about the cause of action. If it had been libel, James Price QC, for the claimant, would have contended that the judge had not only reverted to the old *"mitiori sensu"* criterion rather than arrive at the informed preference which the law now requires but, in founding his choice on article 10, had accorded free expression inappropriate priority over the property right contained in article 1 of the First Protocol to the Convention.'

Thus, according to the Court of Appeal, the single meaning rule is compatible with human rights law and the correct way to balance freedom of expression and the right not to be defamed is not to proceed on the basis of a different meaning that might be what the defendant intended to express.

In *Loutchansky v Times Newspapers Ltd*[97] the court held that a newspaper's freedom of expression in relation to online archive material could be dealt with by the attachment of an appropriate notice, which would normally 'remove any sting from the material' (para 74). The European Court of Human Rights agreed with this approach when the case reached them.[98]

The dissemination of news has always been considered an important aspect of freedom of expression generally, and this reflects the way journalism is treated.[99] However, in the decision in *Delfi AS v Estonia*, the Grand Chamber of the European Court of Justice has held that where Delfi, an Estonian news website, was held liable for defamatory statements made in an un-moderated comment to a news item (which was itself unobjectionable) before they had received a complaint about the comment, that did not amount to a breach of the site's art 10 right.

In reaching its decision, the Grand Chamber balanced Delfi's freedom of expression against the claimant's personality rights, and in doing this took into account the extreme nature of the comments.

The impact of the decision is in the field of human rights, from which it appears that in balancing a news site's freedom of expression against an individual's personality rights, consideration of the freedom of expression of the site may not provide as extensive cover as is provided by UK defamation law.

Apology and offer of amends – Defamation Act 1996, ss 2–4

3.37   If no other defence is available, defendants can limit their exposure as a result of these sections. The defendant must issue an apology and offer to make amends by payment of damages. If the offer is refused and the case proceeds, this will give the defendant a defence.

---

97   Note 71 above at para 74
98   *Times Newspapers Ltd v United Kingdom* (3002/03); *Times Newspapers Ltd v United Kingdom* (23676/03) [2009] EMLR 14, ECtHR.
99   See for example *Goodwin v United Kingdom* n 14 above.

By s 4(3):

'(3) There is no such defence if the person by whom the offer was made knew or had reason to believe that the statement complained of –

(a) referred to the aggrieved party or was likely to be understood as referring to him, and

(b) was both false and defamatory of that party.

but it shall be presumed until the contrary is shown that he did not know and had no reason to believe that was the case.'

This procedure is thus only open to (relatively) innocent defamers, though there is a presumption that all defamers will be innocent. The apology needs to be sufficient to deal with the defamation that occurred.

Defences for disseminators of statements etc

3.38   Since the courts first had to deal with defamation cases, it has been recognised that part of the evil that the law must deal with is the way statements, once made, can spread. The question is, should all those who pass on a statement be treated in the same way as the originator, as defamers in their own right, or should they be given some leeway?

This question is clearly of interest to publishers of printed material, broadcasters, web hosts and internet intermediaries, but can extend to anyone who passes on information. Their status as publishers, or not, of the material has already been discussed under 'the need for publication' above. To the extent that they are publishers, some defences are available to them that are not available to those who initiate publication.

Defamation Act 1996, s 1

3.39   This provides a limited defence for anyone who is *not* an 'author, editor or publisher' of a defamatory statement (s 1(1)(a)). The section states that author 'means the originator of the statement, but does not include a person who did not intend that his statement be published at all'; editor as a person 'having editorial or equivalent responsibility for the content of the statement or the decision to publish it'; and publisher as 'a commercial publisher, that is, a person whose business is issuing material to the public, or a section of the public, who issues material containing the statement in the course of that business' (s 1(2)).

Section 1(3) lists a number of people who are not to be regarded as author, editor or publisher and goes on to state that in other cases 'the court may have regard to those provisions by way of analogy in deciding whether a person is to be considered the author, editor or publisher of a statement'. The list includes printers and sellers of printed material and manufacturers and distributors of films and sound recordings, and 'exhibitors' of them. Of particular interest for this work are those involved:

'(c) in processing, making copies of, distributing or selling any electronic medium in or on which the statement is recorded, or in operating or providing any equipment, system or service by means of which the statement is retrieved, copied, distributed or made available in electronic form;

(d) as the broadcaster of a live programme containing the statement in circumstances in which he has no effective control over the maker of the statement;

(e) as the operator of or provider of access to a communications system by means of which the statement is transmitted, or made available, by a person over whom he has no effective control.'

Thus the defence is clearly intended to apply to internet intermediaries: they would fall under (c) and (e) (intermediaries will provide access to their parts of the network infrastructure even if only to provide transit). Hosts would come under (c).which would also cover operators of websites which allow user-generated content, as their contract with their web host will effectively give them control over part of a system so making them 'operators' of it. ISPs, site operators and hosting companies typically have terms of use which allow them to block or ban users who distribute objectionable material, where the author of a statement is one of their customers. Presumably 'effective control' in (e) refers to an ability to control activities in real time,[100] so this would not exclude ISPs for this reason.

As for s 1(3)(d), the Act does not define 'broadcast': if the definition used in the Copyright, Designs and Patents Act 1988 is used,[101] that would include internet broadcasts, as broadcast is there defined as including any transmission where the time of the transmission is not chosen by the recipient (thus distinguishing a webcast or live stream from on-demand downloadable or streamed content).

But as we have seen, cases since the passage of the 1996 Act have developed the common law concept of publication so it is clear that hosts and intermediaries are not publishers at all unless and until they exercise some control over the content, or become aware that they are hosting defamatory content. In the case of intermediaries, they will also have the benefit of the 'mere conduit' defence under the E-Commerce Regulations (dealt with above). Bearing in mind the 'editorial control' provision of s 1(1), the carve-out from the definition of 'editor' for hosts in s 1(1)(c) would not include hosts which exercise editorial control. The result is that if a host does enough to become a common law publisher, they will also have become an editor and the s 1 defence will not be available to them. The usefulness and application of the s 1 defence to hosts and intermediaries is thus problematical.

The application of this defence to user-generated content was considered in *McGrath v Dawkins*.[102] Amazon did not argue the point that they were not publishers at common law, and the judge held that Amazon were not commercial

---

100 Currently it is not technically possible, or easily possible, to detect the content of material in transit in order to exercise any control over it.

101 In s 6.

102 See n 10 above, in relation to reviews and comments posted by users on the amazon.com website in relation to books that were for sale on it, which did not require pre-approval.

publishers of the reviews (the reviews arose in the course of their book-selling business), nor were they editors (and their procedures for dealing with complaints about posts after they were put up did not change this). The judge noted, however, that the defence might have ceased to be available had Amazon's dispute-resolution process resulted in a human intervention and review of any of the postings. Thus the defence applied, subject to the further requirement to take reasonable care discussed below.

The defence itself only applies if the defendant 'took reasonable care in relation to its publication, and ... did not know, and had no reason to believe, that what he did caused or contributed to the publication of a defamatory statement' (s 1(1) (b) and (c)). Given the variety of different relationships between web hosts and website owners and the content on their sites, the interpretation of this is likely to be critical to many situations. It should also be noted that knowledge or reason to believe is in relation to the statement being defamatory, regardless of whether there would be a defence (eg of truth). By contrast under the E-Commerce Regulations (dealt with above) the service provider must be aware of the *unlawful nature* of the activity (either *ab initio* or by notice). So if a defence of truth (or any other defence) would be available then the defence under the Directive is also available as the material will not be unlawful.[103] Section 1(5) states that:

> '(5) In determining for the purposes of this section whether a person took reasonable care, or had reason to believe that what he did caused or contributed to the publication of a defamatory statement, regard shall be had to –
>
> (a) the extent of his responsibility for the content of the statement or the decision to publish it,
>
> (b) the nature or circumstances of the publication, and
>
> (c) the previous conduct or character of the author, editor or publisher.'

It might be thought that a reasonable approach would be to approve all posts in advance. But as noted above the defence does not appear to be available in such situations as that would amount to the assumption of editorial control. In *McGrath* the judge noted that:

> 'this is an illustration of the notorious "Catch-22" under which an ISP seeking to attract the statutory defence by taking reasonable care may find that it has instead forfeited it by becoming an editor'.

Certainly if material is initially allowed on a site with no prior approval, but moderating action is taken to edit or redact a post, that would amount to an editorial action meaning that the defence is not available for the publication from then onwards. It is thus advisable that moderating activity is restricted to allowing or blocking the content, but even that may amount to the exercise of editorial control. And in any event, the alternative approach of taking no steps to restrict material until a problem emerges also has problems.

---

103 Thus distinction was noted in *Bunt v Tilley*, n 66 above.

In *Godfrey v Demon Internet Ltd*,[104] Morland J considered that, once the defendant knew of the defamatory nature of the material but chose not to remove it, they could no longer have the benefit of the defence (on his pre-*Tamiz* interpretation of common law publication, a defence was needed). HHJ Moloney QC in *McGrath* felt that Amazon's position prior to any problem being notified to it was arguable but unclear, and left to trial its argument that its procedures for dealing with complaints about postings after they had been uploaded did amount to reasonable care. Finally, in *Metropolitan International Schools Ltd v Designtechnica Corpn*,[105] where the 'no initial common law publication' point was accepted, Eady J offered the opinion that it was difficult to see how an operator *who was a publisher at common law* (ie once they had been put on notice) could argue that doing nothing to control what material was included on a website could amount to reasonable care.

It can be argued that, for example, only after the host has become aware (through notice of the work of a moderator) that material is possibly defamatory will there be common law publication and the reasonableness of any steps taken must be determined at the time the host or operator became a publisher at common law and not before. *Metropolitan* indicates that continuing to do nothing would mean that the defence does not apply, but it is possible that the defence would apply to a reasoned decision, taken as part of a reasonable procedure, to leave in place material which is later held to be defamatory, provided it could be argued that this did not amount to taking editorial control. Possibly the defence will allow a period of time within which to make the decision before editorial control is assumed to kick in and the defence is lost. Bearing in mind s 1(5)(c), a site that has a history encouraging scurrilous rumour will not have the benefit of the defence whatever its procedures.

Clearly, the possible availability of the s 1 defence is unclear and thus web hosts and site operators have a cause for concern. A further criticism of it is that most ISPs and hosts would not be interested in investigating whether a statement was in fact defamatory, less still whether the statement might be true, and would just pull the relevant material when any notice was received. This applies to the 'notice and take down' procedure under the Regulations as well. The notice system is thus open to abuse by those without genuine claims who wished to suppress material. This can have the effect of removing completely from the internet whole blogs and websites with campaigning or controversial material. The 2013 Act sought to make the position clearer for hosts.

The defence for web hosts in Defamation Act 2013, s 5

3.40   Section 5 of the Act is a long section, but the main provisions are:

'5.   Operators of websites

(1)   This section applies where an action for defamation is brought against the operator of a website in respect of a statement posted on the website.

104   See n 63 above.
105   See n 8 above.

> (2) It is a defence for the operator to show that it was not the operator who posted the statement on the website.
>
> (3) The defence is defeated if the claimant shows that –
>
> > (a) it was not possible for the claimant to identify the person who posted the statement,
> >
> > (b) the claimant gave the operator a notice of complaint in relation to the statement, and
> >
> > (c) the operator failed to respond to the notice of complaint in accordance with any provision contained in regulations.'

The section goes on to deal with what is and is not a 'notice of complaint', and to give powers to make regulations.

The Act does not define 'website', 'operator' or 'post', so the courts will have to determine what the intention of Parliament was. In technical terms, a website would be any source of information which is connected to the World Wide Web.[106] Thus it will be a matter of interpretation whether systems such as Usenet, which uses the internet and its communication protocols but is not technically regarded as part of the World Wide Web (it pre-dates it), will fall within the ambit of the Act. Certainly, information on communication systems that are outside the internet, such as those that operate solely via the mobile phone network, would not be websites. The status of some systems is unclear and will have to be assessed on a case-by-case basis.[107]

The operator of a website is presumably a person with control over the site's content. In a typical scenario, there may be more than one such person: someone setting up a site will need a web host to put the material on the web, and both the host and the site owner will have the power to remove[108] content. To the extent that the host needs a defence, it would be illogical for them not to have one along with the site owner.

Someone will presumably post information on a site when they upload material to the site (even if it might have to be scrutinised by a human before being allowed to go public). Posting is the term generally used for uploading material to a site or message board with the intention that it be published or read by others. The Act did not use the word 'publish' here, but of course a poster will only need a defence if they are also a common law publisher. By analogy with the cases on publication (see above) someone who uploads material to a server genuinely and reasonably believing that it will not be published or shared (eg to their cloud storage) is not a publisher at all. They will not become one if the host makes it public (whether by error, deliberately or as the result of malicious action). Such uploading would not generally be termed 'posting' in any event.

---

106 See the technical discussion above.

107 For example emails, usenet and messages on popular messaging systems can all be accessed via web-based portals, but the decisive issue is likely to be whether an individual message or post, that might contain defamatory material, can be (and is) linked to from a web page. On that basis, an email host would not be a website operator in relation to the emails kept on its servers.

108 In the sense of rendering it unavailable and thus no longer part of the web.

Section 5(12) clarifies one issue about posting – the position of sites which moderate content. Moderation involves the review of material already published, it is distinguished from the review of material prior to publication, which is not called moderation (it would normally be described as editing or curating). Typically, operators of sites with user-generated content will 'moderate' the content even if they do not vet material prior to making it public.

It is submitted that the process of moderation does not make the moderator a 'publisher' of material unless they modify it in some way, but the site operator will, or may become, a publisher of the content. Section 5(12) makes it clear that the process of moderation does not make the site owner a 'poster' for the purposes of s 5(2), but the scope of this is a little unclear. An uncontroversial core meaning of s 5(12) is that the fact that a site is moderated does not make the operator or moderator a 'poster' of material that remains unaltered, the defence will still be available (presumably whether the material was looked at and considered OK, or not looked at at all). But what of material that is altered or redacted by moderators? The Act contains no definition of 'moderate', but the limits of what can be called 'moderation' are important: if a particular act of modification of a post goes beyond 'moderation' then it will presumably amount to 'posting', and will also be common law publishing of the material, meaning that the defence is not available and the website operator might be liable. It would be odd if a moderator's attempt at making a post non-defamatory that only succeeded in making it less defamatory would attract liability. But if the moderation made things worse, or even rendered the non-defamatory defamatory, then if the defence applied there would be effectively a liability-free defamation.[109] As with s 1 of the 1996 Act, restricting moderating actions to leaving be or blocking totally appears the safest course.

Nevertheless, by talking of 'posting' rather than 'publication', s 5 avoids the problem with s 1 of the 1996 Act that makes giving it a useful meaning so difficult. A site operator may become a publisher at common law (eg when they become aware of defamatory content) but the defence remains available to them so long as they were not the original poster and to not take a step that amounts to re-posting the material (see above). But the strings attached to the defence (notably the notice procedure contained in subsection (3)) are important:

'(3) The defence is defeated if the claimant shows that –

(a) it was not possible for the claimant to identify the person who posted the statement,

(b) the claimant gave the operator a notice of complaint in relation to the statement, and

(c) the operator failed to respond to the notice of complaint in accordance with any provision contained in regulations.'

---

109 This issue was discussed in parliamentary debates on the Bill, and it appears that the ordinary internet meaning noted above was intended. See 'The Defamation Act 2013' (n 32) Ch 6 for a discussion of the legislative history.

The relevant Regulations are the Defamation (Operators of Websites) Regulations.[110] The Ministry of Justice has also published guidance: Complaints about Defamatory Material Posted on Websites: Guidance on Section 5 of the Defamation Act 2013 and Regulations.[111] The scheme is complex, an outline of the process is given in Figure 1 below:

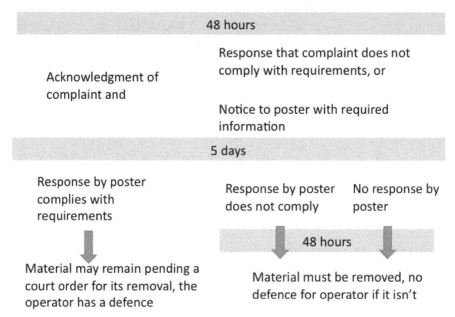

Complaint to site operator

48 hours

Acknowledgment of complaint and

Response that complaint does not comply with requirements, or

Notice to poster with required information

5 days

Response by poster complies with requirements

Response by poster does not comply

No response by poster

48 hours

Material may remain pending a court order for its removal, the operator has a defence

Material must be removed, no defence for operator if it isn't

Important points to note about it are:

● The notice of complaint must set out the defamatory meaning alleged and why any facts in it are untrue, or opinions in it not based on fact. To do this properly, it is submitted that legal advice from a defamation specialist would be needed. However where the notice does not do this the operator must either respond saying how the notice is defective, or comply with the Regulations anyway.

● The claimant only need provide a name and contact email address and can ask for these details not to be forwarded to the poster. There are no particular adverse consequences for claimants seeking anonymity.

● If the poster wishes the material to remain on the site, they must provide a full name and postal address, otherwise the material complained of must be taken down. If 'a reasonable website operator' would think that an address given is false, they can treat it as if the details were not given. The poster

---

110 2013/3028.
111 January 2014, available at www.gov.uk/government/uploads/system/uploads/attachment_data/file/269138/defamation-guidance.pdf.

does not have to agree to their details being provided to the claimant, but the Guidance states that this will not prevent the claimant obtaining a court order requiring the operator to disclose the information.

- If the site owner does not have a contact for the poster (which must include an email address or similar) the material must be taken down.

- If the poster complies with the procedure and does not consent to the material being taken down, then provided the site operator also complies with the procedure, the defence will persist. The effect of this is that (unless the site operator decides unilaterally to remove the material) the material will remain on the site until the claimant obtains a judgment in their favour, when they can obtain an order to remove the material under s 13 of the 2013 Act. The defence will prevent any damages being recoverable from the operator for the period when the material was on the site.

The time limits are short – five days for an initial response by the operator. A court may treat a late compliance with a requirement of the regulations as having been done in time if 'it is in the interests of justice to do so' (reg 5).

According to s 11, 'The defence under this section is defeated if the claimant shows that the operator of the website has acted with malice in relation to the posting of the statement concerned'. The malice must relate 'to the posting of the statement', implying that it does not apply to any action or inaction after that and it is difficult to see how this could arise. For the defence of qualified privilege, malice can only be inferred if the defendant knew the statement was false, or was reckless as to whether or not it was false. Application of these principles to the operator's knowledge of the content of a post is difficult to reconcile with the clear intention behind the defence, which was to protect operators who do not know or care what is put on their site (until a notice is received, when they have to be careful to comply with the Regulations).

The defence will not apply if the operator posts material himself, which will include colluding with others to do so (resulting in becoming a joint tortfeasor by virtue of general principles, but also presumably a joint 'poster' for the purposes of the section).

While useful for website operators, this defence will, in many situations, be subsumed by the defence under s 10 below.

Further protection for non-authors etc – Defamation Act 2013, ss 10 and 13

3.41   Section 10 states:

(1) A court does not have jurisdiction to hear and determine an action for defamation brought against a person who was not the author, editor or publisher of the statement complained of unless the court is satisfied that it is not reasonably practicable for an action to be brought against the author, editor or publisher.

(2) In this section "author", "editor" and "publisher" have the same meaning as in section 1 of the Defamation Act 1996.'

Section 13 gives the court power, after a judgment that a statement has been defamatory, to order website operators to take material containing the statement down and to order people who are not authors, editors or publishers of it to stop distributing it.

A main consideration behind s 10 was to limit 'libel tourism', but there will be situations where it is practicable to pursue an overseas author. The 'not reasonably practicable' requirement raises several unanswered questions.

First, the relationship with the notice procedure of s 5 needs to be noted. The debates on the Bill indicate concern that s 10 would not mean website operators could rely on it and so ignore a s 5 notice.[112] This would mean that, in cases of an anonymous or pseudonymous poster (as would be the case with many contributors to internet discussion boards, or social networking sites) obtaining and enforcing a *Norwich Pharmacal*[113] order against the operator to identify the author may not amount to a reasonably practicable route.

Secondly, the extent to which the circumstances of the defendant, if and when their identity becomes known, are relevant will need to be addressed by the courts. Prima facie, all factors should be taken into account, including the defendant's means to pay compensation and their propensity to repeat the defamatory statement. There may be situations where it is not reasonably practicable to pursue a defendant who is identifiable and within the jurisdiction.

Finally there is the situation of the overseas poster. Where they are in a jurisdiction that would accept jurisdiction over the claim and apply effective defamation law to the case, it may be practicable to sue them. This might apply to countries that are within the EU jurisdictional scheme. But in many situations pursuing overseas defendants will be impracticable.

Websites, web hosts, ISPs and network intermediaries – summary

3.42   An important distinction here is between control exercised over what goes on the site, and control exercised once material is available on the site. Some sites vet all user-submitted content prior to making it live. Anyone involved in taking the decision to add material in this way will be a potential defendant in a defamation claim. But many sites allow users to submit content with no pre-vetting.

A difficult situation is where a moderator edits or partially removes content, but it remains defamatory, or possibly becomes more defamatory (if the moderation was ill-advised). If significant changes are made, the moderator would become akin to a re-publisher of the defamatory statement and would be liable. It might be thought that the way to avoid such difficulties is for moderators to act by just allowing the whole of an article, post or comment to stand, or to remove it completely. This is easier said than done: other site users may have engaged in a discussion about the content and quoted sections of it – that quoted text may also be defamatory. Further, once an item that has been commented on by others has been removed, the comments that remain will look silly and could

112 See n 32 above, Ch 6.
113 See **3.4** above – the only certainty of a *Norwich Pharmacal* procedure would be the cost involved.

theoretically acquire a defamatory meaning in their new context, though it is difficult to think of an example of how this might occur. The point is, a lively site with user-generated content is a complex and highly interconnected thing (ie the whole point of the social element of websites) and tinkering with it can have unexpected consequences.

Overall, the best advice for moderators is to act swiftly and decisively. This will not simply protect the site owner, but also protect users from getting sucked into a debate and repeating defamatory statements themselves, thereby incurring liability. This would mean locking and perhaps deleting a whole thread of discussion where the content started to become risky.

Remedies

3.43   In defamation cases, often the outcome that is most valuable to a claimant is simply a finding in their favour, that they have been defamed. But damages are also available, and where there is a risk of the publication continuing, injunctions may also be awarded.

In cases where special damage or financial loss has to be proved (eg cases of slander and for corporate claimants who trade), damages will be assessed on usual tortious grounds and are not controversial (dealt with in a little more detail in the section of this chapter on negligence). In other cases, the question of damage was left to the jury and high awards in some cases caused controversy and were reduced by the Court of Appeal.[114] The leading case is *John v Mirror Group*[115] in which the Court of Appeal sought to link damages for defamation to damages for personal injury (as to which there is extensive guidance and case law). While that is an exercise in comparing apples with oranges, personal injury awards do set limits for even the most serious injury which will limit defamation damages. In effectively eliminating jury trials in s 11, the 2013 Act has reduced further the possibility of excessive awards, but aggravated and exemplary damages remain available.

A defendant is able to put forward (true) facts in mitigation of damages, even where a defence of truth is not available, for example to show that the defendant's reputation is such that it does not have a great capacity for being damaged.[116]

While final injunctions are awarded as a matter of course where the defendant has not ceased publication, interim injunctions are extremely rare in defamation cases. This is because of concern at infringing the defendant's right to freedom of expression, so such injunctions are only granted where the claimant can show that the statement complained of is plainly untrue.[117]

---

114 In *Tolstoy v United Kingdom* (1995) 20 EHRR 442, the European Court of Human Rights held a high award of damages to be a violation of the right to freedom of expression in art 10 of the Convention. The Court of Appeal has power to reduce damages under s 8 of the Courts and Legal Services Act 1980.

115 [1997] QB 586.

116 *Burnstein v Times Newspapers* [2000] EWCA Crim 338.

117 *Green v Associated Newspapers Ltd* [2004] EWCA Civ 1462, [2005] QB 972.

The international element – jurisdiction and choice of law in defamation

3.44 Curbing libel tourism was one objective of the 2013 Act. The requirement for serious harm to the claimant addresses this issue in part – where the publication in the UK is minor and the claimant's reputation here slight, there may be no serious harm. Another important way the Act dealt with this is in s 9 (below), but that section only applies where an action is brought against a defendant who is not domiciled in the UK or a state that is part of the European Economic Area. Readers are referred to the general schemes set out at **3.7** above. For the purposes of jurisdiction, the place of publication is the place where a communication is received,[118] so material on the internet is published in every jurisdiction where it is read.

Defendants domiciled in the EU or countries that are party to the Lugano Convention

3.45 Under the Regulation, the 'act complained of' will be the publication of a defamatory statement. So where material on the internet is accessible from the UK, an action can be brought if a claim can be made out. However, there still needs to be a *sufficient* publication here for a cause of action in defamation to arise under UK law – this is dealt with under the next heading, though s 9 of the 2013 Act will not apply. If there is not a cause of action for those reasons, the English and Welsh courts may have to apply the defamation law of another state if there is a cause of action under that law.

Defendants domiciled outside the European scheme

3.46 In *Jameel* and *Thornton*[119] the courts required there to be a 'real and substantial' tort within the jurisdiction as a way of filtering out cases where the connection with the UK was tenuous. The requirement for substantial harm (discussed above) imposes a higher standard on such cases.[120] In *Ames v Spamhaus*[121] it was held that claimants resident in California who ran a bulk emailing service from there had a reputation in the UK and were likely to suffer serious harm here as a result of being labelled spammers. It was held that a range of factors had to be taken into account including the nature of the statement, the international nature of internet businesses (by which it is possible to build up a reputation in a foreign country without visiting it) and the possibility of re-publications of the statement occurring. In cases where there is not a sufficient tort within the UK, the courts have struck out the claims as an abuse of process (see the discussion under **3.47** below for the position where there may be an action under foreign law).

In addition, s 9 of the 2013 Act introduces a further requirement in cases where the defendant is not domiciled in the UK, EU or a Convention State:

---

118 *King v Lewis* [2004] EWCA Civ 1329, [2005] EMLR 4.
119 See the discussion at **3.19** above.
120 Recognised in *Ames and Another v Spamhaus Project Ltd*, n 41 above
121 Ibid.

'9. Action against a person not domiciled in the UK or a Member State etc

…

(2)   A court does not have jurisdiction to hear and determine an action to which this section applies unless the court is satisfied that, of all the places in which the statement complained of has been published, England and Wales is clearly the most appropriate place in which to bring an action in respect of the statement.

(3)   The references in subsection (2) to the statement complained of include references to any statement which conveys the same, or substantially the same, imputation as the statement complained of.'

This serves to re-cast the general common law *Spiliada* question (referred to above) so that England and Wales must be considered along with all other jurisdictions and found to be the most appropriate place.

Choice of law in defamation cases

3.47   This issue was not discussed in the general section above as the law of defamation has been excluded from statutory interventions in this area so is governed by the common law. The common law is as follows:

- English and Welsh law applies exclusively to a tort committed in England and Wales.[122] As noted above defamation in respect of a publication read here will be committed here since defamation law regards receipt of a publication as the defining event.

- In the case of torts committed abroad, the 'double actionability rule' applies, meaning that the tort must be actionable both under English and Welsh law and the law of the place where the tort is committed (so foreign law would need to be applied in such cases).[123]

Thus, if defamation claimants wished to restrict their claim to the consequences of publication in England and Wales, they could proceed under domestic law provided the facts supported a claim. If they wished to claim for the consequences of publication overseas, the double actionability rule applied. However, in cases where the European jurisdiction scheme does not apply, in such cases the courts applied *Spiliada* principles and declined jurisdiction. For defendants domiciled within the EU and Convention area, this is not an option and the courts may have to accept jurisdiction and apply both systems of law according to the double actionability rule.

Internet defamation claims – conclusions

3.48   Publication on the internet will generally involve publication, at least in the theoretical sense of availability, on a worldwide basis, with concomitant

---

122 *Szalatnay-Stacho v Fink* [1947] KB 1.
123 *Boys v Chaplin* [1971] AC 356.

damage occurring worldwide also. Prior to the 2013 Act claimants were generally happy to litigate in the UK even if this meant restricting their claim to the consequences of publication in the UK because of the claimant-friendly nature of UK defamation law. While the law is now not quite so friendly, this may still be so. But if the worldwide consequences of publication are serious and the claimant wants to seek redress in respect of them, the position depends on whether the courts have jurisdiction pursuant to the European scheme or the common law: under the European scheme claims can be brought in the UK in respect of publications overseas, under the common law the court will most likely decline jurisdiction in relation to those aspects of the claim.

Possible impact of press regulation on news sites

3.49   As a result of the Leveson Report,[124] a scheme for the regulation of the press has been implemented in UK law. The scheme involves an uber-Regulator, the Press Recognition Panel, which has been set up pursuant to a Royal Charter and which will approve independent press regulators pursuant to the provisions of the Charter. No schemes have yet been approved. Despite the scheme being non-statutory, there are important statutory provisions contained in the Crime and Courts Act 2013 and the Enterprise and Regulatory Reform Act 2013. When a regulator does exist which a 'relevant publisher' of 'news-related material' can join, failure to join a regulatory scheme will result in possible sanction by way of exemplary damages and enhanced costs awards in defamation and other litigation (Crime and Courts Act 2013, s 34). To be approved under the Charter, a regulatory scheme must, *inter alia*, involve low-cost arbitration procedures to handle claims which publishers must use or suffer costs penalties.[125]

Whether websites containing news material are potentially subject to the sanctions for not joining a voluntary regulatory scheme will depend on the definitions of 'news-related material' and 'relevant publisher' in the Crime and Courts Act 2013. In s 42:

'(7) "News-related material" means –

(a) news or information about current affairs,

(b) opinion about matters relating to the news or current affairs, or

(c) gossip about celebrities, other public figures or other persons in the news.'

And in s 41 a relevant publisher 'means a person who, in the course of a business (whether or not carried on with a view to profit), publishes news related material (a) which is written by different authors, and (b) which is to any extent subject to editorial control'. However, small publishers and bloggers probably escape the scheme by virtue of para 8 of Sch 15, which exclude 'micro-businesses'

---

124 The Report of an Inquiry into the Culture, Practices and Ethics of the Press, ordered by the House of Commons to be printed on 29 November 2012 (HC 779).
125 For details of the requirement for schemes see the PRP website at http://pressrecognitionpanel. org.uk/the-recognition-criteria/.

which are defined as businesses which have fewer than ten employees and an annual turnover of less than £2,000,000. There are also exclusions for incidental newsletters, special interest publications, scientific journals and book publishers.

These provisions will thus affect large online newspapers and the online operations of print newspapers but the majority of news-related blogs will be under the micro-business threshold. Membership of an approved regulator must have been available to the publisher for them to suffer sanctions, and this might exclude overseas publishers if membership is not available to them. The sanctions can also be avoided if there were good reasons for not joining a scheme (s 35), which may also apply in the case of an overseas news site, particularly if it is regulated in another jurisdiction.

For press regulation and law generally, readers are referred to specialist texts.

MALICIOUS FALSEHOOD

Overview

3.50   The differences between this and defamation are evident from the following summary of the elements of the tort:

- the defendant must make a statement to a third party that is false;

- maliciously (ie knowing that it is false), or being reckless as to its truth; and

- cause special damage to the claimant.[126]

Thus while this is a tort that can clearly be committed by use of a computer network, the particular problems that arise in defamation because of the liability of network intermediaries will not arise with malicious falsehood: unwitting network intermediaries and publishers will lack the mental element.

Elements of the tort

3.51   The requirement for communication to a third party distinguishes malicious falsehood from deceit (which is the civil cause of action that should be pursued where the complaint is of loss caused by false statements to the claimant, dealt with under the next heading). There can be a single recipient or many, and as with defamation it matters not if the communication was in confidence.

The requirement for the statement to be false does not bring in as much of the baggage of defamation law as might be thought – it has been held that the 'single meaning rule' does not apply.[127] The question of meaning is akin to that in tort – if a substantial (in the sense of not negligible) proportion of recipients of the information understand it in a particular way, then that meaning must be considered when deciding if the other elements of the tort (malice, special

---

126 Though in certain situations statute relaxes this requirement.
127 *Ajinomoto Sweeteners Europe SAS v Asda Stores Ltd*, n 96 above.

damage) have been made out. The meaning becomes a question of fact on which evidence can be led.

Mostly, malicious falsehood actions will concern allegations of fact. They can be based on statements of opinion, but the requirement for malice will mean that only where the opinion stated is not honestly held can the statement be actionable. The requirement for causation will mean that claims are more likely to succeed where the defendant is a person whose opinions are likely to be followed.

The requirement for malice has been held to be the same as in the case of the qualified privilege defence to defamation[128] (ie some kind of improper motive is required). In practice, malice is generally proved by showing knowledge that the statement is untrue, or recklessness as to its truth.

Special damage has the same meaning as in defamation (in those cases where it is required, eg slander) – that is the loss must be pecuniary in nature or capable of being estimated in money: falsehoods that cause anxiety or distress, or which damage reputation, are not actionable unless such loss is caused. So, false statements about a business must be linked to lost business in some way. However, it must be noted that s 3 of the Defamation Act 1952 relieved certain claimants of the requirement to show special damage:

> '(1) In an action for slander of title, slander of goods or other malicious falsehood, it shall not be necessary to allege or prove special damage –
>
> (a) if the words upon which the action is founded are calculated to cause pecuniary damage to the plaintiff and are published in writing or other permanent form; or
>
> (b) if the said words are calculated to cause pecuniary damage to the plaintiff in respect of any office, profession, calling, trade or business held or carried on by him at the time of the publication.'

'Calculated to' means 'likely to have the effect of'.[129] Publishing in writing or permanent form includes broadcasting.[130]

Pecuniary damages are assessed on the usual tortious basis, but are not limited on the grounds of remoteness or lack of foreseeability (as they are for the non-deliberate torts such as negligence and nuisance). Instead, all losses that are the 'natural consequence' of the tort are recoverable as damages.[131] But causation must still be proved, and the mitigation rule also applies.

Examples of malicious falsehoods

3.52   The law is not limited to specific situations, but the phrases 'slander of goods' and 'slander of title' are used to refer to the common situations where one

---

128 *Spring v Guardian Assurance plc* [1993] 2 All ER 273, CA.
129 This is the same as the meaning given those words in the tort of passing-off, and there is New Zealand authority for this in malicious falsehood – *Customglass Boats v Salthouse Boats* [1976] RPC 589.
130 Broadcasting Act 1990, s 166(2).
131 *Smith v New Court*, see n 133 below.

trader disparages another's products, or a person causes someone's ownership of a thing (this is not limited to real property though historically that has been the subject of the cases). It is not difficult to see how malicious falsehood in those areas could be made out.

So, false statements as to the safety or legality of products might damage the business that trades in them. False statements which cause people to question a company's ownership of its intellectual property or the value of its assets could also damage the business by reducing its ability to raise money on the security of its assets, or to sell off assets. In *Spring v Guardian*[132] malicious falsehood was possible in the giving of a job reference, though in that case the judge held there was no malice.

Malicious falsehood and the internet

3.53   In most cases, the fact that a false statement is made using the internet will not affect the application of the law, and can be treated as if it was a statement made by other means. But it must be borne in mind that in many cases internet publication amounts to publication to the whole world, and so the scale of the tort can be large whoever makes the original statement. A publication of a false and damaging statement on a social networking site or internet forum could, if it goes viral, have far-reaching consequences. Bearing in mind the scope of damages (see above) this could result, if a malicious falsehood claim is successful, in very substantial damages being awarded against the original publisher.

In the scenario postulated above, others who pass the malicious statement on will not be liable if they are not themselves malicious in doing so. In the case of a product safety scare, for example, they may be motivated by a (possibly naive) desire to alert people to the danger. However, if they are also malicious in their re-publishing of the falsehood, then they will be liable. As for damages, it is submitted that in such cases the malicious re-publication should be viewed as a new intervening act which breaks the chain of causation back to the original publisher, thus limiting their potential damages liability.

Looking at these situations from the victim's point of view, they will no doubt take a global view on what, if any, steps to take to correct the falsehood. From a purely legal perspective, taking steps to publicly correct the falsehood will have the effect of mitigating damages and also of making it more difficult for re-publishers of the falsehood to deny the allegation of malice.

This leaves open the question of who is a publisher of a statement for this purpose. Having said at the beginning of this section that the requirement for malice eliminated many possible publishers, we can see that there is an area of uncertainty left. What is the position of a website operator who is informed of the falsehood of a statement on a site they control, but takes no action? Bearing in mind the fate of the single meaning rule, it would be unwise to import the defamation approach willy-nilly. But defamation law would hold that they are arguably a publisher of the offending material once put on notice of it, and if they

132 See n 128 above.

are publisher, their publication would be malicious if the facts they are given are sufficiently compelling.

Damages for malicious falsehood

3.54   The defendant does not have the benefit of the rule that damage must be foreseeable, but is liable for all the damage directly flowing from the wrong.[133] Thus, rules of remoteness and contributory negligence do not apply.

Malicious falsehood – the international element

3.55   For the purposes of applying the rules set out at **3.7** above, the damaging event is the making of the false statement (so it takes place where the statement is published from, where the maker makes it) and the damage will occur where actual damage occurs.

OTHER DELIBERATE TORTS

Deceit

3.56   The tort of deceit is also clearly capable of being committed via the internet, indeed the typical 'scam' email that seeks to induce recipients to part with money upfront in the hope of a future return that does not materialise is an example of this. The effect of the internet on this wrong is that it makes it much easier for the scammer to contact a large number of people in the hope of finding one gullible enough to fall for it. The capacity and likelihood of hosts and intermediaries to become liable in deceit appears very limited when compared to malicious falsehood, however.

Assault and harassment

3.57   This is a species of trespass to the person that can occur remotely, so is relevant to the use of the internet. Prior to the Protection from Harassment Act 1997 it was difficult for civil actions to be brought as they had to be framed in trespass or nuisance. The 1997 Act creates a statutory tort of harassment, though its criminal provisions are more widely used.

The wrong is defined in s 1 of the Act:

'1. Prohibition of harassment.

(1)   A person must not pursue a course of conduct –

    (a)   which amounts to harassment of another, and

    (b)   which he knows or ought to know amounts to harassment of the other.

---

133   *Smith New Court Securities Ltd v Citibank NA* [1997] AC 254 (HL), a case in deceit.

(1A) A person must not pursue a course of conduct –

    (a) which involves harassment of two or more persons, and

    (b) which he knows or ought to know involves harassment of those persons, and

    (c) by which he intends to persuade any person (whether or not one of those mentioned above) –

        (i) not to do something that he is entitled or required to do, or

        (ii) to do something that he is not under any obligation to do.

(2) For the purposes of this section or section 2A(2)(c), the person whose course of conduct is in question ought to know that it amounts to or involves harassment of another if a reasonable person in possession of the same information would think the course of conduct amounted to or involved harassment of the other.

(3) Subsection (1) or (1A) does not apply to a course of conduct if the person who pursued it shows –

    (a) that it was pursued for the purpose of preventing or detecting crime,

    (b) that it was pursued under any enactment or rule of law or to comply with any condition or requirement imposed by any person under any enactment, or

    (c) that in the particular circumstances the pursuit of the course of conduct was reasonable.'

This definition is used for both civil and criminal purposes, the civil wrong is created by s 3 which states that 'An actual or apprehended breach of s 1(1) may be the subject of a claim in civil proceedings by the person who is or may be the victim of the course of conduct in question.' Guidance on the meaning of harassment is set out in s 7 which states that it includes alarming a person or causing them distress. Section 7 also says that a course of conduct involves doing something on two or more occasions.

It has been held that a sensible line must be drawn 'between the ordinary banter and badinage of life and genuinely offensive and unacceptable behaviour'.[134] *Ferguson v British Gas Trading Ltd*[135] concerned harassment initiated by a computer: the sending of unjustified bills and threatening letters was held to be harassment (even though the recipient knew they were unjustified). Clearly such behaviour can also be conducted electronically using the internet. Remedies of damages and an injunction are available, but s 3 also envisages quasi-criminal sanctions for breach of an injunction.

The intermediation of the internet does not add many complexities to this wrong and readers are referred to a practitioner work on tort for a more detailed account.[136] A further significance for this rote and its inclusion in this chapter is that since harassment is a recognised means of harm occurring to someone, the

---

134 *Majrowski v Guy's and St Thomas's NHS Trust* [2006] UKHL 34, [2007] 1 AC 224.
135 [2009] EWCA Civ 46, [2010] 1 WLR 785.
136 For example *Clerk & Lindsell*, n 128 below, ch 15 s 4.

liability in negligence of hosts and operators who allow harassment to take place via their sites must be considered, as it is under 'Negligence' below (see **3.75**).

Wrongful interference with property

3.58   Under the tort of wrongful interference with property,[137] any interference with personal property is actionable if that interference is direct and intentional, falling under the heading of trespass to goods. The interference can be simply damaging goods that are in the possession of the claimant. This raises the possibility that intentionally infecting or altering the operation of a computer which the claimant possesses can amount to this tort (for how altering the electronic state of a computer amounts to damage to it, see 'Negligence' at **3.75** below).

However, the requirement for the interference to be direct is not met by actions taking place over the internet, via communications hardware not owned or possessed by the claimant, but only by actions involving physical contact with the computer,[138] although this aspect of the law has received little recent judicial attention.[139] On this basis the only tortious action available for damage to computers caused remotely is in negligence, but given the lack of recent authority it may be worth re-visiting the area in an appropriate case. One reason why there has been no consideration of this in the field of computers and data may be that in some situations the Privacy and Electronic Communications (EC Directive) Regulations 2003 (SI 2003/2426) will apply.

In contrast in the US, an action in trespass is possible in relation to damage to data taking place at a distance.[140]

LIABILITY FOR PATENT INFRINGEMENT

3.59   Its application to computers and related technology is one of patent law's most contentious areas and that can have an impact on internet activities. But there are reasons why those operating on the internet need to be aware of patent law apart from the possibility that the technology used in their operations might be covered by a patent. This section will focus on the possibilities for patent infringement as a result of use of the internet. An overview only of patent law generally will be given.

---

137 Partly codified in the Torts (Interference with Goods) Act 1977, though the main elements still come from the common law.
138 See generally *Clerk & Lindsell on Torts* (21st edition) Ch 17, section 4 and *Hartley v Moxham* (1842) 3 Queen's Bench Reports 701, in which locking someone's possessions up so they could not access them was not trespass to them.
139 *Marco Pierre White v Withers LLP and Another, Marcus Dearle* [2009] EWCA Civ 1122, 2009 WL 3398661, where *Hartley* was referred to, but in that case there was physical contact with the property so the elements of the tort were made out.
140 See eg *Compuserve Inc v Cyber Promotions* Inc 962 F Supp 1015.

The nature of a patent and the patent application process

3.60   Patents are monopolies granted for developments in technology that are capable of industrial action, new and which contain an inventive step over what was known at the time of filing the application for the patent. All of the concepts in the previous sentence are freighted with a depth of legal doctrine that cannot be addressed in a part of a chapter such as this. Only the highlights will be given.

If patent law is to be understood at any level, it must first be understood what a patent is. A patent is a document which:

● gives details of who made the invention and who was granted the patent;

● contains a description which explains to a person skilled in the relevant area of technology how they can put the invention to practical use (thus to someone lacking the relevant technical knowledge it may well be unintelligible);

● contains a series of numbered claims which define the technological scope of the monopoly granted by the patent (each claim is considered separately for the purposes of validity and infringement); together the description and claims are called the specification of the patent.

The main task in applying for a patent is to draft the specification and a qualified patent agent is normally required for this task. The application will then be submitted to a patent office and examined by technically and legally trained officers against the legal requirements for patentability noted above, that is patentable subject matter, industrial applicability, novelty and non-obviousness. In addition there are issues of 'internal validity' of the specification: it must teach the skilled person how to carry out the invention and the claims must be supported by the description, that is are not drawn too widely.

Patent applications must be published before they proceed to substantive examination. After a patent has been granted its validity may be challenged either by application to the office that granted it, or by making an application to the court. In the majority of patent infringement actions, the defendant counterclaims that the patent is invalid and should be revoked.

The claims may cover a thing (product claims) or a method or procedure (process claims). Where a product exists, or a process is being carried out, that falls within the scope of a claim, then if anyone carries on an infringing activity (as defined in the legislation) in relation to that product or process they are infringing the patent. Prima facie therefore, articles of computer technology that operate in particular ways *may* be patented, as *may* processes that involve, or are carried on inside, computers or computer networks. But there are limits on what subject matter can be patented, related to the requirement that patents should protect 'technology' that are relevant in the area of computers and their use.

Patent law – international co-operation and harmonisation

3.61   The only international treaty governing substantive patent law is the TRIPs agreement. This recites the basic requirements for patentability: patents should be granted in 'all areas of technology',[141] for inventions that are capable of industrial application, new, involve an inventive step and where the specification teaches how to put into effect the invention claimed.

In addition, two important procedural treaties must be considered:

• The Paris Convention provides that where a patent is applied for in one state, further applications for the same invention can be made in other Convention States which (if they claim it) will have their priority backdated to the application in the first state, provided the subsequent applications are made within one year of the first. The priority date is important for two reasons:

   – that is the date on which inventions must be new and not obvious;

   – where the patent applied for goes on to be published, the material in it will count as part of the 'prior art' for applications that have a later priority date (the normal rule is that the material will only count as part of the prior art on the date on which it is actually published, which may be many months after the date of filing). This provision deals with competing applications for over-lapping inventions.

• The Patent Co-operation Treaty provides some cost-savings for international applications: While under the PCT applications must still be examined by the offices in each case where protection is sought, only one filing needs to be made and only one search of prior art is carried out, thus saving costs.

More detailed requirements for the granting of patents and how they may be infringed are contained in the European Patent Convention, to which all EU states and other European countries are signatories. In addition to setting out the rules of substantive patent law, the EPC set up the European Patent Office. As a result of this, patents in Europe can be obtained:

• By a single application to the EPO, which must designate which EPC states protection is sought in. This will be examined within the EPO and, if a patent is granted, it will then take effect as a bundle of national patents in each of the designated EPO states. After grant, issues of validity and infringement of these national patents is a matter for the courts and patent offices of those states, subject only to the possibility that the validity of all the component national patents may be challenged by an application for revocation made to the EPO within nine months of the grant of the European patent.

• By separate applications to the individual states. Where these can be combined with an EPO application, the EPO application cannot designate states where a patent for the same invention is being applied for.

---

141 The only permitted exceptions concern the medical field.

An overview of substantive patent law

3.62   This section will address mainly the law as it applies in the EPC states, with reference to US law where it differs.

Patentable subject matter in Europe

3.63   The EPC repeats the 'all areas of technology' definition from TRIPs, but add some detail to that. Article 52 states:

'(1) European patents shall be granted for any inventions, in all fields of technology, provided that they are new, involve an inventive step and are susceptible of industrial application.

(2) The following in particular shall not be regarded as inventions within the meaning of paragraph 1:

(a) discoveries, scientific theories and mathematical methods;

(b) aesthetic creations;

(c) schemes, rules and methods for performing mental acts, playing games or doing business, and programs for computers;

(d) presentations of information.

(3) Paragraph 2 shall exclude the patentability of the subject-matter or activities referred to therein only to the extent to which a European patent application or European patent relates to such subject-matter or activities as such.'

It follows from this that the EPO regards computer programming per se as a non-technical activity.

However, the EPO has consistently held that these 'non invention' things are examples of what is not technical and the list is not exhaustive. In difficult cases, the EPO asks 'does the invention cover technical subject-matter'? There is considerable case law on *how* to identify technical subject matter in an invention, but so far there is no satisfying fundamental doctrinal approach to identifying what is and is not technical.[142]

The EPO since *PBS Partnership/controlling pension benefits system*[143] ('Pensions') has adopted a two-stage approach to identifying technical subject matter:

● When identifying compliance with the 'all areas of technology' requirement and avoiding the excluded things, it does not look at the prior art but simply

142 When identifying compliance with the 'all areas of technology' requirement, it does not look at the prior art but simply identifies, in a relatively mechanistic way, whether the claims are drawn to technical things such as machines (including computers) or things such as networks or data storage hardware. But when examining a claim for novelty and lack of obviousness, it asks 'is the novelty and inventive step of a technological nature or not?'
143 Case T 931/95.

identifies, in a relatively mechanistic way, whether the claims are drawn to technical things such as machines (including computers) or things such as networks or data storage hardware.

● But when examining a claim for novelty and lack of obviousness, it asks 'is the novelty and inventive step of a technological nature or not?'[144]

By contrast the UK courts adopt the test used by the EPO prior to *Pensions* in which technical subject matter is investigated more closely at the first state by asking:

● Does the 'contribution to the art' of the invention lie in an excluded area?

● And if it does, is the contribution nevertheless of a technical nature?

● Novelty and inventive step are then considered separately from the question of patentable subject matter.

In most cases, the end result is likely to be the same. The invention must involve some technical content which goes beyond the excluded areas. The areas that are of interest for the purposes of this work are mathematical methods, schemes, rules and methods for performing mental acts, playing games or doing business, and computer programs.

To give a flavour of the general things that have been held technical and non-technical, the following have been held to represent non-technical subject matter: methods of directing traffic flow; and an automatic self-service machine in which the user could use any machine-readable card he possessed once that card had been recognised by the machine. A television signal and a computer-controlled system for controlling a queue sequence for serving customers at a number of service points have been held to be technical in nature by the EPO. In the field of computer technology per se (rather than other technology that may be computer-implemented), processing language using linguistic rules has been held to be non-technical as have related text-processing applications. Methods of organising the internal operation of a computer that make it perform better have been found to involve technical content as generally the technical constraints of the hardware are a factor in the invention.

A good example of something non-patentable is in *Hitachi/ Auction Method.*[145] A problem with conducting 'live' auctions over the internet is the unpredictable time delay in messages sent over a network. This invention sought to overcome this problem of network latency by changing the auction rules so the problem disappeared. The EPO held, in finding the invention not patentable, that devising auction rules was a business method and not technical, and that there was no technical invention in encoding those rules. On the other side of the divide,

---

144 The EPO position is summarised in *Programs for Computers* Case G3/08, which includes some dust-up with the UK Court of Appeal over the diverging doctrinal approaches.
145 Case T 258/03 [2004] EPOR 55.

schemes for compressing data (such as music and film) have been patented.[146] It might be thought that data compression is a matter of pure maths and so not patentable, but in fact in the case of 'lossy' methods the key lies in using the science of psycho-acoustics to help choose a method in which the distortions are not noticeable. This is also an example of turning science (not patentable) into a patentable technology.

Patentable subject matter in the United States

3.64   US law has swung one way and another on this issue since applications for computer-related inventions were first filed. The statute is not as specific as that in Europe, s 101 of the US Patents Act providing 'Whoever invents or discovers any new and useful process, machine, manufacture, or composition of matter, or any new and useful improvement thereof, may obtain a patent therefor, subject to the conditions and requirements of this title.' US patent law has always held that laws of nature, natural phenomena, and abstract ideas do not fall within s 101, but as we have seen, there remains the question of how and where you look for patentable or non-patentable subject matter.

It is convenient to start the story with a series of cases in which the Court of Appeals for the Federal Circuit held that the US Patent Office (USPTO) was wrong to look into the underlying content of a patent application in order to find if it 'was drawn to non-patentable subject-matter': if a patent claimed a machine that was in fact just a general purpose computer programmed in a particular way, it was patentable – even if what it did was to implement a business method or operate on data. An exemplar is *State Street v Signature*[147] where a method of communicating between branches of a business via a computer network was patented. Thus it was that developments which amounted to programmed business methods became patentable – though the other elements of patentability such as novelty and non-obviousness had to be present.

The US Supreme Court can become involved in this as the right of the state to grant patent monopolies is set out in the US Constitution. They reviewed the position in *Bilski v Kappos*[148] and explained the approach more clearly in relation to discoveries and natural phenomena in *Mayo* (a biotechnology case). This new more restrictive approach was developed further by the Supreme Court in *Alice Corp Pty Ltd v CLS Bank International*,[149] a case (like *Bilski* and *State Street*) about computer-implemented methods in the banking sector. The key differences over the *State Street* approach are that the court first looks at what the claims are directed to, so in *Alice* although the claims described a computer system, they were directed to a business method ('intermediated settlement'), so *prima facie* not patentable as an abstract idea. The next stage was to enquire of the invention:

146 The MP3 sound compression method and format was developed by a number of organisations and patents successfully applied for, though there were disputes between the developers over ownership and infringement. The patents have now expired.
147 (1998) 149 F 3d 1368.
148 561 US 593 (2010).
149 134 S Ct 2347 (2014).

'whether it contains an "inventive concept" sufficient to "transform" the claimed abstract idea into a patent-eligible application. A claim that recites an abstract idea must include "additional features" to ensure that the claim is more than a drafting effort designed to monopolise the abstract idea. Transformation into a patent-eligible application requires more than simply stating the abstract idea while adding the words "apply it".'

(The final words essentially describe the *State Street* approach.) As the claim in *Alice* simply proposed known methods using known computer hardware to achieve the objective, there was no such transformation. This approach has some similarities with the European approach, save that the Supreme Court has avoided defining that which is patentable with reference to the concept of 'technology'; rather it simply looks for things that are not discoveries etc and requires the transformation from the non-patentable to the patentable to involve invention.

Novelty

3.65   Novelty is assessed on a worldwide basis. To be valid a claim must not cover anything that was already known at the priority date of the invention. Known means 'available to the public', which requires there to be some information in the public domain and for that information to enable the skilled person to put the invention into effect. The information can become available in any manner, by a published patent application, a paper on an academic journal, a product on sale or display or a website.[150] In the case of computer technology, or inventions embodied in software, if the source code is public that will place information in the public domain. 'Public' in this context means anyone who is free to pass the information on – so a letter or email to one person could (unless the recipient was under a duty of confidence) be a member of the public for this purpose. It does not actually matter that nobody noticed the information, as long as someone could.

Where scripts which help run a website are run on the client computer (such as embedded Javascript), that code will be in the public domain, as will the other aspects of web-page mark-up. Material which remains on the server, such as the structure of the database underlying the website and the server-side scripts, will not be public, but any aspects of this that can be 'reverse engineered' by a skilled person by observation, and will be public. The effect of this is that some aspects of the technology underlying an internet-based operation will be public when the public have access to it, but some will remain secret.

Inventive step

3.66   In addition to being new, the invention must be sufficiently different from what was known for it to represent an inventive step over it. An inventive step means that the invention was not obvious to the skilled person bearing in mind common general knowledge in the technical field concerned. There are a few different doctrinal approaches to this, but ultimately it is a question of

150 See Availability to the public (G01/92) [1993] EPOR 241.

fact. Patent examiners will rely on their own knowledge of the field in question, whereas courts will rely heavily on expert evidence as to what the state of knowledge of the skilled person at the relevant date was. This is probably the most common area in which a court may rule invalid a patent that has been granted by an examiner – even if no prior art that was not available to the examiner is found, a detailed investigation with expert evidence may result in the invention being held to be obvious. The bar for inventiveness is not set high – the skilled person has been described as a boring nerd.[151]

Internal validity

3.67 The requirements for patentability mentioned so far refer to the invention(s) set out in the patent's claims. But in order for a patent to be granted, the specification must also contain a description that explains the invention in such a way that it can be put into effect by the skilled person and the claims must not be cast more widely than that which is enabled in this way.

Infringement of patents

3.68 As mentioned, the technical scope of the patent monopoly is defined in the claims. The infringing acts are set out in s 60 of the Act. To infringe activity must be carried on in the UK (s 60(1)). Acts that are neither public nor commercial do not infringe (dealt with later). Except in two situations mentioned below, there is no mental element for infringement, no knowledge or intention is required.

For product claims, the infringing acts are making, disposing of, offering to dispose of, using, keeping (whether for disposal or otherwise) or importing the product or keeping it whether for disposal or otherwise. Here 'disposing of' means 'placing on the market'[152] and offering does not carry the technical contract law meaning – so negotiating a sale would be offering for sale.[153] Where products are purchased from sellers who are outside the jurisdiction, the seller is not disposing of the product within it.[154] The person liable for the act of importation of the product will depend on the nature of the contract. Following UK sale of goods law, in the absence of any terms to the contrary, property passes when the goods are delivered to a postal service or courier, where the contract specified delivery by that method, so the purchaser will generally be the importer. If the purchasers operations are private and non-commercial (see next section) they will have a defence, but if that is not the case, then the purchaser will infringe by importing and subsequent using. However, it is possible that the overseas supplier may be liable as a joint tortfeasor if there is a common design to carry out infringing acts in the UK (see **3.6** above).

151 Per Jacob LJ in *Rockwater v Technip* [2004] RPC 919.
152 These are the words used in the Community Patent Convention, with which, by virtue of s 130(7), Patents Act, s 60 must be interpreted.
153 *Gerber v Lectra* [1995] RPC 383 at 411.
154 *Sabaf SpA v MFI Furniture Centres Ltd* [2004] UKHL 45, [2005] RPC 10.

Making, in the case of making something from scratch, is self-explanatory, but acts of repairing or re-manufacturing can amount to infringement by making[155] depending on the nature of the re-manufacturing process. It is submitted that the same principles will apply where a manufacturing process is carried on across jurisdictions, in relation to that part of the manufacture carried on in the UK.

A combination of the 'using' and 'keeping' infringing acts means that having possession of something (unless for private and non-commercial purposes) will likely amount to one form of infringement or another. However, there is a limitation on keeping – the activities of warehousemen and carriers are not keeping or using,[156] there must be stocking for the purpose of a business.[157]

For process claims, using the process, where using means carrying out the process, infringes. Process claims can also be infringed by 'offering the process for use' where the use would be in the UK the offeror knows, or it is obvious to a reasonable person in the circumstances, that its use in the UK without the consent of the proprietor would be an infringement of the patent. Offering a machine for sale has been held to be offering the process for use,[158] but offering to provide a service (eg cleaning windows or vehicles) which includes carrying out the process would also fall within the meaning. This is one of only two situations where there is a mental element to infringement, the other being contributory infringement under s 60(2). It appears from the wording that knowledge of the technical elements of the process and of the fact that the process falls within the claims of a patent is required.

A process patent can be infringed by disposing of, offering to dispose of, using or importing a product made by the process or keeping that product whether for disposal or otherwise. The key here is that the process of making the product could take place anywhere in the world, possibly in a country where the process is not patented, but the patentee will still have a remedy in countries where products of the process end up, though they may not be able to cut the infringing products off at source.

It is also possible to infringe a patent by doing something in relation to a product of process which does not contain all the elements required in a patent claim. Section 60(2) of the Patents Act makes it an infringement to supply or offer to supply in the UK a person other than a licensee or other person entitled to work the invention with any of the means, relating to an essential element of the invention, for putting the invention into effect when the supplier knows, or it is obvious to a reasonable person in the circumstances, that those means are suitable for putting, and are intended to put, the invention into effect in the UK. Note that both the supply and the use must be in the UK. The intention to put the invention into effect is that of the intended end-user of the invention.[159]

---

155 *Schutz (UK) Ltd v Werit UK Ltd* [2013] UKSC 16, [2013] RPC 16.
156 *Smith, Kline & French Laboratories Ltd v RD Harbottle (Mercantile) Ltd.* [1980] 1 CMLR 277, [1980] RPC 363.
157 *McDonald v Graham* [1994] RPC 407 at 431.
158 *Tamglass Ltd Oy v Luoyang North Glass Technology Co Ltd* [2006] EWHC 65 (Pat), [2006] FSR 32.
159 *Grimme Landmaschinenfabrik GmbH & Co KG v Scott (t/a Scotts Potato Machinery)* [2010] EWCA Civ 1110, [2011] FSR 7.

The knowledge required is of both the technical nature of the process and of the intention of the end-user, but not of infringement, and may be actual or the objective knowledge of the reasonable person. The effect of this is that sellers of products or machinery cannot get around patent law by leaving a part out of the thing so that it does not contain all the elements necessary to infringe the claim, or by selling something in kit form.

Finally it should be noted that the general law of joint tortfeasorship applies to patents as it does to copyright and trade marks. Thus, anyone involved in the supply chain might become jointly liable with the end user of a product or process or the importer of a product even if they do not infringe. (They might not infringe because they are overseas, or because what they are doing does not involve the whole product or process or an essential element of it). In the case of overseas joint tortfeasors, jurisdictional rules mean that they can be joined as defendants provided an action can be properly started in the UK against one of the infringers.

Defences

3.69   Anything that is both private and non-commercial will not infringe a patent. So using a patented product or process for commercial ends will infringe even if the use is kept secret. Similarly doing something of a public nature (such as distributing products or software for free) will infringe even though there is no underlying commercial objective. Private individuals acting non-commercially will have the defence, and it should cover private sales by them of products or software (even if conducted in a very public way such as by an online auction).

There is also a defence for research activities – activities conducted for the purpose of investigating the technology of the invention (even if that is done in a commercial context). This would cover dismantling and testing products, de-compiling and running software and so on, but the purpose must be to investigate the technology and not, for example, for marketing or regulatory approval purposes.

EU free movement of goods law applies to patents as it does to other rights. It is a defence to offer for sale or sell a product or import it within the European Economic Area if that product had been placed on the market by or with the consent of the patent owner. This defence does not apply to goods originally placed on the market outside the EEA.

It will be noted that using or keeping a patented product infringes a patent. However, UK patent law applies an internal exhaustion of rights principle: where a product has been sold by the patent owner in the UK without any restriction on its use, the first purchaser has the right to use it for all purposes, and that right is passed on to further purchasers.[160] This will not necessarily apply to products sold abroad.

---

160 *Betts v Willmott* (1871) LR 6 Ch App 239.

Infringement and the internet

Selling products, offering services etc

3.70   Clearly, business that happens to trade via the internet will infringe by selling patented products, or carrying out patented processes, just as much as they would if they conducted business face to face or via mail order. But the internet has had an effect on intellectual property by opening up to consumers and trade customers in the UK a new means of accessing products made in far-off countries where enforcement of rights may be expensive or impossible (in the case of the registered rights, there may be no rights registered there). As noted above, UK contract law would as a default say that where goods are purchased on the internet to be sent by mail or courier to the UK, the purchaser is the importer. Private consumers will not be infringing thereby, but businesses will be infringing by importing and then keeping and using the product. The problem for rights owners is that instead of having a single importer and relatively few container loads of product to deal with, there are numerous customers and many small packages.

It is possible to argue that the overseas seller is a joint tortfeasor with the purchaser, but this may not be so. For there to be a common design the seller would have to do more than simply letting purchasers take the risk, and it must be remembered that there will be sales where no infringement follows.

Where machinery located overseas (such as a 3D printer) is controlled from the UK, there will be no infringement at that stage, though any subsequent importation will infringe (see above). If the overseas manufacture is purely a device to avoid infringement, there may be a strong argument that the manufacturer is jointly liable with the importer/customer for infringement.

Distributing software by download

3.71   First, it should be noted that a supplier of software by this method (ie the operator of the website which offers downloads) may obtain a licence from the patent owner to offer the software. In such cases, the rights which the recipients of the software shall have will probably be determined by licence terms required to be imposed on them by the supplier's licence, and those terms may include terms as to the transferability of the licence. If an analogy with the use of physical goods which have been supplied holds, such end-user licences will be transferrable unless there is a term to the contrary, and in the absence of any end-user licence terms there will be an implied licence to use the software for its intended purpose, and that will be transferrable. The following paragraphs under this heading deal with the position where there is no licence from the patentee at any stage.

Section 60(2) infringement is particularly important in the case of software. As we have seen, most computer-related inventions will not protect software itself, but rather a machine or a way of operating that has software at its core of operation. The patent could cover a way of operating that can be implemented by using standard computer hardware when programmed to operate in a particular way. It is likely that for such patents the software is an essential element of the invention, so anyone who provides the software is providing the means necessary for s 60(2) infringement: the wording of s 60(2) is broad enough to cover supply on physical media or by download. Whether the necessary mental element for s 60(2) infringement is present will depend on the facts, but this can be cured as to future infringements by the patentee putting the supplier on notice.

Thus, the supply of software for a commercial purpose may infringe a patent (the supplier will infringe even if the end users will not infringe because their use is private and non-commercial). A non-commercial supplier will also infringe if their supply is not private. Although there are no cases directly on the point, making software available to the public by download (which is how most Free and Open-Source (FOSS) software is distributed) will fall outside the 'private and non-commercial' defence.[161] The fact that the software is only available in source-code form rather than ready-to-run will not affect this if it can be easily compiled. If the recipients of the software use it in the course of a business, they will be infringing by using it, regardless of the infringing status of the supplier. As with the distribution of physical goods, if the supplier is located outside the jurisdiction, they cannot be infringers in their own right but may be jointly liable with their customers under the law of joint tortfeasorship.

Operating a website and providing cloud services

3.72   As we have seen, using an invention (whether it is claimed as a product, eg computer hardware when programmed in a particular way or a process carried on by a computer) will infringe a patent. However, the process must be carried on within the jurisdiction. This means that it is the location of the computers forming the product, or carrying on the process that matters. For many smaller website operators, these computers will belong to and be operated by a hosting provider, though larger operators may run their own servers.

The operation of a website will involve running a stack of software, each layer of which makes use of the one below it. There will be the basic operating system and the programs necessary to provide internet connectivity. On this will run a web server program, through the internet-specific software elements that provide connectivity and the hosting tools which enable the customers to control their websites, to the 'content management' software on which the site runs to the site-specific scripts and data which the operator has created (or sub-contracted the creation of) which give the site its unique character or functionality (if any). Infringement could occur at any level in the stack. It is not clear if a website operator is a 'user' of the software that runs on the servers operated by their web host in circumstances where they have no control over the choice or operation of that software. The host will be a user, of course.

---

161 There are no cases on what amount to private purposes, but the principle of construing defences narrowly and the wording of art 30 of the TRIPs agreement, which only allows defences which 'do not unreasonably conflict with a normal exploitation of the patent and do not unreasonably prejudice the legitimate interests of the patent owner, taking account of the legitimate interests of third parties' suggest that the operations of a FOSS project is public, not private. This may be distinguishable from a hobbyist's website, who offers software to like-minded individuals.

Computer-related patents in the wild and 'patent trolling'

3.73   As we have seen, approaches to patenting computer-related inventions have changed over the years and patents will be in force that were granted under previous approaches. Furthermore, the process of patent examination is not perfect and there will be patents out there that should never have been granted under any approach to patentability. They may cover non-patentable subject matter or they may in fact be old or non-inventive when all the prior art is considered (the examiner's searches may not have uncovered all relevant prior art). Computer-related inventions are a particular technical area where examiners may not have had all the prior art available to them or the resources to fully examine a patent. Even if there was a patentable invention, it is possible that a patent's claims are cast too widely so that they cover things that are old or not inventive over the prior art.

Of course, such unworthy patents can be opposed and may be revoked upon an in-depth investigation, but until that happens, they are ostensibly valid and enforceable.

Enter the patent troll. Trolls typically invest after grant in patents with a view to enforcing them for profit. The literature labels them as 'non-practising entities', that is owners of patents that have no intention themselves to exploit the technology, but are solely interested in licensing. To be a troll of the objectionable variety requires a bit more though. The successful troll will seek out patents that (unknown to the owner) cover technology that has become widely used and obtain them for a keen price, then seek to enforce them against vulnerable opponents even though the validity of the patent is questionable. But to measure trolling, an objective test is required so the 'non-practising entity' is used as the definition, though some NPE activity may be unobjectionable. Empirical research has shown that there probably was a great increase in litigation by NPEs in the United States between 2003 and 2010, but no explosion between 2010 and 2012 as had often been asserted.[162]

The evidence is that patent trolling is more of a problem in the United States than it is in the UK and that this is a result of the different costs regimes for civil litigation (and not the lack of availability of suitable patents to troll with).[163] The 'loser pays' principle in English and Welsh litigation means that a defendant who forms the view that the claim is worthless can start to defend the claim, whereupon the troll will probably blink first. In the US where costs are only recoverable in 'exceptional circumstances', it will always make some commercial sense for a target business to pay some money to resolve the problem, as even defending a claim successfully will cause expense.

Action has been taken to limit patent trolling in the US. First, in *Octane Fitness, Llc v Icon Health & Fitness, Inc*[164] the Supreme Court ruled that the Federal

---

162   Christopher A Cotropia, Jay P Kesan and David L. Schwartz, 'Unpacking Patent Assertion Entities' (PAEs), 99 *Minnesota Law Review* 649 (2014) provides a comprehensive study of research in this area. Other research cited found that litigation by NPEs has accounted for over half of all US patent suits in recent years.

163   Christian Helmers Brian J Love Luke McDonagh, 'Is There a Patent Troll Problem in the UK?' *Fordham Intellectual Property, Media & Entertainment Law Journal*, Vol 24, at 509, 2014.

164   134 S Ct 1749 (2014).

Circuit's rules for deciding 'exceptional circumstances' in patent litigation were too strict and that it should simply enquire whether the losing party acted in bad faith, vexatiously, wantonly or for oppressive reasons. Secondly, the Innovation Act[165] is before Congress and this seeks to place a greater burden on patent claimants to be specific in their claims and

> 'Requires courts to award prevailing parties reasonable fees and other expenses incurred in connection with such actions, unless: (1) the position and conduct of the nonprevailing party was reasonably justified in law and fact; or (2) special circumstances, such as severe economic hardship to a named inventor, make an award unjust.'

This is not at the time of writing law and may not achieve the necessary bi-partisan support.

In addition to these measures, the impact of the decision in *Alice* is likely to result in US patents that might otherwise be prime candidates for trolling being revoked.

In conclusion, patent trolling will remain an issue for US-based internet operators, though that risk may reduce. It does not appear to be a major issue in the UK or, more widely, Europe.

Jurisdiction and choice of law in patent cases

3.74   The national nature of patent rights limits the scope for jurisdictional issues to arise. Article 22 of Regulation 1215/2012 states that in matters of the validity of patents, the courts of the granting state shall have exclusive jurisdiction. This does not apply to the enforcement of patents, but as the damage will occur in the granting state, patentees will always have the option of suing there as well as in the defendants home jurisdiction (if different).

NEGLIGENCE

3.75   There are a number of ways in which careless actions can cause damage (thereby raising the possibility of an action in negligence) via the internet. The following is one way of organising these that maps onto the legal taxonomy:

- liability for statements (advice, etc) communicated via the internet;

- liability for services delivered via the internet;

- liability for viruses, etc distributed via the internet that damage data on or impair the operation of computer systems;

- liability to users of websites, etc in relation to site content (harassment, etc);

---

165 HR9 – 114th Congress (2015–2016).

- liability for damage to property other than computer systems and data – remotely controlled devices, etc.

The basic elements of the tort are summarised as:

- The defendant must have done something negligently, that is without exercising reasonable care in doing so. The standard of care expected is that of the reasonable man in that context (eg in the case of writing computer code, the standard of care of a reasonably careful programmer).

- The claimant must have been within a class of people to whom the defendant owed a duty of care in relation to the activity that was done carelessly. Only people within the contemplation of the reasonable person (see above) as likely to be affected by their actions and in a relationship of sufficient proximity to them are owed a duty of care.

- The defendant must have suffered loss and damage as a result of the defendant's negligent activities. Normally *pure* economic loss is not recoverable, but some negligent mis-statements and negligent provision of services provide an exception to this rule. However, economic loss flowing from damage to property is recoverable.

- For public policy reasons, some items of damage, although technically caused by the negligence on strict 'but for' test for causation, are nevertheless not recoverable as their connection with the negligent act is considered too remote. Only types of damage that are reasonably foreseeable in the circumstances of the case can be recovered.

- The doctrine of contributory negligence further limits the extent of items for which compensation can be recovered and claimants must mitigate their loss.

Exclusion of liability for negligence is possible but is subject to the Unfair Contract Terms Act 1977, s 2 where the defendant is operating in the course of a business (in relation to notices between traders and consumers, the Consumer Rights Act 2015, s 62 now has the same effect).

'2. Negligence liability

(1) A person cannot by reference to any contract term or to a notice given to persons generally or to particular persons exclude or restrict his liability for death or personal injury resulting from negligence.

(2) In the case of other loss or damage, a person cannot so exclude or restrict his liability for negligence except in so far as the term or notice satisfies the requirement of reasonableness.

(3) Where a contract term or notice purports to exclude or restrict liability for negligence a person's agreement to or awareness of it is not of itself to be taken as indicating his voluntary acceptance of any risk.'

In relation to the reasonableness test, s 11 of UCTA gives some guidance:

'(3) In relation to a notice (not being a notice having contractual effect), the requirement of reasonableness under this Act is that it should be fair and reasonable to allow reliance on it, having regard to all the circumstances obtaining when the liability arose or (but for the notice) would have arisen.

(4) Where by reference to a contract term or notice a person seeks to restrict liability to a specified sum of money, and the question arises (under this or any other Act) whether the term or notice satisfies the requirement of reasonableness, regard shall be had in particular (but without prejudice to subsection (2) above in the case of contract terms) to –

(a) the resources which he could expect to be available to him for the purpose of meeting the liability should it arise; and

(b) how far it was open to him to cover himself by insurance.

(5) It is for those claiming that a contract term or notice satisfies the requirement of reasonableness to show that it does.'

In addition the guidelines in Schedule 2 of UCTA, although expressed to be limited to certain contractual situations, have been held to be generally useful.

Readers are referred to a suitable textbook for an in-depth discussion of the basic elements of the tort of negligence. Detailed issues relating to internet liability are discussed below.

Negligent mis-statement

3.76   The use of the internet does not alter the application of the basic law to a great extent here: the situation when statements are made by email will be similar to statements by letter, and the situation when statements are widely available on a website will be similar to statements published in a newspaper or newsletter.

The law in this area has developed in a line of cases starting with *Hedley-Byrne & Co v Heller and Partners*.[166] Under the *Hedley-Byrne* principal, for liability to arise for a statement there must be a 'special relationship' between claimant and defendant involving the 'assumption of responsibility' by the defendant, and there must be 'reasonable reliance' on the statement by the defendant. The assumption of responsibility need not be explicit, it can be deemed from the circumstances (including the presence or absence of a disclaimer).

It appears that liability can only arise for statements made by a business in a business context. In the case of advice, the defendant does not need to be in the business of giving advice.[167]

Much of the case law in this area concerns the liability of those who give advice to people other than the intended recipient of that advice. The canonical situations are the liability of surveyors, hired by a mortgage lender, to a mortgagee who is shown the report (a duty of care is owed at least to private purchasers of

---

166 [1964] AC 465, [1963 3 WLR 101.
167 *Esso Petroleum v Mardon* [1976] 1 QB 801.

modest properties[168]) and the liability of company auditors, hired by the company to report on its financial health, to potential investors in the company (no duty of care owed[169]). The difference between these situations was summarised by Lord Goff in *Caparo*:

> 'The salient feature of all these cases is that the defendant giving advice or information was fully aware of the nature of the transaction which the plaintiff had in contemplation, knew that the advice or information would be communicated to him directly or indirectly and knew that it was very likely that the plaintiff would rely on that advice or information in deciding whether or not to engage in the transaction in contemplation. ... So also the plaintiff, subject again to the effect of any disclaimer, would in that situation reasonably suppose that he was entitled to rely on the advice or information communicated to him for the very purpose for which he required it.'

By contrast in the auditor type cases:

> 'The situation is entirely different where a statement is put into more or less general circulation and may foreseeably be relied on by strangers to the maker of the statement for any one of a variety of different purposes which the maker of the statement has no specific reason to anticipate. To hold the maker of the statement to be under a duty of care in respect of the accuracy of the statement to all and sundry for any purpose for which they may choose to rely on it is ... also to confer on the world at large a quite unwarranted entitlement to appropriate for their own purposes the benefit of the expert knowledge or professional expertise attributed to the maker of the statement.'

In short, the law is reluctant to hold that anyone is liable for pure economic loss caused by a negligent mis-statement of theirs *other than* liability to specific people who the maker of the statement intended should or knew would reasonably rely on it.

Readers are referred to tort textbooks for a discussion of the somewhat conflicting detailed approaches taken in the case law to deciding where the boundary of liability lies. Here, we will concentrate on how these principles apply to particular aspects of activity on the internet.

In *Patchett v Swimming Pool and Allied Trades Association*,[170] it was held that a trade association was not liable to a visitors to its website for statements made on it. The defendants were a trade association of swimming pool builders, the claimants' prospective clients searching for a contractor to install a swimming pool. They chose a contractor from those listed on the site, but all did not go well with the job and the contractor became insolvent. The SPATA website made statements about the quality of work to be expected from its members, some of which were not true as regards the chosen contractor. There was a disclaimer that visitors should make their own enquiries. There was no issue as to foreseeability

---

168 *Smith v Eric Bush* [1990] 1 AC 831. There was a disclaimer of liability, but it was held to be invalid under s. s 2 of the Unfair Contract Terms Act 1977 as the valuer was a professional and Mrs Smith was paying (albeit indirectly) for his services.
169 *Caparo Industries v Dickman* [1990] 2 AC 605.
170 [2009] EWCA Civ 717.

(clearly it was foreseeable that site visitors might choose a contractor based on those listed), the case turned solely on whether a duty of care was owed, that is whether there was sufficient proximity between claimant and defendant.

The Court of Appeal upheld the trial judge's finding that there was not sufficient proximity and important guidance for site operators can be found in the detailed reasoning. The case was one that lay in between the two extremes exemplified by *Smith* and *Caparo*. The trial judge was right to look at the site as a whole and ask (following *Hedley-Byrne*) if 'SPATA might reasonably anticipate that those reading the statements made on its website would rely upon those statements without making any checks of their own' and to take the whole of the website, not just specific statements on it, into account in answering that question. As the site advised visitors to make their own enquiries and, in addition to giving a list of contractors, offered a checklist for potential clients to use, the answer to that question was no.

It is thus clear from *Patchett* that general advice given on a website, at least if there is a disclaimer that visitors should make further enquiries, or seek specific advice for their particular situation, will not give rise to liability. It is possible that in *Patchett* liability might have arisen in the absence of a disclaimer and if sufficiently unqualified recommendations and promises about contractors listed on the site had been made. One scenario that might occur is if a group or association's web page for individuals or businesses with a specific common interest offered advice to members. In the absence of a suitable disclaimer, liability may arise.

The status of websites which purport to give legal, financial or technical advice to the world generally thus puts them on the 'not liable' side of the line.[171] The presence of suitably worded disclaimers accompanying the advice only reinforces this: it was held in *Smith v Bush*[172] that (where advice is given by a business) UCTA applies in relation to attempts to exclude liability completely, so where, but for the notice, a duty of care would have been found, the notice attempting to exclude liability must satisfy the reasonableness test.

Negligent provision of services beyond static advice

3.77   Services offered over the internet can range from the most basic interactive websites (such as online currency converters) to sophisticated outsourced computing services. Tortious liability for the provision of services can arise. Cases following *Hedley-Byrne* have applied the principles to the provision of services where the defendant 'entrusts the defendant with the conduct of his affairs, in general or particular …'[173] The result is that such cases represent another exception to the general bar on claims for pure economic loss (if the provision of the service damages data or affects computer operation, see

---

171 Similar to the position of authors of textbooks.
172 Note 165 above.
173 Per Lord Goff in *Spring v Guardian Assurance plc* [1995] 2 AC 296 at 318. In *Spring* contractual claims were statute-barred, but the claimants were able to proceed in tort because of a different limitation period.

the following heading). The notion of an 'assumption of responsibility' by the defendant, which is divined from the totality of things said and done by them, is used in the cases on this topic. It can be argued that in many cases where an internet service is offered, there is such an assumption (cloud services, described further below, are an example). Disclaimers of liability are part of the factual matrix in determining liability but are not necessarily determinative.[174]

It must at once be noted that in many cases where a service is provided over the internet, there will be a contract. Even if the service is free, where a user has to create an account and log in to access it, that will generally involve a contract. In return for the service, the user is at a minimum agreeing to terms as to using the service lawfully and almost certainly agreeing to restrictions on liability and providing the site operator with data which can be used to target third-party marketing messages to site visitors, thereby generating advertising revenue for the site.[175] It is thus important to note that the presence of a contract with the defendant does not negate the possibility of tortious liability.[176]

A few years ago it was possible to draw a firm dividing line between the provision of software to run on a customer's computer on the one hand, and the operation of (relatively) passive websites which were accessed by those computers and that software on the other. The divisions are becoming blurred. Many services, though accessed via a website, involve the operation of considerable computing power on the server to process user inputs and may also involve dozens of lines of script in the web page that is delivered to the client browser, which are processed by the client computer. Often for mobile access an app is available for download as an alternative and more device-friendly means of accessing the services. The advent of cloud computing[177] takes things even further. It is possible for most of an organisation's computing requirements to be provided on servers operated by a third party and delivered over the internet and paid for on a subscription model (this is true in some respects of the latest version of Microsoft Corporation's Office suite of office productivity software and is not confined to business users).

Provision of sophisticated internet services will always involve a contract, and the liability of the provider under that contract will be dealt with similarly to the liability of providers of conventional software. Given that this chapter concerns tort, a detailed treatment of the law on contractual liability for defective software is beyond its scope. But as there are no cases on purely tortious liability, the relatively few cases there are on contractual liability do offer some important clues as to what the tortious position will be.

It makes no effective difference whether software is considered as the supply of goods or the provision of services because the drafting of the Supply of Goods

---

174 In the building society surveyor cases noted under the previous heading disclaimers were not effective, but provision of cloud services is a very different situation.

175 Hence the saying 'if you are not paying for the lunch, you are the lunch'. Nevertheless, many users are content with such arrangements and it is likely that few bother to read the terms and conditions they click to accept.

176 *Spring v Guardian* n 70 above.

177 According to Wikipedia 'Cloud computing and storage solutions provide users and enterprises with various capabilities to store and process their data in third-party data centers' see https://en.wikipedia.org/wiki/Cloud_computing accessed on 19/08/2015.

and Services Act 1982 effectively includes the same implied terms as to quality.[178] The SGA provides an implied term, where goods are supplied in the course of a business that they shall be of satisfactory quality, which is defined in s 14 thus:

'For the purposes of this Act, goods are of satisfactory quality if they meet the standard that a reasonable person would regard as satisfactory, taking account of any description of the goods, the price (if relevant) and all the other relevant circumstances.'

There are no liability for defective software cases in the consumer field. Most of the cases that have gone to trial involve bespoke, or at least amended, software supplied under high value contracts. The following principles have emerged:

- Customers must expect some bugs in software, provided they are dealt with in a reasonable time.

- Exclusion of liability for defects clauses can be reasonable as between commercial entities who negotiated the deal on an equal footing and where the party bearing the risk can insure against it: in deciding this, the terms on which software was generally available in the market were considered (terms which did not exclude liability were not generally available).[179]

The requirement for exclusion clauses in contract (in some situations) and tort to meet the reasonableness test means that these principles will apply to the tortious situation. For large customers contracting for cloud services, these cases suggest that an action in tort, if available, will not add anything to a contract claim. For small, individual or private paying customers the situation is less clear as there are no cases. On the one hand, they are in a weak bargaining position, but on the other the services will be generic rather than tailored and there will be no expectation that they will be used in a way that makes them critical for high-value operations. Readers are referred to a text on computer law for a more in-depth discussion of liability for software.[180] It should also be borne in mind that the Consumer Rights Act 2015 places consumers' rights in relation to digital content on a par with their rights in relation to physical products, which might have the effect of raising expectations in this area.

A typical scenario where tortious liability might be a real alternative, or where there is no contract, is where services are made available for free on the internet via a website and that is the scenario which will be addressed here. It is submitted that the level of care expected of the provider will be determined by similar principles to those set out above in relation to reasonable quality of goods and services. The low or non-existent price of the service and the fact that it will be generic rather than specific suggests that very little can be expected – the principle of 'caveat user' will apply. But a distinction should be made between the ability of the service to perform its intended function (it may be useless) and the possibility of it causing damage to the user's system by infecting it with

---

178 *Saphena Comuting Ltd v Allied Collection Agencies Ltd* [1995] FSR 616 at 652.
179 See generally *Information Technology Law* (7th ed, Ian J Lloyd, OUP, 2014) Ch 24.
180 Ibid.

a virus or damaging the system by its own operations (if the service involves accessing the client computer in some way). Liability for this type of damage is addressed under the next heading.

So if there is some possibility of tortious liability for pure economic loss arising out of provision of an internet service (the premise of this section, see the opening paragraph), the question of the enforceability of the exclusion clause that will almost inevitably be sought to be imposed arises. In this respect, the considerations noted above in relation to negligent mis-statement will apply equally.

Liability under this principle could extend to a situation where someone assumes responsibility for managing the content of a website on behalf of someone else. If it is badly done, losses (eg from claims in defamation or for intellectual property infringement or in relation to data protection or privacy) could fall on the operator of the website and would be foreseeable. The requirement that liability only arises in the context of business operations would exclude liability where the services are provided pro bono, even if the person providing them does similar things for pay as part of their day job (which is a common scenario in the case of clubs, societies and so on). Web design and development businesses would need to consider this where they get involved in providing or managing content for their customers in addition to providing the graphical and functional design of the site.

Finally under this heading it should be noted that if the service provided is the storage of data provided by others, then the defence in the E-Commerce Regulations[181] will potentially apply – this is discussed in the context of negligence under the following heading. This defence will not apply where the data provided by the service is generated by the site itself as then the site operator will not have the benefit of any of the defences in the Regulations.

Negligence resulting in damage to computers or data

3.78   The cases following *Hedley-Byrne* only apply as an exception to the general rule that liability does not arise for pure economic loss. In general, there must be some physical damage for liability to arise (though damages of an economic nature flowing from that can be recovered).

The possibility of using computers remotely to make real-world things happen is discussed below. But computers are themselves physical property that can be damaged and the law has held that the memory storage devices on a computer can be damaged just by changing the data on them in a loss-causing way.[182] It is not necessary to scratch a hard disc to damage it, wiping its indexes to make its files unobtainable without specialist help or expensive data recovery operations also amounts to damage.[183] So losses consequential upon data corruption are in principle recoverable through the tort of negligence, and to the extent that

---

181 See **3.3** above 'Over-arching legal topics' above.

182 This was established in the criminal damage case of *R v Whitely* (1991) 93 Cr App Rep 25.

183 At a microscopic level, changing the information stored on a device changes its physical structure.

the negligent operation of an internet service results in such damage to a client computer, this chapter should deal with it. Similarly, sending emails or uploading files for sharing could result in liability. Of course, damage resulting from such actions may be intentional and criminal liability for intentional acts of hacking are addressed in **Chapter 2**. Allowing the propagation of infected material is one way innocent intermediaries might incur liability; the other way is by unwittingly, but carelessly, creating and distributing damaging material themselves.

In such scenarios, the internet intermediary or service provider (normally a website) will be offering a service in a sense, if only by having material available for browsing or download. A distinction needs to be made between services that the user has to sign up to by agreeing to terms and conditions and creating a user account, and services where this is not required (though there may be terms and conditions of use on the site and linked to from relevant pages). In the former case there will almost certainly be a contract, in the latter there will not be as it will be difficult to say any agreement was made. Where there are terms of use, whether contractual or not, it is unlikely they will contain terms advantageous to the site visitor and likely the terms will seek to exclude liability. Cloud services such as data storage[184] will fall into the first category. Most websites that allow user-generated content, such as social networking sites and discussion forums, require user registration before the user can make posts or comments. The conditions that users must sign up to are normally framed as a contract,[185] so the relationship with the site will be governed by contract not tort.

Aside from the special cases where pure economic loss can be claimed noted above, in which cases the claimant can choose to bring an action in contract, tort or both,[186] where the parties have entered into a contract governing their respective liabilities the law of tort will not operate to extend the defendant's duty in respect of economic loss beyond that contained in the contract.[187] So this section will proceed by looking at non-contractual scenarios. This might involve liability in respect of services available just by visiting a website and the liability of internet users to other internet users with whom they do not have a contract. The claimant in such cases will be the owner of the hardware on which the data which is damaged is stored. That will also be the 'owner'[188] of the data where they use their own hardware. However, if the data is stored in the cloud, the data owner will not own the hardware, so if the data is corrupted in some way, any claim by the data owner against a third-party internet user who damaged

---

184 According to Wikipedia 'Cloud computing and storage solutions provide users and enterprises with various capabilities to store and process their data in third-party data centers' – https://en.wikipedia.org/wiki/Cloud_computing accessed on 19/08/2015. In other words, someone else processes or stores the data on their computers which the user accesses via the internet.

185 The consideration from either side being allowing posting on the site and agreeing to abide by the conditions of use respectively. Well-drafted conditions state that they are legally binding, thus indicating an intention to create legal relations.

186 *Henderson v Merrett Syndicates Ltd (No 1)* [1995] 2 AC 145.

187 *Greater Nottingham Cooperative Society v Cementation Piling & Foundations Ltd* [1989] QB 71, [1988] 3 WLR 396, CA.

188 This convenient term will be used for the person who controls the data and has an interest in its well-being, despite there being no property in data, 'data controller' having a special legal meaning that is not intended in this context.

it will be for pure economic loss and so not actionable[189] unless the claim fits under one of the classifications dealt with in the preceding sections where pure economic loss can be claimed. If the cloud service provider is liable to the data owner (either in contract or tort) as a result of this, in theory they might seek to recover from the third party any payments made to the data owner, but whether such payments would be foreseeable in simple cases such as the propagation of an infection may be doubted.[190]

Perhaps surprisingly, there are no cases regarding the liability in negligence of websites, internet users, etc for causing loss to computer systems by allowing damaging material to be browsed to or downloaded. However, there are reasons why successful actions in negligence in this area are unlikely. For a claim to succeed, all the elements of the tort must be made out.

Use of exclusion clauses

3.79   Readers are referred to the sections on negligent advice and provision of services above. The most analogous situation from contract law is the supply of software for consumers, where such clauses routinely exclude liability totally, or for all except the cost of direct replacement of the software. It can be argued that in the case of free online services, the exclusion of liability is reasonable (the fact that the service is free being one of the circumstances of the case): if the consequences are high, a user can always acquire insurance or procure custom software or bespoke services at a price (though the practicality of this in many situations can be doubted).

Duty of care

3.80   A duty of care is likely to be owed to those foreseeably affected by the operation of the site, but is also limited by considerations of fairness, reasonableness and the proximity of the parties to each other.[191] Thus, the duty of a site operator will extend to users who directly access a faulty service or download a defective or infected file from the site, but may not extend to secondary infections. The duty of internet users to each other is more tenuous, but in principle possible where material is uploaded to a site where it is known that it will be downloaded and used.

---

189 *Cattle v Stockton Waterworks Co* (1874–75) LR 10 QB 453 is authority for the principle that a person cannot claim for the economic consequences of damage to the property of another in which he does not have a proprietary interest.

190 *Stockton* was accepted as applying to the train operating companies in *Conarken Group Ltd v Network Rail Infrastructure Ltd* [2011] EWCA Civ 644, but in that case Network Rail, the owners of the tracks which had been negligently damaged, were able to recover damages which included the amounts they had to pay the train operating companies under their contracts with them as these were foreseeable in that situation.

191 *McLoughlin v O'Brian* [1983] 1 AC 410, [1982] 2 WLR 982.

Breach of duty

3.81   Breach of the duty will be a matter of current good practice in the area concerned. The role of the defendant in the communication chain is relevant here. The fault may lie with the site operator, but may alternatively lie with their web host or website designer if those are different. The operator may have behaved reasonably in choosing a host and designer, so escape liability, in which case someone affected will have to chase the guilty party (and demonstrate a duty of care was owed by them).

An illustration of this is with email (emails may infect recipients' computers). A private user of a web-based email system has no control over the server and cannot install disinfection software on it. If they accidentally send an infected file, that may not be down to any lack of care on their part. A commercial concern which operates its own email server might be in breach of a duty to email recipients by failing to operate screening software to eliminate common risks from emails and attachments that its users send via its server.[192]

Of course, once the site operator becomes aware of a problem with their site, or a user of a problem with their file, their duty will extend to dealing with that problem. In general, a duty is likely to be met by using up-to-date software, appropriate anti-virus systems and dealing with problems that emerge promptly. Doing this will not eliminate the possibility of damage occurring, for example in the time between a file being uploaded and the problem coming to the attention of the site operator, so there may be no liability for such damage.

Physical damage and consequential economic loss

3.82   As noted above, altering data on a computer does amount to a physical change to a thing. If loss flows from that, there is a cause of action in negligence. If the case is not one where damages for pure economic loss can be claimed, the only damages that can be claimed are:

- the cost of repairing a damaged computer system or the value of any data destroyed; and

- economic losses flowing from that damage, provided causation can be shown.

The leading case in this area is *Spartan Steel*.[193] The physical damage caused by negligence was the cutting off of a power cable supplying, but not owned by, the defendants. This caused damage to a melt of steel in the claimant's furnace. The claimants could recover the value of that melt and their lost profit flowing from it, but not lost profit from the further melts that could have been processed while the power supply remained down. Had the claimants owned the part of the power supply that was damaged, they would have been able to recover lost profits for

---

192 Some organisations clearly think this kind of liability plausible enough to install checking software and add elaborate disclaimer notices to outgoing emails. Law firms are particularly prone to this.

193 *Spartan Steel & Alloys Ltd v Martin & Co (Contractors) Ltd* [1973] QB 27 (CA).

the down time as that was consequential on the damage to the cable (but not on the damage to the melt). Lord Denning argued that this was either because the unrecoverable losses were purely economic or too remote, but justified the rule on the basis of public policy. An electricity customer wanting a reliable supply can install a back-up generator (and might have a contractual claim if that failed). It would be wrong for tort law to put customers who had not invested in such measures on the same footing as those who had.

The logic can be applied to computer operation. If data is important it should be backed up, and if keeping a system up and running is vital then operators should take steps to minimise down-time by keeping software up to date and virus-free and ensuring that data and operating systems can be restored quickly. Computer operators who have not taken such measures should not be able to use tort law to put themselves in the same position as those who have. This does not mean that no damages are recoverable, but in practice, applying these principles to a complex modern website and establishing what is and is not recoverable will be challenging and might require a detailed technical investigation.

Causation and reasonable foreseeability of the damage will also represent a difficulty for claimants in the scenario of a generic internet service available to all-comers. It is foreseeable that infected computers will need to be repaired, so the cost of carrying that out should be recoverable. But the defendant will not know what the service might be used for; so even if consequential economic losses would pass the *Spartan Steel* test, they may well not be foreseeable. This will depend very much on the nature of the service.

Finally, contributory negligence and mitigation of loss should be considered. Just as site operators should keep their systems up to date and deal with problems promptly, so should internet users. If a free service is used as a critical component of high-value work that itself may amount to contributory negligence, and certainly a user in that situation would be expected to keep back-ups and have contingency plans in operation to deal with outages (thus avoiding contributory negligence) and then to operate such systems competently (thus mitigating its loss).

The defence under the Electronic Commerce Regulations

3.83   See generally the heading at **3.3** above.

If a wide interpretation of 'Information Society Services' is taken, these defences will potentially apply to website operators, but not to internet users who might post material to websites.

The 'hosting' defence will apply where the damage occurs as a result of material hosted on a site that was not put there by the operator and where the operator is unaware of any problem with it. It is difficult to see how liability can arise from being a 'mere conduit' of data in any event, but that defence will apply if needed. But once a host is made aware of the presence of damaging material on their site, the defence will cease to operate.

Negligence resulting in damage to computers or data – conclusions

3.84   From the above matters that a claimant must prove, the difficult issues, which might effectively reduce the value of a claim to zero as distinct from just limiting it, are the probable inclusion of an exclusion clause, the foreseeability of consequential losses and the problems of contributory negligence and mitigation. The cumulation of these factors may be why no successful claims for liability of this type have been reported. But it remains the case that if a site operator does not give prominence to an exclusion of liability and takes no care over their site, even after problems become apparent, they may become liable for some losses if a careful user would suffer them.

Negligence causing injury to internet users

3.85   The law of negligence recognises purely psychiatric illness, not necessarily resulting from any physical trauma, as a type of injury for which liability can arise in the normal way. Thus, provided it was foreseeable to the defendant that their actions might result in such injury to the claimant, they owe a duty of care to the claimant.[194] However, the law draws a line – mere emotional distress cannot found a claim, there must be actual psychiatric illness, which in the context of negligence is also referred to as 'nervous shock'.

The argument would be that a website with social networking functions negligently allowed bullying or harassing behaviour towards a user to go on, as a result of which the user suffered psychiatric illness. There are no cases where liability has been found on this basis, but employers have been held liable to protect their employees from bullying and harassment pursuant to the duty of care they owe. In *Waters v Commissioner of Police of the Metropolis*[195] the court held that in principle the Commissioner (who was not technically an employer) could be liable on this basis and applied general negligence principles of foreseeability to the situation. The website scenario is analogous in the sense that, just as an employer can take actions against employees to restrain bullying behaviour, so a site operator can take action by banning users or providing tools to enable undesirable users to be blocked, etc. Given the increasing prominence in public discussion of harassment and stalking, and the presence of the criminal and civil liabilities for it, harm arising via this route must be foreseeable and site users, at least those who have signed up to an account, might be regarded as sufficiently proximate for a duty of care to be owed (see the discussion in relation to physical damage above). It could be argued that a user can simply walk away from a site that is causing them problems, but that might not always be practical.

In practice, most websites with a social networking element allow users to block other users and have an acceptable use and complaints policy that can result in users (or rather accounts) being banned from the site. The operation of these procedures help to discharge the duty of care. An operator will argue that any issues must be drawn to its attention. Operators are well advised to take these steps to minimise the risk of such an action being successful.

---

194 *Page v Smith* [1995] 2 WLR 644, [1996] AC 155 HL.
195 [2000] 1 WLR 1607 HL.

Negligence resulting in damage beyond data and computer operations

3.86   Clearly computers and networks can form part of the chain of causation leading from someone's actions to physical damage, as computers can cause interactions with the physical world via output devices. A discussion of the general law of negligence as it applies to all such scenarios is beyond the scope of this work and readers are referred to a textbook on the subject. But as the internet can provide a means of causing physical action at a distance without the need for human intervention, it will be considered briefly.

It is now possible for household devices to be controlled, via the internet, remotely from a computer (which may be a smartphone) using devices obtainable off-the-shelf. In future, this is likely to raise novel situations of liability (not just for the operator of the connected devices, but, also potentially for the maker and supplier of the connective hardware and software). It is possible that new models for the apportionment of risk and the provision of insurance will have to be developed to deal with such situations. The internet is not a reliable communication channel as messages can take an arbitrary time or not arrive at all, so it would not be appropriate in all such situations.

Jurisdiction and choice of law in negligence

Readers should refer generally to **3.3** above for the basic elements of the law.

Jurisdiction where the defendant is domiciled in a Convention State

3.87   In *Newsat Holdings Ltd v Zani*,[196] a case of negligent mis-statements, the 'place of the event giving rise to the damage' was the place where the statement was made, rather than where it was received and acted on. It was held that it was not necessary for all the elements of the cause of action to be present for that event to take place. The place where the damage occurs will generally be where the statement is acted on.

In a typical internet scenario, the defendant X may connect to the internet in country A to control the operation of a computer (perhaps a web server) in country B which then has the effect of causing damage to a computer in country C. Clearly the courts of country C have jurisdiction as the place of the damage. If X is also domiciled in country A he can be sued there for that reason; but if he is domiciled in another Convention State E, then the question of the place of the event giving rise to the damage arises. If the chain of causation is to be followed all the way back to X's actions in operating his browser to control the server, the place of the event is country A not country B. In the case where the tort is the uploading of an infected file, the argument for country A is stronger in that the file was started off on its journey by X's computer. Where the cause of

---

196 [2006] EWHC 342 (Comm) 2006 WL 584595.

the damage is the re-configuration of the server in some way without sending an infected file to it, the argument for country B appears stronger.

Where the common law scheme applies

3.88   Generally the operation of CPR rule 6.31 and PD 6B will mean that English and Welsh courts will only accept jurisdiction where the damage occurred in the jurisdiction or 'resulted from an act committed within the jurisdiction'. In *Metall and Rohstoff AG v Donaldson Lufkin & Jenrett Inc*[197] it was held that the court should look at the tort alleged in a common-sense way and ask whether the damage resulted from 'substantial and efficacious acts committed within the jurisdiction'. The focus on acts rather than events makes it easier to see that in the scenario described above, X must be located within the jurisdiction when he is operating the server. If he is outside the jurisdiction at the time, then jurisdiction must be founded on the basis of damage occurring here. However, the operation of *Spiliada* principles might mean that jurisdiction would be declined if the only connection with the jurisdiction was X's fleeting presence here while he remotely operated a server, the server and the damage being located elsewhere.

Choice of law

3.89   This poses fewer problems; the applicable law will be where the damage occurs under the Rome II Regulation. *Hillside (New Media) Ltd v Baasland and Others*[198] was a case involving tort arising from a contractual relationship. An internet gambling company sought a declaration from the English court that a claim against them in negligence by a Norwegian gambler was governed by English law (and therefore could not succeed). The losses claimed occurred by the use of funds deposited in an account which was located either in England, or possibly Gibraltar or the Netherlands Antilles (but not Norway). The court held that the damage was the reduction in value of the account (a chose in action), so happened where the account was located, but the claim was also manifestly more closely connected to England as the claimant was an English company whose operations were located in England and the contractual arrangements were governed by English law.

Following *Hillside* therefore, the place of damage will be the location of the computer that is infected or whose operations were affected by the tort. In cases not involving damage to computers it will be where the assets damaged, or the economic loss occurs. In claims arising from internet transactions generally, the nature of the transaction and the location of its subject matter will need to be investigated.

197 [1990] 1 QB 391.
198 [2010] EWHC 3336 (Comm); [2010] 2 CLC 986.

CHAPTER FOUR

Intellectual property

'[T]he internet is the world's biggest copying machine.'

Marybeth Peters, Register of Copyrights, 1995[1]

4.1   The material stored and transmitted through the internet is intangible and much of it will be protected by intellectual property rights. These rights can protect the intangible but substantial assets of companies and creative products of the mind from damage and unauthorised use. This chapter focuses on two of these rights: trade marks and copyright.

A trade mark or a brand name is forever important to businesses and consumers. For businesses the goodwill built up through sales under a brand can be extremely valuable. For consumers, a trade mark indicates the source of a product and so indicates its quality. It is therefore crucial that where e-commerce takes to the internet, where it is easy to fake an identity, the law protects trade mark owners and consumers from imposters. This is crucial in the area of domain names.

Copyright protects almost all the material used and transferred over the internet and the World Wide Web. This right can protect emails, websites and the programs and content shipped across the internet. It is therefore relevant for users and internet service providers to understand the ambit of these rights and what activities will lead to their infringement.

TRADE MARKS, DOMAIN NAMES AND PASSING OFF

4.2   A webpage provides a business with both a method of advertising and a method of selling to customers. The difference between any other advert and one on a website is that the nature of the internet means that the advertisement can be viewed anywhere by anyone.[2] This provides incredible commercial benefits

---

1   US News and World Report, 23 January 1995, at p 59.
2   Geo-blocking technologies are becoming increasingly effective, and courts are starting to require website providers to institute location-sensitive access. However, the European Commission appears to be against using such technical measures: See Press Release: *Digital Single Market,* 25 March 2015 (IP/15/4653).

to a business, as it no longer has to have any local physical presence to sell to customers. But in both the real world and the virtual world, trade marks and branding are essential. The potentially global reach of the internet, however, makes issues about trade marks far more complicated than was ever previously the case. This first part of the chapter will look at trade marks, in particular how domain names can be used as trade marks. It then moves on to consider passing off and its application to domain names through the instrument of fraud doctrine. It then considers the special arbitration rules which apply to domain names.

Technical rights v legal rights

4.3   As early as 1994, domain name disputes were starting to appear in courtrooms. In *MTV Networks v Adam Curry*,[3] Adam Curry had beaten the famous Music Television Network to a domain name. Before August 1993 he had registered and operated a website with the domain name 'www.mtv.com'. This site provided information about the music business, and dovetailed with the television business of MTV. On 19 January 1994 MTV sought to acquire the domain name. By spring 1994 millions of internet users had accessed the 'www. mtv.com' site. This is a common scenario in domain name clashes. The only right which Adam Curry had over the site was a technical one: he was the owner of the domain name alias: he was not the owner of any legal rights to use the name (or trade mark) MTV.

This problem is also affected by the fact that although there can be only one '.com', there has always been the risk that there may be many variations of the domain name with different suffixes (TLD). For example, in November 1993, Merritt Technologies Inc was granted the domain name 'mit.com'. From 30 December 1993 Merritt used the domain to provide free internet access to the handicapped, disabled and elderly. On 6 May 1996, Merritt received a letter from the Massachusetts Institute of Technology asking Merritt to select an alternative domain name. Their rights to insist upon this were based on their use of the MIT trade mark since 1861, having a worldwide reputation and five registered trade marks in classes unrelated to Merritt's use of the mark. The Institute already owned the domain names 'mit.org' and 'mit.edu'. There was no crossover in fields of activity: the Institute was simply worried that its trade mark was being used at all. This is now a routine occurrence. This is because the naming committees both here and elsewhere are expanding, and will continue to expand, the numbers of suffixes (TLDs) available; but as the late Jon Postel of the Internet Assigned Name Authority (IANA) wrote:[4]

> '[T]he trade mark issue is just a mess. McDonalds is going to want to have mcdonalds.com, mcdonalds.biz, and other domain names involving McDonalds.'

---

3   867 F. Supp 202 (SDNY 1994).
4   Information Law Alert, 02/09/96, 'Antidilution trade mark law gets first court case'.

This chapter looks at the conflict between legal rights in cyberspace, where in most cases little has really changed, and the conflict between technical rights (in domain names) and legal rights (in trade marks).

The nature of trade mark protection

4.4   Trade marks are, like all intellectual property rights, territorial by nature. This means that a person who registers a trade mark at the Intellectual Property Office is entitled to protection for that trade mark only within the United Kingdom and the Isle of Man. Such a person is only entitled to protection in other countries where separate applications are made in those countries. This means that a trade mark can be owned by two entirely separate and unrelated entities in two different countries; for example, one business could own the mark 'DOG' for clothing in the US, and another could own and use 'DOG' on clothing in the UK. The territorial nature of trade marks means that, in the real world at least, there is no overlap of rights as each trade mark owner can operate only within the geographic territory where they have rights.

In addition, a trade mark only grants protection in relation to the goods and services in respect of which it is registered. This means that two traders can use the same mark for different goods in the same marketplace (eg 'Green' used in respect of musical instruments by one trader and in respect of footwear by another) without infringing each other's rights. In such cases, therefore, there is no conflict of rights. It is also possible for two traders to agree between themselves that they can both use the same mark in respect of the same goods in the same (or part of the same) marketplace (co-existence agreements).

Trade marks are not unique. It is possible, therefore, to have conflicts between trade mark rights where two trade mark owners (one from the US, one from the UK) both use the mark on the internet at the same time. The nature of the internet also means that problems may arise in relation to genuine goods which are sold under the trade mark, but which have yet to be put on the market inside the EU (ie parallel imports). This can cause problems when consumers see products (eg jeans) are on sale on a US website for less than they are sold in the UK, and then seek to buy from abroad. The basic questions of trade mark law which these businesses face, however, is little different from real world activities. The nature of the internet raises different matters only in some areas. It is these areas which this chapter concentrates on, but a general introduction to trade mark law is included although those wanting answers to more technical questions should consult a specialist text.

Domain names

4.5   Every computer on the internet has an IP (Internet Protocol) address. These addresses are made up of a series of numbers, which have the form 123.45.678.910.[5] The numbers can be assigned permanently or temporarily

---

5   This is an IP version 4 address of the type used by virtually all networks.

(floating), for example most home users of the internet have a new IP address allocated by their internet service provider every time they log onto the internet. In contrast, businesses often have a permanent IP address for the server; although users of the business's network might have a temporary address.

The problem with IP addresses is that they are not very easy to remember.[6] To remedy this problem a sort of phone directory was set up which assigned a name to every IP address. This meant that instead of typing up to a 12-digit number, users could type a domain name ending with one of the so-called generic top level domains (.com, .org, .net, .biz, .tv) (gTLD) or one of the country code top-level domains (.uk, .fr) (ccTLD). Where a domain name has a ccTLD[7] (eg lawyer.co.uk) it does not necessarily mean that the user of that domain name is in the UK or that the server where the material is stored is in the UK. A postal address necessarily changes whenever one moves from one town to another, but a domain name may remain the same wherever one moves. The only way to locate the owner of a domain name is to geographically locate the internet protocol address.[8]

Domain names, like company names, are not simply taken; they are registered. They are also unique (so www.flower.com is different from www.flowers.com) and so no two people can separately own the same domain name. Most registration companies do not check that an applicant has the right to use a particular name as a domain name and so the registrars allocate them on a first-come, first-served basis. In the UK, this approach was been approved of (or at least accepted) by the court in relation to the domain name 'pitman.co.uk'.[9] It was concluded that because the claimant, Pitman Training Ltd had no rights to proceed for passing off or any other tort, Nominet (responsible for 'co.uk' domain names) was entitled to register domain names as and when they are requested by an applicant and did not have to investigate entitlement in advance.

Trade marks v domain names

4.6   The unique nature of each domain name means that unlike trade marks there is no way to exercise rights independently of each other. There can only be one apple.com despite both Apple and Apple Records both wanting to use the name and, until the launch of iTunes, there being only limited overlap between

---

6   Because the domain name which humans remember and type merely 'refers' to a unique number, it is possible to expand the quantity of IP addresses without having to alert consumers to the change. This is clearly different from telephone numbers where, if extra numbers are required to allow for growth, every existing number must change. At present most IP addresses still use version 4 (which uses 32-bit binary numbers). It is possible for a network to change to using IP addresses using version 6, which is a 128-bit hexadecimal number. Although this format is not widely used, when it is adopted it will not change domain names and most users will be totally unaware of the change.

7   There are also a number of quasi-ccTLDs, such as '.uk.com'. These are not actually ccTLD, but are privately owned sub-domains in the gTLD '.com'. Accordingly, 'uk.com' is registered as a domain name and if there were 'IPlawyer.uk.com' then if the 'uk.com' domain name is not renewed all those relying on sub-domains would lapse at the same time.

8   There are a number of geo-locating websites, which can provide details of where a particular site was accessed from.

9   *Pitman Training Ltd v Nominet UK* [1997] FSR 797.

the businesses. In contrast, Apple can own the trade mark in relation to some goods and services whereas Apple Records can own in relation to others without there necessarily being any conflict of the rights.[10] John Gilmore of the Electronic Frontier Foundation sums up the issue well:[11]

> 'Trade marks are registered in a system that permits many companies to share a name legitimately without interfering with each other, such as Sun Photo, Sun Oil and Sun Microsystems. Domain names only permit one user of a name; there is only one sun.com, which Sun Microsystems registered first. Neither lawyers nor governments can make ten pounds of names fit into a one-pound bag.'

The different nature of domain names and trade marks can lead to commercial, technical and legal problems relating to conflicts between trade marks. If a business owns a trade mark in the UK, can it stop a US company using it as a domain name? This question, and others, will be explored below.

REGISTRATION OF TRADE MARKS

4.7   In the United Kingdom there are three types of registered trade marks, as well as certain protection for unregistered marks and certain well-known[12] marks.[13] First, it is possible to register a mark under the Trade Marks Act 1994,[14] which grants a trade mark only in the United Kingdom; secondly, it is possible to register a Community trade mark[15] under the Community Trade Mark Regulation (No 207/2009) ('the CTM Regulation'),[16] which grants uniform protection across all 28 members of the EU; and finally, it is possible to obtain protection under the Protocol Relating to the Madrid Agreement Concerning the International Registration of Marks ('the Madrid Protocol'). The last of these options enables a single application to be made which grants protection in up to 96 countries[17] by way of 94 separate registrations from a single application.[18]

---

10   Nevertheless, there had been a long-running dispute between the two companies over the right in the name, which was settled in February 2007: see http://news.bbc.co.uk/1/hi/entertainment/6332319.stm.
11   *The Economist*, Letters, 13 July 1996.
12   Protection under art 6*bis* of the Paris Convention (s 56 of the Trade Marks Act 1994).
13   Special protection also exists for other symbols and signs both within and outside the trade mark system. International organisations and states have special protection for their emblems under art 6*ter* of the Paris Convention (which is given effect by ss 57 to 59 of the Trade Marks Act 1994), the Olympic and Paralympic symbols are also given special protection under the Olympic Symbols etc (Protection) Act 1995.
14   This implements Directive 89/104/EEC which has now been codified as Directive 2008/95/EC. There is currently a proposal being considered to revise this codified Directive (as well as the Community Trade Mark Regulation).
15   It is proposed that these will be re-branded as European trade marks as part of the reform package. The Proposals are: COM(2013) 161 final and COM(2013) 162 final.
16   A reform package has been agreed, and at the time of writing is being finalised, which will rename the Community Trade Mark to the European Trade Mark. This chapter will use its current name.
17   As of 31 October 2015.
18   In the UK this is given effect by the Trade Marks (International Registration) Order 2008 (SI 2008/2206).

Whether a mark is registered under the 1994 Act, the CTM Regulation or in accordance with the Madrid Protocol the protection that is granted is the same in scope within the UK and the requirements that the mark must satisfy to be registered are more or less the same.

Signs that can be registered as trade marks

4.8   It is possible for any sign which is capable of graphical representation to be registered as a trade mark[19] provided that the representation is clear, precise, self-contained, easily accessible, intelligible, durable, unequivocal and objective.[20] These requirements will always be met in relation to a word mark, such as a domain name, as it can be written in straight text. Most traditional trade marks can also be represented to this standard; it is only where a mark is unusual (such as smell or sound) that problems arise. However, these unusual marks will not be examined here.[21]

Absolute grounds of refusal

4.9   In addition to the basic requirement that a sign is capable of being graphically represented, there are several other so-called absolute grounds of refusal that lead to an application to register a trade mark being refused. These are, in summary, that the mark is devoid of distinctive character, that it is descriptive, that it has become generic, that it is functional or that it is deceptive or otherwise contrary to public policy.[22] These various grounds will not be examined generally here. Instead this section will look only at the registration using domain names as its working example.

Distinctive and descriptiveness issues

4.10   In general, a trade mark cannot be registered if the relevant public[23] would think that it is devoid of distinctive character.[24] This exclusion is to prevent the registration of a mark which is incapable of fulfilling its essential

19   Trade Marks Act 1994 (TMA), s 1(1); CTM Regulation, art 4.

20   C-273/00 *Sieckmann* [2002] ECR I-11737, [2003] EMTR 37 at para 46. It is part of the reform package that it will be possible to register things which can be contained in digital files (such as sound files or CAD files).

21   See J Mellor *et al*, *Kerly's Law of Trade Marks and Trade Names* (15th edition, Sweet and Maxwell, 2011).

22   TMA 1994, s 3; CTM Regulation, art 7.

23   C-136/02 *Mag Instrument Inc v Office for Harmonisation in the Internal Market (Trade Marks and Designs) (OHIM)* [2004] ECR I-9165, [2005] ETMR 46 at paras 19 and 49; C-218/01 *Henkel KGaA v Deutsches Patent- und Markenamt* [2004] ECR I-1725, [2005] ETMR 45 at para 50. The relevant public is made up of those who might buy the goods or services.

24   TMA, s 3(1)(b); CTM Regulation, art 7(1)(b).

function, namely distinguishing[25] the goods or services of one undertaking from others which have a different origin.[26] In principle, however, even the simplest marks such as a single letter[27] or number[28] may be registered provided they are distinctive.

In addition it is necessary to address whether a mark is descriptive of the goods and services for which the mark is registered.[29] It is not, for example, permissible to register the trade mark COMPUTERS for computers,[30] but it could be registered for bananas. The exclusion from registration of descriptive marks is intended to protect the general[31] (or public)[32] interest so that other traders may use a mark. In considering such an interest it does not matter whether the mark is presently being used descriptively, it is sufficient that it could be used in that way.[33] But the test should not be applied too rigorously as some marks may allude to the function of the goods or services, but in essence are lexical inventions and so cannot be descriptive.[34]

The assessment of whether a mark has acquired distinctive character across the whole of the relevant territory[35] (and whether it remains descriptive) in respect of the goods or services for which registration has been applied for, may take into account the following factors:

(a)   the market share held by the mark;

(b)   how intensive, geographically widespread, and long-standing use of the mark has been;

(c)   the amount invested by the undertaking in promoting the mark;

(d)   the proportion of the relevant class of persons who, because of the mark, identify goods as originating from a particular undertaking; and

---

25   The distinctiveness bar may actually be very low: see C-64/02 *Office for Harmonisation in the Internal Market (Trade Marks and Designs) (OHIM) v Erpo Mobelwerk* [2004] ECR I-10031, [2005] ETMR 58.
26   C-329/02 *SAT.1 Satellitenfernsehen GmbH v Office for Harmonisation in the Internal Market (Trade Marks and Designs) (OHIM)* [2004] ECR I-8317, [2005] ETMR 20 at para 23; C-37/03 *BioID* [2005] ECR I-7975 at para 27.
27   C-265/09 *OHIM v BORCO-Marken-Import Matthiesen* [2011] ETMR 4 at para 38.
28   C-51/10 *Agencja Wydawnicza Technopol* [2011] ETMR 34 at para 31.
29   TMA, s 3(1)(c); CTM Regulation, art 7(1)(c).
30   Similarly, Goldfish is descriptive for pets, but not credit cards: see *O2 Holdings Ltd (formerly O2 Ltd) v Hutchison 3G Ltd* [2006] EWHC 534 (Ch); [2006] ETMR 55 at para 71.
31   C-329/02 *SAT.1* [2004] ECR I-8317, [2005] ETMR 20 at para 25.
32   C-191/01 *Office for Harmonisation in the Internal Market (Trade Marks and Designs) (OHIM) v Wm Wrigley Jr Co (DOUBLEMINT)* [2003] ECR I-12447, [2004] ETMR 9 at para 31.
33   *DOUBLEMINT* [2003] ECR I-12447, [2004] ETMR 9 at para 32.
34   C-383/99 *Procter & Gamble Co v Office for Harmonisation in the Internal Market (Trade Marks and Designs) (OHIM) (BABY-DRY)* [2001] ECR I-6251, [2002] ETMR 3, paras 43 and 44; but note that this decision is probably the absolute high point of protection and, following later jurisprudence, similar marks may no longer overcome the descriptiveness hurdle.
35   C-108/05 *Bovemij* [2006] ECR I-7605 makes it clear that a mark must have become distinctive across the whole of the UK for a UK mark and across the whole of the EU for a CTM.

(e)   statements from chambers of commerce and industry or other trade and professional associations.[36]

Descriptive domain names

4.11   When this approach is put in context it makes more sense. In some industries, it is often better to be listed under one's services than under one's name. For example, it may be more profitable for a chemist to be listed under 'pharmacies' than under his name. It may appear that the same is true for the internet: the domain name, 'flowers.com' may appear to be far more valuable than 'lindasflorist.com'. However, the advantages of such a registration can be greatly overestimated. Most internet users will search the internet using a search engine (such as Google) and searching under 'florist' would bring up both 'flowers.com' and 'lindasflorist.com'.[37] Indeed, there is probably significantly more commercial benefits in being a sponsored link (and so being highlighted at the top of the page) than there is from having a generic web address.

Nevertheless, there is always an advantage from internet users knowing what a website provides without having to access it and so these generic names do provide some commercial benefit. This commercial benefit, however, may not be possible to protect under trade mark law as flowers.com is descriptive of the goods it provides (flowers) and descriptive marks only become registrable where they have become distinctive through use. In other words, it is necessary to show that the mark, although at first blush descriptive, has now become associated in consumers' minds with the relevant business. In contrast, marks like 'lindasflowers.com' are more likely to be distinctive and so could be registered without waiting for it to acquire so-called secondary meaning.

This means that those individuals who are considering acquiring a domain name are advised to use a distinctive name: this has few disadvantages on the web, particularly now search engines are well developed and utilised, but has the obvious advantage of being registrable at the outset.

Registration of 'www' and '.com' etc

4.12   The prevalence of the internet means that many brands only have an online presence. Such businesses may want to register their full domain name as a trade mark to stop others using similar marks (or domain names). In general, at both the Intellectual Property Office and OHIM, it is possible to register trade marks which include the prefix 'www' or with the suffix '.com'/'.co.uk'. However, both this prefix and such suffixes are normally not thought to have any

---

36   C-108 and 109/97 *Windsurfing Chiemsee Produktions- und Vertriebs GmbH v Boots- und Segelzubehor Walter Huber* [1999] ECR I-2779, [1999] ETMR 585, para 51; also see C-25/05 *August Storck (Storck II)* [2006] ECR I-5719.

37   In fact, a simple Google search using 'florist' generates 63,800,000 hits (as at 31 October 2015).

trade mark significance. A recent example of this issue arose when Getty Images tried to register photos.com, as the court explained:[38]

> '... the word mark PHOTOS.COM, considered as a whole, reproduces the characteristic structure of a second-level domain name ("photos") and a TLD [top level domain] ("com"), separated by a dot. ...that mark has no additional features – in particular, graphic features – because the dot is typically used to separate the second level domain from the TLD. Furthermore, the addition of the element ".com" to the word "photos", which is descriptive and devoid of distinctive character, does not render the sign distinctive as a whole .... Accordingly, in the absence of special characteristics peculiar to the sign at issue, the relevant public's perception of that sign will be no different from its perception of the combination of the two words comprising the sign. It follows that ... the relevant public will not be able to distinguish the goods and services covered by the trade mark application from goods and services of a different commercial origin. Consequently, the sign is devoid of distinctive character.'

This decision, which was following an established practice. Means that a mark which is not distinctive or descriptive in itself (eg 'flowers' for flowers or 'photos' for photographs) does not cease to be descriptive simply by the addition of 'www' or '.com'. Secondly, when considering infringement or the relative grounds of refusal 'www' or '.com' might be ignored as having no independent significance.[39] This means that 'www.flowers.com' will usually be considered to be identical to 'flowers' or 'flowers.com'.

Nevertheless, some businesses may wish to register as trade marks their actual domain name, prefix, suffix and all. However, there seems little reason to do so as it will give less rather than more protection. This is because registering as a trade mark the name element of the domain name will also protect the name's use within a domain name.

Example 4.1

David Peters Ltd is a one-man company that specialises in repairing old hi-fi equipment. As the company grows in experience, its owner realises that there is a market in repairing old computer equipment for a pre-determined quotation. The company sets up a website on which restored equipment is offered for sale and on which viewers may enter details of their ailing equipment to receive an emailed repair quotation. The domain name for the site is 'www.compair.com'. To provide added protection for this sign, David Peters Ltd may seek a trade mark registration over the word 'compair' in the appropriate classes. Such a registration is normally sufficient to prevent uses by third parties of the mark www.compair.com as well.

---

38   T-338/11 *Getty Images v OHIM* (21 November 2012) at paras 24 to 28; adopted by the Court of Justice: C-70/13 *Getty Images v OHIM* (12 December 2013) para 25; also see T-117/06 *DeTeMedien v OHIM* (12 December 2007) para 24.
39   Eg *Reed Executive v Reed Business Information* [2004] EWCA Civ 159; [2004] RPC 40, para 36; also see *Compass Publishing BV v Compass Logistics* [2004] EWHC 520; [2004] RPC 41.

Example 4.2

A data recovery company registers the domain name 'data-recovery.co.uk.' It is the only owner of this domain name; it is unique among not only all data recovery companies, but also all domain name owners. This does not mean that the name is capable of distinguishing the services of its owner from any other company. Without more the company will be unable to register a trade mark over the name.

Registering in relation to goods and services

4.13   A trade mark is registered in relation to goods and services and trade mark applicants must indicate on their applications which goods and services in respect of which protection is sought. Accordingly, a trade mark ('flower') which is registered in respect of milk (Class 29) cannot be used to prevent that mark being used by another trader in relation to laundry detergent (Class 3).[40] This means that trade marks are quite different from domain names. A domain name is necessarily unique and so the one person who owns a particular domain name automatically precludes anyone else from using the domain name for whatever goods that second person sells.

Classification

4.14   To assist with both the application for, and searching of, trade marks goods and services are classified in accordance with the Nice Classification.[41] This system is used both by the Intellectual Property Office[42] and the Community Trade Mark Office (OHIM).[43] It has 45 different classes and each class includes a detailed list of goods and services. Practically, there will be few occasions when a registered trade mark proprietor will need to broaden the scope of an existing trade mark registration when beginning to use the name as a domain name. It is wrong to think that because the medium of exploitation is the internet that the trade mark registration needs to be expanded into other classes.

---

40   Unless the mark has a sufficient reputation to be protected under s 10(3) of the TMA or art 9(1)(c) of the CTM Regulation.
41   The Nice Agreement Concerning the International Classification of Goods and Services for the Purposes of the Registration of Marks.
42   Trade Marks Rules 2008 (SI 2008/1797), r 7.
43   Commission Regulation (EC) No. 2868/95, r 2.

Example 4.3

Artsake Ltd is a manufacturer of artists' materials within the UK. It has a trade mark registration in Class 16 to reflect the use of its name Artsake in relation to paper, cardboard goods and other artists' materials. It now wishes to expand its business by setting up a website through which customers can place orders. It chooses the domain name 'artsake.co.uk' and is concerned that it will require additional trade mark protection for the domain. It does not; its existing registration will equally protect its domain name in respect of artists' materials sold over the internet.

There may be times where an individual already has a trade mark registration but is providing new goods or services through a website. In this circumstance there may be a reason to broaden the number of classes or specification for which a trade mark is registered. Some websites are, in trade mark terms, still little more than a digital billboard or leaflet. In contrast, true e-commerce solutions which allow the site to obtain information about the viewer and take payment from a user may lead to an increase in the activities provided through a website. An illustration is where the proprietor of a small local newspaper starts to allow and charge for sophisticated searching of its archives from its website. A change in the nature of the business may be taking place. This proprietor should not simply rely on a registration for paper products, but should widen the specification to include the use of computers to search and access data.

Example 4.4

A car manufacturer that uses its trade mark as a domain name decides to make its website more than merely a digital version of its paper brochures. To do this the dealer includes on its website an applet that acts as a route finder: individuals may type in where they are and where they wish to go and the program generates a map of the quickest route. The map also includes the miles per gallon that the dealer's car would use on the same route, so promoting the fuel economy of the car. The business now involves not only the sale of cars but also the provision of a route-finding service. It would be prudent to broaden the trade mark protection to cover these new services accordingly.

Similarly there will be times where the trade mark owner continues to use the trade mark in a slightly different market of goods or services. For example, a travel agent may well have a trade mark registered in classes including class 39 for travel services. If, however, the agent expands its business to include taking bookings over its website, it may want to consider carefully its existing specification on the trade marks register. In this situation it may be wise to ensure its registration covers the provision of travel services by means of a global network.

It is tempting for internet-related firms to apply for a mark in relation to class 38 which relates to, among other things, telecommunication of information. But in fact, registration in this class is only appropriate for infrastructure providers for the internet and those providing the core activities of internet service providers, such as search engines, hosting chat-rooms, email services and so forth.

Some of the more complex services provided on the internet might, however, be better classified as computer programs (in class 9) and any computer programs which are intended for download should be registered in class 9.

Specifications for computers, databases and other online services

4.15   In general broad specifications or vague terms like 'multi-media services', 'internet services' and 'online services' are unacceptable as the specification must enable the goods and services for which the protection of the trade mark is sought to be identified by the applicant with sufficient clarity and precision to enable the registry and competitors to determine the extent of the protection sought without recourse to other sources.[44] Once an applicant has decided the classes for which a trade mark registration should be obtained, an appropriate specification within that class must be provided.

In *Avnet Incorporated v Isoact Ltd*[45] Jacobs J was required to assess, in trade mark terms, the services offered by internet service providers to those subscribers who use their websites as a means of advertising their businesses. Avnet was the registered proprietor of the 'Avnet' trade mark under class 35 (advertising and promotional services etc, all included within class 35). The defendant was an ISP using 'Avnet' in the course of business as a domain name and trading name. This mark was used to promote its usual ISP services of: providing email addresses and providing server space to customers on which they could host their own websites.

Jacob J found that ISP services did not fall within 'advertising and promotional services' within class 35, even where the ISP allowed its subscribers to use its services for this purpose. This decision, of course, defeated the claim, but it also indicates that ISPs must draft their trade mark specifications with care. Jacob J warned:

> '… specifications for services should be scrutinised carefully and they should not be given a wide construction covering a vast range of activities. They should be confined to the substance, as it were, the core of the possible meanings attributable to the rather general phrase.'[46]

Conversely, in relation to a specification for 'computer database, or a database program, or a telecommunications service' in *Total Ltd v YouView TV*[47] Sales J stated:

> '… it is my view that although there may be some element of uncertainty at the margins about whether something is a computer database, or a database program, or a telecommunications service, there is no significant doubt about the core meaning of those terms and no unacceptable uncertainty regarding their scope of application.'

44   C-307/10 *Chartered Institute of Patent Attorneys* [2012] ETMR 42 at para 49.
45   [1997] ETMR 562; for different reasons, Avnet was denied a transfer of 'avnet.net' by the WIPO Arbitration and Mediation Centre: *Avnet Inc v Aviation Network Inc* Case (WIPO D2000–0046).
46   *Avnet Incorporated v Isoact Ltd* [1997] ETMR 562 at 565.
47   [2014] EWHC 1963 (Ch), [2015] FSR 7 at para 59.

Nevertheless, there is a risk where a specification is too broad or includes terms that are essentially generic terms, 'computer programs' are likely to be viewed as too wide.[48]

Comparison websites

4.16 The easy access to information and data which now exists in the current market place has led to the development of price comparison websites. The complexity of these spans listing retailers selling the same goods and indicating their different prices to enabling insurance premiums to be calculated and compared. In C-420/13 *Netto Marken-Discount AG*[49] the court made it clear that it was possible to register trade marks in relation to such comparison services, but the specification must be formulated with sufficient clarity and precision so as to allow others to know which services the applicant intends to bring together. Thus, a specification must indicate, for example, whether it is for 'bringing together insurance services' or 'bringing together pricing information on computers'.

Opposition and registration

4.17 Once an application has been examined on absolute grounds, assuming it is not found to be wanting, it will be published.[50] Once an application has been published it is possible for the application to be opposed by the proprietor of any earlier trade mark or right, who may oppose the registration on what are called relative grounds of refusal. Essentially, these arise where the mark applied for would infringe the earlier mark or right if it was used in the course of trade. Accordingly, the relative grounds of refusal can be considered along with infringement below.

Once the opposition period[51] is over, or if all opposition proceedings have been withdrawn or decided in favour of the applicant, the mark will be registered.[52] The protection afforded by a trade mark begins at registration, although this is backdated to the date the application was filed.[53]

---

48 In *Second Sight Ltd v Novell Inc and Novell UK Ltd* [1995] RPC 423 an overly wide specification in class 9 for 'computer software' was the cause of a clash between two rights-holders in different fields both asserting rights over the same trade name; also see *Mercury Communications Ltd v Mercury Interactive (UK) Ltd* [1995] FSR 850.

49 [2014] ETMR 52.

50 TMA, s 38(1); CTM Regulation, art 40.

51 The period is usually two months at the Intellectual Property Office, but can be extended to three months where an application is made: Trade Marks Rules 2008, r 17. It is three months at OHIM: CTM Regulation, art 41(1).

52 TMA, s 40; CTM Regulation, art 45.

53 TMA, ss 9(3) and 40(3); different rules apply to the Community trade mark.

REGISTRATION OF DOMAIN NAMES

4.18   The usual way to register a domain name is to use a registrar, which is either an internet service provider or a registration agent; direct registration is possible but requires some technical knowledge. When an online registrar is used the process is incredibly straightforward. A domain name is selected and paid for. There is little more to it, unless the domain is restricted to certain types of undertakings.[54]

There are, however, some things that registrants should take into account. As mentioned previously, domain names are unique. If you want a domain name that is owned by someone else, you have only three choices. First, wait for the domain name to become available if the owner chooses not to renew it;[55] secondly, buy it from the owner; or finally, litigate for it. Domain names still change hands for massive sums of money. The highest price paid to date was $17 million in 2015 for 360.com although the payment of $11 million in 2001 for hotels.com comes close (when inflation is taken into account).[56] It is hardly surprising that so many turn to litigation or dispute resolution under one of the arbitration schemes. These will both be considered below.

Originally, there were seven generic top level domains (.com, .org, .net, .int, .edu, .gov, .mil) and country code top level domains (such as .uk). However, since the liberalisation announced by ICANN in 2008[57] it has been possible to sponsor a TLD,[58] and then register sub-domains within that domain to users. Thus, the TLD '.bike'[59] could allow Teds Cycles to register the domain 'tedscycles. bike'. The massive expansion in domain names has two implications. First, it means that some of the conflicts which existed because there was only one 'cars. com' have dissipated as the multitude of TLDs means that others can get 'cars. biz' or 'cars.london'. Secondly, it means those who own trade marks have more difficulty in preventing third parties getting domain names; so does Coca Cola need to register 'coke.bike' or take action if a third party registers it?

Trying to identify the domain name owner

4.19   The technical nature of domain names is such that, presently, one may not know who owns a domain name. While a Whois search[60] will provide the registration details of a person this is rarely the end of the story. Indeed, even if one knows the owner, pinpointing them on the planet to issue and serve proceedings

---

54   So for example, the '.pro' domain name requires proof the registrant provides professional services (eg legal services).

55   This can happen deliberately or accidentally; for example, in 1999 Microsoft did not renew 'hotmail.com', fortunately somebody external to the company did it on their behalf.

56   See www.europeandomaincentre.com/pages/news-room/domain-management-news/the-top-25-most-expensive-domains-of-all-times.

57   32nd International Public ICANN Meeting 22 to 26 June 2008: see http://archive.icann.org/en/meetings/paris2008/.

58   The current list is at: www.iana.org/domains/root/db.

59   Sponsored by Grand Hollow, LLC.

60   See for example https://who.is.

can be complex.[61] The domain name registrars do not necessarily require, and certainly do not check, whether the name and address of the registrant is correct; although the 'wilful' provision of inaccurate ownership data can be used to trigger domain name cancellation (or transfer).[62] Where, for whatever reason, one cannot locate the defendant, how can one prevent the infringement from occurring? This has been resolved to some extent by injunctions against internet service providers, discussed below.

However, it is also possible, in some cases, to pursue the domain name itself 'in rem'. In England it is not presently possible to file proceedings against a domain name as an action in rem. But in the US it is possible to bring an action against a domain name under the Anti-Cybersquatting Statute.[63] Accordingly, claimants may wish, in some circumstances, to consider filing a claim relating to .com, .net etc domain names in the US, rather than in the UK.

Bad faith registrations

4.20   An application, or part of it, can be refused on the grounds that it was applied for in bad faith.[64] This concept is uniform across the EU[65] and so it does not depend on local factors. Thus, where a person applies to register a word mark (or a domain name mark) it might be possible to oppose the registration. The date for judging bad faith is the date the application was made[66] and when making the judgement whether something is in bad faith an overall assessment is made taking into account all the relevant factors.[67] This includes in particular the subjective intention of the person making the application in light of the objective factors[68] and so it is immaterial that the applicant believes that what he or she is doing is proper.[69] But an intention to prevent a person using the mark is

---

61   It is possible to service claim forms by social media. This first occurred using Twitter in *Blaney v Persons Unknown* (HC unreported, 1 October 2009) and using Facebook in *AKO Capital v TFS Derivatives* (HC unreported, 17 February 2012). In Ireland service over LinkedIn has been permitted: *Re Irish Education Research Institute* (HC unreported, 10 November 2014).

62   *T-Nova Deutsche Telekom Innovations Gesellschaft mbH v TechNova* (T-nova.com) (NAF FA 94646).

63   Lanham Act, s 43(d)(2)(A); cybersquatting in this context means: registering a domain name associated with a protected trade mark either to ransom the domain name to the mark holder or to divert business from the mark holder: *DaimlerChrysler v The Net Inc*, 388 F 3d 201, 204 (6th Cir 2004).

64   TMA, s 3(6), which is derived from Directive 2008/95/EC, art 3(2)(d); bad faith is not a ground of refusal for Community trade marks, but it is a ground of invalidity: CTM Regulation, art 52(1)(b).

65   C-320/12 *Malaysia Diary v Ankenaevnet for Patenter og Varemaerker* [2013] ETMR 36 at para 16.

66   C-529/07 Chocoladefabriken *Lindt & Sprüngli AG v Franz Hauswirth GmbH* [2009] ECR I-4893, [2009] ETMR 56 at para 35.

67   C-529/07 Chocoladefabriken *Lindt & Sprüngli AG v Franz Hauswirth GmbH* [2009] ECR I-4893, [2009] ETMR 56 at para 37.

68   See also, by analogy, C-569/08 *Internetportal und Marketing GmbH v Schlicht* [2010] ETMR 48 at para 45.

69   *Pavel* Maslyukov *v Diageo Distilling* [2010] EWHC 443 (Ch), [2010] ETMR 37 at para 42.

likely to suggest bad faith.[70] The degree of legal protection for a mark may also be a relevant factor in determining bad faith.[71] Nevertheless, establishing that an applicant knew that another person in the marketplace uses an identical or similar sign in relation to the goods is not sufficient to establish bad faith[72] and neither is knowledge that a person uses the mark abroad.[73] In any event, a person who applies to register a mark so that the mark can be sold to the trade mark owner (squatting) will usually be treated as having made the application in bad faith.

TRADE MARK INFRINGEMENT

4.21   Once a trade mark is registered, then within the territories in which it has effect, it grants the proprietor certain exclusive rights. These rights vary between jurisdictions, and just because a particular use of a trade mark would infringe in the US does not mean that equivalent use in the UK would also infringe, and vice versa. The territorial nature of a trade mark also means that it is possible to both have clashes between two legitimate right holders; for example, a trade mark may be owned by different people in Australia and in the UK. Indeed, such clashes could potentially involve a number of different traders, all of whom have rights in relation to identical or similar marks. The US Court of Appeals for the Ninth Circuit warned of the particular problems which occur on the internet:

> 'We now reiterate that the Web, as a marketing channel, is particularly susceptible to a likelihood of confusion since, as it did in this case, it allows for competing marks to be encountered at the same time, on the same screen.'[74]

These clashes of rights have led to an attempt to provide a uniform solution to the problem,[75] but as there has been no international consensus to follow such an approach the rules remain jurisdiction specific.

The basic act of infringement in the UK is set out in s 10 of the Trade Marks Act 1994 (similar rights are granted in relation to a Community trade mark by art 9 of the CTM Regulation). This reads as follows:

> '(1) A person infringes a registered trade mark if he uses in the course of trade a sign which is identical with the trade mark in relation to goods or services which are identical with those for which it is registered.

---

70   The registration of a mark to assist in pending litigation is not a registration in bad faith: *32Red plc v WHG (International) Ltd* [2011] EWHC 62 (Ch), [2011] ETMR 21, [159].
71   C-529/07 Chocoladefabriken *Lindt & Sprüngli AG v Franz Hauswirth GmbH* [2009] ECR I-4893, [2009] ETMR 56 at para 46.
72   C-529/07 Chocoladefabriken *Lindt & Sprüngli AG v Franz Hauswirth GmbH* [2009] ECR I-4893, [2009] ETMR 56 at para 40.
73   C-320/12 *Malaysia Diary v Ankenaevnet for Patenter og Varemaerker* [2013] ETMR 36.
74   *GOTO.com v Disney*, 202 F 3d 1199, 1207 (9th Cir 2000).
75   See *WIPO Joint Recommendation Concerning the Protection of Marks, and Other Industrial Property Rights in Signs on the Internet* (WIPO Publication 845) (2001).

(2) A person infringes a registered trade mark if he uses in the course of trade a sign where because –

    (a) the sign is identical with the trade mark and is used in relation to goods or services similar to those for which the trade mark is registered, or

    (b) the sign is similar to the trade mark and is used in relation to goods or services identical with or similar to those for which the trade mark is registered, there exists a likelihood of confusion on the part of the public, which includes the likelihood of association with the trade mark.

(3) A person infringes a registered trade mark if he uses in the course of trade, in relation to goods or services, a sign which –

    (a) is identical with or similar to the trade mark,

where the trade mark has a reputation in the UK and the use of the sign, being without due cause, takes unfair advantage of, or is detrimental to, the distinctive character or the repute of the trade mark.'

There are, therefore, three classes of infringement: identity, similarity and what might loosely be called dilution. Each of these classes will be looked at in turn, but there are some things which must be shown in respect of each. The first of these was that it was the use of a sign.

Use of a sign in the course of trade

4.22 The two concepts to examine are the simple question of what is 'use' of a sign and then, the more complex concept of what is 'use' of a sign in the course of trade. A person uses a sign in particular when he:

    '(a) affixes it to goods or the packaging thereof;

    (b) offers or exposes goods for sale, puts them on the market or stocks them for those purposes under the sign, or offers or supplies services under the sign;

    (c) imports or exports goods under the sign; or

    (d) uses the sign on business papers or in advertising.'[76]

In relation to a sign being used on the internet the most relevant uses are (b) and (d). The European Court of Justice in *Arsenal v Reed*[77] explained that in the course of trade means that the use of the mark is in the context of a commercial activity with a view to economic advantage, and not as a private matter.[78] A person using a trade mark on a website for non-commercial purposes, for example a fan site for the Rolling Stones,[79] where the words the 'Rolling Stones' are used in relation

---

76   TMA, s 10(4).
77   C-206/01 *Arsenal v Reed* [2002] ECR I-10273, [2003] ETMR 19, para 40; followed C-48/05 *Adam Opel* [2007] ECR I-1017, [2007] ETMR 33, para 18.
78   C-206/01 *Arsenal v Reed* [2002] ECR I-10273, [2003] ETMR 19, para 40; C-48/05 *Adam Opel* [2007] ECR I-1017, [2007] ETMR 33, para 18.
79   CTM No 169680.

to music (class 9) would still not be trade mark infringement as the use of the mark was not in the course of trade. However, if someone was selling Rolling Stones CDs online or even simply for download, this would be use in the course of trade (although not necessarily use in the UK). Furthermore, where, a trade mark is used on a website which is run for a commercial purpose, for example, to generate advertising revenues, this would be use in the course of trade. However, a search engine (such as Google) does not use the mark in the course of trade where it simply displays the trade mark as a search result.[80]

Example 4.5

A website lists various programs for sale under the Microsoft logo and uses the Microsoft logo on the small icons that represent each program itself. The name of each program begins 'Microsoft' or 'MS'. Microsoft is not the developer of any of these programs. It is of little legal consequence that this is on a website: this is use of a sign by exposing and offering goods for sale under a registered trade mark. However, if as a search result Google links to this website, Google are not using the mark in the course of trade.

When is use on the internet use in the UK?

4.23   A question of paramount importance in the global marketplace is whether a person is using a trade mark in the UK (or in the case of a Community trade mark, in the EU) when that person runs a website outside that jurisdiction to sell within it. This problem arises because the 'very language of the internet conveys the idea of the user going to the site – 'visit' is the word'[81] the question is, therefore, when does the availability of the site mean that a business is touting for trade from within the UK?

The English courts have long held that mere access to a website is not enough to constitute infringement,[82] but it is now clear from the Court of Justice that this is correct. In C-324/09 *L'Oreal v eBay*[83] the Court held:

> 'It must, however, be made clear that the mere fact that a website is accessible from the territory covered by the trade mark is not a sufficient basis for concluding that the offers for sale displayed there are targeted at consumers in that territory .... Indeed, if the fact that an online marketplace is accessible from that territory were sufficient for the advertisements displayed there to be within the scope of [the Trade Marks Directive or Regulation], websites and advertisements which, although obviously targeted solely at consumers in third States, are nevertheless technically accessible from EU territory would wrongly be subject to EU law.

---

80   C-236/08 *Google v Louis Vuitton* [2010] ECR I-2417, [2010] ETMR 30, paras 50 to 59.
81   *Euromarket Designs v Peters Crate & Barrel* [2001] FSR 20, para 24.
82   See *1-800 Flowers Inc v Phonenames Ltd* [2001] FSR 20; *Euromarket Designs v Peters, Crate & Barrel* [2001] FSR 20; *Bonnier Media v Smith* [2002] ETMR 86; *Sony v Pacific Game Technology* [2006] EWHC 2509 (Ch); *Dearlove v Coombes* [2007] EWHC 375 (Ch), [2008] ETMR 2.
83   [2011] ETMR 52 at paras 64 and 65; also see C-98/13 *Blomqvist v Rolex* [2014] ETMR 25.

It therefore falls to the national courts to assess on a case-by-case basis whether there are any relevant factors on the basis of which it may be concluded that an offer for sale, displayed on an online marketplace accessible from the territory covered by the trade mark, is targeted at consumers in that territory. When the offer for sale is accompanied by details of the geographic areas to which the seller is willing to dispatch the product, that type of detail is of particular importance in the said assessment.'

The question of whether a particular communication is targeted at the UK (or the EU) or another jurisdiction was discussed in another context[84] in C-585/08 *Pammer and Hotel Alpenhof*:[85]

'The following matters, the list of which is not exhaustive, are capable of constituting evidence from which it may be concluded that the trader's activity is directed to the Member State of the consumer's domicile, namely the international nature of the activity, mention of itineraries from other Member States for going to the place where the trader is established, use of a language or a currency other than the language or currency generally used in the Member State in which the trader is established with the possibility of making and confirming the reservation in that other language, mention of telephone numbers with an international code, outlay of expenditure on an internet referencing service in order to facilitate access to the trader's site or that of its intermediary by consumers domiciled in other Member States, use of a top-level domain name other than that of the Member State in which the trader is established, and mention of an international clientele composed of customers domiciled in various Member States. It is for the national courts to ascertain whether such evidence exists.'

This case was referred to in the *eBay* decision[86] and it has been held by the English courts as the appropriate test as to whether or not a particular website is targeting the UK.[87]

Example 4.6

Finnegan Ltd is an online electrical supplier based in Hong Kong. Its sells, among other things, Daddy plc products. These products were made by Daddy for the Chinese market. Daddy sues Finnegan for infringement in the UK. The website is in English, it is possible to enter UK credit card details and prices are given in sterling. These are good indicators that Finnegan is targeting the UK. However, Daddy plc would be advised to make a test (or trap) purchase from the website to see if the products are despatched.

---

84 It related to whether a court had jurisdiction under art 15 of Regulation (EC) 44/2001 (the Brussels Regulation) (now art 17 of Regulation (EU) No 1215/2012).
85 [2010] ECR I-12527 at para 93.
86 C-324/09 *L'Oreal v eBay* [2011] ETMR 52, para 64.
87 *Stichting BDO v BDO Unibank Inc* [2013] EWHC 418 (Ch), [2013] ETMR 31, paras 105 and 106 (also suggesting that this approach is essential the same as that which was previously adopted by the English courts).

The use of domain names in the course of trade

4.24   While these factors are relevant to whether or not a particular use is targeting the UK, it also falls to be considered whether the use of a domain name, which includes a trade mark, is of itself an infringement of that trade mark. In *BT v One in a Million*[88] the High Court considered when a domain name is used in the course of trade:

> 'The first and most obvious [use] is that it may be sold to the enterprise whose name or trade mark has been used, which may be prepared to pay a high price to avoid the inconvenience of there being a domain name comprising its own name or trade mark which is not under its control. Secondly, it may be sold to a third party unconnected with the name, so that he may do or attempt to do the same thing or to use it for the purposes of deception. Thirdly it may be sold to someone with a distinct interest of his own in the name, for example a solicitor by the name of John Sainsbury or the Government of the British Virgin Islands, with a view to its use by him. Fourth it may be retained by the dealer unused and unsold, in which case it serves only to block the use of that name as a registered domain name by others, including those whose name or trade mark it comprises.'[89]

It is clear that the first three of these 'uses' could be construed as being 'use of a sign in the course of trade in relation to goods or services'. The fourth 'use' is, however, misconceived and was recognised as such by the Court of Appeal. The registration of a domain name does not actually block the brand owner from exploiting its brand name as a domain name. All the claimants had lost was a single domain name which reflected their brand names; they simply wanted to prevent any other confusingly similar domain names from existing. The Court of Appeal puts this as follows:

> 'The registration [of a domain name] only blocks the identical domain name and therefore does not act as a block to registration of a domain name that can be used by the owner of the goodwill in the name.'[90]

It would therefore appear that a domain name could be registered but not 'used' for the purposes of trade mark infringement if it is retained unsold and unconnected to an IP address. Nevertheless it will be difficult to persuade a court that one does not intend to 'use' the domain name having registered it. Despite the prejudicial evidence adduced as to 'One in a Million's' previous conduct,[91] their approaches to the claimants in the action had all been careful

---

88 *BT v One in a Million* [1998] FSR 265 HC.
89 *BT v One in a Million* [1998] FSR 265, 268.
90 *BT v One in a Million* [1999] 1 WLR 903, 923, CA.
91 In September 1996, one of the defendants wrote to Burger King: 'Further to our telephone conversation earlier this evening, I confirm that I own the domain name burgerking.co.uk. I would be willing to sell the domain name for the sum of £25,000 plus VAT. In answer to your question regarding as to what we would do with the domain name should you decide not to purchase it – the domain name would be available for sale to any other interested party.' The threat to sell the inherently deceptive name possibly to a person passing off the trade mark is explicit. It should not be forgotten that Burger King was not a plaintiff in the action (*BT v One in a Million* [1999] 1 WLR 903, 922–3).

to pre-empt any suggestion of illegal use of the domain names. To J Sainsbury plc, one defendant wrote: 'We are not trading under the name Sainsbury nor do we intend to trade under the name Sainsbury. We have merely purchased the internet domain names j-sainsbury.com, sainsbury.com and sainsburys.com as part of our personal collection.'[92] This raises the question of when possession of a domain name becomes its use in the course of trade.

Where a domain name uses (or incorporates) a trade mark and that domain name points to an active website then the use of the domain name is use in the course of trade.[93] This issue is more difficult where the domain name does not point to an active website. For example, the putative claimant can write to the domain name owner asking for his undertaking that he will either sell the domain name to the claimant for the amount of money it cost him to register the domain name or undertake not to sell or transfer it at all. If the domain name owner does not confirm this, or offers to sell it for more than the mere registration cost he is, arguably, threatening to use the domain name in the course of trade. In *Tropical Resorts Management Ltd v Morgan*[94] Mr Morgan did just this. He registered a domain name incorporating the claimant's trade mark 'Banyan Tree'. When approached about the domain name, he tried to bargain for a higher price than the claimants would pay. And when they refused to pay, he threatened to auction the domain name. This case was brought in passing off, but there is no reason to suppose that if the domain name includes a trade mark that this would be used in the course of trade. In *Britannia Building Society v Prangley*,[95] Mr Prangley, having registered the domain name 'britanniabuildingsociety.com' (apparently for the purposes of a new business providing services to British builders in Iran) refused to sell it to the claimants. He did not threaten to sell it to anyone else. In these circumstances, Rattee J was concerned that there was no use of a sign at all, let alone use of a sign in the course of trade.

Example 4.7

RRZ Ltd is a well-known stockbroker with a registered trade mark over the mark 'RRZ' in the appropriate classes. It wishes to register the domain name 'RRZ.co.uk' and instructs a domain name agent accordingly. The agent reports back that RRZ.co.uk is already registered as a domain name but that no website is 'pointed' to the domain name. Without some indication of trade from the domain name owner, RRZ Ltd will have a difficult task to sue the owner for trade mark infringement as the domain name (the sign) does not appear to be being used in the course of trade.

---

92 *BT v One in a Million* [1999] 1 WLR 903, 923.
93 *Bayerische Motorenwerke AG v Ronaynet/A BMWcare* [2013] IEHC 612, [2014] ETMR 29; *Evegate Publishing Limited v Newsquest Media (Southern) Limited* [2013] EWHC 1975 (Ch) at para 119; *Porsche v Van den Berg*, 15 January 2013, Hague Appeal Court.
94 [2001] All ER (D) 38 (Jul).
95 Ch D, June 12, 2000 (unreported).

Use must affect the trade mark functions

4.25   The requirement that the use must affect the function of the trade mark has proved to be very complicated and contradictory. The law in relation to this aspect of the matter had led towards a conclusion that the only function relevant for identity and similarity infringement was the trade mark's essential function, namely guaranteeing origin. The other functions of a trade mark,[96] such as those relating to its advertising and communicative functions, were thought to relate only to dilution type protection. More recently, it appears that the protection afforded to the trade mark in relation to identity type infringement includes some of the trade mark's other functions, such as guaranteeing the quality of the goods or services in question and those of communication, investment, or advertising.[97]

The essential function of a trade mark

4.26   The essential function of a trade mark is its origin function so that the trade mark demonstrates to consumers that all the goods and services bearing it have been manufactured or supplied under the control of a single undertaking which is responsible for their quality.[98] The question is, therefore, whether consumers will interpret the use of the sign as indicating a material link between the goods or services and the trade mark owner.[99] Are consumers likely to interpret the sign as designating or tending to designate the undertaking from which the goods originate (ie a licensee)?[100] If the relevant public[101] (including those confronted with the goods after it has left the third party's point of sale) does not perceive the use of the sign as an indication that the goods or services come from the trade mark owner or an undertaking economically linked to it then that use does not affect the trade mark's essential function.[102]

---

96   These functions seem to be growing rapidly; cf C-487/07 *L'Oreal v Bellure* [2009] ECR I-5185, [2009] ETMR 55 at para 58 with those identified by the Advocate-General in C-482/09 *Budějovický Budvar v Anheuser-Busch* [2012] ETMR 2, fn 26 (the Advocate-General indicated: 'they include, according to legal writing on trade mark law, *inter alia* the coding, guarantee, origin, identification and individualisation, information and communication, monopolising, naming, quality, distinction, confidence, distribution and advertising functions, without the individual functions always having legal relevance in addition').

97   C-487/07 *L'Oreal v Bellure* [2009] ECR I-5185, [2009] ETMR 55 at para 58; C-238/08 *Google France Sarl v Louis Vuitton Malletier SA* (C-236/08) at para 77; C-278/08 *Die BergSpechte Outdoor Reisen* [2010] ECR I-2517, [2010] ETMR 33 at para 31.

98   C-206/01 *Arsenal v Reed* [2002] ECR I-10273, [2003] ETMR 19 at para 48.

99   C-206/01 *Arsenal v Reed* [2002] ECR I-10273, [2003] ETMR 19 at para 56.

100 C-245/02 Anheuser *Busch v Budejovicky* [2004] ECR I-10989, [2005] ETMR 27 at para 60; C-17/06 *Céline* [2007] ECR I-7041, [2007] ETMR 80 at para 27 (which was suggested to be the effect of C-206/01 *Arsenal v Reed* [2002] ECR I-10273, [2003] ETMR 19, paras 56 and 57).

101 The relevant public being the average consumer of the type of goods or services in question: C-251/95 *Sabel BV v Puma AG* [1997] ECR I-6191, [1998] ETMR 1 at para 23.

102 C-48/05 *Adam Opel* [2007] ECR I-1017, [2007] ETMR 33 at para 24.

The other functions of a trade mark

4.27   The existence of the other functions of a trade mark originated in relation to the re-commercialisation of parallel imports. It arose because in certain circumstances it was possible to prohibit parallel imports from within the EU despite the goods sharing the same trade origin. In such circumstances the resale of the legitimate (but parallel) goods did not affect the essential function of the trade mark and so the limited prohibition[103] must have related to another function: the so-called advertising function. This function, along with the other functions of guaranteeing the quality of the goods or services in question, communication and investment, became part of the mainstream of trade mark law more recently.[104] The existence of a broader function for trade marks (or brands[105]) is not problematic as in marketing terms they can remain amorphous concepts. Now that these functions appear to be protected under trade mark law, however, it is necessary to try and determine what they actually cover. Importantly, these functions apply to all types of infringement (identity, similarity and dilution) and they apply not only to marks with a reputation, but all marks[106] (although, not all trade marks are used in such a way as to engage all the potential functions[107]).

The so-called advertising function is that which is said to protect the trade mark proprietor's use of its mark as a factor in sales promotion or as an instrument of commercial strategy.[108] The indications of what it means more precisely are limited. First, another trader's conduct which causes a person to pay more for a better advertising position *does not* affect the advertising function.[109] Secondly, a trader having to intensify its advertising to maintain or enhance its profile does not affect the advertising function.[110] Thirdly, the advantage taken by a person who uses another person's trade mark so as to lend an aura of quality to the first person's business (but which is in other respects honest and fair) probably does not affect the advertising function either.[111] Fourthly, because commercial communications fall within the fundamental right of freedom of expression,[112] the

---

103 Directive 2008/95/EC, art 7(2).

104 Following C-487/07 *L'Oreal v Bellure* [2009] ECR I-5185, [2009] ETMR 55.

105 This appears to be an analogy now drawn by the court: see C-324/09 *L'Oreal v eBay* [2011] ETMR 52 at para 46 of Advocate-General Opinion.

106 C-323/09 *Interflora Inc v Marks & Spencer plc* [2011] ECR I-8625, [2012] ETMR 1 at paras 35 to 40.

107 C-323/09 *Interflora Inc v Marks & Spencer plc* [2011] ECR I-8625, [2012] ETMR 1 at para 38.

108 C-238/08 Google *France Sarl v Louis Vuitton Malletier SA* (C-236/08) at para 92.

109 C-238/08 *Google France Sarl v Louis Vuitton Malletier SA* (C-236/08) at paras 94 and 95; C278/08 BergSpechte [2010] ECR I-2517, [2010] ETMR 33 at para 33; C-558/08 *Portakabin Ltd v Primakabin BV* [2010] ECR I-6963, [2010] ETMR 52 at para 32; C-323/09 *Interflora Inc v Marks & Spencer plc* [2011] ECR I-8625, [2012] ETMR 1, para 56.

110 C-323/09 *Interflora Inc v Marks & Spencer plc* [2011] ECR I-8625, [2012] ETMR 1, para 57.

111 This proposition relates to re-commercialisation under Directive 2008/95/EC, art 7(2); but as this is the origin of the advertising function it is probably correct: in this regard see C-63/97 *Bayerische Motorenwerke AG (BMW) and BMW Nederland BV v Deenik* [1999] ECR I-905, [1999] ETMR 339 at para 53; C-558/08 *Portakabin Ltd v Primakabin BV* [2010] ECR I-6963, [2010] ETMR 52 at para 90.

112 See C-324/09 *L'Oreal v eBay* [2011] ETMR 52 at para 49; and also *L'Oreal v Bellure* [2010] EWCA Civ 535, [2010] ETMR 47 at paras 8 to 13.

advertising function cannot be interpreted in such a way as to trump *legitimate* free expression[113] or to affect the basic practices inherent in competition.[114] Fifthly, using a trade mark to demonstrate to consumers that there are alternative products does not affect that function.[115] Finally, the English courts have suggested that the advertising function relates to the *image* of the goods and so only where that image is tarnished is the advertising function affected.[116] This approach provides a sensible demarcation point protecting all the other functions of the trade mark, but it is yet to be seen whether it is adopted by the Court of Justice.

The so-called investment function relates to where a trade mark is used by its proprietor to acquire or preserve a reputation capable of attracting consumers and retaining their loyalty.[117] Thus, it overlaps with the advertising function (as investment can come from other commercial techniques). The function is adversely affected where the use by the third party substantially interferes with the proprietor's use of its trade mark to acquire or preserve a reputation capable of attracting consumers and retaining their loyalty.[118] But it is not sufficient that the only consequence of that use is to oblige the proprietor of that trade mark to adapt its efforts towards that end.[119] As with the advertising function, the fact that that use may prompt some consumers to switch from goods or services bearing that trade mark cannot be successfully relied on by the proprietor of the mark.[120]

In relation to goods or services

4.28   The sign purportedly infringing the trade mark must be used in relation to goods or services.[121] This question is sometimes mixed up with trade mark use, but it is distinct.[122] In most cases this hurdle is very low, as use is in relation to goods if it concerns the affixing of a sign to the trade mark onto goods and subsequently offering for sale, or stocking, those goods.[123] It is also use in relation

---

113 The trade mark proprietor's rights will be protected as a property right under art 1, Protocol 1 of the European Convention of Human Rights, but this would have to be balanced against free expression if the two rights were in conflict.

114 C-323/09 *Interflora Inc v Marks & Spencer plc* [2011] ECR I-8625, [2012] ETMR 1, para 57.

115 C-323/09 *Interflora Inc v Marks & Spencer plc* [2011] ECR I-8625, [2012] ETMR 1, para 58.

116 *Datacard Corp v Eagle Technology* [2011] EWHC 244 (Pat), [2011] RPC 17 at para 272.

117 C-323/09 *Interflora Inc v Marks & Spencer plc* [2011] ECR I-8625, [2012] ETMR 1 at para 60.

118 C-323/09 *Interflora Inc v Marks & Spencer plc* [2011] ECR I-8625, [2012] ETMR 1 at para 60.

119 C-323/09 *Interflora Inc v Marks & Spencer plc* [2011] ECR I-8625, [2012] ETMR 1 at para 60.

120 C-323/09 *Interflora Inc v Marks & Spencer plc* [2011] ECR I-8625, [2012] ETMR 1 at para 64.

121 See C-245/02 *Anheuser Busch v Budejovicky* [2004] ECR I-10989, [2005] ETMR 27, para 62.

122 As may have happened in *Bravado Merchandising Services v Mainsteam Publishing* [1996] FSR 205; see *British Sugar v James Robertson* [1997] ETMR 118 at 124.

123 C-48/05 *Adam Opel* [2007] ECR I-1017, [2007] ETMR 33, para 20; C-17/06 *Céline* [2007] ECR I-7041, [2007] ETMR 80, para 22; this premise is derived from somewhat more opaque wording in C-206/01 *Arsenal v Reed* [2002] ECR I-10273, [2003] ETMR 19, paras 40 and 41.

to goods or services where a trader uses the sign in such a way that a link is established between the sign which constitutes the business name and the goods marketed or services provided by that trader.[124]

Most websites appear to be purely providing information but usually they also have banners or links to other pages that advertise or provide goods or services. In such cases, the use of the mark would be in relation to goods or services.[125] Few commercial sites are no more than an electronic poster. If the site is used to interact with customers then the domain name would appear to be used in relation to goods or services. Nevertheless, because there is no other route to access the website than by using the domain name,[126] it remains possible that it is not really being used in 'relation' to anything.

Identical sign to registered trade mark

4.29   The most straightforward type of infringement arises where a sign identical to the trade mark is used on identical goods or services in respect of which the mark is registered. In determining whether a sign is identical to the mark it should be considered whether the sign reproduces, without modification or addition, all the elements constituting the mark or where, viewed as a whole, it contains differences so insignificant they may go unnoticed by the average consumer.[127] Nevertheless, certain parts of the mark which have no trade mark significance can be ignored.[128]

Many uses of signs on the internet will be simple straightforward trade mark infringement. A business which sells goods online is no different from any other act of infringement. A website selling books to UK consumers under the name Penguin is little different to selling those books from a shop in Birmingham. It is for this reason that the discussion will concentrate on domain names and the peculiar rules that may apply to them.

It has already been explained in relation to domain names that when registering a mark the prefix 'www' or the suffix '.com' does not make a mark distinctive if it was not otherwise so. Similarly, as neither the prefix nor the suffix have any

---

124 C-17/06 *Céline* [2007] ECR I-7041, [2007] ETMR 80, para 23.

125 See for example: C-62/08 *UDV North America Inc v Brandtraders NV* [2009] ECR I-1279, [2010] ETMR 25.

126 Of course, off the internet, the domain name may be used not in relation to registered goods or services. For instance, a designer of the Harrods website may set up his own website to advertise his previous commissions, including 'Harrods'. The presence on his website of the domain name 'www.harrods.co.uk' would not be the use of the trade mark in relation to goods or services for which Harrods had a trade mark. See *Harrods v Schwartz-Sackin* [1986] FSR 490. In contrast, Harrods were granted an injunction against defendants who registered the domain name 'harrods.com' when Harrods had already registered 'harrods.co.uk' (unreported, Mr Justice Lightman, 9 December 1996).

127 C-291/00 *LTJ Diffusion SA v Sadas Vertbaudet SA* [2003] ECR I-2799, [2003] ETMR 83 at para 54.

128 'Compass Logistics' not identical to 'Compass': *Compass Publishing BV v Compass Logistics Ltd* [2004] EWHC 520, [2004] RPC 41.

trade mark significance, they can be ignored when considering infringement.[129] By extension this may also mean that where a person has 'www.company. co.uk' registered as a trade mark this will be considered to be identical to 'www. company.com', the differences between the two marks being only technical.

Example 4.8

SOUK Ltd have registered the mark SOUK. Southern Orphanages UK Ltd registers the domain name www.souk.co.uk and starts trading from the site. The domain name used is identical to the registered mark and so might be infringing.

Identical goods

4.30   The court will take on the mantle of the relevant customer to assess whether the goods or services in respect of which the mark is being used are identical to those for which it is registered. The views of an expert in the field, on the other hand, are of little relevance because they cannot provide assistance on whether that consumer would consider the goods to be the same or not.[130]

Similar or identical sign with similar or identical goods or services

4.31   Similarity type infringement is the most common before courts and tribunals. The central question is: does the person's use of the sign lead the average consumer to be confused as to the origin of the goods,[131] so that they believe the goods and services sold under the sign come from the same undertaking or one economically linked to it.[132] It is therefore important to know if there is a risk of mistaking the origin of the goods, not whether consumers actually do mistake the origin of the goods or services.[133]

The mark has to be appreciated globally, taking into account all the relevant factors of the case.[134] In particular, the global appreciation of the visual, aural and conceptual similarity of the marks in question must be based on the overall impression given by the marks, bearing in mind their respective distinctive and dominant components.[135] But it must be remembered that the average consumer perceives a mark as a whole and does not break it down into its various details.[136]

---

129 *OCH-ZIFF Management v OCH Capital LLP* [2010] EWHC 2599 (Ch), [2011] ETMR 1 at para 46.
130 *Beautimatic v Mitchell* [1999] ETMR 912; as to the construction of specifications see above at para **4.14**.
131 C-251/95 *Sabel v Puma* [1998] ETMR 1, para 23.
132 C-342/97 *Lloyd Schufabrick Mayer v Kliysen Handel* [1999] ECR I-3819, [1999] ETMR 690, para 17; C-39/97 *Canon v MGM* [1998] ECR I-5507, [1999] ETMR 1, paras 29 and 30.
133 *Thomson Holidays v Norwegian Cruise Lines* [2003] RPC 32, para 26.
134 C-251/95 *Sabel v Puma* [1997] ECR I-6191, [1998] ETMR 1, para 23.
135 C-251/95 *Sabel v Puma* [1997] ECR I-6191, [1998] ETMR 1, para 23.
136 C-251/95 *Sabel v Puma* [1997] ECR I-6191, [1998] ETMR 1, para 23.

Where a more detailed discussion of judging similarity is sought a specialist text should be consulted.

Distinctiveness

4.32 A mark which has become very distinctive is entitled to enhanced protection.[137] Before it is possible to rely on additional distinctiveness it is necessary to provide sufficient evidence that a mark has become that distinctive. This broader protection can be particularly useful for well-known marks as they will be more distinctive and, accordingly, easier to infringe.

Similarity of goods

4.33 The issue of confusion is not merely concerned with a comparison of the two marks. The similarity of the goods or services in relation to which the sign is used by the parties is also important. Indeed, the greater the similarity between the goods the less similarity there needs to be between the marks (and visa versa).[138] Notwithstanding, there still needs to be some similarity of goods or services for infringement. If there is no such similarity then the claim should be made on the basis of dilution. The factors that should be taken into account when assessing the similarity of the goods or services include their nature, their end users and the methods of use and whether they are in competition with, or complement, each other.[139] The nature of the internet is not going to affect this basic determination as it is in most cases only a method of selling.

The average consumer

4.34 The characteristics of average consumers, the centre of any comparison, are that they are reasonably well informed and reasonably observant and circumspect. Such consumers rarely directly compare the two marks and so they will have an imperfect recollection of a mark. They will give more attention to some purchasing decisions than to others[140] (high-volume low-cost goods, for example, would have less attention than other types of goods). But the confusion of the careless and stupid is never enough to make out infringement.[141] As the use made of a trade mark on the internet could be for a wide range of goods and services, the average consumer will vary accordingly.

Initial interest confusion

4.35 In the US there is a concept known as initial interest confusion. This arises where a consumer was confused by a defendant's conduct at the time of

---

137 C-251/95 *Sabel v Puma* [1997] ECR I-6191, [1998] ETMR 1, para 24.
138 C-39/97 *Canon v MGM* [1998] ECR I-5507, [1999] ETMR 1, para 18.
139 C-39/97 *Canon v MGM* [1998] ECR I-5507, [1999] ETMR 1, para 23.
140 C-342/97 *Lloyd Schufabrick Mayer v Kliysen Handel* [1999] ECR I-3819, [1999] ETMR 690, para 26.
141 *Reed Executive v Reed Business Information* [2003] EWCA Civ 159, [2004] RPC 40, para 82.

interest in a product or service, even if that initial confusion is corrected by the time of purchase.[142] This doctrine would be particularly relevant for websites as it might arise where a person searches a term, believes that a search result (or domain name) is linked to a particular undertaking, but when the person arrives at the website it is clear that it is distinct.[143] This doctrine made a temporary appearance in English trade mark law,[144] but was disapproved of by the Court of Appeal in *Interflora v Marks and Spencer*[145] and so this sort of confusion should not be considered material to any assessment.

Dilution protection

4.36   The final ground of infringement, dilution, occurs where a sign is used which is identical or similar to a registered trade mark which has a reputation in the UK (or in the case of a Community trade mark, the EU) and the use of the sign, being without due cause, takes unfair advantage of, or is detrimental to, the distinctive character or repute of the trade mark.[146] The law has now developed to recognise three forms of dilution in the EU.[147] First, protection against blurring (or dilution in the strict sense) is given against uses that entail a danger that the trade mark loses its distinctive character and thereby its value. Secondly, protection against tarnishment means protection against uses that endanger the reputation of the trade mark. Thirdly and finally, protection against free-riding or the taking of unjustified advantage of the reputation or distinctiveness of another's trade mark. In each case the essential function of the trade mark, guaranteeing origin, will not be affected[148] but rather one of the other functions identified above must be affected. It is for the proprietor of the mark to show that there will be injury or likely injury to it,[149] but before dilution protection can be engaged it is necessary for the mark to have a reputation.[150]

The test that the mark must satisfy to show it has a reputation is that the mark is known by a significant part of the public concerned with the goods or

142 *OCH-Ziff Management v OCH Capital* [2010] EWHC 2599 (Ch), [2011] ETMR 1, para 80.
143 Similar to the idea of bait and switch.
144 Following, *OCH-Ziff Management v OCH Capital* [2010] EWHC 2599(Ch), [2011] ETMR 1.
145 [2014] EWCA Civ 1403, [2015] ETMR 5, para 158.
146 TMA, s 10(3) (infringement); s 5(3) (relative grounds); also see C-292/00 *Davidoff & Cie SA v Gofkid Ltd* [2003] ECR I-389, [2003] ETMR 42, C-408/01 *Adidas-Salomon AG v Fitnessworld Trading Ltd* [2003] ECR I-12537, [2004] ETMR 10.
147 See C-323/09 *Interflora Inc v Marks & Spencer plc* [2011] ECR I-8625, [2012] ETMR 1, para 52 and 53 of Advocate-General's opinion; the division of the three types has been acknowledged, by a different name, in C-252/07 *Intel v CPM* [2008] ECR I-8823, [2009] ETMR 13 at para 27.
148 This was stated explicitly in C-323/09 *Interflora Inc v Marks & Spencer plc* [2011] ECR I-8625, [2012] ETMR 1 at para 59. The absence of a requirement of confusion, as stated by the Court, supports this: C-425/98 *Marca Mode CV v Adidas AG* [2000] ECR I-4861, [2000] ETMR 723, at para 36; C-408/01 *Adidas v Fitnessworld* [2003] ECR I-12537, [2004] ETMR 10, at para 30; see the early domestic cases to the contrary: in particular, *Baywatch Production Co Inc v Home Video Channel* [1997] FSR 22.
149 C-252/07 *Intel v CPM* [2008] ECR I-8823, [2009] ETMR 13 at para 37.
150 Directive 2008/95/EC, recital 9.

services in relation to which it is registered[151] and this knowledge must exist in a substantial part of the territory.[152] The greater the mark's[153] reputation, the easier it is to establish that detriment is caused.[154] In assessing whether the mark has a reputation the following should be taken into account: the market share held by the trade mark, the intensity, geographical extent and duration of its use, and the size of the investment made by the undertaking in promoting it.[155] Once it has been established that the mark has sufficient reputation it is necessary to prove lack of any due cause to use the mark.

Due cause

4.37   If a user wants to argue that they had due cause to use the mark it is for them to prove it.[156] The concept of 'due cause' includes both objectively overriding reasons and also the subjective interests of the third party using the sign.[157] It is intended to strike a balance between the rights of the trade mark proprietor and those of the third party and requires the proprietor to tolerate certain uses.[158] The assessment of due cause has two stages. First, such an assessment requires a determination as to how that sign has been accepted by, and what its reputation is with, the relevant public.[159] Secondly, it is necessary to examine the intention of the person using the sign and see whether the use was in good faith.[160] This includes taking account of at least the following factors: (a) how that sign has been accepted by, and what its reputation is with, the relevant public; (b) the degree of proximity between the goods and services for which that sign was originally used and the product for which the mark with a reputation was registered; and (c) the economic and commercial significance of the use for that product of the sign which is similar to that mark.[161] Thus, a person who has used a mark descriptively (or uses a domain name descriptively) for a long period of time probably has due cause to do so.[162]

Similarly, where the owner of a domain name owns a trade mark representing the text of a trade mark in one class, but the more famous mark is used in relation to a different class the using the famous mark would probably be treated as use with due cause.[163] Accordingly, in the MIT case mentioned above (see **4.3**) this was more or less what happened. Merritt Technologies, the owner of the 'mit. com' domain name, was legitimately using the mark and the Massachusetts

---

151 C-375/97 *General Motors v Yplon* [1999] ECR I-5421, [1999] ETMR 950, paras 24 and 26.
152 C-375/97 *General Motors v Yplon* [1999] ECR I-5421, [1999] ETMR 950, paras 28 to 29.
153 The reputation must be in the mark relied upon and not another related mark: *CDW Graphic Design TM App* [2003] RPC 30, para 17 *et seq*.
154 *Premier Brands v Typhoon* [2000] ETMR 1071, 1095 per Neuberger J.
155 C-375/97 *General Motors v Yplon* [1999] ECR I-5421, [1999] ETMR 950, para 27.
156 C-65/12 *Leidseplein Beheer BV* [2014] ETMR 24, para 44.
157 C-65/12 *Leidseplein Beheer BV* [2014] ETMR 24, para 44.
158 C-65/12 *Leidseplein Beheer BV* [2014] ETMR 24, para 45.
159 C-65/12 *Leidseplein Beheer BV* [2014] ETMR 24, para 54.
160 C-65/12 *Leidseplein Beheer BV* [2014] ETMR 24, paras 55 and 56.
161 C-65/12 *Leidseplein Beheer BV* [2014] ETMR 24, paras 57 and 60.
162 *Supreme Petfoods Ltd v Henry Bell & Co* [2015] EWHC 256 (Ch), [2015] ETMR 20, para 192.
163 As noted by Neuberger J in *Premier Brands v Typhoon* [2000] ETMR 1071 at 1091.

Institute of Technology was trying to extend its influence beyond its trading sphere on the grounds that any use of MIT was objectionable. Use for this reason may be both with due cause and justifiable.

Blurring

4.38   The detriment to the distinctive character of the earlier mark is caused by dilution by blurring (or whittling away) when that mark's ability to identify the goods or services for which it is registered and used as coming from the proprietor of that mark is weakened, since use of the later mark leads to dispersion of the identity and hold upon the public mind of the earlier mark.[164] That is notably the case when the earlier mark, which used to arouse immediate association with the goods and services for which it is registered, is no longer capable of doing so.[165] This means, of course, that the relevant public must perceive a link between the registered mark and the mark alleged to be blurring it.[166] The factors which might suggest a link include the following:

(a)   the degree of similarity between the conflicting marks; the more similar they are, the more likely it is that the later mark will bring the earlier mark with a reputation to the mind of the relevant public. But even when they are identical this is not enough to establish a link;[167]

(b)   the nature of the goods or services for which the conflicting marks were registered, including the degree of closeness or dissimilarity between those goods or services, and the relevant section of the public;

(c)   the strength of the earlier mark's reputation; whether it has gone beyond its usual relevant public;[168]

(d)   the degree of the earlier mark's distinctive character, whether inherent or acquired through use;

(e)   the existence of the likelihood of confusion on the part of the public.[169]

It may be that the relevant public for the goods and services in respect of which the mark was registered is completely different from that by which the later mark is used and so it may be that, despite having a reputation, it is not known to the public targeted by the later mark and so no link would be established.[170]

Where a link is found and the mark has been sufficiently blurred it is no longer capable of creating an association in the minds of consumers of the existence of an economic link with a specific commercial source (as so many

---

164 See generally, Frank Schechter 'The Rational Basis of Trademark Protection', 40 *Harvard LR* 813 (1927).
165 C-252/07 *Intel v CPM* [2008] ECR I-8823, [2009] ETMR 13 at para 29.
166 C-252/07 Intel *v CPM* [2008] ECR I-8823, [2009] ETMR 13 at para 30 and 31.
167 C-252/07 Intel *v CPM* [2008] ECR I-8823, [2009] ETMR 13 at para at 44 and 45.
168 C-252/07 Intel *v CPM* [2008] ECR I-8823, [2009] ETMR 13 at para at 53.
169 C-252/07 Intel *v CPM* [2008] ECR I-8823, [2009] ETMR 13 at para at 42; C-320/07 *Antartica* [2009] ECR I-28, [2009] ETMR 47 at para 45.
170 C-252/07 Intel *v CPM* [2008] ECR I-8823, [2009] ETMR 13, at para 48.

users are using the mark that its primary user is no longer seen as such). This means that the very purpose of a trade mark might be affected or destroyed if blurring continued unabated.[171] This could occur where the use leads towards the mark becoming generic for a particular term, for example.[172] Eventually the mark becomes denigrated and can no longer function as it once did. The nature of blurring means that it is unlikely to have any application where the goods and services are the same, such activity being confined to identity or similarity infringement.[173]

In assessing whether injury has been caused by blurring it is necessary to consider the use in the eyes of the relevant public, that is the consumer of the goods in respect of which the mark with a reputation is registered (and not the goods in respect of which the sign is being used by the other trader).[174] The stronger the mark the more likely that the mark would be blurred in the minds of the relevant public[175] but to demonstrate blurring it is necessary to demonstrate a change in the economic behaviour of the relevant public.[176] It is not enough that the user of the later mark derives real commercial benefit from the distinctive character of the earlier mark.[177] A change in economic behaviour probably means that consumers make a transactional decision they would not otherwise have made[178] and this is incredibly difficult to prove.

Dilution by tarnishment

4.39   The second type of dilution is by tarnishment;[179] it is caused when the goods or services for which the identical or similar sign is used by the third party may be perceived by the public in such a way that the trade mark's power of attraction is reduced. To establish dilution by tarnishment a link is required in the relevant public's mind between the famous mark and the later user.[180] The likelihood of such detriment may arise in particular from the fact that the goods or services offered by the third party possess a characteristic or a quality which is liable to have a negative impact on the image of the mark.[181] This ground

---

171 C-323/09 *Interflora Inc v Marks & Spencer plc* [2011] ECR I-8625, [2012] ETMR 1 (AG) at para 80.
172 C-323/09 *Interflora Inc v Marks & Spencer plc* [2011] ECR I-8625, [2012] ETMR 1.
173 C-323/09 *Interflora Inc v Marks & Spencer plc* [2011] ECR I-8625, [2012] ETMR 1 (AG) at para 60, 61, and 82.
174 C-252/07 *Intel v CPM* [2008] ECR I-8823, [2009] ETMR 13, [34] and [35] (note this is different from other forms of dilution).
175 C-252/07 *Intel v CPM* [2008] ECR I-8823, [2009] ETMR 13, at para 67.
176 C-252/07 *Intel v CPM* [2008] ECR I-8823, [2009] ETMR 13 at para 77.
177 C-252/07 *Intel v CPM* [2008] ECR I-8823, [2009] ETMR 13 at para 78.
178 See Directive 2005/29/EC, art 2(e) which defines 'to materially distort the economic behaviour of consumers' to make transactions that would not otherwise be made.
179 There are very few tarnishment cases, examples being T-357/09 *Emilio Pucci* (27 September 2012) (under appeal C-584/12); *Red Bull v Sun Mark* [2012] EWHC 1929 (Ch); *Kappa* (O/192/14).
180 C-320/07 *P Antartica Srl v Office for Harmonisation in the Internal Market (Trade Marks and Designs)* [2009] ECR I-28, [2009] ETMR 47 at para 44; C-252/07 *Intel v CPM* [2008] ECR I-8823, [2009] ETMR 13 at para 31.
181 C-487/07 *L'Oreal v Bellure* [2009] ECR I-5185, [2009] ETMR 55 at para 40.

of dilution is likely to invoke questions of freedom of expression as it is most likely to be used where statements about particular brands are made. Examples might include things like 'sucks' websites or websites which criticise particular companies. Finally, it is not clear whether it is necessary for there to be a change in economic behaviour for tarnishment to be made out, but it is likely to be the case.[182]

Dilution by free-riding

4.40 The third ground of dilution is the most pervasive and in many respects appears to dwarf the importance of the other two. Indeed, the finding of tarnishment or blurring can help support a finding of free-riding or unfair advantage.[183] The meaning of free-riding so as to take unfair advantage is that a person through the use of a sign similar to a mark with a reputation, rides on the coat-tails of that mark in order to benefit from its power of attraction, its reputation, and its prestige, and exploits, without paying any financial compensation and without being required to make efforts of his own in that regard, the marketing effort expended by the proprietor of that mark in order to create and maintain the image of that mark; the advantage resulting from such use must be considered to be an advantage that has been unfairly taken of the distinctive character or the repute of that mark.[184] When making these assessments it is important to acknowledge that the relevant public is different from that for blurring (and probably tarnishment) – it is the consumers of the goods and services of the later user of the mark which must be considered (rather than the goods for which the mark is registered).[185]

Whichever public is used as the barometer, this test is incredibly generous to trade mark proprietors as it appears to remove the word 'unfair' from unfair advantage.[186] As it was explained by the Court of Appeal in *Specsavers International Healthcare Ltd v Asda Stores Ltd*.[187]

> 'The Court [of Justice] may reasonably be thought to have declared, in substance, that an advantage gained by a trader from the use of a sign which is similar to a mark with a reputation will be unfair where the sign has been adopted in an attempt to benefit from the power of attraction, the reputation and the prestige of that mark and to exploit, without paying any financial compensation, and without making efforts of his own, the marketing effort expended by the

---

182 For the reasons set out at in *Jack Wills v House of Fraser* [2014] EWHC 110 (Ch), [2014] ETMR 28, paras 81 to 83.

183 C-487/07 *L'Oreal v Bellure* [2009] ECR I-5185, [2009] ETMR 55 at para 45.

184 C-487/07 *L'Oreal v Bellure* [2009] ECR I-5185, [2009] ETMR 55 at para 49.

185 C-252/07 *Intel v CPM* [2008] ECR I-8823, [2009] ETMR 13 at para 36; C-320/07 *Antartica SRL v OHIM* [2009] ECR I-28, [2009] ETMR 47 at para 48.

186 Darren Meale and Joel Smith, 'Enforcing a Trade Mark when Nobody's Confused: Where the law stands after L'Oréal and Intel' (2010) 5 *Journal of Intellectual Property Law and Practice* 96, 103; cited with approval *L'Oreal v Bellure* [2010] EWCA Civ 535, [2010] ETMR 47 at para 18. It has been described as moving away from the welfare optimal position (as users are prejudiced without benefit to proprietor): see C-323/09 *Interflora Inc v Marks & Spencer plc* [2011] ECR I-8625, [2012] ETMR 1 at para 94.

187 *Specsavers International Healthcare Ltd v Asda Stores Ltd* [2012] EWCA Civ 24, [2012] FSR 19, para 127.

proprietor of the mark in order to create and maintain the mark's image …. But plainly there are limits to this broad principle.'

Those limits are not yet clear and it has been suggested that this very broad approach may only be restricted to goods which are imitations and replicas rather than being of general application to ordinary goods.[188] In relation to normal goods, a more moderate approach has also been suggested whereby the use by a person who without due cause takes advantage of a trade mark is automatically deemed to be unfair.[189] If this approach is adopted then it would suggest that a person who uses the other goods for comparison or description would usually not be acting unfairly. Finally, the English courts, but not yet the Court of Justice, has held that there needs to be a change in economic behaviour for free-riding to be made out.[190]

Metatags, keywords and sponsored links

4.41   Websites include information which cannot normally be seen by the user, some of this information is deliberately concealed, but there is also information which is contained on a website to assist the workings of search engines. This information stored in this 'meta' section of a website is called metatags. These tags are divided into 'keywords' and a 'description' of the website. These mean that a site can be included in web search despite having no obvious connection. This code will be invisible to most visitors to the website[191] and so they will have no indication of why the site has been listed in the search results. For example, the following could be included in the HTML code making up a law firm's website: <META name='keywords' content='law, legal, lawyer, litigation'>. The law firm includes this code to ensure that, even if the words 'law', 'legal', 'lawyer' and 'litigation' are not actually used within any articles on the website, someone entering 'lawyer' into a search engine may still be directed to the firm's website. This issue was observed by Jacob J in *Avnet v Isoact*:[192]

> 'It is a general problem of the internet that it works on words and not words in relation to goods or services. So, whenever anyone searches for that word, even if the searcher is looking for the word in one context, he will, or may, find Web pages or data in a wholly different context … Of course, users of the internet also know that that is a feature of the internet and their search may produce an altogether wrong Web page or the like. This may be an important matter for the courts to take into account in considering trade mark and like problems.'[193]

---

188 Suggested by the Advocate-General in C-323/09 *Interflora Inc v Marks & Spencer plc* [2011] ECR I-8625, [2012] ETMR 1 at para 95.

189 C-487/07 *L'Oreal v Bellure* [2009] ECR I-5185, [2009] ETMR 55, at para AG105-111; again C-323/09 *Interflora Inc v Marks & Spencer plc* [2011] ECR I-8625, [2012] ETMR 1 at para AG97.

190 *Jack Wills v House of Fraser* [2014] EWHC 110 (Ch), [2014] ETMR 28, at para 81 to 83.

191 Some, of course, will use the 'View Source' command from their browser to see this, and other, hidden code.

192 [1998] FSR 16.

193 *Avnet v Isoact* [1998] FSR 16 at 18.

Now that search engines sell sponsored links and otherwise provide search optimisation services, their algorithms have been developed so as to reduce the advantage given by using hidden information in metatags (or indeed white text[194]). Indeed, the trade mark issues which related to metatags – both descriptions and keywords – have largely been overtaken[195] by developments in the law relating to sponsored links (such as Google's Adwords).

The costs of these sponsored links can be very high indeed. How it works is Google are paid a fee whenever a person clicks a particular sponsored link (but not the so called 'natural result', that is the result determined by the algorithm and not the keyword). Thus, following a study by Wordstream Inc,[196] it was found that the highest cost-per-click for a keyword was for 'insurance' at $54.91. Thus, for every consumer who clicks the sponsored link the owner of the top insurance sponsored link paid that sum (whether or not the consumer purchased insurance or not). The top keyword payment for 'Attorney' was $47.07 and for 'Lawyer' $42.51.

These high costs arise because the keywords are essentially part of an ongoing auction. The first person (A) who bids for a sponsored link pays 5 cents. If somebody else (B) wants to be above A's sponsored link they have to pay more say 10 cents. B will then be the first sponsored link. If A wants to become the top sponsored link then it has to pay 15 cents, then B must pay 20 cents and so forth. When it is remembered that there may be many bidders for a keyword this can push the price up substantially. In addition to descriptive words, such as insurance, this also applies to trade marks. Thus, if A, the trade mark owner of the trade mark 'Superstar Chocolate' bids 5 cents, B can bid 10 cents and become the top sponsored link (and above the trade mark owner) unless A ups the bid to 15 cents and so forth. It was this practice of non-trade mark owners bidding to use trade marks and so pushing up the cost of the trade mark owners using their own trade marks as keywords that has been most contentious.

When does the use of keywords and sponsored links amount to infringement?

4.42 The leading case of keyword advertising and sponsored links is C-236/08 *Google France*.[197] Here the Court of Justice indicated that the third party (B in our example) who buys a keywords associated with another's trade mark is using that mark in the course of trade.[198] This on its own is not enough. It was necessary for national courts, on a case-by-case basis, to determine whether a third party (B) use of that keyword (which is never displayed on the website) affects the functions of the trade mark. This might be because the average consumer perceives there is actually an economic link between

194 White text is where a word is used on a webpage, but the font is the same colour as the background so it cannot be seen by the user.
195 For a discussion of the situation before these developments see third edition, paras 4.4.7.1 and 4.4.7.2.
196 See www.wordstream.com/articles/most-expensive-keywords.
197 C-323/09 *Interflora Inc v Marks & Spencer plc* [2011] ECR I-8625, [2012] ETMR 1.
198 C-236/08 *Google France v Louis Vuitton* [2010] ECR I-2417, [2010] ETMR 30, para 51 and 52 (but as explained above, Google was not using it in the course of trade: see para 56).

the trade mark owner and the holder of the sponsored link (which would be infringing) or conversely where the use of the keyword may be so vague it may be difficult for it to constitute infringement.[199] The test of whether the use of the keyword affects the function of the trade mark seems to be the same whether it is identity or similarity infringement.[200]

In C-323/09 *Interflora v Marks and Spencer* the Court of Justice considered the issue of when consumers would be confused:[201]

> 'if the referring court's assessments of the facts were to show that M&S's advertising, displayed in response to searches performed by internet users using the word "interflora", may lead those users to believe, incorrectly, that the flower-delivery service offered by M&S is part of Interflora's commercial network, it would have to be concluded that that advertising does not allow it to be determined whether M&S is a third party in relation to the proprietor of the trade mark or whether, on the contrary, it is economically linked to that proprietor. In those circumstances, the function of the INTERFLORA trade mark of indicating origin would be adversely affected.'

In making this assessment the Court went on to identify three factors:[202] (a) whether the reasonably well-informed and reasonably observant internet user was deemed to be aware, on the basis of general knowledge of the market, that M&S's flower-delivery service was not part of the Interflora network but was in competition with it; (b) should it become apparent that that was not generally known, whether M&S's advertisement enabled that internet user to tell that the M&S service did not belong to the Interflora network; and (c) the fact that the Interflora commercial network was composed of a large number of retailers which varied greatly in terms of size and commercial profile and that, in these circumstances, it might be particularly difficult for the reasonably well-informed and reasonably observant internet user to determine, in the absence of any indication from M&S, whether or not M&S was part of that network. It was clear, however, that the Court of Justice did not consider the use of a third-party trade mark as a keyword to be inherently objectionable.[203] The question is whether a particular use of a keyword leads consumers to conclude there is an economic link between the person behind the sponsored link and the trade mark owner.

---

199 C-236/08 *Google France v Louis Vuitton* [2010] ECR I-2417, [2010] ETMR 30 at para 89 and 90 and 98.

200 C-278/08 *Die BergSpechte Outdoor Reisen und Alpinschule Edi Kobmüller GmbH* [2010] ECR I-2517, [2010] ETMR 33; C-558/08 *Portakabin v Primakabin* [2010] ECR I-6963, [2010] ETMR 52 at paras 51 to 54.

201 C-323/09 *Interflora Inc v Marks & Spencer plc* [2011] ECR I-8625, [2012] ETMR 1 at para 49.

202 C-323/09 *Interflora Inc v Marks & Spencer plc* [2011] ECR I-8625, [2012] ETMR 1 at para 51 and 52 as summarised by *Interflora Inc and Another v Marks and Spencer plc* [2014] EWCA Civ 1403 at para 95.

203 *Interflora Inc and Another v Marks and Spencer plc* [2014] EWCA Civ 1403 at paras 98, 104 and 143.

Defences

4.43   If an action for trade mark infringement exists, the alleged infringer may still come within one of the defences. This section will briefly examine some of those defences and, in particular, look at where they might apply to the internet.

Consent and acquiescence

4.44   The most straightforward defence to trade mark infringement is consent; in fact the absence of consent is not strictly a defence but a missing element of the cause of action (accordingly the burden of proving there was no consent falls on the proprietor of the mark). The nature of consent[204] is such that it can be express or implied and, unlike a licence, does not need to be in writing. It is also a defence to show that the proprietor has granted a licence to use the mark. Of course, if licensees operate outside the scope of their licences they will infringe (and probably also be in breach of contract).

Registered mark and own name

4.45   Section 11 of the Trade Marks Act 1994[205] sets out numerous defences; of those, the defences in sub-ss (1) and (2) are worth setting out in full:

'(1) A registered trade mark is not infringed by the use of another registered trade mark in relation to goods or services for which the latter is registered (but see s 47(6) (effect of declaration of invalidity of registration)).

(2) A registered trade mark is not infringed by –

    (a) the use by a person of his own name or address,

    (b) the use of indications concerning the kind, quality, quantity, intended purpose, value, geographical origin, the time of production of goods or of rendering of services, or other characteristics of goods or services, or

    (c) the use of the trade mark where it is necessary to indicate the intended purpose of a product or service (in particular, as accessories or spare parts),

provided the use is in accordance with honest practices in industrial or commercial matters.'

Section 11(1) makes it clear that it is not an infringement of a registered trade mark to use it in relation to goods and services for which it is registered.[206] The defence requires that the mark is used as registered (and without some variation)

---

204 Consent can also be given during the registration process: see TMA, s 5(5).
205 TMA, s 11(2) is replicated in relation to Community trade marks in art 12.
206 In C-561/11 *Federation Cynologique International* [2013] ETMR 23 it was held that a CTM entitled the proprietor to preclude third parties using the mark even third party's with a later registered CTM; also see *Pinterest Inc v Premium Interest Ltd* [2015] EWHC 738 (Ch). This might suggest that s 11(1) is not compatible with EU law. The reform package will address this issue.

and solely in relation to those goods for which it is registered. This would provide a defence where a trade mark is owned by different traders for different goods and only one of those traders is able to use it as a domain name.

There is also a defence available to traders who trade using their own name[207] (meaning the name by which they are usually known[208]). At present,[209] this applies to individuals but it also applies, in principle, to trade names[210] and company names.[211] This defence may be particularly important in relation to domain names. If a Mr Paul Smith owns and runs a website at www.paulsmith. net then provided his use is in accordance with honest practices in industrial and commercial matters this defence will be available. But it goes further than that; the defence might cover all sorts of companies and traders using domain names which follow their own names.

The other defences under s 11(2) will not be discussed here as they will have little relevance to the internet and where they apply in other cases there is little difference that the conduct is taking place online or in the physical world. In any event, the own name defence (and the other defences in s 11(2)) are only available where use is in accordance with honest practices in industrial and commercial matters.[212] This is an objective test[213] and the court must undertake an overall assessment of all the circumstances, and, in particular, assess whether the other trader might be regarded as competing unfairly with the proprietor of the mark.[214]

The purpose of the proviso[215] is to ensure a trader using another's mark acts fairly in relation to the legitimate interests of the trade mark owner,[216] rather than preventing any possible confusion about trade origin that might arise.[217] The English courts have formulated the question as follows: would reasonable members of the trade concerned say, upon knowing all the relevant facts that the trader knew, that the use complained of is honest?[218] The courts have also indicated that where the use might deceive the ultimate consumer (but not an intermediary) such use may not be honest.[219] The Court of Justice, on the other

---

207 TMA, s 11(2)(a); CTMR art 12(a).
208 See *Mercury Communications v Mercury Interactive* [1995] FSR 850, 860-1; *Reed Executive v Reed Business Information* [2004] EWCA Civ 159, [2004] RPC 40, para 115.
209 The proposal to modify the TMD and CTMR will restrict it to personal names of individuals.
210 C-245/02 *Anheuser Busch v Budejovicky* [2004] ECR I-10989, [2005] ETMR 27, para 81.
211 C-17/06 *Céline* [2007] ECR I-7041, [2007] ETMR 80, para 36.
212 This is based on Paris Convention art 10*bis*(2). The reform package will restrict the own name defence to personal names.
213 *Reed Executive v Reed Business Information* [2004] EWCA Civ 149, [2004] RPC 40, paras 131 and 132.
214 C-100/02 *Gerolsteiner Brunnen* [2004] ECR I-691, [2004] ETMR 40, paras 23 to 26; C-63/97 *BMW v Deenik* [1999] ECR I-905, [1999] ETMR 339, para 61.
215 It is not clear whether as a restriction on a proviso it should be interpreted narrowly or not: but it appears that it probably should be: see the comments of the Advocate General in C-48/05 *Adam Opel* [2007] ECR I-1017, [2007] ETMR 33, para AG 50.
216 C-63/97 *BMW v Deenik* [1999] ECR I-905, [1999] ETMR 339.
217 To this effect see C-100/02 *Gerolsteiner Brunnen* [2004] ECR I-691, [2004] ETMR 40, para 25 (likelihood of confusion is not enough to make use not in accordance with honest practices).
218 *Volvo v Heritage* [2000] FSR 253, 259.
219 L'Oreal v Bellure [2007] EWCA Civ 968, para 51.

hand, has given some indicators of the factors which should be considered when assessing whether a particular use is honest:[220]

- is the mark used in a manner as to give the impression that there is a commercial connection between the other trader and the trade mark;

- does the use affect the value of that trade mark by taking unfair advantage of its distinctive character or repute;

- does the use entail the discrediting or denigrating of the mark;

- what is the overall presentation of the goods marketed by the other trader, in particular the circumstance in which the mark of which that person is not the owner displayed in that presentation;

- what efforts have been made by the other trader to ensure that customers distinguish its goods from those which are licensed by the trade mark owner.

The effect of this proviso is that any attempt to use a mark in a domain name which is not in accordance with honest practices will remain infringing, even if it is using a trader's own name. Finally, it was made clear in C-558/08 *Portakabin*[221] that in general none of these defences can apply to keyword advertising once the factors made out to establish infringement (discussed above) have been satisfied. This is because, at the infringement stage, the keyword advertisement has already been found to lead consumers to perceive a link between their use of the mark and the trade mark holder.[222]

Trade mark infringement remedies

4.46   Some of the remedies for trade mark infringement in the real world are rarely as important in the virtual world. But as with all cases of infringement, it is necessary to examine what remedies should be sought at a very early stage. The usual remedies for trade mark infringement are damages, an injunction, an account of profits, delivery up or erasure.[223]

Usually, the claimant wants more than simply stopping the other party using the domain name, or any similar, but also to take over the domain name.[224] For this reason, in addition to any claim for damages and injunction, claimants should seek delivery up of the infringing materials.[225] These materials are essentially the domain name registration; the actual content of the site may, or may not, be infringing material. Section 17(4) of the Trade Marks Act 1994 defines 'infringing material' to include material bearing a sign identical or similar to the

---

220 C-228/03 *Gillette v LA Laboratories* [2005] ECR I-2337, [2005] ETMR 67, paras 40 to 49; C-17/06 *Céline* [2007] ECR I-7041, [2007] ETMR 80, para 34.
221 [2010] ECR I-6963, [2010] ETMR 52 at para 67 to 72.
222 C-323/09 *Interflora Inc v Marks & Spencer plc* [2011] ECR I-8625, [2012] ETMR 1 at para 88.
223 TMA, ss 14 to 20; Community Trade Mark Regulation 2006 (SI 2006/1027) reg 5.
224 The right to an injunction under the Trade Marks Act 1994, s 14(2).
225 TMA, s 16(1).

infringed mark which either is used for advertising goods or services in such a way as to infringe the registered mark, or is intended to be so used and such use would infringe the registered trade mark.

Under this definition it appears possible that a domain name registration could be delivered up. Nevertheless, a domain name does not fit comfortably into 'infringing materials'. The High Court in *One in a Million* accepted this is not an 'unjust' remedy[226] but, should a court take the view that a domain name cannot constitute 'infringing materials', the claimant should seek an order that the defendant 'takes all steps as lie within its power to release or facilitate the release or transfer or facilitate the transfer to the claimant of the domain name' and appeal to the court's general discretion to grant 'all such relief' to the claimant. It may be also relevant to the court that the High Court in *One in a Million* accepted that 'assigning the domain name' is the equivalent, in this particular context, of the delivery up of infringing goods.[227]

Remedies against internet service providers

4.47   The circumstances when a copyright owner can rely on s 97A of the Copyright, Designs and Patents Act 1988 to obtain an injunction against an internet service provider when its service is being used to infringe copyright is discussed below. There is no similar statutory provision in relation to trade marks[228] however in *Cartier International v British Sky Broadcasting Ltd*[229] after a lengthy and detailed consideration of the issue, Arnold J concluded that the High Court had jurisdiction to grant injunctions against service providers whose services were being used to infringe trade marks. He further held that the threshold requirements for trade mark infringement claims against ISPs are the same as against copyright infringers:

> 'First, the ISPs must be intermediaries within the meaning of the third sentence of Article 11. Secondly, either the users and/or the operators of the website must be infringing the claimant's trade marks. Thirdly, the users and/or the operators of the website must use the ISPs' services to do that. Fourthly, the ISPs must have actual knowledge of this. …As to what constitutes "actual knowledge" in this context, I see no reason to interpret this requirement differently to the manner in which I interpreted it in the section 97A … context.'[230]

---

226 *BT v One in a million* [1999] 1 WLR 903 at 924.

227 *BT v One in a million* [1999] 1 WLR 903 at 924.

228 As to the reasons not to provide an express statutory provision when art 11 of the Enforcement Directive (2004/48) was implemented see the discussion in *Cartier International AG and Others v British Sky Broadcasting Ltd and Others* [2014] EWHC 3354 (Ch) at paras 112 to 120.

229 [2014] EWHC 3354 (Ch); this decision is currently under appeal.

230 *Cartier International AG and Others v British Sky Broadcasting Ltd and Others* [2014] EWHC 3354 (Ch) at para 141.

PASSING OFF

4.48   Where a sign is not registered as a trade mark this precludes an action for trade mark infringement, but it does not mean that the sign owner (or more technically the owner of the goodwill in the sign) has no remedies available. It is possible to bring an action for passing off. Indeed, a passing off claim can, and often should, be brought in conjunction with an action for trade mark infringement. A claim of passing off requires three basic elements to be established: goodwill in the get-up of goods or services; a misrepresentation leading the public to believe the goods supplied by the defendant are those of the claimant; and damage caused by reason of the erroneous belief.[231]

Goodwill of claimant

4.49   The concept of 'goodwill' was succinctly defined by Lord MacNaghten in *IRC v Muller & Co's Margarine Ltd*:

'It is the benefit and advantage of a good name, reputation and connection of a business. It is the attractive force which brings in custom.'[232]

If a company has customers who would think of using its name, or the name of a product, as a domain name, there appears little to suggest that the company does not have goodwill in the domain name. And as businesses have pervaded the world wide web they advertise and provide goods and services to their customers using the internet. This, in turn, increases the chances of a company extending its goodwill from merely its name to the domain name of the company. To demonstrate the existence of this goodwill the claimant would need to provide evidence of sales, advertising expenditure or direct evidence from customers indicating that they believed that goods sold with a particular get-up must come from the claimant, rather than any other person.

Misrepresentation by defendant

4.50   The term 'misrepresentation' does not imply any malice or intention; it is more a statement of the perception of the public.[233] It is actionable to misrepresent that one's business or trade is that of another person or is connected

---

231 *Reckitt & Coleman v Borden* ('Jif Lemon') [1990] RPC 341, 499; also see the five elements identified by Lord Diplock in *Erven Warnink v Townend* ('Advocaat') [1979] AC 731, 742. The author has argued elsewhere that these requirements have changed see: Phillip Johnson and Johanna Gibson 'The "New" Tort of Passing Off' (2015) 131 LQR 476. These arguments will not be explored here.
232 [1901] AC 217 at 223 to 224.
233 Innocence does not provide a defence to an injunction. The court will simply assess whether on an objective basis injury was a reasonably foreseeable consequence of the misrepresentation. See *Taittinger v Allbev Ltd* [1993] 2 CMLR 741 at paras 21 to 25.

with that person in any way likely to cause damage.[234] The misrepresentation must be made to customers of the other's goods or services (ie web users)[235] and it should be judged against how the relevant goodwill was acquired in trade. This means customer confusion is central to the action for passing off.[236] The trading practices of the person making the representation are also relevant and so, for example, where a sign or badge is not used as a 'trade mark' it is unlikely to amount to passing off.[237]

Misrepresentations involving domain name

4.51   Using a domain name may by passing off as is the use of certain telephone numbers:

> 'The defendants are right that a misrepresentation must be established, but are wrong in believing that it requires an express statement. A person who adopts the mantle of another can by his silence misrepresent that he is that other. Thus a person who selects a confusingly similar telephone number or a similar name may well represent that he is that other by either saying so or by failing to take steps when telephoned or called to disabuse the person who is making the telephone call.'[238]

This can be applied to domain names. If instead of Adam Curry setting up the copycat MTV website (see **4.3**) Martin Trevor Vantram had established the site with his initials as a domain name it may be easier to argue that it was a misrepresentation.[239] Indeed in *MBNA America Bank NA v Stephen Freeman*[240] the court was not convinced either way that the abbreviated domain name 'mbna. co.uk' for Mr Freeman's new business 'Marketing Banners for Net Advertising' was a misrepresentation by Mr Freeman of the MBNA America Bank's mark, MBNA.

The Court of Appeal in *One in a Million* goes so far as to rule that: 'The placing on a register of a distinctive name such as www.marksandspencer.com makes a representation to persons who consult the register [a WHOIS search] that the registrant is connected or associated with the name registered and thus

234 *Ewing v Buttercup Margarine* [1917] 2 Ch 1, 11–13; *Clock v Clock House Hotel* (1936) 53 RPC 269, 275 per Romer LJ; *British Telecommunications v Nextcall Telecom* [2000] FSR 679 (where the defendant sold phone services allowing customers to believe that defendant was part of British Telecom found to be actionable).

235 *Erven Warnink v Townend* [1979] AC 731.

236 But confusion per se is not sufficient to found such an action: see *My Kinda Town v Soll* [1983] RPC 407, 418.

237 *Arsenal v Reed* [2001] ETMR 77 (this aspect of the case was not appealed, but doubt was still expressed by Aldous LJ, paras 70 and 71: [2003] EWCA Civ 696, [2003] ETMR 73).

238 *Law Society of England and Wales v Griffiths* [1995] RPC 16 at 21.

239 That this may be a misrepresentation does not mean there is passing off. Indeed, it has been said, 'a man must be allowed to trade in his own name and, if some confusion results, that is a lesser evil than that a man should be deprived of what would appear to be a natural and inherent right': *Marengo v Daily Sketch* (1948) 65 RPC 242 at 251 per Lord Simonds.

240 [2001] EBLR 13.

the owner of the goodwill in the name.'[241] So, unlike mere registration as a trade mark, mere registration of a domain name, for passing off purposes, makes a representation which is false.

Where two domain names are very similar, such as www.southernfarmer.co.uk and www.southernfarmers.co.uk, then only evidence as to confusion between the two domain names would be relevant to this issue and not other incidents of passing off which occurred off-line.[242]

Disclaimer

4.52 This raises the question as to whether anything could be done to disabuse the public of this misrepresentation. Certainly the defendant, in the knowledge that its domain name is confusingly similar to another's name, may seek to distinguish its site from the potential claimants. It may be thought that, by using the words, 'Unofficial MTV Site' the misrepresentation is stopped. In certain circumstances this may be true.

However, it appears that initial interest confusion will not usually apply to passing off as there can be no damage if the misrepresentation is corrected before purchase.[243] Thus, if someone uses a domain name and this misrepresents that it is connected to a third party, but it is clear upon arrival that the site is not linked there is usually no passing off. Nevertheless, in relation to websites where no trade exists until after the site has been viewed – such as a purely advertising website (such as for an event); it is possible that a disclaimer upon arrival is too late. Nevertheless, it will still depend on the circumstances in each case.

Because domain names and their owners are put on a publicly accessible register held on the web by the registration companies, avoiding litigation may be difficult. A defendant may seek to introduce 'true' distance between its site and that of the claimant by using disclaimers. Associations could be avoided, but even so, the domain name and representation is at large on the public register. This said, if concerned, a defendant might be able to persuade the domain name registrar who controls the register to include a disclaimer on the record itself. Of course, there will always be some individuals who will remain confused as to the source of a website because of the domain name, but as Gibson LJ stated bluntly:[244]

> 'It is not right to base any test on whether a moron in a hurry would be confused, but it is proper to take into account the ignorant and unwary.'

---

241 *BT v One in a Million* [1999] 1 WLR 903, 924.

242 *Evegate Publishing Ltd v Newsquest Media (Southern) Ltd* [2013] EWHC 1975 (Ch) at para 119.

243 *Woolley v Ultimate Products Ltd* [2012] EWCA Civ 1038 at para 4; *Moraccanoil Israel Ltd v Aldi Stores Ltd* [2014] EWHC 1686 (IPEC), [2014] ETMR 55. Accordingly, it probably did not exist even before the Court of Appeal objected to its application in trade mark law in *Interflora v Marks & Spencer* [2014] EWCA Civ 1403, [2015] ETMR 5, para 158.

244 *Taittinger v Allbev Ltd* [1993] 2 CMLR 741 at para 20. See *Singer Manufacturing Co v Loog* (1882) [1882] 8 LR App Cas 15 at 18, per Lord Selborne LC.

Damage

4.53   The third aspect of passing off is that the claimant must show that he has suffered, or is likely to suffer, damage to the goodwill because of the misrepresentation. This requirement to show damage, however, is not onerous in quality or quantity.

If the infringing website is selling goods or services, the test will be easy to satisfy. But the internet contains many sites that serve not as shops but as shop fronts. A website under the domain name 'mtv.com' may not provide products and services for payment; it may merely provide useful information such as the latest releases and Top 20 sales. The damage therefore cannot be equated to lost sales but to a 'dilution' in the distinctiveness of the name MTV or harm to the reputation attaching to it. This will have the likely consequence that the goodwill in the name MTV will be reduced. Aldous LJ in *One in a Million* in relation to the famous mark 'Marks & Spencer' held that: '[R]egistration of the domain name including the words Marks & Spencer is an erosion of the exclusive goodwill in the name which damages or is likely to damage Marks & Spencer plc.'[245]

The level of damage need not be high. In fact, the level required is expressed in terms of a presumption that there will be damage unless proved to be de minimis.[246]

Instrument of fraud claim

4.54   The problems associated with cyber-squatting are occasions where an individual with no legal rights over a name acquires a domain name incorporating that name and then offers to sell the domain name to a more bona fide owner. This practice can work where the policy of the domain name registration company permits such arbitrage. Such a practice is common for company names[247] and the Court of Appeal confirms that precedents from that area may be applicable for domain names.

BT v One in a Million

4.55   The defendant in *BT v One in a Million*[248] had registered a number of domain names, which included 'bt.org', 'ladbrokes.com', 'marksandspencer. com', 'virgin.com' and others. The domain names were not active and were not being used (except one, which was accidently activated). The claimants were some of the owners of the trade marks which were incorporated into the domain names. They alleged trade mark infringement and passing off. In its analysis,

---

245 *BT v One in a Million* [1999] 1 WLR 903,924.
246 *Taittinger v Allbev Ltd* [1993] 2 CMLR 741 at para 27 per Gibson LJ.
247 See *Habib Bank Ltd v Habib Bank AG Zurich* [1981] 2 All ER 650; *Exxon Corpn v Exxon Insurance Consultants International Ltd* [1982] Ch 119; *Fletcher Challenge Ltd v Fletcher Challenge Pty Ltd* [1982] FSR 1; *Direct Line Group Ltd v Direct Line Estate Agency Ltd* [1997] FSR 374; *Glaxo plc v Glaxo Wellcome Ltd, Cullen, and McDonald* [1996] FSR 388.
248 *BT v One in a Million* [1998] FSR 265 HC, [1999] 1 WLR 903 CA.

the Court of Appeal looked at two classes of mark: those where the name is 'unique' and those where it is not. In relation to each of these classes the Court of Appeal found infringement both on the grounds of traditional passing off and as an instrument of fraud.

Where a sign denotes one business and nobody else (eg Marks and Spencer), then when a domain name incorporating that sign is registered, it is passing off. The misrepresentation arises because a substantial number of persons who conduct a WHOIS search will think the name of the registrant is connected with the first business. The Court of Appeal held that such a registration erodes the goodwill in the mark and so amounts to straightforward passing off.[249] It also suggested that the conduct of the defendants had amounted to an express or implied threat to trade using the domain name or to transfer it to another to so trade. This, the court held, was a threat to pass off. The Court went further and argued that in such cases the domain name was an instrument of fraud because any realistic use whatsoever would constitute passing off.[250]

Where a sign denotes more than one business (eg Virgin or Ladbrokes) then use of it as a domain name is not inherently deceptive. Nevertheless, the court still concluded that passing off or threatened passing off had been made out on the same basis as before and also on the basis of it being an instrument of fraud:[251]

'The trade names were well-known "household names" denoting in ordinary usage the respective respondent. The appellants registered them without any distinguishing word because of the goodwill attaching to those names. It was the value of that goodwill, not the fact that they could perhaps be used in some way by a third party without deception, which caused them to register the names. The motive of the appellants was to use that goodwill and threaten to sell it to another who might use it for passing off to obtain money from the respondents. The value of the names lay in the threat that they would be used in a fraudulent way. The registrations were made with the purpose of appropriating the respondents' property, their goodwill, and with an intention of threatening dishonest use by them or another. The registrations were instruments of fraud and injunctive relief was appropriate just as much as it was in those cases where persons registered company names for a similar purpose.'[252]

It is clear that what was important to the court was the motivation for registering the domain name and not the use to which the domain name would be put. The 'value' of the domain name in such cases, the court opined, comes from the fact the mark might be used in a fraudulent way. It is clear, therefore, that where a domain name is registered for the purposes of selling it on to trade mark owner this will inevitably lead to a finding of passing off by using it as an instrument of fraud. But mere registration and maintenance is not sufficient.[253]

A word of warning before discussing this in more detail: each case turns on its facts. In *One in a Million* the court was clear the defendants were dishonest. For

249 *BT v One in a Million* [1999] 1 WLR 903, 924 to 925.
250 *BT v One in a Million* [1999] 1 WLR 903, 924–925.
251 *BT v One in a Million* [1999] 1 WLR 903, 924–925.
252 *BT v One in a Million* [1999] 1 WLR 903, 924.
253 See *Global Projects Management Ltd v Citigroup Inc* [2005] EWHC 2663 (Ch); [2006] FSR 39 at para 40.

occasions where the case is not simply one of obvious extortion, the courts may be more conservative.[254]

Later cases

4.56   In *Britannia Building Society v Prangley*[255] the defendant registered the domain name britanniabuildingsociety.com, but had not yet used the domain. The Building Society brought a claim for passing off and was awarded summary judgment. The defendant claimed that he intended to provide the services of British builders to Iranians, but this was rejected by the court. The court found the defendant to be aware of the commercial value of the domain name and concluded:

> 'I regard the evidence as wholly incredible, and I have no doubt that the defendant registered the [domain] name that he did having regard to the fact that it represented the name of the claimant, a very well-known British trading organisation, and the fact that the first defendant regarded such a domain name as being a commercially usable instrument is apparent from ... his particulars of defence ...'

In *Global Projects Management v Citigroup*[256] the claimant registered citigroup. co.uk and, upon receipt of a letter threatening trade mark infringement, sued for making unjustified threats.[257] The defendant counterclaimed for passing off and infringement. The decision was interesting as there was no evidence of any use of the domain name in business or any attempt to sell the mark or anything else and the defendant denied 'cybersquatting'. Nevertheless, the judge concluded that the defendant had no credible reason for holding the domain name and so found it to be an instrument of fraud. Similarly, in *Thomson Ecology v Apem*[258] it was argued that no injunction should be granted because the defendant had agreed before proceedings had started to transfer the domain name he was squatting. Once more the court thought this was not sufficient and as there was a risk that this would not happen an injunction could be granted. Another significant case[259] is *Phones4U v Phone4u.co.uk*[260] where the defendant registered the domain name phone4u.co.uk (among others). At the time the domain name was registered he was not aware of John Caudwell's company Phones4U.[261] After the registration

254   See *Ben & Jerry's Homemade Inc v Ben & Jerry's Ice Cream Ltd* (unreported, 19 January 1995).
255   (Unreported, 12 June 2000).
256   [2005] EWHC 2663 (Ch), [2006] FSR 39, Park J.
257   Under TMA 1994, s 21.
258   [2013] EWHC 2875 (Ch).
259   There are a handful of other cases, including *Metalrax Group v Vanci* [2002] EWHC 167; *Halifax plc and Others v Halifax Repossessions and Others* (unreported, 27 February 2002), Blackburn J; *EasyJet Airline Co Ltd v Dainty* [2002] FSR 6; *Easygroup IP Licensing v Sermbezis* [2003] All ER (D) 25 (Nov); *Bonnier Media v Smith (GL)* [2002] ETMR 86; *Tesco Stores v Elogicom* [2006] EWHC 403 (Ch), [2007] FSR 4; *Lifestyle Management Ltd v Frater* [2010] EWHC 3258 (TCC); *Vertical Leisure Limited v Poleplus Limited, Martin Bowley* [2014] EWHC 2077 (IPEC).
260   [2006] EWCA Civ 244, [2007] RPC 5.
261   At the time of writing, Phones 4U has ceased trading.

of the domain name, goodwill developed in Caudwell's business and by the time the action was commenced it was found by the Court of Appeal that there was no realistic use of the name which would not cause deception.[262] Finally, in common with *One in a Million* the defendants tried to sell the domain name. This final point meant there was no material difference between the two cases as in both the domain name was an instrument of fraud.

The nature of the action means that there is less authority going the other way.[263] One example is *MBNA America Bank v Freeman*, which was an application for an interim injunction.[264] The defendant had registered 'mbna.co.uk', which he claims he did for the purpose of running a 'banner exchange' business (Marketing Banners for Net Advertising). He also produced evidence of use of another web address as a 'banner exchange' covering a period of 18 months. The judge concluded that there was an arguable case that the domain name was registered for an improper purpose and so he granted an injunction pending trial. However, the injunction extended to preventing transfer or dealing in the domain name, but not its use. Another example is *French Connection v Sutton*[265] where the defendant registered the domain name 'fcuk.com' and successfully resisted an interim injunction on the basis that he wanted to use the domain name as web and email address. This was accepted because fcuk is a common alternative on the internet to the word 'fuck' (a word which is often blocked by email and other filters).

The approach in context

4.57 These cases illustrate certain things which should be taken into account. The first is whether or not by reason of the similarity between the domain name and the brand name, there will inherently be passing off. The more famous and distinctive the brand name, therefore, the greater the likelihood that a similar domain name will lead to passing off.

The Court of Appeal's reasoning in *One in a Million* could be taken further and in an undesirable direction. The court seemed to distinguish between signs which could never be used other than as an instrument of fraud (eg Marks and Spencer) and marks which in some cases could be so used. In the former situation, the Court did not seem to be concerned about the defendant's intention or purpose for registration; but in the latter it was the deciding factor. This raises the question of what happens where a person registers a domain name for purposes other than cybersquatting. For example, if the defendant had registered the marksandspencer.com domain name to run a 'sucks' site (where the company is lampooned or criticised) anyone searching on WHOIS will still lead confusion (at least according to the Court of Appeal) as to the connection. But any person accessing the site will know straight away that the site is unconnected to Marks

---

262 *Phones4U v Phone4u.co.uk* [2006] EWCA Civ 244, [2007] RPC 5, para 35.
263 Where there is clearly a genuine interest in the website then the claim will fail: see for example: *Radio Taxicabs (London) Ltd v Owner Drivers Radio Taxi Services* [2004] RPC 19.
264 (Unreported, 17 July 2000), Nicholas Strauss QC.
265 [2000] ETMR 341.

and Spencer; unless a conventional passing off or trade mark infringement case is made out.[266]

The Court of Appeal was clearly concerned about the use and abuse of domain name registration. This concern led to the grant of incredibly broad protection to trade mark owners to resist cybersquatters. The problem is, however, that it might have gone too far if the comments of the Court are used to suggest that where a mark is only used by one business ('it is unique') the intention of the registrant is irrelevant. There is previous authority suggesting that where something could be used as an instrument of fraud it is necessary to look at the context of use or expected use.[267] But this wide, liberal, approach to preventing cybersquatting has largely been followed by the later cases.

The second consideration arises if the domain name does not inherently lead to passing off. In this situation the court may look at the 'wider' issues such as the intention of the defendant, the type of trade and all the surrounding circumstances. Claimants should therefore investigate the past conduct of the defendants. In *One in a Million*, the fact that the defendants had previously offered to sell domain names to Burger King, although not parties to the action, was used to illustrate the defendants' intention to use the domain names for cyber-squatting purposes. Advisors should therefore check to see what other domain names have been registered by the defendants.

Passing off remedies

4.58   Like the remedies for trade mark infringement, the key remedy that the claimant should seek is to restrain the defendant from providing or describing any website, email access or other internet access under or by reference[268] to the relevant trade mark, domain name or anything which is confusingly similar. Where only the domain name is being used to pass off then the injunction is unlikely to be awarded in a form wide enough to prevent the use of the material on the website itself, as long as, subject to the main restraint, it does not use the particular domain name. Whether the court would order the domain name to be transferred to the claimant depends on the circumstances It is not necessary to restrain the passing off, but there are instances of requiring it to be assigned.[269]

Finally it is not clear whether an injunction can be granted against an internet service provider to prevent a third person passing off (as can be granted to prevent trade mark infringement). Different considerations apply as passing off probably does not fall within the scope of the EU Enforcement Directive[270] which, among other things, led to the remedy being available for trade mark infringement.

---

266 Indeed, this is a reason to distinguish between company names and domain names.
267 On this point see the case of *Singer v Loog* [1882] 8 LR App Cas 15.
268 This will include the use of the domain name in a page of links on which viewers click rather than retype into their browser.
269 See for example, *Vertical Leisure Limited v Poleplus Limited, Martin Bowley* [2014] EWHC 2077 (IPEC) at para 25.
270 A passing off is an act of unfair competition and not intellectual property infringement.

PROTECTIVE DOMAIN NAME MEASURES

4.59   There are a series of steps which should be considered by someone considering registering a domain name. As has been discussed, registering a domain name which is protected by another's registered trade mark can lead to problems. Conversely, registering a domain name and then protecting that domain name with a registered trade mark can provide additional security over the domain name. Potential applicants for domain names should therefore first perform some clearance exercise over the name they wish to register as a domain name. Having registered a domain name they may then seek to protect it from third parties and the registration authorities.

Check availability of domain name

4.60   Domain names are not simply taken: they are registered. The number of registrars has increased substantially as the number of gTLD has expanded from the original ones (ie .com, .net, and .org) to include the wide selection now available. For ccTLD, there is usually a national provider and, accordingly, for '.uk', Nominet UK is the provider. All these companies charge a small fee to register a domain name and generally sell the domain names through agents. The difficulty arises because the registrars do not check that an applicant has the right to use a particular name and so allocates them on a first-come, first-served basis. Because of this policy, many names are already registered. The first step is therefore to use online searches to check whether the intended name has been registered. Companies should try to consider variations of their names and attempt to register these also. This can be done using a WHOIS search.[271]

Register domain name

4.61   Increasingly, domain names which are desirable have been registered. This is as a result of the first-come, first-served system. But it is also as a result of the huge increase in domain names being registered each second. This does not lend itself to careful selection and 'mulling over' of a number of possible brands before 'plumping' for the best. Having searched and found that a number of domain names are free, any delay in registering one of them could lead to disappointment if the desired domain name is registered in the meantime.

To be safe, therefore, each possible domain name should be registered (up to a commercially sensible number). Once these 'possibles' are secured, each should then be 'cleared' to reduce the risk of trade mark infringement. As outlined above, the registration of a domain name can give rise to a claim for passing off in certain cases. This is a risk that, unfortunately, must be taken to avoid seeing a 'cleared' brand registered as the domain name during the clearing process. Registrants may therefore like to register the domain name, pre-clearance, in a

271   Eg www.whois.net.

shelf company and then assign the domain out of the limited liability shell when the clearance is positive. This has two advantages. First, thoughtful naming and corporate structuring of the shelf company should ensure that nobody else gets wind of a new product launch or branding strategy before time. Second, if the mere registration does infringe a trade mark, the liability arising from this is restricted.

It is admitted that it is not ideal for a company to spend hundreds, if not thousands, of pounds registering domain names it may not use because of later rejection at the 'clearance' stage. When thousands of domain names are being registered each day, however, registering pre-emptively may be the safest option.

Clear use of domain name

4.62   Registering a domain name does not provide any legal rights over the domain, only technical rights. A company that seeks a particular domain name should search to see whether or not a third party is using the intended domain name as a trade mark. This search must be undertaken in all target markets, but it may be practicable and economically justifiable to search more widely[272] so as to cover other high risk jurisdictions.

Protect domain name with trade mark registration

4.63   As described earlier, an applicant's domain name may already be protected under its existing trade mark registrations. If this is not the case, the domain name owner should seriously consider obtaining a trade mark registration in respect of the trade mark within the domain name. It has been illustrated that a trade mark registration provides significant rights against a user of a commercially impinging domain name. Even without a registration, the use of a domain name may build up trade mark rights in the name. To signify this to the 'world' the domain name can be followed with the ™ symbol on the website content.[273]

'Sunrise' provisions

4.64   As new gTLD and ccTLD are adopted some providers create Rights Protection Mechanisms (RPMs) such as a 'sunrise' procedures. These procedures enable trade mark holders to either object in advance to the registration of domains using their marks or to reserve a mark in advance of the launch of the domain. The approach varies between TLD provider.

272 Particularly now resources like OHIM's TMView enable most jurisdictions to be searched simultaneously.
273 One should pay particular attention to the fact that it is a criminal offence to use in relation to an unregistered trade mark any word, symbol or express or implied reference that the trade mark is so registered. Use of ® should be carefully monitored – it is not akin to misuse of © or TM, for which there is no criminal sanction: Trade Marks Act 1994, s 95.

Consider domain name dispute rules

4.65   Domain names are bought from a commercial third party. These purchase contracts (usually) incorporate an arbitration clause which applies a particular DRS (dispute resolution policy) to any domain name disputes. The policy that applies varies depending on the TLD in question. The main gTLD (.com, .net, .org) and many ccTLD from smaller jurisdictions have adopted the Uniform Domain Name Dispute Resolution Policy.[274] Nominet, which covers the .uk TLD, applies the Nominet DRS[275] and the .eu TLD is governed by a Commission Regulation.[276] There is also a more complicated procedure of objection and arbitration in relation to new gTLDs.

In each case, the policies are limited to deliberate, bad-faith, abusive registrations. Any other dispute is a matter for the court and will not be considered by an arbitration panel. This limited scope of adjudications means that where there are complex legal issues over varying rights the matter is left to the court. The discussion will now turn to that policy. While each of these policies is slightly different there all are largely based around the UDRP. Indeed, there is now a Uniform Rapid Suspension System (URS) which is essentially a quicker version of the UDRP with a much higher standard of proof. As the basic approach is based on the UDRP in each case and so only it will be considered here. However, it is important when objecting to a domain name to apply under the right policy and to the right arbitration centre.

Uniform dispute resolution policy

4.66   The Dispute Resolution Policy regulates how, without resorting to the courts, an applicant may defend the use and ownership of their domain name or trade mark. The main arbitration provider[277] is WIPO where on well over 2,000 cases are heard a year.[278] In 2014, 87.86% of cases resulted in the domain name being transferred, and over the life of the system the figure is 83.71% (and 1.69% cancelled).[279] The system is, therefore, a very effective tool for trade mark owners to reclaim domain names from squatters. It is based on a contractual provision which is incorporated into the agreement between a domain name registry and a registrant. The term typically reads:

> 'The registrant agrees to be bound by ICANN's Uniform Domain Name Dispute Resolution Policy ("UDRP"). Any disputes regarding the right to use your Domain Name will be subject to the UDRP.'

---

274 It is at www.icann.org. This has been in force since 1 January 2000.
275 In relation to registrations after 2008, the 2008 version applies. Earlier registrations which have not been renewed have an earlier version.
276 Regulation (EC) No 874/2004, Chapter VI.
277 Nominet provides its own arbitration service and .eu arbitrations are conducted by the Czech Arbitration Centre.
278 In 2014, it was 2,634 cases.
279 See www.wipo.int/amc/en/domains/statistics/decision_rate.jsp?year=2014.

It is recommended to weigh up the costs and benefits of this grievance procedure with those of the courts. The logistics and timing of the Resolution Policy are as follows:

(a) Any person may complain about the ownership of a domain name by submitting a complaint to any approved Provider.[280]

(b) The complaint must address three types of issue; first, formal issues; second, factual issues; third, legalistic issues.[281]

Formal issues

4.67 The complaint must:[282]

(a) request that the complaint is to be submitted for a decision in accordance with ICANN'S Policy and Rules;

(b) provide the name, postal and email addresses, and the telephone and fax numbers of the complainant and of any representative;

(c) specify a preferred method for communications directed to the complainant in the administrative proceeding;

(d) designate whether complainant elects to have the dispute decided by a single-member or a three-member Panel (and where a three-member panel is selected provide names of three candidates to serve as panellists);

(e) provide the name of the respondent (domain name holder) and all contact information of which the complainant is aware;

(f) state that a copy of the complaint has been transmitted to the respondent, that the complainant will submit to the jurisdiction of a mutually specified jurisdiction to challenge any arbitration award; and

(g) state verbatim the waiver of all claims against the dispute resolution panelists, registrar, ICANN and their representatives and officers.

Factual issues

4.68 The complaint must:[283]

(a) specify domain names subject to the complaint;

(b) specify the Registrar with whom the domain names are registered;

(c) specify, with supporting evidence, the trade mark or service mark upon which the complaint is based;

---

280 Rules for Uniform Domain Name Dispute Resolution Policy (2009), para 3(a).
281 Rules for Uniform Domain Name Dispute Resolution Policy (2009), para 3.
282 Rules for Uniform Domain Name Dispute Resolution Policy (2009), para 3(b).
283 Rules for Uniform Domain Name Dispute Resolution Policy (2009), para 3 (remainder).

(d) specify the goods or services with which the mark is used or is intended to be used;

(e) identify any other legal proceedings that have been commenced or terminated in connection with the domain names.

Legal issues

4.69 The complaint must describe the three grounds on which the complaint is made, in particular:

(a) the manner in which the domain name is identical or confusingly similar to a trade mark or service mark in which the complainant has rights;[284]

(b) that the domain name holder has no rights or legitimate interests (other than technical ownership) in the domain name;[285] and

(c) the domain name has been registered in bad faith and is being used in bad faith.[286]

Finally, the claimant must set out the remedy sought (eg transfer or cancellation).[287]

Trade mark or service mark

4.70 First, one must address what is encompassed by a 'trade mark or service mark'.[288] Having established this, one can consider when a domain name is 'identical' and when it is merely 'confusingly similar'. The cases on the ambit of a 'trade mark or service mark' show that the panellists view the term generously and, furthermore, licensees can bring claims in appropriate cases.[289] It is usually the case that a registered trade mark falls within its scope,[290] even where the trade mark is registered in one jurisdiction but the respondent was in another.[291] Beyond registered trade marks, the panellists have also accepted unregistered rights protected under the common law,[292] but generally not trade

---

284 Rules for Uniform Domain Name Dispute Resolution Policy (2009), para 3(b)(ix)(1).
285 Rules for Uniform Domain Name Dispute Resolution Policy (2009), para 3(b)(ix)(2).
286 Rules for Uniform Domain Name Dispute Resolution Policy (2009), para 3(b)(ix)(2).
287 Rules for Uniform Domain Name Dispute Resolution Policy (2009), para 3(b)(x).
288 In the United Kingdom there is no longer a distinction between a trade mark and a service mark.
289 See *Teva Pharmaceutical USA v US Online Pharmacies* (adipex-p.com) (WIPO D2007-0368); *Toyota Motor Sales USA Inc v J Alexis Productions* (lexusmichaels.com) (WIPO D2003-0624). The *Avenue v Guirguis* (sizeunlimited.com) (WIPO D2000-0013).
290 But occasionally, panellists go behind the registration: eg *PC Mall v Pygmy Computer Systems* (mobile-mail.com) (WIPO D2004-0437) (prior rights existed); *Advance News Service v Vertical Axis* (religionnewsservice.com) (WIPO D2008-1475) (registration on supplemental register not the same as main register); *Jet Marques v Vertical Axis* (jeettour.com) (D2006-0250) (unexamined rights need more consideration).
291 *Bennett Coleman & Co v Long Distance Telephone Co* (thetimesofindia.com) (WIPO D2000–0015); also see *Infospace v Infospace Technology* (microinfospace.com) (WIPO D2000-0074).
292 *CBS Broadcasting v Vanity Mail Service* (48hours.com) (WIPO D2000–0379).

mark applications.[293] Further, where the registration is a device mark or word and device mark it is necessary to prove this covers rights in the word comprised in the domain name.[294]

Where a right in a mark is claimed (particularly where it is unregistered) then it may be necessary to establish that the mark is distinctive,[295] similarly it is necessary to show entitlement to geographic names.[296] Difficulties have arisen where celebrities have been concerned that their names have been used as a domain name. Here, it would appear, the more uncommon the name, the more likely it is for the panellists to deem the name is a trade mark or service mark. So, for example, Julia Roberts,[297] Jimi Hendrix[298] and Jeanette Winterson[299] (or their estates) were able to assert their common law rights in their names. The pop singer Sting, however, was not able to assert his common law rights because his name 'is in common usage in the English language, with a number of meanings'.[300] It is also necessary to show that a person exploits their name commercially; fame is not enough.[301]

Is the domain name identical or confusingly similar to the mark?

4.71 Once a trade mark or service mark has been established, it must be determined whether the domain name is identical or confusingly similar to it. The basic test is confusion as to commercial origin between the mark, the domain name and the relevant goods and services.[302] The exact application of this test depends on the legal background of the panellists.

Originally, those from a US law background relied heavily on the decision of the Court of Appeals for the Ninth Circuit in *AMF v Sleekraft Boats*[303] with its list of eight factors to be taken into account: (a) strength of the mark; (b) the proximity of the goods; (c) similarity of the marks; (d) evidence of actual confusion; (e) marketing channels; (f) types of goods and the degree of care

293 *Microsoft Corp v SL Mediaweb* (usdocuments.com) (WIPO D2003-0538).
294 See for example *Borges SA v English* (borges.com) (WIPO D2007-0477) (denied on other grounds).
295 See *Fine Tubes v J & J Ethen* (fine-tubes.com) (WIPO D2012-2211) for an example where the mark was not found to be distinctive.
296 Thus, the New Zealand government could not claim rights in the country name: *HM Queen v Virtual Countries* (newzealand.com) (WIPO D2002-0754); and similar *BAA v Larkin* (gatwick. com) (WIPO D2004-0555).
297 *Julia Roberts v Boyd* (juliaroberts.com) (WIPO D2000–0210).
298 *Experience Hendrix v Hammerton* (jimihendrix.com) (WIPO D2000-0364).
299 *Jeanette Winterson v Hogarth* (jeanettewinterson.com) (WIPO D2000–0235).
300 *Gordon Sumner v Urvan* (sting.com) (WIPO D2000–0596); also see *Scorpions Musikproductions und Verlagsgesellschaft MBH v Alberta Hot Rods* (scorpions.com) (WIPO D2001-0787).
301 *RE, Ted Turner Properties v Fahmi* (tedturner.com) (WIPO 2002-0251); *Asper v Communication X* (leonardasper.com) (WIPO D2001-0539); *Hebrew University of Jerusalem v Alberta Hot Rods* (alberteinsterin.com) (WIPO D2002-0616); cf *Irvine v Talksport* [2002] FSR 60, [2003] FSR 35, CA (for passing off the claimant need to be in the business of endorsements).
302 *Diageo v Zuccarini* (guiness-sucks.com) (WIPO D2000-0996); *Wal-Mart Stores v Walmarket Puerto Rico* (walmartcandasucks.com) (WIPO D2000-0477).
303 599 F 2d 341 (9th Cir 1979).

likely to be exercised by the purchaser; (g) defendant's intent in selecting the mark; and (h) likelihood of expansion of the product lines.

However, the application of this test has led some panels to consider some matters which it is suggested are not relevant. The first, and most obvious, of these are considerations of the goods and services sold under the mark/domain name.[304] A domain name, in contrast to a trade mark, can only be used once. This means that simply because a domain name is used for different goods does not mean that it is not cybersquatting. The relevance of whether the goods are the same or different, it is submitted, should only come into play when considering whether the holder of the domain name has any legitimate interest in the mark. If the holder has a pre-existing trade under the domain name (or something similar), then it is relevant that this is conducted lawfully (ie not infringing any trade mark) or if the domain name has developed a sufficient business to make the use of the domain name legitimate then the fact that they are similar goods might be relevant, but in neither case is it relevant to confusion.

Similarly, consideration of marketing channels misses the point. The channel for both businesses will be the internet and the territorial nature of real world marketing channels does not work when considered in the context of the global reach of the internet. Only where the domain name holder has taken steps to exclude the domain name's use from a particular jurisdiction (such as geo-blocks), blocking orders etc, should marketing channels have any impact on an arbitration decision as to confusion. This is why most panellists today adopt a different, more straightforward, approach.

Such an approach was set out in *Mejeriforeningen Danish Dairy Board v Cykon Technology*:[305]

> 'the question ... is simply whether the alphanumeric string comprising the dispute domain name is identical to the Complainant's mark or sufficiently approximates it, visually or phonetically, so that the dispute name on its face is "confusingly similar" to the Complainant's mark.'

Thus, it is not confusion in a trade mark sense (confusion as to source), but whether the domain name is sufficiently similar standing alone to move onto other elements of a claim for cybersquatting.[306] Nevertheless, many issues of trade mark law still pop up in domain name arbitrations. So for example, the addition of a generic term to a trade mark will not usually be sufficient to stop a domain name being confusingly similar. Thus, the addition of the word 'fragrance' to 'Beyoncé' in the domain name 'Beyoncefragrance.com' was still confusing to the name of the well-known singer.[307]

304 *Busy Body v Fitness Outlet* (efitnesswarehouse.com) (WIPO D2000-0127).
305 *Mejeriforeningen Danish Dairy Board v Cykon Technology* (lurpa.com) (WIPO D2010-0776).
306 *Nikon Corp v Technilab Inc* (nikondealer.com) (WIPO D2000-1774); *F Hoffmann-La Roche v P Martin* (alli-xenical.com) (WIPO D2009-0323); *Sermo v Domains by Proxy Inc* (sermosucks.com) (WIPO D2008-0647) (consideration should be devoid of marketplace factors).
307 *Beyoncé Knowles v Sonny Ahuja* (beyoncefragrance.com) (WIPO D2010-1431); also see *Volvo Trademark Holdings v Nicklas Uvelov* (volvovehicles.com) (WIPO D2002-0521); *Bayerische Motoren Werke AG v bmwcar,com* (bmwcar.com) (D2002-0615).

Initial confusion and disclaimers

4.72   The application of real world concepts to domain name disputes has led to some decisions finding on the basis of 'initial confusion', this is where there is confusion when the domain name is typed in, but once the site is accessed no confusion remains.[308] In relation to domain names, the importance of this is that once someone is brought to the site the objective is achieved even if once a person is there they are aware there is no connection.[309] Where this sort of approach is adopted it means that disclaimers[310] and the content of the website[311] are irrelevant to confusion. In most cases, initial interest confusion is raised by complainants in relation to sites which are critical[312] or a parody[313] relating to the brand behind the trade mark. This is why when where a domain name includes a brand and the addition of "sucks" or other derogatory terms, panels have found that the mark is confusingly similar.[314] Indeed, because not everybody speaks English the addition of pejorative terms after a trade mark might not be understood by non-English speakers (or whatever the language may be) as distancing the domain name from the trade mark proprietor.[315] Thus, issues of legitimate criticism or parody are not usually considered at the confusion stage, but later on in the analysis (see **4.76**).

Irrelevant changes – typo-squatting

4.73   The panellists accept that the '.com' or suffix should be disregarded when comparing the domain name with the trade mark.[316] Similarly, 'typo-piracy' (where the deliberate misspelling to a domain name is used to attract those with spelling or typing deficiencies) means that minor typographical differences are usually ignored.[317] Thus, in *Draw-Tite Inc v Broderick* the panel held that the addition or deletion of a hyphen or a space does not necessarily affect the confusing nature of the domain name and mark.[318] Where, however, the domain name and trade mark are not alphanumerically identical but are phonetically similar under a particular language, the panel will doubtlessly seek to rely on trade mark law of the relevant jurisdiction. This view is supported by the fact that the panel is able to decide a complaint using any rules and principles of law that

308 *Six Continents Hotels, Inc v Hotel Partners of Richmond* (holidayinnhotelreservations.com) (WIPO D2003-0222).
309 *Mahamayavi Bhagavan 'Doc' Antle v Domains by Proxy* (docantle.com) (WIPO D2014-1793).
310 *Las Vegas Sands v The Sands of the Caribbean* (carsands.com) (WIPO D2001-1157); *CIMCities v Atonce Americans Specialists* (insideeneworleans.net) (WIPO D2001-0449).
311 *Arthur Guinness & Son v Dejan Macesic* (guinness.com) (WIPO D2000-1698).
312 *Mahamayavi Bhagavan 'Doc' Antle v Domains by Proxy* (docantle.com) (WIPO D2014-1793) (critical of complainant's (Doc Antle's treatment of rare animals).
313 *CFA Properties Inc v Domains By Proxy* (chickfilafoundation.com) (WIPO D2012-1618).
314 *Société Air France v Mark Allaye-Chan* (airfrance-suck.com) (WIPO D2009-0327); *Sermo v Domains by Proxy Inc* (sermosucks.com) (WIPO D2008-0647); *Air Austral v Tian Yi Tong Investment* (airaustraliasucks.com) (WIPO D2009-0020).
315 *Vivendi Universal v Sallen* (vivendiuniversalsucks.com) (D2001-1121); *Red Bull GmbH v Snyder* (betterthanredbull.com) (WIPO D2007-0915).
316 See *KCTS Television v Get-on-the-Web Limited* (kcts.com) (WIPO D2001–0154).
317 *Louis Vuitton Malletier v Net-Promotion* (luisvuitton.com) (WIPO D2000-0430); *Diageo plc v Zuccarini* (guinnes.com) (WIPO D2000-0541).
318 *Draw-Tite Inc v Broderick* (drawtite.com) (WIPO D2000–0017).

it deems appropriate.[319] Descriptive terms are also widely ignored by consumers when considering similarity of marks, but only where those terms lack trade mark significance. Complainants and their advisors are therefore well-advised to support all their legal arguments with court decisions from, it would appear, any relevant jurisdiction to regulation confusion.

Domain name holder has no rights or legitimate interests in the domain name

4.74   The complaint must prove that the domain name owner has no rights or legitimate interests in the domain name.[320] The difficulty of proving that someone has no interests in a site is mitigated by the guidance provided on how to demonstrate one's rights to and legitimate interest in the domain name. There are three non-exhaustive issues that should be discussed and they must be proved by the complainant. The following discussion will explain how such interests can be established, of course, someone challenging a domain name will need to prove that they are not shown.

Use of the name granting prior rights.

4.75   The ownership and use of a relevant trade mark relating to a domain name is usually a legitimate interest in that domain.[321] Therefore, prior to the dispute, the domain name holder should have used or made preparations of use of the domain name in connection with a bona fide offering of goods or services.[322] The use of a name on a product (even if not used as a trade mark) may be adequate to grant rights, and legitimate interests, in a name.[323] Only in rare circumstances will offering to sell the domain name to the complainant be considered a bone fide use of the domain name.[324] In the main, unless the domain name is particularly descriptive or generic, offering to sell the domain will negate the respondent's responsibilities.

Where the mark is not registered then the domain name holder must prove to be commonly-known by the domain name. This can apply to any individual's name, for example, Anand Ramnath Mani registered the domain name 'armani.com'. This matched his business cards which, since 1982, displayed the name 'A. R. Mani'. The owners of the Armani fashion brand complained to the WIPO panel and lost.[325] The panel stated: 'This is therefore not a case of the type sometimes

---

319 Rules for Uniform Domain Name Dispute Resolution Policy (2009), para 15(a). See *American Vintage Wine Buscuits v Brown* (americanvintage.com) (WIPO D2000–0004) and *Ellenbogen v Pearson* (musicweb.com) (WIPO D2000–0001).

320 Rules for Uniform Domain Name Dispute Resolution Policy (2009), para 4(a)(ii).

321 *BSB v Global Access* (skytravel.com) (WIPO D2009-0817); *Chemical Works of Gedeon Richter v SL Covex Farma* (cavinton.com) (WIPO D2008-1379).

322 Rules for Uniform Domain Name Dispute Resolution Policy (2009), para 4(c)(i); rights acquired after knowledge of the dispute are disregarded: see *ISL Marketing v European Unique Resource* (euro2000.com) (WIPO D2000-0230).

323 *CellControl Biomedical Laboratories GmbH v Mike Flowers* (cellcontrol.org) (WIPO D2000-1257) (use as title of software product); *Religious Technology Center v Freie Zone* (scientologie.org) (WIPO D2000-0410) (use as title of book).

324 See the oft-cited, rarely followed decision in *Allocation.com* (WIPO D2001–0537).

325 *GA Modefine SA v AR Mani* (armani.com) (WIPO D2001–0537).

encountered, where an opportunistic registrant adopts a name which is intended to give a spurious air of legitimacy to an otherwise questionable registration.' It can also apply to a person's nickname,[326] provided they have evidence they are known by the name.[327] Having unregistered rights, even as against a complainant's registered rights may constitute 'rights' under this section.[328]

Where the domain name holder is not actually using the trade mark which is the subject of the domain name, he or she may still have an interest where the use made of the domain name is a legitimate non-commercial or fair use.[329]

Critical and parody sites

4.76   Parody or criticism is often relied upon by those who register domain names with the trade mark followed by the word 'sucks' to criticise the company or product. It may come as no surprise that 'natwestsucks.com' and 'dixonssucks.com' were domain names registered, apparently, to condemn those companies.[330] These sorts of cases attract a mixed response from the panels depending on the origin of the panellists and parties. When there is a connection to the US, the view has generally been taken that provided the criticism is non-commercial[331] and a 'fair use' it should be permitted.[332] Where panellists or parties are from other countries a view is often taken that there is no need to use the trade mark to criticise or engage with a brand.[333] In some cases a test is applied to determine which side of the line a particular site falls.[334] It is:

(a)   Has the domain name been registered and is it being used genuinely for the purpose of criticising the owner of the mark?

(b)   Does the registrant believe the criticism to be well founded?

(c)   Does the registrant have intent for commercial gain?

(d)   Is it immediately apparent to Internet users visiting the website at the domain name that it is not a website of the owner of the mark?

(e)   Has the respondent registered all or most of the obvious domain names suitable for the owner of the mark?

326 *Penguin Books Limited v Anthony Katz* (penguin.org) (WIPO 2000-0204).
327 *Redbull GmBH v Harold Gutch* (redbull.org) (WIPO 2000-0766).
328 *Digitronics Inventioneering Corporation v @six.net* (sixnet.com) (WIPO D2000–0008).
329 Rules for Uniform Domain Name Dispute Resolution Policy (2009), para 4(c).
330 This provision has no equivalent in the TMD or CTMR.
331 Banner ads can make a site commercial: *Travis Hill v Needalife.com* (mediaenforcer.com) (NAF FA 95345).
332 See for example, *Sutherland Institute v Continuative LLC* (sutherlandinstitute.com) (WIPO D2009-0693); *Sermo v Domains by Proxy Inc* (sermosucks.com) (WIPO D2008-0647); but see *HBT Invetmsnets v Bussing* (valleygoldminesucks.com) (WIPO D2010-1326).
333 *1066 Housing Association v Morgan* (1066ha.com) (WIPO D2007-1461); *Paul McManni v McEachern* (paulmcmann.com) (WIPO D2007-1597); *Anastasia International Inc v Domains by Proxy Inc* (anastasia-international.info) (WIPO D2009-1416).
334 Summarised in *Midland Heart Ltd v Uton Black* (midlandheart.com) (WIPO D2009-0076) based on *Fundacion Calvin Ayre Foundation v Erik DeutschDomains/Registration Private/ByProxy.com* (calvinayrefoundation.org) (WIPO D2007-1947).

(f)   Where the domain name is one of the obvious domain names suitable for the owner of the mark, is a prominent and appropriate link provided to the latter's website (if any)?

(g)   Where there is a likelihood that email intended for the complainant will be sent using the domain name in issue, are senders immediately alerted in an appropriate way that their emails have been misaddressed?

Fan sites

4.77   The other side of the coin from a critical site is a fan site. These are sites where a fan of a person or product creates a site to tell the world about their interest (or sometimes to bring fans together). Once more there are two views on this issue. On the one hand, some panels have held that non-commercial site[335] is permitted provided it is clear that it is a fan site and not the official site.[336] The other view is that fans need not use the trade mark to attract people to the site, and where the website is actually the name of the person or thing it lauded as it might actually preclude the trade mark owner using the relevant site.[337] This final argument may become decreasingly relevant as the number of TLDs increase (and it would seem untenable in relation to the .fan TLD).

Registration in bad faith

4.78   The final requirement is that the complainant demonstrates that the registration was in bad faith.[338] There are a number of examples of what amounts to bad faith registrations set out in the policy:[339]

'(i)   circumstances indicating that you have registered or you have acquired the domain name primarily for the purpose of selling, renting, or otherwise transferring the domain name registration to the complainant who is the owner of the trademark or service mark or to a competitor of that complainant, for valuable consideration in excess of your documented out-of-pocket costs directly related to the domain name; or

(ii)   you have registered the domain name in order to prevent the owner of the trademark or service mark from reflecting the mark in a corresponding domain name, provided that you have engaged in a pattern of such conduct; or

(iii)   you have registered the domain name primarily for the purpose of disrupting the business of a competitor; or

---

335   See *The Jennifer Lopez Foundation v Jeremiah Tieman* (jenniferlopez.net) (WIPO D2009-0057) where the revenues received were considered to make the site commercial.

336   *Estate of Francis Newton v Zwyx.org* (fnsouza.com) (WIPO D2007-0221); *Estate of Gary Jennings v Submachine and Joe Ross* (garyjennings.com) (WIPO D2001-1042).

337   See *Russell Peters v George Koshy* (russelpeters.com) (WIPO D2009-0173).

338   This usually cannot be shown where the domain name was registered before the trade mark: see for example *Collective Media Inc v CKV* (collectivemedia.com) (WIPO D2008-0641); *Meeza QSTP LLC v Torsten* (meeza.com) (WIPO D2009-0943). But where the domain name was obtain in anticipation of brand being established (reverse domain name hijacking) this might be different.

339   UDRP, para 4(b).

(iv) by using the domain name, you have intentionally attempted to attract, for commercial gain, Internet users to your web site or other on-line location, by creating a likelihood of confusion with the complainant's mark as to the source, sponsorship, affiliation, or endorsement of your web site or location or of a product or service on your web site or location.'

Registration for the purposes of selling

4.79   The most obvious example, and the first listed above, is where the registration is in circumstances indicating that it was primarily for the purposes of selling, renting or otherwise transferring the domain name to the owner of a trade mark for a sum greater than the out-of-pocket expenses to acquire it. Thus, where such offers are made it will almost automatically lead to an inference of bad faith.[340] Domain name registrants are therefore advised to be careful when negotiating the sale of a domain name. Even though they may have registered it in good faith, a high offer to sell it will indicate bad faith. Nevertheless, it will be particularly difficult to prove bad faith if there was a long period of honest use by the domain name owner before the offer to sell was made.[341]

Where there are negotiations to sell a domain name these can sometimes be used to establish bad faith.[342] Importantly, there are differing views as to whether 'without prejudice' communications can be used to establish bad faith or not[343] and so some panels may allow settlement negotiations to be considered.[344]

Registration to prevent registration by trade mark owner

4.80   Where a person registers in order to prevent the owner of a trade mark from reflecting the mark in a corresponding domain name or to disrupt a business (the second and third examples) this can represent bad faith. Indeed, the incorporation of a well-known trade mark into a domain name without any plausible reason for doing so can, in itself, constitute bad faith.[345] It is also possible that 'parking' a domain name – holding it passively – might be evidence

---

340 Of course, where a domain name owner has legitimate rights to a domain name, offering to sell it for more than out-of-pocket expenses may, nevertheless, be acting in good faith: *Avnet v Aviation Network* (avnet.net) (WIPO D2000–0046).

341 *The One Retail Network v DynaComware Taiwan* (theone.com) (WIPO D2004-0528); similarly with generic names: *3Z Productions v Globaldomain* (eshow.com) (NAF FA 94659).

342 *SAFA v Fairfields Tours* (bafanabafana.com) (WIPO D2009-0998) (originally asked for large sum of money, but in response said not after money).

343 Inadmissible: *Donna Karan Studio v Donn* (dknyjeans.com) (WIPO D2001-0587); *London Marathon v Website brokers* (thelondonmarathon.com) (WIPO D2001-0157); *Motorola v Newgate Internet* (talkabout.com) (D2000-0079) (dissent); Admissible: *Spirit Airlines v Spirit Airlines* (spiritairlines.com) (WIPO D2001-0748); *Maxol Direct v Web Names* (maxol.com) (WIPO D2004-0078); *Magnum Piering v Wilson* (magnumpiering.com) (WIPO D2000-1525).

344 See *NB Trademarks v Domain Privacy* (aliensport.com) (WIPO D2008-1984).

345 *Veuve Clicquot Ponsardin v The Polygenix Group* (veuveclicquot.org) (WIPO D2000-0163); *GE v CPIC NET* (gehoneywell.org) (WIPO D2001-0087); *Microsoft Corp v Montrose Corp* (microsoft-office-2000.com) (WIPO D2000-1568); *Intel v Pentium Group* (pentiumgroup.net) (WIPO D2009-0273).

of bad faith in certain cases.[346] Where this is coupled with other conduct (such as providing inaccurate contact information) then the case becomes stronger still.

The requirement of a 'pattern of conduct' (Example b) can be evidenced where a respondent has had multiple cases with similar factual situations[347] or a single case with multiple domain names. It usually requires more than two examples of bad faith registrations,[348] however, to amount to a pattern of conduct.

Another relevant consideration is whether the domain name holder knew of the trade mark.[349] This usually requires something close to actual knowledge of the mark's existence.[350] Thus, it is usually the case that constructive notice as to the existence of a particular trade mark (eg its registration) is not enough.[351] However where the domain name owner should have known (or was wilfully blind) this is usually enough to satisfy the requirement of bad faith.

Example 4.9

Arrgh Inc is the owner of a registered trade mark, 'Arrgh', which it licenses to its European-based group of pain therapists. It also owns the domain name 'Arrgh.com'. Since registering the trade mark a competitive anaesthetist has registered the domain name, 'Arrh.com', and publishes at that website distressing stories of why pain therapy can be damaging. Arrgh.com have a right to dispute the ownership of 'Arrh.com'. Trade mark holders and their advisors should note that disruption of business is not merely concerned with disruption of business but disruption by a competitor of that business.

Example 4.10

Ladybird Ltd runs an extremely successful children's book-publishing business and catches on, perhaps a little late, that it could use its reputation and warehouse for an e-commerce website. It has a registered trade mark which covers its activities and attempts to register the domain name. It discovers that Ladybird.com, Lady-bird.com, LadyBird.com and many other such variants have been registered by a pornographic website. Despite the perception of the damage caused by children accessing 'Ladybird.com', Ladybird Ltd will have difficulty in proving the bad faith requirement, particularly as it does not compete with Ladybird.com.

---

346 *Telstra Corp v Nuclear Marshmallows* (telstra.org) (WIPO D2000-0003); *Polaroid v Strommen* (polaroidporn.com) (WIPO D2005-1005); *Ferrari v American Entertainment Group* (ferrariowner.com) (WIPO D2004-0673) (sporadic use considered similar to parking).

347 See for example, *Wikimedia Foundation v Kevo Ouz* (wikipeadia.com) (WIPO D2009-0798); *Playboy Enterprises v Baert* (playboys.mobi) (WIPO D2007-0968).

348 Registering a lot of domain names in itself is not problematic for a course of conduct: see *Investone Retirement Specialists v Ohno* (investone.com) (WIPO D2005-0643).

349 Some panels, where both parties are located in the same jurisdiction, have used a trade mark registration as constructive knowledge of its use: *Barney's v BNY Bulletin Board* (barneysnewyork.com) (WIPO D2000-0059).

350 See *Michelman v Internet Design* (michelman.com) (WIPO D2007-1369); *Align Technology v Web Reg* (aligntechnology.com) (WIPO D2008-0103).

351 *Aspenwood Dental Associates v Wade* (coloradodentalimplantcenter.com) (WIPO D2009-0675) (constructive notice rarely applied); an example where it is applied see *American Funds Distributors v Domain Administration Ltd* (amercanfunds.com) (WIPO D2007-0950).

Registration for commercial gain from use of domain name

4.81   A domain name which is used in an intentional attempt to attract, for commercial gain, internet users to the website or another online location, by creating a likelihood of confusion with the complainant's trade mark as to the source, sponsorship, affiliation or endorsement of the website or locating or of a product or service on the website or location amount to bad faith. This is a significant requirement: the domain name must not merely be registered but also used (passive use is not enough[352]).

When considering the activity of a website the use of robots.txt (which prevent archiving of a website)[353] or privacy shield[354] as to the registrant's details or proxy settings can be evidence that conduct is trying to be concealed. As can failure to carry out a trade mark search[355] and stockpiling of domain names.[356] Importantly, these are a factor in the wider picture of conduct and should not be considered sufficient on their own.

Example 4.11

2L8.com is a company which registers the '.com' domain names of newly merged companies. Websites are not established for each domain name. 2L8.com lists all the domain names it has for sale and conducts auctions as soon as each corporate merger is officially announced. Even though the domain names are not pointed to operating websites, this is use of the domain names and use in bad faith.

Other matters that need to be included in a complaint

4.82   Once the legal basis for the complaint has been spelt out, the remedies sought must be stated.[357] These are either cancellation of a domain name or transfer of the domain name to the complainant. It is rare that a complainant does not wish for the transfer of the domain name but would rather cancel it. This is because cancelling a registration leaves open the chance that another usurper will register the name.

Finally, the complainant must specify any legal proceedings connected with the domain name.[358] Where there are existing legal proceedings, the panel may in its absolute discretion decide not to proceed to its decision or suspend or terminate its proceedings.[359] Clearly, it is in the interests of any domain name holder to initiate declaratory legal proceedings prior to a trade mark holder starting a complaint under the Rules. This may dissuade or delay the panel from adjudicating over the domain name.

---

352   *Jupiters Ltd v Hall* (jupitercasion.com) (WIPO D2000-0574).
353   *The iFranchise Group v Jay Bean* (ifranchise.com) (WIPO D2007-1438).
354   See for example, *Ustream.TV v Vertical Axis* (ustream.com) (WIPO D2008-0598); *Süd-Chemie AG v Tonsil.com* (tonsil.com) (WIPO D2000-0376).
355   *Kate Spade v Darmstadter Designs* (jackspade.com) (WIPO D-2001-1384).
356   *TV Globo v Green Card Transportes* (redeglobo.net) (WIPO D2000-0351).
357   Rules for Uniform Domain Name Dispute Resolution Policy (2009), para 3(b)(x).
358   Rules for Uniform Domain Name Dispute Resolution Policy (2009), para 3(b)(xi).
359   Rules for Uniform Domain Name Dispute Resolution Policy (2009), para 18(a).

Timing of the arbitration

4.83   The arbitration under the UDRP will follow a standard timetable (the URS has a faster timetable). This begins with the provider reviewing the complaint and then either:

(i)   within three calendar days, forwarding the complaint to the respondent ('commencement date');[360] or

(ii) informing the complainant and respondent that the complaint is administratively deficient, allowing the complainant five calendar days to correct the deficiencies.[361]

The timeline after this decision is as follows:

(a)   within 20 days of the commencement date, the respondent must submit a response akin in all requirements to the complaint;[362]

(b)   within 5 further days of receiving the response the panel is appointed (where a panel of three is requested then the fees for three panellists has to be paid and the panel is appointed based on the lists provided by the parties);[363]

(c)   within 14 days of its appointment (except in exceptional circumstances) the panel will decide the dispute and inform the provider;[364]

(d)   within three days of the provider receiving the decision the provider informs the parties of the decision.[365]

Once the parties have been informed of the decision, assuming the complainant wins and the domain name is to be cancelled or transferred, the domain name holder will implement the decision. This procedure means that decisions can take around 45 days if they are straightforward. Where this is too slow, it is possible to apply under the URS where adjudications can be in a matter of weeks. However, it is necessary to satisfy a higher burden of proof in respect of the relevant conditions.

COPYRIGHT

4.84   Most material on the internet is protected by copyright. It protects emails sent from one person to another and usually protects all the elements of an intricate website including all its mini-programs or executable code. Copyright can also protect the underlying material beneath that which appears on a screen: it protects say the original drawings which were converted into a digital animation on a home page. This width and depth of protection means that everyone using

---

360 Rules for Uniform Domain Name Dispute Resolution Policy (2009), para 4(a).
361 Rules for Uniform Domain Name Dispute Resolution Policy (2009), para 4(b).
362 Rules for Uniform Domain Name Dispute Resolution Policy (2009), para 5(a).
363 Rules for Uniform Domain Name Dispute Resolution Policy (2009), para 6.
364 Rules for Uniform Domain Name Dispute Resolution Policy (2009), para 15(b).
365 Rules for Uniform Domain Name Dispute Resolution Policy (2009), para 16(a).

the internet should be aware of their rights as creators of copyright works and their obligations as users of others' works.

This section considers the extent of copyright protection of material on the internet. It examines the copyright in emails and postings to websites including user-generated content, and the copyright that protects websites. This examination of websites reveals that, although copyright protects the whole website, its constituent elements are also protected: a separate copyright attaches to the text, the graphics, and more active elements such as animations and sounds. Copyright even protects the complex executable programs embedded within a website.

Having discussed that copyright protects most material on the internet, this section goes on to show that most material on the internet is copied on a regular basis. This width of copying results in a simple conclusion. Copyright disputes involving the internet will rarely turn on the existence of copyright or if copying took place

This book considers only English copyright law although the rules of English law are increasingly harmonised in line with other EU Member States and so some of this discussion will be of wider application.

Copyright protection

4.85   There are two important questions that must be answered at the outset. First, is the work itself protected by copyright at all? Second, who owns the copyright? This is a query that is always relevant to a copyright issue, but particularly relevant for the internet. More than any other medium, the internet allows many individuals to interact to produce a copyright work. Taking the most simple of examples: a website company selling books hosts a Comment section on its website to which customers may post reviews, about which other customers may comment. This is repeated over many days creating a thread that is shown on the website and stored on its internet service provider's server. What rights have the individual customers who have posted up their reviews and comments? What rights has the website owner in relation to the entire thread, and the individual postings? These questions, and many more like them, will be examined but first there must be some analysis of what works are protected by copyright.

Protected works

Types of work

4.86   The Copyright, Designs and Patents Act 1988, s 1(1) specifies eight different types of work that can qualify for protection as a copyright work.[366] These are:

---

366 It is possible, following, C-393/09 *BSA v Ministry of Culture of the Czech Republic* [2010] ECR I-13971, [2011] ECDR 3, that the close subject list of subject matter is no longer relevant and any 'work' is protectable.

'(a) original literary, dramatic, musical or artistic works,

(b) sound recordings, films or broadcasts, and

(c) the typographical arrangement of published editions.'

It is important to remember that the work that appears on the screen of someone viewing a website is not usually one copyright work, it is a collection of works, some side-by-side and some underlying the work shown on screen. For example, a home page consisting of graphics, text and which plays a recorded tune has at least four discrete copyright works that are evident and others underlying those. Separate copyrights will attach to the text on the page, the graphics and the sound recording. In addition, the copyright that protects computer programs may protect the entire home page. However, deeper than this is the protection that may attach to the musical score that was composed to play the recorded tune. Controllers of websites in particular must therefore understand that their servers are not holding simply one copyright work, but a montage of works. They should ensure that they have the right to use all the works and understand that a visually small aspect of a website may represent an entire copyright work. A requirement for most copyright works distributed over the internet is that they are fixed in a material form; if a work is not fixed, even indirectly, then no copyright can subsist.[367]

Functionality/ideas vs expression

4.87 Copyright does not protect ideas; it protects the creativity exercised in converting an idea into something tangible. Merely recording an idea, however, does not provide protection over that idea. Indeed, international treaties[368] as well as the Software Directive[369] specifically state that copyright protection does not extend to ideas.

Example 4.12

Four individuals use a special instant messaging service which allows them to type messages to each other in real time; they can see one another's typing on their own screen as each letter key is pressed. The controller of the website realises that one of the individuals is a famous actor and keeps a copy of everything typed by the actor with a view to publishing it. Without a licence or assignment, the controller does not have the copyright to do this; the actor's typing is a copyright work that was formed when he converted his ideas into expressions through his keyboard.

The distinction between ideas and their expression is particularly tricky in the area of computer programs which underlie internet sites and services.

---

367 Copyright, Designs and Patents Act 1988, s 3(2). Fixation is not expressly required for artistic works, but it is inherent in the nature of such works at least as they exist on the internet.
368 WTO Trade Related aspects of Intellectual Property Agreement, art 9(2); WIPO Copyright Law Treaty, art 2.
369 Computer Software Directive 2009/24/EC, art 1(2).

The difference between ideas and expression, and functionality in computer programs was explored by the Court of Justice in C-406/10 *SAS Institute v World Programming*[370] and by the Court of Appeal on its return.[371] The Advocate General explained functionality as 'the set of possibilities offered by a computer system, the actions specific to that program. In other words, the functionality of a computer program is the service which the user expects from it.'[372] It is the different ways of achieving the same functionalities that are protected by copyright; or put more accurately the code which provides that functionality; whereas the functionality itself is not protected at all.[373] Even the selection of functionalities by the developer (ie which functions to include or select in the final product) is simply the selection between ideas and so is not protected.[374]

An example referred to by the Advocate General, was the English case of *Navitaire v Easyjet Airline Company and BulletProof Technologies Inc*[375] which related to ticketless airline booking software. The functionality was expressed as the following steps: 'check flights–check availability of seats–reserve–take passenger details–take payment details–record transaction. The seats thus sold must be made unavailable for future passengers, and that may be done at a number of stages in the transaction (including the initial grab: they can be returned to stock if the transaction is ultimately not proceeded with).'[376] These various functions could be copied freely as they are unprotectable ideas, provided the code for putting them into effect was not copied. Thus, a developer is free to *independently* come up with the same code to achieve those unprotected functions.

Authorship

4.88   Every copyright work has an author.[377] The person who is the author of a work is the person who creates it and it is a work of joint authorship where a work is produced by the collaboration of two or more authors in which the contribution of each author is not distinct from that of the other authors.[378]. Generally, the first owner of a copyright work is its author[379] This is, however, a

---

370 [2013] RPC 17; the issue had been explored by the English courts in early cases (*Navitaire Inc v Easyjet Airline Co Bulletproof Technologies Inc* [2004] EWHC 1725 (Ch), [2006] RPC 111 and *Nova Productions Ltd v Mazooma Games Ltd and ORS* [2007] EWCA Civ 219).

371 *SAS Institute v World Programming* [2013] EWCA Civ 1482, [2014] RPC 8.

372 C-406/10 *SAS Institute v World Programming* [2013] RPC 17 at [52]. The Court of Justice did not define functionality itself, but the Court of Appeal assumed that had used the Advocate General's definition: *SAS Institute v World Programming* [2013] EWCA Civ 1482 at [48].

373 See to this effect C-406/10 *SAS Institute v World Programming* [2013] RPC 17 at [39].

374 *SAS Institute v World Programming* [2013] EWCA Civ 1482, [2014] RPC 8 at [45].

375 *Navitaire Inc v Easyjet Airline Co Bulletproof Technologies Inc* [2004] EWHC 1725 (Ch), [2006] RPC 111; AG at [22].

376 *Navitaire Inc v Easyjet Airline Co Bulletproof Technologies Inc* [2004] EWHC 1725 (Ch), [2006] RPC 111 at [117].

377 Copyright, Designs and Patents Act 1988, s 9.

378 Copyright, Designs and Patents Act 1988, s 10.

379 Copyright, Designs and Patents Act 1988, s 11(1).

general statement and those who work for others in creating websites and online graphics should be aware that works made in the course of employment are first owned by their employer, subject to any prior arrangement.[380] Particular care is needed, however, where contractors or third-party developers are used to create websites or content. Without addressing the assignment of copyright in such works to the customer, the supplier will be the author and owner. Nevertheless, in some circumstances a commissioning contract may include by implication an equitable assignment to the commissioner or alternatively some form of licence.[381]

Example 4.13

A designer is employed by a bank for general design work and is asked to create a website for the bank: the site looks like the inside of a bank with graphics of cashiers counting money, help-desks and other features. Some months later the designer resigns from his post and starts working as a freelancer. He is asked to design a similar website for a building society. He reuses the graphics of the cashiers and help-desks. Unless this is provided for in his contract, he does not own the copyright in those graphics. He may be the author of the works, but having created them during his employment, the bank is the copyright owner.

Original works

4.89   Most copyright works must be original to be protected. A work is original if it is the author's own intellectual creation.[382] This new standard originates from the Court of Justice in C-5/08 *Infopaq v Danske Dagblades Forening*[383] and it replaces[384] the lower standard of "skill labour and judgment" previously used by the English courts.[385] The Court of Justice has indicated that originality requires the exercise of creative freedom[386] or making creative choices[387] which for some works at least requires the "stamp of the personality" of the author.[388] The requirement of originality means that the "mere" copying of a work is not protected by copyright.

---

380 Copyright, Designs and Patents Act 1988, s 11(2).
381 See *Ray v Classic FM* [1998] FSR 622; followed in *Griggs v Evans and Others* [2005] EWCA Civ 11, [2005] FSR 31.
382 C-5/08 *Infopaq v Danske Dagblades Forening* [2009] ECR I-6569, [2010] FSR 20.
383 [2009] ECR I-6569, [2010] FSR 20.
384 The English courts are now often applying the test without comment: eg *Ukulele Orchestra of Great Britain v Clausen & Oths* [2015] EWHC 1772 (IPEC) at [99].
385 *SAS Institute v World Programming* [2013] EWCA Civ 1482, [2014] RPC 14 at [37]; but see *T v A Textiles and Hosiery v Hala Textile* [2015] EWHC 2888 (IPEC) at [16].
386 C-403/08 *FA Premier League* [2011] ECR I-9083, [2012] FSR 1
387 C-145/10 *Painer* [2011] ECDR 13 (AG), [2012] ECDR 6 (Court).
388 C-145/10 *Painer* [2011] ECDR 13 (AG), [2012] ECDR 6 (Court); this is a photography case and it is possible the 'stamp' requirement only relates to photographs rather than more generally as it originates from a reference to photographers in the Term Directive 2006/116/EC, recital (16).

Example 4.14

A budding journalist 'cuts' an article he finds on a website (by pressing two keys) and 'pastes' it into an email. He sends this email to an editor of a newspaper claiming to have written the article. The editor publishes the article without paying the journalist. The journalist, however, may not be entitled to payment: he had no copyright in the email sent to the editor as it did not originate with him.

Scope of copyright protection

4.90   Copyright provides copyright owners with protection in the form of economic rights. These differ slightly for each particular category of copyright work but can be broadly summarised as follows: the owner of the copyright in a work has the exclusive right to copy it, issue it to the public in any form (therefore including issuing copies, lending and renting and performing or showing or playing the work in public), communicate the work to the public and adapt the work. In addition the authors of certain types of copyright work enjoy moral rights which protect the integrity of the work and the right to be identified as the work's author. The implication of these rights on the internet will be discussed in the context of key aspects of the internet below.

Qualification requirements

4.91   There are three alternative routes for a work to qualify as protected under the Copyright, Designs and Patents Act 1988: (a) in relation to its country of first publication; (b) by reference to its author; (c) where applicable, by reference to the place from where it was broadcast.[389] If any one of the routes is satisfied, the work benefits from protection.

Place of publication

4.92   The question of where the work (other than broadcasts) is first published[390] is complicated in an internet environment. It is made available simultaneously throughout the world but where is it published? To address this question it is initially important to understand the stages in creating and 'publishing' a website.

When people speak of 'designing a website' they are technically creating a computer program. Either the designer creates the program by typing commands or uses another program visually to design the site and then allows that program to generate the appropriate commands. These programs that represent websites are written in special computer languages, such as HTML, Java, Flash and XML. For copyright purposes, these languages describe to a computer what a particular web page should look like and how it should operate. The program is then 'run'

---

389 Copyright, Designs and Patents Act 1998, s 153.
390 Copyright, Designs and Patents Act 1998, s 153(1)(b).

through a viewer's browser (maybe thousands of miles away) which interprets the commands and converts these back into a visual layout for the website. Similarly, any executable code embedded in the code is written on the designer's computer and then interpreted by the viewer's. For example, a designer may create some executable code in the form of a Java applet. This is stored on the designer's computer in and interpreted on the viewer's computer.

The 'publication' of a website occurs only when a viewer's computer is provided with a copy of the code from the server computer and the viewer's browser program converts this into a visual representation.

So a website is not published as such; it is made available on a server for the public to access over the internet. It is published by means of an electronic retrieval system rather than an electronic distribution system. This is however taken to be 'publication'[391]. However, this still leaves open the issue of where that publication takes place. It is submitted that the old principles apply and that publication takes place not in the place of receipt[392] of a copy but where the publisher invites the public to view the copies. Were this not the case, 'a periodical which is offered to the public by postal subscription and has 10,000 subscribers would have 10,000 places of publication'.[393] Applying this to the web, the relevant place is from where the site material is made available.[394] If this is located in the UK or in another country in respect of which UK copyright is granted,[395] then the site will be protected. This important question of place of publication for a website is therefore answered by where the server is located as this is where the information is made available for the public. This will be the physical location of the web server which may be located by reference to its internet protocol address (the unique number which has a domain name as its alias).

Example 4.15

A non-British individual establishes a website, stored on a server based in his own country, to publish anti-English propaganda aimed at his own countrymen living in England. This propaganda is printed, verbatim, in a scathing newspaper article in an English newspaper. It will not be deemed to have been first published in England, even if the only accesses to the website are from England. England is the place of receipt; the individual's homeland is the place of first publication under English law.

---

391 Copyright, Designs and Patents Act 1998, s 175(1).
392 See the Canadian case, *Grossman v Canada Cycle* [1901-4] Mac CC 36.
393 *British Northrop Ltd v Texteam Blackburn Ltd* [1974] RPC 344, Ch D at 66.
394 See *McFarlane v Hulton* [1899] 1 Ch 884; and *British Northrop Ltd v Texteam Blackburn Ltd* [1974] RPC 344 as applied in *Television Broadcasts Ltd v Mandarin Video Holdings* [1984] FSR 111. This also accords with the definition that both 'publication' and 'commercial publication' refer to the issuing of the work to the public: Copyright, Designs and Patents Act 1988, s 175(1)(a) and (2)(a).
395 Copyright, Designs and Patents Act 1988, ss 155 and 157. The Act extends to countries where the Act becomes the law of that Country (until recently, this was the case in Gibraltar). The Act applies to works or authors from foreign countries (eg France).

In view of the conclusion that the place of the server is the place of publication it is vital to address how this rule works for a website on more than one server. These are called 'mirror sites' and are server computers holding identical copies of the website code so allowing more people to access the code at once. Website designers who wish to benefit from the English copyright regime must ensure that their porting of website code to such servers will not constitute first publication outside the requisite countries.

There is a rule which covers so called simultaneous publication, but this appears to be reserved for when two separate distribution channels exist in separate countries. This will be the situation for two or more mirror sites. The rule that applies to this situation is simple: as long as material on one server inside a requisite country was made available within 30 days of the site's publication on another server, the site will qualify for copyright protection.[396]

Example 4.16

An individual establishes a website based on a server outside the qualifying countries. After a couple of months the popularity of his site has grown so much as to warrant renting space on a server based in London. Unfortunately, one week after establishing this mirror site, a copycat site springs up also in London. The individual has missed by one month having his work qualify for protection.

The lesson of this is obvious: it makes little practical difference where a website is hosted. The server can physically be based anywhere in the world. Those web designers outside the requisite countries can, therefore, be advised to publish simultaneously their site material on two servers, one within a requisite country. It is hard enough preventing worldwide infringement, but it is easier if rights over the work are gained in as many countries as possible.

Author qualification

4.93   There is another method to qualify for copyright protection: if at the time the work was created its author was a 'qualifying person'.[397] This covers British citizens and bodies incorporated in the UK as well as any citizen of a country that qualifies under the Copyright and Performances (Application to Other Countries) Order 2013.[398] Essentially, this covers almost every industrialised country in the world.[399]

---

396 Copyright, Designs and Patents Act 1988, s 155(3).
397 Copyright, Designs and Patents Act 1988, s 154.
398 SI 2013/536; as amended by SI 2015/216
399 There are some variations for broadcasts, sound recordings and performances where a country is not party to the Rome Convention for the Protection of Performances, Producers of Phonograms and Broadcasting Organisations (such countries include the United States). However, these are not really relevant to the internet.

Example 4.17

An American web designer does not get a chance to publish her work before it is copied onto a London-based server. The copyright work in question has not been published but the author is resident and domiciled inside one of the qualifying countries. The work is, therefore, protected in the UK.

Broadcasts

4.94   A broadcast will qualify if it is made or sent from the UK or another country to which the Act has applied[400] it is defined in section 6 in wide terms encompassing any:

'electronic transmission of visual images or other information which –

(a)   is transmitted for simultaneous reception by members of the public and is capable of being lawfully received by them, or

(b)   is transmitted at a time determined solely by the person making the transmission for presentation to members of the public.'

There is a specific carve-out of an internet transmission being deemed a broadcast unless it is:

'(a)   a transmission taking place simultaneously on the internet and by other means,

(b)   a concurrent transmission of a live event, or

(c)   a transmission of recorded moving images or sounds forming part of a programme service offered by the person responsible for making the transmission, being a service in which programmes are transmitted at scheduled times determined by that person.'

This was intended so that transmissions over the internet will only constitute broadcasts where they, in effect, replicate more traditional television broadcasts.[401] Live or other streaming of programming delivered at scheduled times will therefore constitute a broadcast. Accordingly, where a third person captures a streamed programme and re-transmits it at a later time, the re-transmission is a new broadcast requiring a copyright licence. This is the case even where the content was originally streamed to viewers without payment (eg free to air television).[402] So, for example, copying a freely available YouTube clip and posting that clip on your own website requires a licence from the copyright owner.[403]

---

400   Copyright, Designs and Patents Act 1988, s 156.
401   It appears from C-279/13 C *More v Lindus Sandberg* (26 Mar 2015) that this distinction is permissible.
402   See C-607/11 *ITV v TV Catchup* [2013] ECDR 9.
403   The current UK You Tube licence (9 Jun 2010) provides at Cl 8 that you licence others to use your work through the service (wider rights are licenced to YouTube itself). Accordingly, you are not licensing them to use it off the service.

Term of protection

4.95   The term of copyright varies for different works and when they were made.[404] Websites contain a variety of different works (music, film, text) which need to be considered in terms of their constituent parts:

(i)   Literary, dramatic, musical or artistic works: 70 years from the end of the year in which the author dies.

(ii)   Broadcasts: 50 years from the end of the year in which the broadcast was made.

(iii) Sound recordings: 50 years from the end of the year in which the work was made or 70 years from when it was first published or communicated to the public.

(iv)   Films: 70 years from the end of the year in which the last of the following persons dies: the principal director, the author of the screenplay, the author of the dialogue or the composer of the music specifically created for and used in the film.

Exhaustion

General rules

4.96   The rules regarding free movement of goods are particularly relevant where tangible goods are involved.[405] In summary, the exclusive rights granted to right holders include the right to prevent the importation or distribution of infringing goods, this is restricted where the goods are genuine. Where a right holder sells goods (bearing or incorporating his or her copyright) to a third party based in the EEA[406] the goods have been placed on the market by the right holder for the purposes of exhaustion.[407] If legitimate (or infringing) goods are put on the market by someone other than the right holder then no rights are exhausted. The operative moment for determining whether the right holder consents is the point at which the goods are put on the market.[408] The consent must relate to each and every item in respect of which exhaustion is raised[409] and it must be given by the

---

404 Copyright, Designs and Patents Act 1988, ss 12 to 15. The term of various types of copyright work has been extended a few times since the coming into force of the 1988 Act. Thus, the Duration of Copyright and Rights in Performances Regulations 1995, the Copyright and Related Rights Regulations 2003 and the Copyright and Duration of Rights in Performances Regulations 2013 all include transitional provisions. These will not be explored here.

405 Arts 34 and 36 of the Treaty on the Functioning of the European Union; see generally Peter Oliver, *Oliver on Free Movement of Goods in the European Union* (5th Ed, Hart, 2010).

406 This means any of the twenty-seven Member States or Liechtenstein, Norway, or Iceland (but not Switzerland any more).

407 C-16/03 *Peak Holding AB v Axolin-Elinor AB* [2004] ECR I-1 1313, [2005] ETMR 28, [39].

408 Case 78/70 *Deutsche Grammophon v Metro* [1971] ECR 487, [1971] CMLR 631.

409 C-173/98 *Sebago Inc v GB Unic SA* [1999] ECR I-4103, [1999] ETMR 681, [22].

right holder[410] or someone economically linked to that person. Where the goods were put on the market outside the EEA it is for the parallel importer to prove that the right owner consented to the subsequent sale within the EEA.[411] Whereas if a right holder cannot prove that the goods were first sold outside the EEA (and there is a real risk that the right holder is trying to partition the market) it is for the right holder to prove that the goods were not put on the market within the EEA.[412]

Where the goods are legally put on the market by a third person in one Member State the right holder's consent is still needed to market them in another where the rights subsist.[413] This is likely to occur in two circumstances. First, where a person sells goods incorporating intellectual property rights which that person owns (eg a trade mark is owned by different traders in different Member States); and secondly, where a person sells goods in a country where the relevant intellectual property right does not subsist (eg the trade mark is not registered).[414] In neither case is the intellectual property right of the right holder exhausted and so sale within a Member State where the right subsists can still be prevented.

Software and downloadable content

4.97   These general rules are modified in the online world. Indeed, there are different rules of exhaustion for software[415] and for other content.[416] The rule for software was explained in C-128/11 *Usedsoft*.[417] Oracle, the database maker, sold block licences of 25. Thus, if a company had 23 employees and so wants 23 licences, it actually had to buy 25 licences (and have two left over). Usedsoft's business was buying these left over licences and reselling them to other people. Oracle alleged that this was infringing their copyright. Oracle argued that they had provided the software "free" to customers who had bought their services and that they had granted only a licence to use the software. Accordingly, it had not been sold. The Court of Justice, however, considered that the downloading of the software and the purchase of the user licence was an "indivisible whole" which

---

410 As to where the facts lead to a finding of consent see *Mastercigars Direct Ltd v Hunters & Frankau Ltd* [2007] EWCA Civ 176, [2007] ETMR 44, [45] et seq.

411 C-414/99 to 416/99 *Zino Davidoff SA vA & G Imports Ltd* [2001] ECR I8691, [2002] ETMR 9, [54].

412 C-244/00 *Van Doren & Q GmbH v Lifestyle Sports & Sportswear Handelsgesellschaft mbH* [2003] ECR I-3051, [2003] ETMR 75, [41].

413 This was not always the case; see David Keeling, *Intellectual Property Rights in EU Law: Volume 1—Free Movement and Competition Law* (Oxford: Oxford University Press, 2003), 88–9 which suggests that this rule is limited to trade marks; also note *Bolton Pharmaceutical Co 100 Ltd v Doncaster Pharmaceuticals Group Ltd* [2006] EWCA Civ 661, [2006] ETMR 65 (Court of Appeal indicated that it might be necessary to see why intellectual property rights were divested).

414 In relation to this latter scenario see Case 341/87 *EMI Electrola GmbH v Patricia Im- und Export Verwaltungsgesellschaft mbH* [1989] ECR 79, [1989] 1 FSR 544 (copyright expired in one Member State, but not another; cannot buy goods from third person in Member State where copyright expired and sell in Member State where copyright subsists).

415 Computer Software Directive 2009/24/EC, art 4.

416 Information Society Directive 2001/29/EC, art 4.

417 [2013] RPC 6.

were intended to make the software available to the customer permanently: it was thus a sale. This meant that Oracle could not prevent the resale of the left over licences by Usedsoft. It appears, therefore, that even where a copyright owner thinks it is merely licensing software it may be that in fact a sale is taking place; and the subsequent resale cannot be prevented. It remains unclear whether this can be avoided where the work is "rented" or the licence is time limited.

It appears that there are different rules for content (eg films or music sold online). In C-419/13 *Art & Allposter*[418] it was held that exhaustion only applies to where a tangible copy of a work has been put on the market.[419] Thus, it appears, it does not apply to a digital copy (or intangible copy). This means that where an executable programme which runs a film is licenced perpetually to a user two different rules of exhaustion apply. The executable program is transferable (and the copyright owner cannot stop it) whereas the film itself is not transferable (and a third person buying it on the second hand market via download swaps would be infringing). This appears to be a somewhat unsatisfactory outcome, particularly as the code and content are not always clearly separate.

Internet examples

4.98   This section takes the principles of copyright and applies them to the most common internet scenarios.

Emails

4.99   Electronic mail will be protected as a literary work if it is original. Typing, in any language, even using symbols, would be a 'writing' and so a literary work. And this may be by hand or otherwise regardless of the fixing medium. This presumably includes the use of 'emoticons' which are little pictures made from the characters of the email viewed from the side.[420] It will also encompass an email which is not written but dictated to a voice recognition or dictation system. If the author is an employee creating the email in the course of employment, the first owner will be deemed to be the employer.

The basic rule is that, unless there are agreements to the contrary, sending an email to someone does not alter its copyright owner or its owner's rights over that copyright. The copyright remains with the author/sender.[421] Accordingly, a recipient of an email should not forward the email to others, unless there is some form of licence (implied or express) or copyright exception permitting them to do so.

The forwarding of an email one is not simply performing the equivalent of putting a letter in another envelope (which would not constitute a breach of

---

418   [2015] ECDR 7 (AG) and 8 (Court).
419   This is based on an agreed statement in the WIPO Copyright Treaty.
420   For example, ;-) is a smiling, winking man when turned sideways.
421   The rule as it applied to letters is ancient and is found in *Pope v Curl* (1741) 2 Atk 342, 26 ER 608.

copyright, but perhaps only one of confidence). It involves copying and an issuing of copies to the public and, absent a licence, infringes copyright.

Forums

4.100 A 'forum' is the term used here to encompass newsgroups, commercial bulletin boards controlled by internet service providers and website-based chat rooms and social networking services. Forums contain a variety of digital information. Some contain only postings and replies from members (here we will refer to this as a conversation thread) whereas others allow users to post digital sound, picture and video files (user-generated content, or 'UGC'). These two types of posting will be considered separately.

Conversation threads

4.101 A conversation thread is a collection of postings by individuals collected together as a written conversation. An individual, instead of sending an email to another person, sends a message to the forum and a particular thread. Anyone else who also accesses the particular thread may then read this message. These readers can either reply to the public message or can simply read it and the replies. Over time, sometimes minutes, a conversation thread emerges in which questions are asked and answered and those answers prompt other questions.

The controller of the thread may 'moderate' it. This means that the controller, or his agent, takes an active part in the management of the thread: certain parts of messages or whole messages may be deleted and certain conversations may be 'steered' in their content. The controller acts as an editor. At the other extreme, the controller does not manage or oversee the content of the thread in any way. The controller, in such a system, is simply providing a storage system for a group of individuals' messages.

Therefore, the controller is probably not the copyright owner as any claim would fall at the first hurdle: originality. The thread is simply a copy of others' messages and so not the work of the controller at all. However, if the controller undertakes substantial moderation by editing the content of the messages themselves then there might be enough originality. Further, it is just about possible that the decision to accept or reject a message in the thread is sufficient selection or arrangement for the collector to own copyright in a database.[422] For an unmoderated conversation thread, however, there is no originality upon which to base any claim for copyright.

UGC forums

4.102 In the same way as some controllers simply store messages, others store and publish the files of members (for example, Youtube). These may be

---

422 Copyright, Designs and Patents Act 1988, s 3A(1); also see C-604/10 *Football Dataco v Yahoo!* [2013] FSR 1 (which suggests that compilation copyright, which existed under UK law and may previously have granted the moderator a right, may no longer be permissible under the Directive).

sound recordings or movies clips (usually. in a compressed format such as MP3, MP4 or DivX) that a member wishes to share with others. In some cases the files themselves are infringements of copyright as the uploader has no licence in relation to the work at all and this raises the question of what liability the controller may have over such postings (considered below). For the same reasons as mentioned in relation to threads there is probably no copyright protection owned by the controller in relation to the content stored by third parties.

Accordingly, if a controller[423] wishes to prevent others copying the collection they must rely upon establishing a contract[424] with their users that prevents this copying or create something worthy of database right protection. Such a contract, as all, suffers from the limitation on privity: it may serve to restrict contractually primary copiers, but those who duplicate the copy will not be bound by the contract. They, and the controller, may also be restricted by the copyright vested in the individual files themselves.

Websites

4.103   Websites are the most legally complicated of all works on the internet. Websites consist of many overlapping and adjacent copyright works each of which may have protection separate from the whole and each of which may have a different owner. To appreciate these many copyright works it is perhaps useful to outline how one creates a website.

Creation of a website

4.104   To most website designers what is important is how the site looks, how it interacts and how quickly it can be displayed.[425] The first stage is usually to create a scheme that shows how each of the different pages of a site fit together. This may be created on paper or using one of the many web design programs now available. A website may include frames, which allow some information to remain on the screen even though the viewer chooses a new page (useful for contents sections and legal disclaimers).

The second phase of the site's design is the preparation of the individual pages. A designer must be aware of where every element of a page will be placed. This is because the language used to store the site eventually is a layout language, and like all computer programming languages demands certainty.

Designers do this 'storyboarding' either on paper (converting it subsequently by eye into programming commands), or on a computer screen using a special program that performs the conversion.

A page may consist of many discrete, individually designed elements. The most basic of these is the text: this is the line of characters from the first letter

---

423   As opposed to the person who uploaded the work who will own the copyright and can exercise it against others.

424   See C-30/14 *Ryanair Ltd v PR Aviation BV* [2015] ECDR 13 (which is discussed below).

425   This section refers extensively to web designers in the sense of a person or company, who creates the code to put on a server. The legal conclusions reached, however, are equally applicable to anyone who designs a website whether for themselves or their company.

to the last, rather than the layout that is concerned with how the characters are portrayed, in which typeface[426] and in which format. The other common element is graphics. These are digitally stored pictures but it is crucial to realise that their digital nature refers only to the method of storage. A picture on a website could just as easily have been an oil painting on canvas as a digitally created picture made using a computer-painting software package. Each graphic is stored on the website and 'anchored' into the page at the correct place. Unlike a newspaper, the graphics are stored and are accessible separately from the main page. All the page holds is a link to the graphic.

Certain websites use a particular script or include an executable program which allows interaction with the viewer of the site. At its simplest, viewers can enter their name and other details to receive information. More involved scripts allow certain areas of the screen to become 'hotspots' which respond to a viewer's clicks on those parts.

The most complex element to websites is executable code. These 'apps'/'applets' and 'objects' are, in short, whole computer programs that are automatically run whenever a website is viewed or an event is triggered. Some executable code may perform a simple task such as playing a three-note tune. Other code is more intricate and displays animations and allows viewers to play games. For instance, some websites will allow their viewers to draw pictures, others to write letters. Those dealing with ecommerce may ensure that an entered credit card is both valid and subsequently debited. Of course the effort which goes into coding one applet may be extensive involving the work of many people including designers and programmers.

Having explained this factual background it is now possible to examine the copyright that will, inevitably, protect not only the whole website, but also its constituent parts.

Preparatory material

4.105 The preparatory design materials for a computer program are protected as a literary work[427] and any artwork developed in those design materials may be an artistic work.[428] This means that the visual chart of how the website fits together, even though not on computer, if fixed and original, will be protected by copyright. Each of the individual graphics, even as rough sketches, is protected as original artistic works.

This underlying protection cannot be ignored: if the designer is not the owner or the licensee of the underlying protected works, he will probably infringe their copyright by incorporating them into a website. What should be noted is that those who design websites cannot simply scan, say, a photograph[429] from a magazine and legally use it on their website without being the owner or licensee

---

426 Also known as 'font'.
427 Copyright, Designs and Patents Act 1988, s 3(1)(c),
428 Copyright, Designs and Patents Act 1988, s 4(1)(a) interwoven with s 4(2)(a) and (b).
429 See *Bauman v Fussell* [1978] RPC 485.

of the copyright in the photo.[430] Similarly, as demonstrated by *Hoffman v Drug Abuse Resistance Education*[431] the taking of a copyright work from a website and reusing it is an infringement even if the person honestly believed that they had permission to do the act. Accordingly, it is important to be very careful about the sourcing of any material used on a website.

A particular issue for web designers is that they cannot hide their work, as most websites are available for viewing by anyone who wants to type the corresponding URL. Designers must be wary of using infringing works as they can easily be spotted.

Example 4.18

Many websites use a backdrop that gives each page a patterned background. One designer decides that the patterned wallpaper on his office walls would be appropriate for a particular background. He uses a digitised version as the backdrop. Although he may have incorporated the graphic and designed the other portions of the site, he is not entitled to use the textured background to the site. The wallpaper can be protected as an original artistic work and he may face infringement proceedings for copying it.

Text

4.106   The text that is used on a website is clearly a literary work and as such will probably be protected by copyright. The web designer, by simply retyping the text, gains no copyright over it (and probably infringes).

Example 4.19

A web designer is employed to create a site for a law firm. As to be expected, the firm supplies a page of carefully drafted disclaimers to put on the site in a frame. Months later the designer is approached to design a site for an accountancy firm and offers them a site, 'including web-specific disclaimers'. If the designer uses the same disclaimers on the accountant's site, without permission from the lawyers, he is copying a literary work protected by copyright. He may be sued for doing so.

Graphics

4.107   Web designers are often approached by persons who already have graphics to put on their site. These may include logos and photographs which have already been used. It may be that the modifications needed to digitise the images (lighting, cropping etc) may be sufficient to be original and so attract copyright. However, this should not be confused with the right to copy the original

---

430 In *Antiquesportfolio.com v Rodney Fitch & Co* [2001] FSR 23 the defendant used small copies of the photographs to form icons and other graphics from a well known antiques encyclopaedia without consent of the author. The claimant was entitled to summary judgment on the basis that there was copyright in the photographs which had been infringed by the claimant.
431 [2012] EWPCC 2 at [18].

photograph: the designer's right is in the modifications made and incorporated in the digitised version and not in the underlying photograph. The designer should, therefore, seek explicit permission if he seeks to reuse the digitised photograph on another website.

Example 4.20

A well-known petrol company commissions a web designer to produce a website for it. It supplies the designer with its logo which is a small yellow fish. The designer sets about writing an app that will appear to rotate this fish in three-dimensions on the screen. Sometime later the designer is approached by a high-class seafood restaurant which also wants a website. The designer, rather than 'reinventing the wheel' colours the fish grey and uses the same app on the restaurant's site. If copyright subsists in the fish logo, the designer can be prevented from displaying the copy even though his intellectual creation went into the production of the animating applet.

Music and sounds

4.108   Websites often play or 'stream' music and so allow a sound recording to be played. Copyright can subsist in that sound recording provided that it is not a copy of another recording.[432] Nevertheless, the technical conversion from a musical score to a recording or MP3 file should not be confused with any copyright over that underlying original musical score.[433] A right in the sound recording does not include a right to reproduce the tune of a musical score included in that recording. A web designer must look to the owners of the rights in the underlying musical work for permission to reproduce it before using it again on another website.

It is more common on websites to hear sounds and recordings than music, however. For example, a site advertising a new film set in space may open with the sound of laser fire. The 'sound' is recorded in a digital format called a 'sample'. This sample is sent from the website server to the client computer. The browser program on that computer then interprets the sample's series of binary codes as pitch and amplitude variations and will play the sound back in perfect quality.

This sample will be a sound recording in a copyright sense[434] as sound recordings include both digital recordings on a computer, stored in a digital format, and a MP3 file, storing the music in a special musical notation that allows the computer to 'play' the music directly. This sample may also be an infringement of the copyright in the copied recording.

432 Copyright, Designs and Patents Act 1988, s 5(2).
433 Copyright, Designs and Patents Act 1988, s 1(1)(a).
434 Copyright, Designs and Patents Act 1988, s 5(10).

Example 4.21

The owner of a news website decides to use a sound recording of Big Ben chiming one o'clock. The owner digitally records BBC Radio's use of the same chime on its one o'clock news programme. The website owner not only may have infringed the copyright in the BBC's own recording, but also, the owner has no copyright in his own recording. If the owner had stood beside Big Ben and digitally taped the chiming himself, he would have a copyright in the sound recording.

Commercial issue

4.109   This discussion of the individual elements of a website serves two purposes. First, it shows that website designers should be careful to form explicit arrangements with their commissioners. They should ensure that they are indemnified from any copyright infringement by virtue of using material supplied to them by the commissioners. Conversely, the commissioner should ensure the agreement makes clear what rights are to pass back to the commissioner and what is to remain vested in the designer.

There are a number of cases,[435] albeit not concerned directly with the internet, which indicate the necessity of explicitly specifying which party owns what works and what each party is entitled to do with the works. As Lightman J said in *Ray v Classic FM plc*[436]

> 'This litigation springs from the failure of the parties (and more particularly the advisors who were then acting for them) at the time that the parties entered into the Consultancy Agreement to consider, or provide for, the intellectual property rights that would arise in the course of the engagement of the [claimant]. This expensive lesson of this litigation is the vital necessity for provision for these rights in such agreements.'

The second purpose of looking at the copyright that subsists in the elements of a website is that it is easy for infringers to copy only one of those elements. When it comes to infringement it is easier to show the entirety of a graphic has been copied then a substantial part of a website which comprises many different works.

Websites as computer programs

4.110   The content of a website is built up from a number of elements, but the website itself is the code held on a server which sets out how that content is to be displayed and run. This code, as a computer program, is a literary work.[437] As with other types of copyright work, a computer program is only protected if it is the

---

435 *Pierce v Promco SA* [1999] ITCLR 233; *Fylde Microsystems Ltd v Key Radio Systems Ltd* [1998] FSR 449.

436 *Ray v Classic FM plc* [1998] FSR 622; another example is *Laurence John Wrenn and Integrated Multi-Media Solutions Limited v Stephen Landamore* [2007] EWHC 1833 (Ch).

437 Copyright, Designs and Patents Act 1988, s 3(1)(b).

author's own intellectual creation.[438] Computer programs include the preparatory design material, but otherwise what they are is not defined.[439] However, the words computer program probably cover both the whole program and sub-programs that make up that program (eg sub-routines).[440]

Copyright protects the program at two levels: one, the actual words, symbols and numerals of the code[441] and two, the compilation of the various smaller programs or elements within the whole; these are both literary works. The entire coding from the first instruction to the last is protected as a pure literary work. In addition, the individual programming elements (such as individual procedures or routines) are also protected as smaller literary works. This becomes particularly important for websites that use a considerable amount of executable code. If a person copied one small app without licence there is an argument that, in relation to the whole HTML or XML listing, it is insubstantial and so its copying is not infringement. If the programmer can claim that the copyright work is not the whole website, but is the copied app only, then copying the entire app is clearly a substantial taking.

Example 4.22

An insurance company establishes a website over which it conducts business. One aspect of the site is a form to fill in one's personal details. The website has over 200 graphic-rich pages of information taking up 200Mb of storage space; the form takes up half a page and less than 1Mb. The form is copied. If the company claims copyright in the whole site the taking of the form may not be held to be substantial by the court. The company might, however, be able to claim a separate literary copyright in the code for the form. Its taking is clearly substantial.

Joint authorship of website

4.111 The Copyright, Designs and Patents Act 1988 is of little guidance in this area, demanding only that joint authorship requires both collaboration and contributions that are indistinct.[442] Nevertheless, it appears that are four requirements: (i) the collaborator must make some sort of contribution; (ii) that contribution must have been significant;[443] (iii) the contribution must have been

---

438 In contrast to most other sorts of work, this is set out in a Directive: the Computer Software Directive 2009/24/EC, art 1(3).
439 Computer Software Directive 2009/24/EC, art 1(1). This definition is not expressly set out in the Copyright, Designs and Patents Act 1988, but it clearly represents the position: see *SAS Institute v World Programming* [2013] EWCA Civ 1482, see **4.105**.
440 It was so held in *Ibcos Computers Ltd v Barclays Mercantile Highland Finance Ltd* [1994] FSR 275, but it is not clear how far this would be followed if the matter were referred to the Court of Justice.
441 Some might use the word 'source code' to refer to this listing. This is perhaps not strictly accurate as the distinction between source and object code for HTML and XML code is not as pronounced as for compiled computer languages.
442 Copyright, Designs and Patents Act 1988, s 10(1). There is an additional class of works call works of co-ownership (see s 10A) these apply only to works which are the combination of music and lyrics.
443 See *Brighton v Jones* [2004] EWHC 1157 (Ch), [2005] FSR 16 at [34(1)].

original; and (4) it must have been a contribution to the creation of the work. *Cala Homes (South) Ltd v Alfred McAlpine Homes East Ltd*[444] demonstrates the issues that arise. In that case, the draftsmen of some architectural drawings followed very closely a brief written by a Mr Date but, for the drawings in question, Mr Date did not 'move the pen on the paper'.[445] This was not the question as the court made clear it is who contributed to the production of the work not who physically drew it which is important. It was put simply in *Fylde Microsystems Ltd v Key Radio Systems Ltd,*[446] what is important is that the contribution was of the right sort (going towards its originality) and that it was 'big enough'.

Hyperlinks

4.112   The question of whether a hyperlink is an original work is difficult. While it was held in *Shetland Times v Wills*[447] that a hyperlink could be an original work, this was based on the old standard of originality (skill, labour and judgment) and so there was no requirement of creativity. In *Shetland Times,* Lord Hamilton took the view that news headlines were protectable so hyperlinks should be as well. The protection of some news headlines as original literary works is now clear,[448] but many hyperlinks are quite different from a headline. Indeed, much of the content of a hyperlink relates to the roots of the folders where the particular webpage is stored. There is therefore little creativity in the hyperlink itself. Thus, it may be that a more appropriate method of protecting a hyperlink is not in its own right, but the protection as a database of the structure and arrangement of the various directories. Nevertheless, if the hyperlink includes a news headline within it, then that phrase may well be protected.

Databases

4.113   There are two separate types of protection for databases: copyright protection for the structure and arrangement of the data and a sui generis right database right which protects the investment in creating the database.

Copyright in databases

4.114   A database is defined as a collection of independent works, data or other materials which are arranged in a systematic or methodical way, and are individually accessible by electronic or other means.[449] Most websites store a

---

444   [1995] FSR 818 at 834 to 836.
445   [1995] FSR 818 at 833.
446   [1998] EWHC Patents 340.
447   [1997] FSR 604.
448   *Newspaper Licensing Agency v Meltwater Holdings* [2011] EWCA Civ 890 [22], C5/08 *Infopaq* [2010] FSR 20.
449   Copyright, Designs and Patents Act 1988, s 3A(1).

lot of data in a systematic or methodical way. Indeed, most large websites use content management systems or other applications to arrange the content from their site into a database (in the computer sense). It is also relevant that a database may be more than merely text or digits. It may also encompass sounds, images, and other data.[450]

The required originality in a database probably cannot arise from a database which is automatically generated by a computer program and so more than mundane arrangement is required.[451] A more obvious category which may not qualify consists of databases based on simple organisation, for example a list of customer contact details or postings structured in alphabetical order. Here neither the contents themselves (which are simply names and addresses and postings given by customers themselves), nor their arrangement, can be said to be the website owner's own intellectual creation.

Database rights

Scope of the database right

4.115   A database is protected by a database right (regardless of whether it also qualifies for copyright protection as a literary work) provided there has been a substantial investment in obtaining, verifying or presenting the contents of the database.[452]

It is vital here to appreciate that the maker of a database takes the initiative and risk of investing in the database, but not necessarily its contents. A database is a collection of other works and data. The maker of the database may have had no hand in the creation of these underlying elements and it is not necessary that the elements are actually copyright works themselves.[453] To be a maker of a database one needs only to have taken the initiative and risk of obtaining, verifying or presenting the underlying data.[454] Databases are about protecting the investment in 'contents pages' and 'indexes' rather than the creativity in chapters and sentences.

The concept of investment is wider than mere financial investment. It also includes human or technical resources.[455] Many complex websites utilise the skills of database architects and other computer programmers to ensure that the database supporting a website functions correctly. This is an ongoing and expensive task; most websites, in particular e-commerce websites, have a continually changing structure and appearance to keep both stock and the look of the website fresh.

---

450 Database Directive 96/9, recital 17.
451 The computer programme which created it might be protected, and in some instances if it can be shown to be creative then the author of the computer program may also be the author of the database: Copyright, Designs and Patents Act 1988, s 9(3).
452 Copyright and Rights in Databases Regulations 1997 (SI 1997/3032), reg 13(1).
453 Database Directive 96/9, art 7(4).
454 Database Directive 96/9, recital (41); Copyright and Rights in Databases Regulations 1997, reg 14(1).
455 Copyright and Rights in Databases Regulations 1997, reg 12(1).

In *British Horseracing Board v William Hill*[456] it was held that the substantial investment must be in the creation of the database itself and that the investment can be either qualitatively or quantitatively substantial (or both).[457] It must, however, be in one or more of the following three types: verification of data, obtaining data and presenting data.

The investment in *verifying* the contents refers to the resources used to ensure the reliability of the information, or to monitor the accuracy of the materials collected when the database was created and during its operation. Resources used for verification during the stage of creation of the data (which were subsequently collected in a database) cannot be taken into account to assess whether there was substantial investment.[458]

The investment in *obtaining* the contents of a database only includes the resources used to seek out existing independent materials and collect them in the database. It does not cover the resources used for the creation of materials which make up the contents of a database.[459]

The investment in the *presentation* of the contents of the database concerns, for its part, the resources used for the purpose of giving the database its function of processing information, that is to say those used for the systematic or methodical arrangement of the materials contained in that database and the organisation of their individual accessibility.[460]

Term of protection

4.116   The database right protects the database for 15 years from the end of the calendar year in which the making of the database was completed or, if earlier, 15 years from the end of the calendar year in which the database was first made available to the public. In addition, a new 15-year period will commence if there are any substantial changes made to the contents of a database, including a substantial change resulting from the accumulation of successive additions, deletions or alterations, which would result in the database being considered to be a substantial new investment.[461]

---

456 C-203/02 *British Horseracing Board v William Hill* [2004] ECR I-10415, [2005] RPC 13.
457 Copyright and Rights in Databases Regulations 1997, reg 12(1); Database Directive 96/9, art 7(1).
458 C-203/02 *British Horseracing Board v William Hill* [2004] ECR I-10415, [2005] RPC 13; also see C–46/02 *Fixtures Marketing v Oy Veikkaus Ab* [2004] ECR I-10365, [2005] ECDR 2 at [49].
459 C-203/02 *British Horseracing Board v William Hill* [2004] ECR I-10415, [2005] RPC 13.
460 C-46/02 *Fixtures Marketing v Oy Veikkaus Ab* [2004] ECR I-10365, [2005] ECDR 2 at [37].
461 Copyright and Rights in Databases Regulations 1997, reg 17; C-203/02 *British Horseracing Board v William Hill* [2004] ECR I-10415, [2005] RPC 13.

MORAL RIGHTS AND THE INTERNET

4.117   In addition to economic rights, authors and directors[462] also have moral rights connected to their works.[463] These rights include the right to be attributed as author of a copyright work, the right to object to derogatory treatment of a copyright work and the right not to be falsely attributed as the author of a copyright work. This section considers the first two of these rights: the so-called rights of 'paternity' and of 'integrity'.

The two rights do not apply to computer programs or computer-generated works,[464] so much of the work on the internet is excluded from protection. The rights attach only to literary, artistic, musical and film works. This does not mean that a site on the internet cannot infringe a work's moral rights. What this means is that those who construct web pages, and those that control forums, should be wary of infringing the moral rights in one of the works they are using.

Paternity

4.118   The author of a literary work has the right to be identified as the author of that work whenever it is published commercially, performed in public, communicated to the public or included in copies of a film or sound recording which are issued to the public.[465] The author of an artistic work has the right to be identified as the author of that work whenever the work is published commercially, exhibited in public or communicated to the public.[466] It has been discussed that making a work available on a website will constitute commercial publication; money does not need to change hands.[467]

To rely on the right, an author needs first to assert it.[468] This is achieved in relation to general or specific acts on an assignment of copyright or by an instrument in writing[469] signed by the author.[470] A relevant question for those who

---

462 Performers also get moral rights, in relation to performances given since February 2006, see Part 2 of the Copyright, Designs and Patents Act 1988.

463 The rights do not apply where the work was created by an employee in the course of employment: Copyright, Designs and Patents Act 1988, ss 11(2), 79(3), 82(1)(a).

464 Copyright, Designs and Patents Act 1988, ss 79(2) and 81(2).

465 Copyright, Designs and Patents Act 1988, s 77(1) and (2)(a).

466 Copyright, Designs and Patents Act 1988, s 77(4)(a).

467 See 4.100, above.

468 Copyright, Designs and Patents Act 1988, s 78(1). See *Christoffer v Poseidon Film Distributors* [2000] ECDR 487 per Park J.

469 The term 'writing' is widely defined as including any form of notation or code, whether by hand or otherwise and regardless of the method by which, or the medium on, in or on which, it is recorded: Copyright, Designs and Patents Act 1988, s 178. Cf Law of Property Act 1925, s 40 which is silent on what may constitute 'writing' forcing a court to rely, therefore, on the Interpretation Act 1978, Sch 1. This provides that '[w]riting includes typing, printing, lithography, photography and other modes of representing or reproducing words in a visible form ...'.

470 Copyright, Designs and Patents Act 1988, s 78(2).

see their works commercially published on the internet is, therefore, whether this right can be asserted over the internet. In absence of specific requirements for paper copies or manual signatures, there is no such specific restriction and even an email clearly sent by an individual may potentially prove sufficient provided it can be considered to have been 'signed'.[471] Given the importance of evidence in relation to copyright, whether that be assertion, waivers or assignments, many may be reluctant to take the risks of relying on anything other than traditional manual signatures.

Example 4.23

An individual posts a poem to a forum and ends the email with the words 'This author asserts his right to be identified as the author of this work under the Copyright, Designs and Patents Act 1988'. This is problematic as a valid assertion since, although in writing, it is not clearly signed and could be open to challenge. Subject to copyright infringement, the forum and others using the forum may reproduce his email without reference to his authorship.

Artistic works may have their paternity right asserted simply by being identified on the original or copy of the work in relation to a public exhibition.[472] For this method of assertion it appears likely that the assertion may be made over the internet. Most websites that show artistic works may be considered as public exhibitions and it is easy to include on a digital copy of a work a typed or 'signed' name.

Example 4.24

A website serves as an advertising medium for young artists. One artist posts up on the site a computer-generated graphic that he designed. He includes on the graphic his name and is perturbed when he sees his work republished on a website without payment and without acknowledgment. He may well have a strong case of copyright infringement. He would have a similarly strong case of infringement of his moral rights but there are no moral rights over computer-generated artistic works. A hand-generated work digitised and posted on the internet, in contrast, could be protected by a paternity right.

The right of paternity applies to the whole or any substantial part of the work[473] and it is infringed where the work is commercially published or exhibited without the author's identity being brought to the notice of a viewing person.[474]

---

471 See discussion in **Chapter 2**.
472 Copyright, Designs and Patents Act 1988, s 78(3)(a).
473 Copyright, Designs and Patents Act 1988, s 89(1).
474 Copyright, Designs and Patents Act 1988, s 77(7)(c).

Integrity

4.119   In appropriate circumstances, the author of any literary or musical work has the right not to have the work subjected to derogatory treatment.[475] Similarly, in appropriate circumstances, the author of any artistic work has the right to object to any derogatory treatment of a copyright artistic work in a commercial publication or public exhibition.[476] In comparison to the right of paternity, the right of integrity is far more powerful: it does not need to be asserted, it applies to any part of the work and not merely substantial parts[477] and it has far wider scope for infringement.

A 'treatment' of a work means any addition to, deletion from or alteration to or adaptation of the work. It does not include a translation of a literary work or a transcription of a musical work involving no more than a change of key or register.[478] As should be apparent, this is a very wide definition. It may include the re-colouring of an artistic image to look appropriate on a website with a limited palette.[479] It will also include the reduction in size of an artistic work, or cropping of an artistic work to fit in a particular space on a website. More technically, an artistic work will also be 'treated' where it is converted into a digital format with a lower resolution so that the picture appears more grainy or 'pixelated'.[480] Literary works may be treated by over-zealous editing or 'snipping' as it is termed in conversation threads. Obviously, literary works are also 'treated' when they are blatantly altered.

A treatment is derogatory if it amounts to distortion or mutilation of the work or is otherwise prejudicial to the honour or reputation of the author.[481] The terms 'honour' and 'reputation' should probably be given the same meaning as there are in relation to defamation.[482] However, a distortion appears to have been set at a much lower bar. In *Emma Delves-Broughton v House of Harlot*[483] it was held that change of the background (and some other minor orientation changes) to a photograph was sufficient to be a distortion of the work. Thus, it infringed the right to prevent derogatory treatment even though the court took the view that it did not affect the honour or reputation of the author.

---

475   Copyright, Designs and Patents Act 1988, s 80(1).
476   Copyright, Designs and Patents Act 1988. s 80(4)(a).
477   Copyright, Designs and Patents Act 1988, s 89(2).
478   Copyright, Designs and Patents Act 1988, s 80(2)(a).
479   See the analogous French judgment of *Angelica Houston v Turner Entertainment* [1992] ECC 334.
480   See *Harrison v Harrison* [2010] EWPCC 3, [2010] FSR 25 where it was held to be a treatment where changes were made to a second edition of a book; and *Confetti Records Ltd v Warner Music UK Ltd* [2003] EWHC 1274 (Ch); [2003] EMLR 35 where it was held adding a line to a song was a treatment.
481   Copyright, Designs and Patents Act 1988, s 80(2)(b).
482   Copinger and Skone James, *Copyright* (16th ed, Sweet and Maxwell, 2011) at [11-45].
483   [2012] EWPCC 29.

Waiver of rights

4.120   The uncertainty and scope of moral rights should make every user of another's copyright on the internet think carefully about obtaining a waiver from each contributing author. It is not an infringement of the moral rights if the author waives those rights.[484] Unlike assertions, a waiver does not have to meet any formal requirements and can be in relation to any works for any purposes.[485] The waiver can also be made conditional or unconditional.[486]

Web designers would therefore be wise to obtain such a waiver in respect of any work that they use for a site and internet service providers can also be advised to obtain a waiver on all works submitted by their members. Finally, the terms and conditions for any site should include an express wavier in relation to any posting.

Copyright and database right infringement

4.121   A copyright infringement occurs where one of the acts reserved for the right of the property owner are carried out or authorised by a person without a licence or defence for doing so in relation to the whole or a substantial part of a copyright work. Therefore, if one has the licence to copy a copyright work, one does not infringe it. If one copies only an insubstantial part of a copyright work, one does not infringe the copyright in the work. These two non-infringing methods of copying are particularly relevant. This is because the only way to use the internet involves copying. It is not only unlicensed substantial copying that infringes a copyright; visually presenting a work in public may also infringe the copyright in the work.[487] One also infringes copyright by authorising anyone to perform an act restricted by copyright.[488] In addition the law provides for secondary infringements where one deals in a restricted way with an infringing copy of a work, but secondary infringement is outside the scope of this work.[489]

COPYRIGHT PROHIBITED ACTS

4.122   The acts reserved for copyright owners are set out in s 16(1) of the Copyright Designs and Patents Act 1988 as follows:

'(a) to copy the work;

(b) to issue copies of the work to the public;

---

484 Copyright, Designs and Patents Act 1988, s 87(1).
485 Copyright, Designs and Patents Act 1988, s 87(3)(1).
486 Copyright, Designs and Patents Act 1988, s 87(3)(b).
487 Copyright, Designs and Patents Act 1988, s 19(2)(b).
488 Copyright, Designs and Patents Act 1988, s 16(2).
489 Copyright, Designs and Patents Act 1988, ss 22 to 26.

(ba) to rent or lend the work to the public;

(c) to perform, show or play the work in public;

(d) to communicate the work to the public;

(e) to make an adaptation of the work or do any of the above in relation to an adaptation.'

The traditional English terminology, set out in s 16, must now also be read in light of the EU terminology used in the various copyright directives.

Copying

Technical copying

4.123 Technically, a copy is made each time one views a website, or accesses a forum, or even forwards an email. This is because, unlike the postal system, any material of any form that is sent over the internet or viewed over it is copied. What occurs is that the viewer's computer transmits a request to the server computer to forward a duplicate of some particular material it is storing. This duplicate material is not passed directly to the viewer's computer. It is broken into packets, each with a delivery address, and sent across the internet. It is passed from one computer on the internet to another until all the packets are eventually received at the viewer's computer. In reality, each of these intermediary computers has made a copy of the packet that it received and forwarded.

When the material is finally received by the viewer's computer it is stored in the computer's memory – another copy. This transfer does not physically alter the information held by the server, rather it reproduces in the memory of the viewer's computer the material held by the server. The material on the server remains unchanged. The material now held in the viewer computer's memory is then 'interpreted'[490] or 'executed'.[491] This will allow the viewer to experience the website. However, this is the result of another copy.

Notwithstanding the extensive copies made most are not infringing as there is a specific exception to copyright infringement for making temporary copies.[492] In *PRCA v Newspaper Licensing Agency*[493] the Supreme Court felt[494] that the purpose of this exception was to ensure that websites were treated like books. In other words, a person reading an infringing book online (but not downloading to the hard drive) would not be infringing copyright; in the same way as a person who buys a pirated book would not be infringing copyright when it is taken home to read.

---

490 For pure HTML or XML.
491 For executable code.
492 Copyright, Designs and Patents Act 1988, s 28A.
493 [2013] UKSC 18, [2013] RPC19.
494 Also the Court of Justice did not demur: see C-360/13 *PRCA v Newspaper Licensing Agency* [2015] RPC 13.

Issuing copies to the public

4.124   The issuing of copies of the work to the public is also an infringement. This would probably cover the sending of an email attachment of a digital work. One of the difficulties with the issuing of works to the public, particularly where it is downloaded from a website, is determining whether the website operator is infringing.

A German website operator is providing ebooks on its website for free download. The operator has a licence to distribute these ebooks in Germany, but not elsewhere. A person in Britain downloads the ebook. Is the German website operator responsible? The answer to this is depends on whether the operator is targeting the United Kingdom.

When determining whether a website operator is targeting a work to the public a number of factors should be considered such as: the language of the website, the content and distribution channels of the advertising materials and where deliveries are made (particularly of tangible goods).[495] The rules which apply when something is targeted as part of a communication to the public would likewise apply to the issuing of copies to the public.

Finally, it appears that the right to prevent the issuing of copies to the public includes a right to prohibit advertisements being targeted to the United Kingdom of the original or a copy of that work even where the advertisement does not lead to the purchase of the work by any British buyer.[496]

Renting or lending to the public

4.125   This rights in relation to rental and lending of literary, dramatic, musical and artistic works and the requirement for the return of the work means that it is less likely to be of relevance in the context of internet infringements. For example, where music or other infringing copies are made available, even where there are conditions on, say, the amount of time for which it may be viewed, there will not be an expectation of a return of the file, it will simply be deleted and duplicate copies used elsewhere.[497]

Performing, showing or playing in public

4.126   The right of public performance in the United Kingdom applies to literary, dramatic or musical works only but encompasses any mode of visual or acoustic presentation of such a work (including broadcasts or sound recordings). In addition, the section makes the showing or playing of a broadcast, film or

---

495   C-5/11 *Donner* [2012] ECDR 18; also see C-98/13 *Blomqvist* [2014] ECDR 10.
496   C-516/13 *Dimensione Direct Sales* [2015] ECDR 12.
497   On issues of libraries, digitisation of works, availability to the public on terminals and also whether the public may download or upload from there to USBs, see C Morgan, 'On the Digitisation of Knowledge: Copyright in the Light of *Technische Universitat Darmstadt v Eugen Ulmer KG*' (2015) 37 EIPR 107.

sound recording a separate act of infringement. The showing of an image on a monitor is only a public performance where the monitor is in a public place and viewed by the public, such as in a bar or club. It would not cover an individual seeing it on a monitor at home.[498] Accordingly, it is of limited relevance to the conventional internet context.

Communication to the public

4.127 The exclusive right which is most relevant to the internet is the communication to the public right. This covers both traditional broadcasts, but also 'making available of the work by electronic transmission in such a way that members of the public may access it from a place and at a time individually chosen by them.'[499] This right, particularly in terms of broadcasting, presents difficult questions as to what constitutes the public.[500] However, whether the reception of a broadcast is by the public or not is rarely relevant to the internet (unless the screen were in a public place and displayed) and so it will not be explored here. In relation to works, other than broadcasts,[501] the right is completely harmonised across the EU and so there is only one EU standard which applies.[502]

In relation to the internet, there are two key questions. The first is whether the work is targeted at a particular public and the second is whether it is being communicated to a 'new' public. In *EMI v BSB*[503] the factors from C-585/08 *Pammer and Hotel Alpenhof*[504] were applied to determine whether an internet site was targeted at the United Kingdom. The *EMI* claimants relied upon the following as indicating that the communication to the public was targeted at the UK: a large number of users in the UK; a substantial proportion of the visitors to the websites were from the UK;, the recordings listed on each websites include large numbers of both recordings by UK artists and recordings that are in demand in the UK; the default language of the websites was English; and prices were being displayed in sterling. The Court agreed that this was sufficient to show that there had been targeting.

The second key question is whether a communication has been received by a 'new' public. This concept is explained easily in relation to hyperlinks. In

---

498 However, the boundary between public performances and communications to the public appears to have blurred a little: *FA Premier League v QC Leisure* [2012] EWCA Civ 1708, [2013] FSR 20.
499 Copyright, Designs and Patents Act 1988, s 20.
500 It also varies its meaning between Directives: see C-89/04 *Mediakabel* [2005] ECR I-4891, C-306/05 *SGAE v Raphel Hotels* [2006] ECR I-11519, [2007] ECDR 2; C-135/10 SCF [2012] ECDR 16; C-162/10 *Phonographic Performance (Ireland) Ltd v Ireland* [2011] ECDR 22 (AG), [2012] ECDR 15 (Court); C-403/08 *Premier League* [2012] FSR 1; C- 351/12 *OSA* [2014] ECDR 5 (AG) and 25 (Court).
501 In relation to broadcasts, Member States may grant a higher standard of protection: C-279/13 C-More Entertainment *v Sanberg* [2015] ECDR 15.
502 C-466/12 *Svennson* [2014] ECDR 9. Thus, Member States cannot give more (or less) protection than provided by the Directive.
503 [2013] EWHC 379 (Ch).
504 [2010] ECR I-12527 at para 93.

C-466/12 *Svennson*[505] the Court of Justice explained that a person who provides a hyperlink on a webpage is making a communication to the public of the web. The question was whether a third person using the hyperlink was communicating the wok to a new public or the same public as before.

Example 4.25

Sunny Website provides a webpage which sets out a news story about a popular celebrity. The website has no access controls and so anyone can access it – its public is the whole world. Star Website provides a hyperlink to Sunny Websites news story. Star Website is communicating that news story to the public, but it is the same public to whom the original communication was made. It is therefore not restricted by copyright.

This rule also means that where a person 'frames' another freely available website within their own website, this is not an infringement of the communication to the public right.[506] This is because the framed content is already available to the public on the first website and the fact that you provide the same content within your own website does not amount to it being communicated to any *new* public.[507]

Making or acts in relation to an adaptation

4.128 The right of adaption applies to literary, dramatic and musical works only. In relation to computer programs, an adaptation includes an arrangement or altered version of the program or a translation of it and its translation a conversion into or out of computer language or code into a different computer language or code.[508]

DATABASE INFRINGEMENT

4.129 A person infringes database right if, without the consent of the owner of the right, he or she extracts or re-utilises all or a substantial part of the contents of the database.[509] Whether something is a substantial taking can be judged quantitatively or qualitatively or a combination of both[510] and should be judged against the entirety of the database.[511] However, the repeated taking of an

505 [2014] ECDR 9.
506 C-348/13 *Bestwater* (20 October 2014).
507 There is a pending reference: C-160/15 GS Media (7 April 2015) which asks what happens where a hyperlink is used to a website which is not available to the public already (ie closed).
508 Section 50C of the Act prevents standard, lawful use of software being an automatic infringement as considered in 4.147; there is also a defence in relation to decompilation: s 50B.
509 Copyright and Rights in Databases Regulations 1997, reg 16(1).
510 Copyright and Rights in Databases Regulations 1997, reg 12.
511 C-203/02 *British Horseracing Board v William Hill* [2004] ECR I-10415, [2005] RPC 13.

insubstantial part so that the total taken becomes a substantial part is sufficient to create liability.[512]

Extraction

4.130   The word 'extracts' means the permanent or temporary transfer of those contents to another medium by any means or in any form.[513] In general, the on screen display of the contents of a database should be taken to require the authorisation of the database right owner.[514] However, the mere consultation of a database is not an extraction[515] and for these purposes a consultation is where the person accessing the information has interest in that information himself or herself[516] (and not an interest in providing to any third party). The extraction will usually mean the transfer of data[517] whether it is temporary or permanent.[518]

Re-utilisation

4.131   Extracted data can therefore be contrasted with 're-utilised' data which means making the database contents available to the public by any means.[519]

Where a database is made available on-line, it is necessary to be able to localise where the infringements are taking place – that is in which EU Member State. There are likely to be many acts involved in the reuse of the database which will range from placing of the database on the website, to making it available to members of the public, to the actual transmission of data to members of the public in response to a request. The mere act of putting the database on a website is not, in itself, sufficient to infringe the re-utilisation right.[520]

In C-173/11 *Football Dataco v Sportradar*[521] the Court of Justice indicated that where a transmission takes place across national borders it is necessary to see whether the intention was to target a particular Member State. This intention may be gathered from evidence that: (a) the database is potentially of interest to persons in the recipient territory; (b) the right of access to the website is regulated by a contract which shows that the operator of the website service must have been aware of the specific destination of the data (particularly where any contractual payment takes account of such users); and (c) the language used shows an intention to target users in the recipient territory.[522]

As to what must be re-utilised it is necessary to show that the investment has been taken. In C-202/12 *Innoweb v Wegener* the Court of Justice considered

---

512 Copyright and Rights in Databases Regulations 1997, reg 16(2).
513 Copyright and Rights in Databases Regulations 1997, reg 12.
514 Database Directive 96/9, recital (44).
515 C-203/02 *British Horseracing Board v William Hill* [2004] ECR I-10415, [2005] RPC 13.
516 C-202/12 *Innoweb v Wegener* [2014] Bus LR 308 at [47].
517 C-304/07 *Directmedia Publishing v Albert-Ludwigs* [2008] ECR I-7565, [2009] RPC 10.
518 C-545/07 *Apis-Hristovich EOOD v Lakorda* [2009] ECDR 13.
519 Copyright and Rights in Databases Regulations 1997, reg 12(1).
520 C-173/11 *Football Dataco v Sportradar* [2013] FSR 4.
521 [2013] FSR 4.
522 It is likely that similar factors to those for communicating a copyright work to the public will be relevant.

re-utilisation in the context of meta-search engines. A meta-search engine is designed to use search engines on other sites and transfers queries from it to those other search engines (unlike search engines such as Google). The Court concluded that it was an impermissible re-utilisation. Essentially this was because the original websites would lose revenue from the database being interrogated by the meta-search engine without the original websites advertisements being displayed.[523] This is turn would reduce the money available to invest in the original database and so make it less extensive.[524] Indeed, the court said such search engines came close to manufacturing a competing product.[525]

Finally, a lawful user of a database which has been made available to the public in any manner is entitled to extract or re-utilise insubstantial parts of the contents of the database for any purpose.[526]

A substantial part

4.132 To infringe a copyright work by copying it one must not only have no licence to copy the work, but also the copy must be of a substantial part of the claimant's work.[527] The test of whether a taking is substantial is now a matter of EU law[528] and originates from C-5/08 *Infopaq*.[529] Accordingly for a taking to be substantial the parts taken must contain elements which are the expression of the intellectual creation of the work.[530] Thus, it is important to look not at how much of the defendant's work is made up of material taken from the claimants, but whether the work taken is sufficient to reach the threshold. This adoption of this new EU test means that much of the older English case law now has to be read with caution. In contrast to many types of comparison, for the purposes of assessing whether there has been a substantial taking of computer software, the court may require expert evidence to determine how much was actually taken.[531]

Defences

4.133 Even if it can be established that a particular activity is an infringement of copyright, there are a large number of exceptions to infringement and other defences. However, only those exceptions to infringement which are particularly

523 C-202/12 *Innoweb v Wegener* [2014] Bus LR 308 at [41].
524 C-202/12 *Innoweb v Wegener* [2014] Bus LR 308 at [43].
525 C-202/12 *Innoweb v Wegener* [2014] Bus LR 308 at [48] referring to Database Directive 96/9, recital (42).
526 Copyright and Rights in Databases Regulations 1997. reg 19(1).
527 Copyright, Designs and Patents Act 1988, s 16(3)(a).
528 See *SAS Institute v World Programming* [2013] EWCA Civ 1482, [2014] RPC 8 at [38].
529 [2009] ECR I-6569, [2010] FSR 20.
530 C-5/08 *Infopaq* [2009] ECR I-6569, [2010] FSR 20 at [39].
531 *Ibcos Computers Ltd v Barclays Mercantile Highland Finance Ltd* [1994] FSR 275 at 301.

relevant to the internet will be examined here and those seeking to consider other exceptions (including, private study and research, reporting current affairs, criticism and review and so forth) should consult a specialist text.[532]

Licences

4.134 It will be recalled that it is not an infringement to copy the whole or a substantial part of a copyright work with licence from the copyright owner.[533] A licence does not need to take any particular form and an implied licence may be inferred by the courts from the circumstances in which the copyright work or part of it is transferred.[534] However, caution should be employed when seeking to rely on an implied licence[535] and it is always more prudent to rely on an express written licence rather than an implied one.

Temporary copies

4.135 There is a copyright exception[536] for making temporary copies of works which are transient or incidental and an integral and essential part of a technological process. The defence has five elements: (a) the act is temporary; (b) it is transient or incidental; (c) it is an integral and essential part of a technological process; (d) the sole purpose of that process is to enable a transmission in a network between third parties by an intermediary of a lawful use of a work or protected subject-matter; and (e) the act has no independent economic significance.[537]

When determining whether something is an integral and essential part of a technological process it is necessary to decide whether the temporary acts of reproduction to be carried out entirely in the context of the implementation of the technological process and, therefore, not to be carried out, fully or partially, outside of such a process.[538] Furthermore, the technological process must not be able to function correctly and efficiently without the acts of reproduction concerned.[539] Finally, to have an independent economic significance the economic advantage derived from the implementation of the technological measures must not be either distinct or separable from the economic advantage derived from the lawful use of the work concerned and it must not generate an additional

---

532 For example, Copinger and Skone James, *Copyright* (16th Ed, Sweet and Maxwell 2011).
533 Copyright, Designs and Patents Act 1988, s 16(2).
534 *Springfield v Thame* (1903) 89 LT 242; *Hall-Brown v Iliffe & Sons Ltd* (1928–35) Macq Cop Cas 88; *Blair v Osbourne & Tomkins* [1971] 2 QB 78; *Solar Thomson Engineering Co Ltd v Barton* [1977] RPC 537 at 560 to 561; *Roberts v Candiware* [1980] FSR 352; *Anvil Jewellery Ltd v Riva Ridge Holdings Ltd* (1985–87) 8 IPR 161.
535 Note that in *VLM Holdings Limited v Ravensworth Digital Services Limited* [2013] EWHC 228 (Ch), the court held that a software sub-licence survived termination of the head licence under which it had been granted.
536 Copyright, Designs and Patents Act 1988, s 28A.
537 C-5/08 *Infopaq v Danske Dagblades Forening* [2009] ECR I-6569, [2010] FSR 20 at [54].
538 C-302/10 *Infopaq v Danske Dagblades Forening* ('Infopaq II') (17 January 2012) at [30].
539 C-302/10 *Infopaq v Danske Dagblades Forening* ('Infopaq II') (17 January 2012) at [37].

economic advantage going beyond that derived from that use of the protected work.[540]

While it is clear that the display on the screen of material from the internet is temporary and falls under this exception,[541] it has also been confirmed that copies made in an end users internet cache[542] is covered by the exception as well[543] (even where the cache may not be cleared for some time).

Text and data analysis

4.136 The internet provides access to massive amounts of data and textual information. The easy availability of this data makes certain sorts of research possible which were not previously feasible (so called 'big data' research). This has led to the introduction of a new research exception for the purposes of analysing this sort of data. This exception[544] permits this sort of analysis where it involves making a copy of a work by a person who has lawful access to the work does not infringe copyright in the work provided that the copy is made in order that a person who has lawful access to the work may carry out a computational analysis of anything recorded in the work for the sole purpose of research for a non-commercial purpose and there is sufficient acknowledgement. This defence is likely to be of use for academics, but as it is restricted to non-commercial uses it is unlikely to be of wider assistance.

Caricature, parody or pastiche

4.137 The use of social media, and the provision and accessibility of movie editing and other software, has led to a wide range of parodies being produced and disseminated on the internet. Sometimes these go 'viral' and will be seen by millions of people. There is an exception that provides fair dealing with a work for the purposes of caricature, parody or pastiche does not infringe copyright in the work; and this exception cannot be excluded by contract.[545] In C-201/13 *Deckmyn*[546] the Court of Justice indicated that the essential characteristics of parody, are, first, to evoke an existing work, while being noticeably different from it, and secondly, to constitute an expression of humour or mockery.[547] In addition, it is necessary to show that the parody does not conflict with a normal exploitation of the work and does not unreasonably prejudice the legitimate interests of the copyright owner.[548]

---

540 C-302/10 *Infopaq v Danske Dagblades Forening* ('Infopaq II') (17 January 2012) at [50].
541 *PRCA v Newspaper Licensing Agency Ltd* [2013] UKSC 18, [2013] RPC 19 at [2].
542 The internet cache stores material locally on hard drives to make browsing easier. It does not clear automatically and is usually overwritten as it fills.
543 C-360/13 *PRCA v Newspaper Licensing Agency* [2015] RPC 13.
544 Copyright, Designs and Patents Act 1988, s 29A.
545 Copyright, Designs and Patents Act 1988, s 30A.
546 [2014] ECDR 21.
547 C-201/13 *Deckmyn* [2014] ECDR 21 at [20].
548 Directive 2001/29/EC, art 5(5).

Back up copies

4.138   Some users believe that a website comes complete with an implied licence to take a backup copy, on disk rather than the normal memory only.[549] Indeed, the 'offline viewing' facility standard with some internet browsers makes it easy to create these copies. There are also useful websites that allow one to make a perfect copy of a website and to hold that copy on its servers. Such conduct is unlikely to be permitted by implied (or express) licences.

There is, however, a copyright exception which allows lawful users of a computer program to not infringe copyright by making a backup copy of it which it is necessary for him or her to have for the purposes of his or her lawful use.[550] But it will rarely be necessary to take a backup copy of a website. In the usual course of things, the code on the website is constantly available and so it will not be necessary to have you own copy. It must be remembered that the content of the website (eg news stories) are not software and so do not fall within the backup right it, is only the software which runs behind website.[551]

Increasingly, however, websites have explicit restrictions on copying in certain situations. Viewers and users of websites should be cautious of these restrictions which may be found in the context of a positive licence. Some prevent viewers from even making a printed copy of a site. Other sites prevent the use of their graphics.[552] These explicit licences are not added on sites as rhetoric. If contravened they will have the result that the viewer has infringed copyright. If this infringement is then 'advertised' by, say, posting a copied graphic on one's own website, the copyright owner may well take action.

Decompilation

4.139   It is not an infringement of copyright for a lawful user of a computer program to decompile it to see how it works. Decomplilation is changing code from a low level language (eg object code – a series of 0s and 1s) to a high level language (such as BASIC or C++).[553] Decompliation is only allowed for the permitted objective that is it is necessary to decompile the program to obtain the information necessary to create an independent program which can be operated with the program decompiled or with another program.[554] Further, the information so obtained is not used for any purpose other than the permitted objective.[555] Finally, it is not permitted to decompile the software where the information necessary to achieve the permitted objective is available (ie the source code has

---

549   A website viewed but not saved will not be available for re-viewing after the computer is switched off and then on again. A website saved to disk will be re-viewable even after the computer has been switched off.

550   Copyright, Designs and Patents Act 1988, s 50A.

551   Some might argue that the display of the content requires it to be part of computer software, but the Court of Justice appears to see a distinction between software and digital content (see the discussion of exhaustion at **4.97**).

552   The popular browsers allow users to copy a graphic to be used as the computer screen's backdrop; even this may be infringement by the viewer.

553   Copyright, Designs and Patents Act 1988, s 50B(1).

554   Copyright, Designs and Patents Act 1988, s 50B(2)(a).

555   Copyright, Designs and Patents Act 1988, s 50B(2)(b).

been published), the acts as are not necessary to achieve the permitted objective, the person supplies the information obtained by the decompiling to any person to whom it is not necessary to supply it in order to achieve the permitted objective or the person uses the information to create a program which is substantially similar in its expression to the program decompiled or to do any act restricted by copyright.[556]

Observing, studying and testing of computer programs

4.140   There is also a further exception which provides that it is not an infringement of copyright for a lawful user of a copy of a computer program to observe, study or test the functioning of the program in order to determine the ideas and principles which underlie any element of the program if he or she does so while performing any of the acts of loading, displaying, running, transmitting or storing the program which he is entitled to do.[557]

In addition, it is not an infringement of copyright for a lawful user of a copy of a computer program to copy it provided that it is necessary for his lawful use and doing so is not prohibited by contract.[558] As a website is a computer program and the only way to 'use' the website is to copy it, it is implied that a lawful viewer of a website and the intermediaries working on behalf of the website owner are entitled to copy it.

Database rights exceptions

4.141   There are certain exceptions to the *sui generis* database right. Most of these relate to public administration,[559] but where a database has been made available to the public in any manner database right is not infringed by fair dealing with a substantial part of its contents if the part is extracted from the database by a person who is a lawful user of the database, and it is extracted for the purpose of illustration for teaching or research and not for any commercial purpose, and the source is indicated.[560] Thus, outside public administration, the defences to database infringement are very limited indeed and, essentially, extend only to teaching and research.

The internet defences

4.142   The Electronic Commerce (EC) Regulations 2002 provides some general partial defences for internet service providers, which also apply to copyright infringement. These defences apply to those acting as mere conduits, those caching and those hosting.

---

556 Copyright, Designs and Patents Act 1988, s 50B(3).
557 Copyright, Designs and Patents Act 1988, s 50BA.
558 Copyright, Designs and Patents Act 1988, s 50C.
559 Copyright and Rights in Databases Regulations 1997, reg 20(2) and Sch 1.
560 Copyright and Rights in Databases Regulations 1997, reg 20(1).

Mere conduit

4.143   The internet is made up of many servers, computers and electronic communications providers transmitting material over which they have very little control. Therefore, there is a defence for an internet service provider where they are a mere conduit for other people's (infringing) data. Accordingly, an internet service provider is not liable for damages, other pecuniary remedies or criminal sanctions where as the result of a transmission where they did not initiate the transmission, and did not select the receiver of the transmission and did not select or modify the information contained in the transmission. In other words, they are a mere conduit.[561] This is clarified further by it being stated that the transmission includes the automatic, intermediate and transient storage of the information and this takes place for the sole purpose of carrying out the transmission in the communication network, and the information is not stored for any period longer than is reasonably necessary for the transmission.[562] In contrast to the other internet immunities, it does not end with actual knowledge of the infringement. However, an injunction can be granted to prevent infringement (see the discussion of blocking injunctions at **4.170**).

Caching

4.144   A web cache is a computer with vast storage capacity which holds copies of the most popular pages on the internet. If this cache is located on the local network, users can be saved the delay of gaining access to the over-burdened site. It also means that the network can restrict access to the internet, thus reducing the risk from hacking and viruses.

Commercially, a web cache may be unwelcome for a website owner, few companies publish on the web out of charity; they wish to advertise, to sell to and to find the demographics of those who visit their site. A web cache may hide this information from companies. Companies whose sites are cached may be unable to establish exactly how many people are 'hitting' their site, and also they cannot find out who makes up their audience. These statistics are an attractive aspect of the internet and are relevant for selling advertising.

In addition to the specific copyright defence, there is also a defence under the Electronic Commerce (EC) Regulations 2002[563] which provides that the intermediary is not liable for damages or for any other pecuniary remedy or for any criminal sanction as a result of the storage and subsequent transmission of a cache. It remains, however, possible for a person to get an injunction even where a person acts within the exception. There are five conditions.

First condition: nature of activity

4.145   This defence applies where the copyright work in question is both the subject of automatic, intermediate and temporary storage and where that storage is for the sole purpose of making more efficient onward transmission of the work

---

561   Electronic Commerce (EC Directive) Regulations 2002, reg 17(1).
562   Electronic Commerce (EC Directive) Regulations 2002, reg 17(2).
563   Electronic Commerce (EC Directive) Regulations 2002, reg 18.

to other recipients of the service upon their request.[564] In essence, therefore, the storage of the copyright work must not be an end in itself; the work must be stored automatically to transmit it to others.

Example 4.26

ForeverThere.com spots a gap in market for search engines. It realises that other search engines' index of websites become inaccurate in a matter of weeks because websites continually update the web addresses on which they store pages. This leads to 'broken links' where an individual is unable to relocate the page indexed by the search engine. As a strategy, ForeverThere.com takes full copies of websites as it indexes them to allow its users to locate the information requested, even if the website moves the page in question. This may be automatic and intermediate but it is not temporary; ForeverThere. com may not be able to rely upon the caching defence.

Second condition: proper use

4.146   This second condition is that the service provision must be a proper use. This includes a number of requirements. First, the service provider must not modify the 'information'.[565] The second is the service provider must comply with conditions on access to the information.[566] An example of second requirement would be where a password is required to access the copyright work and the web cache stores a copy of the pages beyond the password point; as a result this website would allow those without passwords to access the copyright work. Such a tactic would bring the intermediary outside the scope of the defence.

Third condition: service provider must comply with any rules regarding the updating of the information

4.147   The third requirement is service provider must comply with any rules regarding the updating of the information, specified in a manner widely recognised and used by industry.[567] Some websites include 'objects' which cannot be cached as they are defined as 'PRAGMA:No Cache' or must be dynamically retrieved each time they are accessed, say, from a database. If a web cache were to circumvent these well-known strategies, it would, again, lose the benefit of the defence.

Fourth condition: service provider does not interfere with the lawful use of technology

4.148   The fourth requirement is that the service provider does not interfere with the lawful use of technology, widely recognised and used by industry, to obtain data on the use of the information.[568] Again, certain websites are concerned

---

564 Electronic Commerce (EC Directive) Regulations 2002, reg 18(a).
565 Electronic Commerce (EC Directive) Regulations 2002, reg 18(b)(i).
566 Electronic Commerce (EC Directive) Regulations 2002, reg 18(b)(ii).
567 Electronic Commerce (EC Directive) Regulations 2002, reg 18(b)(iii).
568 Electronic Commerce (EC Directive) Regulations 2002, reg 18(b)(iv).

with the number of visits that they receive. There are certain ways of allowing the majority of one's website to be cached but ensure that a small element is required to be accessed from the original site. This allows the website to be cached but still to be able to know how many visits there have been to the site. Interference with this important data will be enough to prevent the cacher from relying on the defence.

Fifth condition: service provider must act expeditiously on obtaining actual knowledge

4.149   The final condition to permit legal temporary copying is that the service provider must act expeditiously to remove or to disable access to the copyright work he has stored upon obtaining actual knowledge of the fact that the information at the initial source of the transmission has been removed from the network, or access to it has been disabled, or that a court or an administrative authority has ordered such removal or disablement.[569] Whether a service provider has actual knowledge is discussed below in relation to hosting.

Hosting defence

4.150   The final defence is the hosting defence. It is intended to ensure that the service provider who has not played an active role such as to give it knowledge or control over the data is immune from liability.[570] Depending on the circumstances the defence can apply to both search engines (such as Google[571]) as well as online marketplaces (such as eBay[572]).

Essentially, the hosting defence provides immunity from damages, pecuniary remedies and criminal sanctions and extends to services consisting of the storage of information provided by a recipient of the service and the service provider does not have actual knowledge of unlawful activity or information and, where a claim for damages is made, is not aware of facts or circumstances from which it would have been apparent to the service provider that the activity or information was unlawful or upon obtaining such knowledge or awareness, acts expeditiously to remove or to disable access to the information, and the recipient of the service was not acting under the authority or the control of the service provider.[573]

Neutrality

4.151   What is important for determining whether the hosting defence is available is the need for neutrality.[574] Neutrality means that the hosting service is technical, automatic and passive and points to a lack of knowledge or control of the data. Where the host is involved in the process it becomes active and ceases to be neutral. The best guide to whether a host is involved (and so active)

---

569   Electronic Commerce (EC Directive) Regulations 2002, reg 18(b)(v).
570   C-236/08 to C-238/08 *Google France* [2010] ECR I-2417, [2010] RPC 19 at [114 and 120].
571   C-236/08 to C-238/08 *Google France* [2010] ECR I-2417, [2010] RPC 19 at [120].
572   C-324/09 *L'Oreal v eBay* [2011] RPC 27 at [110 and 111].
573   Electronic Commerce (EC Directive) Regulations 2002, reg 19.
574   C-236/08 to C-238/08 *Google France* [2010] ECR I-2417, [2010] RPC 19 at [113] and [114].

is C-324/09 *L'Oreal v eBay*.[575] In that case, the court indicated that a website operator who has provided assistance which entails, in particular, optimising the presentation of the offers for sale of goods or promoting those offers, is playing an active role (and so is not neutral).[576] Once that neutrality is lost the service provider has knowledge and thus cannot rely on the hosting defence.

Knowledge and notifications

4.152   Where the hosting service does not play an active role, it may still have knowledge where it uncovers, as the result of an investigation undertaken on its own initiative, an illegal activity or illegal information, or where it is notified of the existence of such an activity or such information.[577] Where it is notified, the court should consider whether it was sent through the proper channel, the extent to which it includes the full name and address of the sender, details of the location of the information in question and the details of the unlawful nature of the activity or information in question.[578] Further, a notification must be sufficiently precise and adequately substantiated to give rise to the necessary knowledge. The question is whether the "diligent" person should have identified the illegality from the information they had.[579] The requirement that the notice be precise and adequately substantiated means it must be more than simply a bold assertion of infringement. It must enable the service provider to consider the validity of the claim and any possible defences.[580]

No monitoring

4.153   Article 15(1) from the Electronic Commerce Directive[581] states that:

> 'Member States shall not impose a general obligation on providers, when providing the services covered by [the] Articles [concerning mere conduit, caching and hosting], to monitor information which they transmit or store, nor a general obligation actively to seek facts or circumstances indicating illegal activity.'

This article is not explicitly implemented in the Electronic Commerce (EC) Regulations 2002 as it is not usual practice to legislate not to regulate. Nevertheless, it follows that the Regulations do not, in effect, force those who cache or take temporary copies for other justifiable reasons to monitor for changes on the websites they copy from, to be able to benefit from the defence.

---

575 C-324/09 *L'Oreal v eBay* [2011] RPC 27.
576 C-324/09 *L'Oreal v eBay* [2011] RPC 27 at [116].
577 C-324/09 *L'Oreal v eBay* [2011] RPC 27 at [122].
578 Electronic Commerce (EC Directive) Regulations 2002, reg 22.
579 C-324/09 *L'Oreal v eBay* [2011] RPC 27 at [122].
580 *Tamiz v Google Inc Google UK Ltd* [2012] EWHC 449 (QB) at [59] (a libel case) (the issue was not considered on appeal: [2013] EWCA Civ 68).
581 Also see C-275/06 *Promusicae v Telefónica de Espana* [2008] ECR I-271, [2008] ECDR 10.

Contractual restrictions

4.154 Where intellectual property rights fall short, in other words where something is not protected by copyright or database right, the question arises whether or not it is possible to use contractual terms to prevent the use of information. This issue arose in C-30/14 *Ryanair Ltd v PR Aviation BV*[582] which related to an airline price comparison website. The comparison website used data from various airline websites, including Ryanair. It was found that there was neither copyright nor database right in the information taken by the comparison site. However, Ryanair had a contractual condition prohibiting the use of its website or the information for selling flights. The Court of Justice felt that there was nothing in the Database Directive to prohibit national law allowing contractual conditions to be enforced which prohibited the use of the information in the Ryanair database. Thus, it is important to ensure there are robust contractual conditions in place, particularly where it is not clear that intellectual property rights exist in the relevant respect.

Creative Commons licences

4.155 Creative Commons is a project which provides a novel form of licensing structure of particular interest and application on the internet. The aim of the project is to build a layer of reasonable, flexible copyright licensing to exist alongside traditional licensing models. It is widely used by internet content users.

Taking inspiration from the Free Software Foundation's GNU Public Licence, Creative Commons has developed a web application that purports to allow people to dedicate their work to the public domain[583] or retain their copyright while licensing the work for certain uses, encouraging the practice of 'remixing' which involves artists using the past works to create new works.

Like Open Source software, Creative Commons does not mean the removal of intellectual property rights. Both involve the use of licences which still set contractual parameters on the permitted uses of the applicable code or works. Creative Commons provides a set of six key licences which allow the use and distribution of works providing the user abides by certain conditions chosen by the author, with different levels of restriction:

Attribution non-commercial, no derivatives

4.156 Permit others to copy, distribute, display, and perform the work and derivative works based upon it only if they credit the author and the work cannot be changed in any way or used commercially.

---

582 [2015] ECDR 13.
583 Phillip Johnson 'Dedicating copyright to the public domain' (2008) 71 MLR 587.

Attribution non-commercial share alike

4.157   Similar to above but remixing and changes to the work are permitted providing there is a credit to the author and the new work is licensed on identical terms.

Attribution non-commercial

4.158   The same as attribution non-commercial share alike, but without the restriction requiring licensing on identical terms.

Attribution no derivatives

4.159   Permit others to copy, distribute, display and perform only verbatim copies of the work, not derivative works based upon it.

Attribution share alike

4.160   Permit others to distribute and create derivative works only under a licence identical to the licence that governs the work.

Attribution

4.161   Allows others to distribute and create derivative works as long as the author is credited.

The licences are expressed in three ways: (a) 'Human readable commons deed'; (b) 'Lawyer readable legal code'; (c) Machine-readable metadata that can be used to associate creative works with their public domain or licence status so that it is searchable and so that a link can be used to link from the website containing the work to the licence.

Stepping outside the boundaries of such a licence constitutes a potential copyright infringement in the normal way.

COPYRIGHT INFRINGEMENT AND THE INTERNET: EXAMPLES

4.162   In this section we consider some specific infringement scenarios in the context of the internet.

Email

4.163   This section considers what might constitute infringement of the copyright in someone's email or message on social media. It is assumed that there is copyright in the email. When an email is received, it has already been copied; it is copied into the memory and probably the hard disk drive of the receiver's machine. This will be permitted by an implied licence (and, usually, the temporary copying exception) as it is necessary for business efficacy and can be implied by sending it over the internet rather than, say, by post. What is not implied is for an individual (rather than a server because that is likely to be an essential part of a technological process) to forward the message without either an express or implied licence to do so. A good example of this is any email that is headed 'Private & Confidential'.

Example 4.27

Paul sends an email to Robbie. It ends, 'Actually, you should tell Charlotte about this.' Robbie forwards the email to Charlotte who then replies to Paul. Paul is upset that Charlotte read the email, but he has no legal redress in copyright. His endnote was an implied licence that Robbie would not infringe the copyright by copying the whole message to Charlotte. Charlotte also does not infringe Paul's copyright; her licence is implied by the common law.

4.164 By way of licence an internet service provider may legally hold a copy of all its member's emails until they are collected by the member. However, many modern email services now retain the emails for much longer. Internet service providers are advised to alert members to this additional copying and storage by including such a statement in their terms and conditions. This ensures that retaining customer's sent emails is not infringing, but it will not cover the emails sent to its customers as there is no contractual relationship between the senders of the email to the account.

In relation to well-known email services (such as gmail), it is reasonable to assume that people sending an email to such an email account must be aware how the email will be used and so there is an implied licence. Additionally, even where the service is not well know there might be a licence implied by reason of custom and usage – as the storage of email is now so commonplace. Of course, the internet service provider can also usually rely on the hosting defence.

Infringement by social media and forums

4.165 There are two discrete issues concerned with controllers of forum and social media. The first is the issue of what the controller can do with copyright material owned and posted by its members. The second issue is the liability a controller of a forum has in respect of copyright material not owned by its members but nevertheless posted on the forum.

Every message posted by its author to a forum, bulletin board or conversation thread carries with it an implied licence (which can, of course, be expressly revoked). In addition, the hosting defence provides additional buttressing when there is an unwitting infringement. This licence and defence permits the copying of the message on the server itself and also onto any other viewer's computer that is legitimately permitted by the controller to access the email.

Example 4.28

Mr Smith is a contributor to We Love Cats and ends all his postings with 'Not for reposting or redistribution on any other groups.' Ms Jones reposts one of his messages which describes cats being tortured to a forum dealing with animal cruelty. That reposting constitutes an unlicensed copy of the whole of a copyright work; it is an infringement of Mr Smith's copyright.

Human 'requests' to infringe

4.166   When a message is posted to a forum, re-tweeted on Twitter or placed on a Facebook wall, it is placed at the 'request' of a human and the usual rules apply.

Example 4.28

Mr Smith uploads a film he makes of his cat (Ginger Rogers) playing with his dog (Fred Astaire) – onto his Facebook page. Ms Jones copies it and includes it on her page and asks her friends to share it.

Example 4.29

Mr Smith finds an unknown person's mobile phone which includes a film on it of a cat dancing. He also uploads this onto his page. Ms Jones finds it really funny and posts it on her page and asks her friends to 'share' it.

Mr Smith can licence others to use his own picture on Facebook[584] and so, provided it is in accordance with the terms and conditions, Ms Jones can copy it and include it on her own page. However, Mr Smith had no permission to post the cat dancing film (as the copyright owner is the person who directed and produced the film – probably the unknown owner of the phone). So he would have been infringing copyright when he uploaded the material. He also is in no position to grant a licence to anyone else (and so the websites terms and conditions are irrelevant). Accordingly, Ms Jones, even if she believed Mr Smith owned the video, would also be infringing when she placed the cat dancing film on her page. She may also have been authorising other people's infringement when she asked people to share it.

---

584   The current terms and conditions (30 January 2015) of Facebook all Facebook to use the work and allow other people to use your work (clause 2.4).

Server 'response' to infringe

4.167   As soon as Ms Jones clicked the 'send' or 'OK' icon to post Mr Smith's message or film, this message was sent to the page automatically. Many computers were involved in the request. These include: the first internet service provider; possibly a second internet service provider hosting a copy of the forum; all the other internet service providers hosting a copy of the forum and the intermediary servers acting as conduits between the previous three 'families' of server.

We have seen that the posted message or film infringes Mr Smith's copyright. It can also be said with reasonable certainty that each of these computers has copied a substantial part of the work without licence from Mr Smith. However, the hosting defence will provide a defence for the host in respect of any unwitting infringement until they receive a possible complaint from Mr Smith or are otherwise put 'on notice'.

Infringement using peer-to-peer networks

4.168   There was some debate over whether and how peer-to-peer networks infringed copyright.[585] The development of the jurisprudence relating to blocking injunctions (discussed below), has made it clear how these networks might infringe. In *Dramatico Entertainment v British Sky Broadcasting*[586] Arnold J explored the role of the users involved in peer-to-peer networks and whether they infringed. He indicated that the users of the peer-to-peer network infringed by: (a) copying; and (b) communication to the public. The former arises when the user selects a copy on someone else's network and downloads it.[587] The latter arises because the users have made available the recordings online and further that have made it available to a 'new public'.[588] More recent Court of Justice case law[589] might suggest that it is made available to a new public only where more users can access the work after it has entered the downloading user's network than could enter it before.

A copies the song 'If More People Join In'[590] to A's hard drive. All the songs available on A's hard drive are available to everyone else on the peer-to-peer network. B downloads 'If More People Join In' to B's hard drive. It then is available on the P2P network to the same people as A's copy of the song (unless B is part of two networks). It is therefore arguable that B is not communicating it to a 'new' public.

The flaw with this example, however, is that the original communication was not authorised; and it appears that *Dramatico* has been upheld as right following

---

585   See Third Edition of this work.
586   [2012] EWHC 268 (Ch), [2012] RPC 27.
587   *Dramatico Entertainment v British Sky Broadcasting* [2012] EWHC 268 (Ch) , [2012] RPC 27 at [40].
588   *Dramatico Entertainment v British Sky Broadcasting* [2012] EWHC 268 (Ch) , [2012] RPC 27 at [69 and 70].
589   See C-466/12 *Svennson* [2014] ECDR 9.
590   A song from the TV Show Family Guy, episode Friends Without Benefits (Seth MacFarlane).

the developments before the Court of Justice.[591] Accordingly, re-communicating an unauthorised work which has already been made available illegally is infringing notwithstanding the new communication communicates to the same 'public'.

Turning to the operators of the website, they are clearly communicating the work to the public. The issue is whether they target the United Kingdom.[592]

The operators may also be authorising the infringement of the users. For these purposes, authorises means the grant or purported (express or implied) grant of the right to do the act complained of and it does not extend to mere enablement, assistance or even encouragement.[593] In relation to supplying a product or service, such as a peer-to-peer software, Kitchin J stated in *Twentieth Century Fox Film Corporation v Newzbin Ltd*[594] that the relevant circumstances for an authorisation by supply include:

> '...the nature of the relationship between the alleged authoriser and the primary infringer, whether the equipment or other material supplied constitutes the means used to infringe, whether it is inevitable it will be used to infringe, the degree of control which the supplier retains and whether he has taken any steps to prevent infringement. These are matters to be taken into account and may or may not be determinative depending upon all the other circumstances.'

Most cases involving the application of these factors[595] are for blocking injunctions and the cases brought in that context have tended to be sites clearly set up to share copyright works. There has not been any which fall on the borderline. Finally, the web site operator might be a joint tortfeasor with the infringing user.[596] In most cases, a joint tortfeasor will also be authorising the infringement and so it rarely takes the matter further.

Infringement by streaming

4.169 The streaming of film or music is now commonplace. It involves data being copied from a remote server to the local computer. Usually, there will be a cache which holds some of the data in advance of it being played on the local computer. The work being played is not (usually) downloaded to the local computer first and so it differs from peer-to-peer sharing.[597] In this scenario, the

---

591 *Paramount Home Entertainment & Anor v British Sky Broadcasting & Ors* [2014] EWHC 937 (Ch) at [33 and 34].

592 *EMI Records Ltd & Ors v British Sky Broadcasting Ltd & Ors* [2013] EWHC 379 (Ch), [2013] FSR 31 at [40 to 51].

593 *Twentieth Century Fox Film Corporation v Newzbin Ltd* [2010] EWHC 608 (Ch), [2010] FSR 21 at [90].

594 [2010] EWHC 608 (Ch), [2010] FSR 21 at [90].

595 Eg *EMI Records Ltd & Ors v British Sky Broadcasting Ltd & Ors* [2013] EWHC 379 (Ch), [2013] FSR 31 at [52 to 70].

596 The law on joint feasorship was recently considered by the Supreme Court in *Sea Shepherd v Fish & Fish* [2015] UKSC 10.

597 However, to make streaming quicker there are often peer-to-peer connections on the network. This is a different meaning of peer-to-peer however.

person providing the film or music is communicating the work to the public. The only question is whether or not that person is targeting the United Kingdom or not (and if there is no targeting there is no infringement). Further, notwithstanding that a temporary copy is made on the user's computer, the making of this temporary copy in the cache falls under a copyright exemption.[598] Therefore, it appears that the user is not infringing copyright either.

Imagine Minsk TV provides its TV service by streaming. They obtain a licence to show a James Bond film (with Russian subtitles) in Belarus. All the adverts on the stream are targeted at a Belarus audience. Minsk TV is not targeting the UK and so is not communicating to the public the work in the United Kingdom. Peter, who lives in London, watches the stream of the James Bond film, Peter can rely on the copyright exception (s 28A) provided his watching does not have an independent economic significance.

Whether Peter's copy has an independent economic significance depends on whether his use is either distinct or separable from the economic advantage derived from the lawful use of the work concerned.[599] As copyright is territorial, it is arguable that the use of the work in a different (unlicensed) jurisdiction is distinct and separate from the use in the licensed jurisdiction and so Peter watching James Bond would have an independent economic significance. In any event, Minsk TV would not be infringing only Peter would. This would be enough, however, to obtaining a blocking injunction. The outcome would probably be the same even if Minsk TV were not a legitimate television station but a pirate.

Blocking

4.170   The issue of website blocking has been contentious[600] for a number of years.[601] Section 97A of the Copyright, Designs and Patents Act 1988[602] provides

---

598   Copyright, Designs and Patents Act 1988, s 28A; see C-360/13 *PRCA v Newspaper Licensing Agency* [2015] RPC 13; PRCA v Newspaper Licensing Agency Ltd [2013] UKSC 18, [2013] RPC 19.

599   C-302/10 *Infopaq v. Danske Dagblades Forening* ('Infopaq II') (17 January 2012) at [50].

600   In C-314/12 *UPC Telekabel v Constantin Film* [2014] ECDR 12, the Court of Justice held that these sorts of injunctions are compatible with EU law provided: that '(i) the measures taken do not unnecessarily deprive internet users of the possibility of lawfully accessing the information available and (ii) that those measures have the effect of preventing unauthorised access to the protected subject-matter or, at least, of making it difficult to achieve and of seriously discouraging internet users who are using the services of the addressee of that injunction from accessing the subject-matter that has been made available to them in breach of the intellectual property right, that being a matter for the national authorities and courts to establish.'

601   See, for example, P Savola, 'Blocking Injunctions and Website Operators' Liability for Copyright Infringement for User-Generated Links' (2014) 36 EIPR 279. KT O'Sullivan, 'Enforcing Copyright Online: Internet Service Provider Obligations and the European Charter of Fundamental Rights', (2014) 36 EIPR 577. J Smith, A Moir and R Montagon, 'ISPS and Blocking Injunctions: *UPC Telekabel Wien v Constantin Film Verleih GmbH and Wega Filmproduktionsgesellschaft mbH'*, (2014) 36 EIPR 470.

602   The Digital Economy Act 2010, s 17 was to provide a power to grant blocking injunctions (in addition to s 97A). This section was repealed (before it came into force) by the Deregulation Act 2015, s 56.

a right to copyright owners to obtain an injunction to block access to particular websites where copyright is infringed. The case law in this area has developed rapidly in recent years[603] and now there are some settled principles as to when an injunction will be granted. In *EMI Records Ltd & Ors v British Sky Broadcasting Ltd*[604] Arnold J set out the criteria that need to be established to obtain such an order:

> 'In order for this Court to have jurisdiction to make the orders sought by the Claimants, four matters must be established. First, that the Defendants are service providers. Secondly, that users and/or the operators of the Websites infringe copyright. Thirdly, that users and/or the operators of the Websites use the Defendants' services to do that. Fourthly, that the Defendants have actual knowledge of this.'

The second criterion requires it to be shown that the website operator has communication a work to the public in the United Kingdom or that UK users have copied works from the internet. Finally, the order will only be granted where it is proportionate.[605]

JURISDICTION OVER INFRINGEMENT

4.171   Conflict of laws and intellectual property law has an uneasy coexistence. The mismatch became more pronounced as the internet developed. The first question when it comes to conflict of laws is whether or not a court has jurisdiction (or competence) to hear a particular claim. The second is what law that court should apply to the dispute. These difficulties are compounded by the fact that there are a number of issues which are often conflated into one. A court which has jurisdiction over a defendant will not necessarily apply its own law to a dispute.

---

603   See in particular, *Twentieth Century Fox Film Corp v Newbin [2010] EWHC 608 (Ch), [2010] FSR 21; Twentieth Century Fox Film Corp v British Telecommunications plc* [2011] EWHC 1981 (Ch); *Twentieth Century Fox Film Corp v British Telecommunications plc (No 2)* [2011] EWHC 2714 (Ch); *Dramatico Entertainment Ltd v British Sky Broadcasting Ltd* [2012] EWHC 268 (Ch), [2012] RPC 27; Dramatico *Entertainment Ltd v British Sky Broadcasting Ltd (No 2)* [2012] EWHC 1152 (Ch); *EMI Records Ltd v British Sky Broadcasting Ltd* [2013] EWHC 379 (Ch); *Football Association Premier League Ltd v British Sky Broadcasting Ltd* [2013] EWHC 2058 (Ch), [2013] ECDR 14; *Paramount Home Entertainment v British Sky Broadcasting* [2013] EWHC 3479 (Ch); *Cartier International v British Sky Broadcasting* [2014] EWHC 3354 (Ch), [2015] RPC 7; *1967 Ltd v British Sky Broadcasting Ltd* [2014] EWHC 3444 (Ch), [2015] EMLR 8.
604   [2013] EWHC 379 (Ch), at [20].
605   *Golden Eye (International) Ltd v Telefónica UK Ltd* [2012] EWHC 723 (Ch), [2012] RPC 28 at [116 and 117]; this view of proportionality was approved by the Supreme Court in *Rugby Football Union v Viagogo Ltd* [2012] UKSC 55, [2012] 1 WLR 3333 at [45].

Jurisdiction

4.172   There are two sets of rules determining whether a person can be brought before the English courts. The first set of rules applies where the defendant is domiciled in an EU member state, the second set of rules applies in any other case. Even when an English court has jurisdiction over a matter, it does not mean that it must apply English law, instead under the Rome II Regulation[606] in relation to intellectual property it will apply the law of the country from which protection is sought[607] and in relation to passing off the law where the competitive relations are likely to be affected.[608] Thus, an English person being sued for infringing a German trade mark (in Germany) would have German trade mark law applied by the English High Court (albeit this is 'harmonised' within the EU).

Jurisdiction and EU domiciles

4.173   The rules of jurisdiction are, in relation to those domiciled in the EU, governed by the Brussels Regulation (Recast) (No 1215/2012). The purpose of this harmonised regime, was according to Laddie J in *Coin Control Ltd v Suzo International (UK)*[609] 'to replace the differing domestic rules, at least in relation to forum, by a simple set of rigid provisions forcing litigation into the courts of one country and out of the courts of others'.[610]

E-Commerce Directive

4.174   The rules of jurisdiction should not lead to the conclusion that the Electronic Commerce Directive, and its implementing Electronic Commerce (EC Directive) Regulations 2002, addresses questions of private international law. These rules only apply to those service providers which are established within the EU. Second, the Regulations certainly do not determine which country's courts will decide a particular dispute and certainly not which country's law will apply in a given situation. They merely prevent, in particular circumstances, a service provider established in a member state outside the UK being restricted from conducting activities inside the UK which would have been legal in their member state.[611] In any event, these particular rules do not extend to intellectual property issues.[612] The Electronic Commerce Directive and Regulations therefore

606 Regulation 864/2007 on the law applicable to non-contractual obligation.
607 Rome II Regulation, art 8.
608 Rome II Regulation, art 6.
609 [1997] FSR 660.
610 *Coin Control Ltd v Suzo International (UK)* [1997] FSR 660 at 671.
611 Electronic Commerce (EC Directive) Regulations 2002, reg 7.
612 Electronic Commerce (EC Directive) Regulations 2002, reg 4(4)(1) and art 3(3), Annex, first indent.

have absolutely no influence over the jurisdiction and applicable law rules applied to intellectual property disputes.

Basic rules of jurisdiction

4.175   The Brussels Regulation provides simple rules on where a party can sue when 'choosing' between the member states. Article 4 sets out the primary rule: defendants must be sued in the courts of their domicile unless another article derogates from this rule. In the words of Laddie J, 'ie the [claimant] must play away'.[613] Article 4 thus provides the foundation for jurisdiction over a foreign intellectual property infringement, indeed a multiplicity of infringements, to be brought before the UK courts. Additionally, it is possible for parties to agree that a particular court has jurisdiction over a matter.[614] Thus many websites require registered users to consent to the jurisdiction of particular courts. Where this is a business this consent will usually be upheld by the court and the user may find they have consent to jurisdiction in some distant country (usually the US). Where the user is a consumer as the agreement would not be in a form they would be expected to be aware of, a court might hold that the jurisdiction agreement does not bind them. Further, it is possible for a party to submit to the jurisdiction of a foreign court even where it would not otherwise have jurisdiction.[615]

Exclusive jurisdiction

4.176   Article 24(4) of the Brussels Regulation states that proceedings concerning the validity of patents and other registered rights must be determined in the country of registration; accordingly, a determination of the validity of a UK trade mark must take place before the UK courts even if the defendant is domiciled abroad (as copyright is not registered this provision has no effect). This restriction applies whether the claim was started as an infringement claim (and there was a counterclaim for invalidity) or the claim began as one of invalidity.[616] Therefore, where a claim of UK trade market infringement was started on the basis of jurisdiction under art 4 in France, if invalidity becomes an issue then the case must be stayed and transferred back to the UK courts for the issue to be decided. Notwithstanding this rule it is possible to grant interim remedies where jurisdiction would otherwise exist for such a remedy.[617]

613   *Fort Dodge Animal Health Ltd v Akzo Nobel* [1998] FSR 222.
614   Brussels Regulation, art 25.
615   Brussels Regulation, art 26.
616   C-4/03 *GAT v Luk* [2006] ECR I-6509, [2006] FSR 45.
617   C-616/10 *Solvay SA v Honeywell Fluorine Products Europe BV* (12 July 2012) at para 29 and 30.

This distinction is extremely important for trade mark infringements committed over the internet because infringement of registered trade marks may be treated differently to infringement of unregistered trade marks, such as passing off actions.

Infringement of intellectual property rights across Europe

4.177 A person may be sued in matters relating to tort, delict or quasi-delict, in the courts for the place where the harmful event occurred or may occur.[618] For the purposes of jurisdiction, the assessment of where the damage occurred requires only an allegation of damage to be made; it is not necessary to actually prove there was damage (or that an infringement actually occurred).[619] The meaning of 'tort, delict or quasi-delict' has an autonomous EU meaning, namely a matter which seeks to substantiate the liability of the defendant.[620]

The most important question, when considering art 7(2), is determining where 'the harmful event occurred'. The Court of Justice, in Case 21/76 *Handelskwekerij GJ Bier BV v Mines de Potasse D'Alsace SA*[621] made it clear that this covers both the place where the event giving rise to the damage occurred and the place where the damage itself occurred or may occur, so giving the claimant a choice between the two forums. The Court of Justice re-affirmed this approach in C-68/93 *Shevill v Presse Alliance SA*[622] a defamation case. It went further by holding that where jurisdiction is based on damage within the jurisdiction, the court could only hear those parts of the matter that relate to that damage.[623] Thus, a claimant has two choices, he or she can rely on art 7(2) and sue separately in each Member State where damage was suffered, or he or she can sue in the defendant's domicile and recover for all the damage caused by the tort.

When considering jurisdiction, the court must actually examine where the damage actually took place to determine whether it is within the jurisdiction.[624] For the purposes of an intellectual property right, the harm can only occur where the right is registered (or protected) and so in relation to a claim of infringement

---

618 Brussels Regulation, art 7(2).
619 C-170/12 *Pinckney v KDG Mediatech AG* [2014] FSR 18 at para 43.
620 C-189/87 *Kalfelis v Bankhaus Schroder, Munchmeyer, Hengst & Co* [1988] ECR 5565 at para 17 and 18.
621 [1976] ECR 1735.
622 C-68/93 *Shevill v Presse Alliance SA* [1995] ECR I-415.
623 C-68/93 *Shevill v Presse Alliance SA* [1995] ECR I-415 at para 33; in C-509/09 *eDate Advertising and Martinez* [2011] ECR I-10269 an additional ground of jurisdiction was found to exist for the 'centre of a person's interests'. However, this appears to be confined to personality rights cases.
624 C-228/11 *Melzer v MF Global UK Ltd* [2013] QB 1112, [2013] 3 WLR 883.

of a French trade mark, the only harm that can occur is in France.[625] For these purposes, it is enough that an allegation of infringement is made, even if at the time the allegation was made the intellectual property right has not yet been infringed; provided the harmful event may occur there.[626] Thus, where the infringement was caused in another jurisdiction where the particular defendant did not act, jurisdiction cannot be asserted.[627] Indeed, the Court of Justice has acknowledged that a declaration that something is not a tort (eg a declaration of non-infringement) is sufficient to found jurisdiction for the purposes of art 7(2).[628] Thus, a court has jurisdiction over a trade mark or copyright claim where either the trade mark (or copyright) has (allegedly) been infringed or there is a threat that it might be infringed in the jurisdiction.

Jurisdiction over intellectual property and non-EC domiciles

4.178 The English traditional rules of jurisdiction, which apply where a defendant is not domiciled in the EU, permit jurisdiction over a defendant where they are served with process within the jurisdiction. Where a person cannot legally be served, a court has no jurisdiction over them.[629] In certain circumstances, the English courts also permit process to be served outside the jurisdiction,[630] which is equivalent to granting additional special grounds of jurisdiction. Such service is permitted in particular where the tort is committed, or damage is sustained, within the jurisdiction.[631]

The English courts are also willing to accept jurisdiction over a dispute where the parties have agreed that the court should have exclusive jurisdiction. Further flexibility is provided by the possibility of parties submitting to the jurisdiction. The courts have made it clear that this willingness extends to intellectual property litigation.[632] Despite having personal jurisdiction over a case the traditional rules include some subject-matter restrictions. Before the Supreme Court's decision in *Lucasfilm v Ainsworth*[633] there was some conflicting authority over whether or not an English court has subject matter jurisdiction over a foreign intellectual property case. The Supreme Court ruled that it had such jurisdiction over a copyright case and, in principle, there is no reason this should not apply to other intellectual property rights.

---

625 C-523/10 *Products 4U Sondermaschinenbau GmbH* [2013] Bus LR 150 at para 25 and 28; C-170/12 *Pinckney v KDG Mediatech AG* [2014] FSR 18.
626 C-170/12 *Pinckney v KDG Mediatech AG* [2014] FSR 18.
627 C-387/12 *Hi Hotel HCF SARL v Uwe Spoering* [2014] 1 WLR 1912 at para 40.
628 C-133/11 *Folien Fischer AG v Ritrama SpA* [2013] QB 523 at para 55.
629 Although, English courts now allow what is called substituted service at an address for service: see CPR 6.8; Companies Act 2006, s 1139.
630 These grounds are set out in CPR, PD6B, para 3.1.
631 CPR, PD6B, para 3.1(9); this provision is intended to mirror that in the Brussels Regulation.
632 *Celltech R&D Ltd v Medimmune Inc* [2004] EWCA Civ 1331, [2005] FSR 21.
633 [2011] UKSC 39, [2011] FSR 41.

COPYRIGHT, DIGITAL AGENDA FOR ECONOMY AND EU SINGLE MARKET DEVELOPMENTS

4.179   There are both national developments and EU developments which will impact both the commercialisation and use of copyright as well as infringement and misuse issues.

The Commission has announced the Digital Single Market Strategy for the EU on 6 May 2015.[634] This will introduce cross-border rules for consumers and businesses in e-commerce. This is partly to ensure that barriers do not arise (or continue) which includes copyright barriers to cross-border trade and commerce. The Commission states that it will make a modification covering:

(i)   harmonised EU rules for online purchases of digital content; and

(ii) the application of the trader's national law with a focused set of key mandatory EU contractual rights for domestic and cross-border online sales of tangible goods.

Geo-blocking is also viewed as concern to the single market. Therefore, the Commission will make proposals to end unjustified geo-blocking.

Copyright purchase, sale and use can sometimes be treated differently across Member States, and when purchased in one Member State but intended to be used in another Member State. The Commission states that it:

> 'will make legislative proposals … to reduce the differences between national copyright regimes and allow for wider online access to works by users across the EU, including through further harmonisation measures. The proposals will include: (i) full portability of legally acquired content, (ii) uninhibited access to legally paid for cross-border online services while safeguarding the value of rights in the audiovisual sector, (iii) greater legal certainty for the cross-border use of content for specific purposes (eg research, education, text and data mining) through harmonised exceptions, and (iv) launching a process to modernise the cross-border enforcement of copy right, initially focusing on commercial-scale infringements and the "follow the money" approach'.

VAT AND EBOOKS

4.180   Electronic books have become somewhat contentious in terms of tax as well as location issues and tax generally.

In Cases C-479/13 and C-502/13 *Commission v France and Commission v Luxembourg*,[635] the Court of Justice has supported the EU Commission argument that France and Luxembourg breached the VAT Directive by applying a reduced rate of VAT to ebooks.

---

634 Communication from the Commission to the European Parliament, the Council, the European Economic and Social Committee and the Committee of the Regions, A Digital Single Market Strategy for Europe, 6.5.2015 COM (2015) 192 final.
635 [2015] STC 1714.

The Court of Justice said that a reduced rate of VAT can apply only to supplies of goods and services covered by Annex III of the VAT Directive. That refers in particular to the 'supply of books … on all physical means of support'. The Court concludes that the reduced rate of VAT is applicable to a transaction consisting of the supply of a book found on a physical medium, but not the supply of ebooks.

The VAT Directive excludes any possibility of a reduced VAT rate being applied to 'electronically supplied services' and the Court held that the supply of electronic books is such a service.

CHAPTER FIVE

Crime

'It is easy to run a secure computer system. You merely have to disconnect all
... connections and permit only direct-wired terminals, put the machine and its
terminals in a shielded room, and post a guard at the door.'

Grampp FT and Morris RH, *AT&T Bell Laboratories Technical Journal*[1]

5.1   From the press coverage, one imagines the internet as a breeding
ground for international crime and new ominous sounding 'cybercrimes'
which threaten to steal our identities, assets and children's confidence. A
report from the House of Lords Science and Technology Select Committee
warned that the internet has become a 'criminals' playground'. The Report
criticised the government for exposing the public to the risks and security
threats of a 'wild west' internet.[2] This all suggests that the internet is inherently
insecure and that new and special technical crimes are being perpetrated on a
regular basis. In fact, the overwhelming number of crimes committed via the
internet are traditional crimes. They are now simply being facilitated through
another medium. This is not to diminish the impact internet crimes may have,
however. Figures published by the campaign awareness group Get Safe Online
(a government-sponsored initiative) indicated that 12% of UK internet users
(around 3.5 million people) were victims of online fraud in the previous year.
Each attack, they stated, costs an average of £875, totalling more than £3
billion. However, as a House of Lords report[3] reveals, the fact is that 'figures
on the scale of the problem are hard to come by' and so the exact scale of the
problem remains unknown.

What is clear is that a reference to internet crime or cybercrime oversimplifies
the legal wrongs and potential remedies. To understand the nature of crime over
the internet and the rules which seek to circumscribe and define it, it is useful to
distinguish the different types of criminal activity and offence.

One set of crimes comprises those in which internet and computer networks
provide an essential tool for seemingly new crimes. Examples include email

---

1   UNIX operating system security. *AT&T Bell Laboratories Technical Journal*, 63 (8, Part 2):
      1649–1672, October 1984.
2   BBC news (www.news.bbc.co.uk), Friday 10 August 2007.
3   House of Lords Science and Technology Committee, 5th report of session 2006–2007
      'Personal Internet Security', published on 10 August 2007.

spamming and copyright piracy, many of which have only become possible with technological advances in broadband speeds and the utilisation of peer-to-peer networks. The traditional legislative frameworks have been required to adapt: the data protection regime to deal with unsolicited marketing via electronic communications services; the Copyright Designs and Patents Act 1988 to deal with the circumvention of digital rights management systems and the Regulation of Investigatory Powers Act 2000 to extend phone tapping prohibitions to offences, of interception of communications via any 'electronic communications network'. These types of crimes are considered separately in **Chapters 6** (Data and data protection) and **4** (Intellectual property).

A second set of offences, which forms the statistical majority, are pre-existing crimes which are simply facilitated through the use of computers, networks and the internet. Examples include identity theft and fraud (such as the infamous 'Nigerian' scam), online money laundering, the exchange of paedophilic materials, and harassment (known also by its more fear-inducing name, 'cyber stalking'). As with the first category, these crimes do not have special and separate internet-specific laws dedicated to them. However, they do require that lawyers navigate various pre-existing and occasionally non-technically focused statutes. Some steps have been made to update these laws, and **5.59** to **5.89** of this chapter consider some of the most common crimes and their statutory basis.

A third set consists of crimes which actually target computers and computer networks themselves. These computer misuse offences do require specific and focused legislation, and are the subject of the first section of this chapter.

Even if many of the crimes are not in themselves new, crimes perpetrated over the internet or against computer networks do raise some unique issues which are often the real cause for concern. First, because the internet knows no territorial boundaries, the co-ordination of an approach to such crimes is problematic. UK legislation to counter electronic fraud may be robust, but if a UK user is targeted from a jurisdiction where there are lesser or even no controls, then such user may rightly feel exposed and the enforcement authorities may be powerless. Second, prosecution even within the UK is hampered through the ability of an offender to remain invisible or take on a fake persona and hide the traces of their crime. Internet crime therefore demands new techniques for gathering and preserving evidence, ensuring its integrity and tracing perpetrators.

The internet has also had an effect on the course of proceedings from a privacy and justice point of view. The section on 'Contempt of court' (see **5.90** below) deals with the issue of jurors and the internet, specifically looking at contempt of court proceedings in the context of searching for details about offenders via the internet and posting social media comments about ongoing proceedings.

Legislation for dealing with these problems has developed. Changes draw upon attempts towards greater harmonisation internationally. The EU Framework Decision on Attacks against Information Systems[4] and the Council of Europe Convention on Cybercrime[5] are Europe-wide responses to the increasing severity of the threat from viruses, internet-based fraud and

---

4   The Council of the European Union Framework decision on attacks against information systems, 17 January 2005.
5   European Convention on Cybercrime, Budapest, 23 November 2001.

other computer-based crime. The UK is a signatory to both and is obliged to implement the EU Framework Decision. Both Decision and Convention have, however, had an impact on shaping the changes to the Computer Misuse Act 1990 and extradition arrangements in general in order to fulfil the UK's obligations.

These crimes, and the evidence needed to support their prosecution, are examined as follows.

● When does one commit the computer misuse crime of unauthorised access using the internet?

● How does the more serious computer misuse offence of unauthorised access with ulterior motive address the wrongful interception of credit card numbers or digital cash?

● What are the laws, and how do they control the electronic spread of viruses, logic bombs and other malicious code?

● For crimes committed over the internet, what is the special significance and difficulty of adducing computer-generated evidence?

● Those who gain unauthorised access to computers often follow the same pattern; what are the key legal issues involved in their techniques?

● What is the English courts' jurisdiction over criminals who use the internet, and how may they be extradited?

● What are the criminal laws that apply to obscene digital articles, and more serious indecent photographs?

COMPUTER MISUSE

Introduction

5.2   There are currently three main statutory types of computer misuse. First, there is unauthorised access, or 'hacking'. This is where a person without authority physically or electronically penetrates a computer system. This may be compared with breaking and entering, where no further offence is intended or then committed. The second type of digital crime is the more serious form of unauthorised access. This is where a person without authority accesses a computer with the intention to commit a further offence such as theft. Distinct from unauthorised access is the third type of digital crime, where a person does any unauthorised act in relation to a computer, intending the computer to be impaired or access to it prevented (and once implemented, is reckless as to the impact). A common example of this is a computer virus which may prevent a computer from working.[6] A new, fourth offence concerns the making, supplying

---

6   An action under the Computer Misuse Act may not always be the most appropriate recourse for access or damage caused by viruses. Chapter 3 considers the bases in tort which may be relevant.

or obtaining of articles for use in any of the other offences. Aimed at capturing those who knowingly facilitate computer misuses, this last offence has given cause for concern to many IT professionals who believe it could capture dual-use tools used for highlighting or testing security flaws.

The unique legal question in relation to all these crimes is who or what is actually the victim? Everything which exists in a computer is represented as zeros and ones. These binary digits, or bits, are generally stored using a magnetic medium. So, to destroy a computer file a person may only have to change the state of, say, 100 bits from one, on, to zero, off. Previously, courts were forced to wrestle with older statutes which concerned physical property to fit the misuse of new technology before them.[7] Even where this was successful, there was an obvious need for legislation to take account of computers. Prosecutions were troublesome.[8]

To counter the distrust of computers which was emerging, stemming from the ineffectiveness of the criminal law to deal with computer viruses and hacking, Parliament introduced the Computer Misuse Act 1990; an Act[9] 'to safeguard the integrity – what I call the trustworthiness – of computers'.

The Act introduced three new criminal offences.[10] With computer crime on the increase but convictions under the Act remaining in single figures annually, the Act came under scrutiny. It was accused of containing dangerous loopholes, and insufficient teeth to act as an effective deterrent or to appropriately punish offenders. As a consequence the Act was amended under the Police and Justice Act 2006. This reworked the third offence to give it wider application, introduced a new offence of making, supplying or obtaining articles for use in computer misuse offences, and doubled the maximum sentence for hacking. However, with work in Parliament currently underway in respect of a new Serious Crime Bill (which at the time of writing is before the House of Lords and seeks to introduce new procedures, abolish common law offences of incitement and in its place create new offences in respect of the encouragement or assistance of crime), the Secretary of State has delayed bringing these amendments into force as required pursuant to s 53 of the Police and Justice Act. It is necessary then, to consider both existing and pending legislation. We analyse each section in turn, below.

---

7   For example, Forgery and Counterfeiting Act 1981 in *R v Gold and Shifreen* [1988] 2 All ER 186.

8   In an obvious signal to Parliament, Brandon LJ in *R v Gold and Shifreen* said, 'there is no reason to regret the failure of what [Lord Lane CJ] aptly described as the Procrustean attempt to force the facts of the present case into the language of an Act not designed to fit them' [1988] 2 WLR 984 at 991.

9   Michael Colvin MP, Hansard 166 HC col 1134. Despite statements in April 2001 by the then Home Secretary, Jack Straw, to consider 'whether [the Act] needs to be reviewed, the Computer Misuse Act 1990 remains the United Kingdom's key statute addressing general hacking and malicious code'.

10   Computer Misuse Act 1990, ss 1, 2 and 3.

Section 1: unauthorised access

5.3   The following discussion of hacking over the internet focuses on the Computer Misuse Act 1990. Prosecutions are considered to be in low figures yearly with only five proceedings brought (by way of a criminal offence) under this section in each of 2004 and 2005.[11]

Despite these low figures, it is generally easy to prove the conduct aspect of the offence, the *actus reus*. The structure of the Act is such that, where the internet is involved, it is almost impossible for a defendant to interact in any way with a victim computer without satisfying the physical requirements of the section of 'causing the performance of a function'. The tough burden on the prosecution however lies elsewhere. It is proving the necessary intention and satisfying the rules to admit computer-generated evidence. Before considering these burdens it is necessary to appreciate the ambit of the activity required to satisfy the conduct aspect of the offence.

Conduct or actus reus

5.4   Section 1 creates the summary offence. The details of the *actus reus* are set out in full in s 1(1) of the Computer Misuse Act 1990 as follows (with square bracketed sections indicating the provisions caught by implementation via the Police and Justice Act 2006 as discussed above):

'1.   (1) A person is guilty of an offence if –

(a) he causes a computer to perform any function with intent to secure access to any program or data held in any computer [or to enable such access to be secured];

(b) the access he intends to secure [or to enable to be secured] is unauthorised; and

(c) he knows at the time when he causes the computer to perform the function that that is the case.'

There are three main questions which must be addressed in relation to this section. First, what is meant by a computer, program or data? Second, what is required to cause a computer to perform a function? Third, what is entailed in securing access to (or enabling access to be secured to) any program or data?

Computers, programs and data on the internet

5.5   The conduct element of a s 1 offence is causing a computer to perform any function with intent to secure access to any program or data held in any

---

11 See, for example, figures from RDS Office for Criminal Justice Reform as reported in House of Commons Hansard Written Answers for 20 April 2007: Column 830W.

computer. At an early stage it should be noted that the words 'program', 'data' and 'computer' are not defined by the Act.[12]

Computer

5.6   The Computer Misuse Act 1990 does not define 'computer'. This was intentional on the part of Parliament, following recommendations of the Law Commission to ensure that the legislation would not become restricted in the face of technological advances.[13] The absence of the definition has not caused any difficulties for proving unauthorised access over the internet to date and the All Party Internet Group's review of the Act which helped frame the provisions of the Police and Justice Act 2006 recommended that no further clarification would be necessary or helpful.[14] For a machine to be a victim or conduit of hacking over the internet, that machine must be a computer within any reasonable definition. The very nature of the internet is that it joins together networks of computers.[15] For the purposes of this chapter, therefore, where the hacking is conducted over the internet, the functioning 'machine' and accessed 'machine', as well as the network to which they provide access, will both be considered as computers within the ambit of s 1.

Some considered that digital rights management systems should be specifically included within the definition of computer. This would have strengthened the protection for copyright works. This call was resisted but rightsholders can now find specific protection through the amendments to the Copyright Designs and Patents Act 1988.

Program, data

5.7   The terms 'program' and 'data' within s 1 are also left undefined by the Act for the same reason. That said, it remains crucial for a computer misuse prosecution that the conduct element of the offence, the *actus reus*, is proved and, therefore, that the two terms are understood in a reasonable context.

The main difficulty with these terms is in appreciating what, other than 'a program' or 'data', can be accessed in a computer. The answer is that the two

---

12   Mr Harry Cohen MP did attempt to amend the Act at the Committee Stage with a definition of the word 'computer'. This was unsuccessful. Cf Law Commission No 186 on Computer Misuse at para 3.39: 'it would be unnecessary and indeed might be foolish, to attempt to define computer ... We cannot think that there will ever be serious grounds for arguments based on the ordinary meaning of the term "computer".'

13   Interestingly, the European Convention on Cybercrime refers to a 'computer system' and defines a computer as a device that uses a 'program' to run 'data' but does not go on to define these other terms.

14   Revision of the Computer Misuse Act: Report of an Inquiry by the All Party Internet Group, June 2004.

15   It is not doubted that the future of ecommerce is away from the conception of simply linking computers as such but more towards connecting together 'intelligent appliances' such as personal digital appliances and wireless devices, and even household appliances such as fridges!

terms encapsulate all that can be accessed digitally in a computer. But if the terms were absent from the section, one could commit a s 1 offence by turning off a computer before prising open the casing. Turning off the computer causes it to perform a function, and opening its metal casing would be accessing the computer in the physical sense.

In summary, the absence of definitions should not concern a court where the accused has used the internet to gain access to information which resides in a digital form. In this form, the information will constitute data or a program within the ambit of the relevant section.

Example 5.1

A company runs a mobile phone and WAP-enabled website which tracks business news stories on particular companies. Users pay a subscription fee and, in return, are given a password to grant them access to the site. A hacker attempts to use a password which he has not paid for in order to enter the site to read the stories. The home page is mainly constructed using a computer language called Java, and much of the site's content is data. The hacker is intending to secure access to a program and its associated data without authority.

Held in any computer

5.8   Before examining the remainder of s 1 and its application to the internet, this section analyses the notion of data or programs being 'held in a computer'. A computer can be reasonably thought to include the processing unit, its memory and storage devices. Computers are simple machines; they are so simple that they can purely store and work with two numbers: a zero and a one. But that sentence illustrates one division which exists within a computer: it stores and it works; it executes instructions on those numbers. The central processing unit of a computer is able to store very few of these numbers at one time but is able to process them very quickly: it is where all the real work is performed. However, certain other physical parts of the computer cannot process or work with these numbers: they can only store them. Examples of these are the computer's hard disk drive and its memory. These are purely components of a computer that can store vast quantities of digital information.

Section 17(6) clarifies the phrase 'held in a computer' by providing that it includes references to data or programs held in any removable storage medium which is in the computer for the time being. This particular inclusion refers to the possibility of obtaining access to the data or program which is stored on a floppy disk: these allow the storage of small quantities of data, but are physically small and portable. A CD-ROM is a further example of a removable storage medium. Section 17(6) does not define the term and seeks only to clarify the phrase 'held in a computer' with one example, one inclusion. 'Held in a computer' may therefore also be reasonably read to include data or programs which are stored away from the processing unit of a computer, but accessible by it.

Example 5.2

A hacker uses an authorised person's password to log in to a UK insurance company's computer. The hacker is hoping to gain access to the company's customer details. The computer to which he logs in stores these details in a huge data storage unit which is located elsewhere. The data itself is stored on a magnetic tape. The processing unit of the computer retrieves this information through fibre-optic cables. The computer would be thought to include the magnetic tape, and so the data would still be considered as being 'held in a computer'.

Performing any function

5.9   If it is concluded that any machine which is connected to the internet will fall into the category of 'computer' in s 1(1), it is then necessary to establish how one causes that computer to perform a function. The word 'function' is also undefined within the Act, but the interpretation section of the Act provides some indication of the wide scope of the term. It appears that there is no activity which one can perform in relation to a computer that does not cause a function to be performed. Even typing on a computer's keyboard or using an input device, such as a mouse, will alter the state of the computer's processor. This alteration has been effected by the person causing the computer to perform a function.

Function on any computer

5.10   The computer performing the function does not need to be the same computer on which the data or programs are stored. So, a client computer, being made to perform a function, which is intended to secure access to the server computer, falls within the ambit of s 1(1). Section 1(1) also encompasses the use of a home computer to log in to an internet service provider's server from which the user intends to penetrate another computer. The home computer is caused to perform a function, and so is the internet service provider's computer.

Where a hacker uses the internet to attempt to gain access to a victim computer, signals may pass through many computers, as described in this book's introduction, before reaching the victim. Indeed, when Yahoo.com, one of the busiest sites on the internet, was brought down, it was attacked from a vast number of other computers. Each had been made to act in concert, having been themselves infected with a 'daemon' program. Each of these infected computers was then under the control of a 'master' program (generally without the computer owners' knowledge). In the case of Yahoo!'s attack, the 'master' program probably instructed its 'daemons' to simultaneously bombard Yahoo!'s servers with a flood of requests to be sent data or web pages: a 'SYN flood'. This was probably combined with a set of other attack procedures variously called 'spoofing', 'smurfing' and 'fraggle'. In short, a vast range of computers, all compromised in the same way, were made to focus their attentions on one victim computer, this time Yahoo.com. This so-called 'denial of service' attack illustrates the way in which the computers made to perform the function are often not the same computers on which the data or programs being attacked are stored.

What is important to the prosecution, though, is that each of these intermediary computers is caused to perform a function. And the cause of the performance of this function is the instructions which the hacker has provided to the first computer in the chain. This allows the prosecution to rely on the functioning of any computer in the chain to establish this aspect of the *actus reus*. What is difficult for the prosecution to prove is that the accused was the cause of the performance of this function. This difficulty is considered in greater depth below.[16]

Example 5.3

A hacker uses a set of software tools called a 'root kit' to break into an insecure computer on the internet. A 'master program' is installed onto this computer with a view to controlling a large number of 'daemon' programs installed on other computers. Using a program called 'Tribal Flood Network' the hacker remotely calls on all the 'daemon' computers to launch a distributed attack on a well-known sports site. For a s 1 offence, the prosecution does not need to prove that the hacker's own computer was made to function: all the computers involved, 'daemons' and 'masters' will suffice. The prosecution may have a problem in proving that it was the accused who caused these functions.

Unsuccessful attempts

5.11   The broad drafting of s 1 has the effect that even unsuccessful hackers can be guilty of the offence. Usually, to gain unauthorised access a person must enter a login procedure and masquerade as another, or attempt to bypass the login procedure altogether. In the first instance, if the victim computer rejects the unauthorised login, the person has caused at least two computers to function: his own, and the victim computer. The victim computer has performed a function: it rejected the hacker. Where the hacker attempts to log in with the requisite intention – a guilty mind – despite being unsuccessful, the hacker may have committed the offence.

Of course, the difficulty for the prosecution in such a situation is proving that the victim computer did foil the attempt, and proving that the attempt was made by the accused. This will be hard unless the victim computer maintains a log of all unsuccessful logins as well as successful ones.[17] It is more technically complex to prove the source of an unsuccessful login, weakening further a prosecution.

If the person is somehow able to bypass the standard login procedure, this bypassing itself will constitute the function. If the standard procedure for the victim computer is to ask for login details from each person wishing to gain access, by avoiding this the person must be causing the computer to perform a function.

---

16   See 'Evidence', at **5.84**.
17   Evidence used to convict one hacker consisted of a log which his computer maintained of all functions!

Example 5.4

A hacker oversees a password being entered by someone logging-in to a remote computer. The login prompt specifies that you must be authorised to access the computer. Later, the hacker then attempts to use the password himself. Because the remote computer only allows one login each day, the unauthorised login attempt is rejected by the computer. This would still constitute a s 1 offence: the rejection constitutes a function and this function was caused by the hacker using a password at the wrong time.

Automatic causation of a function

5.12   Many hackers will automate part of the process of unauthorised access. Denial of service attacks rely on automatic co-ordination between computers. As another example, a home page may require two items of information from each of its users to allow them to enter the site. The first may be the person's name, followed by the second, their password, which is say a number seven digits long. To penetrate this site digitally a hacker may write an automatic login program. Its first task is to enter a common name, 'John Smith'. The hacker's program then tries to enter the password. First the password 0000001 is tried. If the victim computer rejects this as being incorrect, the login program will simply move the password number to 0000002. Often after a number of unsuccessful attempts, the victim computer will reject the attempting client.

As automation usually plays some part in hacking, it is necessary to address whether this may constitute a s 1 offence.[18] The key question is whether a computer has been caused to perform a function. The running of the hacker's program would constitute the conduct element of the offence. It is at the point of executing that code that a computer is caused to perform a function, so the physical element of the offence can be made out. Establishing the intention for this automated hacking is less straightforward.

Securing access

5.13   The Computer Misuse Act 1990 prescribes that securing access to a program or data is established where the defendant, by causing a computer to perform a function:[19]

'(a) alters or erases the program or data;

(b) copies or moves it to any storage medium other than that in which it is held or to a different location in the storage medium in which it is held;

---

18   A similar program can be used to search automatically for the vulnerable hosts on the internet, which, once discovered, may be probed further. See Cheswick WR and Bellovin SM, *Firewalls and Internet Security* (Addison-Wesley Publishing Company, Wokingham, 1995) at p 145. Similar programs were used to scan a range of telephone numbers to test whether they were connected to a modem, and were thus potential targets. Such a program is described in the now deleted book, *The Hacker's Handbook* by Hugo Cornwall (Century Communications, London, 1985).
19   Computer Misuse Act 1990, s 17(2).

(c) uses it; or

(d) has it output from the computer in which it is held (whether by having it displayed or in any other manner).'

The purpose of considering this aspect of s 1 is to establish the intention of the defendant to secure access to any program or data held in any computer.[20] That the defendant actually did secure such access, a question of fact, may bolster the case that the defendant has the requisite intention; it is not a prerequisite of proving this intention. The amendments in the Police and Justice Act 2006 will expand this to incorporate enabling the access. In so doing it will no longer be necessary to show actual access or that any of the items under (a) to (d) has been or was intended or attempted to be done by the defendant. A defendant will still be acting unlawfully where the function which they cause the computer to perform allows a third party actually to obtain the access. In this way hackers who only undertake the first steps, leaving the door open for others (or themselves at a later date) to obtain access, are still caught.

Which computer?

5.14   It is helpful to consider to which computer s 1(1)(a) refers. Section 1(1)(a) states 'to secure access to any program or data held on any computer (or, once it is implemented, to enable any such access to be secured)'. Following a judgment of the Court of Appeal in June 2006, it is clear that the access does not need to be directed at a different computer to the one on which the defendant caused performance of the function, but can be programs or data accessed either directly from a computer or indirectly via another computer.[21] It will now be illustrated that the Computer Misuse Act 1990 leaves very little scope for interacting with a computer over the internet without that interaction being classified as securing access or enabling such access to be secured.

Example 5.5

A hacker uses a Telnet connection to attempt to gain unauthorised access to a company's Intranet. Three main computers are used to attempt the access: the hacker's own computer and the computer to which he connected to by Telnet. This 'distance' alone will not prevent a successful hacking prosecution. There are two computers caused to function: the hacker's own and the Telnet computer. That the hacker sought to secure access to data held on a third computer is not a bar to a conviction: it is still 'any computer'.

---

20 The author submits that no emphasis should be placed on the Act's use of the word 'secure'. It is the author's understanding that this verb is introduced because, while using the word 'access' as a verb is grammatically dubious, it also makes the word ambiguous.

21 *Attorney General's Reference (No 1 of 1991)* [1992] 3 All ER 897. This concerned a case in which the defendant keyed instructions into a wholesaler's computer without authority in order to obtain a 70% discount on his purchases. In the initial action, the judge held that, in order to prove the offence, the defendant would have had to use one computer in order to secure unauthorised access to another. This was rejected.

Copying or moving programs and data

5.15   Section 17(2)(b) defines securing access as a person copying or moving data or programs to any storage medium other than that in which it is held or to a different location in the storage medium in which it is held. The word which widens this section dramatically is 'copies'. Computer data and programs cannot even be viewed on a screen without there being copying. To show characters on a screen, the characters making up the program or data are copied from the storage unit, be that memory or a hard-disk drive, to the video memory of the computer. The same is true of a hacker who uses the internet to view the content of programs or data which are held on a victim's computer. By being able to view their content, a part of those data must have been copied into the memory of the hacker's computer. It therefore appears that viewing files which are held on any computer will constitute securing access to those files and, even if the defendant does not himself view the files, enabling this will be sufficient.

Example 5.6

A hacker makes a connection to a secured part of a server. Once within this portion of the server the hacker views the contents of a password data file. To avoid drawing attention to the breach in security, the hacker does not make a digital copy of the data file. Nevertheless the hacker has secured access to the file by having read it: to view the file it must have been copied from the storage unit on the server to the memory of the hacker's computer.

Using a program

5.16   Section 17(2)(c) states that one secures access to a program if one 'uses it'. The Act elaborates on the meaning and context of this word 'use'. Section 17(3)(a) explains, first, that one uses a computer program if the program is executed. This is, pragmatically, covered by subsection (2)(b). Section 17(3) explains that running a program indicates the gaining of access to that program. This will therefore cover programs executed on a client computer, having been copied there, or programs executed on the server computer.

Example 5.7

An employee uses her firm's intranet to attempt to read the online diary of her supervisor. She is unable to read the diary because the program requests her to enter a password which she does not know. That the diary program is able to reject her attempt shows it had, at the least, been executed. The employee did intend to access the diary program.

In *Ellis v DPP*,[22] John Ellis, a graduate of the University of Newcastle appealed to the Divisional Court against three convictions under s 1. He had used computers left logged on by others to access certain websites. The evidence was that he

---

22   [2001] EWHC Admin 362, [2001] All ER (D) 190 (May).

used already-running internet browsers on the computer and that he accessed already-'activated' sites. Nevertheless, and technically correct, the Divisional Court unanimously judged that he did 'use' the computers knowing that use to be unauthorised.

Output of programs or data

5.17   Section 17(1)(d) expands the term 'access' by not only including executing a computer program, but also reading a computer program. A computer program is made up from a list of instructions. Each instruction tells the computer to perform a function. Some functions are imperceptible, such as moving a byte from one storage area to another. Others make a perceptive difference, for example clearing the screen. Section 17(1)(d) defines securing access as including 'ha[ving the program or data] output from the computer in which it is held …'. Section 17(4)(a) refines this section by further defining 'output' as including the instructions of the program being output. So, executing a program over the internet is deemed to be securing access to it. This therefore compromises the 'classic' thin-client where the server executes the program but outputs the results to the client computer. This was explained above.[23] In addition, merely looking at the instructions which make up the program will also be securing access.

It is crucial that a court appreciates the mischief at which this section is aimed. It is concerned with the 'integrity'[24] of programs and data. It is not directed at subsequent use, or utility, of the digital information compromised. For this reason, s 17(4)(b) clearly expresses that the form of output, whether executable or otherwise, is immaterial. This expression applies also to data: it is of no concern that, say, the data is unusable. The fact that it has been output per se is sufficient to constitute securing access.

Example 5.8

A company, worried about data security, encrypts all data held on its network. Each individual who is permitted to gain access to the data is provided, on disk, with a de-encrypting key. The network security is breached and a hacker prints out some of the encrypted data. The hacker has still gained access to that data despite the issue that the output is unreadable. In addition, the data will be deemed to have been copied onto the hacker's computer for printing; this also denotes securing access.

Erasure or alteration

5.18   Subsection (a) of s 17(2) illustrates the final type of access to programs or data: alteration or erasure of programs or data. This would constitute a 'classic' hack: data are deleted and programs are altered. Complex issues of proving the

---

23   See 'Using a program'.
24   See n 9 above.

program has been altered, where the program itself is the source of that proof (an activity-logging program for example), are covered below.[25]

Intention or mens rea

5.19   The prosecution must prove the two limbs of the intention aspects of the offence. The first, that the defendant intended to secure access to any program or data held in any computer (or, once this section is implemented by the Secretary of State, to 'enable such access to be secured'), has been considerably examined above.[26] Nevertheless, a few additional points are mentioned below. The second limb is that at the time of causing the computer to perform the function the defendant knew that the access intended to secure (or enable to be secured) was unauthorised. This can be a difficult intention to prove where the defendant had limited authority, but is accused of operating outside this authority. A common example of this is where the defendant is an employee of a company and is accused of using the company's intranet or other systems outside their authority.

The prosecution need only make out these two limbs and any consideration of the motivations and reasons for securing or enabling such unauthorised access is irrelevant. The case of Dan Cuthbert,[27] a system penetration tester, provides a useful example. On making a £30 charitable donation following the 2004 Asian tsunami via a website run by the Disasters Emergency Committee, Mr Cuthbert was concerned by the slowness of the system in processing his payment. Having read about alleged 'phishing' attempts, he decided to use his skills to check whether the site was in fact vulnerable to security breaches. He tried to breach the system and it did not seem to be weak, and so he thought no more about it. Unfortunately for Mr Cuthbert, his tests triggered an alarm and he found himself facing prosecution under s 1 of the Computer Misuse Act for unauthorised access. His defence centred on the fact that Mr Cuthbert's motivations for the access were innocent, and indeed considered his own and other users' welfare. However, the court found the intention to be irrelevant; he had clearly known that the action was unauthorised and the fact that no damage had been caused was irrelevant in the context of a s 1 offence. 'With regret' the court fined him £400.

Intention to secure access

5.20   Much has been explained about what constitutes securing access; a little needs now to be added to what is an intention to secure access (or, once this amendment is implemented, to enable such access to be secured). First, it should be reiterated that this intention can be directed at any computer. The defendant does not need to have been aware of exactly which computer he was attacking, and nor will he have to make such access himself once the pending amendments

25   See **5.84**.
26   See 'Securing access', at **5.13**.
27   *R v Cuthbert* (unreported, Horseferry Magistrates' Court, 7 October 2005).

are finally brought into force.[28] This suits the internet: often it is complicated to prove that a person intended to log in to a specific computer. This is particularly true where the defendant used a program automatically to check the security, or otherwise, of a computer. The intention to secure access also does not need to be directed at any particular, or particular kind of, program or data. It is enough that an individual intends to secure access to programs and data per se. The section encompasses the hacker who intends to access a computer with no clear perception of what data or programs will be held on the computer.

Unauthorised

5.21   The second limb of intention is focused on the authority of the defendant to secure access. Section 1(1)(b) prescribes that the access the defendant intends to secure (or, once this amendment is implemented, enable) be unauthorised. Section 1(1)(c) makes it clear that the person must have the relevant knowledge that the access is unauthorised at the time the computer is forced to perform a function.

Outsiders

5.22   The question of authority is generally not difficult to prove when an 'outsider' to a system uses the internet to attempt to secure access to any programs or data on the system. Where a person must resort to using 'techniques' to gain access to programs or data, it can be readily inferred that it is an insecure defence to claim he did not know he was unauthorised. The concept of authority is elaborated, but thinly, by s 17(5). This section states that access is unauthorised if the person is not entitled to control access of the kind in question, and the person does not have the consent of the person who does control access.

A person must know that he is unauthorised in this sense. The question of fact as to whether the individual knew the limits of his authority will often be a finely balanced one.

> *Example 5.9*
>
> An art gallery uses a website to advertise forthcoming displays. On its home page it states that the graphics which follow on subsequent pages may not be downloaded to a storage medium. A person saves one of the graphics to his hard disk. The person has authorised access to copy the file to memory, but not to his hard disk. Access was unauthorised; the issue would be whether the evidence would be strong enough to prove that he did not see the limitation to disprove he had the necessary intention.

This raises an issue of relevance for advisers to server operators. Where a server seeks to provide limited authority, say with an extranet site, the boundaries of

---

28   The amendments under the Police and Justice Act 2006 after the Serious Crime Bill is adopted and implemented, as discussed above.

this authority must be clearly stated.[29] If not, it will be doubtful an offence has been committed. If publicly available but subject to a limitation, a court will be unenthusiastic to hold that an offence has been committed. What is more, because the intention must have been formed at the time of causing the function, the stipulations of any limitations should be obvious at all times. An ftp site appears to a user as a catalogue of the files and directories on the particular computer. Unless security is in place, a user can secure access to any file without having to pass through any limitations statement. Similarly, if poorly constructed, it is possible that a person may select a single page of the website to view, missing the opening page altogether.[30] A viewer may not have seen a limitation statement.

Insiders

5.23 The ubiquity of intranets and extranets within organisations creates a potential arena for insiders to secure unauthorised access to programs and data. Disgruntled employees, temporary staff and even happily employed staff may all attempt to read information which is actually out of their authority to view. This is possible where there are various strata within a system each for different users of the network. For example, personnel files may be uploaded to the intranet but only made available to the personnel department. Before considering the problems of an insider's unauthorised access it is necessary to mention how an insider may access the files.

An insider can secure access to unauthorised information held on an intranet through a connected computer, or through the actual server on which the information is held. In the early case of *R v Cropp*,[31] Sean Cropp, without authority, entered a discount into a computerised till to obtain key-cutting equipment at 30% of cost. This is a straightforward example of unauthorised access.

Aglionby J, after consulting the statute, held that there was no case to answer. Section 1(1)(a) refers to:

> 'causing a computer to perform any function with intent to secure access to any program or data held in any computer.'

He construed this wording did not apply where only one computer is used; he felt the word 'any' referred to any other computer. To confirm this interpretation, Judge Aglionby considered s 17 of the Act. Here, a s 3 offence is described as only addressing:[32]

---

29 A website may state the following on its terms and conditions page: 'Permission to use, copy and distribute documents and related graphics available from this server ("Server") is granted, provided that ... (2) use of the graphics available from this Server is for non-commercial purposes ... (4) no graphics available from this Server are used, copied or distributed separate from accompanying copyright notices.' Accessing the site with the intention to use the graphics in a commercial brochure would therefore constitute a s 1 offence, if these disclaimers were known at the time of downloading the graphic.

30 This is a very common occurrence where a person uses a search engine to search for a particular term.

31 *R v Cropp*, unreported, although see [1991] 7 *Computer Law and Practice* 270.

32 Per Aligonby J in *R v Cropp*, transcript of shorthand notes, p 9F. Emphasis added.

'the computer concerned or any other computer … It seems to me to be straining language to say that only one computer is necessary.'

Concern at this decision was so widespread that an opinion on a point of law was sought from the Court of Appeal.[33] The question was asked if, to commit an offence under s 1(1), does the computer caused to perform a function have to be a different computer to the one in which unauthorised access is intended? The Court of Appeal set the Act back on course:[34]

'In our judgment there are no grounds whatsoever for implying, or importing the word "other" between "any" and "computer" …'

This leaves no doubt that, all things being equal, insiders who gain access to unauthorised files through the computer on which they are stored can commit the offence.

For an insider to be convicted, the prosecution has two hurdles to prove intention. The first is that the person intended to secure access to any program or data (or, once this amendment is implemented, to enable such access to be secured). This may not be disputed. What will often be disputed is the second, higher hurdle, that the insider knew that he was unauthorised to secure (or enable) this access at the time of causing the computer to perform a function.[35]

In a perfect organisation, the boundaries of each employee's actions are clear and known. In practice, an employee's role changes over time. This is especially the situation for a temporary worker, who may work for many different sectors of an organisation within a short period. It will therefore often be important for the prosecution to show clear guidelines which were made known to the employee at the time of causing the computer to perform the function.

On this point the Law Commission has provided the following guidance:[36]

'We think there is some importance in requiring the court, in a case where there is a dispute about authorisation, to identify, and to be clear about the status of, the person alleged to have authority to control the access which is in issue.'

Unclear company guidelines, or none at all, in relation to the use of the intranet can only weaken the prosecution's case that a person knew they were acting outside of their authority. Conflicting authorisations will also weaken any case.

---

33 AG's Reference (No 1 of 1991) [1993] QB 94 under s 36 of the Criminal Justice Act 1972. While explaining s 1 offences, in the House of Commons, Michael Colvin MP added: '[The section] is also aimed at insiders who try to get into parts of the system where they know that they should not be' (Hansard 166 HC col 1138). Parliament's intention is confirmed by the unanimous opposition to and later withdrawal of Harry Cohen's amendment proposing that 'any computer' be replaced with 'another computer'.
34 [1992] 3 WLR 432 at 437.
35 A 'bootstraps' approach to this question is to assess whether the ultimate purpose of the access was unlawful. As unlawful, it must, necessarily, have been unauthorised by the controller of the programs or data. That this was known by the defendant remains a question of fact, but an unlawful purpose will indicate such knowledge.
36 Law Commission No 186, para 3.37.

Example 5.10

An employee secures access to the personnel section of her company's intranet. She copies her personnel file using a stolen password. Clearly the employee does not have authority to enter the personnel section of the intranet, but her intention was to gain access to her own personnel file. The relevant knowledge and intent may be inferred from her stolen password.

Without a clear indication of boundaries, the defence is at liberty to question whether the defendant actually knew of these limits.[37]

This discussion highlights the theoretical applicability of the Computer Misuse Act 1990 to insider access, but also the practical difficulty of satisfying the criminal standard of proof in such a case.

The most complex situation concerning insiders is where they are carrying out their duties with 'technical authority' but without 'actual authority'. The *Bignell* case illustrates this concept.

Paul and Victoria Bignell were police officers and lived together. A dispute arose in relation to two cars owned by the new partner of Mr Bignell's former wife. On six occasions the Bignells instructed police computer operators to extract from the Police National Computer details of the two cars. Such instructions would have been perfectly legal were the Bignells discharging genuine police duties. However, they were not.

The respondents were convicted by a stipendiary magistrate and fined under the Computer Misuse Act 1990, s 1.[38] They each appealed against these convictions to the Crown Court. The Crown Court[39] upheld their submission that, even if their use of the police computer was for private purposes, it was not within the definition of 'unauthorised access' under s 17(5) of the Act because the access was with authority, even though the authority was used for an unauthorised purpose.

The DPP appealed, its main question to Pill LJ and Astill J being whether or not it was correct in law to conclude that a police officer does not commit an offence contrary to s 1 of the Computer Misuse Act 1990 if he intends to secure access to the Police National Computer for purposes other than policing.[40]

---

37 This said, the defence should be wary that 'it is always open to the tribunal of fact, when knowledge on the part of a defendant is required to be proved, to base a finding of knowledge on evidence that the defendant deliberately shut his eyes to the obvious or refrained from inquiry because he suspected the truth but did not want to have his suspicion confirmed' (per Lord Bridge, *Westminster City Council v Croyalgrange* Ltd [1986] 2 All ER 353 at 359). This 'wilful blindness' approaches a subjective recklessness threshold of intention. It is the author's opinion that this lower level of intention was not intended by Parliament. Emma Nicholson's Bill, proposed but rejected, included recklessness; the Computer Misuse Act 1990 does not. Further, the proponent of the Act explained, '[Section 1] is also aimed at insiders who try to get into parts of the system where they know that they should not be' (Hansard 166 HC col 1138).
38 On 28 June 1996. In a remarkably similar case, the CPS prosecuted a police officer, David Keyte, of conspiring to commit 'misconduct in a public office'. The officer was found guilty and jailed for two years. See *Computing*, 10 July 1997.
39 The appeals were heard on 19 September 1996.
40 *DPP v Bignell* [1998] 1 Cr App Rep 1.

Mr Justice Astill gave judgment for the court in a systematic manner. Access is unauthorised if it meets the conditions in s 17(5): one is not entitled to control access of any kind in question, and, one does not have consent to access from any person so entitled. Section 17(2)(a) to (d) sets out four ways in which a person secures access, including altering data, copying data, using it, or outputting it. Section 17(5), however, is drafted in terms of access 'of the kind in question'. This, the court judged, referred to the four kinds of access set out in s 17(2) (c) and (d) at least. The court felt this indicated that as the respondents were authorised to secure access by s 17(2)(c) and (d), they had not committed the s 1 offence. In short the respondents had authority to access even though they did not do so for an authorised purpose.

The effects of this ruling would have been devastating. It would suggest that, because all employees have authority to touch the keys connected to a computer, any employee may use the computer to gain unauthorised access to material in the computer without criminal sanction.

The Bignells had instructed that a false 'reason code' be typed into the Police National Computer.[41] Why? They wanted the computer to perform this function to allow them to gain access to data which was 'not necessary for the efficient discharge of genuine police duties'.[42] In other words, they were not authorised in those circumstances to secure access to the data. The offence should have been made out. The reason that the court did not come to this conclusion was because they did not restrict their analysis of the facts to the precise wording of the statute. The Act is drafted in terms of 'causing a computer to perform a function', together with the intention to 'secure unauthorised access to any program or data'. It is therefore an error in law for the court to have provided a judgment littered with references to 'accessing a computer'. The Act does not sanction those who access computers, it sanctions those who use computers to secure access to data and programs.

Unfortunately, this ruling was relied upon by Kennedy, LJ and Blofeld, J in *R v Governor of Brixton Prison ex p Adeniyi Momudu Allison.*[43] Allison was accused by the US government of conspiring when in England with an employee of American Express (then in Florida) to defraud the credit card company. The committal had sought that Allison, within the jurisdiction of the US, conspired with this US employee to secure unauthorised access to the American Express computers with intent to commit theft, forgery and to modify their computers' contents. The employee had access to accounts of American Express cardholders and relayed the secret information about these accounts to Allison. This permitted them to forge credit cards and obtain substantial sums of money.

---

41 A question remains whether when a third party touches the computer this is sufficient for the offence. Certainly, precedent suggests it is: *R v Pearce, Farquharson* (unreported, Croydon Magistrates' Court, 9 December 1993). Mr Farquharson was convicted under s 2 for instructing Ms Pearce to access her employer's computer system to obtain details of numbers and electronic codes which would have facilitated the cloning of mobile phones. Mr Farquharson did not touch the computer.

42 Directions on the use of the Police National Computer, para 3.8.

43 [1999] QB 847.

The court relied upon the ruling in *Bignell*. It decided that the US employee was, under more usual circumstances, entitled to access the data about the American Express accounts. Consequentially, the court determined that the access was not 'authorised' access within the Computer Misuse Act 1990, s 17(5).

The case was appealed from the Divisional Court to the House of Lords.[44] Lord Hobhouse delivered judgment for all five Lords and was clear that the Divisional Court fell into error by relying on the *Bignell* judgment. Indeed, the House of Lords ruled that the *Bignell* case wrongly elided 'kinds of access' and 'kinds of data'. The Act is not concerned with authority to access kinds of data. It is concerned with authority to access the actual data involved. The 'level' of security that an individual has is therefore largely irrelevant; the question is whether, given the circumstances, the individual had authority to access the data.

In short, Allison's accomplices, although no doubt trusted employees of American Express at the time, were not authorised to provide data to third parties to allow frauds to be committed. Similarly, by disapproving of the decision made in *Bignell*, the House of Lords was also impliedly stating that the police officers in that case had accessed data without authority.

Example 5.11

Cleerdz.com operates a credit card clearance system for other websites. It allows a website to offer credit card payment facilities to customers without having the capability themselves. Cleerdz.com is entitled to debit from the entered card where the card's 'fraud score' is below an agreed maximum. An operator at Cleerdz.com re-enters old customer details to pay for a holiday for himself. Even though his usual job and usual level of authority would have permitted him to enter card details, he was not authorised to do so in those particular circumstances. He accessed a computer and data without authority.

Sentencing

5.24   Criticised for a long time for being too lenient, the amendments to the Computer Misuse Act 1990 effected through the Police and Justice Act 2006 will, make the punishments stricter (although lobbyists have been disappointed that the potential sentence was not increased to sit in line with ss 2 and 3).

A person guilty of an offence under s 1 will become liable on summary conviction to imprisonment for a term not exceeding 12 months (six months for Scotland) or a fine not exceeding the statutory minimum and, on conviction on indictment, to imprisonment for a term not exceeding two years or to a fine or both.[45] This increase, allowing the offence to be indictable, means it is now possible to prosecute for criminal attempt.

For the time being, however, liability on summary conviction is to imprisonment for up to six months or to a fine not exceeding level 5 on the standard scale or both.

---

44   [2000] 2 AC 216.
45   Computer Misuse Act 1990, s 1(3).

Section 2: hacking to offend further

5.25   The s 2 offence applies to someone seeking to access a computer for a further criminal purpose. That is, where a s 1 offence has been committed with the further intent to commit a serious criminal offence.[46]

It will be discussed below that this section applies to interception of digital cash and credit card numbers. It also applies to the interception of goods or services which are delivered over the internet, for example software.[47]

Further offence

5.26   If a s 1 offence is made out, the s 2 offence may be proved by establishing that the defendant committed that offence with the intention to commit a further offence. This type of further offence is defined as one punishable by at least five years' imprisonment. This covers theft and fraud, and most other dishonesty offences.[48] Importantly, it now covers an offence of dishonestly obtaining a money transfer by deception.[49]

Example 5.12

A hacker gains unauthorised access to a computer and takes a copy of an encryption key used for internet-safe e-commerce transactions. The hacker then uses the key to pay for services without the permission of the account owner. The hacker may be convicted of the s 2 offence because the s 1 requirements are met and the defendant intended to commit the further offence of obtaining a money transfer by deception.

Intention

5.27   The hacker is not required actually to commit the further offence. Simply committing a s 1 offence with the intention of committing the further offence is sufficient. Where the hacker is accessing encryption keys to digital cash accounts, it seems probable that the secondary intention will be inferred. Gaining access to another's email account though, with no other evidence of intent, would not appear to provide sufficient evidence to make out a conviction.

An individual accessed without authority a database of 300,000 accounts held by CD Universe, a leading online music retailer. The individual demanded

---

46   No exhaustive list of these further offences is provided by the Computer Misuse Act 1990. The offence must carry either a fixed sentence penalty, such as murder, or be punishable with imprisonment of five years or more. This appears to cover the majority of serious offences.

47   The application of the Computer Misuse Act 1990 to such a mischief, however, may not always be possible. In that scenario, the Law Commission has concluded that if a service (not a product) were obtained deceitfully, no offence would be committed because no human mind would be deceived: Law Commission Report on Fraud and Deception, May 1999.

48   In illustration, although Cropp was acquitted for other reasons, Aglionby J stated: 'There is no doubt that false accounting contrary to s 17(1)(a) of the Theft Act 1968 falls within the statutory definition of 'further offence' (*R v Cropp* Transcript of Shorthand Notes, p 7G).

49   Theft Act 1968, s 15A as inserted by the Theft (Amendment) Act 1996.

$100,000 in ransom from the company. CD Universe refused and the individual threatened to post 25,000 credit card account details on the internet. This is a classic example of a s 2 type offence.[50]

If a hacker is found not guilty under s 2, the jury may still find the defendant guilty under s 1.[51]

Future intention

5.28   Section 2(3) states:

> 'It is immaterial for the purposes of this section whether the further offence is to be committed on the same occasion as the unauthorised access offence or on any future occasion.'

This eliminates difficult issues for the prosecution of whether the subsequent offence was sufficiently connected in time with the s 1 offence. It also creates a wider frame of culpability for the defendant: the intention may be to use the data at some time in the future.

Impossible further offence

5.29   Similar to the House of Lords' ruling in *R v Shivpuri*[52] in relation to the Criminal Attempts Act 1981, 'objective innocence' does not save a hacker who attempts a factually impossible crime. A hacker may be guilty of an offence under s 2 even though the facts are such that the commission of the further offence is impossible.[53] But the Computer Misuse Act 1990 is wider than the existing provisions under the Criminal Attempts Act 1981 and, say, the Theft Act 1968. This is because, even under the wider reading of the Criminal Attempts Act 1981 in *Shivpuri*, the defendant must still have done 'an act which is more than merely preparatory to the commission of the offence'.[54] In contrast, under the Computer Misuse Act 1990, an act less than merely preparatory may suffice as evidence of the additional intention needed for a s 2 offence.

Example 5.13

A hacker uses a computer to obtain another person's encryption key with which he intends to access the owner's online bank account. The hacker does not know that the bank will only allow access through its own dial-up connection and not over the web. The hacker's attempt would fail. Despite this, the hacker may have committed a s 2 offence, although he would probably not have made sufficient preparation for a statutory attempt.

---

50   For details, see *The Observer*, 12 February 2000.
51   Computer Misuse Act 1990, s 12(1)(a).
52   [1987] AC 1, especially at 21.
53   Computer Misuse Act 1990, s 2(4).
54   See Lord Bridge, [1987] AC 1 at 21; cf *Anderton v Ryan* [1985] AC 560 at 582–583.

Sentencing

5.30   A person guilty of an offence under s 2 is liable, on summary conviction, to imprisonment for a term not exceeding six months or to a fine not exceeding the statutory maximum or both and, on conviction on indictment, to imprisonment for a term not exceeding five years or to a fine or both. The potential term of imprisonment will be increased to 12 months (six months in Scotland) on summary conviction and up to five years on indictment.[55]

Section 3: unauthorised acts to impair or to prevent or hinder access

5.31   In 1865 Mr Fisher was convicted of damaging a steam engine by plugging up the feed-pipe and displacing other parts to render the engine useless.[56] There was no removal of any part, no cutting and no breaking. Pollock CB upheld the conviction, stating:[57]

> 'It is like the case of spiking a gun, where there is no actual damage to the gun, although it is rendered useless ... Surely the displacement of the parts was a damage ... if done with intent to render the machine useless.'

Malicious computer code is similar to Mr Fisher's feed-pipe plug. Often the victim computer program remains intact, as does the data it generates or uses; what alters is the computer's 'usefulness'. Before the Computer Misuse Act 1990, courts were forced to rely on the Criminal Damage Act 1971 to reason that the value of a computer's storage medium was impaired by altering the storing magnetic particles.[58]

   Prosecutions are more straightforward under s 3 of the Computer Misuse Act 1990. However, since its adoption, this section had come under increasing criticism for perceived problems in failing to address denial of service attacks and interference by authorised users of systems (insiders). This author writes 'perceived problems', since, in fact the previous drafting of s 3 was wide enough to capture these offences. Indeed, in 2006, the first prosecution for a denial of service attack was successfully brought, whilst the amendments to s 3 were still being debated in Parliament.[59] The amendments were nonetheless enacted through the Police and Criminal Justice Act 2006, making the offence even broader.

   The wording of s 3 provides that:

   '3.   (1) A person is guilty of an offence if:

55   Computer Misuse Act 1990, s 2(5). Once the amendments of the Police and Justice Bill 2006 are formally brought into force by the Secretary of State.
56   (1865) LR 1 CCR 7.
57   (1865) LR 1 CCR 7 at 9.
58   See *Cox v Riley* (1986) 83 Cr App Rep 54; also *R v Whiteley* (1991) 93 Cr App Rep 25. The Criminal Damage Act 1971 is no longer applicable owing to the Computer Misuse Act 1990, s 3(6).
59   *Director of Public Prosecution v David Lennon* [2006] EWCH 1201, 11 May 2006.

    (a) he does any act which causes unauthorised modification of the contents of any computer; and

    (b) at the time when he does the act he has the requisite intent and the requisite knowledge.

  (2) For the purposes of subsection (1)(b) above the requisite intent is an intent to cause modification of the contents of any computer and by so doing:

    (a) to impair the operation of any computer;

    (b) to prevent or hinder access to any program or data held in any computer; or

    (c) to impair the operation of any such program or the reliability of any such data.'

As amended, s 3 will read:

'3. (1) A person is guilty of an offence if:

    (a) he does any unauthorised act in relation to a computer; and

    (b) at the time when he does the act he knows that it is unauthorised; and

    (c) either subsection (2) or subsection (3) applies.

  (2) This subsection applies if the person intends by doing the act –

    (a) to impair the operation of any computer;

    (b) to prevent or hinder access to any program or data held in any computer;

    (c) to impair the operation of any such program or the reliability of any such data; or

    (d) to enable any of the things mentioned in paragraphs (a) to (c) above to be done.

  (3) This subsection applies if the person is reckless as to whether the act will do any of the things mentioned in paragraphs (a) to (d) of subsection (2) above.'

Conduct or actus reus

Unauthorised act or modification

Modification

5.32 Any act which causes an unauthorised modification of the contents of a computer can be the necessary conduct for a s 3 conviction.[60] Modification is exhaustively defined as taking place where, by the operation of any function, any program or data held in a computer is altered or erased or is added to.[61] The concept is widened by the clarification that 'any act which contributes towards causing such a modification shall be regarded as causing it'.[62]

---

60 Computer Misuse Act 1990, s 3(1)(a).
61 Computer Misuse Act 1990, s 17(7)(a) and (b).
62 Computer Misuse Act 1990, s 17(7). Emphasis added.

Example 5.14

A programmer is commissioned to write a Java applet which will show an animation on a home page. Without authority he also includes a logic bomb which downloads to each client computer and wishes them 'Happy Christmas' on 25 December. The logic bomb will not directly alter any program or data as it does not attach to other code stored on the computer. On the set date, however, the program will alter the contents of data held in the computer. The applet causes a modification.

Defence counsel should be alive to the fact that it is not unlawful to possess malicious code. Further, it is not prohibited to write it.[63] The hard task for the prosecution is therefore to prove that the defendant distributed or contributed to the release of malicious code. This is the case for two reasons.

First, malicious code is often spread by people other than those who wrote them initially. It can therefore be difficult to prove to the high burden of criminal proof that the source of the infection on the victim computer was the defendant's action. The existence of the virus on other systems prior to the alleged infection can weaken the prosecution's case by suggesting someone other than the defendant caused or contributed to the modification. The second difficulty for the prosecution is that, at present, there is no equivalent of a DNA fingerprint test for computer code. It will often be impossible to state categorically the source of an infection other than by extrapolating the code's dissemination. Occasionally, though, the prosecution will be able to rely on evidence gained from the defendant's own computer. In *R v Pile* the defendant surreptitiously stored programs on his computer which he used to write and distribute the viruses.[64] The FBI was helped by 'globally unique identifiers' (such as the embedding of Ethernet adaptor addresses in Microsoft Office 97 documents) to capture David L Smith, the Melissa virus writer.

Act

5.33   The amended s 3 offence, once in force, will capture any 'unauthorised act in relation to a computer' and therefore creates an even wider *actus reus*. There is no longer any need to demonstrate that the act 'causes an unauthorised modification of the contents of a computer' which will be a welcome amendment for prosecutors given that many forms of malicious code do not actually cause any alteration but just have an impact such as slowing down, jamming or simply making systems behave in a different way.

It has already been shown that 'computer' has a very wide meaning.[65] In addition, 'act', like 'function' in s 1, is not defined, although s 3(5) clarifies that this will encompass not just a single act but also a series of acts and that it also includes 'causing an act to be done'.[66]

---

63 Sadly, there are countless examples of 'macro virus construction kits' for large programs such as Microsoft Office. Use of inchoate offences to prosecute such virus writers, while possible, has never been tested in the UK's courts.

64 Unreported, Plymouth Crown Court, May 1995. See *The Guardian*, 16 November 1995.

65 See the discussion in the context of the s 1 offence at **5.5**.

66 Computer Misuse Act 1990, s 3(5)(a) and (b).

Unauthorised

5.34   For both existing and pending provisions, the concept of 'authority' is central. As for ss 1 and 2, demonstrating that the defendant's act was unauthorised is rarely difficult to prove when the malicious code is spread from outside an organisation. Sometimes within an organisation the act is so obvious that the defence can raise no serious questions of authority. Two real case examples should suffice. A male nurse pleaded guilty to two charges under s 3. He had altered prescriptions and treatment of various patients in his hospital.[67] In *R v Spielman* the defendant, a former employee of an online financial news agency, tampered with and deleted employee emails.[68]

A third case indicates the widening of the court's approach to acts which are deemed to be 'unauthorised'. Teenager David Lennon was fired from his position at Domestic and General after only three months in the job. As an act of revenge, Lennon used a mail bomb program to send up to five million emails to the company, the majority using the human resources manager's email address. A classic, 'denial of service' attack, the program operated by sending email upon email, copying to the employees within the company and increasing the email traffic so as to slow down systems and cause annoyance. The device was set up to keep going until manually stopped by Lennon. The Wimbledon youth court initially held that s 3 did not apply because the sending of emails was authorised. The whole purpose of the recipient's server was to receive email. The quantity was just 'unwelcome rather than unauthorised'. Lord Keen and Mr Justice Jack sitting in the High Court disagreed, concluding that implied consent had limits and the email bombing had to be considered as a whole and not on an email-by-email basis. On this basis, the emails were not sent for the purpose of communication (which was authorised), but to disrupt the systems (which was not).[69]

As stated previously, the more vague the internal guidelines on authority, the more difficult it may be to prosecute an insider who is regarded to have acted outside such authority.[70] Of course, employers may not resort to calling the police when an existing employee can be dealt with internally for gross misconduct.[71]

Intention or mens rea

5.35   The prosecution have several limbs to prove the *mens rea* elements of the offence.

---

67   *R v Rymer* (unreported, Liverpool Crown Court, December 1993). See *The Guardian*, 21 December 1993.
68   Unreported, Bow Street Magistrates' Court, March 1995. See *Computer Weekly*, 2 February 1995.
69   *Director of Public Prosecution v David Lennon* [2006] EWCH 1201, 11 May 2006. The defendant subsequently pleaded guilty and was sentenced to a two-month curfew and electronic tagging.
70   See **5.22**.
71   In *Denco v Joinson* an employee's unauthorised access was stated by the Employment Appeal Tribunal to be gross misconduct [1992] 1 All ER 463.

Currently, there are two limbs of a 'guilty mind' for s 3: the defendant must have the 'requisite intent' and the 'requisite knowledge'.[72] Simply put by the Act, the 'requisite knowledge' under s 3(1)(b) is that any modification intended to be caused is unauthorised. The examination under s 1 of the degree of 'knowledge' is equally relevant for this section.[73] In terms of intention, the defendant must not only have intended to modify the contents of a computer, but also this modification should have at least one of four results set out below.[74] This does not mean that the defendant must have intended one particular kind of modification: an intention to modify is sufficient.[75] These results are considered below with specific reference to potential rogue code which may be spread over the internet. It is not a defence that the results were intended to be merely temporary.[76]

Under the new s 3 there will still be a two-step test. First, the defendant must have known at the time he did the act that it was unauthorised. This issue of authority has been considered at some length above in relation to the s 1 offence, and so is not considered further here. Second, the prosecution must show that the defendant's intention in doing such act was to do one of five things (since a new addition has been made). Alternatively, the prosecution can now prove that the defendant was reckless as to whether the act would do any of these things. Each of these components and options is considered below.

Intent to impair or prevent or hinder access

5.36   In s 3 the motive and intention are tied up together. With s 1, it is enough that a defendant intends to secure unauthorised access; it is irrelevant why or what they then intend to do or permit. With s 3, the unauthorised modification or act must be intended to have some sort of impact namely, to do one of the following:[77]

3(2)(a) To impair the operation of any computer
5.37   To impair the operation of a computer itself, without impairing the operation of any program, would suggest that this subsection caters for a worm. A worm is a program which replicates and grows in size.[78] This reproduction and expansion can cause a computer storage system to run more slowly and can also cause the computer itself to slow down. Legally it is important to note that it does not attach itself to the operating system of the computer, to a program or data it infects; it does not directly impair the workings of a computer. The most infamous example of such a program is Robert Morris's worm. This was released on 2 November 1988 and within a couple of days had almost crashed the entire internet

---

72   Computer Misuse Act 1990, s 3(1)(b).
73   See the *dicta* of Lord Bridge, *Westminster City Council v Croyalgrange Ltd* [1986] 2 All ER 353.
74   Computer Misuse Act 1990, s 3(2).
75   Computer Misuse Act 1990, s 3(3)(c).
76   Computer Misuse Act 1990, s 3(5).
77   Although, as the cases and examples considered below indicate, the intention does not need to extend to the actual full impact of the act.
78   Not to be confused with the acronym WORM.

which existed at the time, including NASA and the US Defense Department. Morris was convicted of violating the Computer Fraud and Abuse Act.[79]

Another example of impairment can be seen in the case of university student Joseph McElroy, who used hacking tools to gain access to vulnerable systems so as to use their storage facility for uploading music, games and software for his own use and by his friends. Unfortunately, the vulnerable system he thought was an academic site, turned out to be owned by the US Department of Energy which is, amongst other things, responsible for the USA's nuclear weapons (although in fact the breach was found to be restricted to several unclassified computers). The storage caused the Department's systems to slow down, thereby impairing its operation. The systems needed to be repaired, costing tens of thousands of pounds.[80] McElroy (only 18) was convicted, but sentenced to just 200 hours of community service.

3(2)(b) To prevent or hinder access to any program or data held in any computer
A worm will hinder access to a program or data, indirectly, but there are three other types of code which will cause this. A virus which obstructs the use of a computer will certainly fall within this section. One of Christopher Pile's viruses, Pathogen, after infecting a computer 32 times, would at a particular time on a Monday evening show a message, 'Smoke me a kipper, I'll be back for breakfast. Unfortunately some of your data won't.'[81] This virus certainly hinders the access to the program being used at the time.

This type of result is also satisfied where a programmer seeks to use a logic bomb to 'lock out' an individual from accessing a program or data. Again, disgruntled employees appear to be the main culprits. Mr Hardy, an IT manager, added a program to his company's system which encrypted stored data, and de-encrypted it on retrieval. One month after he left the firm the program stopped unscrambling the data. This left his former company hindered from accessing its stored information. He pleaded guilty.[82]

Example 5.15

As a joke, a person attaches a virus to a word processing document which he forwards to a friend at work. The virus was intended simply to play a rude sound when the machine was next switched on. Owing to a special sound device attached to the friend's machine, the computer, and then the entire network, crashed. The more limited result intended by the joker is not relevant to the issue of culpability under the old s 3 wording; it may be relevant for sentencing or under the amended wording of s 3 however.

---

79   *United States v Morris* 928 F 2d 504 (2nd Cir) (1991). For additional details see Hafner K and Markoff J, *Cyberpunk* (Corgi, London, 1993).
80   *R v Joseph McElroy* (unreported, Southwark Crown Court, 3 February 2005).
81   See *The Guardian*, 16 November 1995.
82   *R v Hardy* (unreported, Old Bailey, November 1992).

3(2)(c) To impair the operation of any such program or the reliability of any such data

5.38   This subsection focuses on how a program executes when some code has run. The 'operation' can be taken to mean how the program should function without the malicious code. It should not be read narrowly to mean the use that the victim makes of the program. The Melissa virus would automatically 'send itself' to the first 50 addresses listed in the address book of the Microsoft Outlook program. The operation of Microsoft Outlook was impaired on the infected computer.

'Impairing the reliability of data' should be viewed by defence counsel as an objective notion of reliability. It is not enough for an infected computer owner to claim that he now cannot rely on the data because he feels it may be unreliable. The prosecution must prove the alteration or reduction in quality of the data on an objective basis.[83] This approach is supported in a case mainly concerning the extradition of two Kazakh hackers.[84] The facts of the case concerned the hacking of the Bloomberg financial computer system, so allowing the appellants to send messages that appeared to come from someone else; they were, in effect, forging the messages. The Divisional Court was asked whether or not adding new data to a computer system would fall within the section. Mr Justice Wright's terse judgment pointed out that s 17(7) of the Act provides that any addition of data to the contents of a computer amounts to a modification of the contents.

3(2)(d) To enable any of the things mentioned in paragraphs (a) to (c) above to be done

5.39   This provision is added under the Police and Justice Act 2006 and not yet in force at the time of publication. It widens and clarifies the acts which will be caught, meaning that the defendant need not themselves have actually caused the impairment or hindrance. It is sufficient that he intended that this would be enabled (whether by someone else, or by a user simply triggering the harm, for example by opening an attachment).

Example 5.16

A website has a virus which is downloaded secretly and automatically to any computer which accesses the site. This virus reduces the security of any credit card transactions which the user makes using their browser. It is of no importance that the only victims of the virus do not actually use their browser for such a purpose. The operation of the browser, as it was originally designed, has been impaired by the unauthorised modification.

---

83   This approach is confirmed in A-G's Reference (No 1 of 1991) [1993] QB 94. Lord Taylor stated *obiter* that it is questionable whether it is correct to 'giv[e] the word "reliability" the meaning of achieving the result in the printout which was intended by the owner of the computer. It may not necessarily impair the reliability of data in the computer that you feed in something which will produce a result more favourable … than the [owner] intended' ([1992] 3 WLR 432 at 438).

84   *Zezev and Yarimaka v Governor of HM Prison Brixton and Government of the United States of America* [2002] EWHC 589 (Admin) [2002] 2 Cr App Rep 515.

Any computer, program or data

5.40 The intention to modify does not need to be directed at any particular computer, or particular program, data or kind of program or data.[85] The drafting of s 3(4) in this way is essential to encompass fully the mischief which it addresses. Computer viruses and other malicious codes are disseminated in a random manner. The initial release of the code then results in it being passed to, and perhaps replicated by, any number of computers anywhere on the internet. The prosecution would not be able to show a defendant had the intent to infect each victim of his code.[86]

Temporarily

5.41 The pending (at the time of writing) amendment to s 3 at sub-s (5) (c) clarifies that 'a reference to impairing, preventing or hindering something includes a reference to doing so temporarily'.

Recklessness as to act

5.42 The Police and Justice Act 2006 introduces a new sub-s 3 to the s 3 offence which means that a defendant need not have intention but can still be found guilty if they were 'reckless as to whether the act will do any of the things mentioned in paragraphs (a) to (d) of subsection (2)'.

This reintroduces the recklessness element which exists in criminal damage cases, the main basis for action prior to the Computer Misuse Act. The recklessness requirement is objective.

Sentencing

5.43 Currently, a person guilty of an offence under s 3 is liable, on summary conviction, to imprisonment for a term not exceeding six months or to a fine not exceeding the statutory maximum or to both and, on indictment, to imprisonment for a term not exceeding five years or to a fine or to both.

The Police and Justice Act 2006 amendments increase the potential term of imprisonment to up to 12 months (six months for Scotland) on summary conviction and up to ten years on indictment.

Section 3A: making, supplying or obtaining articles for use in computer misuse

5.44 The most controversial of the amendments to the Computer Misuse Act which found its way into the Police and Justice Act 2006 is the inclusion of a new offence of making, supplying or obtaining articles for use in computer misuse.

---

85 Computer Misuse Act 1990, s 3(3)(a) and (b).
86 This is confirmed by the conviction in *R v Pile* (unreported, Plymouth Crown Court, May 1995). Mr Pile's viruses were placed on bulletin boards and then spread by other people. See *The Guardian*, 16 November 1995.

One of the main drivers behind this new provision is art 6 of the Council of Europe Convention on Cybercrime, which requires the criminalisation of the distribution or making of a computer password through which a computer system is capable of being accessed with intent to commit a crime. The Convention was opened for signature at a signing in ceremony in Budapest on 23 November 2001, when 30 countries signed. The terms of the Convention require that it enters into force only once it has been ratified by five countries. Nonetheless, it is clear from the amendments to the Computer Misuse Act, together with other changes in e-crime legislation (including serious crime) that the government has taken its provisions and motivations into consideration.

Section 3A reads:

'(1) A person is guilty of an offence if he makes, adapts, supplies or offers to supply any article intending it to be used to commit, or to assist in the commission of, an offence under section 1 or 3.

(2) A person is guilty of an offence if he supplies or offers to supply any article believing that it is likely to be used to commit, or to assist in the commission of, an offence under section 1 or 3.

(3) A person is guilty of an offence if he obtains any article with a view to its being supplied for use to commit, or to assist in the commission of, an offence under section 1 or 3.'

In this way, three separate offences are created. This section considers the *actus reus* and *mens rea* of each in turn.

Making, adapting, supplying or offering to supply article for commission of an offence

5.45   This offence captures the manufacture, supply, adaptation of or offering (eg advertising) of any equipment for the use in connection with the commission of an offence under s 1 or s 3 of the Act. 'Article' is defined in sub-s (4) as including any program or data held in electronic form and we have already seen above, how wide program and data can be construed.

Although perhaps the simplest of the offences, this section has come under recent criticism for failing to address the real problem of botnets, which are a vehicle typically used for the delivery of spam or denial of service attacks. The House of Lords' 2007 report on Personal Internet Security calls for a gap to be filled in order to cover those persons who purchase or hire botnets and those who sell them regardless of the purpose. The reasoning here is that a botnet is inherently designed for criminal use and 'can only exist by virtue of the criminal acts by those who recruited it'.[87]

Supply of an article to commit or assist in commission of an offence

5.46   This offence only captures the sale or offering of an article but where the defendant believed that it is likely to be used to commit or to assist in the

---

87   House of Lords Science and Technology Committee, 5th report of session 2006–2007 'Personal Internet Security', published on 10 August 2007, para 7.12.

commission of an offence under the Act. The most debated of the changes, particular concerns have been raised over the problem this presents for suppliers of tools which (unlike the issue with botnets) may be used for legitimate as well as illegal purposes. The IT and testing industry have been very alarmed by this development since it means that a risk hangs over them that the sale or offer of code which may be designed or intended for use in penetration testing or the permitted sending of email or distribution of code, could result in prosecution.

The main problem is the inclusion of the words 'believing it is likely to be used'. Programmers and developers are generally all too well aware of the capabilities of their creations or how a password tool could be used if in the wrong hands, say, of a hacker. Although discussed, no definition of what may constitute 'likely' has been included in the Act and attempts to replace this with 'primarily' resisted. Hansard discussions reveal that Ministers intended this to be a high test in practice, with the prosecution needing to prove beyond reasonable doubt that the person supplying the tool knew it would be used for unlawful purposes in most instances. This provides little comfort when the actual wording is around likely belief, rather than knowledge, however.

As the Earl of Erroll stated: 'One is trying to criminalise people who advertise on the internet saying, "Great hacker tool available, derived from such and such, best thing ever, why don't you buy it for X?"'[88] Without clarification in the legislation itself, it is left open to the courts to give its own interpretation to these words in due course.

Obtaining an article for supply or assistance in commission of an offence

5.47 This new offence catches the defendant who has obtained but not yet put to use an article which may be used for the commission of an offence under the Act. In this way it usefully opens the door to preventative action by the authorities. The difficulty, as ever in such possession cases, is in proving the intention where no acts have yet taken place.

Sentencing

5.48 A person guilty of an offence under s 3A is liable, on summary conviction, to imprisonment for a term not exceeding 12 months (six months for Scotland), or to a fine not exceeding the statutory maximum or to both or, on indictment, to imprisonment for a term not exceeding two years or to a fine or to both.[89]

Jurisdiction and extradition

5.49 Jurisdiction and extradition can be fundamental to an internet-based case. The Computer Misuse Act 1990 operates within tight jurisdictional confines.

---

88 Lords Hansard 11 July 2006: Column 581.
89 Computer Misuse Act 1990, s 3(A)(5).

Computer misusers do not. It has been discussed that a hacker will often log in to computers across the globe in a bid to disguise his true location and identity. Malicious code, such as viruses, can spread across the whole internet, and are therefore capable of modifying any data or program in any jurisdiction.

The physical location of the hacker or other misuser is not an indication of where the crime is committed. And what may not be legal here, may well be caught by the laws of another jurisdiction. These other laws are not considered in this chapter, but the rules on extradition to those countries are.

Jurisdiction

5.50   The Computer Misuse Act 1990 provides its rules on jurisdiction in ss 4 to 7.[90] They are complex and apply differently to each of the offences. If the English court does not have jurisdiction over the offence the offender may still face charges from abroad.

Section 1 jurisdiction

5.51   The court will have jurisdiction over a computer misuse offender under s 1 where the offence has at least one 'significant link' with England and Wales.[91] For a s 1 offence, a significant link can be either:[92]

'1. that the accused was in England at the time when he did the act which caused the computer to perform the function; or

2. that the computer containing any program or data to which the accused secured or intended to secure unauthorised access by doing that act was in England at that time.'[93]

The second situation has been replaced by the amendments of the Police and Justice Act 2006 with:

'2. that any computer containing any program or data to which the accused by doing that act secured or intended to secure unauthorised access, or enabled or intended to enable unauthorised access to be secured, was in England or Wales concerned at that time.'

These changes are natural consequences of the amendments to the s 1 offence and do not represent a substantial change.

---

90   Readers unfamiliar with rules as to jurisdiction are warned not to conflate the assessment of jurisdiction with assessment of culpability under the offence itself. The rules described below are necessarily wider than the rules for a conviction. It is perfectly possible that the courts have jurisdiction over a person, who at trial, is found not to be guilty of the offence itself. Nevertheless, the defence should be prepared to fight on jurisdiction, without which there will be no trial in England at all.
91   Computer Misuse Act 1990, s 4(2).
92   Computer Misuse Act 1990, s 5(2).
93   A 16-year-old pleaded guilty to 12 s 1 offences. All the unauthorised accesses were performed from his north London home. The victim computers were top security military computers based in the US. The Senate said that 'he had caused more damage than the KGB': *R v Pryce* (unreported, Bow Street Magistrates' Court, 21 March 1997).

Location of accused

5.52   This is a simple test. Neil Woods and Karl Strickland were convicted and sentenced to six months' imprisonment under s 1. They had used UK computers, mostly academic, to break into databases in 15 countries outside the UK.[94]

Example 5.17

A French postgraduate student at university in England logs in to his former university computer in France. From this computer he runs an automated hacking program which fails to gain access to a further computer in the US. The English court has jurisdiction, even though the computer caused to function was outside England, as was the victim computer. The act causing the function was made while the postgraduate was in England.

Location of victim computer

5.53   The nub of this subsection is that the misuser secured access or intended to secure access to any computer situated in England. It is of no consequence that the hacker was only using an English computer as a 'stop' on the way to a victim computer outside the jurisdiction. Jurisdiction can result from the victim computer or any computer through which the hacker journeys being within England.

Example 5.18

A programmer based in the US has for some time been plotting to hack into an English oil company's computer. He is caught by US police, having secured access to a US computer which has a secure line to the English computer. The English court, perhaps not alone, has jurisdiction over the American. It is sufficient that his intentions were directed to an English computer.

Example 5.19

A hacker based in a country with no extradition treaties gains unauthorised access into a computer with weak security in Bolivia. She uses this computer to plant daemon programs in countless other computers across the globe. Finally, she uses a program called Tribal Flood Network to launch attacks at a UK newspaper's website. It is brought down by the attack in seconds. The English court has jurisdiction over the hacker as her intention was to impair a UK computer.

Section 2 jurisdiction

5.54   The jurisdiction over s 2 offences is wider than that for s 1. Either or both of two rules give the court jurisdiction:

---

94   Unreported, Southwark Crown Court, 21 May 1993.

1. subject to 'double criminality' below if the accused intended to do or facilitate anything outside England which would be a s 2 offence if it took place in England and the offence has a significant link to England for a s 1 offence;[95]

2. if the accused gained unauthorised access to a computer abroad with the intent to commit the further offence in England.

The English courts must view the conduct as falling within the ambit of the offence and the relevant country abroad must also view the conduct as criminal, although the offences here and abroad need not be the same.[96] The further offence must involve the commission of an offence under the law in force where the whole or any part of the further offence was intended to take place.[97]

Defence counsel must note that the onus is on them to serve a notice on the prosecution stating that the double-criminality is not satisfied. Full facts and grounds for that opinion must be included in the notice.[98]

Example 5.20

A US bank protects its records by storing them with an English data warehouse, fully encrypted. From a mobile device, a hacker, at the time in Switzerland, gains access to this data warehouse and appropriates a number of confidential files, still encrypted. After cracking the encryption, the hacker intends to steal electronically from the US bank. The English court has jurisdiction over the hacker, having both a significant link with England, constituting an offence if in England and being punishable in the US.

Section 3 jurisdiction

5.55   The court will have jurisdiction over s 3 misuse where the offence has at least one 'significant link' with England.[99] For a s 3 offence, a significant link can be either:[100]

1. that the accused was in England at the time when he did the act which caused the unauthorised modification; or

2. that the unauthorised modification took place in England.

Again, minor amendments reflect the changes to the s 3 offence pursuant to the Police and Justice Act 2006.

It has been mentioned on numerous occasions that a virus may spread throughout the entire internet. It is possible to affect computers in multiple jurisdictions. An effect of the 'significant link' is to allow the English courts to prosecute a person who disseminates malicious code from England, even if

---

95 Computer Misuse Act 1990, s 4(4).
96 Computer Misuse Act 1990, s 8(4).
97 Computer Misuse Act 1990, s 8(1).
98 Computer Misuse Act 1990, s 8(5) and (9).
99 Computer Misuse Act 1990, s 4(2).
100 Computer Misuse Act 1990, s 5(3).

no computer in England is modified. Also, the significant link contemplates a computer modifier from anywhere in the world being prosecuted for a computer in England being affected.

Location of accused

5.56

Example 5.21

An English public schoolboy uses his school computer to post on a French internet bulletin board a logic bomb which corrupts an important part of any computer it infects. It is of no consequence that the logic bomb is 'defused' before it reaches a computer in England. The act constituting the offence was committed within the jurisdiction.

As previously stated, executable code which is on a website may cause an unauthorised modification or impairment. The act of uploading this code to the website will constitute the relevant act for the purposes of jurisdiction.

Location of victim computer

5.57   The jurisdiction of the court is triggered by any computer situated in England affected by the unauthorised modification or act. It does not matter that the modifier had no intention to infect an English computer.

Extradition

5.58   The law concerning extradition is complex and that readers should consult a specialist text in the field before providing or acting on any advice. The following is a brief indication of the aspects of digital crime over the internet which should be factored into any extradition evaluation.

The rules of extradition are largely governed by way of international treaties and agreements between states.

In the UK, statutory rules (implementing certain of these arrangements) are set out in the Extradition Act 2003 (repealing the Extradition Act 1989). This Act separates out the procedures for extradition to 'category 1 territories', which are part of the European Arrest Warrant Scheme, namely European member states, and 'category 2 territories', which are designated territories which are not. The Act also incorporates controversial arrangements of an extradition treaty with the US, against which alleged hacker Gary McKinnon was fighting. Mr McKinnon gained access to various US government computers specifically out of curiosity, he maintains, as to evidence of UFO attacks, rather than with any terrorist intention. For category 1 territories, the process is now expedited allowing, essentially, for the mutual recognition of warrants issued in one member state in the courts of another. In relation to crimes, of which computer crime is punishable by up to three years' imprisonment, extradition within such territories is therefore intended to be automatic and it is not necessary to consider whether such an offence would be an offence in both relevant territories. In other cases, such dual criminality assessments may still apply. Both ss 2 and 3 of the Computer Misuse Act therefore fall within this automatic category. (Remember of course that extradition is a different matter to the making out of an offence in the UK in the first place for the purposes of s 2, which is considered above, so although seemingly at odds and complex, these are different things.)

For category 2 territories, the 'double criminality test' applies (therefore an offence must be made out in each of the relevant territories although not necessarily the same offence). An order from the Secretary of State is required.

The following discussion of an actual extradition case illustrates the way a hacker from abroad may be extradited to a place where his actions were illegal.

In *R v Governor of Brixton Prison, ex p Levin*, the US government sought the extradition of a Russian expert computer programmer who had gained access to Citibank's computer in New Jersey, in the US.[101] Levin, using his skill as a computer programmer, was able to monitor the transactions of substantial customers and insert unauthorised instructions to make payments from their accounts into those of a Russian accomplice. If the scheme had been successful, sums in excess of $10 million would have been obtained. Levin was detained[102] in execution of a warrant under s 1(3) of the Extradition Act 1989 at the request of the US government. He was accused of having committed in the US offences of wire fraud and bank fraud and of conspiring to commit those offences. No single criminal offence under the law of England and Wales equates to the offence of wire fraud or bank fraud.

The prosecuting authority gave details of acts and conduct which translated into 66 offences under the criminal law of England and Wales, including unauthorised access to a computer with intent to commit or facilitate further offences, conspiracy to commit offences under the Computer Misuse Act 1990 and unauthorised modification of computer material.

The applicant challenged his committal on the main grounds that the computer print-out records could not be admitted under s 69 of the Police and Criminal Evidence Act 1984 since that section did not apply to extradition proceedings, because they were not criminal proceedings within s 72 of the Act.

The Divisional Court and House of Lords held that as the extradition crimes involved conduct punishable under the criminal law, they were criminal proceedings for the purposes of the Police and Criminal Evidence Act 1984. Evidence of the computer print-outs in extradition hearings should be, and rightly in this case, was admitted in evidence under s 69 of the Act.

One of the other grounds was that as the appropriation took place in Russia, where the computer keyboard was situated, the English courts had no jurisdiction. For the purposes of the Theft Act 1968, the Divisional Court had to decide where the actions of Mr Levin took place. They said:[103]

'[T]he operation of the keyboard by a computer operator produces a virtually instantaneous result on the magnetic disk of the computer even though it may be 10,000 miles away. It seems to us artificial to regard the act as having been done

---

101   [1997] QB 65; affd [1997] 3 All ER 289, HL.
102   On 3 March 1995.
103   [1996] 3 WLR 657 at 671.

in one rather than the other place. [T]he fact that the applicant was physically in St Petersburg is of far less significance than the fact that he was looking at and operating on magnetic disks located in [the US]. The essence of what he was doing was done there.'[104]

Mr Levin was extradited to the US.[105] Subsequently Federal prosecutors announced that they had reached a plea agreement with Mr Levin: three years in prison together with $240,000 payable in restitution.

INTERNET FRAUD

5.59   Internet fraud is not a new crime, it just takes traditional scams and schemes and uses new technical means to trap its victims. As the Law Commission had revealed in a comprehensive 2002 report,[106] the previous offences contained in the Theft Act 1968 and 1978 (governing goods and services respectively) were outdated and overly complex and therefore unable to deal with this new development. In particular, the legislation contained a loophole which meant that it was not possible to deceive a machine. This had the natural consequence that a whole raft of computer and internet-based frauds were not in fact criminal, for example the giving of fake credit card details in order to purchase goods fraudulently. As the Law Commission pointed out, the fraud should be the offence, and the means by which it is effected should be immaterial.

The Fraud Act 2006, implemented in line with the Commission's recommendations, creates a general offence of fraud, with three ways of committing it: by false representation; by failing to disclose information; and by abuse of position. The new offence of 'fraud by false representation' carries a maximum sentence of ten years' imprisonment and is drafted broadly so as to encompass fraudulent internet and other online activities such as 'phishing'. Government resisted calls for a specific anti-phishing offence, preferring a broader approach which would capture this and future forms of fraudulent activity.

The Act also requires that the person must make the representation with the intention of making a gain or causing loss or risk of loss to another, regardless of whether the gain or loss actually takes place. A representation is defined as false if it is untrue or misleading and the person making it knows that it is, or might be, untrue or misleading. A representation means any representation as to fact or law, including a representation as to a person's state of mind. It can be stated in words or communicated by conduct. There is no limitation on the way in which the words must be expressed: they could be written, spoken or posted on a website.

---

104 In *Zezev and Yarimaka v Governor of HM Prison Brixton and Government of the United States of America* [2002] EWHC 589 (Admin) [2002] 2 Cr App Rep 515 the Divisional Court also judged that the UK court could extradite two hackers who committed computer misuse from Kazakstan against Bloomberg LP in New York.
105 This took place in September 1997.
106 Law Commission Report on Fraud (Law Com No 276, Cm 5560, 2002).

In respect of the gain, there is no limitation in the Act, which means that this need not be limited to goods or services. This is good news for those increasingly concerned with the appropriation of credit card or identity details across the internet. Confirmation is provided in the Explanatory Notes to the Act, which expressly give internet-based examples. One such example includes that of 'a person who disseminates an email to large groups of people falsely representing that the email has been sent by a legitimate financial institution. The email prompts the reader to provide information such as credit card and bank account numbers so that the "phisher" can gain access to others' assets.' Although a very welcome development, problems still arise in terms of public confidence and the manner of investigation and reporting of internet fraud. The House of Lords has condemned in particular[107] the approach taken by the government, which seeks to discourage the reporting of these sorts of crimes to the police, instead asking those affected to report it to APACS (the UK trade association for payments services and institutions).

OBSCENE AND INDECENT MATERIAL

5.60   It has always been possible to acquire by mail order obscene and paedophilic material from within England or from abroad which is illegal in England. The internet has made this process easier and it may have made this activity more prevalent; it has not, however, altered the legal ramifications of the activity.[108] The Obscene Publications Act 1959, as amended by the Criminal Justice and Public Order Act 1994, covers material which has the effect of depraving and corrupting. Additionally the Sexual Offences Act 2003, which came into force on 1 May 2004, amends parts of the Protection of Children Act 1978 to extend protection in relation to indecent photographs of children of 16 and 17. It also introduces a new offence under s 15, intended to target those who may use the internet for sexual grooming.

This section considers the different liabilities which may arise where a person either publishes indecent or obscene material over the internet, or takes, downloads, distributes or possesses indecent photographs. We then consider the position as regards liability of intermediaries for such content.

Publication over the internet

5.61   An offence is committed under the Obscene Publications Act if a person publishes an obscene article: merely possessing an article is not an offence.[109] Possessing an obscene article for publication for gain is an offence.[110] Often,

---

107 House of Lords Science and Technology Committee, 5th report of session 2006–2007 'Personal internet Security', published on 10 August 2007.
108 See also Telecommunications Act 1984, s 43 and Indecent Displays (Control) Act 1981.
109 Obscene Publications Act 1959, s 2.
110 Obscene Publications Act 1959, s 2.

those who use the internet for these purposes do not pay money for obscene articles; rather, they exchange them for other articles. This too will be seen as 'for gain'.[111] It is for the possessor of the article to prove that it was not for gain.

An amendment to the Act introduced the concept that it is publication to transmit electronically stored data which is obscene on resolution into a viewable form.[112]

Example 5.22

A person sends an email attached to which is an encrypted graphics file depicting an obscene activity. Only the recipient has the unlocking key. The person will have transmitted the obscene material: it does not matter that the data is encrypted; when de-encrypted it will be obscene.

Transmission or retrieval

5.62   Often, obscene material is not transmitted to an individual. It is uploaded to a website or an ftp site. Interested parties download this material by instructing their computer to issue a command to the holding site. It is clearly an important question whether this constitutes transmission, and thereby constitutes publication.

This question was addressed by the Court of Appeal in *R v Fellows; R v Arnold*.[113] The appellants argued that publication within s 1(3) requires some form of active conduct, and that providing the means of access to a website or ftp site is passive only. In short, putting obscene pictures on a website, although no doubt allowing them to be seen by many people, is not publication of those pictures; technically it is each viewer who retrieves the picture.

The Court of Appeal was prepared to accept that some form of activity is required for publication. In this case they thought that there was ample evidence of such conduct. The first appellant:

'took whatever steps were necessary not merely to store the data on his computer but also to make it available world-wide to other computers via the internet. He corresponded by e-mail with those who sought to have access to it and he imposed certain conditions before they were permitted to do so.'

This 'activity' prior to the actual offence appears to have satisfied the court that the storage of the material alone would be distribution.[114]

---

111 Obscene Publications Act 1959, s 1(5). See *R v Fellows; R v Arnold* (unreported, CA, 27 September 1996).
112 Obscene Publications Act 1959, s 1(3), as amended by Criminal Justice and Public Order Act 1994, s 168 and Sch 9.
113 [1997] 2 All ER 548.
114 See also *R v Pecciarich* (1995) 22 OR (3d) 748 at 765.

Publication abroad

5.63 It has been stated that possessing an obscene article is not an offence. However, where a person possesses an article and then transmits this abroad, where it is there published, a question arises as to whether this is an offence.

In *R v Waddon the Crown Court*[115] and Court of Appeal[116] were asked whether a UK resident creating obscene articles in the UK and uploading them to non-UK websites was 'publishing' for the purposes of the Obscene Publications Act. The courts reasoned that 'publishing' an article includes 'transmitting' that data.[117] Transmitting, the Crown Court held, means to send on from one place or person to another. Consequently, the transmission by the defendant to his UK internet service provider took place within the jurisdiction. The Court of Appeal added that there was not one publication, but rather 'further publication when the images are downloaded elsewhere'. The fact that the appellant would not have been directly responsible for any downloads into the UK, so therefore could not have been prosecuted for them, is ignored by the Court of Appeal. This author prefers the arguments of the Crown Court as being a more robust application of the law to the known facts.

In a similar case, *R v Perrin*,[118] the Court of Appeal was asked to consider an appeal to a conviction of publishing an obscene article. The article in question was a sexually obscene web page, able to be viewed by anyone, and a further much larger set of sexually obscene material only viewable by subscribing with a credit card. The site was, in part, managed from outside the UK. The appellant appealed the conviction on a number of grounds. One was that it was necessary for the Crown to show where the major steps in relation to publication were taken. The Court of Appeal rejected this as being a necessary precursor to any prosecution. Instead, they deemed it enough to rely on a strict application of *Waddon*: there was 'transmission' within the jurisdiction.

These cases illustrate the rather parochial (and maybe morally justified) application of the Obscene Publications Act to published material on the internet. Perhaps not unreasonably, in *Perrin*, the appellants sought to convince the Court of Appeal of the legal consequence of 'the sites [being] legal where they were managed'. In effect, the appellants unsuccessfully tried to appeal to the Court's commercial sense: 'Community standards as to what tends to deprave and corrupt are not Europe-wide, and the court should look at the problem from the point of view of a publisher who is prepared to comply with the law.' Of course these arguments are neither novel nor unique to English internet jurisprudence. In the US, the Court of Appeal (Third Circuit) has (reluctantly) judged that only where the 'major' steps in relation to publication take place in the jurisdiction should the court take jurisdiction over a prosecution.[119] The US court in that case noted

---

115 [1999] ITCLR 422, [1999] Masons CLR 396, CC.
116 Unreported, 6 April 2000.
117 Obscene Publications Act 1959, s 1(3)(b), as amended.
118 [2002] EWCA Crim 747, [2002] All ER (D) 359 (Mar). It should be noted that the Court of Appeal also rejected the various pleas that the European Convention on Human Rights, arts 7 and 10, were sufficient to overturn the conviction.
119 *ACLU v Reno (No 3)* [2000] F 3d 162. The case concerned the preliminary injunction against the Attorney-General to prevent the enforcement of the Child Protection Act.

that 'web publishers cannot restrict access to their site based on the geographic locale of the internet user visiting their site'.[120]

It is clear from these cases that the UK criminal courts' jurisdiction in cases of this kind will not be upset by the careful placing abroad of servers or 'management'.[121]

Example 5.23

A woman living in Manchester establishes a Dutch company which operates a series of servers in Holland. The servers host a website which, after a credit card is entered, shows a number of obscene pictures involving sexual acts with animals. These obscene articles are uploaded to the Dutch servers from her home in Manchester. By transmitting the obscene articles from within the UK she is publishing obscene articles in the UK. She will not be able to avoid the jurisdiction of the UK courts by pointing to the 'major' steps being taken outside the UK.

Indecent material

5.64 Section 1(1) of the Protection of Children Act 1978,[122] as amended by the Criminal Justice and Public Order Act 1994 and Sexual Offences Act 2003 (specifically to raise the age of a person considered to be a child from 16 to 18), makes it an offence:

> '(a) to take, or permit to be taken, an indecent photograph of a child (meaning in this Act a person under the age of 18); or
>
> (b) to distribute or show such indecent photographs or pseudo-photographs; or
>
> (c) to have in his possession such indecent photographs or pseudo-photographs with a view to their being distributed or shown by himself or others ...'

Although the circumstances will be rare, there may be occasions where an individual possesses such items without knowledge of them. This is possible because most internet browsers automatically store a copy of every graphic file viewed, called a 'cached' copy. In *Atkins v DPP*[123] the defendant was not convicted of the offence where he was not aware that his computer's cache held copies of the illegal photographs he had once viewed. This can easily be contrasted

---

120 *ACLU v Reno (No 3)* [2000] F 3d 162, at 176. Cf *Groppera Radio AG v Switzerland* (1990) 12 EHRR 321.

121 In *Gold Star Publications Ltd v DPP* [1981] 2 All ER 257, the House of Lords was asked to consider whether thousands of hard-core pornographic magazines due for export from the UK would fall within the jurisdiction of the courts. Only Lord Simon dissented, taking the narrow view that the Obscene Publications Act 1959 should not be interpreted to grant UK courts powers to prevent activities abroad.

122 This legislation remains unaffected by the coming into force of the Human Rights Act 1998, and therefore the European Convention of Human Rights, arts 8 and 10. In *R v Smelhurst*, the Court of Appeal were clear that the exception in art 10(2) covers the Act and it does not contravene the provisions of the Convention.

123 [2000] 2 All ER 425.

with 'making' by downloading and or printing indecent material, which does constitute an offence.[124] Downloading and printing are intentional acts and so may constitute 'making'. Even the deliberate copying of such material in the process of deleting it, may constitute the offence.[125]

Photographs and pseudo-photographs

5.65   The changes brought by the Criminal Justice and Public Order Act 1994 have been implemented to address the use that paedophiles make of computers. The term 'photographs' includes data stored on a computer disk or by other electronic means which is capable of conversion into a photograph.[126] This includes digital graphic images. The court will take a 'purposive approach': if the data can be converted into an indecent image, the data will be classed as a photograph.[127] A 'pseudo photograph' is an image, whether made by a computer graphic or otherwise, which appears to be a photograph.[128] This inclusion, apparently, reflects the practice of paedophiles who use pornographic images of adults and then digitally alter them to look like indecent photographs of children. In *G v DPP*, two paper photographs taped together were not held to be a pseudo-photograph as they did not 'appear' to be a single photograph.[129] This can surely be contrasted with two digital graphic images which, when aligned, do appear as one.

Transmission, retrieval and downloading

5.66   As in the case for obscene material, *R v Fellows* indicated that it will be distribution simply to allow indecent images to be transmitted.

In addition, in considering s 7(2) of the 1978 Act, the court held that a computer file containing data that represented the original photograph in another form was 'a copy of a photograph' for the purposes of that section. Therefore, the downloading of an indecent photograph from the internet constituted the 'making a copy of an indecent photograph', since a copy of that photograph had been caused to exist on the computer to which it had been downloaded.

This decision was taken further in *R v Jayson*,[130] in which the defendant was found to hold child abuse images in the temporary cache created by his internet browser. Although the image was not stored for subsequent retrieval (ie the defendant had just been viewing the images on the internet), the Court of Appeal ruled that 'the act of voluntarily downloading an indecent image from a web page on to a computer screen is an act of making a photograph or pseudo-photograph'.

---

124 *R v Jonathan Bowden* [2001] QB 88.
125 *R v Mould* (unreported, CA, 6 November 2000).
126 Protection of Children Act 1978, s 7(4)(b), as amended.
127 See the US Court of Appeals for the Sixth Circuit, *United States v Thomas* 74 F 3d 701 (1996).
128 Protection of Children Act 1978, s 7(7), as amended.
129 *R v DPP* (unreported, Divisional Court, 8 March 2000).
130 [2002] EWCA Crim 683, CA.

The period of time for which it was held and whether it could be retrieved was judged irrelevant.

'Making' may therefore arise through the copying of an image to removable storage media, where a 'hard copy' is printed out or simply where indecent content is voluntarily viewed on the internet.

Of course the natural consequence of it being an offence to download or copy indecent images from the internet or computer files means that law enforcement and network operators were also potentially liable for copying the contents of suspects files for evidence purposes. This particular issue has been resolved by amendments to include a statutory defence where the making is necessary for the purposes of the prevention, detection or investigation of crime or for the purpose of criminal proceedings, through the Sexual Offences Act.

Liability of internet service providers

5.67   As a starting point, because publication can be 'passive', an internet service provider who facilitates, by storing, the transmission of an obscene file may be culpable as the publisher of obscene material. Similarly, under the Protection of Children Act 1978, mere possession on a server may be an offence under s 1(1)(c).

Internet Watch Foundation

5.68   The high risk of liability where 'blind eyes are turned', together with an interest in the 'common good', led internet service providers to concoct a remarkably impressive system of self-regulation and authority co-operation. The Internet Watch Foundation (IWF) was formed in October 1996. It is an independent self-regulatory body funded by the EU and the online industry and aims (and succeeds) in restricting the availability of criminal content on the internet. It operates a hotline and a 'notice and take down' procedure for internet service providers.[131] The IWF works closely with relevant authorities, forwarding child or adult pornography details on UK servers to relevant British police forces. Child pornography on foreign servers is forwarded to the Child Exploitation and Online Protection Centre, disseminated by Interpol.

Demonstrating the effectiveness of this 'hotline' together with 'notice and takedown' and 'authority notification' is the case of Leslie Bollingbroke. The IWF discovered that an individual using the pseudonym 'Sammy' was posting illegal images of children on the internet and discussing them on newsgroups. The IWF forwarded the information to the Metropolitan Police. 'Sammy' was discovered to be one Leslie Bollingbroke, who was subsequently jailed for four years.

---

131 IWF published statistics; which has resulted in less than 1% of potentially illegal content being hosted in the UK since 2003, down from 18% in 1997.

A second reason for the effectiveness of this 'self-regulation' is the interaction between the Internet Service Providers Association (ISPA) and the IWF. Both are independent bodies, but the ISPA acts, among other objectives, to represent and lobby for ISPs before government and the public. Consequently, most ISPs are ISPA members. However, their Code of Practice[132] obliges members to register with the IWF and receive and act upon 'take down' notices in accordance with the IWF's own Code of Practice. The IWF strengthened its role yet further by recommending to all UK ISPs that they do not carry newsgroups which IWF identifies as regularly hosting child pornography and which have names that appear to advertise or advocate paedophile content or activity.[133] A full IWF member who fails to comply with the Code may be reported to the IWF Executive Committee, receive a formal warning and a report may be filed with the relevant law enforcement authority. Serious breaches may result in suspension.

Electronic Commerce (EC Directive) Regulations 2002

5.69   The Electronic Commerce (EC Directive) Regulations 2002[134] provide internet service providers with a defence to their liability under the Obscene Publications Act 1959 and the Protection of Children Act 1978 together with other criminal statutes.[135] Four conditions must be met: ISP has no actual knowledge; ISP is not aware of unlawful nature; ISP acts expeditiously to remove or disable on knowledge; ISP has no control.[136]

The first condition is that the internet service provider must not have actual knowledge that an activity or information was in breach of any law.[137] This 'actual knowledge' is likely to involve the internet service provider knowing, with some precision, about the activity or information. This precision, particularly relating to the location of the offending material, is essential because the defence envisages the internet service provider needing to 'remove or disable' the information.[138] If the ISP is not able to locate the material, it does not have sufficient knowledge.

---

132 Adopted 25 January 1999.
133 On 15 February 2002. This approach has echoes of the approach taken by New Scotland Yard in 1995 when they, in effect, put all internet service providers 'on notice' of the newsgroups which mainly carry illegal material: *The Independent*, 20 December 1995.
134 Implementing the Directive 2000/31/EC of the European Parliament and of the Council of 8 June 2000 on certain legal aspects of information society services, in particular electronic commerce, in the Internal Market (Directive on electronic commerce) (OJ L178, 17.7.2000, p 1).
135 As discussed elsewhere in this book, such defences only apply in respect of statutes which were in force prior to the adoption of the Regulations or to those enacted after such date where the government has so provided on a case-by-case basis.
136 Regs 19 and 22.
137 Reg 19(a)(i).
138 See below, reg 19(a)(i).

Example 5.24

A very popular UK-based internet service provider has over 500,000 users, most of whom have a website which the ISP hosts. It provides a freephone answerphone for any complaint about the material on these websites. A young girl leaves a message on the answerphone that there are 'horrid pictures of me on a website', bursts into tears and then puts down the phone. While the internet service provider may well have very serious concerns about this complaint, it does not have 'actual knowledge' of any breach of law. It neither knows the nature of the breach nor the identity or location of the complained-of material.

The second condition, wider than the first, is that the ISP is also not aware of facts or circumstances from which it would have been apparent to the service provider that the activity or information was unlawful.[139] The IWF's notification to ISPs of suspicious newsgroups will doubtlessly move ISPs into being in the position of being 'aware of facts or circumstances', from which it will be apparent that information on those newsgroups is unlawful.

The third condition is that upon obtaining such knowledge or awareness, the service provider acts expeditiously to remove or to disable access to the information.[140] There are two issues that arise from this. First, how quickly must an ISP act to ensure that they are removing or disabling 'expeditiously'? Neither the Regulations nor the originating Directive provide a definition. The courts will initially rely on the dictionary definition, if pressed to judge an ISP's 'reaction time'. The dictionary talks of the concept of 'speedily'. The ISP must (despite discussions in respect of a two working day rule, considered in the context of the Terrorism Act 2006 discussed below at **5.70** *et seq*) therefore treat the knowledge or awareness with some urgency and not merely as some 'housekeeping' that can wait.

A second issue arising from the obligation to remove or disable access to the material is the ISP's risk of doing so. What if the 'notice' to the ISP was malicious or plain wrong but, in good faith, the ISP removes the material anyway? The Regulations are silent on this very real possibility. In contrast, this exact situation is considered by the US Digital Millennium Copyright Act. In that Act the ISP has a 'good samaritan' defence to such an act.[141] UK ISPs are therefore advised to state in their contracts with users that they reserve the right to remove or disable access to material in these circumstances. In addition, ISPs must ensure that their contracts exclude any of their liability for so removing or disabling access to such material.

The final condition of the defence, obviously, is that the person responsible for the storage or transmission of the illegal material must not have been acting under the 'authority or the control' of the internet service provider.[142] It may be

---

139 Reg 19(a)(i). See 'Once it is, or should be, appreciated that the material is indecent and its continued retention or distribution is indecent then its continued retention or distribution is subject to the risk of prosecution': *R v Land* [1998] 1 All ER 403 at 407, CA.

140 Reg 19(a)(ii).

141 47 USC §§ 230(c)(2)(A).

142 Reg 19(b).

argued that for an ISP to have 'authority or control' over someone, they would need to have gone further than merely having a usual member contract with the individual. In this sense the concept of 'authority or control' is akin to the concept of 'effective control' in the Defamation Act 1996, discussed in detail in Chapter 3.[143]

ANTI-TERRORISM AND TERRORIST MATERIALS

5.70   The Terrorism Act 2000, which came into force on 19 February 2001 and is amended by the Anti-terrorism, Crime and Security Act 2001 and the Terrorism Act 2006 bolster the Computer Misuse Act 1990 and Fraud Act 2006 for the most serious of computer attacks. As can be seen below, however, the two separate Acts have rather different effects for internet service providers and website owners.

Threat to electronic systems

5.71   The Terrorism Act 2000 addresses, *inter alia*, the use or threat of an '[action] designed seriously to interfere with, or seriously to disrupt an electronic system'[144] where two other conditions are met. First, the use or threat of the action must be 'designed to influence [any] government or to intimidate the public or a section of the public [including public of a country other than the United Kingdom]'.[145] The second precondition which must be met is that the use or threat must be made for the 'purpose of advancing a political, religious or ideological cause'.[146]

Example 5.25

A British-based cult from the UK threatens to disrupt the computer systems and power supplies in every US hospital that carries out abortions. It threatens to do so in accordance with its governing religious doctrine, that 'all life is sacred'. This serious threat, despite being targeted at a non-UK, non-governmental section of society, will fall within the provisions of the Terrorism Act 2000.

This general area is open to legislative change, particularly as regards official data access and data retention. For example, the EU regime for official access and data retention was undermined when the Data Retention Directive (Directive 2006/24/EC, and which amended Directive 2002/58/EC) was struck down in joined cases *Digital Rights Ireland* and *Seitlinger and Others*, Cases C293/12 and C594/12 of 8 April 2014). This has implications for the legality of the UK Regulatory

---

143 Section 1(3)(e).
144 Terrorism Act 2000, s 1(2)(e).
145 Terrorism Act 2000, ss 1(1)(b) and (4)(c).
146 Terrorism Act 2000, s 1(1)(c).

Investigatory Powers Act 2000 (RIPA). The UK responded by enacting updating legislation, namely, the Data Retention and Investigatory Powers Act 2014 (also known as DRIP or DRIPA). However, this was successfully challenged by two MPs in court and the court gave the legislature until early 2016 (31 March 2016 to be specific) to mend its hand in terms of new or amended surveillance legislation (see case of *Davis and Watson v Secretary of State for the Home Department* [2015] EWHC 2092 (Admin) (17 July 2015)).

Liability for terrorist material

Publication of terrorist statements

5.72   The Terrorism Act 2006 introduces, *inter alia*, criminal liability for the encouragement of terrorism. A party is liable if:

'1(2)(a) he publishes a statement to which this section applies or causes another to publish such a statement; and

(b) at the time he publishes it or causes it to be published, he –

(i) intends members of the public to be directly or indirectly encouraged or otherwise induced by the statement to commit, prepare or instigate acts of terrorism or Convention offences; or

(ii) is reckless as to whether members of the public will be directly or indirectly encouraged or otherwise induced by the statement to commit, prepare or instigate such acts or offences.'

A prohibited statement is defined under s 1 of Part 1 of the Act as one which 'is likely to be understood by some or all of the members of the public to whom it is published as a direct or indirect encouragement or other inducement to them to the commission, preparation or instigation of acts of terrorism or Convention offences'.

Publication can be in any form, with the effect that website providers or internet service providers may (subject to a defence being available as discussed below) potentially find themselves liable for such statements which appear on their site.

Dissemination of terrorist publications

5.73   Section 2 of the Act introduces a further offence which is relevant to those providing internet services. Section 2(2) sets out the *actus reus* or conduct element of the offence:

'For the purposes of this section a person engages in conduct falling within this subsection if he –

(a) distributes or circulates a terrorist publication;

(b) gives, sells or lends such a publication;

(c) offers such a publication for sale or loan;

(d) provides a service to others that enables them to obtain, read, listen to or look at such a publication, or to acquire it by means of a gift, sale or loan;

(e) transmits the contents of such a publication electronically; or

(f) has such a publication in his possession with a view to its becoming the subject of conduct falling within any of paragraphs (a) to (e).'

The *mens rea* for the offence is set out in s 2(1) and provides that the offence is committed if:

'(a) he intends an effect of his conduct to be a direct or indirect encouragement or other inducement to the commission, preparation or instigation of acts of terrorism;

(b) he intends an effect of his conduct to be the provision of assistance in the commission or preparation of such acts; or

(c) he is reckless as to whether his conduct has an effect mentioned in paragraph (a) or (b).'

Again, as with s 1, the fact that the wording is technology-neutral means that a website or network provider may be liable if they themselves (or if they permit others to) disseminate terrorist content on their site or via their network. Care must therefore be taken by those who allow advertising or discussions to be conducted on their site. Without the defences which are available as are discussed below, this offence would present a significant threat for intermediaries who, unwittingly have such material posted or sent by third parties.

Defences

Statutory take down regime

5.74   Some comfort is found in respect of both the s 1 and s 2 offences under ss 3 and 4 which provide a form of take down notice procedure. The Act provides that a constable may issue a notice to an internet service provider or hoster, requiring the removal or amendment of a statement, article or record which such constable believes to be 'unlawfully terrorist related'.[147]

On receipt of such a notice, a provider must remove or amend any offending postings from the internet within two working days. Although non-compliance with a notice is not in itself an offence, a failure gives rise to liability under ss 1 or 2 for endorsing or disseminating such statements or material. This would result in the internet service provider being unable to take advantage of the defences which might otherwise be available for such offences under ss 1(6) and 2(9). These sections apply if it can be shown that the statement or publication did not express the defendant's views nor had his endorsement and this was clear in the circumstances.

There is a further risk of liability under s 3(4) in respect of repeat postings of the same material which continue to appear after receipt of the take down notice

---

147 Terrorism Act 2006, s 3(7).

and the initial removal or amendment of the offending statements. This species of liability may arise unless the defendant is able to show that they have 'taken every step he reasonably could to prevent a repeat statement from becoming available to the public and to ascertain whether it does'.[148] This indicates a heavy burden indeed, appearing to impose an obligation on providers to pro-actively check their sites and systems in order to ensure that no repeat publications appear. This de facto monitoring obligation runs contrary to the provisions of the Electronic Commerce Directive, which prevents member states from imposing a general obligation on intermediary service providers to monitor the information which they transmit or store.[149] Government recognised this as a genuine concern during the passage of the Act through Parliament, promising secondary legislation to address the interrelationship of the Act with the provisions of the Directive. This is considered below.

E-commerce defence

5.75   Acting on its promise made during the legislative path of the Terrorism Bill, the government brought into force in June 2007 the Electronic Commerce Directive (Terrorism Act 2006) Regulations 2007. As has been explained elsewhere in this book, the Directive, as implemented through the provisions of the Electronic Commerce (EC Directive) Regulations 2002, only has application in respect of legislation passed before it came into force, with the effect that any legislation brought into force after 2002 must either incorporate or be amended to incorporate the provisions of the Directive on a case-by-case basis.[150]

The 2007 Regulations do several things. First, they respect the country of origin approach of the Directive, meaning that a service provider established in the UK and doing anything in the course of providing information society services in an EEA state other than the United Kingdom which would, if done in a part of the United Kingdom constitute a relevant offence, is liable in the UK for such offence.[151]

Second, and most significant for internet service providers (who, as discussed above, may otherwise have found themselves liable for the dissemination of publication of third-party terrorist materials or statements, specifically in respect of repeat postings), the Regulations mirror the mere conduit and hosting defences available under the general 2002 Regulations for the Terrorism Act offences. There are several interesting points to note in respect of the way in which this defence now fits alongside those under the Act itself.

The Regulations essentially copy out the relevant provisions of the 2002 Regulations. This therefore provides a defence, for hosters, where such a person 'does not have actual knowledge of unlawful activity [and] … upon obtaining such knowledge or awareness, acts expeditiously to remove or to disable access to the information.' Since there is currently no guidance either in the Regulations

---

148   Terrorism Act 2006, s 3(5)(a).
149   Art 15, Directive 2000/31/EC.
150   Another example is the Electronic Commerce Directive (Racial and Religious Hatred Act 2006) Regulations 2007.
151   The Electronic Commerce Directive (Terrorism Act 2006) Regulations 2007, reg 3(1).

or the Directive as to what constitutes 'expeditiously', it is not clear how this tallies with the specific two working days' notice requirement in the Act. This author's view is that it certainly would not be taken to give a longer period of time in order to act, but whether it naturally leads to a two-day period is uncertain. Some suggestions have been made that the Terrorism Act approach provides a strong argument that any action required under either the 2007 Regulations or the more general 2002 Regulations (therefore extending to defamatory or copyright-infringing postings) will be permitted, provided it is done in two working days. It might be suggested that such an assumption is dangerous. Even if terrorist material is acknowledged as lying on the more serious side of any scale of offending content, a proscribed statutory take down notice from an authorised officer is a deliberately different process. Particularly in the case of repeat postings, it is arguable that a shorter period in which to act is appropriate. Internet Service Providers would therefore be well advised not to assume that they always have a two working day window for all unlawful content, and to act as soon as possible in the circumstances.

The other issue to note is that the defence under the Regulations relates to 'actual knowledge' and does not specifically refer to the provision of an official notice. Whilst it is clear that the giving of notice by a constable under the Act would give rise to actual knowledge, it is still possible that other forms of warning or tip-off are sufficient for a provider to acquire knowledge of the material and be required to act under the Regulations. Members of the Internet Service Providers Association (ISPA) lobbied during the drafting of the Regulations for a clarification that 'actual knowledge' would only be deemed to have been acquired where the host or conduit has been given notice of the terrorism-related material by those responsible for giving notices under s 3 of the Terrorism Act, and not where it is given by any other person. The Association's move was resisted by the Home Office on the grounds that it both goes beyond the requirements of the Directive and would unduly limit the effect of ss 1 to 4 of the Act. Service providers will therefore need to act in accordance with their usual procedures for upholding their defence under the Directive's implementing legislation, although with a view to the high penalties and risks presented under the Terrorism Act 2006 in the event of any failure – which is no small detail.

CYBERSTALKING/HARASSMENT

5.76   Stalking is acknowledged to be an increasing phenomenon, with reports in the UK of up to one woman in ten experiencing it at some point during their lifetime.[152] The internet presents another medium via which victims can be found and tracked and targeted. Threatening or abusive messages can be posted anonymously, to an individual alone or in front of a wide audience in a manner which is intended both to offend them and to

---

152 Survey by Leicester University and the Network for Surviving Stalking, as reported by Theresa May, MP on BBC News, Panorama, 12 March 2007.

harm their reputation amongst others. Specific concerns have been raised as to the increasing use of social networking sites and forums for bullying and harassing behaviour, and it is clear that the internet presents unprecedented new and imaginative avenues for harassment. Take, for example, Ms Debnath, who was imprisoned and given a restraining order after a long campaign of 'revenge' against an ex-colleague with whom she had had a one night stand. The defendant employed hackers to infiltrate the claimant's emails and inbox, signed him up to positivesingles.com and to a gay US prisoner exchange, set up a spoof 'A is gay.com' website, and sent countless offensive emails to the claimant and his fiancée.[153]

The legal framework to deal with such crimes encompasses both the general, in the form of the Protection from Harassment Act 1997, and the specific, in the form of the Malicious Communications Act 1988 and Communications Act 2003, which provide separate offences related to the sending of abusive communications via electronic networks. These are considered below.

Another important form of redress which should not be overlooked is the ability for a service provider to enforce its terms and conditions against a member who engages in such behaviour. In this way, if the owner of a website forum receives complaints of bullying or harassment via the site, if it has crafted its terms of membership correctly, it should be able to exercise rights of termination or other action directly against the errant member itself. Further steps may well need to be taken with the most persistent offenders, however, unless the site owner is able to effectively block such person from creating new membership accounts (a difficult task with the age of the anonymous internet café). Issues surrounding contract are considered in Chapter 2.

The Protection from Harassment Act

5.77   The Protection from Harassment Act 1997 introduced welcome new protections. Although aimed at tackling stalking, it is drafted widely and covers a range of different forms of harassing and threatening behaviour. There are two specific prohibitions, each of which is considered below.

Harassment

5.78   The first form of prohibited behaviour is the pursuit of a course of conduct which '(a) amounts to harassment of another, and (b) which he knows or ought to know amounts to harassment of the other'.[154] Knowledge is based on that of a reasonable person in possession of the same information thinking that the course of conduct amounted to harassment.[155]

Action may be taken either by way of criminal proceedings or civil proceedings. Section 2 of the Act makes it a summary offence. Section 3, allows a victim to

---

153 *R v Debnath* [2005] EWCA Crim 3472.
154 The Protection from Harassment Act 1997, s 1(1).
155 The Protection from Harassment Act 1997, s 1(2).

take civil action for damages for (among other things) any anxiety caused by the harassment and any financial loss resulting from the harassment.

Most importantly, injunctions and restraining orders are available, breach of which is also a criminal offence.[156] This often makes the use of this Act, a more attractive option than the Malicious Communications Act or Communications Act, considered below, which do not provide such tools.

Felicity Lowde was convicted[157] of harassment resulting in her imprisonment as well as a restraining order and a five-year anti-social behaviour order. Lowde had launched a vicious campaign against Rachel North, a victim of the 7 July bombings, accusing her, amongst other things, of using her experience for financial gain. Lowde used her own blog as well as email and postings to Rachel's site and blog, when she was finally caught at an internet café in Brick Lane. The prosecution centred on a harassment claim under the Act, but also relied on computer misuse acts, given the modification to email systems which she employed.[158]

Causing fear of violence

5.79   Section 4 of the Act creates an offence where 'a person whose course of conduct causes another to fear, on at least two occasions, that violence will be used against him is guilty of an offence if he knows or ought to know that his course of conduct will cause the other so to fear on each of those occasions'.[159]

Again, knowledge is judged in the basis of the reasonable person in possession of the same information, and injunctions and restraining orders are also available.

A person found guilty of an offence is liable: (a) on conviction on indictment, to imprisonment for a term not exceeding five years, or a fine, or both; or (b) on summary conviction, to imprisonment for a term not exceeding six months, or a fine not exceeding the statutory maximum, or both.

Example 5.26

Hugo joins an alumni networking site run by the university he attended. An ex partner holding a grudge starts responding with nasty comments every time he makes a posting, saying he has sexual perversions and a criminal record. This escalates, until Hugo is receiving scores of abusive emails from her daily, together with postings appearing on the site. Hugo should contact the site administrator to see if her membership can be terminated. Hugo may also wish to report her to the authorities for action to be taken under the Malicious Communications Act, the Protection from Harassment Act or Communications Act, or may also take civil proceedings himself. In relation to the public statements, Hugo may also want to take advice concerning his rights under defamation laws.

---

156 The Protection from Harassment Act 1997, s 5.
157 In June 2007.
158 Between May 2006 and January 2007. See **5.2** *et seq* for a discussion on computer misuse offences.
159 The Protection from Harassment Act 1997, s 4(1).

Social media

5.80   It should be noted that there has been an increase in the number of harassment cases due to the prevalence and uptake in the use of social media. In 2013 responses and conclusions to the Home Office's 'Review of the Protection from Harassment Act 1997: Improving Protection for Victims of Stalking', respondents had raised concerns relating to cyber-stalking conducted via social media.

For the most part, social network site operators seek to adopt responsible positions on most illegal, inappropriate, and offensive content hosted on their sites in the terms and conditions they require for use of their services. Internet service providers and social media also already have a legal obligation to co-operate with the police during investigations of allegations of harassment and stalking.

Malicious Communications Act

5.81   The Malicious Communications Act 1988 has been amended by s 43 of the Criminal Justice and Police Act 2001 to extend offences of sending offensive letters to cover the sending of any indecent or offensive article with intent to cause distress or anxiety. The Act now covers writing of all descriptions, electronic communications (therefore including email or postings to websites), photographs and other images in a material form, tape recordings, films and video recordings. Section 1 reads:

> '1.   Any person who sends to another person
>
> > (a)   a letter, electronic communication or article of any description which conveys
> >
> > > (i)   a message which is indecent or grossly offensive
> > >
> > > (ii)   a threat or
> > >
> > > (iii)   information which is false and known or believed to be false by the sender or
> >
> > (b)   any article or electronic communication which is, in whole or part, of an indecent or grossly offensive nature,
> >
> > is guilty of an offence if his purpose, or one of his purposes, in sending it is that it should, so far as falling within paragraph (a) or (b) above, cause distress or anxiety to the recipient or to any other person to whom he intends that it or its contents or nature should be communicated.'

Given that the offence relates to the sending of the article, it is irrelevant whether it actually reaches the recipient intended. However, what is significant is that the sender must have intended it to cause distress or anxiety to the recipient. Applying this reasoning to the examples contained in the case of Ms Debnath, discussed in the introduction to this section, general postings about the claimant on adult sites he was not a member of, would not be likely to fall under this offence, although the emails to him would.

Following the House of Lords' judgment in *Director of Public Prosecutions v Collins*,[160] it is clear that this crime can be distinguished from an offence under s 127 where, as Lord Brown stated, 'the very act of sending [a] message over … public communications network … constitutes the offence even it if was being communicated to someone who the sender knew would not be in any way offended or distressed by it'.[161]

Restraining orders are not available.

Section 127 Communications Act

5.82 The history of this offence can be traced back to the Post Office (Amendment) Act 1935 which created an offence of sending messages by telephone which are grossly offensive or of an indecent, obscene or menacing character. Similar provisions later appeared in the Telecommunications Act 1984, culminating in s 127(1)(a) of the Communications Act 2003, which reads:

'(1) A person is guilty of an offence if he –

   (a) sends by means of a public electronic communications network a message or other matter that is grossly offensive or of an indecent, obscene or menacing character; or

   (b) causes any such message or matter to be so sent.'

There is a separate offence under s 127(2):

'(2) A person is guilty of an offence if, for the purpose of causing annoyance, inconvenience or needless anxiety to another, he –

   (a) sends by means of a public electronic communications network, a message that he knows to be false,

   (b) causes such a message to be sent; or

   (c) persistently makes use of a public electronic communications network.

(3) A person guilty of an offence under this section shall be liable, on summary conviction, to imprisonment for a term not exceeding six months or to a fine not exceeding level 5 on the standard scale, or to both.'

This captures messages sent via the internet or telephone. The case of *DPP v Collins* considered s 1(a) in detail. The court held that for the offence to be made out, it must be proved that the defendant intended the message or other matter to be offensive to those to whom they related or be aware that they be taken to be so. It is irrelevant whether the message is in fact received or whether those who read or listen to it are themselves offended. What is key is whether reasonable persons in society would find it grossly offensive or not. On this basis, the Lords overturned the ruling of the lower court which had held that racially abusive language used in voicemails left with an MP were not grossly offensive because

160 [2006] UKHL 40, [2006] 4 All ER 602.
161 *Director of Public Prosecutions v Collins* [2006] UKHL 40.

the MP had not found them so and the intention of the defendant was not to grossly offend him.

In *DPP v Chambers*,[162] one of the first substantive social media prosecutions to reach an appeal court, Paul Chambers was prosecuted under the Communications Act 2003 for sending the following tweet: 'Crap! Robin Hood airport is closed. You've got a week and a bit to get your s**t together otherwise I'm blowing the airport sky high!!' This became known as the 'Twitter joke trial.' Mr Chambers subsequently appealed to the Crown Court against his conviction. The appeal was dismissed with Judge Davies stating that the tweet was:

> 'menacing in its content and obviously so. It could not be more clear. Any ordinary person reading this would see it in that way and be alarmed.'

However, Robin Hood Airport had classified the threat as non-credible on the basis that 'there was no evidence at this stage to suggest that this is anything other than a foolish comment posted as a joke for only his close friends to see'. Following an appeal to the High Court in February 2012, the judges who heard the case were unable to reach agreement on the correct interpretation of s 127 and the case was referred for a second appeal. Chambers' conviction was quashed; the approved judgment stated that the appeal against conviction would be allowed on the basis that the 'tweet' could not be usefully taken further. Building upon the judgment of *DPP v Collins*, the court took the view that English law (prior to the Communications Act 2003) had long been tolerant of satirical and even distasteful opinions about matters of both a serious and trivial nature. The court also noted that the 2003 Act predated the advent of Twitter and that the statutory reference to 'menacing' was itself based on the wording of the previous Act of 1935. The Lord Chief Justice, Lord Judge expressed the view that, 'the 2003 Act did not create interference with the … essential freedoms of speech and expression' [2012] EWHC 2157.

In relation to users' understanding of what may constitute criminal activity, it has been a consistent theme that although the posters who have been prosecuted may have few friends on Facebook or followers on Twitter, their posts in many cases were returned on search result engines and thereby brought to the attention of a much wider audience than they might have intended. One of the issues presented by social media is that once the message is posted, the original recipients of the message may copy, re-post, re-tweet or save a copy, thereby bringing the message to a much wider audience even if the author subsequently decided to delete their own post. Another issue presented by such postings is that when search results are returned without their context, it also has the potential to cause significant harm, as those who are interested in the subject are the most likely to make the searches; such examples may include racist statements (*DPP v Collins*[163]) and incitement to commit criminal acts (*DPP v Sutcliffe-Keenan; DPP*

---

162 [2012] EWHC 2157.
163 [2006] UKHL 40.

v Blackshaw[164]), which may not have been the intention of the user when they posted them. This has resulted in different penal ties being applied in different cases and confusion as to when prosecutions will be pursued by the CPS.

Interim Guidelines on Prosecuting Cases Involving Communications Sent via Social Media

5.83   In 2013, the DPP issued final Guidelines on Prosecuting Cases Involving Communications Sent via Social Media ('the Guidelines') via www.cps.gov.uk/ legal/a_to_c/communications_sent_via_social_media/index.html.

The Guidelines are designed to give clear advice to prosecutors who have been asked either for a charging decision or for early advice to the police, as well as in reviewing those cases which have been charged by the police. The Guidelines are primarily concerned with offences that may be committed by reason of the nature or content of a communication sent via social media. However, the Guidance states that where social media is simply used to facilitate some other substantive offence, prosecutors should proceed under the legislation governing the substantive offence in question (eg contempt of court, harassment, public disorder).

EVIDENCE

5.84   The provisions of the Regulation of Investigatory Powers Act 2000 had provisions in relation to the retention of and access to certain computer evidence and records.[165] RIPA, and indeed the Data Retention Directive, have been undermined by the *Digital Rights Ireland* case; and potential new and or amending legislation is understood to be proposed. However, readers are referred to other more detailed texts in relation to these important ongoing issues, and which are in a state of flux. Other ways in which computer evidence can be obtained include the Police and Criminal Evidence Act 1984, together with specific investigatory powers contained in individual legislation such as the Terrorism Act and Data Protection Act 1998. The process for disclosure is governed under English law predominantly by the Criminal Procedure and Investigations Act 1996 (as amended).

This section focuses instead on the nature of computer evidence, how it can be adduced and relied on in court, and the problems of reliance on and seeking to locate it. Evidence is of course crucial in internet-based criminal prosecutions and defences, and yet it holds some inherent weaknesses which impose unique burdens.

---

164 [2011] EWCA Crim 2312.
165 *Director of Public Prosecutions v Collins* [2006] UKHL 40.

Common law presumption

5.85   Prior to the repeal of s 69 of the Police and Criminal Evidence Act 1984 (under the Youth Justice and Criminal Evidence Act 1999) it was necessary to prove through provision of a certificate that a computer was operating correctly and was not used improperly before the computer could be admitted as evidence. This had caused some practical problems and unnecessary administrative hurdles in requiring the examining and certification of all the technical operations of a computer and resulted in some surprising decisions. There was also a risk that a defendant would be prevented from using evidence which could demonstrate his innocence simply on the basis that he was not able to certify the computer on which it was held.

Following recommendations of the Law Commission, this was repealed and not replaced. Consequently, the admissibility of computer records is governed by a common law presumption that the computer was operating properly in the absence of evidence to the contrary (as is the case in other jurisdictions such as Scotland and the US). If however evidence is produced that the computer was not operating correctly, then the party seeking to rely on this evidence is still required to prove its reliability.

The evidential burden

5.86   There are two main issues prevalent in an internet crime case that may create an evidential burden on the prosecution. First, there must be continuity of evidence from the first computer used by a defendant to access content or a second computer; second, defendants rarely use their own names and addresses when perpetrating such crimes. This section analyses some of these problems.

Continuity of access evidence

5.87   To prove beyond reasonable doubt that the defendant was responsible for, say, the unauthorised access of the victim's computer or the dissemination of paedophilic material, the prosecution can be forced to prove continuity of evidence. That is, the prosecution should be able to 'follow' a line of access from the defendant's own computer to the victim's or the other subject of the crime. Any discontinuity may raise the court's reasonable doubt that the defendant in the court was not the person responsible for the action. With hacking, only the most simple cases will feature two computers and an identifiable abuser. More regularly a hacker's commands to his computer will pass through many different computers spread across the internet. It is also usual that a hacker will attempt to disguise his true identity: he is unlikely to attempt unauthorised access using an electronic signifier which can identify him. This poses an evidential difficulty for the prosecution. Similarly, external events or actions may muddy the waters and obscure any clear link between the defendant and his crime. Charges against Karl Schofield of possessing indecent images of children were dropped because experts showed that a Trojan horse infection on his PC could have caused the harm without his knowledge. In another case, *R v Caffrey*,[166] a similar defence to a s 3 charge was used successfully.

Fragmentation of internet hacking

5.88   It has been explained that messages and commands sent over the internet do not pass directly between the sender and receiver computer. Instead the message is broken into small packets, each with a destination address. Each packet is shunted from one computer on the internet to another, and from that computer to the next; gradually moving the packet towards its destination. Eventually, all the packets arrive at their final resting computer in a matter of seconds.

Hackers' messages and commands are no different. Each message will be broken into packets and shunted through many different computers. The prosecution will have to establish that a hacker's message did travel to an unauthorised computer.

In addition, hackers rarely attempt to gain access to their victim computer directly. Their preferred method is to log in to one computer on the internet and from there to log in to another. This process is repeated many times; it is the digital equivalent of speeding around many corners to shake off a chasing police car. And each new login made by the hacker presents another piece of evidence which the prosecution may have to prove to establish continuity from the first to the final unauthorised access.[167]

These computers can be contrasted with the thousands of computers which shunt data from the victim computer to the hacker's computer. In a sense, there are many computers involved with any hacking which merely act as 'conduits' – they do not 'process' the data passed between them. This must be contrasted with computers which carry out functions or process the data involved in a hacking prosecution.

In *R v Waddon* both the Crown Court[168] and Court of Appeal[169] were clear that the many computers involved in the downloading of obscene images by one individual from one website did not necessitate having s 69 certificates for each one. Hardy J referred to the numerous computers in the chain as 'mere post boxes'. The Court of Appeal, giving unanimous judgment through the Vice President, Lord Justice Rose, drew a distinction between the computers that 'produce' the evidence and those that 'transmit' the evidence. Only the former are addressed by the Act.

---

166 (Unreported, Southwark Crown Court, 17 October 2003).
167 *R v Cochrane* [1993] Crim LR 48 illustrates the utility of focusing on one computer in a chain to 'break' the continuity. This must be contrasted with more than one computer 'transmitting' the same evidence but only one computer 'producing' the evidence (*R v Waddon*, unreported, CA, 6 April 2000). In such a case, only the computer 'producing' the evidence is subject to the hurdles of s 69.
168 His Honour Judge Hardy (unreported, 30 June 1999).
169 Unreported, 6 April 2000.

False identification – spoofing

5.89 The situation for the prosecution may be more complex. A hacker logging in to a computer on the way to his victim will often log in under a different identity. This is called 'spoofing'. The hacker is able to do this by having previously obtained actual passwords, or having created a new identity by fooling the computer into thinking he is the system's operator. Whatever the technical method, the legal result remains the same. The prosecution must establish that the hacker at his own computer was the person who has logged in to countless other computers.

CONTEMPT OF COURT

Challenges presented by the digital world

5.90 The creation and now exponential uptake of the internet as a communications tool has brought about a huge change in the way in which people engage with one another. Enormous volumes of material can now be stored, communicated, and redistributed to a mass audience which is now causing real issues in relation to the law of contempt. Historically, newspapers would fade from memory to become 'tomorrow's chip paper'. Now, information on the internet is potentially available forever once it has been posted, and can be found by anyone using a simple search. Social media in particular, which has a viral quality, means that individuals can communicate information to very large numbers of people in a short space of time. The law as relates to contempt has struggled to keep abreast of issues raised which are peculiar to microsites, as individuals posting content may simply view their behaviour as expressing their opinion on topical matters or issues that have affected them privately rather than an attempt to prejudice legal proceedings.

What is contempt of court?

Scope

5.91 Contempt of court is the area of law that deals with behaviour that might affect court proceedings. It takes many different forms, ranging from disrupting court hearings to disobeying court orders, to publishing prejudicial information that might make the trial unfair.

The 'strict liability rule'

5.92 The 'strict liability rule' contained in s 1 of the 1981 Act is narrowly focused, relating only to such conduct as tends to interfere with the course of justice 'in particular legal proceedings'. Section 2 confines the operation of that rule to a publication when 'the proceedings in question' are active, creating the risk of impediment or prejudice to 'the proceedings in question'. Section 2(2) contains a double hurdle. It must first be shown that the possible impediment or prejudice must be 'serious', and secondly that the risk of its occurring must be 'substantial'.

Exclusions from the strict liability rule

5.93   It is suggested that there are exclusions from the rule which may apply to digital content, though the effect of the exclusion is not the same in all cases, which may include, but are not limited to the following:

- Conduct tending to interfere with the justice system in general but not with any particular proceedings is outside the ambit of s 1.

- Conduct during and related to one set of proceedings but likely to prejudice or impede a future set of proceedings. (They may fall within the common law liability for intentional prejudice, or within an order under s 4(2).)

- A publication might not in itself be likely to cause 'serious' prejudice but may form part of a wave of publicity that has that cumulative effect. Section 2(2) would seem to exclude such a publication from liability.

A discussion in a publication as part of a discussion in good faith of public affairs or other matters of general public interest is not to be treated as a contempt of court under the strict liability rule if the risk of *impediment or prejudice* to particular legal proceedings is merely incidental to the discussion (s 5).

The meaning of 'communication'

5.94   In relation to social media, the Law Commission states that contempt can be committed via social networking sites as the definition of communication is widely drafted. The laws relating to contempt would therefore cover almost all of the new media. The Commission states that Facebook postings, tweets, Flickr photographs, videos on YouTube, and words, videos, music or pictures on any other website would fall within the category of communication (Contempt of Court: Summary for non-specialists', Law Commission Consultation Paper No 209 at para [92]).

Application to publications

5.95   The strict liability contempt by publication offence contained in s 1 of Act only applies to publications. The Act defines publication to include speech, writing, programmes (and other similar broadcasts), and any other form of communication. These publications must be 'addressed to the public at large or any section of the public'. The Law Commission states that 'speech' has an obvious meaning, but does state in relation to social media that 'speech' would also include things said on YouTube films. 'Writing' has been defined in law as 'reproducing words in a visible form'. Case law from a different area of criminal law concluded that something on the internet can be considered to have been 'written', as what was on the computer screen was 'in writing'. Presumably, this would also extend to content that could be accessed via Smartphone or tablets, which have internet connectivity (see *Attorney General v Davey; Attorney General v Beard*[170]).

Requirement to be 'addressed to the public'

5.96 To date, there have been few contempt cases involving publications on the internet, so the law on the issue is sometimes unclear. However, a court is likely to examine:

- how many people the publication was addressed to;

- who those people were; and

- why the publication was aimed at them.

A private communication that is only sent to one person (eg an email from one person to another) could not be a publication addressed to the public. By extension, this analysis would likely apply to private messages sent via social networking sites to another individual but not if that message was communicated via private messaging to a number of people, such as a group with many members. In relation to social media factors, the Law Commission Contempt of Court: Summary for non-specialists', Law Commission Consultation Paper No 209 has indicated that factors such as whether the user had turned on their privacy settings so their posting or tweet could only be viewed by a limited number of people would likely be taken into account when reaching a decision.

Contempt by jurors

Section 8

5.97 Section 8 of the CCA 1981 makes it an offence to obtain or to reveal any 'statements made, opinions expressed, arguments advanced or votes cast by members of a jury in the course of their deliberations'. There are some exceptions to this, which means that revealing deliberations to a court will not be considered contempt in certain circumstances. The maximum punishment for contempt under s 8 is a fine or up to two years in prison (CCA 1981, s 14(1)).

Impact of social media upon juror deliberations

5.98 The impact of social media upon juror deliberations has been considered in a number of cases, although prosecutions are sparse. In *Attorney General v Fraill and Stewart*, during the course of a very substantial trial, two previous attempts to conclude a trial had failed and in each case the jury was discharged. Fraill, who was empanelled as a juror, had been on Facebook with the defendant, commenting to the effect that she was pleased that Stewart had been acquitted. As a result of the judge's enquiries, the extent of the contact between Fraill and

170 [2012] EWHC 2157 (Admin), [2013] 1 WLR 1833.

Stewart was investigated. When deciding the sentence to be imposed on Friall, it was noted that her conduct in visiting the internet repeatedly was directly contrary to her oath as a juror and her contact with the acquitted defendant as well, as her repeated searches on the internet, constituted flagrant breaches of the orders made by the judge for the proper conduct of the trial. Moreover the text of the communications between the parties went much further than the expression of a compassionate concern. Fraill was sentenced to immediate custody for a period of eight months. In relation to Stewart, it was noted that the contempt would not have taken place if Fraill had not taken the initiative and contacted her. She responded to the contact made by Fraill in the euphoria of her own acquittal and release from custody, at the same time, knowing perfectly well that her contact was a juror and that conversation about the case was prohibited. Although her conduct was undoubtedly contumacious, she did not take advantage of the contact to make any significant attempt to influence this particular juror's thinking but rather went along with her comments. Stewart was sentenced to a two-month custodial term, suspended for two years.

Jurors conducting their own research on the internet and deliberate disobedience of jury directions

5.99   In *Attorney General v Dallas*,[171] a case where a juror had conducted her own research on the internet, Lord Judge CJ set out four elements that would ordinarily establish the two elements of contempt in cases where there had been deliberate disobedience to a judge's direction or order:

- The juror knew that the judge had directed that the jury should not do a certain act.

- The juror appreciated that that was an order.

- The juror deliberately disobeyed the order.

- By doing so the juror risked prejudicing the due administration of justice.

Materials provided to jurors

5.100   When a person receives their jury summons, they also get a booklet from the court service entitled *Your Guide to the Jury Service*. The booklet is designed to explain to jurors their obligations when sitting on a trial. In the context of social media, the guide explains to jurors that during the trial, they must not 'discuss the evidence with anyone outside your jury either face to face, over the telephone or over the internet via social networking sites such as Facebook, Twitter or Myspace'. It also says that if a juror is 'unsure or uneasy about anything', they can write a note to the judge. The booklet has been mentioned in relation to contempt proceedings in cases such as *AG v Kasim Davey and Joseph Beard*.[172]

---

171 [2012] 1 WLR 991.
172 [2013] EWHC 2317 (Admin) at [11].

Jurors are warned that they 'may also be in contempt of court' if they 'use the internet to research details about any cases' they 'hear, along with any other cases listed for trial at the court'. Presumably, this would therefore include searching for social networking profiles or accounts belonging to those connected with the proceedings. In order to reinforce the message, court staff also warn jurors. The warning that court staff read to jurors now explicitly addresses statements made in relation to the internet and via social networking sites and telephones.

The courts' approach to dealing with technology

5.101 Different courts have different systems for dealing with jurors' electronic devices that can connect to the internet, such as mobile phones, laptops, iPads, iPods, and Kindles. In some courts, jurors are permitted to keep these devices with them in the area where they have lunch and sit during breaks in the trial. However, the devices must be switched off in court, and are removed when jurors are reaching a verdict in the case in the jury room. In other courts, jurors' devices are removed from them for the whole time that they are at court. And in other courts, jurors can keep their devices even when reaching a verdict in the jury room. (Reproduced in 'Contempt of Court: Summary for non-specialists', Law Commission Consultation Paper No 209 at paras [147–148].)

CHAPTER SIX

Data and data protection

'And while serious – very serious – the privacy issues we're dealing with today are trivial compared to what's ahead. What are the implications for individual privacy in a world where millions of people are driving internet-enabled cars that have their movements monitored at all times? What happens to privacy for millions of people with internet-enabled pacemakers?'

Lou Gerstner, Chairman & CEO of IBM[1]

'There is an inherent security issue with many of these online exchanges which is often overlooked. Emails are not particularly secure.'

C Davies, Editorial, *Communications Law* (2012) (17), pp 38–39

INTRODUCTION

6.1   An editorial in the *Computer Law & Security Review* notes that '[p]rivacy and data protection issues are never far from the horizon at the moment. There are waves of discussion in this area … and currently that wave is riding high.'[2] The increasing 'centralisation of information through the computerisation of various records has made the right of privacy a fundamental concern'.[3]

Just at the time of finalising this draft, the decision in the *Schrems EU – US Safe Harbor* case has issued.[4] This has been described as one of the most important case decisions that the ECJ/CJEU has ever issued. It affects fundamental right of citizens, trans-Atlantic relations, politics, business, data transfers affecting millions of individuals and some of the biggest multinationals on the planet (as well as thousands of other companies). There are also inter-EU ripples to this case. The immediate question is whether transfers of EU data to the US will

---

1   eBusiness Conference Expo, New York City, 12 December 2000.
2   Editorial, Saxby, S, *Computer Law & Security Review* (2012) (28), 251–253, at 251.
3   'Personal Data Protection and Privacy', Counsel of Europe, available at http://hub.coe.int/web/coe-portal/what-we-do/rule-of-law/personal-data?dynLink=true&layoutId=35&dlgroupId=10226&fromArticleId=.
4   *Schrems v Commissioner*, ECJ/CJEU. Case C-362/14, referred for a preliminary ruling on 25 July 2014 by the Irish High Court, decision on 6 October 2015. Note also the much commented upon AG Opinion dated 23 September 2015.

have to stop given that the Safe Harbour Agreement has been declared invalid – with no small acknowledgement to the continuing consequences of the Snowden disclosures. (This is discussed in more detail below).

Data protection is important, increasingly topical, and an issue of legally required compliance for all organisations. More importantly it is part of management and organisational best practice. Individuals, employees and customers, expect that their personal data will be respected. They are increasingly aware of their rights. Increasingly they enforce their rights.

Data protection is also increasing in coverage in mainstream media. This is due in part to large numbers of recent data loss and data breach incidents. These have involved the personal data of millions of individuals being lost by commercial organisations but also trusted government entities.

All organisations collect and process personal data. Whether they are big or new start-ups, they need to comply with the data protection regime. Many issues enhance the importance of getting the organisational data protection understanding and compliance right from day one. These include investigations, fines, prosecutions, being ordered to *delete* databases and adverse publicity.

In addition, organisations often fail to realise that data protection compliance is frequently an issue of dual compliance. They need to be looking both *inward* and *outward*. Internally, they have to be data protection compliant in relation to all of their employees' (and contractors') personal data, which traditionally may have related to HR files and employee contracts, but now includes issues of electronic communications, social networking, internet usage, filtering, monitoring, on-site activity, off-site activity, etc.

Separately, organisations have to be concerned about other sets of personal data, such as those relating to persons outside of the organisation (eg customers, prospects, etc). Comprehensive data protection compliance is also required. The consequences are significant for non-compliance.

Substantial fines have been imposed in a number of recent cases. In some instances also, organisations have been ordered to delete their databases. In a new technology start-up situation, this can be the company's most valuable asset.

Until recently the issue of data loss was a small story. More recently, however, the loss of personal data files of millions of individuals in the UK – including from official and non-governmental sources – makes UK data loss a front page issue. There is increased scrutiny from the ICO, and others, and new regulation is forthcoming.

In the UK and elsewhere there are enhanced obligations to report all data losses; as well as discussion to have enhanced financial penalties and in some instances personal director responsibility for data loss. The need for compliance is now a boardroom issue and an issue of corporate compliance. Proactive and complete data protection compliance is also a matter of good corporate governance, brand loyalty and a means to ensuring user and customer goodwill.

The frequency and scale of recent breaches of security, such as Sony Playstation (70 million individuals' personal data[5] in one instance and 25 million

---

5   See, for example, Martin, G, 'Sony Data Loss Biggest Ever', *Boston Herald*, 27 April 2011, available at http://bostonherald.com/business/technology/general/view/2011_0427sony_data_loss_biggest_ever.

in another[6]), TalkTalk, Vodafone, etc, make the topicality and importance of data security compliance for personal data ever more important. (Sony is also central in issues surrounding the hacking of its systems leading to it to pulling the premier of its film *The Interview*, apparently under cyber threat of further retaliation for the film. This is a new escalation in the dangers posed of hacking and its legal and policy consequences.) The largest UK data loss appears to be from the loss by HM Revenue and Customs of discs with the names, dates of birth, bank and address details for 25 million UK individuals.[7]

There are many new UK cases involving substantial fines for data protection breaches. The Brighton and Sussex University Hospitals NHS Trust had a fine of £325,000 imposed by the ICO in relation a data loss incident.[8] Zurich Insurance was fined £2.3 million for losing data in relation to 46,000 individual customers.[9]

National data protection authorities are increasingly proactive and undertake audits of data protection compliance frameworks, as well as incidents of breaches. Facebook internationally has been audited by one of the EU data protection authorities.[10] The ICO is also involved in dealing with personal data issues relating to the phone hacking scandal which is also the separate subject of the Leveson Inquiry.[11] This ICO investigation is called Operation Motorman.[12]

COMMERCIAL IMPERATIVES/PERSONAL PERSPECTIVES

6.2   Businesses demand that their digital presences, including websites, collect and analyse personal data. They collect it, not only to ensure that simple things are performed correctly, such as delivering goods to the right address and managing subscriptions. They also collect to predict their customers' needs. The more sophisticated collect personal data to sell or rent to other businesses to help them predict their customers' needs. In short, businesses view personal data as a critical asset.

---

6   See, for example, Arthur, C, 'Sony Suffers Second Data Breach with Theft of 25m More User Details', *Guardian*, 3 May 2011, available at www.guardian.co.uk/technology/blog/2011/may/03/sony-data-breach-online-entertainment.
7   See, for example, 'Brown Apologises for Record Loss, Prime Minister Gordon Brown has said he 'Profoundly Regrets' the Loss of 25 Million Child Benefit Records', BBC, 21 November 2007, available at http://news.bbc.co.uk/2/hi/7104945.stm.
8   See, for example, 'Largest Ever Fine for Data Loss Highlights Need for Audited Data Wiping', *ReturnOnIt*, available at www.returnonit.co.uk/largest-ever-fine-for-data-loss-highlights-need-for-audited-data-wiping.php.
9   See, for example, Oates, J, 'UK Insurer Hit with Biggest Ever Data Loss Fine', *The Register*, 24 August 2010, available at www.theregister.co.uk/2010/08/24/data_loss_fine/. This was imposed by the Financial Services Authority (FSA).
10   The audit relates to Facebook internationally, outside of the US and Canada. See first stage of the audit report, of 21 December 2011 at http://dataprotection.ie/viewdoc.asp?m=&fn=/documents/Facebook%20Report/final%20report/report.pdf. It is entitled *Facebook Ireland Limited, Report of Audit*, and was conducted by the Irish Data Protection Commissioner's Office. Note also complaints and access requests referred to at Europe Against Facebook, available at http://europe-v-facebook.org/EN/en.html.
11   Available at www.levesoninquiry.org.uk/.
12   Footnote: Available at www.levesoninquiry.org.uk/.

For the customers and other individuals whose information comprises this asset, there is an increasing expectation that businesses will use their data responsibly; that they can retain some control over how it is used and not, for example, have their email inboxes inundated with unwanted marketing communications or their personal details sold or disclosed indiscriminately. In the UK, the Information Commissioner and data protection regime are positioned to ensure that businesses respect the individuals whose data is being harvested, and uphold their rights.

But in an industry where the valuable data of individuals may be collected in ever-increasing number of ways, in ever-more exacting detail, on an ever-increasing scale, continuously, combined and cross-referenced, traded and exchanged outside of the UK in an instant, and spam sent from anonymous sources located in other jurisdictions, such protections have immediately apparent limitations.

From another angle, personal information is valuable not only to the businesses who collect and trade in it, but is also an essential source of evidence for law enforcement and other agencies wishing to build up profiles and details of a suspect's communications, tastes, movements, behaviour and transactions. It increasingly also features in civil law, family law and employment tribunal related cases. Any internet business which may collect or have access to such data therefore becomes a significant law enforcement and investigation resource, and may expect requests for disclosure of information. One of the most interesting and potentially important cases in relation to law enforcement access to personal data held by technology companies involved a case in the US where Microsoft is appealing a non-judicial request for data held in a data centre in Ireland which it says is outside of the normal international protocols and procedures for such access. Various technology companies are supporting Microsoft. The Irish Minister for Data Protection has raised concerns that normal international procedures are not being followed. Various industry commentators feel that if Microsoft were to lose the appeal, there would be a grave adverse affect on the US Cloud services industry.[13] How do these businesses know how to balance their obligations to the data subjects against requests from other regulatory or enforcement bodies?

As criminals become ever more technically savvy, but also dependent on internet communications, and concerns grow about international terrorism and crime, it is clear that the importance and value of such data, and therefore the number of disclosure requests, will only increase. In the UK and throughout Europe, legislation has been developed to put in place a procedural framework for handling and responding to such requests, safeguarding fundamental rights and clarifying when disclosures may be made without fear of legal action. In addition, steps have also been made to require that internet service providers retain minimum communications data precisely so that it can be available for law enforcement purposes.

---

13   See, for example, J O'Connor, 'The Microsoft Warrant Case: Not Just an Irish Issue', *Computers and Law*, Society of Computers and Law, 7 October 2014.

THE LEGISLATIVE LANDSCAPE

6.3   UK legislation on data breaks down into three interrelated areas. First, the basic data regime which upholds individuals' rights in respect of the processing of their data by imposing obligations on those who control it. A second imposes specific obligations on how data may be used for electronic marketing and other value added purposes. The third sets the parameters in which data may be made available for law enforcement purposes. All of these have been introduced to enact European Directives.

The Data Protection Act 1998

6.4   The Data Protection Act 1998 replaces the Data Protection Act 1984. The new legislation was brought into force following a review of data protection across Europe by means of the Second European Convention on Data Protection and the 1995 Data Protection Directive. The new regime introduced new rights and powers of enforcement, prohibitions on transfers of data outside of the EEA to countries with 'inadequate' data protection regimes, and a strengthening of security obligations.

The Act is the starting point for consideration of an internet or website provider's obligations in respect of their customers' and users' personal data. Since its introduction the Information Commissioner's Office (ICO) (which enforces the data protection and freedom of information regimes in the UK) (and which has equivalent national data protection authorities in the other EU member states) also publishes various guidance and codes of practice clarifying the scope of the Act's obligations on those with control over the processing of personal data. (The EU Article 29 Working Party on data protection, which comprises members of the EU national data protection authorities, including the ICO, also publishes sector-specific data protection guidance.) Although many enforcement actions have tended to be at an informal level, the last few years have revealed that increasingly significant fines and prosecutions are arising in the event of data protection breached. This also occurs in the state/official sector as well as the commercial sector. Individuals are also becoming more alert to their rights. The press is also more ready to publicise stories of security breaches and mismanagement of data, as concerns about fraud and identity theft have grown. In parallel, there are now indications that more robust and proactive enforcement may follow. There is an increasing emphasis on director liability issues and board responsibility for data protection compliance.

The Privacy and Electronic Communications (EC Directive) Regulations 2003

6.5   Although the Data Protection Act 1998 contains basic rights and protections for data subjects, European Directives have developed more detailed rules in respect of the sending of unsolicited direct marketing messages using publicly available telecommunications services (eg mobile or fixed telephone, fax and email). In the UK, this legislation was first implemented in March 2000 by way of the Telecommunications (Data Protection and Privacy) Regulations 1999 implementing European Telecoms Directive 97/66/EC. The Directive was implemented differently across Europe, however, resulting in uncertainties as to key definitions and potential bars to harmonisation. A new Directive 2002/58/EC on privacy and electronic communications followed and has been implemented in the UK in the guise of the Privacy and Electronic Communications (EC Directive) Regulations 2003 (PECR).

These Regulations contain clearer rules concerning direct marketing via electronic means, specifically as relates to email or 'spam' marketing, but also regarding the use of website cookies and other tracking devices such as web beacons to harvest users' personal data; and the extent to which users' traffic and billing data may be used after a communication has ended.

The Regulation of Investigatory Powers Act 2000

6.6   The Regulation of Investigatory Powers Act 2000 (best known by its acronym 'RIPA') received Royal Assent on 28 July 2000. Very lengthy and technical in nature, RIPA covers five specific areas. First, it contains prohibitions on the interception of communications in the course of their transmission and defines the circumstances in which this may be authorised and subscriber data may be made available for law enforcement purposes. Second, it contains rules relating to surveillance, proscribing techniques that may be used with a view to safeguarding the public from unnecessary invasions of their privacy. These two parts will be of most interest to those providers or internet networks and services. The latter parts of RIPA cover encryption of data, judicial oversight and the establishment of a tribunal providing redress against those exceeding their powers under RIPA.

Under RIPA sits various secondary legislation. The Regulation of Investigatory Powers (Maintenance of Interception Capability) Order 2002 provides for obligations which the Secretary of State may impose on service providers to establish and maintain system capability for interception in the event that this is required under RIPA. The Order only applies to providers of public telecommunications services offered to more than 10,000 persons in the UK.

The other key secondary legislation is the Telecommunications (Lawful Business Practice) (Interception of Communications) Regulations 2000 which authorises specified interceptions carried out by persons in the course of their business for the purposes relevant to that business (such as monitoring staff email and general running of the system) and using that business's telecommunication system which would otherwise be unlawful under RIPA.

This all needs to be read in conjunction with: (a) the post-Snowden environment and related developments; and (b) the *Digital Rights Ireland* Court of Justice case (*DRI*) (see below) and related cases. Even in the US, the Patriot Act fell by virtue of non-renewal.[14]

---

14   The US Senate a week later in June 2015 did pass the Freedom Act, which is meant to curb some official data collections and data retention.

Post the *DRI* case, the government rushed through the Data Retention and Investigatory Powers Act or DRIPA[15] to cater for data retention issues on a short-term basis. However, this was also challenged.

Two MPs (David Davis and Tom Watson), successfully challenged the Data Retention and Investigatory Powers Act 2014 (DRIPA) in the High Court. The court held that sections 1 and 2 of DRIPA breached rights to respect for private life and communications and to the protection of personal data under Articles 7 and 8 of the EU Charter of Fundamental Rights. The decision gives the Government until March 2016 to rectify the DRIPA problems.

The most recent Queen's speech has also promised a 'snooper's charter' which would replace DRIPA.[16] No doubt argument, debate and research will ensue.[17] It remains to be seen how challenge to DRIPA may transpire, and how courts and policy makers will react. This remains, if anything, a contentious issue.

Anti-Terrorism, Crime and Security Act 2001

6.7   The Anti-Terrorism, Crime and Security Act 2001, introduced following the 9/11 terrorist attacks in the US, provides government with further powers to counter threats to the UK. The provisions of the Act of specific interest to internet providers concern the rights granted to government departments and agencies to require the disclosure of data for national security purposes. The Act itself contains little detail, but Part 11 allows for the development of a voluntary statutory code for retention and contains reserve powers to enable further powers to be brought in if needed.

A Code of Practice for voluntary retention of communications data was drawn up and came into force on 5 December 2003, despite reservations from the internet service provider community. It seeks to encourage service providers to retain types of data which they already hold (as opposed to requiring the restructuring of systems to enable retention of new types of data) for specified periods ranging from four days to 12 months depending on the type of data.

As indicated above in relation to RIPA, this also needs to be read in conjunction with (a) the post-Snowden environment and related developments; and (b) the *Digital Rights Ireland (DRI)* Court of Justice and related cases.

The most recent Queen's speech and referred to legislation may also be relevant.[18]

Readers are advised to consult specialist texts in relation to the unfolding issues regarding if and how the RIPA/DRIPA/Data Retention Directive may be

15   See www.gov.uk/government/collections/data-retention-and-investigatory-powers-act-2014.
16   See T Whitehead, 'Google and Whatsapp will be forced to hand messages to MI5,' Telegraph, 27 May 2015, available at www.telegraph.co.uk/news/politics/queens-speech/11634567/Google-and-Whatsapp-will-be-forced-to-hand-messages-to-MI5.html.
17   See generally TJ McIntyre, 'Cybercrime – Towards a Research Agenda' in Healy, Hamilton, Daly and Butler (eds), *Routledge Handbook of Irish Criminology* (Routledge, 2015).
18   See T Whitehead, 'Google and Whatsapp will be forced to hand messages to MI5', Telegraph, 27 May 2015, available at www.telegraph.co.uk/news/politics/queens-speech/11634567/Google-and-Whatsapp-will-be-forced-to-hand-messages-to-MI5.html.

replaced in light of being undermined by the Court of Justice in the *DRI* (and other) cases and challenges, including in the UK.

Directive 2006/24/EC on data retention

6.8   Data retention is sometimes a controversial topic. Directive 2006/24/ EC on the retention of data generated or processed in connection with the provision of publicly available electronic communications services or of public communications networks is the final key statute. This requires member states to implement measures to require the retention of certain data so that it can be made available to law enforcement authorities and government agencies for the investigation and detection of crime. This is a step forward from the voluntary Code of Practice under the Anti-Terrorism Act discussed above, to provide a compulsory and harmonised minimum level of data that must be retained by communications providers.

The regulation for retention of telephone data is subject to political and legal change, as well as debate.

As mentioned above, data retention is sometimes controversial and has attracted criticism such as on civil liberties, secrecy, overreach, etc. There have been a number of challenges to the Directive and to national measures regarding data retention. In the most significant case, *Digital Rights Ireland*, The Court of Justice struck down the Directive as, *inter alia*, being over-broad.[19] The Directive was held to breach arts 7 and 8 of the European Charter of Fundamental Rights.

It is possible that a new European data protection measure will be drafted in light of the decision. Queries arise in relation to the legality or necessity of data retention by telecoms companies presently. It is understood that at least one telecoms company has decided to delete such data on the basis that there is currently no legal basis to (have to) store the same. Some governments may perceive the need for national emergency legislation. Others may await the new EU data retention measure to replace the Directive which has been struck down. On a general note it should not be underestimated what backdrop effect the Snowden revelations may have had on the decision. The UK government feels the need for such emergency data retention legislation.[20]

DATA PROTECTION

6.9   Before investigating the application of the Data Protection Act 1998 to the internet, it is vital to set out the main aspects to the legislation. The Act is particularly definition-based: to appreciate the responsibilities of a data user

---

19   Joined Cases C-293/12 and C-594/12 *Digital Rights Ireland* Judgment of 8 April 2014. *Digital Rights Ireland Ltd (C-293/12) v Minister for Communications, Marine and Natural Resources and others and Kärntner Landesregierung (C-594/12) and others.* Available at http://curia. europa.eu/juris/liste.jsf?language=en&num=C-293/12.
20   See, for example, 'Emergency phone and internet data laws to be passed', BBC, 10 July 2014, available at www.bbc.com/news/uk-politics-28237111.

one must appreciate a great number of separate concepts: data, personal data, relevant filing system, processing of data, data subject and recipient. For ease of understanding, therefore, this section attempts to simplify the legislation by referring to these issues. This section describes each of these issues with specific internet examples; the following sections consider the application of these issues to commonplace e-commerce transactions and activities on the internet.

Personal data

Data

6.10   The Act applies only to personal data and those dealing with it. Assessing whether information is personal data is the starting point for all data protection questions. The word, 'data', is circularly defined with reference to further defined terms which themselves refer to 'data.'[21]

This wide definition is:

'information which:

(a)   is being processed by means of equipment operating automatically in response given for that purpose;

(b)   is recorded with the intention that it should be processed by means of such equipment;

(c)   is recorded as part of a relevant filing system or with the intention that it should form part of a relevant filing system; or

(d)   does not fall within paragraph (a), (b) or (c) but forms part of an accessible record as defined by s 68 [including health records, education records and accessible public records].'

In this way 'data' encapsulates information processed by equipment, either automatically or that is intended to later be processed by equipment. One example would therefore be information collected from individuals by way of physical paper forms which are to be later transferred into computer files. 'Equipment' is not defined in the Act and is deliberately technology-neutral. A computer would be an obvious example of equipment caught by both (a) and (b) above (others would include cameras, dictaphones, PDAs, etc). Therefore, any website or internet server is unlikely to be caught by section (a).[22]

Although unlikely to be relevant to the internet, the definition also captures non-digitally processed data which remains in manual files, but only if these

21   Data Protection Act 1998, s 1(1). This definition is not drawn from the body of the Directive but rather its preamble.

22   The case of *Smith v Lloyds TSB Bank* [2005] EWHC 246 held that the issue of whether information was personal data had to be answered at the time of the request. At that time Lloyds did not hold any information about Smith wholly or partly on automatic equipment. The reference to and definition of a relevant filing system in s 1(1) would be meaningless if any documents capable of being converted into a digital format were to be treated as if they were in a computer database.

form a part of a 'relevant filing system'. 'Relevant filing system' is defined by s 1(1) as:

> 'any set of information relating to individuals to the extent that although the information is not processed by means of equipment generating automatically in response to instructions given for that purpose, the set is structured as by reference to individuals or by reference to criteria relating to individuals, in such a way that specific information relating to a particular individual is readily accessible.'

This is a possible qualification, highlighted in the case of *Durant v Financial Services Authority*.[23] This means that unsophisticated records such as those which are structured purely by date rather than by name, for example, are unlikely to be caught. Unfortunately for internet providers, although relevant filing system is not stated as applying solely to manual records, the fact that computer records and internet files will be caught by limb (a) of the definition of data means that this caveat is not available. Although a digital record may be difficult to search against an individual, a controller will not clearly be able to rely on this in the same way as the Financial Services Authority did in relation to Mr Durant's paper files. This case has, however, been criticised and is distanced in discussions by other Data Protection Authorities. On a separate note, the Leveson Inquiry notes that judges (as well as others) need to become more familiar with data protection law.

Example 6.1

RemCom gathers salary data from recruitment agents to allow prospective employees to gauge their potential remuneration package in a given job. When an employee gains employment they are encouraged to feed back into RemCom their new salary and benefits package. Even though some of this information is taken from the happy employees by telephone operators, before it is inputted into RemCom's database, it will be classified as data.

Personal data

6.11   The word 'personal' refers to the data:[24]

> 'which relate to a living individual who can be identified:
>
> (a) from those data; or
>
> (b) from those data and other information which is in the possession of, or is likely to come into the possession of, the data controller and includes any expression of opinion about the individual and any indication of the intentions of the data controller or any other person in respect of the individual.'

While this definition is fundamental to whether or not one has data protection obligations, personal data may not be fundamental to a successful internet or e-commerce initiative.

---

23 [2003] EWCA Civ 1746.
24 Data Protection Act 1998, s 1(1).

Example 6.2

An individual repeatedly visits a website and always downloads from it the latest screensaver of a particularly attractive tennis star. Because the individual has entered data into an on-screen form, the website 'knows' four items of data about the individual. The individual is male, between 25 and 35 years of age, earns over £45,000 a year and likes tennis. Each time the individual visits the site, the site confirms it is him by placing on his computer a small file containing a unique identifier. The site, therefore, 'knows' what he looks at, what he downloads, how often he visits etc. All this data is useful and helps the site target the individual with new relevant screensavers when he visits. Without more, however, the site holds no personal data. The Act is not applicable therefore but the Privacy and Electronic Communications (EC Directive) Regulations 2003, are.

This technique of using 'non-personal' data has led e-commerce businesses to explore whether or not they can entirely avoid the obligations of the Act.[25] To consider this avoidance of the Act, one first needs to appreciate the scope, and purposive interpretation, of the definition. Key elements are as follows.

Relate to an individual

6.12　Previously it was thought that the Act concerns the data rather than the individual to whom it relates. This view is rebutted by the Court of Appeal's ruling in *Durant v Financial Services Authority*.[26] The court in this case focused on when data can be said to 'relate to an individual'. The court held that data could only be said to be 'personal' if it 'is information that affects [a person's] privacy, whether in his personal, or family life, business or professional capacity'. It went on to give two ways in which this might be determined. The first was whether or not the information is 'biographical in a significant sense', meaning that it goes beyond just mere recording of data to require some kind of personal connotation. The second appears to go further still, being that the data should have the individual as its focus rather than some other individual.

The Information Commissioner has clarified this interpretation as meaning that the simple fact that 'an individual is referred to in data does not make the information personal data about that individual unless it affects their privacy'.[27] Commentators and national Data Protection Authorities may not fully endorse the perhaps restrictive view of *Durant*.

Even if the decision in relation to relevant filing systems does not help those holding internet or other computer records (see **6.10** above), this part of the judgment does. Indeed the court specifically stated that 'not all information retrieved from a computer search against an individual's name or unique identifier, constitutes personal data'.[28] Obvious examples may include, in certain

---

25　Of course, companies still need to ensure they comply with the Act in relation to their other personal data: personnel, suppliers, contacts, etc.
26　[2003] EWCA Civ 1746.
27　'The "Durant" case and its impact on the interpretation of the Data Protection Act 1998', guidance note of the Information Commissioner issued in February 2006.
28　Ibid.

circumstances, an email which a person is simply cc'd in on. However, a record which shows what a person bought, their payment records or address would do. Most website transaction records and even log records which show what pages and services an individual was using are still likely to be caught therefore. The *Durant* ruling forces one to analyse what personal data is and is thereby caught by the Act. Rather than assuming that any data which can be related back to an individual is, one must assess whether the data does actually relate to and affect an individual. A cautious approach to overreliance on *Durant* is advised however.

A common scenario concerns an email address. Most email addresses incorporate the actual name of an individual and therefore relate to that individual, but this does not mean that it is automatically personal data. If I am simply cc'd in on a chain of emails discussing someone else, then it may be (in the *Durant* view) that my email in that context or the email itself does not constitute personal data. One can see from just this example that the analysis required varies on a case-by-case basis and demands some thought. In most cases controllers will want and need to err on the side of caution in discharging many of their obligations, treating emails with care. However, when it comes to data subject to access requests (as discussed later), controllers may wish to consider this more closely, rather than simply handing over and redacting quantities of information and material.

The *Durant* ruling has been followed in the case of *Ezsias v Welsh Ministers*,[29] concerning information to be provided pursuant to a data subject access request. The High Court held that only information relating to Mr Ezsias, as opposed to that relating to, say, his complaints, had to be provided. Further, to use the provisions of the Act to seek disclosure of documents generated as the result of the applicant's own complaint, in order to further a legal claim of the applicant against a third party is a legal abuse.

Many national data protection authorities would not necessarily take the perceived restrictive view of the *Durant* case. The Court of Justice case of *Commission of the European Communities v The Bavarian Lager Co Ltd*, annulled a Commission decision rejecting an application for access to the full minutes of the meeting, containing all of the names,[30] which is also arguably more in line with interpretations of what is personal data than the *Durant* view.[31] One view may be that a possibly restrictive *Durant* interpretation has received a more mainstream interpretation in the *Bavarian* case. Records of employees' working

---

29   [2007] All ER(D) 65.
30   *Commission of the European Communities v The Bavarian Lager Co Ltd*, Case C-28/08 P. Note also another ECJ/CJEU case which held that 'Article 2(a) of Directive 95/46/EC … must be interpreted as meaning that the data relating to an applicant for a residence permit contained in an administrative document, such as the "minute" at issue in the main proceedings, setting out the grounds that the case officer puts forward in support of the draft decision … and, where relevant, the data in the legal analysis contained in that document, are "personal data"'. In *Joined Cases C-141/12 and C-372/12 YS (C-141/12) v Minister voor Immigratie, Integratie en Asiel, and Minister voor Immigratie, Integratie en Asiel (C-372/12) v M, S*, 17 July 2014.
31   In relation to redacted and bombardised access disclosures, see for example, *Common Services Agency v Scottish Information Commissioner* [2008] UKHL 47. Also see *Webster and others v the Governors of the Ridgway Foundation School* [2009] EWHC 1140 (QB).

time is personal data.[32] In the *Halford* case, where an employee's UK telephone calls relating to a discrimination case were being recorded, the ECHR held, *inter alia*, that art 8 of the Convention is applicable to complaints concerning both the office and the home telephones; and that that there has been a violation of art 8 in relation to calls made on the applicant's office telephones.[33] The author JK Rowling was concerned to take a case under privacy and personal data grounds in relation to surreptitious photographs taken by certain media of her children.[34] The *Von Hannover* case also relates to protection from certain types of media photography.[35] Recently, the scope of the so-called (individual processing) or household exemption to the ambit of the data protection regime has been considered in the context of CCTV footage. The Court of Justice held that 'the operation of a camera system, as a result of which a video recording of people is stored on a continuous recording device such as a hard disk drive, installed by an individual on his family home for the purposes of protecting the property, health and life of the home owners, but which also monitors a public space, does not amount to the processing of data in the course of a purely personal or household activity' within the exception to applicability.[36]

Living individual

6.13   As long as the individual is living and is not a body corporate, the Act can apply. This includes all individuals, whether resident abroad or of foreign nationality.

Example 6.3

A foreign national enters his personal details into an online form required to access a UK newspaper's website. The individual is now concerned that these personal data are being misused. All things being equal, he has rights under the Act to prevent this misuse because he is a living individual and the data held are personal. The individual's nationality is largely irrelevant to the newspaper's obligations.

The definitions of personal data in both the Act and Directive refer to 'person' and 'individual' and not 'people' and 'individuals'. A question therefore arises

---

32 See *Worten – Equipamentos para o Lar SA v Autoridade para as Condições de Trabalho (ACT)*, ECJ/CJEU Case C-342/12, 30 May 2013.

33 *Halford v UK Halford v UK*, ECHR (1997), IRLR 471 (1997) 24 EHRR 523. See also *Copland v The United Kingdom*, ECHR (Application no 62617/00) 3 April 2007.

34 See *Murray v Big Pictures (UK) Ltd* (CA) [2008] EWCA Civ 446; [2008] 3 WLR 1360; [2008] EMLR 399, [2008] EHRR 736, [2008] 2 FLR 599, [2008] HRLR 33, [2008] UKHRR 736. Another example of surreptitious photographs were certain holiday pictures taken of Kate Middleton in what was expected to be a private setting.

35 The ECHR held that there was a breach of art 8 of the Convention. *Von Hannover v Germany (No 1)* ECHR (2004), (application no 59320/00), [2005] 40 EHRR 1. Note also later case of *Springer and Von Hannover v Germany (Von Hannover No 2)*, 07.02.12 [2012] EMLR 16. Also note *Axel Springer AG v Germany* (application no 39954/08) relating to the issue of national law.

36 *František Ryneš v Úřad pro ochranu osobních údajů*, ECJ/CJEU, Case C-212/13, 11 December 2014.

whether or not the Act applies to processed data about 'joint' individuals. Certainly, joint bank account holders are likely to be considered each as an individual under the Act, as are joint tenants of property.

Example 6.4

A well-known department store establishes an online wedding site for couples to create a 'micro-site' before their happy day. As well as displaying directions to the venue and a ceremony of service, the micro-site also provides the chance for guests to make purchases from the couple's gift list. Together with their address and wedding day, the department store does possess data relating to an individual.

However, there is at least academic and the Article 29 Working Party discussion on whether some data protection interests should survive death.[37]

Possession of other information

6.14   The definition of 'personal' data refers to identification in conjunction with other information in possession or likely to come into the possession of the data controller.[38] The Directive's recital 26 illustrates the likely width of 'possession'. It states:

> 'To determine whether a person is identifiable, account should be taken of all the means likely reasonably to be used either by the controller or by any other person.'

It follows that it is still possible to have 'possession' of data permitting identification for the purposes of the Act, even if one does not actually have physical possession of it. When assessing whether or not one is processing personal data, one must therefore examine data which is publicly available (which would 'confirm' the identity of the individual) and data available from a third party under contract or other relationship. This ties in closely with scenarios in which a company may believe that its data is not caught because it is anonymous. Since the key to decrypt or encode the data may be available, the data is still caught.

Another common example concerns IP addresses. An IP in itself appears as a number. This identifies a computer or log on point, rather than an individual. However, if a controller holds account details for an individual including their IP address and uses an IP address to collect further information (eg tracking which pages are read on a website), the information so collected becomes personal data since it can be related back to the individual and says something about them. This is the case even if the IP collected information and the account data is held in separate files. The fact that it could be linked causes the problem.

---

37   See, for example, Article 29 Working Party, Opinion No 4/2007 on the concept of personal data (2007) WP 136, available at http://ec.europa.eu/justice/policies/privacy/docs/wpdocs/2007/wp136_en.pdf. See discussion at 22.
38   Data Protection Act 1998, s 1(3).

Example 6.5

SecuriFirst and Last is a security firm which generates digital 'safes' for people who wish to store digital data off their own hard drives. To do so, one must provide one's first name, date and place of birth to SecuriFirst and Last. One pays for the safe through a third party which takes one's full name and residential address. This third party then provides a password to enable 'unlocking' of the safe. The third party clearly can identify each customer using information in its possession; SecuriFirst and Last also is likely to come into possession of this information because of its relationship with the third party.

Opinions on individuals

6.15   The final test to establish whether data is personal data is to ascertain the nature of the data: if the data is an expression of opinion or indication of intention about the individual, then the data can be personal.

The definition also includes an intention being expressed by a third party. For this reason, repeating the intention of another with respect to a living individual will still fall within the definition; the data may still be personal.

Anonymous data

6.16   The Data Protection Directive explicitly states that: 'the principles of protection shall not apply to data rendered anonymous'.[39] In addition, the Act refers only to living individuals who can be identified from the data processed. This has led many website operators and e-commerce businesses to seek to force (technically or legally) their data into being anonymous and so avoid the regulation of the Act. This is easier said than done. This is particularly so in the era of profiling, connecting information data and big data.

When businesses talk of 'anonymised', 'aggregated', 'generic', or even 'neutered' data, they may be referring to a number of situations. Common explanations of anonymous data include:

1.   'My business cannot identify living individuals from information we have in our possession. If we wanted to obtain extra information to do so, we could.' This business only possesses anonymised information. It will still be classified as personal data because reasonable enquiries would enable them to turn the anonymised data into identifying data.

2.   'My business cannot identify living individuals from information we have in our possession. We have come to an arrangement with a third party; they hold the personal data, we merely hold a unique identification number which allows them to resolve the identities.' This business only possesses anonymised information. Unless their contract with the third party is unambiguous, it is likely that their relationship will allow them to resolve

---

39   Recital 26.

the identification number into identifying a living individual. It is likely that the business will be classified as possessing personal data.[40]

3.   'My business can no longer identify living individuals from information we have in our possession. We have stripped out any information from our data which would allow us directly or indirectly to identify any living individual. Even other data sources would not assist us to identify particular individuals.' If the business truly has destroyed the identifiable features of its data, and even with reasonable enquiries, could not identify individuals, then it is no longer able to be classified as processing personal data. The key words, however, are 'no longer'. The Act and Directive do not apply to anonymised data but the process of anonymising the formerly identifiable data would have been considered to be processing it under the Act. All the usual preconditions would have applied to such processing. One such pre-condition may well be 'consent' by the individuals to allow their personal data to be anonymised.[41]

Example 6.6

A survey firm makes sure it removes all names and addresses from the survey results it collects. It does this on the understanding that this means it will not be classed as a data controller processing personal data. This is not correct. It should not collect any personal data in the first place if it wants this to be the case. The initial collection and the anonymising activity will themselves constitute processing of personal data.

In *R v Department of Health, ex p Source Informatics*, Source Informatics alleged that it was entitled to anonymise patient prescription data gained from general practitioners to sell to pharmacists. No supplied data could identify patients. Latham J in the Queen's Bench Division considered, *inter alia*, the Data Protection Act 1998 and suggested Source's use of the anonymised data was contrary to the Act.[42] On appeal, Simon Brown LJ, for a unanimous Court of Appeal, disagreed. He stated that the Directive does not apply to anonymised data.[43]

4.   'My business does not even collect identifiable data from individuals; our systems even ensure that the collected data is insufficient to permit us to combine the data with other data to identify any individual.' This

---

40   On 11 November 2000, The *Economist* wrote: 'Unlike DoubleClick's data, which is entirely anonymous, Abacus had 88m real names and addresses. Mr O'Connor [the chairman and founder of DoubleClick] realised that, by marrying the two, he could identify individual web users and not only track, but also predict their behaviour – making online advertising even more science than art …'. Had this integration of anonymised and identifiable personal data occurred, DoubleClick would have had personal data. Similar issues have faced Google, which has made an offer to acquire DoubleClick. Google, like Abacus, has personal data which it could link to DoubleClick's anonymous data.

41   A consent of this type should be included in privacy policies to ensure such anonymisation is permitted.

42   [1999] 4 All ER 185 at 192.

43   [2000] 1 All ER 786 at 198–199.

challengeable statement means that the Act does not apply to this particular dataset; the Act will apply to other datasets such as credit card processing, order or service fulfilment.[44]

In another case it was decided that low cell count statistics can amount to personal data.[45]

It is also important to remember that the actual act of rendering data anonymous will itself constitute an act of processing personal data since something needs to be done to it in order to make it that way.

Processing

6.17   It will be recalled that the Act only impinges on certain activities in relation to data with a particular quality: it must be personal. Having defined personal data, any processing of that data which is undertaken is caught by the Act.

The Act defines processing as performing one of a defined set of operations on personal data. Section 1(1) states that processing:

'in relation to information or data, means obtaining, recording or holding the information or data carrying out any operation or set of operations on the information or data, including:

(a)   organisation, adaptation or alteration of the information or data;

(b)   retrieval, consultation or use of the information or data;

(c)   disclosure of the information or data by transmission, dissemination or otherwise making available; or

(d)   alignment, combination, blocking, erasure or destruction of the information or data.'

The above list of what constitutes processing is non-exhaustive. The Directive's definition uses the magic words 'such as' and the UK's definition the similarly widening word 'including'. It is therefore difficult to imagine what operations or activities in relation to personal data would not constitute processing it.

However, one important 'gap' has been identified. In 2007 in *Johnson v Medical Defence Union*[46] the Court of Appeal considered whether the basis for a decision to terminate Mr Johnson's membership and professional indemnity services provided by his union constituted unfair processing of his personal data.

---

44   Google openly admitted that its new toolbar application permitted Google to monitor the sites frequented by its toolbar users. It stated 'By using the Advanced Features version of the Google toolbar, you may be sending information about the sites you visit to Google.' Google spokesman David Krane said: 'We're looking at data en masse, not going record by record' (ZDNet News, 11 December 2000). Google's revised general 2005 privacy policy does not, however, contain this wording.

45   *Department of Health v (1) Information Commissioner (2) Pro Life Alliance*, EA/2008/0074, Court Information Tribunal.

46   [2007] EWCA Civ 262.

The decision to terminate the membership had been made in accordance with the union's policy, which involved the review of Johnson's cases which were held in manual and computer records by a risk assessor who then summarised each case and produced a score sheet. This score sheet was then itself recorded using a computer. The Court of Appeal reversed the High Court ruling which had held that the risk assessor's selection of material and inputting of the report constituted 'processing'. The majority decision in the Court of Appeal was that the extent of the broad definition of processing has to be limited in scope by the definition of data. This means that processing is limited to either processing wholly or partly by automatic means or processing of data in relation to a relevant filing system. To this extent, the selection by the risk assessor of the computer records and the choice as to which information to put into an automatic system involved neither. It was an exercise of judgment which was not automatic at all, but a matter of human judgment.

This is a significant qualification, which demands that practitioners consider the interplay between these definitions and the place of any human intervention in any processing activities which may prevent them from being 'automatic'. It may also narrow the previously case of *Campbell v MGN Ltd*[47] which had given a very wide interpretation to the meaning of processing. That case concerned the publication of information and photographs which were alleged to infringe the privacy of Ms Campbell; processing was held to encompass any set of operations including obtaining and using information. Although each operation in itself was not necessarily an activity which could amount to processing, overall the set constituted an activity linked to automated processing at the instigation of the data controller. The Court of Appeal in *Johnson*, distinguished this case. The Appeals Court held that *Campbell* concerned publication of data which had already been processed automatically and was concerned with privacy as the prime interest of the Act and Directive. The court there had not considered 'pre-processing' stages where information had not previously been processed automatically as in the case it was considering.

Cheryl Cole's husband recently received damages in a privacy and data protection case in relation to a case stemming from a *Target* magazine story revealing private details.[48]

In the context of the internet, one of the key activities which is clearly encompassed by the concept of processing, is disclosure. The internet, especially the World Wide Web and email, is heralded for the ease with which information can be disclosed to others. The novel legal issue for the internet is whether there is disclosure and therefore automatic processing when information is not actively distributed but is merely 'left' on a server for collection.

Disclosure of data occurs where the data or information from the data is divulged to another person or recipient.[49]

---

47 [2003] QB 633.
48 See R Greenslade, 'Magazine pays "substantial" damages to husband of Cheryl Fernandez-Versini', *Guardian*, 21 October 2014, available at www.theguardian.com/media/greenslade/2014/oct/21/magazines-medialaw.
49 Defined in s 70.

> *Example 6.7*
>
> An Internet Service Provider maintains a log of its members' log-in times. The Provider allocates each member a unique number and stores log-in times in conjunction with this number; in another database, the Service Provider stores a list of the unique numbers for each member. The Service Provider seeks to use this log to inform the local telephone networks of the most popular access times. It will be a disclosure for the Service Provider to supply only the log to the network, even when the members' numbers database remains unseen. The ISP is disclosing the information gleaned from the personal data.

One of the keys to the commercial success of the internet is that it is very cheap to 'distribute' information to many recipients. There are two main ways: first, using a mailserver to emailshot a list of email addresses; the second way is to 'leave' information in a readily accessible area of the internet, be that as an upload on an ftp site or published on a website. The commercial difference is that in the second scenario, it is the receiver of the information who acts to retrieve that information; the provider remains passive. Receivers may pay the online or connection charges to locate and download the posted information. By contrast, when emailing the provider takes the active role, by sending the information, the recipients cannot help but receive it, they remain passive.

It is now almost beyond doubt that disclosure is effected by publishing personal data on a web page or uploading it to an ftp site. In the case *R v Brown*, Lord Goff considered the concept of 'disclosure' under the 1984 Act, albeit then with reference to a definition to assist his interpretation. He said:[50]

> '[I]t may be readily inferred that the person effecting the transfer was inevitably therefore disclosing the data to another person or persons who, as he well knew, would retrieve the information from the second database and so have the information disclosed to him.'

Although 'disclosure' is not defined in the 1998 Act, this is immaterial since it is encapsulated by the concept of processing. The European Court of Justice case of *Lindqvist*[51] confirms this. The case concerned a woman who was prosecuted in her home state for processing (as opposed specifically to disclosing) personal data by automatic means by composing a web page about some of her fellow parishioners on her computer and placing it on an internet server. The Court of Justice held that the loading of the page on to the server meant that the process has been performed 'at least in part, automatically'. Although here the prior selection of such information on the parishioners was manual and involved some judgment (much akin to the case of *Johnson* considered above), this ruling is still consistent with the *Johnson* ruling, despite first appearances. *Johnson* concerned the actions which were taken prior to the assessor's report being placed on the computer (and whether this processing was unfair). In *Lindqvist*, the court was considering just the question as to whether the uploading of the page (ie the disclosure and publication)

50   [1996] 1 All ER 545 at 549.
51   *Bodil Lindqvist v Kammaraklagaren* (2003) (Case C 101/01), ECJ.

was itself processing. (In *Johnson*, it was not in dispute that the final report itself, when placed on computer was data able to be processed as disclosed.)

These cases and issues show that it is essential when considering whether or not an action involving the internet or computers constitutes processing, that the different stages and any human involvement be analysed separately. Information held or transmitted via the internet will inevitably involve data and processing. However consideration must still be had of any prior actions undertaken where it is the alleged processing which is in dispute.

Example 6.8

A UK firm of advisers to wealthy individuals seeks to advertise its work for clients. It chooses to use a website featuring lists of clients, each with a link to a further page describing the nature of the work undertaken for the person. Notwithstanding issues of professional conduct and confidentiality, the firm will be disclosing this personal data.

Processors and controllers

6.18 Even a company that processes personal data may not be subject to the provisions of the Act. This is because the key provisions of the Act only apply to those persons who are defined as 'data controllers'. Persons who are simply 'data processors' may not be directly regulated (other than by virtue of certain separate criminal offences contained in the Act) but, because they are processing data, must be kept in check by the controller who instructs them. Understanding this distinction is therefore important, since a company that uses a third-party processor cannot automatically rely on such processor's compliance with the provisions of the Act. They will, therefore, need to be responsible for the imposition of obligations (likely to be contractual) on their processor to safeguard the integrity of the data, the data subjects' rights and the controller's own risk of liability under the Act. It is also essential to appreciate that, even though a party may be described as a data processor, this is not conclusive and the actual actions that they undertake may make them a data controller even so. Both concepts are considered below. Also, depending on the activities, an organisation can be a data controller (eg its own activities; its own employees' personal data) and also a data processor (eg outsource activities for a customer data controller).[52]

Data controller

6.19 A data controller is[53]:

'a person who (either alone or jointly or in common with other persons) determines the purposes for which and the manner in which any personal data are, or are to be processed.'

---

52 In relation to outsourced data processing outstanding account activities by a telecoms company and the nature of the contracts in place, see the ECJ/CJEU case of *Josef Probst v mr.nexnet GmbH*, Case C-119/12, ECJ/CJEU, 22 November 2012.
53 Data Protection Act 1998, s 1(1).

It is necessary to deconstruct two of the conditions listed above. First, determining the purposes and the manner of processing; second, alone or jointly.

Determines

6.20   The first of two conditions of being a data controller is that one determines the purposes and manner in which the personal data are or are to be processed. This determination may be joint or in common with others.

Determination of purposes and manner of processing

6.21   'Determining' can be distinct from processing. It is possible that one person compiles personal data, another formats and filters it and a third person then uses the data. This differentiation separates data controllers from data processors: data controllers (potentially with others) make the final decision as to the purpose of processing the personal data and how it is to be processed. Of course, where a data controller delegates any decisions to a third party, as is often the case with third party database architects, that third party becomes a data controller too. Because the statutory obligations are on data controllers it is important to understand what the Act means by 'determines'. If an internet service provider is doing more than only processing personal data, and is actually deciding the ways in which it is processed, he may be committing a criminal offence by acting as an unnotified data controller. The relevant criterion, therefore, is not what a person or body does with the data or the means he uses, but their capacity to make decisions in relation to the purposes and means of the processing.

Example 6.9

A UK bookseller maintains a website which allows customers to read rated reviews of selected books online and then place an order if desired. The bookseller seeks to establish whether there is any correlation between placing an order and reading a highly rated review. To establish this, the bookseller divulges all the data to a market researcher. The bookseller determines the purposes of the data and their use but is unlikely to know how the data will be correlated and analysed. The market researcher will, being the expert, determine the manner in which the customer data is processed. Both therefore have the relevant capacity to make decisions.

Key issues then concern the level of autonomy in deciding what actions are taken and any powers or management control that a person may have. The analysis of actions taken by SWIFT (a major co-operative providing a system for sending payment instructions between banks) by the Article 29 Working Party (the EU data protection watchdog) provides a useful analysis of the activities various national data protection regulators deem may constitute those of a data controller. This analysis provides a persuasive indication of the view which may be considered by national courts in any future action. In such case, although SWIFT was an intermediary between banks and presented itself as a mere processor, it had in fact taken on responsibilities which went beyond the duties and instructions incumbent on a processor, and therefore did have liability under data protection legislation.[54]

Jointly or in common

6.22 The terms 'jointly' and 'in common' broaden the ambit of 'determine' not only by including data that are under the absolute control of the data controller, but also by including the data partially under the instruction of the data controller. Similarly, where many persons share one collection of data (eg a database of contact details), each person will be classed as determining the use of that collection in common. The inclusion of these terms is particularly relevant to the internet because it is rare that only a single entity will deal on the internet with data: most organisations use one person to design a website, another to host it and perhaps even a third to provide access to the server.

Example 6.10

A UK business rents space on a website to a number of retailers and service providers, rather like a shopping mall. The website collects personal data on each of the entrants to the mall. At the end of each day, the business provides to its 'tenants' a full list of each of the entrants to the mall. Each of the tenants uses the data at its discretion. The business and each of its tenants are data controllers in common.

Of course, use for a collection of data may vary with time. It is conceivable that a person who previously had no input over the content of data or processing of data, could begin determining issues as trust between the parties develops and expertise grows. The varying involvement of a web designer who takes an administrative role is one example. This variance of determination creates uncertainty: those individuals who consider that they only process data under instruction, without discretion, should maintain careful records of their activities to ensure that they can justify their position as a mere data processor.

Example 6.11

An airline already using an online reservation system seeks to research the use of its system. To do this, it provides a list of its users' email addresses to a market researcher for the purposes of sending out a questionnaire. The market researcher reasons that geographical and age data will be useful to focus the questions. If the reasoning is accepted, the researcher has contributed to the content of the data and so may have determined the purposes of the data and manner of processing controlled and so used the data jointly with the airline.

---

54 Opinion 10/2006 on the processing of personal data for *Worldwide Interbank Financial Telecommunication (SWIFT)*, adopted on 22 November 2006.

Actual or potential processed data

6.23   Where a data controller has a specific intention to reprocess the data (having processed it already), he will continue to process that data. This remains the case even if the data are converted into another format.

If the Information Commissioner were to class say, a web developer, as processing personal data but the developer is not notified as a data controller, the developer may be prosecuted. The scope of processing is therefore significant and should also not merely be considered once; a change in circumstances may change an activity into processing.

Jurisdictional scope

6.24   Section 5 contains details of those to whom the Act applies. It applies to data controllers both established and not established in the UK under different circumstances. First, therefore, one must determine whether or not a data controller is established in the UK. Depending on the place of establishment, one must then determine details relating to the processing taking place. These complex issues need to be examined in detail. There is a two-stage test to assess whether the Act applies in situations with a foreign element. First, where is the data controller established; second, what is the nature of the processing.

There are four specific situations where a data controller will be deemed established in the UK. In addition, it is submitted there is a general test of establishment which is wider in interpretation than the specific situations amalgamated. The specific situations are: an individual who is ordinarily resident in the UK; a body incorporated under the law of, or of any part of, the UK; a partnership or other unincorporated association formed under the law of any part of the United Kingdom, and, any person who does not fall within the previous three situations but maintains in the UK a regular practice or office, branch, agency through which he carries out any activity.

In the case of *Vidal-Hall v Google Inc*[55] in a case relating to *inter alia* misuse of private information and internet tracking without consent, an appeal against service of proceedings outside of the jurisdiction failed. It was arguable that there was personal data and private information; that permission could be given to serve out of the jurisdiction in claims for libel demonstrated that damage was not confined to physical or economic harm; damage occurred in England where the claimant's servers were accessed; it was the courts' preliminary view that damage in the form of stress and anxiety could amount to damage sufficiently serious to engage the claimants' rights under art 8 of the European Convention on Human Rights and that their claims were not bound to fail absent any claim for pecuniary damage.[56] This was on preliminary aspect prior to a full trial. It is understood that these issues may be appealed. Note also the recent case of *Weltimmo sro v Nemzetti Adatvédelmi és Információszabadság Hatóság*, Case C-230/14, Court of Justice, 1 October 2013.

---

55   *Vidal-Hall v Google Inc* [2014] EWHC 13 (QB), [2014] FSR 30.
56   Ibid.

A partnership or other unincorporated association formed under the law of any part of the UK

6.25   While the first three concepts of 'residence', 'incorporation' and partnership or 'unincorporated association' are relatively straightforward legal constructs, the final concept needs investigation. For example, if a US company has no employees in the UK, and no equipment in the UK, but has a group of UK-established individuals who work on the company's behalf, does the US company come under the jurisdiction of the Act?

It is submitted that to answer this question one must refer to both art 4 and recital 19 of the Directive. These clarify that the concept of 'establishment' is not determined by legal 'personalities' but by 'effective and real exercise of activity through stable relationships'. It follows that the US company mentioned above is likely to be seen as being 'established' (for the purposes of this but maybe no other Act) in the UK.

Finally, it is possible for one data controller to be deemed established in more than one member state. In that situation (likely for multinationals), the controller must ensure that its establishment complies with the local national law.

Example 6.12

A US corporation houses all its servers, bar one, in the United States. The non-US server sits in Telehouse in London, and processes the credit card transactions for the corporation. Its work is generated from the US and no UK company or individual has the right to access the data stored on the server. The US company is established in a non-EEA state but uses equipment in the UK to process its data. It must comply with the Data Protection Act 1998.

Established in the UK

6.26   If the previous test determines that the data controller is established in the UK, one further test is applied to determine whether the controller is fully within the jurisdiction of the Act. Consider also, *Google Spain, Vidal Hall, Weltimmo, DRI, Schrems*, etc. This second test is whether or not the data are processed in the context of that establishment. The word 'context' is not defined by the Act, nor by the Directive. Taking the ordinary meaning of 'context', it is difficult to conceive of processing being carried out by a UK establishment that would not be in the 'context' of that establishment. One interpretation is that 'context' means that the data and processing should relate to UK data subjects or related activities. For example, if a US company has US customers, but its UK subsidiary holds such data on its own servers in the UK, is such processing activity 'processed in the context of that establishment'? The position is by no means clear, and no guidance has been issued on this point. Caution should be exercised and data controllers established in the UK should generally consider that all of their activities could be caught.

Established outside UK and other EEA states

6.27   Where a data controller is deemed to be established outside the UK and other EEA states, they may still fall within the jurisdiction of the Act. These data controllers fall within the jurisdiction of the Act where they also meet a second 'equipment' test. This 'equipment' test is that the foreign controller must use equipment in the UK for processing data otherwise than for the purposes of transit through the UK. The first issue to address is that this 'equipment' may be automated and that would be enough to bring the foreign controller within the ambit of the Act. The second issue is that 'mere transmission' equipment (such as routers and switches) will not bring the controller under the auspices of the Act.

Example 6.13

A US Internet service provider prides itself on allowing its members to access their accounts from anywhere in the world, on any computer they choose. For resilience and speed, the provider has a server in every major jurisdiction of the world, each with a complete set of data. One of the features of the system is that its members do not store their address book of email addresses on their computer, but on the provider's servers. This has the result that its members can process personal data using the provider's equipment. If one of the servers is in the UK, the provider will be resident here and will be governed by the Data Protection Act 1998.

Data processors

6.28 As discussed, the Data Protection Act 1998 applies to data controllers who process personal data. Those individuals who either allow users access to their equipment to process data, or perform the processing for them, are data processors and need not notify their activities to the Commissioner. More specifically, a person is a data processor if he:

1. not being an employee of the data controller;

2. processes data on behalf of the data controller.[57]

The following provides some internet-specific examples of data processing and the demarcation between controlling and processing in practice.

Archives and data warehousing

6.29 A mere provider of equipment for backing up a data controller's data will be a data processor. This is because it is usual that the data are stored and are also accessible by the data user if there is a breakdown or emergency. This access is likely to fall within the broad scope of processing; as such, the owner of a data warehouse (a company providing data storage services) is processing data on behalf of the data controller. It is rare that those persons will determine the nature of the data processing. In addition, the means of processing have arguably been determined by the data user in selecting that provider. Those who merely archive are therefore more likely to be data processors rather than controllers.

Another common scenario is that the owner of a data warehouse, on request, will perform actions on the data on the data controller's behalf. For example,

---

57   Data Protection Act 1998, s 1(1).

where a data controller urgently requires a list of names and addresses from a particular database, the owner of the data warehouse will usually, on request, provide these data. In doing so, that person is taking on the role of data processor. The person is performing processing on behalf of the data controller but should take care not to go beyond the controller's instructions, and should refer back for further instructions or confirmation where necessary.

The short and important point is that when storing another's data, one should carefully assess whether one is acting as a data processor. The difficulty with such an assessment is that processing, as has been discussed, is a subjective term and who 'determines' is more a matter of opinion than fact.

Example 6.14

An email provider holds emails for each of its members until the member logs in. At this point the member is informed that mail is being stored and is given a choice: either continue to store the mail, or, download the information. On choosing to download the mail, the mail is deleted from the provider's server. One copy only ever exists. Because the provider cannot determine the processing of the data, but requires its members' instructions, the provider will not be a data controller but merely a data processor.

Servers

6.30 Many online companies provide their customers with an area of storage space which could be used to store personal data. In itself, such storage makes these companies data processors. The companies are likely also to hold personal data on those customers who use their service making them a data controller for this purpose.

In the *Google Spain* case, the Court of Justice held that:

'Article 2(b) and (d) of Directive 95/46/EC … are to be interpreted as meaning that, first, the activity of a search engine consisting in finding information published or placed on the internet by third parties, indexing it automatically, storing it temporarily and, finally, making it available to internet users according to a particular order of preference must be classified as "processing of personal data" within the meaning of Article 2(b) when that information contains personal data and, second, the operator of the search engine must be regarded as the "controller" in respect of that processing, within the meaning of Article 2(d).

Article 4(1)(a) of Directive 95/46 is to be interpreted as meaning that processing of personal data is carried out in the context of the activities of an establishment of the controller on the territory of a Member State, within the meaning of that provision, when the operator of a search engine sets up in a Member State a branch or subsidiary which is intended to promote and sell advertising space offered by that engine and which orientates its activity towards the inhabitants of that Member State.'[58]

---

58   *Google Spain SL and Google Inc v Agencia Española de Protección de Datos (AEPD) and Mario Costeja González*, Case C-131/12, 13 May 2014, available at http://curia.europa.eu/juris/liste.jsf?pro=&nat=or&oqp=&dates=&lg=&language=en&jur=C%2CT%2CF&cit=none%252CC%252CCJ%252CR%252C2008E%252C%252C%252C%252C%252C%252C%252C%252C%252C%252C%252Ctrue%252Cfalse%252Cfalse&td=%3BALL&pcs=Oor&avg=&page=1&mat=or&parties=google%2Bspain&jge=&for=&cid=511372.

Remote manipulation

6.31 Many companies provide facilities for remotely manipulating data. Clients may choose this because the remote computer is extremely powerful and is able to perform tasks far more quickly than the client computer. There are various ways in which this manipulation can be performed: one, where the client computer communicates directly with the remote computer, giving instructions over the internet or using a direct line; another way, owners of the remote computer are actually given instructions as to how to manipulate the data. It should be clear that the risk of a security breach is lower in the first way than the second. Where the owner of a computer does permit remote access and manipulation, it may fall within the ambit of a data processor.

Example 6.15

Wonderlandweekend.com is a holiday company. It pays a commission to clients who send out mailings to their customers advertising Wonderlandweekend's luxury short breaks which generate sales. Clients give Wonderlandweekend their customer list to send out the mailings on their behalf. Wonderlandweekend does so acting solely on the client's instructions and can only use the data for the specified, one-off mailing purpose. It is likely that Wonderlandweekend is acting as a data processor when using such data. If a recipient then signs up with Wonderlandweekend to purchase a break, further processing of the customer's personal data will be undertaken by Wonderlandweekend in its own right, for its own purposes and at its discretion. Wonderlandweekend will be acting as a data controller in respect of this processing. Care should be taken in any contract between client and Wonderlandweekend to clarify the demarcation of responsibility and any relevant controls.

Data protection notification

6.32 The impact of the Data Protection Act on users of the internet has been shown to be great. All information sent over the internet will constitute data, and if personal, providing those data over the internet will be viewed as processing. Data controllers are required to register with the Information Commissioner. If a person should notify but does not, this constitutes a criminal offence.[59]

Notifications must be submitted along with a fee. The notification period is one year. Renewals do not occur automatically unless it has been arranged for the renewal fee to be paid by direct debit payment. Otherwise, the renewal notification and fee must be submitted prior to the expiry date of the entry. Although the Information Commissioner's office sends out reminder notices before the expiry date of a notification, it is essential to be alert to this date and to have arrangements in place to effect the necessary administration. Where a notification has passed its expiry date, notifications cannot be renewed and data controllers will be obliged to make a new notification.

---

59   Data Protection Act 1998, ss 17(1) and 21(1).

Any changes to a notification must be notified within a period of 28 days from the date on which the entry becomes inaccurate or incomplete. Failure to do so is a criminal offence. Changes can be made free of charge by post using the specific form to add an additional purpose or a second form covering other amendments. These forms are available from the website, http://www.ico.gov.uk.

Notification exemptions

6.33 Certain data controllers are not required to notify, as they are exempt. Nevertheless, they may notify voluntarily[60] and in all cases are still bound by the other provisions of the Act.[61] The main exemptions extend to processing only for:

1. personal, family or household affairs;[62]

2. maintaining a public register;[63]

3. a non-profit organisation processing only for establishing or maintaining membership or providing or administering activities for individuals who are members of the organisation;[64] or staff administration, or, advertising, marketing and public relations, or, accounts and records but no other processing at all.[65]

Contents of a notification

6.34 A notification is a publicly available document explaining in standard terms the processing activities of a data controller. Notifications can be completed either by following a template available from the Information Commissioner's website at http://www.ico.gov.uk, or by creating a bespoke notification by selecting the relevant categories of information that apply.

Data controllers should pay attention to any partially completed template received from the Information Commissioner. This delineates the responsibilities of the data controller to its subjects. Data controllers should also ensure that their application includes 'free-text' references to the internet, where appropriate. If this section does not accurately describe the ambit of a data controller's purpose for processing the data, that may expose the data controller to prosecution.

---

60 Data Protection Act 1998, s 18(1).
61 Voluntary notification is not available to the following exempt persons, being those who: hold personal data for personal, family or household affairs; hold personal data exempt under national security exemptions; hold personal data exempt under transitional provisions for payroll, unincorporated members' clubs and mailing list usage. Data Protection Act 1998, Part IV.
62 Data Protection Act 1998, s 36.
63 Data Protection Act 1998, ss 17(4) and 70.
64 Data Protection (Notification and Notification Fees) Regulations 2000, Sch, para 15.
65 Data Protection (Notification and Notification Fees) Regulations 2000, Sch, paras 1–4.

Example 6.16

A UK company currently uses one free-standing computer to store and process the biographical details of its staff. Now that the company is expanding out of the UK, it wishes to port these data onto a website, to allow any member of the overseas operation to access the details. The company's notification should reflect this. For, say, the purpose of 'Maintaining and publishing biographical details of staff', the description should be expanded to stress this is 'over the Internet and World Wide Web'. An example of needing to amend the description of a purpose is where the Internet is integral to the purpose.

The notification breaks down information about data processing activities provided for each of the disclosed purposes the data controller processes personal data for. For each of these purposes, the data controller must then state: the data subjects of such data; the data classes (ie the types of data which are processed); data disclosees (the persons to whom data may be disclosed); and whether or not the data is to be transferred outside the EEA. The data controller is then required to sign a declaration and provide certain contact details and confirmation as to whether or not certain specific training and security requirements have been met (not compulsory).

Highlighting the importance of the seventh principle (discussed below), data controllers must also give a general description of the security measures to be taken to protect against unauthorised or unlawful processing of personal data and against accidental loss or destruction of, or damage to, personal data. Often this description will be very sensitive for the data controller and, as a consequence, is not published in the public register. Data controllers need to provide the necessary comfort regarding physical security, technical security and organisational security. Further details relating to security are discussed below in relation to the seventh data protection principle.

Example 6.17

An online UK car retailer has always sold its customer details to car insurance companies; appropriately, its registration notification included the purpose of trading in personal information. Previously, it provided its lists of personal data to the insurance company on disk. To keep the lists more up to date, it has now installed a server which acts as an ftp site for any person with the correct password. Despite this purpose remaining the same, the retailer should update the relevant description to reflect the change in provision.

Principles of data protection

6.35   All data controllers must abide by the eight principles of data protection which are set out in Sch 1 to the Act as follows:

1. Personal data shall be processed fairly and lawfully and, in particular, shall not be processed unless:

      (a)   at least one of the conditions in Sch 2 is met, and

      (b)   in the case of sensitive personal data, at least one of the conditions in Sch 3 is also met.

2.   Personal data shall be obtained only for one or more specified and lawful purposes, and shall not be further processed in any manner incompatible with that purpose or those purposes.

3.   Personal data shall be adequate, relevant and not excessive in relation to the purpose or purposes for which they are processed.

4.   Personal data shall be accurate and, where necessary, kept up to date.

5.   Personal data processed for any purpose or purposes shall not be kept for longer than is necessary for that purpose or those purposes.

6.   Personal data shall be processed in accordance with the rights of data subjects under this Act.

7.   Appropriate technical and organisational measures shall be taken against unauthorised or unlawful processing of personal data and against accidental loss or destruction of, or damage to, personal data.

8.   Personal data shall not be transferred to a country or territory outside the European Economic Area unless that country or territory ensures an adequate level of protection for the rights and freedoms of data subjects in relation to the processing of personal data.

First principle: processed fairly and lawfully and satisfies additional conditions

6.36

'The information to be contained in personal data shall be obtained, and personal data shall be processed, fairly and lawfully.'

This principle will be particularly relevant for those who use their websites or other digital activities to collect and then utilise personal data from visitors. In short, the principle attempts to ensure that those individuals who access a service or send information understand, and consent to, what will happen to their personal data. One must bear in mind that 'processing' encompasses the stages of first 'obtaining' data and then utilising it, by, say, organising, consulting or disclosing.[66] It is, therefore, important to consider, initially, whether a site is 'obtaining' data fairly and lawfully and then consider the method of fuller exploitation. The Act also specifies that '[i]n determining ... whether personal data are processed fairly, regard is to be had to the method by which they are obtained ...'.[67]

Data obtained fairly

6.37   There is no one test to establish that a data user has fairly obtained information from personal data, but there are a number of factors that the

---

66   Data Protection Act 1998, s 1(1).
67   Data Protection Act 1998, Sch 1, Pt II, para 1(1).

Commissioner will take into account. One key factor prescribed by the Act is that the individual was not deceived or misled about the purpose for the data.[68] A data controller should try to indicate to the data subject the full potential use of that information. It is not enough to direct the subject to the notification or to assume that the subject knows the scope of a data controller's notification. To be safe, a data controller must make explicit the purpose to each potential data subject at the point of collection: a data user may breach this principle even where the data subject was misled unintentionally.[69] Unless it is obvious from the method to obtain the information, data controllers should inform their subjects of the potential disclosures and transfers of the information, and the purpose for processing that information.

A good, albeit US, example of the concept is the US Federal Trade Commission Complaint against Geocities.[70] Geocities operated a website consisting of 'virtual communities' of free and fee-based personal home pages. At the time of the complaint, it had more than 1.8 million members. Each member had the option to enter certain personal data with the various provisos that:[71]:

> 'We will not share any information with anyone without your permission'

> '[W]e will NEVER give your information to anyone without your permission'

> 'We assure you that we will NEVER give your personal information to anyone without your permission'

Despite such assurances, Geocities did disclose the personal information to third parties. They, in turn, used the information to target Geocities members. In its consent order with the Federal Trade Commission (FTC), Geocities admitted these 'facts' as true. This blatant misrepresentation as to the use of personal data should amount to 'unfair' obtaining under the first principle. Under the US FTC codes, Geocities settled the complaint.

A UK example concerning unfair obtaining of personal data is the enforcement notice against B4U Business Media Limited; the first such enforcement action against a UK website. The site B4USearch.com provided online access to directory enquiries and electoral roll information. The Information Commissioner held that this was unfair processing. It was unfair for individuals to be compelled to provide information under statute (as part of the electoral roll) where that information was then available for resale without restriction. It was also unfair because B4U was deliberately using old data, knowing that later regulations had been brought in[72] to enable individuals to opt out of having their data made available for other uses. B4U's use of the earlier data unfairly undermined the wishes of those who later chose to opt out. This case also highlights the misconception of assuming that information obtained from a

---

68 Data Protection Act 1998, Sch 1, Pt II, para 1(1).
69 This was decided in the *Innovations (Mail Order) Ltd v Data Protection Registrar Data Protection Tribunal* case DA/92 31/49/1.
70 File No 9823015, 1998.
71 Respectively: New Member Application Form Privacy Statement, Geocites Free Member E-mail Program Privacy Statement, World Report Newsletter 1997.
72 The Representation of the People (England and Wales) (Amendment) Regulations 2002.

person with statutory authority to supply such information provides immunity. The processor must still comply with para 2, Part II of Sch 1 (ie information and data notices must still be provided).

Identity of data user

6.38   Potential data subjects should be made aware of to whom they are providing their personal data. The seamless way that a viewer of a website can move between different websites may cause data protection problems. For example, many commercial sites outsource any payment mechanisms to a third party, who also operates a website. A viewer of the commercial site will be taken through the various stages of choosing a product to purchase. The final stage in this process is for the viewer to enter his personal details and payment particulars. To do this the viewer will often be instructed to click on a certain icon, perhaps labelled 'Payment'. At this point, unbeknown to the viewer, the viewer is connected with the payment website. The only way for the viewer to discover this, unless it is made clear, may be to watch the URL alter at the top of their browser. Where framing or imbedded applications are used, even the URL may not alter.

It is certainly unfair obtaining of data where the provider of that data is not alerted to the identity of the person obtaining the data. Controllers of websites that interact with others for the collection of personal data should make it clear to their viewers that this is the case. It is particularly important that data controllers at the very least make this information 'readily available' to the potential data subject.[73]

Non-obvious purposes

6.39   Often, a data controller will have more than one contemplated purpose for personal information. Where a purpose could not reasonably be expected, the data user must inform the subject prior to obtaining the data. Data controllers must give each individual the informed chance to refuse to become a data subject.[74] This issue of unanticipated uses (and new uses) is a frequent problem in practice.

Data controllers should assume that there is a need to inform the data subject of the intended use. Data controllers should alert their data subjects to any processing prior to obtaining. This is the case even where the data, once obtained, will be used solely by the data controller.

When and how to inform

6.40   A data controller's obligations are not to deceive or mislead the user about the likely processing of the data prior to processing the data or disclosure to a third party.[75] In practice this is likely to entail the data controller informing the potential subjects of all relevant information prior to obtaining the data.

---

73   Data Protection Act 1998, Sch 1, Pt II, para 2(1)(a).
74   This is specifically discussed below at **6.41**.
75   Data Protection Act 1998, Sch 1, Pt II, para 2(2).

Otherwise, the data controller will be obliged to conduct the embarrassing and costly activity of re-contacting data subjects to ask their permission to exploit their data in a new undisclosed manner.

For commercial and legal reasons, therefore, data controllers are advised to inform their potential data subjects of all relevant information before the subject has opportunity to enter their data. A US import to achieve this is the 'privacy policy' which is often used to explain the 'who, why, what and where' of processed data. The Information Commissioner states that privacy policies are 'good practice.'[76] They are a now almost ubiquitous way of ensuring that prior to obtaining the data, the data controller has 'made available' to the subject all the relevant information.

The information that must be given is set out at para 2(3), Part II of Sch 1 to the Act. Those drafting these notices or a privacy policy should also be mindful of the information requirements under the Electronic Communications (EC Directive) Regulations 2003 and Electronic Commerce (EC Directive) Regulations 2002. The information in the notice or privacy policy should include a general description of all the purposes for which the data may be processed.

Where a data controller needs to do this, to broaden its purposes, silence should not be taken to be a data subject's consent. In *Midlands Electricity plc v Data Protection Registrar*[77] it was made clear to Midlands Electricity that:

> 'For the avoidance of doubt ... consent shall not be inferred from the failure of any person to return any other documentation containing an opportunity to opt-out.'

This clarification is also repeated in the undertakings made by London Electricity plc[78] and Thames Water Utilities Ltd,[79] both given to avoid the Commissioner enforcing its sanctions. Data controllers would be prudent not to rely upon a data subject's silence.

Example 6.18

An online pencil procurement website has fairly collected the email addresses and personal data of the stationery budget holders in the country's largest companies. Pressure from its venture capitalist investors leads it to expand into advertising conferences and jobs in the procurement field. It emails all its customers explaining this expansion and asking them to return the email if they have any objections to this new processing. Merely because no one returned an objection does not mean that the site's personal data is now fairly obtained for this new purpose.

Often a data controller will obtain personal data with one intention in mind, and then later decide to use the information for another purpose. Unless this new

---

76 Internet: Protection of Privacy, Data Controllers, Version 4, January 2000. This document is published by the Office of the Information Commissioner.
77 Final form of the enforcement notice (as approved by the Data Protection Tribunal) 20 July 1999, at para 9.5.
78 London Electricity plc Undertaking, 1 January 2001.
79 Thames Water Utilities Ltd Undertaking, 1 January 2001.

purpose is within the scope of the purpose reasonably contemplated or disclosed to the data subject, strictly speaking, the data user should seek a new consent.

Prior consent

6.41 In the fiercely competitive e-commerce sector, it is important to keep open one's options for future business ventures. Unfortunately, it is not advisable to attempt to keep open one's options of dealing with personal data. A data controller cannot try to get around this by making the initial description of the purposes vague in order to encompass future purposes for which they may later choose to use the data. Data controllers must make their intentions clear to potential data subjects before soliciting their personal data.

Example 6.19

Fat?No!, a web-based health and fitness magazine informs its online subscribers that their personal data is held in order to 'send you details of competitions, events and articles that may be of interest to you and for any other related purposes'. The company is not generating enough income through advertising revenues on its site. It approaches a sponsor who requires that they directly send subscribers weekly promotions for its range of fat-free ice cream. This is not within the scope of the original purposes stated, and even without this new purpose, the original notice is arguably unfair.

In *Innovations (Mail Order) Ltd v Data Protection Registrar*,[80] under the 1984 Act, the appellant collected individuals' names and addresses for completing order requests by them. After completing the order Innovations sent an acknowledgement on the back of which was a statement informing the customer that Innovations rents out its names and addresses. The company gave an address to its customers to write to if they objected to their data being used in this way. The Data Protection Tribunal held that this was too late: to be fair, data users must give their subjects the chance to consent to the use of personal information before it is taken. It upheld the enforcement notice served by the Registrar on 9 April 1992.

Surreptitious obtaining

6.42 One quality of the internet is that a data controller may technically collect personal data without a data subject being aware. 'Cookies' can be deposited on a data subject's hard drive which, when combined with personal data knowingly entered by the subject, can create new personal data. If a site 'records' all the movements one makes within a site, and is able to link those movements to data identifying a living individual, it is obtaining personal data about use of its site. Controllers must only obtain such covert data, albeit valuable, where the data subject has been given clear information about the use and purpose of cookies. The Electronic Communications Directive (as implemented into UK legislation via the Privacy and Electronic Communications (EC Directive) Regulations

---

80 DA/92/31/49/1.

2003) addresses this issue. It prohibits the use of cookies or other similar devices, regardless of whether or not they actually involve the processing of personal data, unless data subjects are given 'access to clear and comprehensive information' about the cookies and other information[81] and provided with a means of disabling such device.

Example 6.20

A successful version of browser software allows each site visited to store a small quantum of data about the visitor accessing the site. This data, or 'cookie', is stored on the visitor's hard disk and is used to compile data about each visitor when they revisit any site. If the visitor has no knowledge of this surreptitious method of obtaining information, be it stored at the client or server, it may be unfair obtaining of data. If the server then processes the information, again, without the client's tacit consent, this may also be a breach of the first data protection principle as unfair processing.

The photographs in the JK Rowling case which related to the privacy and personal data relating to her children were apparently surreptitious.[82]

Disingenuous consent

6.43   It is likely to be unfair where a data subject has no choice but to provide consent to additional uses of his personal data. This is the situation where the data controller informs all potential subjects that their order or transaction will not be processed unless they agree to the secondary uses of the data. While the data subject does still have a nominal choice, to stop dealing with the data user, for certain dominant data controllers it will not be a genuine choice.

Information obtained lawfully

6.44   The first hurdle for the Information Commissioner to prove unlawful obtaining is to prove that the obtaining of the information was in breach of a law. Possible candidates for grounds for unlawful obtaining in the normal course of dealing with personal data are breach of confidence and breach of contract. In the internet sphere the most likely law to be broken is not civil, but criminal: the Computer Misuse Act 1990.[83] Unauthorised access, an offence under the Computer Misuse Act 1990, may result in the obtaining of information unlawfully under the Data Protection Act 1998. Along with these more general laws by which data users must abide, certain data users are bound by rules specific to their industry. *British Gas Trading Ltd v Data Protection Registrar*[84]

---

81   Art 5, para 3, also see recital 25. See Agreement between the Attorney General of the States of Arizona, California, Connecticut, Massachusetts, Michigan, New Jersey, New Mexico, New York, Vermont and Washington and Doubleclick Inc, 26 August 2002.
82   See *Murray v Big Pictures (UK) Ltd* (CA) [2008] EWCA Civ 446, [2008] 3 WLR 1360. Another example of surreptitious photographs were certain holiday pictures taken of Kate Middleton in what was expected to be a private setting.
83   See Chapter 5 on Crime.
84   [1998] Info TLR 393.

is a good illustration of this. In this case the Registrar (as then was) viewed the use of customer data to provide non-gas services was *ultra vires*. The Tribunal disagreed but concurred with the concept of an *ultra vires* act of a corporation being 'unlawful' under the first principle.

Whatever the unlawful activity alleged, it will always be open to the data subject or Information Commissioner to argue that, in the alternative, even if the obtaining was not unlawful, it was nevertheless unfair.[85] The protection for data subjects under the first principle of data protection is certainly broader when the accusation is unfair obtaining as compared with unlawful obtaining.

Data processed fairly

6.45   Fair processing is directed at protecting data subjects from treatment that may be described in a data controller's notification but is, nevertheless, prejudicial use of the personal data. The first question is necessarily to establish that processing itself has occurred. It will be recalled that 'processing' is a wide and far-ranging concept but that it is also important to consider the actual activity undertaken at the time of the alleged 'unfair' processing. This is because, as in the *Johnson* case considered above, where this concerns processing that is not automated or in respect of a relevant filing system, the question as to whether or not any action was unfair may become immaterial. As has also been discussed, the concept of 'fairly' is also very wide. Despite such a 'catch-all' provision, the Act further raises the hurdle for a data controller.

Additional conditions necessary for the first principle

6.46   The first principle stipulates both that data shall be processed fairly and lawfully 'and, in particular, shall not be processed unless … at least one of the conditions in Schedule 2 is met'. The additional conditions are discussed below in the context of internet data controllers.

Data subject has given his consent to the processing

6.47   The consent condition under Sch 2 should not be confused with the specific requirement to obtain consent where data is being put to certain uses, as for example under the Privacy and Electronic Communications (EC Directive) Regulations 2003 in relation to direct marketing (see below). The factors in considering how this consent can be obtained over the internet are the same, however.

On the internet, just as in the offline world, one may consent in a number of ways. One may 'positively' consent by continuing to conduct oneself in a particular way. One may also actively consent by signing a particular document at a particular place.

---

85   There will be many situations where obtaining is both unfair and unlawful under the Unfair Terms in Consumer Contracts Regulations 1994/9 which make certain unfair contractual terms unenforceable against a consumer. A contracting party which by its unequal bargaining power is able to coerce a consumer into agreeing to supply personal data may be acting unfairly under the Regulations. The obtaining of those data may be outside the enforceable terms of the contract and classed as unlawful and, by virtue of the disparity in bargaining strength, unfair.

On a website, data controllers and their web designers are faced with the difficulty of 'what is consent?' Is it an opt-in box, pre-ticked? Is it an opt-out box[86] in a small font size and 'below the fold'?[87] There is no definition of 'consent' in the Act. In the House of Lords debate on the Act Lord Williams was adamant that there was no need to include a definition as existing law and the courts were enough.[88]

Further guidance can be drawn from the Act's spawning Directive at art 2(h). This states a person's consent is 'freely given, specific and informed indication of his wishes by which the data subject signifies his agreement to personal data relating to him being processed'. It is worthwhile considering the elements of this definition in the internet context.

Freely given

6.48   This will rarely be a difficult challenge for most data controllers. Even if a data subject must provide consent as an obligation under the contract with the data controller, the data subject does not need to enter into the contract. Consequently, it is acceptable to deduce the 'consent' was freely given. Difficulties can arise where, without acting in an anti-competitive or collusive way, a great number of organisations within a particular sector require consent to process certain data. In such a situation, a data subject may be unable to enter this type of contract with any supplier without giving 'consent'.[89]

Example 6.21

A large group of airlines that fly from London to Paris each have websites and independently choose to allow bookings to be taken only over their respective websites. Each ticket sale contract includes a term to the effect of 'You agree that we may use your personal data to provide you with details of great hotel offers during your flight'. There is no opt-out box. Because it is impossible to fly directly to Paris without giving this 'consent' it may be deemed not to be freely given.

Specific

6.49   This aspect of 'consent' is the one which causes most clashes between the marketing team behind a site and its legal advisors. Specific means just that; general is not enough and reaching a form of statement next to a consent mechanism that is informative but also commercial and not unduly alarming can be a challenge. Explaining the temporary or permanent nature of the activity is also an integral aspect of being specific.

---

86   See discussion on the meaning of opt-in and opt-out consent below.
87   The hidden part of the current web page which is available for viewing by scrolling down the web page. This is, in part, a factor of the resolution of the viewer's screen.
88   Vol 586, No 108, col CWH 15, 23 Feb 1998.
89   See Mr Lamidey's (Assistant Registrar under the 1984 Act) concern at high street bank practices: *Financial Times*, 2 February 1993.

Example 6.22

A fireplace installer establishes a website which allows customers to design and order their fireplaces. The 'fair collection' notice states: 'By ordering this fireplace you will also agree to allow one of our group of companies to contact you by email, yearly, to enquire only whether or not you require your chimney to be swept for your comfort and safety.' Such a notice is specific and leaves the data subject in no doubt as to the precise purpose of collecting their data.

Informed

6.50   Allied to 'specific' is the concept of 'informed': simply put, one cannot consent unless one knows what one is consenting to. For data protection purposes online, companies have taken to producing 'privacy policies'. These detail every possible activity that may be contemplated in relation to the data. Despite their almost viral, widespread usage across websites, there is a risk that they do not fulfil their intended effect. This is not down to their content wanting; it is because their position and incorporation is often so hidden that they are not immediately visible. Websites with unusual uses of personal data would be advised not merely to include details of the uses in their privacy policy. They must also bring the policy to a user's attention, not bury it at the bottom of a web page and/or in terms and conditions.

Example 6.23

An individual complains to the Information Commissioner that a certain website has used their personal data in a non-obvious manner. When approached, the website's owner directs the Commissioner to click on a tiny 'Terms of Use' link at the base of the home page followed by a further link on that page to the 'Privacy Policy'. The page on which personal data was collected has had no such links. Whatever the contents of the privacy policy, it is likely that its hidden position will mean no informed consent was given.

Indication and signifies

6.51   These two terms have been prised out of the Directive's definition to support the Information Commissioner's view that:

> 'Data controllers cannot infer consent from non-response to a communication, for example by a customer's failure to return or respond to a leaflet.'[90]

This approach to 'silence' is endorsed by the undertakings given by London Electricity plc and Thames Water Utilities Ltd[91] in relation to alleged breaches of the first principle. In both undertakings the statement is made:

---

90   The Data Protection Act 1998 – An Introduction, Office of the Data Protection Registrar, October 1998, at p 10.
91   7 January 2001 and 11 January 2001.

'consent shall not be inferred from the failure of any person to return any leaflet or other document containing an opportunity to opt out.'[92]

Similarly, in the Final Form of the Enforcement Notice (as approved by the Data Protection Tribunal on 20 July 1999) against Midlands Electricity plc consent is stated to include where:

'[the individual customers] have returned a document to the [data] user or, by other means of communication received by the data user have indicated that they consented to, or by not filling in an opt-out box or other means have indicated that they do not object to such processing.'[93]

These cases do show that the Information Commissioner believes (and just as important, the Tribunal supports the view) that silence or acquiescence is unlikely to be an 'indication' of consent. The commercial lesson to draw from this is simple. Wherever possible, ensure that a data subject has to 'do' something having read the privacy policy or fair collection notice. The consent provisions of the Privacy and Electronic Communications (EC Directive) Regulations 2003 have provided further clarification on consent requirements in the context of marketing communications. See section **6.133** below for details.

Evidence of consent

6.52   If 'consent' is being relied upon to comply with Sch 2, websites should ensure that they retain evidence of this consent. If a database contains only the email address of data subjects, how can this be used to prove that all their owners did consent, by say, ticking a box? If a privacy policy contains some unusual uses for data, how can its website owner prove that there was a specific, informed indication of the data subject's consent?

To answer these questions, the customer database needs to be constructed to record not merely the collected personal data but also the data relating to the consent itself. In addition, with websites under constant redesign flux, data users should maintain a secure, date-stamped copy of the main data protection aspects of the site to allow them to prove how the site was configured at the time that a data subject keyed in their details and consent.

Processing necessary for the performance of or entering into a contract[94]

6.53   At first glance, a data user could be forgiven for assuming that all that is needed to satisfy this paragraph is publishing an appropriate term in the data subject's contract. The correct focus, however, is on the word 'necessary'. An ancillary use of the data will not be necessary for the performance of the contract. The word necessary must be construed very narrowly and objectively.

---

92   Paras 1.5(iii) and 5(3) respectively.
93   Cl 9.2(ii)(bb).
94   Data Protection Act 1998, Sch 2, para 2.

Example 6.24

NeuPub2 is a radical new type of online publisher: writers submit their manuscript and NeuPub2 distributes their work having edited the manuscript to include 'product placement' from well-known brand names. In return, NeuPub2 pays its writers a royalty on copies sold. For writers that do not sell well, NeuPub2 states: 'From time to time we will pass your details to experienced writing coaches who can help your next project be even more successful.' Processing the data for this ancillary purpose is not necessary for the performance of the contract.

Processing necessary for compliance with a data user's non-contractual legal obligation

6.54   This paragraph of Sch 2 relates to a statutory obligation on the data user to process the data in a particular manner. Owners of websites should take specific sectoral legal advice before relying only on this paragraph to satisfy their compliance with Sch 2.

Processing necessary for data subject's vital interests

6.55   It is clear both from the recitals to the Directive[95] and the Commissioner's guidance[96] that this condition is concerned with life and death situations for the data subject.

Processing necessary for public functions

6.56   This related to the administration of justice, functions of the Crown, minister, government department and related functions of a public nature exercised in the public interest. Again, this is narrowly construed because of the limiter 'necessary'. This condition should not concern private bodies and should not be confused with non-contractual obligations.

Processing necessary for a data controller's legitimate interests

6.57   This is an ambiguous condition. It requires the Information Commissioner, Tribunal and possibly the courts to balance the data user's legitimate interests with those legitimate interests of the data subject,[97] particularly his right to privacy[98] and other rights and freedoms provided for under the European Convention for the Protection of Human Rights and Fundamental Freedoms and the Human Rights Act 1998.

This condition may not allow in, through the back door, anything that a private body does for profit because 'profit making is a legitimate interest'. Legitimate interest in this context must mean those interests protected by the Treaty of Rome and other enabling provisions. It does not mean, in effect, any *vires* act a company chooses to conduct.

---

95   Recital 31.
96   '[R]eliance on this condition may only be claimed where the processing is necessary for matters of life and death ...'
97   Data Protection Act 1998, Sch 2, para 6.
98   Directive 95/46/EC of the European Parliament and of the Council, arts 7(f) and 1(1).

Even if such a wide interpretation were afforded to this condition, one must not forget why the condition needs to be met. To comply with the first principle, first the data must be processed fairly and then also it must satisfy one of the conditions.

Web businesses and their advisors are warned not to trust this condition as their way unfairly to process data and to avoid providing the data subject with the 'specific information' relating to the processing. In addition, all analysis and decision must be conducted on a case-by-case basis, which demands that the interests of one data subject are not assumed to apply for another.

Example 6.25

SpamMethods Ltd is established as a company whose sole function is to harvest Director-level email addresses from corporate websites and then sell access to these email addresses to financial advisors. Such harvesting and processing, without the data subjects' knowledge, is obviously unfair. That the activity is the only reason SpamMethods was established does not make it a 'legitimate interest'. And, even if it were a 'legitimate interest', being 'unfair processing' it remains illegal.

Example 6.26

A manufacturer creates a sophisticated home page that records the number of hits to its site and the email addresses of its members who view the site. This information is then analysed and certain addresses are targeted with 'follow-up' emails. Without a method for an individual to avoid being included in the emailshot, the processing, and obtaining, may be unfair, and therefore a breach of the first data protection principle.[99]

Data processed lawfully

6.58   An obligation to process lawfully is narrower than fair processing and the fact that a data controller has satisfied at least one of the Sch 2 conditions does not, of itself, mean that the requirement for lawful processing is necessarily satisfied. If processing breaches another legal duty, including both criminal and civil duties, or would lead to such a breach, then it will also be a breach of the first data protection principle. The Registrar under the 1984 Act indicated three areas of law particularly relevant to breaches of the first principle of data

---

99   It is a moot point, and discussed earlier, whether simply processing an email address can constitute processing under the Act as personal data must relate to a living individual. An email address may not actually relate to an individual and may not permit identification of the living individual. A similar point was raised by Equifax in a Data Protection Tribunal inquiry. Equifax processed purely in relation to an address. The Tribunal gave a purposive answer to the point saying that one should look to the purpose of the processing. Where that processing was to determine information in relation to the living individual, the processing will fall within the definition of the word in the Act.

protection.[100] It is submitted the same areas will be considered under the 1998 Act:

> 'Confidentiality, arising from the relationship of the data user with the individual;
>
> The *ultra vires* rule and the rule relating to the excess of delegated powers, under which the data user may only act within the limits of its legal powers;
>
> Legitimate expectation, that is the expectation of the individual as to how the data user will use the information relating to him.'

Example 6.27

A data subject supplies to a data controller personal data encrypted using a public key. This encryption may be enough to give the subject the legitimate expectation that the personal data will be used by only the holder of the private key. Wider processing may be unlawful and constitute a breach of the first data protection principle.

Second principle: obtained for specified and lawful purposes

6.59

> 'Personal data shall be held only for one or more specified and lawful purposes.'

Obtained for specified purposes

6.60   To comply with this second principle is simply a matter of ensuring that all purposes for which a data controller obtains data are properly and accurately notified to the Commissioner,[101] and are properly specified to the data subject in accordance with the first principle.[102] Data controllers should be vigilant over their databases and appreciate that including an additional field against a set of personal data or using a database in a new way may constitute a new purpose which their notification to the Commissioner and specification to the data subject must reflect. A data controller must also be aware that obtaining is widely encompassing: newly received personal data may alter the capacity in which other data are being processed. And, the Interpretation Schedule of the Act states that 'regard' has to be had to the intended processing[103] when determining compatible obtaining. These other data may then become part of a collection of data which are intended to be processed. As such, these data will fall within the scope of data held.

---

100 Data Protection Guideline 4, para 1.18.
101 Data Protection Act 1998, Sch 1, Pt II, para 5(b).
102 Data Protection Act 1998, Sch 1, Pt II, para 5(a).
103 Data Protection Act 1998, Sch 1, Pt II, para 6.

Example 6.28

A university has a list of academics who have applied for a new post. To gain more information on them, it enters each academic's name into a search engine that searches both the World Wide Web and Usenet. From these additional data, the university appends to its database two new entries: first, personal details gleaned from the search; second, opinions on the nature of each academic's postings on Usenet. To comply with the second data protection principle the university must check that their current notification and method of obtaining covers the newly held data.

Obtained for lawful purposes

6.61   As for the first data protection principle, the word 'lawful' relates both to criminal and civil laws. Depending on the intention for obtaining the data, it is feasible that an accurate notification is still in breach of the second data protection principle for being unlawful. It would, for example, be unlawful for an online travel agent to compile names and addresses of its customers to provide those details to criminals to burgle the customers' properties while they are on holiday.

Value of personal data database, including on insolvency

6.62   Increasingly, corporations are realising (in both senses of the word) the value of personal data. Personal data allows marketers to target more accurately products and services at individuals. The more a marketer 'knows' about an individual, the higher likelihood that the individual will be interested in the offering. This necessarily increases the return on (marketing) investment. Because of this real value, corporations are also beginning to understand the utility of their customers' personal data to other corporations.

There may be various reasons why personal data is now viewed as a commodity. First, on the internet, as the good joke tells 'no-one knows you are a dog'. In other words, unlike in the corner shop, the website cannot tell whether you are a regular customer, a new customer or even a troublesome schoolchild with no pocket money to spend. Consequently, websites have been forced into collecting information about a visitor to ensure they can greet them appropriately and even recommend purchases to them based upon previous interactions. The second main reason is that many websites have subsisted only on advertising revenues, not direct revenues. As detailed here, the more a marketer knows about an audience and its individuals, the higher price it will pay to access those 'eyeballs'. The third, and more recent, reason is the increasing demise of 'dot com' companies; investors, insolvency practitioners and creditors are needing to extract the greatest possible value from a company's assets. One such asset is the personal data database. And, for the first two reasons, this database has a value well worth paying for (or worth selling). Companies and their advisors or insolvency practitioners are, however, worried that the 'open market' value of the database may not be accurate; the company may be prevented by data protection law from selling the database at any price.

The second principle prevents a company from obtaining data and then, without having told the individual, processing it for the purposes of selling it to a third party. This absolute prohibition applies whether the selling company is on the verge of insolvency or not. The Toysmart bankruptcy is a good US illustration.

Toysmart.com had posted a privacy policy stating 'When you register with Toysmart.com, you can rest assured that your information will never be shared with a third party'. Toysmart had officially ceased operations having run into dire financial difficulties. It was prompted to sell its principal remaining asset, its customer information database. The Federal Trade Commission had blocked the sale to 'any' buyer saying: 'Customer data collected under a privacy agreement should not be auctioned off to the highest bidder'. The FTC were only prepared to permit the entire website and data to be sold off to the 'highest bidder' who operates a 'family-orientated website'.

It is submitted that, under the UK's regime, the Commissioner would construe the word 'never' as just that. The ICO would likely determine that the Toysmart data, having been obtained for processing by Toysmart, could not merely, because of bankruptcy, be transferred to another entity. The second principle would have been breached. Indeed, the US FTC's Commissioner Swindle, in the minority, was of the strong opinion that:

> 'I do not think that the [Federal Trade] Commission should allow the sale [of Toysmart customer data]. If we really believe that customers attach great value to the privacy of their personal information and that consumers should be able to limit access to such information through private agreements with businesses, we should compel businesses to honor promises they make to customers to gain access to this information ... In my view, such a sale should not be permitted because "never" really means never.'

In a twist of fate, no appropriate buyers came forward for Toysmart. Eventually, a Walt Disney company subsidiary bought the company for $50,000 but was forced to destroy the customer records as the FTC had indicated.

Advisors and data controllers (and banks who believe they have security over customer databases) should be particularly guarded against use of phrases such as 'we will never' in collection notices and policies. It is this author's strong belief that once the word is uttered in a fair collection notice or privacy policy, no other processing changes may be introduced without clear data subject consent to the contrary. Each and every customer would have to be contacted for permission to 'purpose creep' and, on the basis of the principles of consent analysed above, their silence would not mean that they had consented. Very few privacy policies should not allow for the transfer of personal data to a third party who will operate under the same privacy policy and terms and conditions. This, at least, allows consensual transfer to a third party seeking to continue to operate the business of the data controller. The third lesson is for those who lend money to companies taking security over customer databases. Conduct detailed due diligence to ensure that this database could have a value to a third party.

Third principle: adequate, relevant, not excessive

6.63

> 'Personal data shall be adequate, relevant and not excessive in relation to the purpose or purposes for which they are processed.'

The Act does not define the limits of this principle and does not interpret it. In relation to the similar principle under the 1984 Act, the Registrar (as then titled) suggested that one method of determining the correct quota of data is to decide the absolute minimum amount of data needed to achieve the registered purposes. The Data Protection Tribunal has established that it will look closely at exactly what information is necessary for the specified purpose.[104] Information should not be held simply on the basis that it might come in useful one day with no clear idea how and when. Frequently, organisations may engage in overreach in gathering as much personal data as possible, as opposed to just such data as is relevant to the service or activity.

Example 6.29

A sports website runs a competition to win two tickets to an important football game. The winner will be selected at random from the correct answers received to three simple questions. Email answers must be sent by contenders on the standard email form stating the dates on which they would be available for travel and the name of the individual who would accompany them if they win. This is excessive, since the company would only need this information from the winner.

Living individual focus

6.64   It is wrong to assume that the necessary quantum of data can be assessed purely in relation to the purpose. The principle applies to each living individual on which the data user holds personal data. What might be the minimum quantum of data for one individual may be excessive for another. To establish a breach, the Commissioner may well examine the data held on each individual for each purpose as specified. This assessment is conducted from an objective viewpoint; it is of little relevance to a breach whether a data controller had reasoned it was holding acceptable amounts.[105]

Example 6.30

An online software supplier uses a standard online form for its customers to complete their order details. Owing to programming technicalities each field of the form must be filled in before the user can select the 'Okay' button to complete the order. This has the result that all users are required to include their home address, even users who will be sent the software by downloading it directly from the site. The supplier will be holding excessive data on all customers who wish their software to be delivered online: a breach of the third data protection principle.

---

104   The Tribunal held that it was excessive for the Community Charge Registration Officers of the local authority of Rhondda to hold the date of birth of an individual. This seemingly innocuous piece of datum was sufficient to warrant the Tribunal deciding that the local authority had breached the relevant data protection principle: Case DA/90 25/49/2.
105   See Part A of 1984 Guidance Note 25.

P3P

6.65   The World Wide Web Consortium continues to promote the Platform for Privacy Preferences (P3P). This allows a user to set maximum criteria for the personal data his browser will share with any website. For example, this author may be happy to allow a website automatically to feed cookies onto their browser and automatically to store their name, but no more.

This technology is a great advance in solving privacy problems; it is not, unfortunately, the data controller's way of avoiding obtaining excessive personal data. Whether data is excessive or not is an objective test and not subjective for either the data controller or data subject. (See also Privacy by Design (PbD) at **6.180** below.)

Future business models

6.66   The web lends itself to flexing and changing business models. This creates a tendency and a temptation to 'hedge one's bets' when collecting personal data and to collect personal data in case it may be useful at some point in the future. From a commercial prospective this makes sense: ask for all a person's personal data in one go; having collected the data, then decide how it can be utilised. Such a policy for obtaining personal data will be a breach of the third principle. One must have, at the time of obtaining, a view as to how the personal data will be used.

Example 6.31

Office@Home sells high-quality home office furniture for home workers. Its Marketing Director observes that many of their purchasers are actually high-powered office executives who are buying office furniture for their studies at home. Office@Home changes its sign-up page to also collect details of the purchaser's work address, status and work type. Office@Home risks this additional data being viewed as excessive for the purposes of selling furniture for use at home.

Fourth principle: accurate and up to date

6.67

'Personal data shall be accurate and, where necessary, kept up-to-date.'

Accurate personal data

6.68   The definition of 'accuracy' is:

'[D]ata are inaccurate for the purposes of this section if incorrect or misleading as to any matter of fact.'[106]

This definition excludes a mere opinion which does not include, or purport to be, a statement of fact. This may appear to be an onerous requirement for data

---

106 Data Protection Act 1998, Sch 1, Pt II, para 7.

users, especially using the internet, where one search engine may provide links to reams of personal data, each of which would have to be checked independently. However, the interpretative schedule to this principle excludes the data obtained and accurately recorded from a third party, including the data subject, under two circumstances.[107] These are that the data controller has taken reasonable steps to ensure the accuracy (with regard for the purpose or purposes for which the data were obtained and further processed) and, if relevant, the data user records an appropriate indication of the data subject's notification of alleged inaccuracies. So, a data controller must be careful when trawling, say, the internet for personal data to buttress an existing data record. One should certainly record details of the source of the data.

Internet data sources and locations

6.69   Particularly on the World Wide Web, the location of data may be only one aspect of its source. For example, the data held on the home page at www.allserve.com/ourhome/coolhome are stored on the Allserve server in the coolhome directory that is within the parent directory, ourhome. This is its location. Its source, in contrast, will include the person who uploaded that data onto the home page. This will probably be the owner of the Allserve account, coolhome. This person's identity, together with the URL, will form the source of the information.

The reason for insisting on this distinction is twofold. First, the relevant section refers to receiving or obtaining data from the 'data subject or a third party'.[108] Both these terms refer to natural or legal persons. The source required under the section is therefore not the place where the data are stored, or from where they are retrieved, but the person who supplied the data to the data user. In illustration, if a data user obtains personal data from a particular book, it will not be enough to include as its source its location in a library; the publisher and author will be its source. By analogy, if personal data are obtained from a particular home page, it will not be enough to include as the source the URL on the internet; the controller and creator of the home page will be the source.

The second justification for the source to be the person not the URL is that it is trivial to alter a URL. Indeed, the greatest difficulty for home pages on the web is that their links to other sites may become outdated. The person who created the site is therefore a more stable and certain source than the location of the data in question.

Notification of inaccuracy

6.70   If a data subject finds personal data inaccurate they may commence an action under s 14 for the court to order rectification, blocking, erasure or destruction of the data. The court may also order a verification enquiry, a supplementary statement and/or a communication order.

In the *Google Spain* case, the ECJ/CJEU held that:

107 Data Protection Act 1998, Sch 1, Pt II, para 7.
108 Data Protection Act 1998, Sch 1, Pt II, para 7(a).

'Article 12(b) and subparagraph (a) of the first paragraph of Article 14 of Directive 95/46 are to be interpreted as meaning that, in order to comply with the rights laid down in those provisions and in so far as the conditions laid down by those provisions are in fact satisfied, the operator of a search engine is obliged to remove from the list of results displayed following a search made on the basis of a person's name links to web pages, published by third parties and containing information relating to that person, also in a case where that name or information is not erased beforehand or simultaneously from those web pages, and even, as the case may be, when its publication in itself on those pages is lawful.'[109]

Database construction

6.71 This section of the book concentrates only on the final three remedies. What is relevant is the need with any of the section's orders to be able to identify all data relating to an individual from that individual's details. Databases, simple, relational, object-orientated or whatever type, must therefore be carefully constructed. It must be trivial for any of the data relating to an individual to be able to be:

(i)   rectified (ie corrected without necessarily deleting the previous data);

(ii)   blocked (ie presented in the database structure but obscured from viewing or processing unless under certain restrictive conditions);

(iii) erased (ie erasure of reference to data and also erasure of data itself);

(iv)   verified (ie investigation of the source of the data being queried by the data subject; certainly contentious data must be recorded together with its source);

(v)   communicated to third party recipients (ie the data controller may be required to alert all subsequent recipients of the queried data as to the inaccuracy; this order, made under extreme circumstances, blocks the 'flow' of inaccurate data).

Reliability of internet sources

6.72 One of the advantages of the internet over other information sources is that it is quick and simple to retrieve vast quantities of data about almost any subject, including living individuals. There is no quality control, however, over this data. It is as easy for individuals to publish unsubstantiated personal data on the World Wide Web as it is for organisations who prudently vet their data. It is therefore unwise, and probably unreasonable, for a data controller to compile data about individuals using unsubstantiated material from the internet.

---

109 *Google Spain SL and Google Inc v Agencia Española de Protección de Datos (AEPD) and Mario Costeja González*, Case C-131/12, 13 May 2014, available at http://curia.europa.eu/juris/liste.jsf?pro=&nat=or&oqp=&dates=&lg=&language=en&jur=C%2CT%2CF&cit=none%252CC%252CCJ%252CR%252C2008E%252C%252C%252C%252C%252C%252C%252C%252C%252C%252C%252Ctrue%252Cfalse%252Cfalse&td=%3BALL&pcs=Oor&avg=&page=1&mat=or&parties=google%2Bspain&jge=&for=&cid=511372.

This reinforces the issue that the important details about data extracted from the internet are the actual sources, which can be checked for the unreliability, potentially under a verification enquiry, not simply the URL of the material on the internet. The issues of online abuse, revenge porn, sextorting, etc heighten the importance of the virtue of digital forgetting, the Right to be Forgotten (TtbF) and the *Google Spain* case.[110]

Up to date, where necessary

6.73   The fourth data protection principle does not require that data users keep all their data up to date at all times; they must do this if it is necessary.

There will be circumstances where data held on an individual does need to be updated. Under the 1984 Act, the Registrar included data used to decide whether to grant credit or to confer or withhold some other benefit.[111] These are examples where what is required is a reflection of the data subject's current status or circumstances.

Example 6.32

An online cinema-ticket agency establishes an account for each new customer. To set up an account a data subject must enter, among other details, his age in years and months on 1 January next. If the purpose of these data are to ensure that customers do not attend films under the required age, it must be updated each month to ensure that these data do not exclude individuals who have had a recent birthday.

Fifth principle: kept no longer than necessary

6.74

> 'Personal data processed for any purpose or purposes shall not be kept any longer than is necessary for that purpose or those purposes.'

Data users should be diligent in deleting data when they have already served their purpose. Each set of data should have a lifespan. At the end of this time, the data should be reviewed and assessed against the specified purpose for holding that data. If the data no longer appear necessary to complete or continue the purpose, data users have one of two options. They can either delete the data, or they can obtain consent from the data subject and amend their notified purposes to reflect the reason for extending holding the data.

---

110 See, for example, P Lambert, *International Handbook of Social Media Laws* (Bloomsbury, 2014); P Lambert, *Social Networking: Law, Rights and Policy* (Clarus Press, 2014); V Mayer-Schönberger, *Delete: the Virtue of Forgetting in the Digital Age* (Princeton University Press: Princeton, 2009); *Google Spain SL and Google Inc v Agencia Española de Protección de Datos (AEPD) and Mario Costeja González*, Case C-131/12, 13 May 2014, available at http://curia.europa.eu/juris/liste.jsf?pro=&nat=or&oqp=&dates=&lg=&language=en&jur=C%2CT%2CF&cit=none%252CC%252CCJ%252CR%252C2008E%252C%252C%252C%252C%252C%252C%252C%252C%252C%252Ctrue%252Cfalse%252Cfalse&td=%3BALL&pcs=Oor&avg=&page=1&mat=or&parties=google%2Bspain&jge=&for=&cid=511372.

111 Data Protection Guideline 4, para 5.3.

As detailed in **6.135** *et seq*, a provider may in fact be required to hold certain data for specific periods under anti-terrorism or other legislation. Depending on the nature of the business, there may be other legal requirements to hold data which are relevant, for example financial service rules. It is essential that companies understand that these legal justifications are not blanket exemptions to the fifth principle. Real care must be taken to ensure that any justification is approached narrowly and with constant attention to the Act. For example, a requirement to hold data for, say six years, under separate legislation may in some circumstances still be complied with once the records have been anonymised or superfluous details removed.

Multiple purposes

6.75   There will be many occasions when one set of data is held for more than one purpose. Consequently, there will be occasions when, for one purpose, a data user should delete data, but for other purposes the data remain necessary and relevant. The principle's use of both the singular 'purpose' and the plural 'purposes' clearly envisages this situation. The solution is to attempt to segregate the use of the data into their various purposes and to ensure that all data which are not necessary for a purpose are deleted.

Example 6.33

A firm publishes biographical data about its employees on its home page. One of these employees leaves the firm. The firm is able to hold on an internal database the necessary information about the former employee for many years for, say, legal claims. In contrast, it should, to comply with the fifth data protection principle, remove the personal data being held on the home page as soon as the employee leaves.

The ease with which data may be published and obtained on the World Wide Web acts also as a reason continually to check the relevance of data published on the World Wide Web. Data users should regularly check their website and other internet sites to delete data which has served its purpose and is past its lifespan. It is therefore not simply good commercial practice to update one's website; it may be required under data protection, and possibly other, laws.

Holding historical data

6.76   Data users are at liberty to hold indefinitely data that they will purely use for historical, statistical or research purposes.[112]

No one or fixed rule

6.77   Too often, a general 'purge rule' is set for a personal data database. This cannot be correct unless all the data serves the same purpose and all the

---

112 Data Protection Act 1998, s 33(3).

data subjects have an identical relationship with the data controller. Databases need to be constructed to allow deletion at particular times of particular types of data relating to particular types of data subject. No one or fixed rule can be adequate.

Sixth principle: process in accordance with data subject rights

6.78 'A person is to be regarded as contravening the sixth principle if, but only if:

    (a) he contravenes [a data subject's right to access personal data];

    (b) he contravenes [a data subject's justified right to prevent processing likely to cause damage or distress];

    (c) he contravenes [a data subject's right to prevent processing for the purposes of direct marketing];

    (d) he contravenes [a data subject's justified rights in relation to automated decision making].'

Data subject access

Validity of requests

6.79 If a subject access request is ignored or is incorrectly complied with within the usual 40-day period,[113] the Information Commissioner may make an access order forcing the data controller to reveal the data held on the subject. What is more serious, though, is that the Information Commissioner may also inspect the data held by the controller.

A valid subject access request must be made in writing[114] and to any valid address for the data controller. The request need not be in any particular form or style, and, data controllers may not impose a special format upon a data subject. The request is valid only when the appropriate fee is paid (being no more than £10.00, unless medical records are concerned).

Example 6.34

A website is concerned that its staff may 'miss' a data subject access request being sent to them and so devise an online form, to allow requests to be made. Despite the form, an elderly gentleman sends a request (together with a £10 cheque) on paper to the website owner's registered office where it is ignored for two months. The website owner is at risk of an action, even though the gentleman utilised another medium to make his requests.

---

113 Data Protection Act 1998, ss 7(8) and 7(10) subject to any variation by the Secretary of State under s 7(11).
114 Data Protection Act 1998, s 7(7).

Data controllers need also only process a request where the data subject supplies him with the appropriate information both to satisfy himself as to the identity of the requesting person and the information being sought.[115]

Example 6.35

An online secure spreadbetting site updates its 'credit risk' analysis on each of its members every 20 minutes. This allows it to extend the maximum line of credit to its customers at all times. Phillip makes a subject access request and within two days of making the request, he discovers that the site has now deemed his credit line to be zero. Bearing in mind the nature of the data, why the data is processed and the frequency of updating, it would be reasonable for Phillip to make a further request to discover what had changed.

When to provide data

6.80 Data controllers must supply to the data subject the relevant information under s 7 promptly, but at least within 40 days from receiving a request.[116]

Data users should pay respect to this sixth principle by ensuring that, on constructing and programming their database, there is a simple way of extracting all the data relating to one individual. It is important for data users to note that merely because a particular record has no reference to an individual's name does not mean that the information should not be provided to the subject. If the data user possesses sufficient information, wherever held or stored, to identify the individual, then the data can be classed as personal data, and so be requested by its subject. Where the data held on individuals are spread throughout many databases, throughout many buildings, it can be expensive and time-consuming to locate all the necessary data within the period set by the Act. This said, 40 days is the maximum period and so systems should be established early which allow a request to be processed rapidly.

Information disclosed on other individuals

6.81 A problem may arise where a data controller in complying with a subject access request would be disclosing information relating to an individual other than the individual making the request. The Act recognises this problem. In such circumstances a data controller is obliged to comply with the subject access request in only two situations. The first is where the other individual has consented to the disclosure of the information. The second situation is where it is reasonable in the circumstances to comply with the request without the consent of the other individual. Alternatively, of course, it may be necessary to redact any references to third parties.

---

115 Data Protection Act 1998, s 7(3).
116 Data Protection Act 1998, s 7(8) and (10). This 40-day period begins on the first day on which the controller has both the fee and request.

Example 6.36

Teenze FM, a website for teenage girls, runs a feature called 'nightmare date of the month'. It invites its members to send in photographs and stories of disastrous dates to be posted on the site. June's 'winner' is horrified to see his picture appear on the site together with a totally fictitious story. He submits a subject access request in order to find out who nominated him without his knowledge. The site would be breaching data protection rules if it disclosed the nomination email containing these details without the consent of the sender.

What to provide

6.82   Data controllers cannot simply 'print out' their database entry for an individual. Indeed, doing merely this, complies with only one of seven requirements. These are listed and described below, but first it will be important to consider carefully whether the subject matter of the request does in fact concern 'data'. One should consider the decisions in *Durant* and *Ezsias*, as summarised at **6.12** above, and noting wider European and national data protection authorities' views,[117] in particular as to whether information not held on computerised records which have been automatically processed, fall within the definition of a relevant filing system. If not, the data may not be disclosable and the following may not apply.

(i) Data controller to inform subject whether or not processing is being carried out in relation to data subject

6.83   In effect, the data controller must reply to a data subject whether or not they are holding or processing data. Because of potential difficulties involving misspelt or mis-typed names, it may be safer for a data controller not merely to search on the precise details given by the subject, but also to use 'fuzzy logic' to search more widely.[118]

Example 6.37

Jane Isaacs is worried that an auction site has retained her personal details. She sends an email from her home email address together with £10 to constitute a subject access request. The data protection officer at the company incorrectly searches for the name 'Jane Isaac' and for her home email address; both searches return a negative result. The auction site would have been better advised to reply to Jane, seeking, as they are entitled under s 7(3) the reasonable information they need to search for Jane's personal data.

(ii) Data controller to give subject description of personal data

6.84   This can be thought of as a requirement to 'put the data into context'. It is an obligation to explain what the data 'means' to the data controller.

---

117 For example, see *Commission of the European Communities v The Bavarian Lager Co Ltd*, Case C-28/08 P.
118 Data Protection Act 1998, s 7(1)(a).

(iii) Data controller to give subject description of purposes for which data is processed

6.85 'Processing' is described earlier in this chapter and readers may want to refresh their memories before responding to this element of a data subject access request. What is crucial is to describe not merely what the data is, but how it is being utilised and processed.

Example 6.38

An online photo developing company allows anyone to store digital images and other files on their servers. Revenue to support this flows from advertising and printing. Its research suggests that men tend to use the storage facilities to store pornographic material. They therefore target 'relevant' advertising at those of its members who are male with many image files stored. To comply with a subject access by a male, the company must therefore include details of this processing and not merely report the member's sex and number of files held.

(iv) Data controller to describe to subject recipients or classes of recipients of personal data

6.86 A recipient is defined as being any person, even an employee of the data controller, to whom data is disclosed in the course of processing the data. Data controllers do not need to disclose those recipients of data who receive it pursuant to a legal power, such as a police enquiry. Data controllers should be aware, therefore, that the suggested recipients of data in a fair collection notice or, privacy policy and notification can be confirmed by a data subject. Data controllers cannot hide their true processing of data.

Example 6.39

TCI collects data from its membership and, for financial reasons, exports it for processing in Russia. A Russian company will therefore be a recipient of the data. This can consequently be discovered by any data subject. TCI will not be able to covertly send the data to Russia (potentially in breach of the eighth principle), without risk of it being discovered by any subject.

(v) Data controller to communicate to data subject in intelligible form the information constituting the personal data

6.87 The key aspect of this obligation is 'intelligible' form. Sending the data subject a series of zeros and ones may well provide the data to the subject; it does not provide the information underlying or surrounding the data. Data controllers must be prepared to disclose 'what the data means to them' not merely the data that has been recorded.

> *Example 6.40*
>
> A business user of an online travel agency makes a valid subject access request. The agency provides a response detailing the user's name and address, the flights he has booked and a reference to 'cookie data' being 'AC8924EA29BBE'. To comply with the subject access request, the site should have resolved this cookie data into information making it clear what it means to the site.

(vi) Data controller to communicate to the data subject any available information on the sources of the data

6.88   Unlike under the 1984 Act, the sources of data do not need to be specified to the Commissioner in the data controller's notification (then registration). The information to be provided as to the sources of the data is only that which is available to the data controller. Clearly, a 'scorched earth' policy of destroying all source information would leave the controller unable to provide any information to the data subject.

Data controllers must be warned, however, that with no information about the source of personal data they may find it more difficult to defend an action brought under the first principle. Similarly, unless the source's information is retained, it will be difficult for the data controller to prove that they took reasonable steps to confirm the accuracy of the data, under the fourth principle.

(vii) Data controller to inform data subject as to any logic involved in automated significant decision-taking, subject to the information being a trade secret

6.89   This applies only where the decision being automatically taken is the sole basis of something which may significantly affect the data subject. It is therefore safe to opine that, automatic processing of a cookie to determine which adverts to show or which books to recommend, will not fall within the remit of this section. Conversely, decisions taken relating to a person's creditworthiness are more likely to be deemed to be significant.

> *Example 6.41*
>
> A car manufacturer establishes a site at which prospective customers may enter their name, telephone number and postcode to receive a telephone call from their nearest dealer. In truth, they also utilise the postcode to decide the potential affluence of the customer and prioritise their enquiry appropriately. This automated decision-taking is unlikely to be significant enough to justify needing to inform the data subject.

Preventing direct marketing, including emails

6.90   In the context of the internet, a significant right is to prevent processing for direct marketing, at any time. Even where the relevant 'tick' boxes have been 'ticked' (or 'unticked') an individual may change their mind and prevent further direct marketing at any time. Databases must be constructed to allow such processing to be stopped at any time.

Direct marketing is widely defined as:

> 'the communication (by whatever means) of advertising or marketing material which is directed to particular individuals.'[119]

This definition will certainly encompass emails and instant messages whether sent automatically or processed individually by a human.

Example 6.42

Forex4X.com uses cookies to enable its site to show particular information based on previous uses by the particular member. It does not send out emails or faxes to its members. Nevertheless, its members are entitled to prevent Forex4X from processing their data for the purposes of customising the site they view.

The subject's right is framed in terms of ceasing processing for the purposes of direct marketing. It is therefore a substantially wider right than one which merely prevents direct mail being sent subject to certain requirements. The right, once activated, will prevent all data manipulation and mining activities, even where this processing does not result in material being sent.

Unlike many other provisions in the Act, data controllers cannot rely upon any exemptions. If they do not comply with a written request within a reasonable period,[120] the subject may request that the court orders that the notice is complied with.[121] Data-intensive companies must ensure that the architecture of their databases is sophisticated enough to block this type of processing.

Example 6.43

E-masp is an Application Service Provider which facilitates companies in targeting and sending relevant emails to their customers. In the usual course of events, any individual who indicates that they do not consent to receive mailings is simply not included in the final, compiled, list. Their details are, in contrast, still analysed and processed. E-masp must refine its database to ensure it is able to exclude blocked individuals from even the first batch processing well prior to any mailing itself.

Preventing automated processing

6.91 There can be little doubt that computers are incredibly valuable when used to process personal data. Indeed, a whole sector of the IT industry, customer relationship management, is fundamentally concerned with capturing, processing and better utilising personal data. These sophisticated 'back office' systems are increasingly utilised to process data on visitors to websites. They allow regulars to be greeted appropriately, orders to be tracked and requests pre-empted. In the broadest terms, they make automated decisions relating to personal data.

---

119 Data Protection Act 1998, s 11(3).
120 Data Protection Act 1998, s 11(1).
121 Data Protection Act 1998, s 11(2).

Controllers of data need to consider whether this processing is 'solely' used to make decisions which 'significantly affect' an individual. If their systems do make such decisions, while no doubt very efficient, they are prone to subjects exercising their right under s 12 of the Act to prevent decisions being taken in that manner.

Significant effects

6.92   The Act and Directive provide a non-exhaustive list of significant issues. These include 'performance at work', 'creditworthiness', 'reliability' and 'conduct'.

Sole basis for decision

6.93   This aspect of the Act[122] and art 15 of the Directive is aimed at preventing computers making important decisions without humans being involved. Consequently, any human input into the decision, even where supported by volumes of automatically processed quantitative data, will bring the processing outside the ambit of s 12.

Example 6.44

A busy recruitment department in a management consultancy builds a new online recruitment section to the firm's website. It requires that each candidate wanting to attend an open day enters their answers to a series of questions to create their VCV (Virtual Curriculum Vitae). To save reviewing certain applications by hand, the system automatically sends (a few hours later) a polite rejecting email to any candidate acknowledging less than a 2:2 in their first degree. Any candidate will be entitled to prevent the firm from taking such decisions in this way.

Exemptions

6.94   Automated decisions are exempt from the application of s 12 where they fall into one of a number of categories. These are where the effect of the decision is to grant the data subject a request relating to:

(a)   considering whether to enter a contract with the subject;

(b)   with a view to entering such a contract;

(c)   in the course of performing such a contract.

Alternately, as long as the legitimate interests of the data subject are safeguarded, for example, permitted representations like an 'appeal', automated decisions can also be taken in relation to (1), (2) and (3) above.[123]

---

122 Data Protection Act 1998, s 12(1).
123 Data Protection Act 1998, s 12(6) and (7).

Example 6.45

RideLiketheWind is a 'name your price' website for businesspeople who would prefer to travel by private jet rather than traditional airlines. Financing deals are available to allow one to travel today and pay off the cost over a subsequent number of months. An individual becomes convinced that his requests to obtain credit are automatically refused because of his home postcode. Even if such an automated decision is significant enough, the decision is exempt because the individual is making the request of the website with the view to entering into the contract to buy a seat on credit.

Procedure to prevent

6.95   A subject must write to a data controller asking them not to take such an automated decision.[124] As soon as reasonably practical, the controller must reply confirming (or not) that the decision was so taken.[125] Within 21 days, the individual may then demand that a new, non-solely automated decision is taken.[126] A further 21 days may lapse before the controller must explain how they now intend to re-consider the decision.[127] The court can force the data controller to comply with the individual's request.[128]

Example 6.46

A data subject requests from a data user relevant information under the seventh principle and s 7. The data controller duly retrieves the pertinent data from the various relational databases and then realises that more data are held than has been notified or consented to by the data subject. If the data controller supplies all the data to the subject they are admitting processing data illegally. If the data user supplies the data only mentioned in the notification, they can be forced to comply with s 7(1)(a) which demands that all the data held by the controller must be supplied to the subject. The data controller must immediately contact the Commissioner and the data subject to rectify the data held and widen the notification if necessary for further processing.

Principle 7: kept secure

6.96

'Appropriate technical and organisational measures shall be taken against unauthorised or processing of personal data and against accidental loss or destruction of or damage to personal data.'

This seventh data protection principle demands lawyers understand, at the least, the basics of computer security. Complying with this part of the Act can be

---

124 Data Protection Act 1998, s 12(1).
125 Data Protection Act 1998, s 12(2)(a).
126 Data Protection Act 1998, s 12(2)(b).
127 Data Protection Act 1998, s 12(3).
128 Data Protection Act 1998, s 12(8).

expensive. It is, however, essential that these controllers of personal data employ appropriate technological and supervisory methods to secure their subjects' data.

Security under the seventh principle

6.97   This principle tackles one of the most obvious tensions between the internet and data protection. Back in the Data Protection Registrar's annual report of 1995, it is stated that:

> '[i]n connecting to the Internet [data users and computer bureau operators] are entering an open environment which exists to facilitate the exchange of and the publication of information. It is inherently insecure.'

This remains the case today. In contrast, data protection legislation attempts to ensure that personal data are not left in open environments but are stored in controlled, private environments. The seventh principle takes the idea of a controlled environment to its logical extreme by demanding that data are not simply secure from unauthorised or unlawful processing but also from alteration, destruction, damage and loss.

Appropriate

6.98   In the abstract it is difficult for a lawyer or security consultant to advise on the appropriate level of security for personal data. The Act's interpretation of this seventh principle highlights that one must have regard to 'state of technological development and cost of implementing the measures' appropriate to ensure a level of security taking into account the possible 'harm' and 'nature of data to be protected'.[129] The level of the security should be in proportion to the nature of the data and the harm which would ensue should there be a breach in security. For example, the Commissioner is likely to distinguish between personal data compiled from readily available sources, such as a list of names and addresses, and data which are sensitive[130] or are acquired in confidence.[131] Eli Lilly, the pharmaceutical manufacturer of Prozac, settled a claim with the US FTC relating to sensitive data held on Prozac takers. It had established in March 2000 an email reminder service for those recovering from depression using Prozac. It sought to tell all its subscribers by email that it was cancelling the service. Instead of sending each an individual email, or using the BCC field, an employee sent a group email to all the subscribers. Each was therefore able to see who else took Prozac. Not surprisingly, there were complaints about this disclosure of sensitive data and an investigation began. The lesson for those needing to observe the seventh principle is simple. Even the greatest security systems can be useless if those using them are inappropriately qualified and trained.

---

129 Data Protection Act 1998, Sch 1, Pt II, para 9(a), (b).
130 Personal data that may be seen as sensitive are defined in s 2(3). These include: racial origins; political opinions, or religious or other beliefs; membership of a trade union; physical or mental health or sexual life; and criminal convictions or alleged offences.
131 1984 Data Protection Guideline 4, para 8.3.1

A case addresses a finding of inadequate security regarding a person's sensitive health-related data.[132] There appears to be a growing concern in relation to health-related data and devices collecting health data, and it is forecast to be an increasing focus for the ICO and courts.

Data controllers and data processors must make their own decisions as to the adequacy of their data security, but they should consider their obligation to the data subjects and the possibility of a compensation claim by a data subject.

Appropriate outsourcing

6.99   Data controllers do not shirk their responsibilities under this principle by shunting off their data to a third-party processor such as an outsourcing company or application service provider for example. In fact, the data controller must not only carry out due diligence to check the processor provides sufficient guarantees as to security but also take reasonable steps to ensure compliance with the technical and organisational measures.[133] Further, data controllers are obliged to enter into a written contract with the processor under which the processor will only act under instructions from the data controller and under which the data processor will comply with equivalent obligations to those of the data controller.[134]

Unauthorised

6.100   The seventh data protection principle stresses that security measures must be in place preventing unauthorised and unlawful processing of personal data. This does not refer solely to outsiders such as hackers; it is referring also to insiders who are acting outside the scope of their authority, potentially unlawfully. Controllers and processors should consider this authority from two angles: technical authority and social authority.

Technical authority

6.101   All equipment which stores, processes, transmits or discloses personal data must have passwords which only authorised people know. These passwords must not be the same for all aspects of data security within the organisation. Data controllers and data processors must treat distinctly those aspects of their equipment which they will use for activities relating to personal data.

To stop as early as is possible any security compromise it is advisable that each person granted the authority to access the personal data has an individual password. This, combined with an audit trail of all personal data, can permit a data controller or data processor to 'trace' the human source of compromised data, and so prevent its reoccurrence. It is essential that this technical authority is granted by providing individuals each with a unique password, not by allocating one password for 'all personal data activities'. This latter method does not allow

---

132 Case of *I v Finland* ECHR (Application no 20511/03) 17 July 2008. A further breach regarding health data was held in the case *of LH v Latvia*, ECHR (Application no 52019/07) 29 April 2014.

133 Data Protection Act 1998, Sch 1, Pt II, para 11(a), 11(b).

134 Data Protection Act 1998, Sch 1, Pt II, para 12(a), 12(b).

a data user to trace the source of a security leak as easily and results in one password being known by more people.

Social authority

6.102 Establishing a strict regime with passwords is not adequate unless there is also a strict regime over who has these passwords and how they are used. Data controllers and processors must give proper weight to the discretion and integrity of members of staff who are to have these passwords. They should be given adequate technical and data protection training; they should be made aware of the seriousness of their responsibilities. They should not process data outside of the appropriate consents and obligations of the data controller. If a member of staff leaves the department, or is found to be unreliable, the data users must immediately 'lock out' that member from the system. There should be no 'old' or 'general' password for accessing personal data.

Processing

6.103 The obligation to take appropriate measures to prevent unauthorised and unlawful processing is obviously a wide obligation because of the all-encompassing definition of 'processing'. Some aspects of 'processing' are described below.

Organisation, adaptation or alteration

6.104 Certain data should be 'read-only': that is, the data cannot be altered or even deleted without appropriate authority. This authority is generally in the form of a password that allows the password-user to alter the 'read-write' properties of the data.

Example 6.47

An Internet Service Provider allows its members to sign up to various services using an online form. As well as address and surname, one field of this form is the forename of the member. Unless it is clearly appropriate this particular field should retain a 'read-only' status. If it is freely able to be overwritten, it is feasible an accidental alteration will result in another member of the same family, at the same address, being treated as the data subject.

As stated below, the safest solution is to have 'read-only' status both for data and the database structure along with regular, archival backups. If the backup is archival it will highlight any changes in data since the previous backup, so alerting a data user to a potential alteration. It will also allow the data user to regenerate an unaltered copy of the data, if necessary, from the previous backup. It is also recommended that only a limited set of reports and processes are available over a series of data.

Entitled deletion and backups

6.105   The fourth data protection principle entitles a data subject to delete data which it is inappropriate for a data user to continue holding. This required deletion will include both the personal data on the usual storage system and any backup copies of the data on whatever medium. Data users must therefore ensure that their archival backup system is sufficiently sophisticated to allow them to remove data fields without compromising the security of the remaining data which may breach the seventh data protection principle.

Destruction

6.106   The same security considerations apply to avoiding destruction, accidental or not, of data and avoiding alteration of data. Data users should classify as much data as possible as 'read-only' and maintain regular and frequent backups of the data. In this way, if data are destroyed on the main system, it is an easy task to regenerate those data. As above, data users should ensure that their backup facilities, while secure, do not prevent the deletion of personal data where this will be necessary to comply with a data subject's request.

Internet security issues

6.107   Connecting a computer to the internet is easy and commonplace. But, with present levels of standard internet security, going onto the internet will result in the personal data held on the computer online becoming less secure. Data controllers and data processors must not rely on the inherent security on the internet if they wish to avoid possible breaches of the seventh data protection principle.[135] Increasingly there are arguments for encryption/strong encryption to maintain privacy, data protection and security. One of the tensions is the position of national security and police authorities that encryption is fine, so long as there is a back door access left in encryption for national security and terrorism related investigations.

Automatic-answer modems

6.108   A modem connected to the internet that is set to accept incoming calls will weaken security. The mere fact that an outsider can access a computer which is holding personal data reduces the security of that data. Data controllers or data processors should take expert advice from the manufacturers of their automatic-answer software on how to partition securely certain aspects of their storage system from third parties. They should also investigate how to encrypt the personal data left on the connected system.[136]

---

135 Data controllers and data processors should take specialist advice; the comments on data security within this chapter are intended only to illustrate possible methods of improving security. The comments should not be implemented before checking with a security adviser that they are appropriate for the equipment and data in question.

136 The key to de-encrypt the data must not be stored on the computer storing the encrypted data.

Remote access

6.109   One of the advantages of the internet and related networks is that it has made it possible for individuals easily to access computers from remote locations. This may be through a simple website, a Virtual Private Network (VPN), a bulletin board, an ftp site, a Telnet connection, or even a standard dial-up connection. All these methods, without tight security measures, can as easily allow an individual to leave data on the remote computer as to copy data from the computer.

Security should therefore be in place which, unless it can be justified otherwise, does not permit remote users to access all the personal data on the system: a firewall. The passwords and logins used by remote users should be 'rolled' on a frequent basis. Remote users should not use an automated login procedure that stores the login details and password on their computer. With this set-up, if someone steals the computer the entire security of the personal data is at risk.

Email transactions

6.110   If a data controller or data processor uses the email system to send personal data he should be aware that a standard email system is not completely secure. He must not rely on the security of the internet itself. Again, a good policy is to use encryption on all emails which contain personal data. It must also be remembered that any email is both a transferral and a disclosure of personal data or information. Data controllers should appropriately notify for such an activity.

Web servers

6.111   A web server is connected to the internet. As much as is possible, these computers should not be used for storing data collected from the World Wide Web. The use of an online form on a home page to collect personal data from, for example, customers, should generate data which is either encrypted on the server or is transmitted automatically to a further computer beyond a firewall. Users of the web to collect personal data must also enlist expert advice to ensure that while such an online form is being transmitted to the server from the customer-client, the most stringent safety measures are in place. The transferral of personal data between the subject and the data user is the most insecure time for the subject's personal data. Subjects must be informed of this risk before they transmit the data particularly to websites not utilising standard encryption methodology. Some sites 'pop up' a window allowing the subject to choose to transmit the data or to disconnect from the website.

Viruses

6.112   The internet allows its users to 'view' documents on their screen, but it is also used to download material into the client computer. Sometimes this is with the knowledge of the user: he requests a file to download. At other times, the user may be unaware that the site on the internet is accessing the user's computer and may be storing files and running programs on his computer. There is a real risk that with any file downloaded there will have been a computer virus in tow. Viruses generally attach to programs, but have been found incubating in word processing documents and even innocent looking pictures.[137]

To take appropriate security measures, data processors and controllers must install virus scanning software set to screen regularly for viruses.

Network or intranet

6.113   All the above security issues are equally, if not more, relevant where an internal network or intranet is connected to the internet. This may be through one computer connected to one modem or an established gateway, available to all users. The two scenarios pose risks to any personal data held on the network or intranet.

One computer to internet

6.114   The ease with which one may connect a computer on an internal network to the internet is almost inversely proportional to the risk involved with such a connection. That the connected computer does not hold or process personal data does not greatly reduce the threat to the personal data stored on the network. Because the computer is connected both to the internet and the internal network it can act as a conduit for hacking attempts and the promulgation of viruses, network-wide. Data controllers and processors should therefore periodically check that no computer on an internal network is connected to the internet without their knowledge. If one computer is to be connected, an appropriate technical and social security regime must exist.

Technically, the single computer should be appropriately firewalled from the main network; if it is not, it can form a very weak link in the data security of the network. The social security measures relate to the responsibility of those persons who will use the connected computer. Employers should give employees clear guidelines about whether they are permitted to download software; it is safer not to download. Employees should have clear instructions never to divulge any internal passwords to any other individual using email or any other means.

Network hacking

6.115   Hacking into the internal network from the internet is always a great threat where any computer on the network is connected to the internet. In this situation, a hacker can attach directly into the connected computer and, from there, may be able to penetrate the internal security of the network. Clearly this poses a substantial risk to any personal data on the network, previously treated as being secure. The risk from hacking is currently not as significant, however, as the threat from viruses and other rogue programs.

---

137 '[Digital signatures] are clearly of great importance for executable code on the web': Tim Berners-Lee, W3C Director, viewed as the creator of the World Wide Web; 'Industry embraces Microsoft's Internet digital signature', Microsoft Press Release, PR1382/14 March 1996.

Network viruses

6.116   Every user who has access to the internet will be tempted to download a file. In doing so, as described above,[138] the user risks introducing a virus to the client computer. But where this computer is connected to an internal network, the virus can spread throughout the network threatening the destruction and alteration of any personal data held within the network. Operators at a data controller and processor should install and update anti-virus programs throughout the network, and where possible utilise virus antidote software to screen for viruses as software and emails are being downloaded from the internet.

Eighth principle: prohibition against data transfers

6.117

> 'Personal data shall not be transferred to a country or territory outside the European Economic Area, unless that country or territory ensures an adequate level of protection for the rights and freedoms of data subjects in relation to the processing of personal data.'

The harmonisation of data protection rules in the EU aims to ensure the free movement of information including personal data between member states whilst at the same time ensuring a high level of protection for any person concerned. In the case of non-EEA countries, Directive 95/46/EC therefore requires member states to permit transfers of personal data only where there is 'adequate protection' in a particular country for such data, unless one of a limited number of specific exemptions applies. There are accordingly a number of ways available in order to facilitate transfers of personal data avoiding the prohibition of the eighth principle which are detailed below. A French ruling suggests that enforcement action against companies who fail to comply with such rules may be on the increase. In this case the French data protection authority imposed a fine on a company, Tyco, for sending human resources data to the US (a common practice) but without adequate protections. Companies should heed this warning.

However, it is first important to establish whether or not a transfer, subject to the default prohibition in fact arises. In some situations and particularly relevant in an internet context, data may only transit or be routed through a third country and not be deemed to have transferred there.

In the case of *Bodil Lindqvist v Kammaraklagaren*,[139] the Court of Justice held that the loading of data onto a website in a member state did not amount to a transfer of data to a third country, even though the website could be accessed potentially round the world. However, the court did state that a transfer would have occurred if the data was then actually accessed in a third country. The fact was in this case that the local church website was not in a third country. The significant factor that the court distinguished, and which the UK Information Commissioner has subsequently emphasised, is that there was no intention for the data to be so

---

138 See the section relating to viruses in Chapter 3.
139 (2003) (Case C 101/01), ECJ/CJEU.

accessed. The outcome of this case should prompt care rather than comfort on the part of website publishers. In many cases there will be an intention to access a worldwide audience. In such case it is immediately apparently that many of the options set out below to ensure that the eighth principle is not breached simply will not be possible. For example, on a basic level there simply may not be a processor or controller in a third country with whom to enter into model contract clauses. In these situations, it is essential to ensure that consent is obtained before placing pictures or other personal data on a website.

EU publication of a country's adequacy

6.118   The European Commission has the authority to publish findings that a regime in a particular state ensures an adequate level of protection for the rights and freedoms of data subjects. Transfers to such states will therefore be treated in the same way as transfers to an EEA state. At the time of writing, Switzerland, Argentina, Guernsey, Isle of Man and Canada (although not in the case of the latter in relation to all types of personal data) have been approved in this manner.

EU-US Safe Harbour Scheme

6.119   As for the countries listed above, the Information Commissioner has made a specific finding of adequacy where transfers of data are made to an entity in the US which is subject to the US Safe Harbour Scheme. Under this self-regulatory scheme, US companies signed up to the scheme and complying with the rules issued by the US Department of Commerce are recognised[140] as offering adequate protection.

Example 6.48

A UK-based advertising company is considering using a third party company to manage its personnel databases. It is choosing between companies based in Norway, Holland, Canada, the US and New Zealand. The transfer to the US will contravene the eighth principle unless the company has signed up to the Safe Harbor Scheme or one of the other exemptions applies. Another exemption must apply with respect to New Zealand, but an automatic assumption of adequacy exists in relation to the other jurisdictions.

However, there is now a serious doubt about the operation and legality of the Safe Harbour regime as a legitimising mechanism for the transfer of personal data from the EU to the US. This is despite the fact that the scheme is specifically negotiated and agreed between the EU and US and that it has been in operation since 2000. In a further ripple of the Snowden NSA disclosures, a legal case has reached the Court of Justice which challenges the Safe Harbour agreement. This is, inter alia, on the basis that disclosures to the US of EU citizens' personal data are not adequately protected and are subject to mass surveillance activities in the US. The Advocate General in the case, the *Schrems v Commissioner* case, urged the court to determine that the EU – US Safe Harbour personal data transfer

---

140 European Parliament resolution of July 2000.

agreement is invalid.[141] Lawyers, policymakers as well as the international technology sector were keenly waiting on the full Court of Justice decision. Advocate General Bot had said that the agreement is invalid, which would have the effect of invalidating the transfer of personal data from the EU to the US – at least by way of the Safe Harbour regime. In a very quick turnaround the Court of Justice issued its decision on 6 October 2015, less than a month after the AG's Opinion.[142]

The Court of Justice held that national Data Protection Authorities (DPAs) are obliged to investigate complaints regarding the breach of fundamental rights regardless of what the official position may be regarding a treaty type arrangement negotiated between the EU Commission and other nation states.

In terms of the Safe Harbour agreement itself, the court held that this was invalid, and thus is not a legitimising mechanism to transfer data to the US from the EU. In particular it was important that the US legal regime did not afford protection for EU data and EU citizens whose personal data is transferred to the US. Indeed, this was acknowledged by the Commission itself in argument at the court and by the fact that the Commission was already seeking to renegotiate the Safe Harbour agreement give the shortcomings.

This has major legal, commercial as well as political implications. Arguably, no other case has had the potential to impact as many people. In addition, over 4,000 companies currently rely on the Safe Harbour agreement. The AG's Opinion states that the Safe Harbour agreement is in breach of the Data Protection Directive as well as the Charter of Fundamental Rights of the EU. The court has agreed with the AG, and deemed Safe Harbour invalid.

Many in the US and EU, as well as further afield, await to find out if: (a) transfers must be halted on foot of an official investigation; (b) whether the Commission can renegotiate a more robust Safe Harbour agreement with the US, and the consequences and nuances of what would happen if a Safe Harbour 2.0 cannot be agreed; (c) whether the court's decision also has implications for the other legitimating mechanisms for the transfer of EU data to the US, such as model contracts and binding corporate rules (BCRs); (d) what will happen in Ireland given that when the case was referred back to the Irish High Court after the Court of Justice decision, the Irish Data Protection Commissioner agreed to investigate the original *Schrems* complaint. It also remains to be seen if the agreement being deemed invalid per se, as opposed to from the date of the decision, will have particular consequences. Another consequence, is that the role of national Data Protection Authorities (such as the ICO) appears be enhanced. This could run counter to the aim of the proposed EU Data Protection Regulation which refers to a one-stop-shop mechanism of DPAs. Clearly, this case will require very careful analysis. The immediate consequences have yet to fully show themselves and the long term consequences are significant regardless of what happens in official negotiations and official investigations at DPA level. In the meantime, many companies are in a difficult position as to whether to move data back, stop transferring, locate data centres in the EU, consider the alternative

141 *Schrems v Commissoner* Case C-362/14, AG Bot, 23 September 2015, available at http://eur-lex.europa.eu/legal-content/EN/TXT/?qid=1395932669976&uri=CELEX:62014CC0362.
142 *Schrems v Commissoner* Case C-362/14, ECJ/CJEU, 6 October 2015.

transfer mechanisms, consider the legality of the alternative mechanisms, brace themselves for what queries may arise from users and privacy advocates.

Own assessment of adequacy

6.120 Data controllers are open to make their own findings as to whether the level of protection afforded by all the circumstances of a particular case is adequate (having regard to both legal and general adequacy criteria) when weighed against the potential risks to the rights and freedoms of data subjects which may arise.

Although this may sound an easy option it carries grave risks and will demand that each transfer is considered carefully on a case-by-case basis. Unsurprisingly, the Information Commissioner warns in official guidance on the subject[143] that a data controller is likely to consider the other options instead since self-assessment is a time-intensive exemption with no guarantee of being correct and significant sanctions if the conclusion is incorrect.

For businesses with branches in several different European jurisdictions, the key problem is that national data protection authorities apply their own interpretations of the concept of 'adequacy'. This makes it extremely problematic to establish a suitable and practical transfer procedure which can be used again and again from several countries within the EU.

Standard contractual clauses

6.121 EU data protection authorities are obliged[144] to recognise that transfers have adequate protection where the model clauses approved by the EU Commission are used.

There are three different sets of model clauses:

(1) Controller to Processor, for the transfer of personal data from data controllers in the EU to processors (subcontractor) established in non-EU countries[145] under which the data exporter instructs its subcontractor to treat the data with full respect of the EU data protection requirements and guaranteeing that suitable technical and security measures are in place in the country to which they are sent.

(2) Controller to Controller Set I, for the transfer of data from a data controller in the EU to another data controller outside the EC.[146]

---

143 'The Commissioner's legal analysis and suggested good practice approach to assessing adequacy including consideration of the issue of contractual solutions' first issued in July 1999.

144 Except in exceptional circumstances eg where a competent authority has established that the data importer has not respected the contractual clauses or there is a substantial likelihood that the standard contractual clauses are not being or will not be complied with and the continuing transfer would create an imminent risk of grave harm to the data subjects.

145 The European Commission adopted a Decision on 29 December 2001 effective from 3 April 2002.

146 As contained in the European Commission Decision on Standard Contractual Clauses for the transfer of personal data to third countries under Directive 95/46/EC.

(3) Controller to Controller Set II, being an alternative set of model clauses for transfers between data controllers which provide greater flexibility and give more discretion to the data importer as to how they comply with data protection laws.[147] They also differ from the other model contract clauses in that a data subject is only able to enforce its rights against the breaching data controller, in contrast to Set I above, where exporter and importer are jointly and severally liable.

Use of the model clauses offers an attractive pan-European approach to businesses but does not offer room for flexibility. Parties are free to agree to add other clauses where they do not contradict, directly or indirectly the standard contractual clauses. The model contracts may not however be changed in other ways. Essentially, data controllers are required therefore to follow the clauses word for word 'filling in the blanks'. Where businesses may seek to amend the clauses to suit their own business needs (even where this does not alter the meaning or effect of any clause), the Information Commissioner has stated that this will not amount to authorised use under[148] the Act. In such a situation, it would then be up to the data controller to take its own view that either the transfer gives data subjects sufficient safeguards with the resulting risks that this brings. Alternatively, it should seek individual approval for that contract.

Given that the Safe Harbour regime is now undermined by the *Schrems* Safe Harbour case, the agreement being deemed invalid (see above), it may be that the standard contractual clauses become more popular.

Approval on a case-by-case basis

6.122 Under art 26(2), Directive 95/46/EC, national authorities may authorise on a case-by-case basis specific transfers to a country outside the EEA where the data exporter in the EU is able to demonstrate that adequate safeguards are in place to protect the personal data protection rights of the data subjects. This is usually through a contractual arrangement made between the exporter and the importer which are then submitted to the national authority for approval.

This is a lengthy and difficult process which is not suitable for organisations which will be regularly sending data abroad. This option is particularly cumbersome since each EU Data Protection Authority has a different procedure for granting such approval, different timescales, formalities and grounds for assessment.

Binding corporate rules

6.123 Binding corporate rules have been established to assist multinationals to transfer data outside of the EEA but still within the corporate group. Unlike the model contract clauses these rules must be submitted for prior authorisation before the UK Information Commissioner. The Information Commissioner will only give authorisation if he believes that adequate safeguards are in place. Such a

---

147 Commission Decision 2005/915/EC17 dated 27 December 2004.
148 Sch 4, para 9.

potentially costly and time-consuming process is therefore unattractive; only a few organisations were known to have taken such a path and obtained authorisation in the UK. These may increase.

The advantage of binding corporate rules is that a multinational need not seek authorisation in every country in which it has a group presence. Instead, the group is able to select one authority to act as the main point of contact which then co-ordinates with the other relevant bodies. The lead authority is likely to be the country in which the headquarters are or otherwise where most decisions relating to data transfers are taken.

The binding corporate rules could also be considered more in light of the *Schrems* Safe Harbor case above.

Other derogations

6.124 Under art 26(1), Directive 95/46/EC, data may be transferred to a country outside of the EEA where:

(1) the data subject has given his consent unambiguously to the proposed transfer; or

(2) the transfers necessary for the performance of a contract between the data subject and the controller or the implementation of pre-contractual measures taken in response to the data subjects request; or

(3) the transfer is necessary for the conclusion or performance of a contract concluded in the interests of the data subject between the controller and a third party; or

(4) the transfer is necessary or legally required on important public interest grounds, or for the establishment, exercise or defence of legal claims; or

(5) the transfer is necessary in order to protect the vital interests of the data subject; or

(6) the transfer is made from a register which according to laws or regulations is intended to provide information to the public and which is open to consultation either by the public in general or by any person who can demonstrate a legitimate interest, to the extent that the conditions laid down by the law for consultation are fulfilled in the particular case.

In practice, the first two of these will be the most attractive to data controllers. It will be relatively straightforward for a data controller to incorporate consent provisions at the point of data capture and at the time that other consents are being obtained (eg for direct marketing). Careful attention will have to be had to properly informing individuals what they are consenting to, however, in order to ensure that their consent is 'unambiguous'. Data controllers must also remember that consent can always be revoked at any time and that a clear audit trail evidencing such consent will be needed. In practice, therefore, model contract clauses, or 'safe harbor' status, in the case of the US, will usually be a more prudent and robust approach.

Data controllers relying on derogation (b) must also remember that the threshold for demonstrating that processing is 'necessary' for the performance of a contract is a high one. In illustration, this may not always be an attractive option for multinational companies transferring employees' personal data to other branches.

Example 6.49

Mexican Bliss is an online travel agent. It specialises in honeymoons and arranges everything for the happy couple from transfers to and from the airports to champagne on arrival. It is obviously necessary that Mexican Bliss transfers the names of the honeymoon couple to the hotel in Mexico.

There is a clear message in this discussion. There is no obvious or automatic method for transferring personal data outside the EEA. Transfers are not impossible but the needs of a data controller, the purpose and scope of the transfer and therefore the exemptions to the eighth principle must be considered on a case-by-case basis. One caveat to consider, however, is the extent to which the *Schrems* case, while in theory limited to Safe Harbour, may call into question other routes to legitimate trans-border data flows to the US.

Enforcement

6.125   The eight principles are enforced by the Commissioner serving an enforcement notice.[149] Unlike the bizarre situation under the 1984 Act, the Commissioner may now bring such enforcement proceedings against any data user, and not merely those who have registered (now 'notified'). In short, there is no longer a protective loophole for those who breach the principles. This said, the Commissioner must at least take into account whether the breach has caused or is likely to cause damage or distress to any person.[150] Non-compliance with an enforcement notice is an offence.[151] Subject to a limited defence of 'due diligence', non-compliance with such a notice can result in prosecution. The bad publicity generated by any action taken against a company could, of course, be one of the most damaging effects.

Individuals are also entitled to take proceedings where their data protection rights are infringed.[152]

DIRECT MARKETING

6.126   In addition to a data subject's underlying right to prevent the sending to them of direct marketing messages and the principle of fair collection under the

---

149 Data Protection Act 1998, s 40.
150 Data Protection Act 1998, s 40(2).
151 Data Protection Act 1998, s 47.
152 An example of a court application failing in the context of competing politicians and an election leaflet is the case of *Quinton v Peirce* [2009] EWHC 912 (QB); [2009] FSR 17.

Act, those wanting to send such mailshots must also comply with the consent and information requirements of certain other legislation. This includes the Electronic Commerce Regulations 2002 and The Privacy and Electronic Communications (EC Directive) Regulations 2003 (PECR).

Transparency requirements

6.127   The Electronic Commerce Regulations place obligations on service providers to ensure that commercial communications provided by them (therefore including website content as well as marketing emails or text messages that may be sent) contain information to enable the recipient to identify them, clarify that the message is commercial in nature and clearly explain details of any promotion, game or competition that is the subject matter of the communication. Unsolicited communications sent by electronic mail must be 'clearly and unambiguously identifiable as such'.[153]

Similar obligations appear in the PECR which prohibit the concealment of the identity of the person sending or instigating the transmission of direct marketing emails or other electronic mail and require that the recipient be given a valid address to which they can send a request that such communications cease (reg 23).

It is also important to note that additional obligations in the PECR apply to the use of software devices (such as web beacons, clear gifs and cookies) which may be included in marketing communications or on websites to track the success of campaigns. As with cookies, providers must ensure that users are clearly alerted to the presence of such devices and what they are used for, and given an opportunity to disable them.

These provisions seek to protect consumers from unclear and misleading promotions whilst also ensuring that the sender is identifiable in the event of a problem arising. The principles and requirements are also to be found in certain UK marketing rules.

Consent requirements

6.128   In the UK, the consents required for the sending of unsolicited marketing messages by email are covered by the PEC Regulations which implement Directive 2002/58/EC concerning the processing of personal data and the protection of privacy and electronic communications. This legislation fills the gap previously left by the Telecoms (Data Protection and Privacy) Regulations 1999 (implementing Directive 97/66/EC), which referred only to 'calls' and 'called lines' and therefore left ambiguity as to how email and text messages should be dealt with.

Ensuing differences of approach across member states, and lack of uniformity of trade practices, necessitated a change. Article 13 of the later Directive gave

---

153 Regs 7 and 8.

member states no option. Unsolicited emails are now not to be allowed 'without the consent of the subscribers concerned'.

The key rule to remember in terms of consent is that the form of consent that is required from the recipient depends on the medium by which the communication will be sent, not the medium through which the consent was captured. In this way, the consent that is needed to send a promotional flyer by post is different from that required to send competition details by text or for a cold call via telephone. Promoters need to be alert to this. They should also consider, in obtaining consents initially, whether cross-promotional campaigns may be considered in the future. If that is the intention, different tick boxes will be needed to obtain the different consents that may be required. Alternatively, a promoter may need to move to the highest common denominator of consent needed in order to capture all required.

In terms of email promotions, as will be considered here, the next step is to then consider to whom the communication will be sent and to whom it will be sent since this, in turn, will affect the consents which need to be obtained.

Marketing via electronic mail to individual subscribers: opt-in requirements

6.129   Regulation 22(2) provides that marketing communications may not be sent by email, video or text message[154] to individual subscribers unless 'the recipient of the electronic mail has previously notified the sender that he consents for the time being to such communications being sent by, or at the instigation of, the sender'. 'Individual subscriber' here means a living individual, but also includes an unincorporated body and therefore not just relating to consumers but also sole traders and non-limited liability partnerships. There is one exception to this general rule, detailed in **6.130** below.

Example 6.50

A US online fashion house launches a UK site run out of its London branch. To rely on the 'soft opt-in' marketing consent mechanisms, only the UK entity will be able to send marketing emails to UK customers about its products. Cross-marketing by the US company will not be possible unless express consent is obtained.

The general rule is almost universally referred to as an 'opt-in' requirement, although this term is not used in any of the legislation itself. By 'opt-in' it is meant that the individual must have actually done something positive to indicate their consent. Therefore, a failure to de-select a pre-ticked box, or a failure simply to state that they did not want to receive such communications, will not

---

154   The PECR refer to 'electronic mail', defined as 'any text, voice, sound or image message sent over a public electronic communications network which can be stored in the network or in the recipient's terminal equipment until it is collected by the recipient and includes messages sent via a short message service', which the Information Commissioner has stated in his November 2003 guidance to the PEC Regulations would also apply to voicemail/answerphone messages although not to live phone calls.

fulfil such criteria. A common way of capturing such consent will be the use of a tick box which the individual can choose to tick. Likewise, actively responding with a text message or email saying 'Yes' or otherwise to indicate that one wants to receive further communications would work.

This is not the only way, however. The Information Commissioner has stated in his guidance to the PEC Regulations[155] simply that 'there must be some form of communication whereby the individual knowingly indicates consent. This may involve clicking an icon, sending an email or subscribing to a service.' This last example may be key to providers. The use of a clear, unambiguous and strategically placed statement next to a subscribe button or signature for a service may be sufficient where the individual then knows that in taking a positive step to subscribe, they are also giving their consent to receive email marketing communications. This author believes that real caution must be taken with such an approach, not least in the positioning and choice of words used but also in view of the fact that the Information Commissioner's guidance is non-binding and it is possible to see an argument that a positive step in relation to a contractual commitment cannot fairly append other conditions. If this approach is taken then at the very least the provider should also provide a clear facility for the subscriber to choose not to take this option.

Marketing via electronic mail to individual subscribers: the soft opt-in exception

6.130   There is one key exception to the 'opt-in' requirement which is contained in reg 22(3) and is frequently referred to as the 'soft-opt in' option. This permits the sending of electronic mail marketing messages to individual subscribers, but only where the following conditions are all[156] met:

(i)   The recipient's contact details (ie email address) were obtained in the course of a sale or negotiations or the sale of a product or a service to that recipient (eg where a purchase was made online).

(ii)   Given that the wording of reg 22(3) applies the exemption to the person or instigator of the marketing message who collected the contact details under (i), this prevents the use of the exemption by any third party including, importantly, any group company. This means that a promoter will always have to seek 'opt-in' consent to either send marketing materials itself which relate to third-party products, or pass its list to third parties for their use and it will not be able to rely on soft-opt consents acquired by a third party when using contact details obtained by them.

(iii)   The marketing is in respect of similar goods and services. This is not defined, and therefore a pragmatic approach should be taken; for example, if the contact details were obtained in the context of a sale of, say, groceries online, permission would not extend to marketing in relation to insurance, even if offered by the same provider.

---

155 Information Commissioner guidance for marketers, dated November 2006.
156 There is a misconception that the exception may be relied upon where any of these conditions is satisfied. This is not the case. The Regulation specifically makes this a cumulative list.

(iv)   The recipient must have been given an opportunity (free of charge) to refuse the use of their contact details for marketing purposes when the details were collected, and each time a communication is sent. This requires the use of an 'opt-out' mechanism not just when the initial sale was made but each time a marketing email is sent, for example by providing a link or email to say no to further communications in the future.

Marketing via electronic mail to corporate subscribers

6.131   Where a recipient of a marketing communication is not an individual subscriber (therefore they are a corporate subscriber), the consent requirements do not apply and only the transparency requirements need be followed (see **6.127** above).

This creates an odd position in which depending on whether one receives the same spam message seeking readers to enter into a dubious competition during the day whilst at work, or when one logs onto a personal home email account, differing rights may be available. This is the case even though the competition may be totally unrelated to the recipient's employment.

At the same time, however, one may have rights of redress, given that a work email address often contains personal data. However, here redress is not pursuant to the PEC Regulations but the Data Protection Act itself where one can rely on rights as a data subject and the controller's obligations under the sixth principle (for which see **6.90** above).

Penalties and enforcement

6.132

Example 6.51

Tunz4U sells games for mobile phones from its website. It cold-calls previous phone customers who have not expressed any objection to receiving such calls and intends to follow this up with a demo sent to them by email attachment. Tunz4U will need also to ensure that the customers have not objected to being contacted directly by email and that residents of countries with an opt-in requirement are asked directly whether they can be contacted in this way.

The PECR obligations apply to senders and instigators of commercial communications, the Data Protection Act to data controllers, and action against these persons may therefore be taken for any contravention.

There has been widespread cynicism as to the effectiveness of the PECR to tackle spam in the UK. The problems fall into two camps. Firstly, much spam comes from companies based outside the UK and even Europe. The Data Protection Act only imposes obligations on data controllers who are based in or have equipment for processing in the UK. The PECR do not have any specified jurisdiction (the marketing-specific requirements relating simply to 'a person'), but the difficulties of bringing an action outside of the UK are obvious.

The second concerns the enforcement action which may be taken itself. The PECR provide for the following form of redress.

PECR

6.133 A person who suffers damage may bring court proceedings compensation (and, pursuant to the Supreme Court Act 1981, for an injunction).

As with the Data Protection Act itself, the problem here is that damages claimed are unlikely ever to be substantive and the deterrent effect therefore limited. Three actions have been brought since the PECR came into force in 2003. The first was brought by Nigel Roberts against internet marketing company Media Logistics (UK), in which the judge of the Colchester small claims court found in Mr Roberts' favour, leading to a settlement award of just £270. The second was brought by an individual against Transcom, which resulted in an award of £750 by the Edinburgh Sherriff's Court (the maximum which could be claimed in the Scottish small claims courts). See further example at **6.185**.

Although not likely to be an attractive route for individuals, for network operators, there may be more appeal, not least given the potential availability of injunctions. In this respect the third case provides an important precedent. The case concerned an action for summary judgment by Microsoft Corporation against Paul Martin McDonald who operated a website offering lists of emails for sale for marketing purposes, which the defendant claimed had opted in to receiving marketing communications, including a large quantity of hotmail addresses. Microsoft claimed that as a result of such actions it had suffered loss of goodwill and had also had to purchase additional servers to cope with the volume of spam which was sent via its networks to its subscribers. The court held that the policy underlying the PECR and the Directive was the protection of subscribers and electronic communications networks themselves. Therefore, Microsoft had a direct action itself falling within the class of persons for whom the statute sought to benefit.

In addition, this case clarifies that the seller of such email lists can be a defendant, since such action will be deemed to constitute the 'instigation' of such commercial communications.

Data Protection Act

6.134 The Information Commissioner may exercise his enforcement functions pursuant to Part V of the Data Protection Act; this may be at the request of OFCOM or an aggrieved individual. The Information Commissioner imposed enforcement notices on several companies for making unsolicited calls to individuals who had specifically requested that they not be contacted. Initial action will first be a public warning, however. Until an enforcement notice is actually breached, no offence is made out.

In the UK, a potentially more likely route of enforcement is through the numerous self-regulatory and other codes which have adopted the PECR rules.

For example, the Advertising Standards Authority took action against World Networks to require it to pre-clear future adverts, following complaints that its opt-out provisions contained in a text message promotion were unclear. The CAP Code which the ASA enforces has incorporated consent requirements which echo those of the PECR. Likewise, the ICSTIS code which regulates providers of premium rate telephone services, and the Direct Marketing Association policing of the consent requirements they have set out in their respective codes of practice.

DATA RETENTION AND DISCLOSURES FOR LAW ENFORCEMENT

6.135 Sitting alongside the provisions of the Data Protection Act which protect the privacy of individuals in respect of the processing of their personal data, is further legislation which contains prohibitions on access to and interception of communications made over electronic networks, except in prescribed circumstances. Many of the exceptions concern the access that law enforcement and government bodies may wish to have for the purpose of investigation of crimes and national security.[157] The scope of what access is needed, and what data should be made available, has received greater focus in recent years in line with the attention on the growing threat of terrorism and international crime which may use or rely on such networks, at least in part.

All network operators and many website owners may therefore find themselves the recipient of a request for email or IP addresses or other information from official bodies which extends beyond the requests for data subject access or from solicitors acting for clients that they may be used to pursuant to the Data Protection Act or be concerned as to how the principles under this Act may tie in with such requests and growing obligations under new statutes. This section sets out the high-level principles and obligations relevant to such issues.

Restrictions on interception of communications

6.136 The Regulation of Investigatory Powers Act 2000 (RIPA) seeks to ensure that investigatory powers concerning electronic networks are conducted in accordance with human rights, but also concerns obligations and prohibitions which will be relevant on a day-to-day basis. A significant caveat must be advised to readers. The issue of interception and even storage of communications is highly charged and political at present. This is true both nationally as well as internationally. Examples include the Snowden revelations, the DRI case above challenging the Data Retention Directive, as well as the successful challenge in

---

157 On the separate issue of disclosure of official secrets and official information, see for example *Attorney General v Guardian Newspapers Ltd (No 1)* HL 13 August 1987; *AG v Guardian (No 2)* [1990] 1 AC 109; [1990] 1 AC 109 HL; *AG v Observer and others*; *AG v Times and another* [on appeal from *AG v Guardian (No 2)*]; *Case of Observer and Guardian v UK*, ECHR (application no 13585/88) (Spycatcher case) and also *Baker v Secretary of State for the Home Office (Information Tribunal)* [2001] UKHRR 1275 where a Ministerial certificate that certified personal data as national security-sensitive quashed.

Schrems Prism case and the other successful challenge in the DRIPA (proposed RIPA replacement) case in the UK High Court. The government is again seeking to advance new legislation. While the details are not fully known at this stage, it is still instructive to review the position under RIPA below, but with the caveat that this does not (or at least is not meant to) reflect the current position given the national and EU challenges.

The key starting point in RIPA is Part 1. This makes it an offence for any person to intentionally and without lawful authority intercept communications in the course of their transmission via a public postal or public or private telecommunications system (unless they have consent for such interception). It also creates the right for a civil action by a sender or recipient of a communication that is intercepted by or with the consent of the controller of a private telecommunication system if such interception is without lawful authority.

A person will have lawful authority to intercept a communication (which can include any form of modification or interference or monitoring which makes any of the contents of such communication available to a person other than the recipient or sender and therefore does not impact on any actions taken solely in relation to traffic data[158]) in several ways. The most relevant reasons for providers are likely to be: (i) the consent of recipient and sender has been obtained; (ii) it is an interception undertaken in accordance with the Lawful Business Practice Regulations for purposes connected with the provision and operation of that system (ie day-to-day facilitation of the service itself); (iii) where the provider is expressly provided with a warrant to provide access to an authorised person to cause an interception. Access in this way is considered below.

Obligations to provide access to data

6.137 Although RIPA has detailed provisions in relation to encryption and surveillance, there are two key provisions which enable certain bodies to obtain access to data and place obligations on providers to provide such access which must be understood.

The first, under [Part 1, Chapter I], relates to the warrants which may be obtained in order to secure an interception of communications, assistance in respect of such an interception or the disclosure of intercepted material and related communications data. These warrants are therefore required if the contents of communications may need to be intercepted or disclosed; as a consequence, the process for obtaining such a warrant is onerous, and most providers are unlikely to ever be provided with such a warrant. Warrants may only be issued if proportionate and also necessary, either in the interests of national security, for the purposes of preventing or detecting serious crime, safeguarding the economic wellbeing of the UK, or giving effect to a mutual agreement (ie pursuant to an international warrant). Such warrants are issued by the Secretary of State and

---

158 'Traffic data' is defined in ss 9 and 10, Part 1, and includes information for the purposes of identification of the apparatus, origination or location of the transmission, data comprised in signals which effect the transmission and identifying data as comprised in or attached to a communication.

may only be applied for by a very restricted list of persons and bodies (Director of GCHQ etc).

The second, under [Part 1, Chapter II], relates to notices which may be issued in order to obtain access to communications data as opposed to the contents of communications. 'Communications data' means traffic data or other information which does not contain the contents but is about the use made by a person of the system in question or is otherwise held by the service provider. The circumstances in which such a notice may be obtained are wider and extend to purposes of the prevention and detection of crime or of preventing disorder (as opposed to 'serious' crime for a warrant), public safety or health, tax, preventing harm or injury to a person in an emergency. Such notices may also be issued by designated persons of a police force as well as by Commissioners of Customers and Excise, Inland Revenue, intelligence services and certain public authorities.

A provider in receipt of such a notice or warrant is obliged to comply with it and, in so doing, is exempted from obligations which might otherwise apply in relation to action or any processing of personal data which might otherwise apply pursuant to the Data Protection Act. It is important that such a provider should understand the limits of such devices, however, and not, for example, provide more data than is requested and, in particular, appreciate that a notice does not permit the provision of the transcripts of calls, emails or online communications.

The issue of an access request and a refusal on grounds that disclosure of the psychologist's report was likely to cause serious harm to heath as an exemption was considered in *Roberts v Nottinghamshire Healthcare NHS Trust*.[159] The refusal was upheld. The role of the court was to review the decision of the data controller rather than act as primary decision maker.[160]

Obligations to retain data

6.138 In addition to obligations to disclose data, there are various grounds upon which a service provider can find itself required to actually retain data, the common basis being that such data needs to be retained so that it can be made available to law enforcement authorities, regulatory authorities or government agencies.

There are three broad categories of data retention obligation which must be considered: (i) those that apply specifically because a service provider is in the business of providing internet services or access or conducts business via the internet; (ii) those which apply to their specific line of business (ie under financial services or health authority rules); and (iiii) those which apply following the receipt of a specific order, notice or warrant received from a relevant person, for example a court order, or pursuant to RIPA as considered above and as considered in further detail in Chapter 5. This section focuses on the first of these.

159 *Roberts v Nottinghamshire Healthcare NHS Trust* [2008] EWHC 1934 (QB); [2009] FSR 4.
160 Ibid.

Voluntary retention of communications data

6.139   Currently, service providers are not legally required to systematically retain internet-specific traffic or contents data (such as IP addresses or emails) for law enforcement purposes.

A Code of Practice has been developed pursuant to the Anti-Terrorism, Crime and Security Act 2001 (as outlined at **6.7** above) which sets out suggested data retention periods for service providers. It also provides a framework for the Secretary of State may enter into voluntary agreements with individual public communication service providers (ie providers of any telecommunications service which is offered or provided to a substantial section of the public in any one or more parts of the UK). The purpose is to clarify the data retention practices which such communications provider agrees to adhere to so that those authorities seeking access to such data under RIPA have knowledge and comfort that data will be available to them and not deleted. The Code characterises this agreement as a kind of service level agreement which supplements and expands on the requirements under the Code.

Data types

6.140   The Code specifies the minimum of data that must be retained by providers. As a result, all providers must analyse their existing data capture to ensure that their data sets include at least: traffic data, service data and subscriber data.

Purposes of retention

6.141   Much of the communications data usually held by providers will be for business purposes. Under both human rights and data protection legislation it is rarely legitimate to retain data indefinitely. It follows that in the normal course of events, after a period of time, providers would be advised to destroy or anonymise data.

In contrast, under the Code, communications data must be retained for an extended period for the purposes of national security. It follows that at a point in time, communications data being held by providers will move from being classified as both business and national security data into merely national security data. At that point, a provider must not access the data for its own purposes. This older data therefore needs to be put in a 'silo' so that it may be accessed, but only for national security purposes.

Period of data retention

6.142   Unless otherwise directed, the following retention periods apply:

- subscriber information: 12 months

- email data: 6 months

- ISP data: 6 months

- web activity logs: 4 days.

Communications data (other than SMS, EMS and MMS data) shall be held for a maximum of 12 months unless either directed to retain for longer, or, where destroying that data would compromise the analysis of other data. Of course, as mentioned above, there may be good, legitimate business purposes for retaining the data for longer. If this is the case, the data may only be retained if justified under human rights and data protection legislation.

Costs of retention

6.143 Where for business purposes the same types of data are otherwise being retained for the same 12-month extendable period, the costs shall be borne by the communications provider. However, where new types of data are to be held or any data is to be retained for significantly longer than for business purposes, the Secretary of State will contribute a reasonable proportion of the marginal capital or running costs as appropriate. Clearly, 'significantly' longer in relation to a 12-month retention stipulation would mean that the data would otherwise have been retained for only a few months. The issue of costs can be negotiated to some extent, but these negotiations should take place prior to the signing of the contract.

Moving to compulsory data retention

6.144 The UK government is (again) seeking to move to a regime of compulsory service provider data retention. At the time of writing, this is an area which is in flux and the current and future legal regimes are yet to be properly mapped out. Readers should consult more detailed texts as appropriate.

EU DP review and update

6.145 The EU data protection regime is being fundamentally updated and expanded.[161] Many things have changed since the introduction of the DPD95. Data processing activities have changed as well as increased in scale and complexity. The EU undertook a review of the data protection regime. Partly on foot of the review, it was decided to propose a legal update to the DPD95. This has culminated in the drafting and publication of a proposed new EU General Data Protection Regulation (GDPR). Indeed, the Council of Europe Convention on data protection[162] which pre-dated the DPD95 and which was incorporated into the national law of many EU and other states (40 plus) prior to the DPD95, is also planning to review and update the Convention.[163]

---

161 Graham, R, 'Prepare for European Data Protection Reform', *SCL Computer and Law*, 30 November 2011.

162 Convention for the Protection of Individuals with regard to Automatic Processing of Personal Data, Council of Europe (1982), available at http://conventions.coe.int/Treaty/en/Treaties/Html/108.htm.

163 See Kierkegaard, S, *et al*, '30 Years On – The Review of the Council of Europe Data Protection Convention 108', *Computer Law & Security Review* (2011) (27), pp 223–231.

The WP29 also referred to the need for future data protection measures in its opinion regarding *The Future of Privacy*.[164] Indeed, there have also been calls for greater political activism in relation to particular data protection issues.[165]

Others[166] have also highlighted new problematic developments in relation to such things as location data and location-based services, which need to be dealt with.

Formal nature of Regulations and Directives

6.146   The GDPR is still currently a draft. However, it is important to note that an EU Regulation differs from a Directive under formal EU law.[167] A Regulation is immediately directly effective in all EU member states – without the need for national implementing laws. Once the Regulation is passed, it will apply in the UK. It will also change the UK data protection regime as well as the UK. The reform will be 'comprehensive'.[168]

Review policy

6.147   Rebecca Wong refers to some of the areas of concern which the DPR is proposed to address.[169] These include:

● the data protection regime in the online age;

● social networking;

● cloud computing;

● minimum/maximum standards; and

● the data protection principles.[170]

The Commission states[171] that the policy in reviewing the data protection regime is as follows:

● modernise the EU legal system for the protection of personal data, in particular to meet the challenges resulting from globalisation and the use of new technologies;

---

164 The Future of Privacy, WP29, referred to in Wong, R, 'Data Protection: The Future of Privacy,' *Computer Law & Security Review* (2011) (27), pp 53–57.

165 Ripoll Servent, A, and MacKenie, A, 'Is the EP Still a Data Protection Champion? The Case of SWIFT', *Perspectives on European Politics & Society* (2011) (12), pp 390–406.

166 Cuijpers, C, and Pekarek, M, 'The Regulation of Location-Based Services: Challenges to the European Union Data Protection Regime', *Journal of Location Based Services* (2011) (5), pp 223–241.

167 Generally see, for example, Biondi, A, and Eeckhout, P (eds), *EU Law after Lisbon* (2012); Foster, N, *Foster on EU Law* (2011); O'Neill, A, *EU Law for UK Lawyers* (2011); Steiner, J, *EU Law* (2011).

168 In Brief, *Communications Law* (2012) (17), p 3.

169 Wong, R, 'The Data Protection Directive 95/46/EC: Idealisms and Realisms', *International Review of Law, Computers & Technology* (2012) (26), pp 229–244.

170 See ibid.

171 Reform of Data Protection legal Framework, Commission, Justice directorate, available at http://ec.europa.eu/justice/data-protection/review/index_en.htm.

- strengthen individuals' rights, and at the same time reduce administrative formalities to ensure a free flow of personal data within the EU and beyond;

- improve the clarity and coherence of the EU rules for personal data protection and achieve a consistent and effective implementation and application of the fundamental right to the protection of personal data in all areas of the Union's activities.[172]

It should also enhance consumer confidence in ecommerce.[173] In addition, it should also bring comprehensive savings to organisations as the compliance obligations of complying with somewhat differing national data protection regimes will be reduced if not eliminated.[174]

The review process has been ongoing for some time.[175] It further summarises the need for new data protection rules, as follows:

'The current EU data protection rules date from 1995. Back then, the internet was virtually unknown to most people. Today, 250 million people use the internet daily in Europe.

Think how that has changed our personal data landscape through the explosion of ecommerce, social networks, online games and cloud computing.

The European Commission has therefore adopted proposals for updating data protection rules to meet the challenges of the digital age. In particular, the proposals will strengthen protection of your personal data online.

These proposals will now be debated by the Council and the European Parliament before they can become law.'[176]

Commentators describe the draft proposed GDPR as 'a long (and ambitious) text'.[177] In addition, the process which has arrived at this stage is also described as being herculean.[178]

Some key changes

6.148   While amendments are still being finalised at the time of writing, some key changes are referred to below. In some respects these could also be seen as advantages of the new GDPR data protection regime.

---

172 Ibid.
173 In Brief, *Communications Law* (2012) (17), p 3.
174 See ibid.
175 See details of some of the steps and consultations at http://ec.europa.eu/justice/data-protection/review/actions/index_en.htm, accessed on 17 August 2012.
176 See Commission, Why Do We Need New Data Protection Rules Now?, available at http://ec.europa.eu/justice/data-protection/minisite/index.html.
177 De Hert, P, and Papakonstantinou, V, 'The Proposed Data Protection Regulation Replacing Directive 95/46/EC: A Sound System for the Protection of Individuals', *Computer Law & Security Review* (2012) (28), pp 130–142. Note also, Walden, IN, and Savage, RN, 'Data Protection and Privacy Laws: Should Organisations be Protected?', *International and Comparative Law Quarterly* (1988) (37), pp 337–347.
178 Ibid.

- administrative costs are to be reduced with a single EU-wide set of rules and obligations;

- there may be less need to interact with the IPO as more responsibility and accountability is passed to the organisational level;

- the consent requirement has been clarified as to mean explicit consent (whereas previously there were references to different categories of consent);

- rights are improved with easier access to personal data, as well as its transferability;

- the enhanced right to be forgotten will improve the position of data subjects and the ability to delete it;

- the EU data protection will apply to non-EU entities operating with regard to EU personal data and EU citizens;

- the national authorities will be able to impose fines of €1,000,000 or up to 2% of global turnover.[179]

The ICO is reported as welcoming the GDPR and stating that:

> 'In particular its strengthens the position of individuals, recognises important concepts such as privacy by design and privacy impact assessments and requires organisations to be able to demonstrate that they have measures in place to ensure personal information is properly protected.'[180]

DDPR: definitions

6.149 The DPR sets out new definitions, such as for, 'personal data breach', 'genetic data', 'biometric data', 'data concerning health', 'main establishment', 'representative', 'enterprise', 'group of undertakings', 'binding corporate rules', and 'supervisory authority'.

DPR recitals

6.150 The Recitals to the proposed DPR are also instructive. They include:

Data protection/fundamental right

6.151 Recital (1) states that the protection of natural persons in relation to the processing of personal data is a fundamental right. Article 8(1) of the Charter of Fundamental Rights of the European Union and art 16(1) of the Treaty lay down that everyone has the right to the protection of personal data concerning him or her. Recital (2) states that the processing of personal data is designed to serve man; the principles and rules on the protection of individuals with regard to the processing of their personal data should, whatever the nationality or residence of natural persons, respect their fundamental rights and freedoms, notably their right

---

179 In Brief, *Communications Law* (2012) (17), p 3.
180 Referred to in In Brief, *Communications Law* (2012) (17), p 3.

to the protection of personal data. It should contribute to the accomplishment of an area of freedom, security and justice and of an economic union, to economic and social progress, the strengthening and the convergence of the economies within the internal market, and the well-being of individuals.

Need for stronger data protection regime framework

6.152   Recital (6) states that these developments require building a strong and more coherent data protection framework in the Union, backed by strong enforcement, given the importance to create the trust that will allow the digital economy to develop across the internal market. Individuals should have control of their own personal data and legal and practical certainty for individuals, economic operators and public authorities should be reinforced.

Internet

6.153   Recital (24) states that when using online services, individuals may be associated with online identifiers provided by their devices, applications, tools and protocols, such as Internet Protocol addresses or cookie identifiers. This may leave traces which, combined with unique identifiers and other information received by the servers, may be used to create profiles of the individuals and identify them. It follows that identification numbers, location data, online identifiers or other specific factors as such need not necessarily be considered as personal data in all circumstances.

Rectification

6.154   Recital (53) states that any person should have the right to have personal data concerning them rectified and a 'right to be forgotten' where the retention of such data is not in compliance with this Regulation. In particular, data subjects should have the right that their personal data are erased and no longer processed, where the data are no longer necessary in relation to the purposes for which the data are collected or otherwise processed, where data subjects have withdrawn their consent for processing or where they object to the processing of personal data concerning them or where the processing of their personal data otherwise does not comply with this Regulation. This right is particularly relevant, when the data subject has given their consent as a child, when not being fully aware of the risks involved by the processing, and later wants to remove such personal data especially on the internet. However, the further retention of the data should be allowed where it is necessary for historical, statistical and scientific research purposes, for reasons of public interest in the area of public health, for exercising the right of freedom of expression, when required by law or where there is a reason to restrict the processing of the data instead of erasing them.

Enhancing right to be forgotten

6.155   Recital (54) states that to strengthen the 'right to be forgotten' in the online environment, the right to erasure should also be extended in such a way that a data controller who has made the personal data public should be obliged to inform third parties which are processing such data that a data subject requests them to erase any links to, or copies or replications of that personal data. To ensure this information, the data controller should take all reasonable steps, including technical measures, in relation to data for the publication of which the data controller is responsible. In relation to a third-party publication of personal data, the data controller should be considered responsible for the publication, where the controller has authorised the publication by the third party.

Right to object

6.156 Recital (56) states that in cases where personal data might lawfully be processed to protect the vital interests of the data subject, or on grounds of public interest, official authority or the legitimate interests of a data controller, any data subject should nevertheless be entitled to object to the processing of any data relating to them. The burden of proof should be on the data controller to demonstrate that their legitimate interests may override the interests or the fundamental rights and freedoms of the data subject.

Security

6.157 Recital (66) states that in order to maintain security and to prevent processing in breach of this Regulation, the data controller or data processor should evaluate the risks inherent to the processing and implement measures to mitigate those risks. These measures should ensure an appropriate level of security, taking into account the state of the art and the costs of their implementation in relation to the risks and the nature of the personal data to be protected. When establishing technical standards and organisational measures to ensure security of processing, the Commission should promote technological neutrality, interoperability and innovation, and, where appropriate, co-operate with third countries.

Data breach

6.158 Recital (67) states that a personal data breach may, if not addressed in an adequate and timely manner, result in substantial economic loss and social harm, including identity fraud, to the individual concerned. Therefore, as soon as the data controller becomes aware that such a breach has occurred, the data controller should notify the breach to the supervisory authority without undue delay and, where feasible, within 24 hours. Where this cannot achieved within 24 hours, an explanation of the reasons for the delay should accompany the notification. The individuals whose personal data could be adversely affected by the breach should be notified without undue delay in order to allow them to take the necessary precautions. A breach should be considered as adversely affecting the personal data or privacy of a data subject where it could result in, for example, identity theft or fraud, physical harm, significant humiliation or damage to reputation. The notification should describe the nature of the personal data breach as well as recommendations for the individual concerned to mitigate potential adverse effects. Notifications to data subjects should be made as soon as reasonably feasible, and in close co-operation with the supervisory authority and respecting guidance provided by it or other relevant authorities (eg law enforcement authorities). For example, the chance for data subjects to mitigate an immediate risk of harm would call for a prompt notification of data subjects whereas the need to implement appropriate measures against continuing or similar data breaches may justify a longer delay.

Recital (68) states that in order to determine whether a personal data breach is notified to the supervisory authority and to the data subject without undue delay, it should be ascertained whether the data controller has implemented and applied appropriate technological protection and organisational measures to establish immediately whether a personal data breach has taken place and to inform promptly the supervisory authority and the data subject, before a damage to personal and economic interests occurs, taking into account in particular the nature and gravity of the personal data breach and its consequences and adverse effects for the data subject.

Recital (69) states that in setting detailed rules concerning the format and procedures applicable to the notification of personal data breaches, due consideration should be given to the circumstances of the breach, including whether or not personal data had been protected by appropriate technical protection measures, effectively limiting the likelihood of identity fraud or other forms of misuse. Moreover, such rules and procedures should take into account the legitimate interests of law enforcement authorities in cases where early disclosure could unnecessarily hamper the investigation of the circumstances of a breach.

Impact assessments

6.159   Recital (72) states that there are circumstances under which it may be sensible and economic that the subject of a data protection impact assessment should be broader than a single project, for example where public authorities or bodies intend to establish a common application or processing platform or where several data controllers plan to introduce a common application or processing environment across an industry sector or segment or for a widely used horizontal activity.

Recital (73) states that the data protection impact assessments should be carried out by a public authority or public body if such an assessment has not already been made in the context of the adoption of the national law on which the performance of the tasks of the public authority or public body is based and which regulates the specific processing operation or set of operations in question.

Recital (74) states that where a data protection impact assessment indicates that processing operations involve a high degree of specific risks to the rights and freedoms of data subjects, such as excluding individuals from their right, or by the use of specific new technologies, the supervisory authority should be consulted, prior to the start of operations, on a risky processing which might not be in compliance with this Regulation, and to make proposals to remedy such situation. Such consultation should equally take place in the course of the preparation either of a measure by the national parliament or of a measure based on such legislative measure which defines the nature of the processing and lays down appropriate safeguards.

Compensation

6.160   Recital (118) states that any damage which a person may suffer as a result of unlawful processing should be compensated by the data controller or data processor, who may be exempted from liability if they prove that they are not responsible for the damage, in particular where he establishes fault on the part of the data subject or in case of *force majeure.*

Penalties

6.161   Recital (119) states that penalties should be imposed to any person, whether governed by private or public law, who fails to comply with this Regulation. Member states should ensure that the penalties should be effective, proportionate and dissuasive and should take all measures to implement the penalties.

Sanctions

6.162   Recital (120) states that the in order to strengthen and harmonise administrative sanctions against infringements of this Regulation, each supervisory authority should have the power to sanction administrative offences. This Regulation should indicate these offences and the upper limit for the related administrative fines, which should be fixed in each individual case proportionate to the specific situation, with due regard in particular to the nature, gravity and duration of the breach. The consistency mechanism may also be used to cover divergences in the application of administrative sanctions.

GDPR: processing not allowing identification

6.163   Article 10 refers to processing not allowing identification, and provides that if the data processed by a data controller do not permit the data controller to identify a natural person, the data controller shall not be obliged to acquire additional information in order to identify the data subject for the sole purpose of complying with any provision of this Regulation.

GDPR: health data

6.164   Chapter IX of the DPR makes provisions relating to specific data processing situations. Article 81 refers to processing of personal data concerning health.

GDPR: employment data

6.165   Article 82 refers to processing in the employment context. Article 82(1) provides that within the limits of the DPR, member states may adopt by law specific rules regulating the processing of employees' personal data in the employment context, in particular for the purposes of the recruitment, the performance of the contract of employment, including discharge of obligations laid down by law or by collective agreements, management, planning and organisation of work, health and safety at work, and for the purposes of the exercise and enjoyment, on an individual or collective basis, of rights and benefits related to employment, and for the purpose of the termination of the employment relationship.

6.166   Chapter III of the DPR refers to rights of the data subject. Section 1 refers specifically to transparency. Article 11 is headed Transparent information and communication. Under art 11(1) the data controller shall have transparent and easily accessible policies with regard to the processing of personal data and for the exercise of data subjects' rights. Under art 11(2) the data controller shall provide any information and any communication relating to the processing of personal data to the data subject in an intelligible form, using clear and plain language, adapted to the data subject, in particular for any information addressed specifically to a child.

Article 12 refers to procedures and mechanisms for exercising the rights of the data subject. Article 12(1) provides that the data controller shall establish procedures for providing the information referred to in art 14 and for the exercise of the rights of data subjects referred to in art 13 and arts 15 to 19. The data controller shall provide in particular mechanisms for facilitating the request for the actions referred to in art 13 and arts 15 to 19. Where personal data are processed by automated means, the data controller shall also provide means for requests to be made electronically (art 12(2)).

Article 12(2) provides that the data controller shall inform the data subject without delay and, at the latest within one month of receipt of the request, whether or not any action has been taken pursuant to art 13 and arts 15 to 19 and shall provide the requested information. This period may be prolonged for a further month, if several data subjects exercise their rights and their co-operation is necessary to a reasonable extent to prevent an unnecessary and disproportionate effort on the part of the data controller. The information shall be given in writing. Where the data subject makes the request in electronic form, the information shall be provided in electronic form, unless otherwise requested by the data subject.

Under art 12(3), it is provided that if the data controller refuses to take action on the request of the data subject, the data controller shall inform the data subject of the reasons for the refusal and on the possibilities of lodging a complaint to the supervisory authority and seeking a judicial remedy.

Under art 12(4) the information and the actions taken on requests referred to in paragraph 1 shall be free of charge. Where requests are manifestly excessive, in particular because of their repetitive character, the data controller may charge a fee for providing the information or taking the action requested, or the data controller may not take the action requested. In that case, the data controller shall bear the burden of proving the manifestly excessive character of the request.

Article 13 refers to rights in relation to recipients. It provides that the data controller shall communicate any rectification or erasure carried out in accordance with arts 16 and 17 to each recipient to whom the data have been disclosed, unless this proves impossible or involves a disproportionate effort.

'Personal data breach' is defined to mean a breach of security leading to the accidental or unlawful destruction, loss, alteration, unauthorised disclosure of, or access to, personal data transmitted, stored or otherwise processed.

GDPR: impact assessment

6.167 Section 3 of the DPR refers to data protection impact assessment and prior authorisation. Article 33 is headed data protection impact assessment. Article 33(1) states that where processing operations present specific risks to the rights and freedoms of data subjects by virtue of their nature, their scope or their purposes, the data controller or the data processor acting on the data controller's behalf shall carry out an assessment of the impact of the envisaged processing operations on the protection of personal data.

Under art 33(2) the following processing operations in particular present specific risks referred to in paragraph 1:

- a systematic and extensive evaluation of personal aspects relating to a natural person or for analysing or predicting in particular the natural person's economic situation, location, health, personal preferences, reliability or behaviour, which is based on automated processing and on which measures are based that produce legal effects concerning the individual or significantly affect the individual;

- information on sex life, health, race and ethnic origin or for the provision of health care, epidemiological researches, or surveys of mental or infectious diseases, where the data are processed for taking measures or decisions regarding specific individuals on a large scale;

- monitoring publicly accessible areas, especially when using optic-electronic devices (video surveillance) on a large scale;

- personal data in large-scale filing systems on children, genetic data or biometric data;

- other processing operations for which the consultation of the supervisory authority is required pursuant to point (b) of art 34(2).

In accordance with art 33(3) the assessment shall contain at least a general description of the envisaged processing operations, an assessment of the risks to the rights and freedoms of data subjects, the measures envisaged to address the risks, safeguards, security measures and mechanisms to ensure the protection of personal data and to demonstrate compliance with the DPR, taking into account the rights and legitimate interests of data subjects and other persons concerned.

Under art 33(4) the data controller shall seek the views of data subjects or their representatives on the intended processing, without prejudice to the protection of commercial or public interests or the security of the processing operations.

If the data controller is a public authority or body and where the processing results from a legal obligation pursuant to point (c) of art 6(1) providing for rules and procedures pertaining to the processing operations and regulated by Union law, paragraphs 1 to 4 shall not apply, unless member states deem it necessary to carry out such assessment prior to the processing activities (art 33(5)).

GDPR: Data Protection Officer

6.168   Section 4 of the GDPR refers to the data protection officer. Article 35 is headed the designation of the data protection officer. Article 35(1) states that the data controller and the data processor shall designate a data protection officer in any case where.

- the processing is carried out by a public authority or body; or

- the processing is carried out by an enterprise employing 250 persons or more; or

- the core activities of the data controller or the data processor consist of processing operations which, by virtue of their nature, their scope and/or their purposes, require regular and systematic monitoring of data subjects.

In the case referred to in bullet two a group of undertakings may appoint a single data protection officer (art 35(1)).

Where the data controller or the data processor is a public authority or body, the data protection officer may be designated for several of its entities, taking account of the organisational structure of the public authority or body (art 35(3)).

In cases other than those referred to in paragraph 1, the data controller or data processor or associations and other bodies representing categories of data controllers or data processors may designate a data protection officer art 35(4)).

Under art 35(5) the data controller or data processor shall designate the data protection officer on the basis of professional qualities and, in particular, expert knowledge of data protection law and practices and ability to fulfil the tasks referred to in art 37. The necessary level of expert knowledge shall be determined in particular according to the data processing carried out and the protection required for the personal data processed by the data controller or the data processor (art 35(5)).

The data controller or the data processor shall ensure, in accordance with art 35(6), that any other professional duties of the data protection officer are compatible with the person's tasks and duties as data protection officer and do not result in a conflict of interests.

Also, art 35(7) provides that the data controller or the data processor shall designate a data protection officer for a period of at least two years. The data protection officer may be reappointed for further terms. During their term of office, the data protection officer may only be dismissed, if the data protection officer no longer fulfils the conditions required for the performance of their duties.

The data protection officer may be employed by the data controller or data processor, or fulfil his or her tasks on the basis of a service contract (art 35(8)).

The data controller or the data processor shall communicate the name and contact details of the data protection officer to the supervisory authority and to the public (art 35(9)).

Article 35(10) provides that data subjects shall have the right to contact the data protection officer on all issues related to the processing of the data subject's data and to request exercising the rights under the DPR.

Also, under art 35(11) the Commission shall be empowered to adopt delegated acts in accordance with art 86 for the purpose of further specifying the criteria and requirements for the core activities of the data controller or the data processor referred to in point (c) of paragraph 1 and the criteria for the professional qualities of the data protection officer referred to in paragraph 5.

Article 36 refers to the position of the data protection officer. Article 36(1) provides that the data controller or the data processor shall ensure that the data protection officer is properly and in a timely manner involved in all issues which relate to the protection of personal data.

Article 36(2) provides that the data controller or data processor shall ensure that the data protection officer performs the duties and tasks independently and does not receive any instructions as regards the exercise of the function. The data protection officer shall directly report to the management of the data controller or the data processor. Under art 36(3) the data controller or the data processor shall support the data protection officer in performing the tasks and shall provide staff, premises, equipment and any other resources necessary to carry out the duties and tasks referred to in art 37.

Article 37 refers to the tasks of the data protection officer. Under art 37(1) the data controller or the data processor shall entrust the data protection officer at least with the following tasks:

- to inform and advise the data controller or the data processor of their obligations pursuant to the DPR and to document this activity and the responses received;

- to monitor the implementation and application of the policies of the data controller or data processor in relation to the protection of personal data, including the assignment of responsibilities, the training of staff involved in the processing operations, and the related audits;

- to monitor the implementation and application of the DPR, in particular as to the requirements related to data protection by design, data protection by default and data security and to the information of data subjects and their requests in exercising their rights under the DPR;

- to ensure that the documentation referred to in art 28 is maintained;

- to monitor the documentation, notification and communication of personal data breaches pursuant to arts 31 and 32;

- to monitor the performance of the data protection impact assessment by the data controller or data processor and the application for prior authorisation or prior consultation, if required pursuant arts 33 and 34;

- to monitor the response to requests from the supervisory authority, and, within the sphere of the data protection officer's competence, co-operating with the supervisory authority at the latter's request or on the data protection officer's own initiative;

- to act as the contact point for the supervisory authority on issues related to the processing and consult with the supervisory authority, if appropriate, on his/her own initiative.

6.169   Chapter IV refers to data controllers and data processors, or data controllers and data processors. Section 1 sets out general obligations. Article 22 refers to the responsibility of the data controller.

The data controller shall adopt policies and implement appropriate measures to ensure and be able to demonstrate that the processing of personal data is performed in compliance with the DPR (art 22(1)).

The measures provided for in paragraph 1 are set out in art 22(2), and shall in particular include:

- keeping the documentation pursuant to art 28;

- implementing the data security requirements laid down in art 30;

- performing a data protection impact assessment pursuant to art 33;

- complying with the requirements for prior authorisation or prior consultation of the supervisory authority pursuant to art 34(1) and (2);

- designating a data protection officer pursuant to art 35(1).

Under art 22(3), the data controller shall implement mechanisms to ensure the verification of the effectiveness of the measures referred to in paragraphs 1 and 2. If proportionate, this verification shall be carried out by independent internal or external auditors (art 22(3)).

DPR: Data protection by design (DPbD)

6.170   Article 23 of the DPR refers to data protection by design and by default. This is an increasingly important area in data protection. Article 23(1) introduces this topic by saying that having regard to the state of the art and the cost of implementation, the data controller shall, both at the time of the determination of the means for processing and at the time of the processing itself, implement appropriate technical and organisational measures and procedures in such a way that the processing will meet the requirements of the DPR and ensure the protection of the rights of the data subject.

Under art 23(2), it is provided that the data controller shall implement mechanisms for ensuring that, by default, only those personal data are processed which are necessary for each specific purpose of the processing and are especially not collected or retained beyond the minimum necessary for those purposes, both in terms of the amount of the data and the time of their storage. In particular, those mechanisms shall ensure that by default personal data are not made accessible to an indefinite number of individuals (art 23(2)).

In addition, under art 23(3), the Commission is empowered to adopt delegated acts in accordance with art 86 for the purpose of specifying any further criteria and requirements for appropriate measures and mechanisms referred to in paragraph 1 and 2, in particular for data protection by design requirements applicable across sectors, products and services.

Furthermore, under art 23(4) the Commission is also empowered to lay down technical standards for the requirements laid down in paragraph 1 and 2.

Those implementing acts shall be adopted in accordance with the examination procedure referred to in art 87(2) (art 23(4)).

GDPR: Non-EU data controllers

6.171   Article 25 of the GDPR refers to representatives of data controllers not established in the EU. Article 25(1) provides that '[i]n the situation referred to in Article 3(2), the [data] controller shall designate a representative in the [EU].'
    Article 25(2) explains that this obligation shall not apply to:

- a data controller established in a third country where the Commission has decided that the third country ensures an adequate level of protection in accordance with art 41; or

- an enterprise employing fewer than 250 persons; or

- a public authority or body; or

- a data controller offering only occasionally goods or services to data subjects residing in the EU.

Under art 25(3) the representative shall be established in one of those member states where the data subjects whose personal data are processed in relation to the offering of goods or services to them, or whose behaviour is monitored, reside.
    Article 25(4) also provides that the designation of a representative by the data controller shall be without prejudice to legal actions which could be initiated against the data controller itself.

GDPR: data processors

6.172   Article 26 of the GDPR refers to data processors. Article 26(1) provides that where a processing operation is to be carried out on behalf of a data controller, the data controller shall choose a data processor providing sufficient guarantees to implement appropriate technical and organisational measures and procedures in such a way that the processing will meet the requirements of the DPR and ensure the protection of the rights of the data subject, in particular in respect of the technical security measures and organisational measures governing the processing to be carried out and shall ensure compliance with those measures.
    Under art 26(2) the carrying out of processing by a data processor shall be governed by a contract or other legal act binding the data processor to the data controller and stipulating in particular that the data processor shall:

- act only on instructions from the data controller, in particular, where the transfer of the personal data used is prohibited;

- employ only staff who have committed themselves to confidentiality or are under a statutory obligation of confidentiality;

- take all required measures pursuant to art 30;

- enlist another data processor only with the prior permission of the data controller;

- insofar as this is possible given the nature of the processing, create in agreement with the data controller the necessary technical and organisational requirements for the fulfilment of the data controller's obligation to respond to requests for exercising the data subject's rights laid down in Chapter III;

- assist the data controller in ensuring compliance with the obligations pursuant to arts 30 to 34;

- hand over all results to the data controller after the end of the processing and not process the personal data otherwise;

- make available to the data controller and the supervisory authority all information necessary to control compliance with the obligations laid down in this article.

Article 26(3) also sets out obligations whereby the data controller and the data processor shall document in writing the data controller's instructions and the data processor's obligations referred to in paragraph 2.

Under art 26(4), if a data processor processes personal data other than as instructed by the data controller, the data processor shall be considered to be a data controller in respect of that processing and shall be subject to the rules on joint data controllers laid down in art 24.

GDPR: Processing under authority

6.173　Article 27 refers to processing under the authority of the data controller and data processor and provides that the data processor and any person acting under the authority of the data controller or of the data processor who has access to personal data shall not process them except on instructions from the data controller, unless required to do so by Union or member state law.

Enforcement

6.174　Article 63 refers to enforcement. Art 63(1) provides that an enforceable measure of the supervisory authority of one member state shall be enforced in all member states concerned. In addition, art 63(2) provides that where a supervisory authority does not submit a draft measure to the consistency mechanism in breach of art 58(1) to (5), the measure of the supervisory authority shall not be legally valid and enforceable.

Importance

6.175　Costa and Poullet indicate that once the DPR 'comes into force, the document will be the new general legal framework of data protection, repealing [DPD95] more than 27 years after its adoption'.[181] The DPR as well as art 8(1)

181　Costa, L, and Poullet, Y, 'Privacy and the Regulation of 2012', *Computer Law & Security Review* (2012) (28), pp 254–262, at 254.

of the EU Charter of fundamental rights of 2000 and art 16(1) and reassert the importance of privacy and data protection 'as a fundamental right'.[182] '[E]ffective and more coherent protection' is required.[183]

In terms of policy as between modernising via a Directive or via a Regulation 'in order to ensure a full consistent and high level of protection equivalent in all the EU member states, a Regulation was judged as the adequate solution to ensure full harmonisation'[184] throughout the EU. The Commission may also oversee and monitor the national data protection authorities (DPAs).[185]

Individuals are rarely aware about how their data are collected and processed while they are surfing on the internet at home, using their mobile phones, walking down a video-surveyed street or with an TFID tag embedded in their clothes and so on.[186] There is a need for greater transparency. As regards data processing, 'transparency translates the widening of the knowledge about information systems ... coupled with fairness'.[187]

Transparency

6.176 Article 5 of the GDPR provides that personal data shall be 'processed lawfully, fairly and in a transparent manner in relation to the data subject'. Transparency 'requires greater awareness among citizens about the processing going on: its existence, its content and the flows generated in and out by using terminals.

Transparency also relates to security of data and risk management.[188]

Some commentators have suggested the GDPR could go further. It is suggested that 'the greater the flow of information systems the more opaque it becomes in modern information systems and with new ICT applications. In that case the right to transparency must increase alongside these new processes.'[189]

Discussion

6.177 Commentators have indicated that parts of the GDPR contain particular 'legislative innovation'.[190] Some examples of this innovation are indicated to include:

- data protection principles;

- data subjects' rights;

- data controllers' and data processors' obligations; and

- regulation issues regarding technologies.[191]

---

182 Ibid, at 254.
183 Ibid.
184 Ibid, at 255.
185 Ibid.
186 Ibid, p 256.
187 Ibid.
188 Ibid, pp 254–262, at 256.
189 Ibid, pp 254–262, at 256.
190 Ibid, pp 254–292.
191 Ibid.

It has been noted that while the DPD95 emphasises protection for the fundamental right and freedoms of individuals 'and in particular their right to privacy', the DPR in arts 1 and 2 stresses the need to protect the fundamental right and freedoms of individuals 'and in particular their right to the protection of personal data'.[192] Further references also emphasise data protection as a stand-alone concept from privacy, such as data protection assessments and data protection by design (DPbD)

There is a new consistency mechanism whereby the national data protection authorities are obliged to co-operate with each other and with the Commission (Chapter VII, section 10).[193] Two examples given include data protection assessments and also obligation in terms of notifying data subjects in relation to data breaches.[194]

The obligations in terms of insufficient security and data breaches are more detailed in the DPR than previously.[195] The obligations are now more detailed than the obligation in relation to telcos and ISPs in the ePD.[196] Data breaches are referred to in arts 4 and 9 of the DPR. In the event of a data breach the data controller must notify the ICO (art 31). In addition the data controller must also communicate to the data subjects if there is a risk of harm to their privacy or personal data (art 32).

Data portability is a newly expressed right. It 'implies the right of data subjects to obtain from the [data] controller a copy of their personal data in a structured and commonly used format (art 18(1)) ... data portability is a kind of right to backup and use personal information under the management of the data controller. Second, data portability grants the right to transmit personal data and other information provided by the data subject from one automated processing system to another one (art 18(2)) ... therefore the right to take personal data and leave.'[197]

The DPD95 stated that data controller must not process personal data excessively. However, this is now more limited. The GDPR states that data collection and processing must be limited to the minimum.

Broader parameters are contained in the GDPR in relation to consent. The definition and conditions are broader than previously. The inclusion of the words freely given, informed and explicit in art 4(5) is more specific than the previous unambiguously' consented.

The DPD95 art 15 protection in relation to automated individual decisions 'is considerably enlarged'[198] regarding profiling in GDPR art 20. The use of, *inter alia*, the word 'measure' in the DPR as opposed to 'decision' in the DPD95 means the category of activity encompassed within the obligation is now much wider.[199] There is greater data subject protection. While there were previously

192 Ibid, p 255.
193 Ibid, pp 254–262, at 255.
194 Ibid.
195 Ibid, pp 254–262, at 256.
196 Ibid.
197 Ibid, p 15.
198 Ibid, pp 254–262, at 258. Also see Council of Europe Recommendation regarding profiling, 25 November 2010.
199 Ibid, pp 258–259.

two exemptions, in terms of contract and also a specific law, the GDPR adds a third in terms of consent from the data subject. However, data controllers will need to ensure a stand-alone consent for profiling separate from any consent for data collection and processing per se.[200]

The GDPR also moves significantly further than the DPD95 in terms of creating obligations, responsibility and liability on data controllers.[201] Appropriate policies must be implemented by data controllers, as well as complaint data processing, secure data processing, the undertaking of data protection impact assessments, shared liability as between joint data controllers, appointing representatives within the EU where the data controller is located elsewhere and provisions regarding data processors.[202]

While the DPD95 imposed compensation obligations on data controllers in the case harm to data subjects, the GDPR extends liability to data processors.[203] In addition, where harm is suffered by data subjects any joint data controller and or data processors shall be 'jointly and severally liable for the entire amount of the damage'.[204]

The concepts of data protection by design, data protection by default and impact assessments all emphasise the ability of the data protection regime to become involved in standard setting and the regulation of particular technologies and technical solutions.[205] The Ontario Data Protection Commissioner, Anne Cavoukian, refers to data protection and privacy by design.[206] The GDPR describes it as follows in DPR art 23(1), by indicating that:

> '[h]aving regard to the state of the art and the cost of implementation, the data controller shall, both at the time of the determination of the means for processing and at the time of the processing itself, implement appropriate technical and organisational measures and procedures in such a way that the processing will meet the requirements of the [G]DPR and ensure the protection of the rights of the data subject' (art 23(1)).

Data protection by default is referred to and defines in art 23(2) as follows:

> 'The data controller shall implement mechanisms for ensuring that, by default, only those personal data are processed which are necessary for each specific purpose of the processing and are especially not collected or retained beyond the minimum necessary for those purposes, both in terms of the amount of the data and the time of their storage. In particular, those mechanisms shall ensure that by default personal data are not made accessible to an indefinite number of individuals' (art 23(2)).

---

200 Ibid, p 259.
201 Ibid.
202 Ibid.
203 Ibid.
204 Ibid.
205 Ibid.
206 For example, Anne Cavoukian, DPA Ontario, Privacy Guidelines for RFID Information Systems, at www.ipc.on.ca, says the privacy and security must be built into the solution from the outset, at the design stage. Referred to ibid.

These accord with the general principle of data minimisation, whereby non-personal data should be processed first and where the collection and processing of personal data is required, it must be the minimum data as opposed to the minimum data which is so processed. This is referred to in art 5(c).

Data subjects have more control over their personal data. In the context of social networks, 'individual profiles should be kept private from others by default'.[207]

The concept of PbD and data protection by default as provided in the DPR are predicted soon to impact upon organisational contracts and contracting practices relating to data processing activities.[208]

As mentioned above, one of the new areas is the obligation to engage in data protection impact assessments. Article 33(1) provides that that:

> '[w]here processing operations present specific risks to the rights and freedoms of data subjects by virtue of their nature, their scope or their purposes, the data controller or the data processor acting on the data controller's behalf shall carry out an assessment of the impact of the envisaged processing operations on the protection of personal data.'

This is particularly so where the envisaged processing could give rise to specific risks.

One further addition is the possibility of mass group claims or claims through representative organisations. This is referred to as 'collective redress' and allows data protection and privacy NGOs to complain to both the ICO and to the courts (see arts 73(2), 74, 75 and 76(1)).[209] 'Civil procedure rules'[210] may also need to be introduced.

The regime as regards trans-border data flows or TBDFs will be 'significantly altered'.[211] These are included in arts 40 and 41.

Enhanced provisions

6.178 One of the more important extensions and enhancements relates to the right to be forgotten; the 'right to be forgotten and to erasure, which consists of securing from the [data] controller the erasure of personal data as well prevention of any further dissemination of his data'.[212] (It is also said to interface with the new right to data portability.[213])

---

207 Ibid, at p 260, and referring to European Data Protection Supervisor on the Communications from Commission to the European Parliament, the Council, the Economic and Social Committee and the Committee of the Regions, 'A Comprehensive Approach on Personal Data Protection in the European Union', at p 23.

208 Ibid, at p 260.

209 See also Commission on a common framework for collective redress, http://ec.europa.eu/consumers/redress_cons/collective_redress_en.htm.

210 Costa, L, and Poullet, Y, 'Privacy and the Regulation of 2012', *Computer Law & Security Review* (2012) (28), pp 254–262, at 261.

211 Ibid.

212 Ibid, at pp 254–262, at 256.

213 Ibid.

The RtbF is even more enhanced in instances where the personal data was originally disclosed when the data subject was a child. Some commentators refer to the option of an entire 'clean slate.'[214]

> 'The use of data from social networks in employment contexts is a representative example. Personal data such as photos taken in private contexts have been used to refuse job positions and fire people. But forgetfulness is larger. It is one dimension of how people deal with their own history, being related not only to leaving the past behind but also to living in the present without the threat of a kind of "Miranda" warning, where whatever you say can be used against you in the future. In this sense the right to be forgotten is closely related to entitlements of dignity and self-development. Once again, privacy appears as the pre-requisite of our liberties, assuring the possibility to freely express ourselves and move freely on the street …'[215]

The RtbF is most clearly associated and related to the following in particular:

- where the personal data is no longer necessary in relation to the purposes for which they were originally collected and processed (and the associated finality principle);

- where the data subject has withdrawn their consent for processing;

- where data subjects object to the processing of the personal data concerning them;

---

214 Ibid, at pp 254–262, at 257. In terms of criminal convictions and the issue of deletion note the case of *Chief Constable of Humberside v Information Commissioner and another* [2009] EWCA Civ 1079 where a deletion request was refused, largely on crime policy issues. However, the ECHR has held that there was a breach in the context of an historical disclosure of a person's caution record in the context of an employment application. In this instance there was also an intervening change in weeding policy and certain police records which were previously weeded, were no longer weeded. The ECHR held that '[t]he cumulative effect of these shortcomings is that the Court is not satisfied that there were, and are, sufficient safeguards in the system for retention and disclosure of criminal record data to ensure that data relating to the applicant's private life have not been, and will not be, disclosed in violation of her right to respect for her private life. The retention and disclosure of the applicant's caution data accordingly cannot be regarded as being in accordance with the law. There has therefore been a violation of Article 8 of the Convention in the present case.' *Case of MM v The United Kingdom*, ECHR (Application no 24029/07) 13 November 2012, para 207. The ECHR also held a violation in relation to the retention of fingerprint and DNA samples of persons acquitted of offences, in Case of S and *Marper v The United Kingdom*, ECHR (Applications nos 30562/04 and 30566/04) 4 December 2008. See also *Goggins and others v The United Kingdom*, ECHR (Applications nos 30089/04, 14449/06, 24968/07, 13870/08, 36363/08, 23499/09, 43852/09 and 64027/09), 19 July 2011; Protection of Freedoms Bill and Protection of Freedoms Act 2012; Police and Criminal Evidence Act 1984 (PACE); Retention Guidelines for Nominal Records on the Police National Computer 2006 drawn up by the Association of Chief Police Officers in England and Wales (ACPO); Human Rights Act 1998; *R (on the application of GC) v The Commissioner of Police of the Metropolis* and *R (on the application of C) v The Commissioner of Police of the Metropolis* ([2011] UKSC 21 on 18 May 2011.

215 Costa, L, and Poullet, Y, 'Privacy and the Regulation of 2012', *Computer Law & Security Review* (2012) (28), pp 254–262, at 257.

- where the processing of the personal data does not comply with the DPR.[216]

The DPR and the right to be forgotten 'amplifies the effectiveness of data protection principles and rules'.[217]

Data subjects can have their data erased under the right to be forgotten when there is no compliance as well as where they simply withdraw their consent.[218] User control and data subject control are, therefore, enhanced.

The GDPR and RtbF create the following compliance obligations, namely:

- erasing personal data and not processing it further;

- informing third parties that the data subject has requested the deletion of the personal data;

- taking responsibility for publication by third parties under the data controller's authority[219] (arts 17, 2 and 8).

The DPR also enhances and expands the various powers of the national authorities, such as the ICO.[220]

Comment

6.179   All organisations need to become very familiar with the DPR. While not yet finalised, the current draft is close to final. It reflects the shape of the new and expanded EU data protection regime. While in some instances the current compliance mechanisms are continued, there are many new requirements to compliance. Organisations need to start now in terms of ensuring compliance. Indeed, the most prudent organisations will continually adopt best practice, and data protection compliance is an area where best practice has positive benefits above and beyond mere compliance.

As indicated above, there are still certain amendments being made to the text of the Regulation. These include from the Parliament and the Council. The Council has issued the most recent consolidated version.[221] An outline timetable for further amendment and finalisation of the GDPR has also been issued.[222]

Privacy by design

6.180   It has been suggested that 'law should play a more active role in establishing best practices for emerging online trends'.[223] Privacy by design

---

216 Costa, L, and Poullet, Y, 'Privacy and the Regulation of 2012', *Computer Law & Security Review* (2012) (28), pp 254–262, at 257.
217 Ibid.
218 Ibid.
219 Ibid.
220 Costa, L, and Poullet, Y, 'Privacy and the Regulation of 2012', *Computer Law & Security Review* (2012) (28), pp 254–262, at 260.
221 See Version 21/04/15 – Council's Consolidated Version of March 2015. Available at www.statewatch.org/news/2015/apr/eu-council-dp-reg-4column-2015.pdf.
222 See www.eppgroup.eu/fr/news/Data-protection-reform-timetable.
223 McGeveran, W, 'Disclosure, Endorsement, and Identity in Social marketing', *Illinois Law Review* (2009) (4), pp 1105–1166, at 1105.

is a prime example. One of the most important and developing areas of data protection is the concept of privacy by design or PbD. Originally developed as a follow-on from the data protection legal regime, it is now being recognised more widely, and is also being explicitly referred to and recognised in primary legislation itself.

The concept of PbD is complementary to data protection law and regulation. The idea is acknowledged to start with Dr Ann Cavoukian, the Information and Privacy Commissioner for Ontario, Canada. She states that:

> 'the increasing complexity and interconnectedness of information technologies [requires] building privacy right into system design ... the concept of Privacy by Design (PbD), ... describe[s] the philosophy of embedding privacy proactively into technology itself – making it the default.'[224]

The Information and Privacy Commissioner for Ontario refers to seven principles of PbD.[225] These are set out below.

1. Proactive not reactive; preventative not remedial

    The Privacy by Design (PbD) approach is characterised by proactive rather than reactive measures. It anticipates and prevents privacy invasive events before they happen. PbD does not wait for privacy risks to materialise; nor does it offer remedies for resolving privacy infractions once they have occurred – it aims to prevent them from occurring. In short, Privacy by Design comes before the fact, not after.

2. Privacy as the default setting

    We can all be certain of one thing – the default rules! Privacy by Design seeks to deliver the maximum degree of privacy by ensuring that personal data are automatically protected in any given IT system or business practice. If an individual does nothing, their privacy still remains intact. No action is required on the part of the individual to protect their privacy – it is built into the system, by default.

3. Privacy embedded into design

    Privacy by Design is embedded into the design and architecture of IT systems and business practices. It is not bolted on as an add-on, after the fact. The result is that privacy becomes an essential component of the core functionality being delivered. Privacy is integral to the system, without diminishing functionality.

4. Full functionality – positive-sum, not zero-sum

    Privacy by Design seeks to accommodate all legitimate interests and objectives in a positive-sum 'win-win' manner, not through a dated, zero-sum approach, where unnecessary trade-offs are made. Privacy by Design

---

224 Available at http://privacybydesign.ca/about/.
225 Available at www.privacybydesign.ca/content/uploads/2009/08/7foundationalprinciples.pdf.

avoids the pretence of false dichotomies, such as privacy vs security, demonstrating that it is possible to have both.

5. End-to-end security – full lifecycle protection

    Privacy by Design, having been embedded into the system prior to the first element of information being collected, extends securely throughout the entire lifecycle of the data involved – strong security measures are essential to privacy, from start to finish. This ensures that all data are securely retained, and then securely destroyed at the end of the process, in a timely fashion. Thus, Privacy by Design ensures cradle-to-grave, secure lifecycle management of information, end to end.

6. Visibility and transparency – keep it open

    Privacy by Design seeks to assure all stakeholders that whatever the business practice or technology involved, it is in fact, operating according to the stated promises and objectives, subject to independent verification. Its component parts and operations remain visible and transparent, to users and providers alike. Remember, trust but verify.

7. Respect for user privacy – keep it user-centric

    Above all, Privacy by Design requires architects and operators to keep the interests of the individual uppermost by offering such measures as strong privacy defaults, appropriate notice, and empowering user-friendly options. Keep it user-centric.[226]

DPD95 Recital 46 states that the protection of the rights and freedoms of data subjects regarding the processing of personal data requires appropriate technical and organisational measures be taken, both at the time of the design of the processing system and at the time of the processing itself. This is particularly in order to maintain security and to prevent any unauthorised processing. It is incumbent on the member states to ensure that data controllers comply with these measures. These measures must ensure an appropriate level of security, taking into account the state of the art and the costs of their implementation in relation to the risks inherent in the processing and the nature of the data to be protected.

DPD95 Recital 53 states that whereas, however, certain processing operations are likely to pose specific risks to the rights and freedoms of data subjects by virtue of their nature, their scope or their purposes, such as that of excluding individuals from a right, benefit or a contract, or by virtue of the *specific use of new technologies*; whereas it is for member states, if they so wish, to specify such risks in their legislation.

DPD95 Recital 54 states that whereas with regard to all the processing undertaken in society, the amount posing such specific risks should be very limited; whereas member states must provide that the supervisory authority, or the data protection official in cooperation with the authority, check such processing

---

226 Ibid.

prior to it being carried out; whereas following this prior check, the supervisory authority may, according to its national law, give an opinion or an authorisation regarding the processing; whereas such checking may equally take place in the course of the preparation either of a measure of the national parliament or of a measure based on such a legislative measure, which defines the nature of the processing and lays down appropriate safeguards.

The Commission proposed an enhanced data protection regime including PbD.[227] Article 23 of the GDPR refers to data protection by design and by default. This is an increasingly important area in data protection. Article 23(1) introduces this topic by saying that having regard to the state of the art and the cost of implementation, the data controller shall, both at the time of the determination of the means for processing and at the time of the processing itself, implement appropriate technical and organisational measures and procedures in such a way that the processing will meet the requirements of the DPR and ensure the protection of the rights of the data subject.

Under art 23(2), it is provided that the data controller shall implement mechanisms for ensuring that, by default, only those personal data are processed which are necessary for each specific purpose of the processing and are especially not collected or retained beyond the minimum necessary for those purposes, both in terms of the amount of the data and the time of their storage. In particular, those mechanisms shall ensure that by default personal data are not made accessible to an indefinite number of individuals (art 23(2)).

In addition, under art 23(3), the Commission is empowered to adopt delegated acts in accordance with art 86 for the purpose of specifying any further criteria and requirements for appropriate measures and mechanisms referred to in paragraphs 1 and 2, in particular for data protection by design requirements applicable across sectors, products and services.

Furthermore, under art 23(4) the Commission is also empowered to lay down technical standards for the requirements laid down in paragraph 1 and 2. Those implementing acts shall be adopted in accordance with the examination procedure referred to in art 87(2) (art 23(4)).

PbD is embraced by the ICO in the UK. The ICO refers to PbD by saying that 'Privacy by Design is an approach whereby privacy and data protection compliance is designed into systems holding information right from the start, rather than being bolted on afterwards or ignored, as has too often been the case.'[228] It provides[229] the following documents and guidance:

- Privacy by Design report;[230]

227 See DPR, Spiekermann, S, 'The Challenges of Privacy by Design', *Communications of the ACM* (2012) (55), pp 38–40; Spiekermann, S, and Cranor, LF, 'Engineering Privacy', *IEEE Transactions on Software Engineering* (2009) (35), pp 67–82.

228 ICO website, available at www.ico.gov.uk/for_organisations/data_protection/topic_guides/privacy_by_design.aspx.

229 Ibid.

230 *Privacy by Design*, Information Commissioner's Office (2008). Available at www.ico.gov.uk/for_organisations/data_protection/topic_guides/privacy_by_design.aspx.

- Privacy by Design implementation plan;[231]

- Privacy Impact Assessment (PIA) handbook;[232]

- ICO technical guidance note on Privacy Enhancing Technologies (PETs);[233]

- Enterprise Privacy Group paper on PETs;

- HIDE (Homeland security, biometric Identification and personal Detection Ethics);

- Glossary of privacy and data protection terms;

- Privacy Impact Assessments – international study (Loughborough University).

The ICO report on Privacy by Design Foreword notes that:

> 'The capacity of organisations to acquire and use our personal details has increased dramatically since our data protection laws were first passed. There is an ever increasing amount of personal information collected and held about us as we go about our daily lives … we have seen a dramatic change in the capability of organisations to exploit modern technology that uses our information to deliver services, this has not been accompanied by a similar drive to develop new effective technical and procedural privacy safeguards. We have seen how vulnerable our most personal of details can be and these should not be put at risk.'[234]

In the report, Toby Stevens, Director, of the Enterprise Privacy Group, adds that:

> 'This report is the first stage in bridging the current gap in the development and adoption of privacy-friendly solutions as part of modern information systems. It aims to address the current problems related to the handling of personal information and put into place a model for privacy by design that will ensure privacy achieves the same structured and professional recognition as information security has today.'[235]

The report describes PbD as follows,

> 'The purpose of privacy by design is to give due consideration to privacy needs prior to the development of new initiatives – in other words, to consider the impact of a system or process on individuals' privacy and to do this throughout

---

231 Available at www.ico.gov.uk/upload/documents/pdb_report_html/pbd_ico_implementation_plan.pdf.
232 Available at www.ico.gov.uk/for_organisations/data_protection/topic_guides/privacy_impact_assessment.aspx.
233 *Privacy by Design, An Overview of Privacy Enhancing Technologies*, 26 November 2008. Available at www.ico.gov.uk/for_organisations/data_protection/topic_guides/privacy_by_design.aspx.
234 *Privacy by Design*, Information Commissioner's Office (2008). Available atwww.ico.gov.uk/for_organisations/data_protection/topic_guides/privacy_by_design.aspx.
235 Ibid, p 2.

the systems lifecycle, thus ensuring that appropriate controls are implemented and maintained.'[236]

The report refers to the various lifecycles that arise in an organisation.[237] These can be products, services, systems and processes.

'For a privacy by design approach to be effective, it must take into account the full lifecycle of any system or process, from the earliest stages of the system business case, through requirements gathering and design, to delivery, testing, operations, and out to the final decommissioning of the system.

This lifetime approach ensures that privacy controls are stronger, simpler and therefore cheaper to implement, harder to by-pass, and fully embedded in the system as part of its core functionality.

However, neither current design practices in the private and public sectors, nor existing tools tend to readily support such an approach. Current privacy practices and technologies are geared towards 'spot' implementations and 'spot' verifications to confirm that privacy designs and practices are correct at a given moment within a given scope of inspection.'[238]

The ICO report makes a number of recommendations in relation to PbD practice in the UK.[239] These are set out below:

'Working with industry bodies to build an *executive mandate for privacy by design*, supported by sample business cases for the costs, benefits and risks associated with the processing of personal information, and promotion of executive awareness of key privacy and identity concepts so that privacy is reflected in the business cases for new systems.

Encouraging widespread use of *privacy impact assessments throughout the systems lifecycle*, and ensuring that these assessments are both maintained and published where appropriate to demonstrate transparency of privacy controls.

Supporting the development of *cross-sector standards for data sharing* both within and between organisations, so that privacy needs are harmonised with the pressures on public authorities and private organisations to share personal information.

Nurturing the development of *practical privacy standards* that will help organisations to turn the legal outcomes mandated under data protection laws into consistent, provable privacy implementations.

Promoting current and future research into PETs that deliver commercial products to manage consent and revocation, privacy-friendly identification and authentication, and prove the effectiveness of privacy controls.

Establishing more rigorous compliance and enforcement mechanisms by assigning responsibility for privacy management within organisations to nominated individuals, urging organisations to demonstrate greater clarity in

---

236 Ibid, p 7.
237 Ibid.
238 Ibid, pp 7–8.
239 Ibid, summarised at p 3, and in detail at pp 22–31.

their personal information processing, and empowering and providing the ICO with the ability to investigate and enforce compliance where required.

The government, key industry representatives and academics, and the ICO are urged to consider, prioritise and set in motion plans to deliver these recommendations and hence make privacy by design a reality.'[240]

The report highlights the need and context for PbD in relation to the many instances of data loss in the UK (and internationally). It states that:

'Consumer trust in the ability of public authorities and private organisations to manage personal information is at an all-time low ebb. A stream of high-profile privacy incidents in the UK over the past year has shaken confidence in the data sharing agenda for government with associated impacts on high-profile data management programmes, and businesses are having to work that much harder to persuade customers to release personal information to them.'[241]

PbD is part of the solution whereby 'the evolution of a new approach to the management of personal information that ingrains privacy principles into every part of every system in every organisation'.[242]

Organisations need to address many key privacy and data protection issues, such as:

'assessing information risks from the individual's perspective; adopting transparency and data minimisation principles; exploiting opportunities for differentiation through enhanced privacy practices; and ensuring that privacy needs influence their identity management agenda (since identity technologies are invariably needed to deliver effective privacy approaches).'[243]

PbD is one of the more important innovations in data protection generally. This is reflected in the DPR. All organisations will need to apprise themselves of the concept and the regulatory compliance issues. The above Google requirement to implement PbD is also timely and reflects the importance that enterprise, both large and small, needs to engage the benefits, as well as the requirements, of PbD.

Privacy impact assessments[244] are also referred to in the DPR and may also be relevant in the context of PbD. PbD, privacy impact assessments are also relevant in the context of developing cloud services.[245] Cloud services also

---

240 Ibid, note emphasis in original.
241 Ibid, p 6.
242 Ibid.
243 Ibid.
244 Wright, D, 'The State of the Art in Privacy Impact Assessments', *Computer Law & Security Review* (2012) (28), pp 54–61.
245 Cloud and data protection reliability and compliance issues are referred to Clarke R, 'How Reliable is Cloudsourcing? A Review of Articles in the Technical Media 2005–11,' *Computer Law & Security Review* (2012) (28), pp 90–95. Kind and Rajy also research the area of the protections of sensitive personal data and cloud computing, see King, NJ, and Raja, VT, 'Protecting the Privacy and Security of Sensitive Customer Data in the Cloud', *Computer Law & Security Review* (2012) (28), pp 308–319.

raise important data protection and security considerations and these should be carefully considered by customers as well as providers.[246]

As the GDPR comes to be rolled out, we will increasingly hear of PbD, Privacy Impact Assessments, privacy engineering, data quality, data governance, data due diligence, risk assessments, security assessments, data security and data breach incident response plans and even careers in privacy.

Piracy and identifying users

6.181 Internet-related copyright piracy has been a thorny issue for a number of years. Some of the legal efforts have included litigation to identify individual end-users alleged to be involved in copyright infringement. More recently, the push for identification in large numbers is somewhat moderated by an alternative strategy of having internet access providers notify users on a graduated basis, escalating to potential cutting off of services. This is sometimes known as 'three step' graduated responses or warnings. To some extent it might be argued that this involved a more restrained and proportionate use of individuals' personal data.

Some have suggested that copyright and online infringement can sometimes be over-zealously enforced.[247] Others also criticise the (over) criminalisation of online infringement and also the over-zealous attempts at seeking court orders to identify individual end user infringers.[248] There is a growing argument for other or additional solutions.[249]

Big Data

6.182 The many issues emanating from the (late) arrival of Big Data[250] will come to create many new services, models and legal queries. This will cross the corporate business worlds, as well as the home and everything in between. Data protection is one issue. A related issue is security.

---

246 See, for example ICO, *Guidance on the Use of Cloud Computing*, available at www.ico.gov. uk/for_organisations/data_protection/topic_guides/online/cloud_computing.aspx; Article 29 Working Party, *Opinion 05/2012 on Cloud Computing*, WP 196, 1 July 2012; Lanois, P, 'Caught in the Clouds: The Web 2.0, Cloud Computing, and Privacy?', *Northwestern Journal of Technology and Intellectual Property* (2010) (9), pp 29–49; Pinguelo, FM, and Muller, BW, 'Avoid the Rainy Day: Survey of US Cloud Computing Caselaw', *Boston College Intellectual Property & Technology Forum* (2011), 1–7; Kattan, IR, 'Cloudy Privacy Protections: Why the Stored Communications Act Fails to Protect the Privacy of Communications Stored in the Cloud,' *Vandenburg Journal of Entertainment and Technology Law* (2010–2011) (13), pp 617–656.
247 See for example C hui Yun Tan, '*Lawrence Lessig v Liberation Music Pty Ltd*: YouTube's Hand (or Bots) in the Over-Zealous Enforcement of Copyright', EIPR (2014) (36) 347.
248 See P Sugden, 'The Power of One! The Failure of Criminal Copyright Laws (Piracy) to Blend into the Greater Cultural Consciousness!' EIPR (2014) (26) 376. Also note generally KT O'Sullivan, 'Enforcing Copyright Online: Internet Service Provider Obligations and the European Charter of fundamental rights,' EIPR (2014) (36) 577.
249 S Gorbylev, 'Fighting Online Copyright Piracy: Are There Any Alternatives to Traditional Litigation?' EIPR (2014) (36) 413.
250 T Hoeren, 'Big Data and the Ownership in Data: Recent Developments in Europe,' EIPR (2014) (36) 751.

Internet of Things

6.183 The potentially unlimited nature of new data collections and data uses which results from connecting home compliances (from fridges to curtains to TVs) and body wearable clothing and devices to the internet also creates issues. Data protection and security are some of the foremost issues. This also adds to the Big Data mountain.

Deletion, rectification, right to be forgotten

6.184 The field of deletion of online materials will continue to gather pace. One aspect of this relates to the deletion of personal data. While the *Google Spain* case has received a lot of attention,[251] both academic and media, this merely reflects existing law under the DPD 95, not the forthcoming GDPR. Arguably the GDPR expands this deletion or TtbF requirement. However, given the existing DPD95, one can query the level of surprise at the decision. There is also merit in querying the pursuit of moonshot (or speculative) litigation in this instance. Moonshot litigation does not always work and can sometimes backfire. While corporates do indeed face difficult questions from time to time and litigation might sometimes be necessary, but certain litigation should also be avoided. The contentious and non-contentious messages coming from corporates in this space can sometimes be more positive, nuanced and improved.

Damages

6.185 One of the most important developing issues is the ability of individuals to sue for damages for breach of their data protection rights. Arguably, a perceived inhibitor on such litigation to-date is not so much that there have been no instances where an infringement has taken place, but rather that some have felt it difficult to show, or show sufficient, monetary damages.

The recent case of *Vidal-Hall v Google*[252] may change this perception. In addition to dismissing the frequent jurisdictional objection, the Court of Appeal made it easier for individuals to make data protection damages claims. The decision means that a claim for monetary damages is possible independent of showing financial loss by virtue of the data protection infringement. While the decision is only on certain intermediary issues and not the full hearing, Google has sought leave to appeal the decision to the Supreme Court.

A cautionary note might be that the brokered settlement in the US of $19 million was rejected as not being sufficient. This relates to the Target data breach incident.

An additional cautionary example is a data protection fine against the government for an error relating to a single letter. The fine was £8 million.

---

251 J Jones, 'Control-Alter-Delete: The "Right to be forgotten" – Google Spain SL, Google Inc v Agencia Espanola de Proteccion de Datos', EIPR (2014) (36) 595.
252 [2015] EWCA Civ 311.

Sample of ICO data loss/data breaches, fines and convictions

Issue	Date	Party	Breach	Penalty
Unsolicited marketing texts. PECR.	2 December 2014	Parklife Manchester Limited	Company behind Manchester annual festival the Parklife Weekender. Fined for sending unsolicited marketing text messages. Texts to 70,000 people who had bought tickets to last year's event. Appeared on recipients' mobile phone as sent by 'Mum'.	£70,000
Data breaches	18 November 2014	NHS Grampian	NHS Grampian ordered to ensure patients' information is better protected. Six data breaches within 13 months. Papers containing sensitive personal data abandoned in public areas of the hospital. In one case information was found at a local supermarket.	Enforcement notice
Unlawful accessing	13 November 2014	Pharmacist/ West Sussex Primary Care Trust	Former pharmacist at West Sussex Primary Care Trust prosecuted for unlawfully accessing medical records of family members, work colleagues and local health professionals. Harkanwarjit Dhanju was fined.	Fined £1,000, ordered to pay a £100 victim surcharge and £608.30 prosecution costs
Company director. Fine. Illegally accessing database.		Matthew Devlin	Company director Matthew Devlin fined after illegally accessing Everything Everywhere's (EE) customer databases. Devlin used details of customers due a mobile phone upgrade to target them with services offered by his own telecoms companies.	Fine

Issue	Date	Party	Breach	Penalty
Data breach	31 October 2014	Worldview Limited	Hotel booking website fined for a serious data breach where a vulnerability on the company's site allowed attackers to access the full payment card details of 3,814 customers.	£7,500
Data breaches. Seventh data protection principle. Undertaking.	24 October 2014	Gwynedd Council	An undertaking to comply with the seventh data protection principle signed by Gwynedd Council following two breaches of the Data Protection Act.	
Nuisance calls	29 September 2014	EMC Advisory Services Limited	Devon marketing firm responsible for hundreds of nuisance calls fined. 630 complaints to the ICO and the TPS between 1 March 2013 and 28 February 2014. Failed to make sure that those registered with the TPS, or who had previously asked not to be contacted, were not being called.	£70,000
Undertaking. First, third and seventh data protection principle.	25 September 2014	Norfolk Community Health & Care NHS Trust	An undertaking to comply with the first, third and seventh data protection principle signed by Norfolk Community Health & Care NHS Trust. This follows an investigation involving the inadvertent sharing of data with a referral management centre.	
			The data which was provided in error consisted of referrals from health care services and affected 128,842 data subjects.	

Issue	Date	Party	Breach	Penalty
Harassing calls. 214 complaints to ICO and Telephone Preference Service (TPS). PECR. Consent. Staff training.	22 September 2014	Kwik Fix Plumbers Limited (previously Boiler Shield Limited)	Boiler insurance firm fined for harassing elderly victims with nuisance calls.	£90,000
Breaches. Prisons.	20 August 2014	Ministry of Justice	A monetary penalty notice served on the Ministry of Justice for £180,000 over serious failings in the way prisons in England and Wales handled people's information.	£180,000
Banker. Unlawful access.	22 August 2014	Dalvinder Singh/ Santander	Birmingham banker fined after admitting reading colleagues' bank accounts. He worked in Santander UK's suspicious activity reporting unit at their Leicester office. His role investigating allegations of money laundering meant he was able to view customer accounts. Used his access to look at 11 colleagues' accounts, to learn how much their salaries and bonuses were.	
Unsolicited calls	24 July 2014	Reactiv Media Limited	ICO has served, Reactiv Media Limited, with a £50,000 fine after an investigation discovered they had made unsolicited calls to hundreds of people who had registered with the Telephone Preference Service (TPS).	£50,000

Issue	Date	Party	Breach	Penalty
Website. Breach. Hacking.	23 July 2014	Think W3 Limited	An online travel services company served with a monetary penalty after a serious breach of the Data Protection Act revealed thousands of people's details to a malicious hacker.	£150,000
Owner of company. Failure to notify changes.	15 July 2014	Jayesh Shah	Owner of marketing company trading as Vintels prosecuted for failing to notify ICO of changes to notification. Jayesh Shah was fined £4,000, ordered to pay costs of £2,703 and a £400 victim surcharge.	£4,000, £2,703 and £400
Blagging. Unlawful access.	24 April 2014	Barry Spencer	A man who ran a company that tricked organisations into revealing personal details about customers ordered to pay a total of £20,000 in fines and prosecution costs, as well as a confiscation order of over £69,000 at a hearing at Isleworth Crown Court.	£20,000 plus confiscation order of over £69,000
Unsolicited marketing calls	1 April 2014	Amber UPVC Fabrications Ltd (T/A Amber Windows)	Home improvement company Amber Windows served £50,000 ICO fine after unsolicited marketing calls to people who had registered with the Telephone Preference Service (TPS).	£50,000
Security. Lost data. Breach.	17 March 2014	Kent Police	Kent Police fined after highly sensitive and confidential information, including copies of police interview tapes, were left in a basement at the former site of a police station.	£100,000
Security. Data loss. Hacking. Threats.	28 February 2014	British Pregnancy Advice Service	British Pregnancy Advice Service fined. Hacker threatened to publish thousands of names of people who sought advice on abortion, pregnancy and contraception.	£200,000

Issue	Date	Party	Breach	Penalty
Blagging. Prosecution. Conviction.	24 January 2014		Six men who were part of a company that tricked organisations into revealing personal details about customers sentenced for conspiring to breach the Data Protection Act.	
Data loss. Breach. Security.	14 January 2014	Department of Justice Northern Ireland	A monetary penalty notice on Department of Justice Northern Ireland after a filing cabinet containing details of a terrorist incident was sold at auction.	£185,000
Spam texts.	16 December 2013	First Financial (UK) Limited	A monetary penalty notice served on First Financial (UK) Limited after the payday loans company sent millions of spam text messages.	£175,000
Prosecution. Unlawful access.	3 December 2013	Steven Tennison	A former manager who oversaw the finances of a GP's practice in Maidstone prosecuted by the ICO after unlawfully accessing the medical records of approximately 1,940 patients registered with the surgery. Steven Tennison was prosecuted under section 55 of the Data Protection Act at Maidstone Magistrates' Court.	
Unencrypted memory device. Data loss. Breach.	15 October 2013	North East Lincolnshire Council	A monetary penalty notice served on North East Lincolnshire Council after the loss of an unencrypted memory device containing personal data and sensitive personal data relating to 286 children.	£80,000
Personal data emailed in error	15 October 2013	Ministry of Justice	A monetary penalty notice served on the Ministry of Justice for failing to keep personal data securely, after spreadsheets showing prisoners' details were emailed to members of the public in error.	£140,000

Issue	Date	Party	Breach	Penalty
Personal data uploaded in error	27 August 2013	Aberdeen City Council	A monetary penalty notice served on Aberdeen City Council after inadequate homeworking arrangements led to 39 pages of personal data being uploaded onto the internet by a Council employee.	£100,000
Personal data uploaded in error	20 August 2013	Islington Borough Council	Monetary penalty notice served on Islington Borough Council after personal details of over 2,000 residents were released online via the What Do They Know (WDTK) website.	£70,000
Personal data faxed in error	30 July 2013	Bank of Scotland	Monetary penalty notice served on the Bank of Scotland after customers' account details were repeatedly faxed to the wrong recipients. The information included payslips, bank statements, account details and mortgage applications, along with customers' names, addresses and contact details.	£75,000
Sensitive personal data. Hard drives sold on online auction site.	18 June 2013	NHS Surrey	Monetary penalty notice served on NHS Surrey following the discovery of sensitive personal data belonging to thousands of patients on hard drives sold on an online auction site.	£200,000
Unwanted marketing calls. PECR.	5 July 2013	Tameside Energy Services Ltd	Monetary penalty notice served on Tameside Energy Services Ltd after the Manchester-based company blighted the public with unwanted marketing calls.	£45,000

Issue	Date	Party	Breach	Penalty
Google's Street View. Collection of payload data.	11 June 2013	Google Inc	ICO served an enforcement notice on Google Inc following a serious breach of Data Protection Act relating to the collection of payload data by Google's Street View cars in the UK. The ICO's decision follows the reopening of its investigation into the Google Street View project in 2013.	
Unsolicited calls.	17 June 2013	Nationwide Energy Services and We Claim You Gain	Monetary penalty notices served on Nationwide Energy Services and We Claim You Gain – both companies are part of Save Britain Money Ltd based in Swansea. Over 2,700 complaints to the Telephone Preference Service or reports to the ICO using its online survey, between 26 May 2011 and end of December 2012.	£125,000 £100,000
Personal data faxed in error	11 June 2013	North Staffordshire Combined Healthcare NHS Trust	Monetary penalty notice served on North Staffordshire Combined Healthcare NHS Trust, after several faxes containing sensitive personal data were sent to a member of the public in error	£55,000
Loss of two unencrypted laptops	4 June 2013	Glasgow City Council	Monetary penalty notice served on Glasgow City Council, following the loss of two unencrypted laptops, one of which contained the personal information of 20,143 people	£150,000
Unlawful disclosure	30 May 2013	Halton Borough Council	Monetary penalty notice served on Halton Borough Council. Home address of adoptive parents was wrongly disclosed to the birth family.	£70,000

Issue	Date	Party	Breach	Penalty
Security. Unlawful disclosure.	30 May 2013	Stockport Primary Care Trust	Monetary penalty served on Stockport Primary Care Trust following the discovery of a large number of patient records at a site formerly owned by the Trust.	£100,000
Unwanted calls	18 March 2013	DM Design Bedroom Ltd	Monetary penalty served on DM Design Bedroom Ltd. The company was the subject of nearly 2,000 complaints to the ICO and the Telephone Preference Service. The company consistently failed to check whether individuals had opted out of receiving marketing calls and responded to just a handful of the complaints received.	£90,000
Loss of three DVDs of personal data. Not encrypted.	1 February 2014	Nursing and Midwifery Council	Monetary penalty served on the Nursing and Midwifery Council. The council lost three DVDs related to a nurse's misconduct hearing, which contained confidential personal information and evidence from two vulnerable children. An ICO investigation found the information was not encrypted.	£150,000

Issue	Date	Party	Breach	Penalty
Data breach. Hacking.	14 January 2013	Sony	Monetary penalty served on the entertainment company Sony Computer Entertainment Europe Limited. Serious data breach. The penalty comes after the Sony PlayStation Network Platform was hacked in April 2011, compromising the personal information of millions of customers, including their names, addresses, email addresses, dates of birth and account passwords. Customers' payment card details were also at risk.	£250,000
Data loss. Train. GP and police reports. Allegations of sexual abuse and neglect.	12 December 2012	London Borough of Lewisham	Monetary penalty served on London Borough of Lewisham after a social worker left sensitive documents in a plastic shopping bag on a train, after taking them home to work on. The files, which were later recovered from the rail company's lost property office, included GP and police reports and allegations of sexual abuse and neglect.	£70,000
Unlawful disclosure. Sensitive data.	10 December 2012.	Devon County Council	Monetary penalty served on Devon County Council after a social worker used a previous case as a template for an adoption panel report they were writing, but a copy of the old report was sent out instead of the new one. The mistake revealed personal data of 22 people, including details of alleged criminal offences and mental and physical health.	£90,000

Issue	Date	Party	Breach	Penalty
Unlawful access. Customer financial data. Bank employee.	6 November 2012	Lara Davies	Bank employee obtained unlawfully access to bank statements of her partner's ex-wife. Court prosecution. Pleaded guilty to 11 DPA offences.	Court conviction. Fined. Lost job.
Spam	28 November 2012	Christopher Niebel and Gary McNeish, joint owners of Tetrus Telecoms.	ICO monetary penalty issued. The company had sent millions of unlawful spam texts to the public over the past three years.	£300,000. £140,000.
Data Loss/ Data Breach. Unlawful disclosure. Sensitive data.	22 November 2012	Plymouth City Council	ICO monetary penalty issued for a serious breach of the seventh data protection principle. A social worker sent part of a report relating to family A, to family B due to printing issues. The photocopied report contained confidential and highly sensitive personal data relating to the two parents and their four children, including of allegations of child neglect in on-going care proceedings.	£60,000
Incorrect storage and processing. Potential loss and damage. Financial Institution.	6 November 2012	Prudential	ICO monetary penalty issued after a mix-up over the administration of two customers' accounts led to tens of thousands of pounds, meant for an individual's retirement fund, ending up in the wrong account.	£50,000
Data Loss/ Data Breach. Unlawful disclosure. Sensitive data.	25 October 2012	Stoke-on-Trent City Council	ICO monetary penalty issued following a serious breach of the Data Protection Act that led to sensitive information about a child protection legal case being emailed to the wrong person.	£120,000

Issue	Date	Party	Breach	Penalty
Data Loss/ Data Breach. Police.	16 October 2012	Greater Manchester Police	ICO monetary penalty issued after the theft of a memory stick containing sensitive personal data from an officer's home. The device, which had no password protection, contained details of more than a thousand people with links to serious crime investigations.	£150,000
Data Loss/ Data Breach. Charity.	10 October 2012	Norwood Ravenswood Ltd	ICO monetary penalty issued after highly sensitive information about the care of four young children was lost after being left outside a London home. This was a charity which was fined.	£70,000
Data Loss/ Data Breach	11 September 2012	Scottish Borders Council	ICO monetary penalty issued after former employees' pension records were found in an over-filled paper recycle bank in a supermarket car park.	£250,000
Unlawful disclosure. Sensitive data.	6 August 2012	Torbay Care Trust	ICO monetary penalty issued after sensitive personal information relating to 1,373 employees was published on the Trust's website.	£175,000
Unlawful disclosure. Sensitive data.	12 July 2012	St George's Healthcare NHS Trust	ICO monetary penalty issued after a vulnerable individual's sensitive medical details were sent to the wrong address.	£60,000
Data Loss/ Data Breach	5 July 2012	Welcome Financial Services Limited	ICO monetary penalty issued following a serious breach of the Data Protection Act. The breach led to the personal data of more than half a million customers being lost.	£150,000

Issue	Date	Party	Breach	Penalty
Data Loss/ Data Breach. Sensitive data.	19 June 2012	Belfast Health and Social Care Trust	ICO monetary penalty issued following a serious breach of the Data Protection Act. The breach led to the sensitive personal data of thousands of patients and staff being compromised. The Trust also failed to report the incident to the ICO.	£225,000
Unlawful disclosure. Sensitive data.	6 June 2012	Telford & Wrekin Council	ICO monetary penalty issued for two serious breaches of the seventh data protection principle. A social worker sent a core assessment report to the child's sibling instead of the mother. The assessment contained confidential and highly sensitive personal data. Whilst investigating the first incident, a second incident was reported to the ICO involving the inappropriate disclosure of foster carer names and addresses to the children's mother. Both children had to be re-homed.	£90,000
Unlawful disclosure. Sensitive data. Security.	1 June 2012	Brighton and Sussex University Hospitals NHS Trust	ICO monetary penalty issued following the discovery of highly sensitive personal data belonging to tens of thousands of patients and staff – including some relating to HIV and genito urinary medicine patients – on hard drives sold on an internet auction site in October and November 2010.	£325,000

Issue	Date	Party	Breach	Penalty
Unlawful disclosure. Sensitive data.	21 May 2012	Central London Community Healthcare NHS Trust	An ICO monetary penalty issued for a serious contravention of the DPA, which occurred when sensitive personal data was faxed to an incorrect and unidentified number. The contravention was repeated on 45 occasions over a number of weeks and compromised 59 data subjects' personal data.	£90,000
Data Loss/ Data Breach. Sensitive data.	15 May 2012	London Borough of Barnet	ICO monetary penalty issued following the loss of sensitive information relating to 15 vulnerable children or young people, during a burglary at an employee's home.	£70,000
Unlawful disclosure. Sensitive data.	30 April 2012	Aneurin Bevan Health Board	ICO monetary penalty issued following an incident where a sensitive report – containing explicit details relating to a patient's health – was sent to the wrong person.	£70,000
Unlawful disclosure. Sensitive data.	14 March 2012	Lancashire Constabulary	ICO monetary penalty issued following the discovery of a missing person's report containing sensitive personal information about a missing 15-year old girl.	£70,000
Unlawful disclosure. Sensitive data.	15 February 2012	Cheshire East Council	ICO monetary penalty issued after an email containing sensitive personal information about an individual of concern to the police was distributed to 180 unintended recipients.	£80,000
Data Loss/ Data Breach. Sensitive data.	13 February 2012	Croydon Council	ICO monetary penalty issued after a bag containing papers relating to the care of a child sex abuse victim was stolen from a London pub.	£100,000

Issue	Date	Party	Breach	Penalty
Unlawful disclosure. Sensitive data.	13 February 2012	Norfolk County Council	ICO monetary penalty issued for disclosing information about allegations against a parent and the welfare of their child to the wrong recipient.	£80,000
Unlawful disclosure. Sensitive data.	30 January 2012	Midlothian Council	ICO monetary penalty issued for disclosing sensitive personal data relating to children and their carers to the wrong recipients on five separate occasions. The penalty is the first that the ICO has served against an organisation in Scotland.	£140,000
Unlawful disclosure. Sensitive data.	6 December 2011	Powys County Council	ICO monetary penalty issued for a serious breach of the Data Protection Act after the details of a child protection case were sent to the wrong recipient.	£130,000
Unlawful disclosure. Sensitive data.	28 November 2011	North Somerset Council	ICO monetary penalty issued for a serious breach of the Data Protection Act where a council employee sent five emails, two of which contained highly sensitive and confidential information about a child's serious case review, to the wrong NHS employee.	£60,000
Unlawful disclosure. Sensitive data.	28 November 2011	Worcestershire County Council	ICO monetary penalty issued for an incident where a member of staff emailed highly sensitive personal information about a large number of vulnerable people to 23 unintended recipients.	£80,000

Issue	Date	Party	Breach	Penalty
Unlawful disclosure. Sensitive data.	9 June 2011	Surrey County Council	ICO monetary penalty issued for a serious breach of the Data Protection Act after sensitive personal information was emailed to the wrong recipients on three separate occasions.	£120,000
Unlawful disclosure. Sensitive data. Security.	10 May 2011	Andrew Jonathan Crossley, formerly trading as solicitors firm ACS Law	ICO monetary penalty issued for failing to keep sensitive personal information relating to around 6,000 people secure.	£1,000
Data Loss/ Data Breach. Laptop. Encryption.	8 February 2011	Ealing Council	ICO monetary penalty issued following the loss of an unencrypted laptop which contained personal information. Ealing Council breached the Data Protection Act by issuing an unencrypted laptop to a member of staff in breach of its own policies.	£80,000
Data Loss/ Data Breach. Laptop. Encryption.	8 February 2011	Hounslow Council	ICO monetary penalty issued following the loss of an unencrypted laptop which contained personal information. Hounslow Council breached the Act by failing to have a written contract in place with Ealing Council. Hounslow Council also did not monitor Ealing Council's procedures for operating the service securely.	£70,000

CHAPTER SEVEN

Taxation

> 'The big issue is that it will make it more difficult for government to collect taxes.'

Milton Friedman, on the internet

7.1   The vast growth in online activities over the past decade and the ability of multinational enterprises to carefully structure the location of their profits has highlighted weaknesses in the application of the current tax rules. Due to multinational enterprises taking advantage of gaps in the interaction of different tax systems, or the application of treaty provisions, certain income may either be left untaxed or taxed at a very low rate. Globalisation has also provided opportunities for multinational enterprises to move from country-specific operating models to more integrated global models where certain activities are centralised. The resulting new business models combined with the growth of digital products and the growth of the services market means that enterprises need not locate near to their customers. Some multinational companies have also turned to more aggressive tax planning by artificially shifting profits to low tax jurisdictions where they have limited economic activity. Several high-profile companies such as Starbucks, Google and Amazon have been the subject of investigation regarding the low level of taxes paid in certain jurisdictions.[1]

To combat threats to their tax base and the consequences of profit shifting certain countries have started to implement changes in their domestic law to capture this lost profit and on an international level the OECD has been re-evaluating the tax rules to address artificial profit shifting and tax base erosion. While in 1998 the OECD considered that existing international tax treaty rules could be applied to e-commerce activities, nearly two decades later the OECD are proposing some fundamental changes.[2]

Although traditional mail order still forms a healthy part of the digital economy the growth in digital products and the services market has led to new ways of

---

1   'Google, Amazon Starbucks: The Rise of "Tax Shaming"', www.bbc.co.uk/news/magazine-20560359.
2   OECD Electronic Commerce: Taxation Framework Conditions, A report by the Committee on Fiscal Affairs as presented to Ministers at the OECD Ministerial Conference, 'A Borderless World: Realising the Potential of Electronic Commerce' on 8 October 1998. BEPS Action Plan on Base Erosion and Profit Shifting 9/07/13 www.oecd.org/tax/beps-reports.htm.

generating value. Business taxes are levied not by reference to the methods by which business is conducted, but by the financial results of business. The concepts of profit and loss apply equally to online businesses as to bricks and mortar business and, as a result, online businesses face similar tax concerns to their traditional counterparts.

Consequently, this chapter addresses the following questions:

1. What are the tax considerations of starting an internet business? In particular, in what (legal) form should that business be set up?

2. Because the internet is transnational, what international tax issues need to be considered? Or, more simply, in what countries will the business be liable to tax?

3. How does value added tax (VAT) apply to supplies made over the internet?

The internet has shaped the way in which tax laws have evolved in recent times. In the same way, evolving tax law has shaped online trading behaviour. The more 'virtual' an online business, the more readily it can be set up in, or migrated to, a tax haven. This ability to transport an online business (when coupled with the requisite personnel being prepared to move with it) has seen online businesses in certain sectors move offshore. Such migration has been countered with changes to tax law with either anti-avoidance measures or promises of low-tax to tempt taxpayers back to where certain governments consider they belong.

Early in 2015 the UK introduced a new diverted profits tax aimed at preventing MNEs from artificially diverting profits from the UK.[3] This measure prevents foreign companies from exploiting the rules on permanent establishment to avoid creating a tax base in the UK and also applies where a UK or foreign company with a UK taxable presence uses artificial transactions or entities that lack economic substance to reduce their tax burden. The latter targets arrangements whereby companies divert profits to low tax jurisdictions through payments such as royalties. Tax at a rate of 25% applies to any such diverted profits from April 2015.

The UK also introduced General Anti-Abuse Rules (GAAR) in 1 April 2013 to counteract tax advantages arising from abusive tax avoidance arrangements.

In relation to VAT, the rules have undergone significant changes with the introduction of the VAT package in 2010. At the beginning of this year the rules on the application of VAT to B2C electronic services were also amended to provide a more level playing field for service providers by eliminating the advantages of establishing in those member states with a lower rate of VAT.

UK TAX – GENERAL

7.2   Liability to tax in the UK is, in the main, imposed by a series of Finance Acts following the Budget each year. Periodically Finance Acts and other taxing

---

3   See www.gov.uk/government/uploads/system/uploads/attachment_data/file/385741/Diverted_ Profits_Tax.pdf.

statutes are consolidated and, in recent years, much of the tax legislation has been rewritten in plain English as part of the tax law rewrite project. Recent Acts which form part of this project are the Income Tax (Earnings and Pensions) Act 2003 (ITEPA), the Income Tax (Trading and Other Income) Act 2005 (ITTOIA), the Income Tax Act 2007 (ITA), the Corporation Tax Act 2009, the Corporation Tax Act 2010 and the Taxation (International and Other Provisions) Act 2010. All of this legislation is amended frequently.

Direct tax is administered by HM Revenue & Customs ('HMRC') under the Taxes Management Act 1970. The basic system is that a taxpayer (or his accountant) completes a self-assessment tax return in which the taxpayer calculates his own tax liability. Both individuals and companies are subject to a system of self-assessment.

Following submission of a taxpayer's self-assessment return, HMRC have a period of time within which to open enquiries into that return. Where HMRC consider that a taxpayer's self-assessment of his liability is incorrect, they will seek to agree or impose an appropriate change to the taxpayer's self-assessed liability. An appeal against an assessment or a decision of a tax officer may be made. The appeals process was amended by the Tribunals, Courts and Enforcement Act 2007 when a two-tier tribunal structure was introduced. The lower-tier tribunal, the Tax Chamber of the First-tier Tribunal will hear most tax appeals. With permission an appeal can be made to the second-tier tribunal, the Finance and Tax Chamber of the Upper Tribunal, on questions of law. Decisions of the Upper Tribunal are subject to a right of appeal to the Court of Appeals and Supreme Court.

Tax appeals tend to be on questions of law, usually ones of statutory construction. From such decisions, a body of judge-made law has evolved which complements the tax statutes. For example, the line of cases dealing with tax avoidance and statutory interpretation, culminating in the decisions in *Barclays Mercantile Business Finance v Mawson* and in *Scottish Provident Institution v Commissioners of Inland Revenue*, are an important component of the UK's tax laws.[4]

The tax year for individuals runs from 6 April to 5 April in the following year. For companies, it runs from 1 April to the following 31 March.

Individuals pay income tax on their year's income at the basic rate up to a threshold and, to the extent that such threshold is exceeded, a higher rate of income tax applies. In addition to income tax, individuals are liable to pay capital gains tax ('CGT') on capital profits.

Sole traders (ie individuals trading as such) are liable to income tax on the income profits, and to CGT on the capital profits, arising from their business. Partners in a partnership are also taxed as individuals, although some special rules apply.

Companies pay corporation tax on both income and capital profits. Corporation tax is calculated in respect of each accounting period of a company. Accounting periods usually last one year, but do not have to coincide with the tax year.

---

4   [2005] STC 1 and [2005] STC 15.

Where an individual derives income from being an employee or director, income tax is deducted at source under the PAYE scheme and, where appropriate, primary class 1 (or 'employee's') national insurance contributions ('NICs') are deducted from each payment of salary. It is mandatory for UK employers to operate the PAYE scheme. Employers are also liable to pay secondary class 1 (or 'employer's') NICs, which are payable in addition to the salary. From an employer's perspective, therefore, the total cost of paying a salary is the aggregate of the gross salary and the employer's NICs payable in addition to that salary. Such payments will ordinarily, however, be deductible from a business's taxable profits for the purposes of income or corporation tax (as applicable).

SOLE TRADER, PARTNERSHIP OR COMPANY?

7.3 When setting up a new business, a crucial decision will be the type of legal structure (or 'vehicle') to use. In general, the choice is threefold:

1. sole trader;

2. a company; or

3. a partnership.

Although there are a number of factors to be considered in choosing the appropriate vehicle, tax is generally a key driver.

A limited company is perhaps the most common vehicle for businesses. Of its principal attractions, the benefit of limited liability and the fact that it is such a familiar business vehicle are two of the strongest.

Sole traders and partners in a general partnership cannot rely on limited liability. Accordingly, they may be better served by setting up business as a limited liability partnership (or 'LLP'). An individual can achieve this by creating an LLP between himself and a company that he owns, with the latter participating in the partnership to only a small extent (eg 1% of profits and gains).

It should, of course, be borne in mind that the protection offered by limited liability may be illusory where shareholders of a company or partners of an LLP are, in practice, required to personally guarantee the debts of the business.

From a tax perspective, however, the relative attractiveness or otherwise of each vehicle should be considered in relative terms in light of the expected profits or losses of the business and the extent to which cash will be extracted from the business or reinvested.

A move from one vehicle to another is always a possibility. It is relatively easy to commence trading as a sole trader or a partnership and then 'incorporate' the business at a later date by transferring the business to a company. Whilst the reverse is possible, it is not so easy to achieve in a tax-efficient manner.

The principal difference between a company and a partnership is that the former is itself a taxable entity whilst the latter is not.

Since a company has separate legal personality, tax is potentially payable on two separate occasions. Corporation tax is payable by the company on its profits and, thereafter, the shareholders are charged to income tax on profits distributed to them as a dividend.

In contrast, since a partnership is not a taxable entity, tax is only payable in the hands of the partners. The profits of the partnership are divided between the partners in accordance with the partnership agreement and taxed as the partners' income on an arising basis (ie regardless of whether the profits of the partnership are actually distributed to them). Partners in an LLP and a general partnership are taxed in the same way. Sole traders are taxed in broadly the same way also.

An advantage of a company is that retained profits are subject only to corporation tax, which is generally levied at a lower rate than income tax (ie if profits are to be retained in the company and reinvested, and so are not distributed to shareholders, those profits are only subject to tax once). Where profits are expected to be retained, therefore, a company may be more tax-efficient than a partnership.

Where profits are not of an amount sufficient for the top rates of income tax (on amounts distributed to shareholders) to be applicable and/or where a shareholder looks to extract income from a company by way of salary (which gives a corresponding deduction from taxable profits), the relative tax merits of the different legal structures can change. In addition, with recent Chancellors tinkering with the rates of tax on an annual basis, one structure may be the tax-efficient choice one year but not the next.

Determination of the most appropriate vehicle will ultimately depend on a number of factors including the relevant tax benefits.

BUSINESS PROFITS

7.4   A taxation question commonly of concern to businesses is whether items of expenditure are deductible in computing the amount of taxable profits.

In general, income expenditure which is wholly and exclusively laid out or expended for the purposes of the trade will be deductible from the profits of the business for tax purposes.

Expenditure incurred on creating a website to advertise a business, or through which e-commerce is to be transacted, is likely to have been incurred wholly and exclusively for the purposes of the trade and thus should be deductible from a business's taxable profits. This should remain the case even where the material provided online is free of charge to users, if such expenditure has been incurred in order to market products or otherwise to provide publicity for the business.

Save where a 'capital allowance' is available, expenditure on capital items used in the business is not deductible from taxable profits. Accordingly, in determining the taxable profits of a business from the net accounting profit figure in the business's profit and loss account, accounting depreciation of capital assets has to be added back.

The system of capital allowances does permit certain deductions to be made from taxable profits, as a form of 'tax depreciation', in respect of expenditure on a capital asset over a period of years.

Capital allowances are given in respect of expenditure on plant and machinery. These words are not defined in the legislation, but 'plant' has been held to include 'whatever apparatus is used by a businessman for carrying on his business'.[5] Allowances are most commonly given at a fixed rate, on an annual basis, on a pool of qualifying expenditure.

Expenditure on computers, servers, telecoms equipment and other electronic apparatus is likely to qualify for capital allowances. Expenditure on computer software is also eligible for capital allowances and, for such purposes, is treated as plant. This should apply to all software, whether an off-the-shelf package, software bundled with hardware or bespoke software.

Although not part of the capital allowances regime, if a UK company incurs expenditure on 'intangible fixed assets' it can obtain relief from corporation tax. This would include expenditure incurred on the creation, acquisition or licence of any patent, trade mark, registered design, copyright or design right. The tax relief available is given in line with the depreciation of such intangible assets in the company's accounts (in accordance with generally accepted accounting practice) or, by election, at the rate of 4% per annum.

UK RESIDENCE

7.5   UK taxation is based on a person's place of residence.

Individuals who are resident in the UK are taxed on their worldwide income and gains. Prior to 2008, the UK did not tax individuals who were UK resident on income derived from a non-UK source, where such income was not remitted to the UK, unless they were also UK domiciled (ie broadly they have made the UK their permanent home). Since 2008 non-domiciled individuals must choose either to pay UK tax on foreign income over £2,000, or claim the remittance basis. If choosing the remittance basis they would only pay income tax on income brought into the UK but they must pay an annual charge of £30,000 if they have been a UK resident for at least seven out of the previous nine years (rising to £50,000 once resident for 12 out of the previous 14 years). For an individual, 'residence' means 'to dwell permanently or for a considerable time, to have one's settled or usual abode, to live in or at a particular place'.[6]

A company which is treated as being resident in the UK will be taxed on its worldwide income and gains. A company will be treated as resident in the UK for the purposes of taxation if either it is incorporated in the UK, or if its central management and control is effected in the UK.

There is no statutory definition of central management and control. The UK courts have held that central management and control means the highest form of control and direction of a company's affairs, as distinct from the management of the company's day-to-day operations. The location of a company's central management and control is a question of fact in each particular case.

---

5   See *Yarmouth v France* (1887) 19 QBD 647.
6   *Levene v IRC* [1928] AC 217, HL.

In *De Beers Consolidated Mines Ltd v Howe*[7] it was held that a South African incorporated company was resident in the UK because a majority of the directors lived in London and the board meetings, by which the operations of the company worldwide were controlled and managed, were held in London. This was held to be the case even though shareholders' meetings were held in South Africa and the registered office and head office were located in South Africa. More recently, the Court of Appeal in *Wood v Holden8* confirmed the test in *De Beers* as the relevant test, and went on to emphasise that in determining the place of a company's central management and control, it was necessary to decide whether effective decisions were taken by the company's board of directors or whether those decisions were taken by someone else.

In summary, therefore, it is the place where the people who take the company's key strategic decisions are physically located when they take those decisions that will determine the place of a company's central management and control.

Unlike common law countries (such as the UK), in civil law countries a company is usually taxable only in its country of domicile; namely, where it is incorporated. The US takes a similar approach. In such jurisdictions, the territory from which the company is managed and controlled becomes irrelevant.

THE SOURCE OF PROFITS AND TAXABLE PRESENCE

7.6   Since one can be resident or have a taxable presence in more than one country, it is thus possible for income to be potentially taxable in two countries simultaneously. This situation may be mitigated by a double taxation treaty between the two countries in question which aims to ensure that tax is charged only in one or other of the two countries that have agreed the treaty or, sometimes, that part only of the profits or gains in question are taxed in each country. The UK, which has treaties with more than one hundred countries, has the most extensive network.

A non-UK-resident company will only be subject to UK tax on its profits and gains if such a liability arises under UK domestic law and a relevant double tax treaty does not override the UK domestic law position.

Under UK domestic law, a company not resident in the UK will be subject to income tax to the extent that it carries on a trade 'within' (rather than 'with') the UK; that is, the business is actually carried on from within the UK rather than the business merely entering into transactions with UK customers. If a non-resident company's presence in the UK constitutes a 'permanent establishment' (see below), it will be within the charge to UK corporation tax (again pursuant to UK domestic law) to the extent that it carries on a trade through that UK permanent establishment.

Most of the UK's double tax treaties provide that the UK only has the right to tax the profits of a company (or other entity) resident in the other contracting state (ie the country with which the UK has signed the treaty), if that non-UK resident

7   [1906] AC 455, 5 TC 198, HL.
8   [2006] STC 443.

company is carrying on a trade or business through a 'permanent establishment' in the UK (thus the concept of 'permanent establishment' is found both in the UK's domestic legislation and in its double tax treaties). Accordingly, where a company, which is resident in a country with which the UK has a double tax treaty, is trading 'within' the UK (and so potentially has a UK income tax liability under UK domestic law) but its trading presence is something less than a UK permanent establishment (as defined in the applicable treaty), the UK domestic law may be overridden by the treaty with the result that no UK tax liability will arise.

UK PERMANENT ESTABLISHMENT

7.7   Although not identical, the definitions of a permanent establishment for UK domestic law purposes and the definition used in its double tax treaties are very similar.

A non-UK resident company will have a permanent establishment in the UK if it has a fixed place of business (ie something physical, such as an office) in the UK through which its principal business activities (being matters which are not merely ancillary to its business) are wholly or partly carried on (the 'physical test').

A non-UK company will also have a permanent establishment in the UK if a dependent agent acting on its behalf has, and habitually exercises, authority to enter into contracts, or otherwise does business, on its behalf while in the UK (the 'agency test').

In theory, therefore (and by way of example), the physical test could be applied to a server on which a website is hosted in circumstances where the website allows customers to download telephone ringtones for payments made via an online payment facility. If the server is owned by the foreign company and is both located and physically fixed (ie has a degree of permanence) in the UK then, since the business of the foreign company is carried on through it (eg the selling of ringtones), the server could (without more) arguably constitute a UK permanent establishment. Were this to be the case, all profits derived from the website hosted on the server would be subject to UK tax.

In the UK, HMRC's published practice is that a website, of itself, is not a permanent establishment and that a server is, of itself, insufficient to constitute a permanent establishment of a business that is conducting ecommerce through a website on that server.

Other jurisdictions (particularly other OECD member states) do not, however, take this view. Accordingly, the tax effects of the location of servers should be carefully determined when companies or other entities (wherever resident) are considering locating servers outside of their country of residence.

WITHHOLDING TAXES

7.8   In many jurisdictions, certain payments may be subject to deduction of income tax at source, otherwise known as withholding tax. The most common are payments of royalties, interest and dividends.

The UK levies no withholding tax on dividends paid by UK-resident companies. The UK does, however, levy withholding taxes on certain payments of interest and royalties.

Some payments of annual interest between UK-resident persons are subject to withholding tax. For example, where a UK-resident company makes a payment of interest to an individual, tax at the basic rate is required to be withheld. In contrast, however, payments between UK-resident companies are not subject to withholding tax.

Most payments of interest by UK borrowers to non-UK lenders are subject to withholding tax under UK domestic law. This can, however, be effectively overridden by the EC Interest and Royalties Directive or a relevant double tax treaty (both of which are discussed below) which may eliminate the UK withholding tax liability entirely or, in the case of a double tax treaty, reduce it to a lower amount.

Save in the case of certain patent royalties, withholding tax liabilities do not arise under UK domestic law in respect of royalty payments made by UK licensees to UK licensors.

In relation to royalties paid to non-UK licensors, however, a withholding tax liability will usually arise under UK domestic law in respect to royalties paid for the use of certain patents, copyrights, design rights and registered designs. Copyright royalties that are subject to withholding tax do not include video recordings, films or, where not separately exploited, their soundtracks.

Thus video on demand and video streaming services provided via the web are likely not to be caught, so long as it can be established that the copyright exploited is a copyright in a video recording or cinematograph film. In contrast, payments for audio streaming, the download of music tracks and software licences are potentially caught. HMRC's practice, however, has been that payment for a licence to give the user only a limited right to use the software in question should not be subject to withholding tax. Accordingly, an obligation to withhold should only arise where payment is made to acquire a right of reproduction to make many copies or to otherwise exploit the original.

A requirement to withhold tax under UK domestic law may be removed or varied if either the EC Interest and Royalties Directive applies or if a relevant double tax treaty applies.

The EC Interest and Royalties Directive will apply where the payer is a UK company or a UK permanent establishment of an EU company and the recipient of the payment is a company in a different member state and both companies are 25% associates (ie one company holds at least 25% of the capital or voting rights in the other or a third company has such a holding in both companies). Where the Directive applies, the payment can be made free of withholding tax.

Where a withholding liability exists under UK domestic law and the EC Interest and Royalties Directive does not apply, a double tax treaty between the UK and the country of residence of the recipient of the royalty may reduce or eliminate the withholding liability. Some treaties (eg the treaty between the UK and the US) provide that royalties and/or interest arising in one country which are beneficially owned by a resident of the other country are taxable only in that other country. This, in effect, reduces the withholding tax liability to zero. In other treaties, a reduced rate of withholding tax on payments is prescribed.

If the person paying a royalty in the UK has a reasonable belief that the non-UK payee is entitled to benefit under a double tax treaty, the reduced rate of withholding in the treaty can be applied without seeking advance clearance from HMRC. If this reasonable belief is misplaced, however, the payer remains liable for the full withholding liability and so seeking advance clearance often remains the prudent approach. Note that this rule does not apply to payments of interest.

Many multinational groups of companies implement structures to minimise taxes on royalty income. A typical structure would involve a group company based in a low-tax jurisdiction owning intellectual property and licensing that intellectual property to other companies in the group. Such a structure may route the royalty payments via an intermediary group company based in a country with an extensive network of treaties which impose beneficial rates of withholding tax so as to eliminate or materially reduce withholding tax liabilities on royalty payments flowing back to the owner of the intellectual property.

It is, however, becoming increasingly common for tax treaties to contain specific provision to counter 'treaty shopping'; namely, the practice of establishing an entity in a particular jurisdiction for the primary purpose of taking advantage of the favourable tax treatment offered by a treaty between that jurisdiction and another. In addition, the decision of the UK's Court of Appeal in *Indofood International Finance Limited v JP Morgan Chase Bank NA*[9] has cast doubt on the efficacy of certain international structures which use an intermediate finance entity. Although HMRC have published guidance on the decision, it remains to be seen whether they will use the decision to attack treaty-based structures where they can argue that an interposed entity does not have the requisite 'beneficial ownership' of the relevant payment to benefit from the treaty.

The last few years have seen various companies including Apple, Google, Amazon and Starbucks coming under fire for their use of creative tax planning schemes. Popular approaches have involved routing royalty payments to tax havens through intermediary jurisdictions using a combination of Irish and Dutch subsidiary companies. Such arrangements rely on taking advantage of specific national provisions and also EU rules on taxing royalty payments. The Netherlands has since introduced measures to combat the use of Dutch entities for such schemes.

OECD AND G20 DEVELOPMENTS

7.9   International concern over reduced taxes and shifting of profits led to the OECD and G20 countries' Action Plan on Base Erosion and Profit Shifting (BEPS) in 2013.[10] The aim of the project is to ensure profits are taxed where economic activities generating the profits are performed and where value is created. It will also provide certainty and predictability for businesses as to where

---

9   [2006] STC 1195.
10   OECD (2013), Action Plan on Base Erosion and Profit Shifting, OECD Publishing. See http:// dx.doi.org/10.1787/9789264202719-en.

they will be taxed. The resulting recommendations will create a comprehensive and coherent international tax framework which will include changes to international principles in the model tax treaty and transfer pricing guidelines and also recommendations for changes to domestic law.

The work includes action plans on 15 key areas including the digital economy. Reports on seven of these areas were published in 2014 with the rest to follow this year.[11]

The BEPS report to 'Address the tax challenges of the digital economy' (Action plan 1) published in 2014 recommended that there should not be a separate digital tax regime at this point and concluded that the OECD work undertaken in other areas including transfer pricing and permanent establishment would address existing concerns. The report raised the issue of the difficulty of attributing value created from the generation of data through the provision of digital services and the question of how to characterise it under tax rules.

Key points in the other reports include neutralising hybrid mismatch arrangements (where companies exploit the differences in tax rules in different jurisdictions to avoid or reduce tax) through new treaty provisions, addressing treaty shopping, ensuring transfer pricing results reflect value creation by revising rules on intangibles and countering harmful tax practice particularly in the areas of IP regimes and tax rulings. These recommendations will remain in draft form until the rest of the reports are published later this year.

The practical implementation of these changes has also been considered with steps towards negotiating a multilateral instrument to streamline implementation, the implementation of country-by-country reporting to help tax authorities collect information on the global activities, profits and taxes on MNEs by 2016 and government-to-government exchange mechanisms due to start in 2017.

The reports due this year include Action plan 7 'Preventing the artificial avoidance of permanent establishment status'. Although the report has not yet been completed the discussion draft raises the issue of amending the current exceptions applied to permanent establishments which include activities such as maintenance of stock of goods for storage, display, delivery or processing and purchasing. Whereas these activities would have been considered preparatory or auxiliary when the model tax treaty provisions were developed with internet sales these activities may form the key part of businesses activity.

The next couple of years will prove interesting in the tax arena, as the OECD reforms of the international tax framework are implemented through BEPS. The proposals will provide greater certainty for business and will address the distortion of competition between domestic businesses and those operating on a global level and taking advantages of the gaps in the interaction of the tax systems. This international approach may also help to curb the further development of unilateral steps taken by countries to preserve their tax base.

11   See www.oecd.ord/beos-2014-deliverables.htm.

VAT

Introduction

7.10   Value added tax is an indirect tax on consumers imposed by all EU member states.

The primary EU legislation is EC Council Directive 2006/112 of 28 November 2006 (the 'VAT Directive'). Member states are required to enact domestic legislation giving effect to the VAT Directive. Since in certain areas the VAT Directive permits member states to choose which of a number of provisions to adopt in their domestic legislation, VAT laws across the member states are not completely aligned. An example is the standard rate of VAT itself, which is at the discretion of each member state so long as it is at least 15%. As a consequence, VAT rates vary across the EU from 15% to 25%.

VAT is imposed on supplies of goods and services provided for a consideration (money or something of value exchanged for the goods or services) in the course of a business. Accordingly, VAT is not payable in respect of items supplied between unconnected parties for free (eg free downloads). Where payment is made in a non-cash form, VAT is payable on the value of the non-cash consideration provided.

The VAT system effectively taxes the final consumer of goods and services. In general terms, those businesses in the supply chain that create or add value to those goods or services merely collect and account for VAT to the tax authorities on the value added by them in the supply chain. Accordingly, save where the suppliers are exempt (see below), they do not bear the cost of VAT as they are able to recover any VAT which they have themselves been charged on any goods or services they have used to make their own supplies.

For an example, a company selling chart music in digital form and charging VAT on the services it provides to its customers would be able to reclaim any VAT incurred on buying computers necessary to run the business, on the cost of constructing, maintaining and hosting its website and on royalties that it has to pay to artists. In respect of any VAT accounting period, it would only be required to account to the tax authorities for the difference between the VAT arising in respect of supplies that it has made to its customers (its 'output tax') and the VAT which it had itself been charged on the goods and services it had consumed in order to make those supplies (its 'input tax').

Although the end consumer bears the burden of paying VAT on taxable goods and services, it is the supplier of goods or services who is legally responsible to account for the VAT charged. VAT is deemed included in a price unless expressly stated otherwise. Accordingly, if a supplier omits to charge his customers VAT he is nonetheless liable himself to account for the VAT to the tax authorities. In order to make supervision of the system of deducting input tax possible, a business can only reclaim VAT on its inputs if it holds an invoice from its supplier to show that VAT is payable.[12]

---

12   In *Future Phonics Ltd v Revenue & Customs Commissioners* (2013) UKFTT 169 (TC), HMRC rejected the taxpayer's claim of £1.3 million of input tax as the purchase invoices did not describe the goods supplied.

Exempt and zero-rated supplies

7.11   There are two special categories of supplies:

1.   exempt supplies; and

2.   reduced and zero-rated supplies.

The supplier of an exempt supply is not required to charge VAT on those goods or services. Categories of exempt supply include financial services, insurance services, certain supplies of land, betting and gaming and education.

A trader making exempt supplies cannot, however, recover as input tax any VAT charged to him on supplies which have been used as components of an exempt supply. Thus, he is effectively treated as the final consumer of those components. For example, since the services of an online bookmaker are exempt, he could not reclaim any VAT incurred on the setting up of a website to provide online betting services.

The supplier of a zero-rated supply is required to charge VAT, but at the reduced rate of 0%. Reduced rates of VAT are applied differently in different member states. In the UK, categories for zero-rating include foodstuffs, passenger transport services, and books and newspapers.

Although for the purchaser of a zero-rated supply there is no practical difference from an exempt supply (because no VAT is in fact charged), zero-rating is advantageous to the supplier as he is able to deduct input VAT incurred in respect of the components of the supply. For example, a publisher of physical works (note that the supply of digital works is not exempt) will often have no output tax to pay, due to all his supplies being zero-rated, but will nevertheless have incurred input tax in respect of purchases of paper, inks, binding materials, office equipment, etc. Accordingly, provided that he has registered for VAT, the publisher will actually receive repayments of VAT from HMRC at the end of each VAT period.

The VAT system in the UK

7.12   The rate of VAT in the UK is currently 20%.

In the UK, VAT is imposed by the Value Added Tax Act 1994 (VATA 1994), as amended by annual Finance Acts following the Budget. Secondary legislation often contains important provisions; for example, the Value Added Tax Regulations 1995 contain much of the law relating to administration and collection of VAT in the UK.

Collection of VAT is the responsibility of HMRC. All persons making taxable supplies (ie supplies other than exempt supplies) whose turnover from taxable supplies which are not zero-rated exceeds a certain threshold[13] must register for VAT. In respect of each period (usually three months, but exceptionally one month or 12 months) the taxable person is obliged to complete a VAT return and

---

13   £82,000 for the 2015/16 tax year.

to pay any VAT due. Businesses are also required to maintain proper records and to supply customers who are themselves registered or required to be registered with a VAT invoice in respect of taxable supplies.

There is a right of appeal from certain decisions of HMRC to the First-tier Tribunal (Tax). With permission further appeal may be made on questions of law to the Upper Tribunal (Tax and Chancery), the Court of Appeal and ultimately the Supreme Court. Since VAT is a European tax, points of European law often arise and it is not uncommon for questions to be raised as to whether the UK legislation, or the way in which HMRC seek to implement it, exceed what is permitted under the European legislation. Both the Tribunals and the higher courts hearing VAT appeals are, therefore, able to refer questions for decision to the European Court of Justice in Luxembourg.

VAT and supplies made via the internet

7.13 The principal difficulty surrounding the VAT treatment of supplies made via the internet is jurisdictional or, more accurately, determining where the supplies in question are made for VAT purposes.

Supplies are treated as being subject to UK VAT if they are treated as being supplied 'in the UK'. If they are not treated as being supplied in the UK, they will not be subject to UK VAT but may be subject to VAT in another EU member state or other value added or goods and services taxes outside the EU (eg sales taxes in the US or GST in Australia).

Accordingly, in determining the VAT treatment of any particular supply, one must first determine where that supply is treated as being made.

There are specific rules which determine where, for VAT purposes, a supply is treated as being made with different rules applying to goods and different rules applying to services. As the next step, therefore, one must determine whether a specific supply is a supply of goods or a supply services.

For VAT purposes, with a few exceptions, goods are anything tangible. Services, therefore, are everything else.

Supplies of goods via the internet

7.14 Where the internet is simply used as a form of mail order for physical goods, one must consider the place of supply rules relating to goods (ie the normal VAT rules applicable to such transactions continue to apply regardless of the means of ordering them).

The VAT place of supply rules relating to goods differ depending upon:

1. the place where the supplier belongs;

2. the place where the recipient belongs; and

3. whether the supply is a supply to a VAT-registered person (ie 'business to business' or 'B2B') or a supply to a person who is not registered for VAT (ie 'business to consumer' or 'B2C').

UK to UK (B2B or B2C)

7.15   Where goods are ordered over the internet by a UK purchaser (whether on a B2B or B2C basis) from a UK VAT-registered business, UK VAT will usually have to be accounted for in the normal way.

Outbound – UK to non-EU (B2B or B2C)

7.16   Supplies of goods made by UK businesses to customers outside of the EU are zero-rated provided that the UK supplier retains appropriate evidence that the goods have been exported outside of the EU. This is the case whether the supply is on a B2B or B2C basis. In these circumstances, the supplier would still be able to recover the input VAT on any component costs of the supply.

Outbound – UK to EU (B2B)

7.17   Supplies of goods made by UK VAT-registered businesses to customers within the EU are zero-rated if they are supplied to a person registered for VAT in another member state, the supplier obtains his customer's VAT registration number and shows this on his VAT invoice and if he holds appropriate documentary evidence that the goods have been removed from the UK.

Outbound – UK to EU (B2C)

7.18   If the EU-based customer is not registered for VAT, the UK-registered supplier must charge VAT at the UK rate. However, once B2C supplies made by the UK-registered supplier to any particular EU country exceed an annual threshold set by that country for VAT distance selling purposes (which can be either 35,000 euros or 100,000 euros or the relevant currency equivalent), the supplier must register for VAT in that country and then charge VAT at the rate applicable in the country of destination.

Inbound – non-EU to UK (B2C)

7.19   VAT is payable by the purchaser on the entry of those goods into the UK. For example, where goods are ordered by a UK private customer over the internet from a non-EU website and sent by mail, the Post Office will require payment of the VAT due from the purchaser before delivery will be made. However, small value (less than £15) items are tax- and duty-free at import. This means, for example, that there is no VAT to pay on a single CD ordered over the internet by a UK customer from a supplier based in the Channel Islands.

Inbound – EU to UK (B2C)

7.20   Where non-VAT registered UK customers acquire goods from suppliers in other EU member states, those private customers will be charged VAT at the rate applicable in the other member state, unless the supplier is also registered for VAT in the UK under the UK's distance selling rules referred to above, in which case UK rates of VAT would be charged. Under the UK's distance selling rules, EU suppliers must register for VAT in the UK if the annual value of supplies made to the UK exceeds £70,000.

Inbound – EU or non-EU to UK (B2B)

7.21   Acquisitions of goods from other member states and imports from non-EU member states are subject to VAT at the UK rate if the customer is VAT-registered in the UK. Thus, a VAT-registered UK customer will have to account for UK VAT on such purchases.

Supplies of services via the internet

7.22   In December 2007 the Council of Europe reached agreement on changes to the rules governing place of supply of services. Extensive changes to the place of supply rules came into force 1 January 2010 with the implementation of the 'VAT Package' across the EU.[14] The changes were brought in to simplify and harmonise the treatment of VAT across the EU and to levy VAT at the actual place of consumption of the services. They also create a more level playing field between service providers by reducing the previous advantages for service providers of locating in member states with lower VAT rates. In broad terms, more supplies of services will be treated as taking place where the customer belongs.

The new general rule for place of supply of services depends on the nature of services provided and the status of the customer. A B2B supply of cross-border services will be taxed where the recipient belongs and for B2C supplies the place of taxation will remain in the country where the supplier belongs. For B2B cross-border supplies the recipient will use the reverse charge mechanism to account for the EU VAT in its jurisdiction. Where a B2C transaction has taken place the place of supply will be where the supplier belongs and therefore the supplier must charge VAT at the rate in its own country.

In addition there are several categories of service where special rules apply which will reflect the principle of taxation in the place of consumption. These categories include restaurant and catering services, hiring of means of transport, cultural, sporting and entertainment services and telecommunications, broadcasting and electronic services supplied to customers. Services will fall under the general rule only if they do not fall within one of the other categories.

The VAT package also included the introduction of an electronic procedure for reimbursement of VAT incurred by EU business in other member states to replace the previous paper-based system.

The new rules on the place of supply for intra EU B2C telecoms, broadcasting and electronic services supplied at a distance came into effect on 1 January 2015. The new place of supply rule provides that these services will be taxed in the country where the customer is established, has a permanent address or usually resides. The supplier will therefore have to account for VAT at the rate applicable in a country other than his own; namely, that where his customer is established. To ease the administration of this change, a 'one-stop' system has been established so that EU-based service providers can register for VAT in their home states and comply with all their VAT obligations in that jurisdiction only.

---

14   The VAT package includes Directive 2008/8/EC, the mini one-stop-shop for telecom, broadcasting and e-commerce services, Directive 2008/9/EC and Regulation 282/2011.

In practice, however, a supplier of relevant services to non-business customers throughout the EU will have to account for VAT at the rates applicable in up to 28 member states. Under the 'one-stop' system, VAT revenue not belonging to the supplier's home state will be transferred from that state to that of the customer. The rules apply to all suppliers of electronic services and not only to suppliers who are already registered for VAT as there is no minimum threshold.

The new rules eliminate the advantages for suppliers of locating in certain member states with lower rates of VAT. Prior to 1 January 2015 the place of supply for intra EU B2C supplies of such services was the place of the supplier and therefore Luxembourg with its relatively low rate of VAT was a popular location for businesses to establish. This change also aligns intra-EU supplies with the post-1 July 2003 treatment of B2C electronic services (discussed below) supplied into the EU from traders based outside the EU (thereby completely levelling the playing field and eliminating the potential price disadvantages for B2C suppliers of electronic services based outside of the EU). Since 1 July 2003, many non-EU suppliers of electronic services have re-established their businesses in member states with low rates of VAT to take advantage of the pre 2015 rules.

In order to ease the impact that this change will have on certain member states there is a transition period of four years. The member state where the supplier is established will be entitled, for an initial period, to retain a fixed proportion of the VAT receipts collected through the one-stop scheme (ie a 'halfway house' of sorts). The proportion will be 30% from 1 January 2015 until 31 December 2016, 15% from January 2017 until 31 December 2018 and 0% from 1 January 2019.

The four-year transition phase represents a compromise to deal with concerns of member states with lower VAT rates, notably Luxembourg. These member states anticipated a loss of VAT receipts under the new general regime since many providers of B2C electronic services have registered in those states; particularly those who were previously established outside of the EU and have re-established themselves in Luxembourg since the introduction of the VAT on Ecommerce Directive.

EU suppliers of B2C electronic services will now face the same hurdles in determining where their customers are established and accounting for VAT as non-EU suppliers have been required to do since 2003. The regulations provide information on how to identify the location of the customer in order to determine the correct rate of VAT.[15] In order to provide a level of certainty the regulations include a number of presumptions which will apply. These include the presumption that where suppliers are providing electronic services at a fixed location such as a wi-fi hot spot, an internet café or a hotel lobby the place of supply will be presumed to be at that location, if the physical presence of the recipient is needed in order to provide the service. For electronic services supplied through mobile networks the presumption will be that the place of supply is the member state of the mobile country code of the SIM card used when receiving the service. If no presumption applies the supplier will need to obtain two pieces of evidence to support the country of residence. The possible forms of evidence

---

15   Regulation 1042/2013.

include the billing address of the customer, the IP address of the device used, bank details and billing address, the mobile country code stored on the SIM, the location of the customer's fixed landline where used or other commercially relevant information.

Prior to 1 July 2003, B2C electronic supplies made by non EU suppliers to customers in the EU could be made without charging VAT giving them a significant pricing advantage over their EU competitors. This was illustrated by the well-publicised dispute between the UK-based company, then called Freeserve (now part of Orange Home UK plc), whose supplies of internet access to UK customers were subject to UK VAT, and the US-based company, AOL (now part of TimeWarner Inc), whose supplies to UK customers were free of UK VAT. The VAT on Ecommerce Directive 2002/38 was introduced to level the VAT playing field in this area as a consequence.[16]

The place of supply of electronic services by businesses established outside of the EU to non-business customers resident in a member state was changed to the place where the non-business customer resides. This change of law was innovative since it created a VAT liability for suppliers who are outside the EU and, therefore, beyond the jurisdiction of the taxing authorities of the member states who collect and administer VAT.

To make compliance easier for non-EU-based suppliers making supplies of electronic services to non-business customers in a member state, a special accounting scheme was introduced allowing non-EU suppliers to register in one member state and account for all their supplies there instead of registering for VAT in each member state.

Electronic services are defined to include services which are provided over the internet, or an electronic network, and the nature of the supply is essentially automated and involving minimal human intervention and impossible to provide in the absence of information technology. The implementing regulations give guidance on the types of paid-for service which are included – supply of video, music, games, lotteries and other games of chance, website services, software services, supply of distance teaching and provision of text, images and databases.

Where the internet is merely being used as a means of delivery, the fact that this method of communication has been chosen will not alter VAT treatment of the underlying supply (eg a lawyer sending his legal advice via email must account for VAT on the basis that he is making a supply of legal advice and not a supply of an electronic services). Supplies of services which are merely delivered by electronic means are outside the scope of this chapter.

The rules described below set out the different ways in which the place of supply of services rules can apply to electronic services. The results below assume that the supplies being made are neither exempt nor zero-rated for UK VAT purposes and that advertising is only supplied on a B2B basis.

UK to UK (B2B or B2C)

7.23   An electronic service supplied by a UK-based supplier to a UK-based customer will be treated as made in the UK and so is subject to UK VAT.

16   2002/38/EC, 7 May 2002 as amended.

Outbound – UK to non-EU (B2B or B2C)

7.24   Supplies of electronic services that are made by a UK supplier to a person outside of the EU (whether on a B2B or B2C basis) are not subject to UK VAT and are expressed to be 'outside the scope of VAT'.

Outbound – UK to EU (B2B)

7.25   Supplies of electronic services that are made by a UK supplier to a business customer within the EU are allowed to be 'zero rated' provided that the UK supplier obtains and retains the EU VAT number of the customer.

Outbound – UK to EU (B2C)

7.26   Supplies of electronic services made by a UK supplier to an EU-based non-business customer are treated as made in the country of the customer and VAT at the rate applicable in the country of the customer must be applied and collected by the supplier.

Inbound – EU or non-EU to UK (B2B)

7.27   Business customers established in the UK receiving electronic services from suppliers in another country (whether or not a member state) have to account for UK VAT via the reverse charge mechanism. The reverse charge mechanism essentially requires the business customer receiving the services to self-assess for the input VAT and then, to the extent that he can (ie depending upon whether the services received are a component part of an exempt supply), seek to recover that input VAT.

The exception to this rule is in relation to ESS that are supplied for business purposes (ie on a B2B basis) where those supplies are 'effectively used or enjoyed' outside of the EU; in which case they are not subject to UK VAT.

Inbound – EU to UK (B2C)

7.28   Supplies of electronic services that are made by EU suppliers to non-business customers within the UK are treated as being made in the UK and so will be subject to UK VAT.

Inbound – non-EU to UK (B2C)

7.29   Supplies of electronic services by non-EU suppliers to EU-based business are treated as being made where the recipient belongs and so are subject to VAT at the rate applicable in the country where the recipient belongs.

As discussed at the start of this chapter the next few years will see many developments in the field of digital taxation. Already VAT rules on place of supply for services have been amended to provide a level playing field for suppliers of electronic services and the work by the OECD and G20 will also result in important changes to international tax law and national law in the coming months.

CHAPTER EIGHT

Competition law and the internet

'The Court has upheld a landmark Commission decision to give consumers more choice in software markets. That decision set an important precedent in terms of the obligations of dominant companies to allow competition, in particular in hightech industries. The Court ruling shows that the Commission was right to take its decision. Microsoft must now comply fully with its legal obligations to desist from engaging in anti-competitive conduct.'

Neelie Kroes, European Commissioner for Competition

'In light of the United States' own antitrust case and judgment against Microsoft, and the importance of the computer industry to consumers and to the global economy, the United States has a particular interest in today's CFI decision. ... We are, however, concerned that the standard applied to unilateral conduct by the CFI, rather than helping consumers, may have the unfortunate consequence of harming consumers by chilling innovation and discouraging competition.'

Thomas O Barnett, US Department of Justice
Assistant Attorney General for Antitrust

8.1　　In principle, the internet should be enormously pro-competitive. It is highly innovative and constantly changing. It facilitates market entry and is a highly transparent sales channel which brings us closer to the economists' utopia of perfect competition. The application of competition law to internet-related business should be considered against this background.

The development and functioning of online markets is essential both for cross-border trade and allowing consumers to compare prices and offerings. There has been increasing enforcement activity against and a renewed focus on online sales in recent months across a number of EU jurisdictions.

However, ordinary competition law still applies to internet-related business just as it does to bricks and mortar business. As with any industry, there are ways in which internet businesses develop or operate which may raise competition concerns. Anyone involved in the business of the internet needs to know how competition law can affect them and how it can be used to their own advantage – Microsoft and Sun Microsystems can testify to that.

This chapter examines the impact of the following competition law provisions for internet-related business.

Relevant legal provisions

Domestic provision	European provision	Focus
Competition Act 1998, Chapter I prohibition	TFEU art 101	Anti-competitive agreements
Competition Act 1998, Chapter II prohibition	TFEU art 102	Abuse of a dominant position
Enterprise Act 2002, Part 6	Not applicable	Cartel offence
Enterprise Act 2002, Part 3	EC Merger Regulation	Merger control
Enterprise Act 2002, Part 4	Council Regulation 1/2003 (Art 17)	Market investigations/ sector inquiries

INTRODUCTION TO COMPETITION LAW

8.2   Competition law can be seen as a sophisticated form of consumer protection. While unfair contract terms legislation tries to prevent consumers from being bound by unjust conditions, competition law tries to ensure that markets operate competitively, so that consumers benefit from lower prices, better service and wider choice. It assumes that the natural state of markets is not necessarily to move towards increasing competition. As Thurman Arnold, the one-time head of the US Department of Justice Anti-Trust Division,[1] explained: '[t]he maintenance of a free market is as much a matter of constant policing as the flow of traffic on a busy intersection. It does not stay orderly by trusting to the good intentions of the drivers or by preaching to them.'

However, just because competition law controls certain types of behaviour does not mean that it tries to make markets cosy places. On the contrary, a key aim of competition law is to prevent cosiness between competitors. Another important role of competition law is to ensure that companies that have market power do not use it to suppress competition. Nevertheless, it should not be assumed automatically that 'big is bad', in competition law terms. Although being big can give companies the power to be bullies, it can also simply be a sign of success. Companies grow big when they do things well.

Just as big is not necessarily bad, so small is not necessarily good. Although we might feel sympathy for small businesses who try hard and do not succeed against larger competitors, competition law should have no such sentiment. If larger organisations can deliver products and services more efficiently, then competition law should offer no protection to the small guys who suffer as a result. Competition law, as its name suggests, should protect competition, not competitors. When European regulators and courts take a more expansive view of competition law than their US counterparts (as in the case of the Microsoft investigation), they are often charged with straying beyond protection of competition and, ultimately, consumers, to protection of competitors.

---

1   1939–43.

THE LEGAL FRAMEWORK

Anti-competitive agreements and abuse of a dominant position

8.3   Articles 101 and 102 of the Treaty on the Functioning of the European Union (the 'TFEU') are the foundation of European competition law and prohibit anti-competitive agreements and abuses of a dominant position respectively, provided that they have an appreciable effect on trade between EU member states.

Most member states also have national laws that prohibit anti-competitive agreements and behaviour that have an effect within member states. Most of these are based on arts 101 and 102. Chapters I and II of the Competition Act 1998 replicate arts 101 and 102 for restrictions of competition with an effect in the UK, such that companies face effectively the same set of rules whether a competition issue arises at a domestic or European level. Although the Competition Act has been in force only since 1 March 2000, s 60 of the Competition Act requires national competition authorities, sectoral regulators and courts to interpret the Competition Act so as to avoid inconsistency with European competition law. In other words, the Competition Act largely incorporates the long-standing jurisprudence of European competition law.

Articles 101 and 102 have historically been enforced principally by the European Commission. However, since the Modernisation Regulation[2] came into force on 1 May 2004, national competition authorities, sectoral regulators and courts have been empowered to enforce the provisions in full, in addition to national competition law. The European Commission has also retained jurisdiction to enforce arts 101 and 102. Chapter IV of the Modernisation Regulation provides that the European Commission will co-operate with national competition authorities, sectoral regulators and courts regarding the application of arts 81 and 82 and the European Commission has issued a Notice which sets out the principles for the allocation of cases between the Commission and national competition authorities and sectoral regulators.[3]

Since it is intended that arts 101 and 102 of the TFEU and Chapters I and II of the Competition Act should be congruent, they are discussed alongside one another in this chapter. Only where there are specific differences between the regimes are they dealt with separately.

UK cartel offence

8.4   Separately from the Competition Act prohibitions (and with no parallel under European law), the Enterprise Act 2002 introduced a criminal cartel offence in the UK, which came into force on 20 June 2003. This is enforced by the Competition and Markets Authority (the 'CMA') which took over the functions

---

2   Council Regulation 1/2003 on the implementation of the rules on competition laid down in arts 81 and 82 of the EC Treaty (known as the 'Modernisation Regulation').

3   Commission Notice on cooperation within the Network of Competition Authorities (2004/C 101/03).

of the Office of Fair Trading (the 'OFT') and the Competition Commission (the 'CC') from 1 April 2014 under the Enterprise and Regulatory Reform Act 2013 ('ERRA 2103').

Market investigations

8.5   In addition, the Enterprise Act introduced a new UK market investigation regime, replacing the previous regime under the Fair Trading Act 1973. The ERRA 2013 also made some significant changes to the statutory deadlines for within which market investigations must be completed by the CMA. Final decisions on market investigations are taken by the CMA rather than a member of the government (other than in exceptional circumstances) and the test is based on competition law issues rather than a more general public interest. The Modernisation Regulation referred to above also formalised, from 1 May 2004, a regime for market investigations undertaken by the European Commission.[4]

Merger control

8.6   The final change to UK competition law introduced by the Enterprise Act was the replacement of the previous UK merger control regime under the Fair Trading Act 1973. Consistent with the changes to the market investigation regime, under the new regime final decisions are taken by the OFT or Competition Commission rather than a member of the government (other than in exceptional circumstances) and the test is based on competition law issues rather than a more general public interest. As is the case with market investigations, the ERRA 2013 introduced procedural changes to the merger regime, which are considered in more detail below.

Sector-specific legislation

8.7   Although there is no internet-specific competition law, there are specific regimes, at both domestic and European level, governing electronic communications and broadcasting. It is beyond the scope of this chapter to explore these regimes, but it is notable that in the electronic communications field, the UK Office of Communications ('OFCOM') has the power to control prices, set minimum quality and service standards and impose 'interconnection' obligations requiring infrastructure owners to allow third-party access to their system (following a market review and a finding of market power). OFCOM can also, and has, set 'General Conditions of Entitlement' which include consumer protection obligations, service requirements, technical obligations and numbering arrangements. These conditions may in some cases apply to internet service providers. ISPs offering voice over internet protocol ('VOIP')-based

---

4   Article 17.

services, other than strictly peer-to-peer, may for example be subject to a number of consumer protection obligations. If any internet-related agreement, merger or potentially anti-competitive behaviour involves issues of line pricing or access in a relevant market where so-called SMP (significant market power) obligations have been imposed, it is important to consider the effects of the relevant electronic communications legislation and the possible reactions of OFCOM. Also, as noted above, the Competition Act confers upon the sectoral regulators, including OFCOM as regards electronic communications and broadcasting, the power to apply the Chapters I and II prohibitions concurrently with the CMA.

ANTI-COMPETITIVE AGREEMENTS[5]

8.8   The most important operative part of the Competition Act Chapter I prohibition (s 2(1)) provides that:

'... agreements between undertakings, decisions by associations of undertakings or concerted practices which –

(a) may affect trade within the United Kingdom, and

(b) have as their object or effect the prevention, restriction or distortion of competition within the UK,

are prohibited unless they are exempt in accordance with the provisions of this Part ...'

A prohibited agreement is void unless it is exempted. Article 101 is in almost identical terms – the key difference with Chapter I is that in order to be contrary to art 101, an agreement or concerted practice must have a European dimension; more particularly it must have an appreciable, actual or potential effect on trade between EU member states.[6] The following sections will consider the constituent parts of the Chapter I prohibition.

Undertakings

8.9   Any entity capable of carrying on commercial or economic activities in relation to goods or services will be considered an 'undertaking' for the purposes of the Competition Act. This means that either natural or legal persons can be undertakings, whether they are companies, partnerships, sole traders, co-operatives or even charities.

Although a wide range of entities can be undertakings, where two undertakings form part of a single economic unit (eg parent and subsidiary companies),

---

5   See also OFT Guideline 401 on Agreements and Concerted Practices.
6   Save for this difference between the Chapter I prohibition and art 81, the interpretation of the two provisions is the same (in the light of s 60 of the Competition Act 1998). Throughout the remainder of the chapter, references to the Chapter I prohibition should be read as references to both it and art 81 unless otherwise specified.

agreements between them are not relevant for the purposes of Chapter I. This means that arrangements between subsidiaries and parents can include provisions which, if they formed part of an agreement between independent companies, would fall foul of Chapter I.[7]

Agreements and concerted practices

8.10   Just as the term 'undertaking' is widely drawn, so is the term 'agreement'. In fact, it is hard to distinguish from the European case law what is an agreement and what is a concerted practice. Since nothing hinges on identifying arrangements as one or the other, trying to draw a clear distinction is a sterile exercise.

It is clear that for the purposes of Chapter I, 'agreement' includes far more than just enforceable contracts as defined by English law; gentlemen's agreements are also covered. More informal co-operation or understandings between undertakings also fall within the scope of the Chapter I prohibition, although they are usually referred to as concerted practices. The breadth of these terms reflects the fact that anti-competitive behaviour may be arranged by a 'nod and a wink', rather than through laboriously drafted contracts. As Adam Smith observed in his oft-quoted comment, 'people of the same trade seldom meet together, even for merriment and diversion, but the conversation ends in a conspiracy against the public, or in some contrivance to raise prices'.[8]

When the CMA considers whether there is a concerted practice between undertakings, it will look at whether there have been contacts between the parties; regular gatherings of competitors in obscure hotels, and frequent emails marked 'Private and Confidential', tend to raise suspicions rapidly. It will also consider whether the behaviour of the parties has affected the market in which they are operating in ways that might not be dictated by market forces. Deciding whether this is the case tends to depend on a relatively complex analysis of the nature of the market, the type and number of competitors, their cost structures and their overall pricing behaviour. Inferences can be drawn from competitor meetings followed by parallel actions.

Decisions of associations of undertakings[9]

8.11   Both 'association of undertakings' and 'decision' are broadly applied and the scope of the provision is not limited to any particular form of membership structure or to any particular type of resolution by the members. This element of the prohibition covers trade associations and other standard-setting bodies that have trade members. The decisions in question may be parts of the constitutions

---

7   See Case 22/71 *Beguelin Import v GL Import Export* [1972] CMLR 81.
8   Adam Smith, *The Wealth of Nations*, Book 1, Ch X.
9   See also OFT Guideline 408 Trade Associations, Professions and Self-Regulating Bodies.

of these associations or may be mere recommendations which, although not enforced, are generally applied. The key issue is whether the decision in question limits the freedom of the members in relation to some commercial matter.

In industries, such as those associated with the internet, where standard-setting may be important and may be achieved by associations of companies which are otherwise direct competitors, it is important to note that competition law applies just as it would to bilateral agreements between the individual companies. Of course, agreements to create truly open standards are generally highly pro-competitive. Therefore, even if they fell within the scope of the Chapter I prohibition, they might well be exempted.

May affect trade

8.12   This requirement is often a key threshold over which small agreements do not pass in the context of European law, where it is necessary to show that trade between EU member states is affected and that the repercussions are not simply domestic. However, this is less significant since the introduction of the Competition Act for agreements with purely domestic effects.

Jurisdiction

8.13   Although the Chapter I prohibition is a domestic law provision, it applies to any agreement or arrangement which 'is, or is intended to be, implemented in the United Kingdom'[10] (or part of it). This means that even if the parties to the arrangement are not situated within the UK, or the agreement is not governed by UK law, it can still fall foul of the Chapter I prohibition.

If companies are based outside the UK but the anti-competitive arrangement relates to supplies of goods or services made in the UK, such an arrangement will be prohibited. In the context of the global internet industry, the nature of the UK courts' jurisdiction is important. Even if you are based in California and you enter into an agreement with a company in Moscow, but which is implemented in the UK, your agreement may be caught. A similar approach to jurisdiction is adopted at European level – if the agreement in question affects trade within the EU, it can be caught by art 81. This extended jurisdiction reflects the judgment of the European Court of Justice in the *Woodpulp* case.[11]

Object or effect

8.14   It is sufficient that an agreement have either an 'object' or an 'effect' that is anti-competitive: it need not have both. Consideration should first be given to

---

10   Competition Act 1998, s 2(3).
11   See Cases 114, 125-129/85 *Ahlstrom v EC Commission (Woodpulp)* [1988] ECR 5193.

the object of the agreement in the economic context in which it is to be operated. An agreement that is never implemented may still be held to infringe Chapter I if it has a clearly anti-competitive object, for example a price-fixing or market-sharing agreement.

Where, however, the analysis of the object of the agreement does not reveal an obvious anti-competitive objective, it is then necessary to look at its effect, taking account of all surrounding factors and, in particular, the economic context of the agreement. Factors in such an analysis include the market shares of the parties in the relevant markets, whether the agreement is part of a network of similar agreements, and the state of competition in the market in the absence of the agreement in question.

Prevention, restriction or distortion of competition

8.15   What constitutes an illegitimate constraint on competition is a question at the heart of all competition law systems. Most agreements are pro-competitive, in that they facilitate economic activity. The Chapter I prohibition and art 101 provide identical lists of examples of behaviour which may be caught:

Directly or indirectly fixing purchasing or selling prices

8.16   Fixing purchasing or selling prices is almost certain to infringe the prohibition. Formation of a price cartel is a serious infringement under this head, but prices can also be fixed by, for example, agreement to adhere to published price lists or to forewarn competitors of intended price rises. Similarly, prices may be indirectly affected by agreeing to limit discounts or credit terms or charges for transportation.

Where companies exchange price information (or other relevant data such as their strategies) so that uncertainties in the market are removed, such arrangements may also be contrary to the prohibition. Whether such information-sharing has an anti-competitive effect will depend upon the nature of the market in question and the information exchanged – where there are a small number of competitors in a market for relatively undifferentiated products and sensitive sales information is exchanged, the authorities are likely to consider it unacceptable.

It has been suggested by some that internet 21st century – the places where competing undertakings get together, share information and collude, in particular, on pricing. In principle, the regulatory authorities treat the possibility of cartel-like behaviour in B2Bs in the same way as in any other industry. They consider the structure of the arrangement, the levels and types of information passing between the members and, in the context of price fixing, the levels of prices being charged and the basis upon which changes occur.

In none of the cases that has come before the European Commission in relation to B2Bs (whether under art 101 or the EC Merger Regulation) has there been any finding of collusion between parties. That, of course, is not surprising since the European Commission was scrutinising the arrangements at their outset before they had been put into practice.[12] Nonetheless, in the *Volbroker*[13] case the European Commission required that conditions be complied with to prevent unnecessary risk of collusion or information-sharing before an agreement between major banks to establish a foreign exchange B2B could be approved.

Volbroker.com was created through an agreement between subsidiaries of six major banks which were market makers in the market for foreign currency options. It provided the first brokerage service to bring automated trading in foreign currency options for banks. The parent banks sought clearance under art 81 from the European Commission (note that since the Modernisation Regulation came into force on 1 May 2004, notifications for clearance under art 81 have not been available – contractual parties must generally 'self-assess' their agreements' compatibility with art 81, assisted by their advisers). The parent banks secured a comfort letter (informal clearance) for the arrangements on the basis of the following assurances:

1.   none of Volbroker.com's staff or management would have any contractual or other obligations towards any of the parent banks (and vice versa);

2.   Volbroker.com's staff and management would be in a geographically distinct location;

3.   the representatives of the parent banks who sat on Volbroker.com's board of directors would not have access to commercially sensitive information relating to each other or to third parties;

4.   the parents would not have access to the information technology and communication systems of Volbroker.com; and

5.   the parent banks would ensure that staff and management understood the importance of keeping commercially sensitive information confidential and that sanctions for breach were spelt out.

Limiting or controlling production, markets, technical development or investment

8.17   In economic terms, limiting output has a similar detrimental effect to raising prices. Output restrictions are, therefore, treated with similar severity to price fixing arrangements. In the context of high-technology internet-related business, agreements to restrict the development of new products and innovations could clearly inhibit competition and retard the development of the market. Although in many circumstances agreements between undertakings to set standards may reduce waste and consumers' search costs, such agreements can restrict competition by reducing the scope for innovation.

---

12   See, for example, COMP/M 1969 *UTC/Honeywell/i2/myaircraft.com* decision of 4 August 2000.

13   See Commission Press Release 31 July 2000, IP/00/896.

Sharing markets or sources of supply

8.18   Where competitors divide up markets, whether into geographical sectors or by types of customer, this means that there is in principle a loss of competition. A customer in a particular area (or particular group) has less choice and the incumbent supplier is insulated from competitive pressures which would drive down prices, increase levels of service or increase choice of products.

In the US, a challenge was brought (under US antitrust law) against the 'Baby Bell' telecoms companies[14] for their alleged formation of a cartel to dominate the internet yellow pages market.[15] The key allegations were that: (a) the various telecoms companies had agreed amongst themselves to share geographical markets across the US and control essential points of access to the internet; and (b) major ISPs had made agreements with the telecoms companies to exclude competitors, including GTE New Media, by giving prominence to their own yellow pages on the ISPs' guides. The matter was settled before it came to court, but it illustrates how market sharing arrangements may be challenged in the context of internet-related activity.

Discriminating between customers

8.19   Whether on the basis of price or the conditions of sale, discriminating between customers may place certain customers at a competitive disadvantage and thereby distort the operation of the market. In particular, where a trade association or other association of undertakings sets prices or conditions for sales between its members different from those it sets for non-members, the arrangement may infringe the prohibition.

Attaching supplementary obligations unconnected to the subject of the agreement

8.20   This may also infringe the Chapter I prohibition. In other words, burdening companies with obligations which are irrelevant to the subject-matter of the principal transaction may be anti-competitive.

Appreciability

8.21   The arrangements in question must not just affect competition in the relevant market; they must affect competition to an appreciable extent.[16]

The European Commission notice on agreements of minor importance[17] sets out a 'safe harbour' for appreciability based on the market shares of contracting parties: 10% combined market share if they are actual or potential competitors, and 15% market share for either party if they are not actual or potential competitors.

---

14   The regional companies which resulted from the break-up of certain parts of AT&T ordered in 1984.
15   *GTE New Media Services Inc v Ameritech Corpn* (DDC complaint filed 6 October 1997).
16   See, for example, *Volk v Vervaecke* case 5/69 [1969] ECR 295.
17   Notice on agreements of minor importance which do not appreciably restrict competition under art 81, OJ [2001] C 368/13.

The CMA follows the same approach to appreciability when applying Chapter I.[18] The thresholds are reduced to 5% if there are parallel networks of similar agreements operating in a substantial part of the market. In addition, the safe harbours do not apply to agreements containing 'hardcore restrictions', ie (a) competitors directly or indirectly fixing prices, sharing markets or limiting production or (b) suppliers restricting resellers' ability to determine resale prices or the customers to, or territories in which, they sell. Furthermore, in applying these tests, it is often difficult to decide what is the 'relevant market'.

Market definition

8.22   Market definition is a vexed question which has bedevilled the application of competition law throughout the world. There is, however, a general consensus between US, European and UK competition authorities as to how the analysis should generally be carried out.[19]

A market has two key dimensions: product and geography. It is necessary to identify the group of products with which the products at issue compete, and the geographical area within which they compete. Formally, these dimensions are identified by applying what is known as the 'hypothetical monopolist' test. This works as follows: you define the smallest group of products (and geographical area) which, if it was controlled by a single (hypothetical) company, would allow that company to raise prices by a small but significant amount (5–10%) for the foreseeable future.[20]

If the hypothetical monopolist can raise prices by 5–10% for the foreseeable future that means that: (a) consumers do not consider other products to be substitutes for the products over which there is a monopoly (demand-side substitution); and (b) new suppliers would not enter the market to produce the products which the monopolist controls (supply-side substitution). If consumers could switch to other products then the hypothetical monopolist could not sustain higher prices (and maintain his profits). Similarly, if new suppliers could enter the market, the new suppliers could charge lower prices and again, the hypothetical monopolist could not impose prices 5–10% above competitive levels.

In order to run the test it is necessary to consider whether there are any substitutes for the product or service at issue in the eyes of customers, and whether a rival supplier of similar products or services could enter the market if prices were raised so that the hypothetical monopolist was making excessive profits. This is where the nice neat test becomes rather difficult to apply, for two reasons: first, it is often difficult to gather evidence to support a particular result of the thought-experiment; second, if the company at issue is already charging monopoly prices then when you run the experiment you might consider that

18   See OFT Guideline 401 on Agreements and Concerted Practices, paras 2.16–2.21.
19   See OFT Guideline 403 market definition, Commission Notice on the definition of the market for the purposes of Community competition law [1997] OJ C 372/5; and the Department of Justice and Federal Trade Commission Horizontal Merger Guidelines 1992.
20   This test is sometimes referred to as the 'SSNIP' test – Small but Significant, Non-transitory Increase in Price.

people are switching to substitute products when in fact they are just giving up on that product and turning to different activities. From the subject matter of the US case in which this latter problem first arose, this is known as the 'cellophane fallacy'.[21]

The European Commission has considered the nature of the relevant market in a number of cases involving the internet, a number of them mergers. Although each case must be considered on its own merits and there is no formal system of precedents with competition authority decisions, the following examples are useful illustrations of how internet-related markets have been defined.

The *Worldcom/MCI* merger[22] was only approved on the undertaking that MCI divest itself of its internet business. Initially, the parties argued that other forms of data transmission were a substitute in the eyes of consumers for internet services. The Commission quickly rejected this suggestion because customers purchasing an internet access service do so in the expectation that they will be able to access the full range of services available on the internet and make contact with all other users. While one-to-one data transmission systems might enable customers to perform certain tasks outside the internet, it would not provide 'the permanent, unfettered access to the community of internet users which is the main purpose of buying the service'.[23] Accordingly, on the demand-side there was no substitute for the internet.

The Commission then went on to consider whether these two large telecoms companies, which had substantial fibre networks carrying internet traffic, were in a narrower market than that for internet access services. The Commission held that the structure of the market was in fact hierarchical: there was a tier of top-level ISPs, a group of ISPs with smaller networks and then ISPs who simply resell access to other ISPs' networks. If top-level ISPs raised the prices of their internet connection services by 5%, resellers would have to keep using their systems and so would pay the increase and, in due course, pass it on to consumers. Smaller ISPs would also have to continue to deal with the top-level ISPs if a price rise was imposed and so would not act as a competitive constraint on the top-level ISPs.

In terms of geography, the Commission found that for top-level ISPs the market was global because, although they were based in the US, they operated at an international level providing services throughout the world.

The Commission has recognised that different internet-related services can constitute different product markets. In the *Telia/Telenor/Schibsted* case[24] it distinguished the market for internet access from those for paid-content (eg

---

21 *United States v Dupont (cellophane)* (351 US 377 (1956)).

22 IV/M 1069 *Re Concentration between Worldcom Inc and MCI Communications Corpn* [1999] 5 CMLR 876.

23 IV/M 1069 *Re Concentration between Worldcom Inc and MCI Communications Corpn* [1999] 5 CMLR 876 at 894.

24 IV/JV 1 *Telia/Telenor/Schibsted* (27 May 1998, unreported). See also IV/JV 5 *Cegetel/Canal+/ AOL/Bertelsmann* (4 August 1998, unreported); *IV/JV 11 @Home Benelux* (15 September 1998, unreported); and *DeTeOnline/Axel Springer/Holtzbrink/Internet Corpn* (12 October 1998, unreported).

games, special news services and for internet advertising). It also recognised the weight of the parties' argument that website production services may be a sufficiently technical and specialised activity to constitute a separate market.

In addition to distinguishing between different internet-related services, the Commission has also distinguished the internet provision of services from other channels. The *Bertelsmann/Mondadori*[25] case concerned two major publishing enterprises wishing to create a joint venture to combine their respective book club activities.[26] Although the Commission did not have to reach a final conclusion on market definition, it considered that it might be possible to distinguish between 'distant selling' of books (including book club sales, mail order and internet sales) and the retail sale of books. This reasoning follows the earlier decision in *Advent/EMI/WH Smith*,[27] where a similar distinction between the distant selling and retail selling of books was drawn. Were a distinction between internet and traditional sales channels to be sustained, it could have a profound impact upon the competitive analysis of internet retailers: if the internet is a separate market from retail, internet retailers will be considered to have far larger market shares than would otherwise be the case.

However, the above cases can be contrasted with the more recent views of the OFT and the Competition Commission (the predecessors to the CMA) in the UK on the *HMV/Ottakar's* merger – while the OFT noted only a limited degree of competitive constraint exercised by internet retailers on traditional retailers, principally in relation to pricing, on referral the Competition Commission went significantly further in ruling that no separate market for online book retailing exists.[28] It is already apparent, both at UK and European level, that where price sensitivity is a particular feature of a market, it is becoming more likely that internet sales channels may be found to exercise competitive restraints on traditional channels – see, for example, the Commission decision in *Karstadtquelle/Mytravel*[29] (package holiday retail), and the OFT decisions in *Staples/Globus Office World*[30] (office supplies) and *O2/The Link*[31] (mobile phone retailing). Conversely, where the consumer experience is fundamentally different between the online and offline worlds, as the OFT found in a number of gambling-related cases (see *William Hill/Stanley Leisure*[32] and *Gala Group/ Coral Eurobet*[33]), distinctions between the different channels may endure.

---

25 IV/M 1407 *Bertelsman/Mondadori* OJ C 145 26/05/1999.
26 In relation to the geographical extent of the market, emphasis was placed on language barriers and the market limited to Italy. See also Case No IV/M 1459 *Bertelsmann/Havas/BOL* (6 May 1999, unreported).
27 IV/M 1112 *Advent International/EMI/WH Smith* OJ C 172 06/06/1998. See also, in the context of catalogue sales, IV/M 0070 *Otto/Grattan* OJ C 093 11/04/1991.
28 OFT, *Anticipated acquisition by HMV Group plc, through Waterstone's Limited, of Ottakar's plc*, 6 December 2005, and Competition Commission, Proposed acquisition of Ottakar's plc by HMV Group plc through Waterstone's Booksellers Limited, 12 May 2006.
29 COMP/M.4601 *Karstadtquelle/Mytravel*, 04/05/2007.
30 OFT, *Proposed acquisition by Staples Inc of Globus Office World plc*, 21 July 2004.
31 OFT, *Completed acquisition by O2 UK Limited of the Link Stores Limited*, 10 October 2006.
32 OFT, *Completed acquisition by William Hill plc of the licensed betting office business of Stanley plc*, 1 August 2005.
33 OFT, *Completed acquisition by Gala Group of Coral Eurobet Group*, 10 January 2006.

In the *myaircraft.com case*,[34] which concerned the creation of a B2B market place for aircraft parts and attendant services, the parties argued that the provision of aircraft parts and services over the internet was part of the general market for aircraft parts and services: 'e-commerce should be considered as one segment among the many modalities by which companies transact business'. Although the Commission did not find it necessary to make a definitive finding upon the relevant market, the competitive assessment of the arrangements takes into account the position of the participants in the general market for aircraft parts and services, not just internet-based sales.

Google's proposed acquisition of internet advertising sales house DoubleClick had just been notified to the European Commission.[35] Google argued its online search advertising business and DoubleClick's online graphical advertising activities belong to separate markets, and as such their merger would not alter the position in either of those markets. Conversely, a finding of a wider market for online search advertising in general might lead to the creation or strengthening of a dominant position by Google/DoubleClick. (The EU Commission cleared this transaction under the EU Merger Regulation after an in-depth phase 2 investigation. The Commission concluded that the transaction would be unlikely to have harmful effects on consumers, either in ad-serving or in intermediation on online advertising markets.)

Convergence

8.23   A particular manifestation of the way in which the internet changes the competitive structure of other industries is seen in what is referred to in the jargon as 'convergence'. Televisions, computers and telephones are increasingly able to perform similar functions as digital technology develops. We can access the internet through our televisions and mobile phones and equally access television and make phone calls through our computers.

From the competition law point of view, the key issue is that those people wanting to provide television programming, telecommunications links or online shopping will have a variety of routes by which they can reach the consumer. The result is that different infrastructure systems may be competing against one another for business.

When considering whether the activities of internet businesses are anti-competitive it may be necessary to consider not just the market for internet provision of the relevant services or products but also other distribution mechanisms. Equally, it means that agreements or mergers between businesses which have little or no overlap in their existing activities require close scrutiny

---

34   COMP/M 1969 *UTC/Honeywell/i2/myaircraft.com decision* of 4 August 2000.
35   COMP/M.4731 Google/DoubleClick, notified 21 September 2007.

because each set of activities reinforces the other in the convergent world.[36] A particular example of this was provided by the acquisition by BSkyB, nominally a satellite TV broadcaster and channel supplier, of retail broadband provider Easynet. The OFT noted the opportunity presented to BSkyB to begin to provide 'triple-play' services, and leverage its dominance in premium TV content to its advantage in the market for internet service provision, in part by providing its content over the internet.[37]

British Interactive Broadcasting (which traded as 'Open') was a joint venture whose parents were BSkyB, British Telecom, HSBC and Matsushita. It was established to provide digital interactive television services to consumers in the UK. Using BSkyB's digital satellite broadcasting system and BT's telecommunications network, consumers were able to access a range of interactive services, including home banking, home shopping and a limited 'walled garden' of websites. Upon review of the joint venture, the European Commission found that there was a separate market for the supply of interactive services via the television as distinct from via computers or indeed through high street retailers.[38] It is unsurprising that the supply of services (and goods) from high street retailers was not considered a substitute for interactive services accessible from the comfort of your own home using the television.

Rather more surprising is the distinction between interactive services accessed through a computer and those accessed through the television. The Commission concluded that a small but significant increase in the prices of interactive television services could be sustained. The possibility of accessing such services through a computer would not constrain prices for two reasons: first, only 25% of households in the UK had computers; and secondly, the cost of switching between television and computer is high because a whole PC system had to be bought. A further reason adduced was that TVs are traditionally found in the living room and are a focal point of family life, whereas computers are tucked away elsewhere. The characteristics of the use of the television therefore meant that people would not start using computers as a substitute.

As convergence continues, this may be found to be an untenable distinction in future cases. The traditionally defined roles of the television and computers are rapidly eroding, and people are increasingly using computers for receiving films and other entertainment. At a certain point, substitution will be sufficient to widen the relevant market. As above, the BSkyB/Easynet merger presages the possibility of premium content (eg a BSkyB sports channel, being delivered

---

36 The Time Warner/AOL merger is the most poignant example of this phenomenon. Time Warner had relatively limited internet interests but was a major broadcaster with access to substantial valuable content. AOL had large numbers of people to whom they were ISP and to whom they wished to provide content. By merging, Time Warner was able to provide content which AOL lacked to AOL's subscribers using internet technology. See below and Commission Press Release IP/00/1145 of 11 October 2000, 'Commission gives conditional approval to AOL/Time Warner merger'.

37 OFT, *Anticipated acquisition by BSkyB Broadband Services Limited of Easynet Group plc*, 30 December 2005.

38 IV/36.539 *British Interactive Broadcasting/Open* [1999] OJ L312/1. See also comment upon the decision by Andres Font Galarza in the Competition Policy Newsletter [1999] No 3 October.

by a number of different delivery methods). Note also the interventions by the European Commission to break up the sale of football rights, including requiring the separation of broadcasting rights over the different platforms of traditional television, internet and mobile phone and, in the case of the UEFA Champions League rights, enforcing the simulcasting of matches over the internet.[39] The capacity for substitution between the different platforms is bound to grow as the technological capabilities of the new media develop and catch on among consumers.

A more sustainable distinction might be that which the Commission drew between interactive television services, pay television and free-to-air television.[40] The idea that free-to-air television does not constrain the pricing of pay television is widely accepted (although not uncontroversial) – it is easy to argue that if free-to-air TV was a substitute for pay TV, everyone would watch free TV because everyone prefers not to pay. The distinction drawn between pay TV services, which are principally entertainment services, and interactive TV services, which are largely transactional or information-providing, is perhaps more interesting. The Commission considered that interactive TV was a complement to pay TV, not a substitute.

Note also in the context of the pay television market that the Commission distinguished between the wholesale supply of films and sports channels and other pay TV content. Films and sports channels are often referred to as 'premium' channels due to their higher pricing as compared with basic channels. This higher pricing itself tends to indicate a separate market for such services.[41] It also vindicates the hackneyed new media saying that 'content is king'.

Finally, the Commission considered the infrastructure market. Commentators have suggested that cable networks have had a significant technological advantage over satellite broadcasting systems since satellite systems lack a simple 'return path' – a route by which the viewer can easily communicate with the broadcaster. By linking BSkyB's satellite broadcasting system to the narrowband telephone network, Open was able to compete against the UK cable system by providing a return path which enabled interactivity between consumers and the service providers. The Commission concluded that Open was, therefore, competing in an infrastructure market which included the BT copper wire network and the fibre cable network. Notably, mobile networks were excluded from the market definition.

---

39 See COMP/C.2-37.398 – *Joint selling of the commercial rights of the UEFA Champions League*, COMP/C.2-38.173 and 38.453 *Joint selling of the media rights of the FA Premier League on an exclusive basis*, and COMP/C.2/37.214 – *Joint selling of the media rights to the German Bundesliga*.
40 Free-to-air: programming that customers do not have to pay a subscription for such as ITV1 and BBC1.
41 A similar distinction was drawn by the UK Monopolies and Mergers Commission in its report on the proposed merger between BSkyB and Manchester United [1999] Cm 4305, in particular, paras 2.25–2.51.

Exemptions[42]

8.24   Article 101(3) provides that certain agreements which meet the above criteria (ie they appreciably prevent, restrict or distort competition, can be exempted from the adverse consequences of falling foul of the prohibition). There are two types of exemption available under European law: individual exemptions and block exemptions. The Chapter I prohibition has a parallel system of exemptions.

Individual exemptions

8.25   An agreement which appreciably prevents, restricts or distorts competition will nevertheless benefit from an individual exemption from art 101 and Chapter I if it meets the following art 101(3) criteria:

1.   contributes to the improvement of production or distribution or promotes technical or economic progress;

2.   provides consumers with a 'fair share' of these benefits;

3.   does not impose on the parties restrictions which are not indispensable to the attainment of the objectives specified; and

4.   does not eliminate competition in respect of a substantial part of the products in question.

Although this test is stringent, it is essentially carrying out a balancing exercise: do the pro-competitive aspects outweigh the restrictions of competition, and are all the restrictions included in the agreement necessary to achieve the pro-competitive ends?

As noted above, since the Modernisation Regulation came into force on 1 May 2004, it is no longer possible to apply to the European Commission or UK CMA for a formal or informal individual exemption (although they may give informal advice in cases resolving novel or unresolved questions of law) – contractual parties must generally 'self-assess' their agreements' compatibility with art 101, assisted by their advisers.

The creation by several airlines of the online travel website Opodo generated complaints to the European Commission. As part of a settlement to close the case, the shareholders of Opodo gave various undertakings in order to satisfy the art 101(3) criteria:[43]

1.   they should not discriminate against other travel agents in favour of Opodo;

2.   access to Opodo should not be restricted to shareholder airlines, and Opodo should treat all airlines equally: ie Opodo should not favour shareholder

---

42   These exemptions are subject to 'clawback' provisions which enable the relevant authorities to remove their protection in certain circumstances.
43   Comp/A.38.321 TQ3/OPODO.

airlines over non-shareholder airlines (unless there is an objective commercial basis for doing so); and

3.   the shareholders of Opodo should deal with Opodo on a strictly commercial basis, ie commercially sensitive information should not flow between the shareholders of Opodo through Opodo.

Block exemptions

8.26   There is a range of block exemptions covering, amongst other things, exclusive distribution, exclusive purchasing and franchising (all vertical agreements),[44] research and development,[45] specialisation[46] and technology transfer agreements.[47] These block exemptions provide 'safe harbours' as long as certain criteria are met. Most importantly, the agreements must not contain certain specified 'hardcore restrictions'. The block exemption will not apply to the agreement if such clauses are included. Furthermore, in most instances such clauses will be deemed to restrict competition and will not benefit from an exemption and therefore will infringe art 101 or Chapter I.

The vertical agreements block exemption covers a wide range of agreements between parties at different levels in the production and distribution chain. Agreements containing restrictions on resale prices or 'passive sales' (sales where the customer approaches the supplier, rather than where the supplier has touted for the customer's business) are not covered by the block exemption and would be considered hardcore. Furthermore, where the supplier (or, in certain circumstances, the buyer) has 30% or more of the relevant market for the products at issue, it cannot benefit from block exemption protection.

The guidelines accompanying the block exemption indicate that the use of the internet to advertise or sell products is, in general, considered a form of passive sales insofar as the website is not directed towards a territory or customer group exclusively allocated to another distributor. Agreements which prevent any use of websites would therefore generally not benefit from the protection of the vertical restraints block exemption and such a restriction would be considered hardcore. However, there are exceptions: internet sales can be banned if there is an objective justification, such as perhaps health and safety grounds; and the use of links or on-site advertising which specifically target customers allocated to other distributors are permissible.[48] In addition, a supplier may restrict internet sales by imposing quality standards, particularly when it has established a 'selective distribution' system (ie where the supplier has selected its distributors on the basis of objective criteria, such as service quality or nature of premises). The Commission has in the past accepted a prohibition on internet-only distributors

---

44   Commission Regulation on the application of art 81(3) of the EC Treaty to categories of vertical agreements and concerted practices [1999] OJ L336/21 and accompanying guidelines, [2000] OJ C 291/1.
45   Reg 417/85.
46   Reg 418/85.
47   Reg 772/2004.
48   *European Commission Vertical Agreements Guidelines* [2000] OJ C 291/1, para 51.

for luxury goods.[49] However, the Commission has also fined Yamaha 2.56 million euro for various infringements of competition law, including an obligation on its dealers to notify Yamaha before exporting any of its products via the internet.[50]

ANTI-COMPETITIVE CONDUCT

8.27   The preceding section of this chapter (see **8.8**) considered the prohibitions against anti-competitive agreements contained in art 101 of the EC Treaty and Chapter I of the Competition Act. This section considers the prohibitions against anti-competitive conduct contained in art 102 and Chapter II. The Chapter II prohibition (s 18) provides that:

> 'any conduct on the part of one or more undertakings which amounts to the abuse of a dominant position in a market is prohibited if it may affect trade within the United Kingdom.'

The only significant difference between this provision and art 102 is that art 102 refers to a dominant position 'within the common market or in a substantial part of it', and requires an effect on trade between member states. Under domestic law, a dominant position means a dominant position within the UK or part of it.[51]

Dominance

8.28   The definition of a dominant position which has been applied in European case law and, by virtue of s 60 of the Competition Act, also applies under UK competition law, was given in the *United Brands* case,[52] where the European Court of Justice stated that a dominant position is:

> 'a position of economic strength enjoyed by an undertaking which enables it to prevent effective competition being maintained on the relevant market by affording it the power to behave to an appreciable extent independently of its competitors, customers and ultimately of its consumers'.

'Dominance' is assessed in the context of a particular market, therefore the issue of market definition raises its ugly head again. The market definition considerations discussed at **8.22** above in the context of Chapter I/Art 101 apply equally in the context of Chapter II/Art 102.

Market share

8.29   CMA guidance notes the (rebuttable) presumption of dominance under both EU and UK law, where a market share remains persistently over 50%. CMA

---

49   *Yves Saint Laurent Parfums*, European Commission press release of 17 May 2001, IP/01/713.
50   *PO/Yamaha*, COMP/37.975.
51   Competition Act 1998, s 18(3).
52   Case 27/76 *United Brands v EC Commission* [1978] ECR 207 at 277.

guidance also states that it is unlikely that a market share of below 40% would amount to (single firm) dominance, although this also depends on other factors.[53] Much will depend upon the structure of the market in question – for example, if the undertaking in question is the only large player in the market and competition comes from far smaller players, it is more likely that a finding of dominance will be made. Countervailing buyer power and the existence of barriers to entry and expansion by competitors are also key factors.

Growth and innovation

8.30　In addition to considering market shares, it is important to look at the nature of the market for the products or services in question. If there are low barriers to entry for new competitors and there is a great deal of innovation in the market, a company with a large market share at any particular moment might quickly see it diminished.

Almost all sectors of internet-related activity are highly innovative. The hardware and software which enables people to use the internet evolves rapidly. Processor speeds have increased rapidly whilst prices have fallen. Routers and switching systems manage greater and greater volumes of traffic. Applications software from accountancy packages to browsers is constantly changing and improving.

This rapid change and rapid growth has significant implications for the application of any competition law system. Where products and services are constantly evolving, it tends to be more difficult for any one company to secure the sort of market power which will enable it to distort the proper functioning of the market. Although a product may be very popular at a particular time, the possibility of a new, more advanced, product coming in and replacing it in the near future is higher in dynamic high-technology markets. Although there may be concerns about the manner in which such markets operate from time to time, authorities should be slow to intervene because dynamic markets may well rectify their own problems within a short time.

In addition, there are major practical problems with intervention in dynamic markets. First, it is often hard to gather sufficient quantities of useful data to enable a regulator to gain an accurate picture of how the market is operating. Second, any regulatory intervention tends to take time for consideration and implementation. By the time a conclusion is reached that intervention is necessary, the market may have moved on and, whilst the proposed solution might have been appropriate months or years ago, it may be past its sell-by-date before it can be implemented.

Network effects

8.31　There are certain features of internet-related industries which might incline authorities to intervene. The internet is a network of networks which is dependent upon common language, protocols and applications in order to confer benefits on individuals. As more people adopt a particular standard, the more

53　OFT Guideline 402, paras 4.17–4.20.

value it has to all those using it as a network grows. Each new potential user will have a greater incentive to adopt the standard. The phenomenon is referred to as Metcalfe's Law: the value of a network to its users grows exponentially with the addition of each new user. It is known by competition lawyers as a 'positive network effect'. In practice, it means that if you can be the first to get an application into the market so that you build up a base of users, it is more likely that your application, rather than a competing application, will become the industry standard. In other words, by getting a good start in the market, you can have significant advantages in securing a powerful market position.

Any competition regulator would prefer to stop competition problems before they start. Early intervention to prevent any individual or group of individuals getting undue power in the marketplace is better than waiting until they have market power and actually use it to distort competition. By that time, many potential competitors may have already suffered, and potential entrants will have been deterred. It tends to require government with a very heavy hand, to unravel monopolies. There is, therefore, a temptation for regulators to step in earlier on in the development of a market which exhibits network effects in order to prevent those effects maintaining a monster (in competition terms). The existence of network effects for operating systems was an important motivating factor for the European Commission in investigating Microsoft, which led to an abuse of dominance decision, subsequently upheld on substantive grounds by the European Court of First Instance ('CFI') – see **8.42** below.[54]

Network effects in an internet-related market may be reinforced where the market is in knowledge-based products or services. In such markets marginal costs may be zero. For example, once you have made the effort to produce some software, the cost of producing an additional copy is negligible. Developing the knowledge may have been expensive and the initial investment in exploitation may have been high, but once those investments have been made, further exploitation is cheap. It is therefore extremely easy to scale up your operations quickly. Once a company in a market with network effects has a small advantage, it is able to attract new customers more easily than its nearest rival. The company's attractiveness to customers rapidly increases and so its advantage over its rivals extends, allowing it to bring in new customers easily without incurring significant cost.

Intellectual property rights

8.32 One particular matter which is important to the competition law analysis of so-called knowledge-based industries is the role played by intellectual property rights. Although the possession or use of an intellectual property right is not in and of itself anti-competitive, intellectual property law potentially enables companies to develop significant market power by ensuring that nobody else uses their unique hardware, software, ideas or branding.

The relationship between intellectual property rights and competition law is vexed. A patent, for example, may be seen as a sanctioned monopoly in relation to particular works, products or processes. It is justified on the basis that the

---

54 COMP/C-3/37.792 *Microsoft*, and Case T-201/04 *Microsoft v Commission*.

prospect of winning such a monopoly encourages innovation and endeavour – if there were no such monopolies, writers and inventors would be unable to reap any benefit from their work, since it would be copied as soon as it became public. The extent of these mini-monopolies is limited by competition law. There is therefore a tension between what intellectual property rights can legitimately be used to achieve, and what is anti-competitive. This tension was at the heart of the Microsoft case.

Collective dominance

8.33   Both art 102 and Chapter II refer explicitly to 'one or more undertakings' being dominant. This reflects the possibility that, in certain situations, distinct companies considered together are able to act independently of competitive pressures. This concept of collective or joint dominance has been endorsed by the European Courts.[55] In the *Almelo* case[56] the European Court of Justice held that '[i]n order for ... a collective dominant position to exist the undertakings must be linked in such a way that they adopt the same conduct on the market'. It is clear that contractual links may be sufficient to give rise to a position of joint dominance.

However, other economic links between the parties within a tight oligopoly may be sufficient to result in collective dominance in a market with the appropriate characteristics, in particular in terms of market concentration, transparency and product homogeneity. Where parties are in a position to anticipate one another's behaviour and are therefore strongly encouraged to align their conduct in the market so as to maximise their joint profits by restricting production with a view to increasing prices then collective dominance may exist. In such a context, each trader is party to a 'game' where it is aware that highly competitive action on its part designed to increase its market share (eg a price cut) would provoke identical action by the others, so that it would derive no benefit from its initiative in the long run.[57] Although the possibility of collective dominance existing in markets is recognised, it is in practice difficult to prove[58] and there are very few cases where collective dominance has been found for the purpose of art 102 or Chapter II.

Abuse

8.34   The concept of abuse of a dominant position covers a range of behaviour. As with art 101 and Chapter I, art 102 and Chapter II includes a (non-exhaustive)

---

55   See, in particular, Case T-68/89 *Societa Italiano Vetro v EC Commission* [1992] ECR II-1403.
56   Case C-393/92 [1994] ECR I-1477.
57   See, in particular, Case T-102/96 *Gencor Ltd v Commission* [1999] ECR II–753 where it was suggested that in certain circumstances companies in oligopolistic markets may have a jointly dominant position even without contractual links.
58   See Case T–342/99 *Airtours v EC Commission* [2002] 5 CMLR 317.

list of examples of the types of behaviour which may fall foul of the prohibition.[59] Abuses fall into two broad categories: exploitation of customers ('exploitative abuses') and exclusion of competitors ('exclusionary abuses').

Excessive pricing

8.35   The classic exploitative abuse, and intuitively the most obvious form of abuse of a dominant position, is excessive pricing. Prices are excessively high where they are above the prices which would be charged by undertakings if the market was competitive.

In *Napp Pharmaceuticals v Director General of Fair Trading*[60] the Competition Commission Appeals Tribunal held that the following methods could be used in assessing whether prices were excessive:

- a comparison of prices against costs;

- a comparison of prices against the costs of the next most profitable competitor;

- a comparison of prices against the prices of competitors;

- a comparison of prices against the undertaking's own prices in other markets.

Precisely how much higher prices would need to be above costs to indicate excess is not clear. In fact, excessive pricing is one of the hardest forms of abuse to prove. Referring to profitability in assessing excessive pricing can be highly unreliable. In the OFT Economic Discussion Paper 377 'Innovation and Competition policy', Charles River Associates state: 'Measuring profitability is a poor way of conducting competition policy in standard industries. It is likely to be even worse in high-technology industries. The very high *ex ante* risks of failure mean that the returns to 'winners' in high-technology markets should be very high.' At the time of writing, we are not aware of any decisions or judgments involving exclusionary abuses in the internet/IT sector.

Predation

8.36   An alternative strategy that a dominant firm might adopt, rather than trying to secure higher profits in the short run by pricing excessively high, is to drop prices, to drive competitors out of the market (predatory pricing – an exclusionary abuse). The intention of this strategy is that once the competitors are driven out, the incumbent will be free to increase prices and recover the losses it incurred in dropping the prices and go on to make greater profits overall.

Again, predatory pricing is an abuse which is often difficult to prove. After all, where markets are competitive it would be expected that competitors would drop

---

59   There is no system of exemption for breaches of art 82/Chapter II. Limited exclusions are provided for in s 19 of the Competition Act 1998 – the key area excluded is mergers and concentrations.
60   [2002] Comp AR 13.

prices in order to increase market share. Lower prices may simply be a reflection of increased efficiency.

The general rule historically adopted under art 82 and Chapter II is that where a company prices below its average variable cost of production (ie the average of those costs which vary according to the amount of the product produced), predation is to be presumed. The 2005 European Commission Staff Discussion Paper[61] proposed the slightly different cost benchmark of average avoidable costs (ie those additional costs that the producer incurs by producing the units at the lower price).

However, in high-technology markets, standard price tests are likely to be unhelpful if fixed costs are high and marginal costs are close to zero. As OFT Discussion Paper No 377 points out: 'In one sense, such tests are likely to be far too permissive: they would allow pricing in response to a new entrant that could not possibly be the rational response except for the anti-competitive benefits of exclusion. In another sense such tests are not permissive enough: when competition is for the market, very low penetration pricing may be a perfectly rational and pro-competitive form of competition.'[62]

This 'rational' explanation is often the true state of affairs on the internet. On the internet, much content and software is available at no apparent cost to the end-user. What amounts to predation in such markets may, therefore, be more difficult to identify. It has been suggested that the relevant test should focus upon whether the alleged infringer only took the action because of the anti-competitive (often exclusionary) benefits.[63] Nevertheless, in the *Wanadoo* case,[64] the European Commission found Wanadoo (France Telecom) guilty of predation by reference to average variable costs (and average total costs) in the context of the provision of ADSL-based internet services. Wanadoo was fined 10.35 million euro.

Discrimination

8.37   Price discrimination can be both exploitative and exclusionary. This is most easily identified where undertakings charge materially different prices to different categories of customer without a justification for the distinction. Customers might be divided into regional price categories or by type of activity. It should be noted, however, that the prohibition on discriminatory pricing does not mean that discounting structures are prohibited. Discounts are a form of price competition and so are to be encouraged. It is only where a discount structure is not justified by the economies of bulk buying, but is based on a formula which has the effect of rewarding exclusivity, that it is likely to be found to be abusive. Where a discount structure is put in place which is conditional upon customers buying all or a very large proportion of their needs from a dominant undertaking (what are known as 'fidelity discounts'), they will be prohibited

61   European Commission, DG Competition discussion paper on the application of art 82 of the Treaty to exclusionary abuses, December 2005.
62   Para 1.11.
63   OFT Economics Discussion Paper No 377 at para 1.13.
64   COMP/38.233 *Wanadoo Interactive*.

because they foreclose the market for other sellers competing with the dominant undertaking. In addition to discrimination on the basis of price, discriminatory terms of sale including access to new developments or updates may constitute an abuse. At the time of writing, Intel has been sent a Statement of Objections by the European Commission in relation to the allegedly exclusionary effect of its rebate structure.[65]

Another form of price discrimination is known as a 'margin squeeze'. This is where a dominant vertically integrated company sets a margin between its wholesale and retail prices that is insufficient in the sense that an efficient company competing downstream, which buys raw material at the wholesale price, could not make a reasonable return when competing with the dominant firm's downstream retail prices. This can be achieved by the dominant company overcharging its downstream competitors for the raw material and then using the profits achieved to subsidise a lower retail price for its own products in the downstream market than is sustainable by its competitors. In July 2007, the Commission found Telefónica guilty of a margin squeeze in relation to broadband access for competitors to its downstream retail broadband services.[66] Telefónica's competitors in the retail market were not able to operate profitably in the retail market and therefore faced the choice of incurring losses, exiting the market or choosing not to enter the market at all. Telefónica was fined 151,875,000 euro.

Vertical restraints

8.38   As described above in the context of the art 101/Chapter I prohibition, the authorities adopt a relatively beneficent approach to vertical restrictions. However, arrangements which might otherwise be exempted by a block exemption can still constitute an abuse of a dominant position. The market power of a dominant player can, for example, render exclusive purchasing and distribution arrangements anti-competitive. Where a dominant undertaking enters into such arrangements, they can foreclose the market to competitors.

Tying and bundling

8.39   Tying sales of one product or service to another may also constitute an abuse, particularly if the tie is intended to ensure that the customer takes the full range of the producer's goods when, in fact, the customer would prefer to be more selective. The tying together of products is often referred to as 'bundling'. In the *Microsoft* case, one of the findings was that Microsoft had abused its dominant position by bundling its media player product with Windows (see below).

Refusal to supply

8.40   Although it might be thought that anyone is free to do business, or not do business, with whomsoever they choose, dominance can limit this freedom.

---

65   COMP/37.990 *Intel*.
66   COMP/38.784 *Telefonica SA (broadband)*.

If a dominant undertaking wants to refuse to supply a customer there must be an objective justification for the refusal to supply. Examples of justifications for refusal to supply include a lack of capacity to make the supply, the cost of dealing making the supply unprofitable or the creditworthiness of the customer being extremely dubious. It is generally far harder to justify the termination of supply to an existing customer than it is to justify the refusal of supply to an entirely new one (save in the case of essential facilities, discussed below). In the *Microsoft* case, the other finding of abuse was the refusal by Microsoft to supply (license) source code information required by competitors to develop products that interoperate with Microsoft's Windows operating system (see below).

Access to essential facilities

8.41   It has been suggested that in certain circumstances access to facilities controlled by an undertaking are essential if someone is to compete in a particular market. It is argued that such access is indispensable where it is not possible (or extremely difficult) to duplicate the facility due to physical, geographic or legal constraints. Proving that a facility is essential tends to be a difficult task.[67]

Where an undertaking controls an essential facility, it is likely to be found to be in a dominant position and that refusal to allow access to the facility on fair terms is likely to constitute an abuse. In the context of the internet it may be possible to argue (in certain circumstances) that telecommunications networks are essential facilities. In the *Worldcom/MCI merger* case, although the term 'essential facility' was not used, the reasoning of the Commission decision would tend to suggest that the provision of top-level internet connectivity by ISPs could arguably be an essential facility.

In contrast, in the US, Cyber Promotions, who were sending millions of email advertisements to AOL subscribers, claimed that AOL monopolised the essential facility to advertise to AOL's subscribers using electronic mail.[68] The argument was given short shrift by the court: Cyber could send electronic adverts to AOL subscribers by other means and, in any event, Cyber was not even completely barred from the AOL network. There were no grounds whatsoever for suggesting that the facility was essential. In the *Microsoft* case, the interoperability information was not characterised by the European Commission or the Court of First Instance as an essential facility.

Microsoft

8.42   The most relevant case relating to abuse of a dominant position involving internet-related activities is that brought by the European Commission against Microsoft. In 2004, the Commission found under what is now art 101 that Microsoft had abused its dominant position on the operating system market by: (1) refusing to release its interoperability information; and (2) bundling Windows media player ('WMP') with its Windows operating system. The

---

67   See, in particular, Case C-7/97 *Oscar Bronner v Mediaprint* [1998] ECR I-7791.
68   *Cyber Promotions Inc v America Online Inc* 948 F Supp 456 (ED Pa 1996).

Commission fined Microsoft a record 497 million euro and required Microsoft to license interoperability information and release a version of Windows without WMP (although it is free to sell this at the same price as the bundled version of Windows).[69] In September 2007, the European Court of First Instance ('CFI') rejected Microsoft's appeal against the Commission's decision, affirming all of the Commission's reasoning on the substance of the case.[70] Microsoft did not appeal against the CFI's decision.

Refusal to license interoperability information

8.43 As explained at **8.40** above, failure to supply can be an abuse of a dominant position. The first claim against Microsoft was that it had excluded competitors from the market for work group server operating systems by refusing them interoperability information allowing them to interface with Windows operating system servers. Microsoft argued that the interoperability information was protected by intellectual property rights. For the Commission and the CFI this was debatable, but they took the cautious approach of assuming that the information was protected by intellectual property rights and applied the more stringent regime that applied in such cases (in order to balance the competing needs of protecting competition and stimulating innovation). That regime was established by the European Court of Justice in the cases of *Magill*[71] and *IMS Health*,[72] where it held that a refusal to license an intellectual property right is only an abuse in 'exceptional circumstances', articulated as follows by the CFI in the *Microsoft* case:

1. The refusal relates to a product or service indispensable to the exercise of a particular activity on a neighbouring market. The 'extraordinary feature' of Microsoft's 90% share of the PC operating systems market was central to the CFI's finding that Microsoft was therefore able to impose the Windows domain architecture as the de facto standard for work group computing. The Commission's market evidence suggested that interoperability with that de facto standard was the primary consideration for purchasers of work group server operating systems, notwithstanding that other products might offer enhanced features.

2. The refusal is of such a kind as to exclude any effective competition on that neighbouring market. The CFI relaxed the *Magill* and *IMS Health* approach by equating likelihood of elimination of competition with risk of elimination of competition. Further, the CFI stated that all competition need not be eliminated: 'a marginal presence of competitors remaining on the market does not equate to effective competition'. The CFI was influenced by Microsoft's rapid growth, since a late entry into the market, to 65%

69   COMP/C-3/37.792 Microsoft.
70   Case T-201/04 *Microsoft v Commission*.
71   Joined cases C-241/91 P and C-242/91 *P Radio Telefis Eireann (RTE) and Independent Television Publications Ltd (ITP) v Commission (Magill)* [1995] ECR 743 para 55.
72   Case C-418/01, *IMS Health GmbH & Co OHG v NDC Health GmbH & Co KG* [2004] ECR I-5039.

of market share by 2002 and concluded that its competitors were being confined to marginal positions on the market.

3. The refusal prevents the appearance of a new product for which there is potential consumer demand. In both *Magill* and *IMS Health*, there was a specific new product, for which there was demonstrable consumer demand, and the emergence of which was rendered impossible by the refusal to license the relevant intellectual property. In response to Microsoft's submissions that the Commission had identified no specific new product, and therefore no corresponding consumer demand, the CFI was obliged to pursue a notably broader interpretation of the new product test. The CFI stated its view that the test includes situations where technical development is limited (ie consumer detriment is caused not just by the absence of a specific new product, but by the absence of innovation in general).

4. There is no objective justification for the abusive behaviour. The CFI concluded that Microsoft's abusive behaviour could not be objectively justified, and disagreed that a requirement to supply would disincentivise innovation. Significant by its absence from the CFI's judgment is an explicit weighing of the 'value' of the relevant intellectual property rights against the need to protect competition, which was a feature of the *Magill* and *IMS Health* judgments, as was the particular effort in those cases to diminish the value of the intellectual property rights (copyright) at issue.

The Commission and Microsoft could not agree about the extent of information that competitors required in order to develop interoperating products. The Commission sought a licence of the operating system 'protocols', while Microsoft argued that this would enable competitors to 'clone' the Windows operating system. The CFI confirmed that the Commission had been correct to assess the required level of interoperability as that which was necessary for a competitor to remain viably on the work group operating systems market – fundamentally, competitors had to be able to interoperate with Windows domain architecture on an equal footing with Windows operating systems. For this, the CFI considered that they needed the protocols and reasoned that this would not enable them to clone the Windows operating system because they would not have the source code.

Bundling WMP

8.44 The second claim against Microsoft was that by bundling its WMP product with its Windows operating systems, the market for streaming media players was effectively foreclosed to its competitors. In its consideration of the bundling abuse, the CFI confirmed that the following five elements were present, and therefore that Microsoft had abused its dominant position under art 82:

1. Microsoft was dominant in the market for PC operating systems. This was not disputed by Microsoft.

2. PC operating systems and streaming media players are two separate products. Microsoft argued that media functionality is an integral part

of a PC operating system. At trial, Microsoft's advocates brandished the unbundled version of Windows which had sold just 2,000 copies, mocking the notion that Windows and WMP were separable products. However, the CFI noted the presence of alternative, stand-alone media players such as QuickTime and RealPlayer, as well as Microsoft's development and independent marketing of WMP for other operating systems, as indications of the existence of a separate market for media players. The CFI also confirmed that the relevant date for assessment was May 1999 and acknowledged the possibility that changes in consumer expectations may lead consumers in future to expect an operating system to include native media streaming functionality, and as such operating system and the media player functions may come to constitute one single product.

3. Customers were given no choice to obtain Windows without WMP automatically installed. This deterred OEMs and end users from installing another player, and encouraged the use of WMP at the expense of competing media players, notwithstanding that other players might have been superior.

4. The tying foreclosed competition from alternative streaming media players. Essentially, the CFI agreed with the Commission that the bundling and automatic installation of WMP with Windows guaranteed its ubiquity on personal computers, Windows being installed on 90% of such machines. The effect was to give WMP automatic market penetration without having to compete on the merits with other products. The Commission and the CFI took particular account of RealPlayer's market share, which had been double that of WMP in 1999, and became roughly half that of WMP by 2003. Other media players had no access to a distribution system of comparable efficiency and effectiveness to counterbalance WMP's advantage. The Commission and the CFI also identified significant indirect network effects resulting from the bundling of WMP on the development decisions of content providers and software developers. The desire of such providers to maximise the reach of their own products would favour their writing to the WMP platform, and further consolidate WMP's position as the default streaming media player. The potential which the CFI identified for this to generate knock-on effects on adjacent markets is noted, such as those for media players on wireless devices, set-top boxes, DRM solutions and online music delivery.

5. There was no objective justification for the abusive conduct.

Commentary

8.45   Disputes of a similar nature in the United States (*United States of America v Microsoft Corporation*)[73] were the subject of a settlement in November 2002. In respect of both interoperability and bundling, the US settlement is notably less onerous to Microsoft than the subsequent Commission/CFI rulings in Europe. The difference in approach between Europe and the US to dominance/

---

73 *United States of America v Microsoft Corporation*, Civil Action No 98-1232 (CKK).

monopolisation cases in the internet sector creates an issue for what are often by their nature global markets. The need to comply with local competition law in many different markets presents an unappetising choice: either (1) to pull out of commercially less attractive markets where restrictive enforcement is prevalent, or (2) in the case of restrictive enforcement in commercially critical markets such as Europe, to adopt a 'lowest common denominator' approach by ensuring compliance with the most restrictive jurisdiction in which it operates.

The *Microsoft* judgment is particularly important to technology markets and operators, given the tendency of such markets to coalesce around industry standards. In its response to the CFI ruling, Microsoft stated that the likes of Apple, Google and IBM, being allegedly dominant in other markets of their own, may now be subject to scrutiny by the European regulators, and may be susceptible to accusations of art 82 abuses relating to their existing practices around proprietary software standards, application diversification and so on. At the very least, the *Microsoft* judgment has been a great boost to the European Commission's confidence, at the time of writing encouraging it to continue pursuing art 82 cases against Rambus (for an alleged 'patent ambush' in relation to an industry standard for DRAM chips),[74] Intel (for its rebate scheme which is alleged to exclude AMD)[75] and Qualcomm (for its alleged failure to license on FRAND terms in relation to mobile phone chipsets).[76]

ENFORCEMENT PROCEDURE

Complaints

8.46   An interested party can make a complaint to the CMA or sectoral regulators in relation to alleged infringements of the Chapter I and II prohibitions and arts 101 and 102. In the case of arts 101 and 102, a complaint can alternatively be made to the European Commission. The European Commission has produced a pro forma for complaints,[77] which should include:

- information regarding the complainant;

- details of the alleged infringement and evidence;

- decision sought and the complainant's legitimate interest; and

- information about any proceedings before national courts or competition authorities.

---

74   COMP/38.636 *Rambus*.
75   COMP/37.990 *Intel*.
76   COMP/39.247 *Texas Instruments/Qualcomm*.
77   Form C, Annex to Commission Notice 2004/C 101/05.

Investigation

8.47   The competition and sectoral regulators have wide powers to pursue alleged anti-competitive activity. They can both request information from undertakings and conduct direct investigations. Where an investigation is made without prior notice to the relevant undertaking, it is known as a 'dawn raid'.

Three principles may act as a bulwark against the authorities' investigatory powers: relevance, legal professional privilege, and the privilege against self-incrimination. However, it is for the officials conducting the investigation to determine what the relevant documents to be examined are. They are entitled not only to examine but also to take copies of the books and other business records – undertakings will be reimbursed for reasonable photocopying costs. In particular, the investigating authorities have the power to interrogate computer databases and copy computer files, disks and drives.

An undertaking may consult a legal adviser during an investigation, but the presence of a lawyer is not a requirement for the validity of the investigation. It is extremely important, therefore, for companies to be well prepared to deal with the competition authorities in the event of a dawn raid.

Interim measures

8.48   The competition authorities and sectoral regulators have the power to order interim measures pending their final decisions. These may include positive measures (such as resumption of supply), as well as prohibitory orders. Interim measures can only be taken when it is necessary for the regulator to act urgently to prevent serious irreparable damage to competition.[78]

Orders to terminate infringements

8.49   The competition authorities and sectoral regulators have the power, by a decision, to require an undertaking or an association of undertakings to terminate infringements and to refrain from any similar conduct in future.[79]

Commitments

8.50   The competition authorities and sectoral regulators also have the power and discretion to accept binding commitments from undertakings as an alternative to reaching an infringement decision.[80] The OFT previously indicated

---

78   Modernisation Regulation, art 8; Competition Act 1998, s 35; see also OFT Guideline 407 Enforcement.
79   Modernisation Regulation, art 7; Competition Act 1998, ss 31 and 32; see also OFT Guideline 407 Enforcement.
80   Modernisation Regulation, art 9; Competition Act 1998, s 31A; see also OFT Guideline 407 Enforcement.

that it would only accept commitments for hardcore infringements in exceptional circumstances and the CMA has not made any statement on this issue as at the time of writing.

Fines

8.51   The competition authorities and sectoral regulators have the power to impose fines for infringements of Chapters I or II or arts 101 or 102. Fines are intended to secure implementation of competition policy by suppressing illegal activity and preventing recurrence. They are also used as a general deterrent. Fines are capped at 10% of group worldwide turnover in the preceding business year for the undertaking in question. However, fines rarely reach this cap. The starting point is up to 30% of the revenue generated in the market where the infringement took place, depending upon the seriousness of the offence. This is then subject to many possible adjustments for duration, aggravating and mitigating circumstances that ultimately give the authorities a wide discretion in determining the ultimate level of fine.[81]

Aggravating factors include:

- repeated infringements of the same type by the same undertakings ('recidivism');

- refusal to co-operate with or obstruction of the investigation; and

- instigating or leading the infringement.[82]

Mitigating factors include:

- terminating the infringement immediately upon investigation (except for cartels);

- limited role in the infringement; and

- co-operation beyond legal requirements.[83]

Whistleblowing/leniency

8.52   The European Commission has published a notice on the non-imposition and reduction of fines[84] which is intended to give incentives to participants to blow the whistle on cartels and co-operate with the Commission in its investigation. Those who co-operate will have their fines reduced. The key point to bear in mind is that if you are the first undertaking to approach the Commission and

---

81   Modernisation Regulation, art 23(2); Competition Act 1998, s 36(8); see also OFT Guideline 423 Penalties and European Commission Guidelines on the method of setting fines, 2006/C 210/02.
82   European Commission Guidelines on the method of setting fines, 2006/C 210/02.
83   European Commission Guidelines on the method of setting fines, 2006/C 210/02.
84   OJ [2002] C 45/3.

you co-operate fully, you can secure a 100% reduction in any subsequent fine. The CMA operates a similar system, as set out in its guidelines.[85] The OFT's system was displayed when British Airways was fined £121.5 million for its part in fixing fuel surcharges on passenger and cargo flights, while Virgin Atlantic received total immunity from fines for blowing the whistle.[86] This illustrates the importance of approaching the CMA or the European Commission as quickly as possible if you are involved in anti-competitive activity (the 'grass first premium').

CARTEL OFFENCE

8.53   The Enterprise Act 2002 added a new dimension to the enforcement of competition law in the UK. Since 20 June 2003, the actions of an individual can be investigated and an individual can be subject to criminal prosecution for a substantive infringement of competition law. This 'cartel offence' applies only where the individual is involved in the most serious and damaging forms of anti-competitive behaviour (hardcore cartels).

The cartel offence operates alongside the existing Competition Act regime that imposes civil sanctions on companies that enter into agreements that restrict, distort or prevent competition in the UK or the EC. The cartel offence, however, applies to a much more limited and carefully defined range of activities. The main enforcement body is the CMA. However, when investigating and prosecuting the cartel offence the CMA will generally act under the direction of the Serious Fraud Office (SFO) and will use a new set of investigatory powers granted to it under the Enterprise Act 2002. In December 2007 the CMA's predecessor, the OFT, initiated the first prosecutions and a number of other investigations were underway at the time of writing.

Under s 188 of the Enterprise Act 2002, an individual is guilty of an offence if he dishonestly agrees with one or more other persons to make or implement, or cause to be made or implemented, arrangements whereby at least two undertakings will engage in one or more prohibited cartel activity in the UK. The prohibited cartel activities are: direct or indirect (horizontal) price-fixing; limitation of production or supply; sharing customers or markets; and bid-rigging. A person who is guilty of the cartel offence is liable to imprisonment for up to five years and an unlimited fine.

The CMA's powers under the Enterprise Act 2002 operate in parallel with those under the Competition Act 1998 and arts 101 and 102. It is quite possible that on the same set of facts the CMA/SFO will seek to prosecute individuals for the criminal cartel offence and that the CMA will wish to bring proceedings against the companies involved under the Competition Act 1998.

The CMA will be able to grant 'immunity' from prosecution for individuals in relation to the cartel offence. This is in keeping with the policy adopted in civil cases that there are significant benefits in encouraging cartel participants to come

---

85   OFT Guideline 423 Penalties.
86   OFT press release 113/07.

forward, to confess and to co-operate with an investigation. Unlike in civil cases, however, the application of this 'leniency policy' in criminal cases has statutory recognition.

MERGER CONTROL

8.54   Whilst the Competition Act 1998 and arts 101 and 102 principally operate to prevent anti-competitive behaviour once it has started (*'ex-post* regulation'), merger control effectively gives regulatory authorities the chance to stop such behaviour before it starts (*'ex ante* regulation'). Essentially, the merger control regimes of the UK and EC provide the authorities with the opportunity to prevent the creation of such market power as would jeopardise the proper functioning of the market. Small mergers are not generally of interest to the CMA or the Commission unless the merger gives the new entity significant power in a narrow market. For this reason both the domestic and European regimes contain 'threshold' tests for when a merger qualifies for scrutiny.

When considering whether a merger should be allowed, the factors taken into account will be similar to those considered when assessing whether an arrangement or certain behaviour is anti-competitive under the provisions referred to above. A number of illustrative examples given above in relation to anti-competitive agreements refer to merger decisions.[87] The fundamental test under both the EC and the UK regimes is whether a merger creates or enhances market power, although the substantive test is formulated differently under the two regimes.

It is beyond the scope of this chapter to give a detailed account of merger control in the UK and EC. The following sections indicate the basic tests which should be applied in deciding whether a merger will qualify for investigation and what broad principles are applied in assessing mergers.

EC Merger Regulation

8.55   The EC Merger Regulation[88] is intended to be a one-stop-shop for European merger control. If an arrangement falls within the scope of the Regulation it will not generally be scrutinised by member states' national merger control authorities nor will the merger itself be separately scrutinised under arts 101 and 102 or their national equivalents.

The Merger Regulation requires the prior notification to the European Commission of 'concentrations having a Community dimension'. A 'concentration' is defined by the Merger Regulation as being a situation where two or more independent undertakings merge, or where one or more undertakings acquire the ability to exercise 'decisive influence' over another undertaking. 'Undertaking' has the same meaning as under arts 101 and 102 (and Chapter I

87   See, for example: *MCI/Worldcom;Telia/Telenor/Schibsted; Bertelsmann/Mondadori.*
88   Council Regulation 139/2004 on the control of concentrations between undertakings.

and II). Generally, acquisition of under 20% of the voting rights of a company will not give rise to decisive influence, although the position is more complicated in the case of joint ventures where veto rights over strategic decisions confer decisive influence.

Whether or not a merger has a Community dimension is determined by a series of complex turnover thresholds which relate to aggregate worldwide, EC and domestic turnover. If the aggregate worldwide turnover of the undertakings concerned exceeds 2.5 billion euro and the EC turnover of at least two undertakings exceeds 100 million euro, there may be a Community dimension unless each of the parties achieves more than two-thirds of its turnover in one and the same member state.

If a merger does constitute a concentration with a Community dimension, the merger must be notified to the European Commission in the manner prescribed by Form CO. The Commission will appraise the merger's compatibility with the Common Market on the basis of the following principle: a concentration which 'significantly impedes effective competition in the Common Market or in a substantial part of it, in particular as a result of the creation or strengthening of a dominant position' should be prohibited (or remedies sought to overcome the competition concerns).

UK Enterprise Act

8.56 The Enterprise Act 2002 is the legislative basis for the UK merger control regime. A transaction is reviewable under the Enterprise Act 2002 if a 'relevant merger situation' has been created in the preceding four months or will be created (and the EC Merger Regulation does not apply). There is a relevant merger situation if two or more enterprises 'cease to be distinct' and certain thresholds are met. Where enterprises cease to be distinct, the Chapter I and II prohibitions will not apply to that agreement.

The concept of enterprise under the Enterprise Act 2002 is similar to that of undertaking under EC competition law and the Competition Act. Enterprises cease to be distinct if one acquires at least the ability materially to influence the policy of another. This concept is not defined in the Enterprise Act 2002, but the CMA provides guidance. Material influence can occur with voting rights as low as 10%, and will generally arise with voting rights of more than 25%. It is generally recognised to be a lower threshold than the concept of decisive influence under the EC Merger Regulation. The additional thresholds referred to above are alternative (ie only one needs to be met). They are as follows: (i) the merger will create or enhance a 25% or greater share of the purchase or supply of any goods or services in the UK or a substantial part of the UK; or (ii) the annual UK turnover of the target is £70 million or more.

The CMA and the Secretary of State for Business, Enterprise and Regulatory Reform have decision-making powers under the Enterprise Act merger control regime. Both phase 1 and phase 2 merger investigations are conducted by the CMA. The CMA has a duty to refer mergers to phase 2 where it believes that there is, or may be, a relevant merger situation that has resulted, or may be expected to result, in any substantial lessening of competition ('SLC') in the

UK. Alternatively, the CMA may accept undertakings from the merging parties in lieu of a reference. If a merger is referred to phase 2, the CMA must decide whether a relevant merger situation has been or will be created and, if so, whether the situation results or may be expected to result in an SLC within any market in the UK. If so, the CMA must also decide what (if any) remedies (including prohibition or divestment) should be imposed. In cases involving public interest issues (limited to national security and media at the time of writing), the Secretary of State may refer a merger to the CMA on public interest grounds and take the final decision based on the CMA's report.

Notification of mergers under the UK regime is voluntary, and mergers may be completed without merger control clearance even if they are reviewable. Nevertheless, in practice many mergers are notified for reasons of legal certainty because the CMA has the power to impose remedies even where the merger has been completed, including forced divestment. A notification to the CMA can be by informal submission or by a formal merger notice. In addition it is possible to seek confidential or informal guidance from the CMA.

MARKET INVESTIGATIONS

8.57   The European Commission and the UK competition authorities and sectoral regulators have the power to conduct investigations into markets or sectors that are perceived not to be functioning properly (as opposed to specific alleged infringements of competition law by particular undertakings or individuals).

The European Commission powers are contained in art 17 of the Modernisation Regulation. However, this is in practice merely an information-gathering exercise, as the European Commission has no power to impose fines or remedies unless the sector inquiry also reveals an infringement of arts 101 or 102. None of the European Commission sector inquiries at the time of writing has focused on internet-related activities.

The position is different in the UK. The Enterprise Act 2002 and the Enterprise and Regulatory Reform Act 2013 allow the CMA and sectoral regulators to conduct investigations into the workings of a market, and for them (or, in certain cases, the Secretary of State), to refer a market to the for further detailed investigation and a decision on whether any features of the market have an adverse effect on competition. The CMA may impose remedies in relation to markets which are not operating competitively but where this is not the result of a breach of either of the Chapter I or II prohibitions and/or arts 101 or 102. Similarly, the CMA or sectoral regulators may accept remedies in lieu of a reference.. Additionally, these provisions can be used where the only way to prevent continued breach of the Competition Act prohibitions is to require structural changes to the relevant market.

The CMA has a wide discretion as to the type of remedies by which it may seek to address any adverse effects on competition that it identifies. The types of remedies that it might consider include:

● structural remedies designed to make a significant and direct change to the structure of the market, such as divestment of a business or assets;

- structural remedies that affect the market structure less directly by reducing entry barriers or reducing switching costs (eg by requiring the licensing of know-how or intellectual property, introducing industry-wide technical standards or recommending changes to regulations which limit entry to the market);

- behavioural remedies directing companies to act in a certain way (eg giving notices of price changes or displaying prices and terms and conditions of sale more prominently) or to restrain conduct (eg the imposition of a price cap); and

- monitoring remedies, for example, a requirement to provide the CMA with information on prices or conduct.

At the time of writing, none of the market investigations under the Enterprise Act had focused on internet-related activities.

CHAPTER NINE

Regulation of networks, services and consumer contracts[*]

'Life is a metaphor for the Internet'

Douglas Coupland

9.1   Until now, our focus in this book has been on describing the laws that apply to activities that take place on the internet; the formation of contracts, the conduct of e-commerce, tort liability, cybercrime, protection of intellectual property, data protection, competition law, and the application of VAT to goods and services purchased electronically. In this chapter, we shift to an examination of the laws that regulate ISPs and access to and use of the complex array of networks that constitute 'the internet' itself. We also examine some specific features of the regulatory framework not considered earlier in this book.

REGULATION OF ELECTRONIC COMMUNICATIONS NETWORKS AND SERVICES

Application of General Conditions of Entitlement to ISPs and VoIP providers

9.2   ISPs are not required to obtain any form of licence or similar authority to operate,[1] but insofar as they act as providers of electronic communications networks ('ECN') or electronic communications services ('ECS')[2] they are required to comply with the General Conditions of Entitlement ('GCE') set by

---

1   The use of wireless devices generally requires a wireless telegraphy licence, but WiFi systems and personal devices such as mobile phones, tablets, and the like, are normally exempt.
2   The terms 'ECN' and 'ECS' are defined in the Communications Act, 2003 ('CA') s 32. The 'provider' of an electronic communications network for the purposes of a condition is the organisation which has control over the facilities to which the condition relates. The provider is typically the organisation that has the contract with the end-user, or where the service is provided on a wholesale basis, with the reseller or intermediary.

*   Michael H. Ryan, Arnold & Porter (UK) LLP. I would like to thank my partner Tim Aron for contributing the section on financial services at **9.22**. This chapter draws significantly on the corresponding chapter of the 3rd edition prepared by Elle Todd.

Ofcom.[3] There are 23 GCE, although not all apply to all ISPs. For the purposes of the GCE, providers of ECN and ECS can be divided into three overlapping categories. The category or categories into which a particular ISP falls determines which of the GCE it must comply with.

The first category of providers is the widest. It includes all persons that provide ECN or ECS and therefore embraces providers of private as well as public networks and services. Providers of internet networks and services are covered. So are providers of other types of ECN and ECS such as fixed and mobile voice telephony, data and video networks and services. The following is a list of the GCE with which ISPs in this first category must comply:

Figure 9.1A: Summary of GCE applicable to providers of ECN and ECS	
GCE 1.2 and 1.3	*General access and interconnection obligations* Any information obtained by providers of ECN and ECS from another Communications Provider in the course of negotiations for network access or interconnection must be kept confidential and used solely for the purpose for which it was supplied. In *British Telecommunications plc v Ofcom*,[4] the Competition Appeals Tribunal ('CAT') ruled that BT had contravened GCE 1.2 by using customer-specific information supplied by another Communications Provider in a request for the provision of carrier pre-selection to the customer. BT had used the information to make a 'save call' marketing BT's own services to the customer.
GCE 2	*Standardisation and specified interfaces* Providers of ECN or ECS must comply with any relevant compulsory standards/specifications listed in art 17 of the EU Framework Directive. In the absence of any compulsory standard, they must take account of any voluntary standards/specifications adopted by the European Standards Organisation; and, in the absence of compulsory and voluntary standards/specifications, recommendations adopted by the International Telecommunication Union, the European Conference of Postal and Telecommunications Administrations ('CEPT'), the International Organisation for Standardisation or the International Electrotechnical Committee.

3 The GCE are available at: stakeholders.ofcom.org.uk/telecoms. See also Ofcom, *General conditions guidelines*, undated. The following discussion of the GCE is based on the GCE as revised to 26 February 2015.

4 Case no. 1025/3/3/04, 9 December 2004. In relation to regulation of the customer migration process. See also GCE 22, later adopted by Ofcom.

GCE 17	*Allocation, adoption and use of telephone numbers* Providers of ECN or ECS may not adopt numbers from the national telephone numbering plan unless such numbers have been allocated to them or the provider has been authorised to adopt them. The provider is required to have a numbering plan for all its allocated telephone numbers and, except where Ofcom consents in writing, this must conform with the National Numbering Plan.[5]
GCE 18	*Number Portability* Providers of ECN or ECS are required to provide Number Portability[6] within the shortest possible time, on reasonable terms, including charges, to any of its subscribers who so requests. The provider is also required to provide Portability (other than Paging Portability) as soon as is reasonably practicable in relation to a request by another provider on reasonable terms. In relation to the porting of mobile numbers where the request is for the porting of fewer than 25 mobile telephone numbers, the numbers are required to be ported within [one] business day. Any charges for the porting of numbers must be in accordance with this condition.[7]
GCE 19	*Provision of directory information* Where a person who provides ECN or ECS has been allocated Telephone Numbers in accordance with GCE 17, the provider is required to meet all reasonable requests from any person to make available the directory information of its subscribers and any other end-user assigned a number originally allocated to the provider. Where a provider has been authorised to use a telephone number allocated to another person, it is required on request to supply the directory information for the subscribers using those telephone numbers.
GCE 20	*Access to numbers* Where a provider of ECN or ECS adopts non-geographic numbers (such as numbers starting 0845), it shall, where technically and economically feasible, ensure that end-users in the European Community are able to access those numbers, although access may be limited if the subscriber so chooses.

5   Available at http://stakeholders.ofcom.org.uk/telecoms/numbering/
6   'Number Portability' is not to be confused with 'Portability.' The first refers to the ability of a PATS customer to change service providers without changing his telephone number. 'Portability,' on the other hand, refers to the obligation on *all* service providers to assist providers of publicly available telephone services ('PATS') with the porting of customers' numbers.
7   Concerning portability of VoIP numbers, see Ofcom, *Regulation of VoIP services*, 29 March 2007, Chapter 5.

Figure 9.1A: (continued)	
GCE 22	*Service migrations and home moves* Ofcom has adopted a detailed set of rules that regulate migration of customers of fixed line telephone and broadband services provided within Openreach's network and KCOM's access network. These rules include a mis-selling prohibition, a requirement to provide certain information at point of sale, customer termination rights, and requirements to retain records to secure records of customer consent, and to provide of written advice to the customer. Where a provider who is losing a customer communicates with the customer in order to comply with this condition, it must not make any marketing statements or representations in its communication which may induce the customer not to migrate to a new provider. Annex 3 regulates the issuance of 'MAC' or 'Migration Authorisation Codes' (used to identify a broadband service that is intended to be transferred from one Communications Provider to another Communications Provider) and more generally the MAC Broadband Migrations Process.

The second category of providers is a subset of the first but includes only providers of *public* electronic communications networks ('PECN') and services ('PECS'). It does not include providers of *private* networks and services. ISPs in this second category must comply with the following conditions in addition to the GCE applicable to providers in the first category:

Figure 9.1B: GCE applicable to providers of PECN and PECS	
GCE 1.1	*General access and Interconnection obligations* Persons who provide a PECN must negotiate interconnection agreements with other EU communications providers within a reasonable time on a good faith basis. Ofcom has ruled that the obligation to negotiate interconnection does not impose an obligation to negotiate a particular technical means of providing interconnection.[8]
GCE 4	*Emergency call numbers* Providers of ECS (excluding those providing a click-to-call service; that is, a VoIP service that may be selected on a website or other application that connects the user only to a limited set of numbers pre-selected by the provider or user) must ensure that any end-user can access emergency organisations by using the emergency call numbers '112' and '999' at no charge and, if access is provided through a pay telephone, without having to use coins or cards.

---

8   *Ofcom Determination to resolve a dispute between Hay Systems Ltd and T-Mobile UK about SS7 – based network access for SMS terminations*, 6 November 2006.

	In addition, providers of Public Telephone Networks must, to the extent technically feasible, make caller location information for all calls to the emergency call numbers available to the emergency organisations handling those calls.[9]
GCE 9	*Requirement to offer contracts with minimum terms* Providers of PECN and PECS must offer to enter into a contract or vary an existing contract with that consumer which specifies the following minimum requirements:
	(a) the identity and address of the Communications Provider;
	(b) the services provided, including in particular whether or not access to Emergency Services and Caller Location Information is being provided, and any limitations on the provision of access to Emergency Services;
	(c) information on any other conditions limiting access to and/or use of services and applications (where such conditions are permitted under national law);
	(d) details of the minimum service quality levels offered, namely the time for initial connection and any other quality of service parameters as directed by Ofcom;
	(e) information on any procedures put in place by the undertaking to measure and shape traffic so as to avoid filling or overfilling a network link, and information on how those procedures could impact on service quality;
	(f) the types of maintenance services and customer support services offered, as well as the means of contacting these services;
	(g) any restrictions imposed by the provider on the use of terminal equipment supplied;
	(h) the Subscriber's options as to whether or not to include his or herpersonal data in a directory, and the data concerned;
	(i) details of prices and tariffs, the means by which up-to-date information on all applicable tariffs and maintenance charges may be obtained, payment methods offered and any difference in costs due to payment method;

9   Concerning the application of this condition to VoIP services, see *Guidelines on the application of PATS obligations to VoIP service providers* in Ofcom, *Regulation of VoIP services*, 29 March 2007, Annex 5, paras A5.57 et seq.

Figure 9.1B: (continued)		
	(j)	the duration of the contract, and the conditions for renewal and termination of services and of the contract, including:
		(i) any minimum usage or duration required to benefit from promotional terms;
		(ii) any charges related to portability of numbers and other identifiers; and
		(iii) any charges due on termination of the contract, including any cost recovery with respect to terminal equipment;
	(k)	any applicable compensation and/or refund arrangements which will apply if contracted quality service levels are not met;
	(l)	the means of initiating procedures for the settlement of disputes in respect of the contract; and
	(m)	the type of action that might be taken by the Communications Provider in reaction to security or integrity incidents or threats and vulnerabilities.
	Providers of fixed telecommunications and broadband services to consumers and small businesses must not renew customer service contracts after an initial commitment period without express consent.	
GCE 11.1 & 11.2	*Metering and billing* Providers of PECS must render accurate bills to end-users. Providers must retain such records as may be necessary to comply with this obligation provided that nothing in these paragraphs can oblige the retention of records for more than 15 months.	
GCE 14	*Price transparency for non-geographic calls, codes of practice and dispute resolution* A person who provides PECS must, among other things: • produce a basic code of practice, in plain English, for its domestic and small business customers which sets out at the very least where customers may obtain the information required under GCE 10 (see Annex 3 to GCE 14) and a code of practice for handling complaints (see Annex 4); • produce a code of practice for Premium Rate Services (see Annex 1), Number Translation Services, calls to 0870 numbers and calls to Personal Numbers (see Annex 2), if any such are being provided;	

	• implement and comply with a dispute resolution scheme, including any final decision of the dispute resolution body, for the resolution of disputes between providers and their domestic and small business customers. This scheme must be approved by Ofcom.
GCE 21	*Quality of service* Providers of PECS must, at Ofcom's direction, publish comparable, adequate and up-to-date information for end-users on the quality of their services. This condition is intended to allow consumers to compare the quality of service of different providers.

The third category of provider is a subset of the second and includes only providers of public telephone networks ('PTNs') and publicly available telephone services ('PATS'). ISPs in this category are subject to the most stringent regulation. They must, in addition to complying with all of the preceding conditions, comply with the following GCE:

Figure 9.1C: GCE applicable to providers of public telephone networks and PATS	
GCE 3	*Proper and effective functioning of the network* Providers of PATS and Public Communications Networks over which such a service is provided must take all reasonable steps to ensure:[10] (a) the proper and effective functioning of the Public Communications Network provided by them at all times; (b) the availability of the Public Communications Network and PATS provided by them in the event of catastrophic network breakdown or *force majeure*; and (c) uninterrupted access to emergency services as part of any PATS offered.
GCE 5	*Emergency planning* Providers of PATS and/or Public Communications Networks must, upon request by relevant government or emergency organisations, make and implement arrangements for the provision or rapid restoration of such communications services as are practicable and may reasonably be required in disasters. The Communications Provider is permitted to recover the costs incurred in making or implementing such arrangements (whether from the relevant government or emergency organisation or its customers) and to make the implementation of such arrangements conditional upon being indemnified by the person for whom the arrangements are being implemented.

10 Concerning the application of this condition to VoIP services, see *Guidelines on the application of PATS obligations to VoIP service providers, supra,* Annex A, paras A5.75 et seq.

Figure 9.1C: (continued)	
GCE 6	*Public pay telephones* (Applies only to Providers of Public Pay Telephones)
GCE 7	*Must carry obligations* (Applies only to providers of networks which are used by a significant number of people as their principal means of receiving television programmes)
GCE 8	*Operator assistance, directories and directory enquiries* Providers of PATS must ensure that any end-user can access operator assistance services and, for a reasonable charge, a directory enquiry facility containing directory information on all subscribers in the UK who have been assigned Telephone Numbers by any communications provider, except those Subscribers who have exercised their right to have their Directory Information removed. Providers of PATS who assign telephone numbers to their Subscribers must ensure that each of those subscribers is, on request and for a reasonable charge, supplied with a directory containing directory information on all Subscriber who have been assigned telephone numbers in the Subscriber local area. Subscribers who require directories containing directory information for subscribers assigned telephone numbers by any communications provider outside of the local area must be supplied such directories by the communications provider on request and for a reasonable charge.
GCE 10	*Transparency and publication of information* A person who provides end-users with access to and use of PATS, except public pay telephones, must ensure that clear and up-to-date information on their applicable prices and tariffs (excluding bespoke or individual prices and tariffs) and on their standard terms and conditions is published. Certain specified information must be included. Publication of the information must be effected by sending a copy of this information to end-users upon request and placing the information on the provider's website or their major offices for inspection free of charge by members of the general public
GCE 11.3–11.6	*Metering and billing* Providers of PATS whose relevant turnover exceeds £40 million, must, in addition to complying with the general obligation concerning billing and records imposed on Providers of PECS under paragraphs 11.1 and 11.2, above, obtain approval of their metering and billing system from a relevant approval body.
GCE 12	*Itemised bills* Except when service is provided on a pre-paid basis or where the subscriber has a free alternative means of adequately monitoring their usage and expenditure, Providers of PATS must provide to their subscribers, on request, and either at no extra charge or for a reasonable fee, a basic level of itemised billing.

GCE 13	*Non-payment of bills* Where a subscriber to fixed PATS has not fully paid the bill for such services, any measures taken by the provider to effect payment or disconnection must: (a) be proportionate and not unduly discriminatory; (b) give due warning to the subscriber beforehand of any consequent service interruption or disconnection; and (c) except in cases of fraud, persistent late payment or non-payment, confine any service interruption to the service concerned, as far as technically feasible. The provider must publish details of measures it may take to effect payment or disconnection by sending a copy of this information to end-users upon request and placing the information on their website
GCE 15	*Special measures for end users with disabilities* Providers of PATS must comply with a number of special obligations regarding end-users with disabilities, including a duty to consult with the Ofcom 'Consumer Panel' to ensure that the requirements and interests of disabled end-users are fully taken into account
GCE 16	*Provision of additional facilities* Providers of Public Telephone Networks must, subject to technical feasibility and economic viability, provide dual-tone multi-frequency ('DTMF') dialling and calling line identification ('CLI') facilities, unless Ofcom directs that this obligation shall not apply in all or part of the UK on the basis that there is already sufficient access to these facilities in the relevant areas.
GCE 23	*Sales and marketing of mobile telephony services* (Applies only to mobile telephony services)

ISPs that provide VoIP may, depending on their individual characteristics, fall into any one of the three preceding categories or none of them. Ofcom has distinguished four types of VoIP voice call service for regulatory purposes:[11]

- Type 1: peer-to-peer services to make and receive voice calls over the internet only, usually within the same application community;

- Type 2: VoIP Out services to make voice calls over the internet to the PSTN (Public Switched Telephony Network, the standard public phone network), but not to receive calls from the PSTN;

11   Ofcom, *Regulation of VOIP Services: Access to the Emergency Services*, 5 December 2007, paras 3.5 and 3.19.

- Type 3: VoIP In services to receive voice calls over the internet from the PSTN, but not to make calls to the PSTN. Customers can be allocated an ordinary geographic number or a VoIP number (056); and

- Type 4: VoIP In and Out services to receive voice calls over the internet from the PSTN and to make voice calls over the internet to the PSTN. Customers can be allocated an ordinary geographic number or a VoIP number (056).

Ofcom considers that Type 1 VoIP services are unlikely to constitute an ECS (with the result that none of the GCE would apply to them). Type 2 and Type 3 VoIP services are likely to be regarded as PECS (and providers of those services would therefore be in the second category). Type 4 VoIP services are likely to be PECS or, if they meet the PATS gating criteria, PATS (and providers of those services would therefore be in the second or third category).

Obligation to provide internet connectivity

9.3   ISPs do not have a general obligation to provide internet connectivity to potential customers, but Ofcom has imposed a specific obligation on BT to provide 'universal service' throughout its operating territory (the UK except Kingston upon Hull) and a similar obligation on KCOM (the provider of local telephone services in Kingston).[12] The universal service obligation requires BT and KCOM to provide basic 'telephony services' on request at a uniform affordable price. 'Telephony service' includes for these purposes the provision of 'functional internet access'. Ofcom defined 'functional internet access' in 2006 as a narrowband connection of 28.8 kbps.[13] That is no longer adequate for many purposes, but rather than revise the obligation to require the provision of a faster connection, Ofcom has preferred to promote deployment of broadband.

Ofcom has also imposed a special 'access-related condition' under which BT has an obligation to deliver traffic to users of other service providers' networks to ensure 'end-to-end connectivity'.[14] This condition covers VoIP.

Net neutrality

9.4   Should an ISP be allowed to block or degrade traffic of high-volume users; or to charge for prioritising the traffic of certain ISPs; or to provide a guaranteed quality of service to certain customers? These are among the issues that arise in the ongoing debate over 'net neutrality'. Proponents of net neutrality regard it as vital to the protection of the internet as a forum for open public

---

12   See Oftel, *Designation of BT and Kingston as universal service providers, and the specific universal service conditions,* 22 July 2003. The conditions were amended in 2011 and 2012.
13   See Ofcom, *Review of the Universal Service Obligation,* 14 March 2006, Annex 7.
14   See Ofcom, *End-to-end connectivity,* 13 September 2006.

communication.[15] They would prohibit traffic blocking, traffic throttling and paid prioritisation of traffic. Others take a different view and argue, for example, that it is fair to ask those that use more network capacity to pay more and thereby make a bigger contribution to development of the network, and to permit service providers to pay a premium for priority delivery services.

In the US, net neutrality has been the subject of a sometimes passionate debate for many years. In Europe, however, the issue received comparatively little attention until 2009. The telecoms legislative reform package adopted in that year embraced the principle that national regulatory authorities ('NRAs') should promote the ability of end users to access and distribute information or run applications and services of their choice,[16] gave NRAs authority to set minimum quality of service standards to discourage downgrading of service levels,[17] and introduced transparency requirements so that operators must disclose their traffic management practices to consumers and provide information concerning their impacts on quality of service.[18]

In April 2014, the European Parliament gave first reading to a regulation that would instate the concept of net neutrality in EU law. However, the regulation did not receive the necessary approval of the Council of Ministers before Parliamentary elections intervened and caused the measure to lapse. As of the end of 2014, it is unclear whether or in what form the regulation might be resurrected. The proposed regulation stipulated that '[p]roviders of internet access to end-users shall not discriminate between functionally equivalent services and applications'. It also provided that traffic management measures would be permitted only if they are 'justified' and *not* to the extent that they 'block, slow down, degrade or discriminate against specific content,

15 The following statement is representative of this view:
    'When we log onto the Internet, we take a lot for granted. We assume we'll be able
    to access any Web site we want, whenever we want, at the fastest speed, whether it's
    a corporate or mom-and-pop site. We assume that we can use any service we like ...
    watching online video, listening to podcasts, sending instant messages ... anytime we
    choose. What makes all these assumptions possible is Net Neutrality.'
    http://www.savetheinternet.com/frequently-asked-questions
16 The EU Framework Directive, Directive 2002/21/EC, as amended, includes a requirement that
    NRAs 'promote the interests of the citizens of the European Union' by *inter alia* 'promoting
    the ability of end users to access and distribute information or run applications and services of
    their choice.' See art 8, para 4(g).
17 The 2009 telecoms legislative reform package gave NRAs the power to set minimum quality
    of service standards (subject to Commission oversight) to discourage downgrading: Universal
    Service Directive, Directive 2002/22/EC, art 22, para 3.
18 The 2009 telecoms legislative reform package gave NRAs the power to require that consumer
    contracts disclose (i) any limitations on access to and/or use of services and applications, and
    (ii) any measures that operators might take to measure and shape traffic to avoid congestion
    and how these procedures impact service quality: Universal Service Directive, art 20, para
    1(b), second and fourth indents.
      GCE 9 provides that any contract between an ISP (or other relevant 'Communications
    Provider' to which the condition applies) and a 'Consumer' shall specify 'in a clear,
    comprehensive and easily accessible form' ... '(e) information on any procedures put in place
    by the undertaking to measure and shape traffic so as to avoid filling or overfilling a network
    link, and information on how those procedures could impact on service quality.' The ISP must
    also supply that information on request to any 'End User' who requests it.

applications or services or specific classes'. 'Justified' in this context was defined as 'technically necessary, transparent, proportionate and non-discriminatory' and not 'maintained longer than necessary'. But the proposed legislation also included a provision allowing the introduction of 'specialised services' that could be provided at a premium price so long as 'network capacity is sufficient to provide [specialised services] in addition to internet access services and [specialised services] are not to the detriment of the availability or quality of internet access services'.

In November 2011, Ofcom affirmed its support for net neutrality but declined to adopt *ex ante* regulation for that purpose. Ofcom said that it will rely instead on *ex post* competition law remedies to address net neutrality issues. Ofcom said that the types of situations that could trigger intervention include where ISPs prioritise managed services in a manner that leaves insufficient network capacity for access to the open internet on more or less equal terms for all; where ISPs apply traffic management in a manner that discriminates against specific alternative services (as opposed to broad categories of traffic), as this could have a similar impact to outright blocking; and where insufficient information is available to adequately inform consumers about the quality of the services they are purchasing.[19]

Codes of conduct

2010 Voluntary code of practice: broadband speeds

9.5   The Communications Act directs Ofcom to have regard in performing its duties to 'the desirability of promoting and facilitating the development and use of effective forms of self-regulation' (amongst other things).[20] In 2010, Ofcom published a code of practice relating to advertisement of broadband speeds intended to serve as a voluntary self-regulatory measure for ISPs.[21] Ofcom noted that 'there has been a noticeable trend for some ISPs to advertise their products based on faster and faster headline speeds' but that 'the evidence from Ofcom's research indicates that these headline speeds are rarely achievable in practice by the majority of consumers that buy them'. Ofcom suggested that 'this disparity between actual throughput speeds and headline speeds may have led to some consumers feeling confused and frustrated'. 'With consumers' interests in higher broadband speeds likely to rise,' Ofcom continued, 'it is important to remedy this mismatch in their expectations to avoid such confusion and frustration'.[22]

The 2010 Code establishes eight principles dealing with the following matters:

19   *Ofcom's approach to net neutrality*, 14 November 2011.
20   CA s 3(4)(c).
21   Ofcom, *2010 Voluntary Code of Practice: Broadband Speeds, 2010* ('2010 Code'). The 2010 Code is a revised version of a code adopted by Ofcom in 2008.
22   2010 Code, paras 10 and 11.

- training of representatives involved in selling or promoting broadband products and services;

- the provision of accurate and meaningful information on broadband speeds at point of sale;

- accuracy of information on access line speeds provided by ISPs;

- management of customers' speed-related problems;

- presentation of broadband information on ISP websites, including information on fair usage policies and usage limits and traffic management and traffic shaping;[23]

- timescales for implementation of the Code;

- monitoring of compliance with the Code;

- consumers' awareness of ISPs' adoption of the Code.

The 2010 Code applies to all fixed line access broadband ISPs who sign up to it. A list of signatories is kept on Ofcom's website.

ISPA code of practice

9.6   In 1999, members of the Internet Service Providers Association ('ISPA') adopted a code of practice (amended in 2007) with which all members of the association are required to comply. The code requires members to use 'reasonable endeavours' to ensure that their promotional materials comply with UK law; that services (excluding third-party content) and promotional materials comply with principles of decency and honesty; that, in their dealings with consumers and other business and each other, they act fairly and reasonably; and that promotional materials comply with the provisions of the British Codes of Advertising and Sales Promotion and certain other codes identified in the ISPA code.[24] The code also addresses matters such as clarity of pricing, data protection and transfer of domain names. Furthermore, the code requires ISPA members, if notified that internet sites they host contain material which the Internet Watch Foundation ('IWF') considers to be illegal child abuse images, to remove the specific web pages or, if it is not technically possible to do so, to notify the IWF of the reasons.[25] The code establishes a complaints procedure which applies when a customer or other third party makes a complaint to a member alleging that it has acted in breach of the code.

23   In relation to these matters, see also **9.1.3**.
24   On this subject, see also **9.3**.
25   Concerning the IWF, see also **Chapter 5**.

REGULATION OF AUDIOVISUAL MEDIA SERVICES

On-demand programme services[26]

Definition of ODPS

9.7   'On-demand programme services' ('ODPS') must comply with certain content and advertising standards and other regulatory requirements. A service is an ODPS if it meets the following criteria:[27]

- The 'principal purpose' of the service is the provision of 'television-like' programmes, whose form and content are 'comparable' to the form and content of programmes normally included in television programme services. Determining how this criterion applies is not always straightforward, particularly where the relevant on-demand programmes form part of a broader offering.

- The service can be accessed on-demand. Access to a service is 'on-demand' if users are able to access the service via an electronic communications network, select the programme they want and watch that programme at the time of their choosing (even if this has to be within a limited period set by the service provider).

- There is a person who has editorial responsibility for the service. The person who has general control over the programmes available via the service and the manner in which those programmes are organised within the service has 'editorial control.' If no-one exercises such control, the service falls outside the regulatory framework.

- The service is made available to members of the public. Subscription services meet this criterion if it is open to members of the public to subscribe.

- The service provider falls under UK jurisdiction for the purposes of the AVMS Directive. A service provider is under the jurisdiction of the UK if it is 'established' in the UK or uses a satellite uplink situated in the UK or satellite capacity appertaining to the UK. For example, if a service provider has its head office in the UK and the editorial decisions for the relevant on-demand service are also taken in the UK, the service provider is 'established' in the UK. There are provisions in the AVMS Directive that will be used to determine the place of establishment in more complex cases

---

26   The regime described in this section reflects the requirements of the EU Audio-Visual Media Services Directive 2007/65EC ('AVMS Directive'). The UK implemented the requirements relating to the provision of on-demand programme services in the Audiovisual Media Services Regulations 2009, SI 2009/2979 ('AVMS Regulations 2009'), which came into force on 19 December 2009. These added a new Part 4A to the Communications Act 2003. The Audiovisual Media Services Regulations 2010, SI 2010/419 ('AVMS Regulations 2010'), which came into force on 18 March 2010, contained further implementation measures. Additional requirements relating to distribution of pornography were adopted in the Audiovisual Media Services Regulations 2014, SI 2014/2916 ('AVMS Regulations 2014').

27   CA, s 368A(1).

(eg if the service provider has its head office in one EU member state, but editorial decisions are taken in another member state).

BBC iPlayer is an example of an ODPS.

Ofcom is ultimately responsible for the regulation of ODPS in the UK, but it has the power to designate co-regulators.[28] Ofcom has given the Authority for Television on Demand ('ATVOD') responsibility for determining who is an on-demand programme service provider and for monitoring the compliance of ODPS providers with the relevant standards. Decisions made by ATVOD can be appealed to Ofcom. ATVOD and Ofcom have rendered several decisions interpreting and applying the definition of ODPS.[29]

An ODPS provider does not require a licence, but must notify ATVOD in advance of launching, significantly changing or closing down an on-demand service.[30]

Content standards

9.8   ODPS are required to comply with content standards set out in the Communications Act. These standards resemble, but are in some respects less restrictive than those applicable to conventional television services.

Harmful material

9.9   ODPS must not contain material likely to incite hatred based on race, sex, religion or nationality. If an OPDS contains material which might seriously impair the physical, mental or moral development of persons under the age of 18, the material must be made available in a manner which secures that such persons would not normally see or hear it.[31] (This requirement is an example of how regulation of ODPS is less restrictive than regulation of programming distributed by conventional radio or television because the broadcast of such material on radio or television would be prohibited.) ATVOD has issued guidance on the application of these requirements to ODPS.[32]

Additional requirements aimed at controlling the online distribution of pornography were adopted in 2014. Under these requirements, an OPDS must not contain videos that are not suitable for a classification certificate issued by the British Board of Film Classification, or other material which, if contained in a video, would not be suitable for a classification certificate (referred to as

---

28 See Contracting Out (Functions Relating to Broadcast Advertising) and Specification of Relevant Functions Order 2004. It has used the same authority to designate the BCAP and ASA as co-regulators in relation to other matters. See the later discussion.

29 ATVOD has published guidance on the factors and criteria that it applies when determining whether a service falls within the definition of an 'on-demand programme service' ('ODPS') and is therefore subject to the regulatory framework for VOD. See ATVOD, *Guidance on who needs to notify*, Edition 4.0, 5 February 2014.
    ATVOD posts its Determinations on its website, www.atvod.co.uk

30 CA, s 368BA.

31 CA, s 368E.

32 See ATVOD, *Statutory Rules and Non-Binding Guidance for Providers of On-Demand Programme Services (ODPS)*, Edition 3.0, 5 May 2015.

'prohibited material').[33] It is further provided that an on-demand programme must not contain a video work to which the British Board of Film Classification has given (or it is reasonable to expect would give) an R18 certificate, or other material that might seriously impair the physical, mental and moral development of persons under the age of 18 (referred to as 'specially restricted material') unless the material is made available in a manner which secures that such persons would not normally see or hear it.[34]

ODPS providers are also subject to rules regulating advertising,[35] sponsorship[36] and product placement.[37] These rules are described below.

Advertising

9.10   Advertising of cigarettes and tobacco products and prescription medicine is prohibited, as is advertising aimed at persons under 18 or which encourages excessive drinking.

Advertising that is 'included' in an OPDS must comply with certain requirements. (Advertising is 'included' in the relevant sense if it can be viewed by a user of the service as a result of the user selecting a programme to view.[38]) Advertising must be readily recognised as such and may not employ any subliminal or surreptitious techniques. Furthermore, advertising must not:

(a)   prejudice respect for human dignity;

(b)   include or promote discrimination based on sex, racial or ethnic origin, nationality, religion or belief, disability, age or sexual orientation;

(c)   encourage behaviour prejudicial to health or safety;

(d)   encourage behaviour grossly prejudicial to the protection of the environment;

(e)   cause physical or moral detriment to persons under the age of 18;

(f)   directly encourage such persons to persuade their parents or others to purchase or rent goods or services;

(g)   exploit the trust of such persons in parents, teachers or others; or

(h)   unreasonably show such persons in dangerous situations.

Ofcom has designated the Advertising Standards Authority ('ASA') as a co-regulator in relation to advertising included in ODPS. The ASA is authorised to take the steps that appear to it to be best calculated to ensure that the statutory requirements applicable to advertising described above are complied with. The ASA has the power to decide what constitutes advertising included in an ODPS, to make rules which ensure providers of ODPS comply with the relevant

33   See CA, ss 368E(2) and (3).
34   CA, ss 368E(4) and (5).
35   CA, s 368F.
36   CA, s 368G.
37   CA, s 368H.
38   CA, s 368R(3).

requirements, and to determine if a provider is contravening or has contravened those requirements.[39]

Sponsorship

9.11 An ODPS must not be sponsored for the purposes of promoting cigarettes or tobacco products or prescription medicine. In addition, sponsorship of news and current affairs programmes is prohibited.

All sponsored ODPS must conform to the following restrictions:

- the sponsoring must not influence the content in a way that affects the editorial independence of the ODPS provider;

- where a service or programme is sponsored for the purpose of promoting goods or services, the service or programme must not directly encourage the purchase of the goods or services, whether by making reference to them or otherwise;

- where a service or programme is sponsored for the purpose of promoting alcoholic drinks, the service or programme and sponsorship announcements must not be aimed at under 18s or encourage immoderate consumption;

- the sponsor's name and logo must be displayed at the beginning or end of a sponsored programme; and techniques that may promote a product or service in a subliminal or surreptitious manner may not be used.

A sponsorship announcement must conform with the same standards as advertising, as described in items (a) to (h) above.

Product placement

9.12 Product placement is prohibited in children's programmes. Placement of tobacco products and prescription medicines is also prohibited. Product placement is otherwise permitted in films and series, sports programmes and light entertainment programmes provided that various conditions are met. Many of these conditions track the types of restrictions that apply to sponsorship described above; for example, the product placement must not influence the content of the programme in a way that affects the editorial independence of the ODPS provider.

Programme copy retention

9.13 ODPS providers must keep copies of all programmes for at least 42 days after the day on which the programme ceases to be available for viewing.[40]

---

39 The ASA's CAP Code, referred to in section 9.3, includes rules that mirror the statutory requirements applicable to advertising by on-demand services. See *CAP Code: The UK Code of Non-broadcast Advertising, Sales Promotion and Direct Marketing*, Appendix 2.
40 CA, s 368D(3)(zb).

Regulation of 'television licensable content services'

Licensing

9.14   For regulatory purposes, there is an important distinction drawn between 'push' technologies and 'pull' technologies. Push technologies send content to viewers without the viewer specifically requesting it at a certain point in time. Conventional television and radio broadcasting (whether distributed over the air or by cable) is a classic example of a push technology. The World Wide Web is based on 'pull' technologies; the user seeks out the content he wants and downloads or streams it. Generally speaking, services provided via push technologies require a licence and those provided via pull technologies do not. However, the matter is not quite as simple as that: some types of content provided online that resemble conventional television services are subject to a licence requirement. A person who distributes content via the internet must obtain a licence from Ofcom if the content constitutes a 'television licensable content service' ('TLCS');[41] that is, a service distributed via an electronic communications network (including services broadcast over the internet or by cable) or broadcast by satellite or radio multiplex service that:

- consists of, or has as its principal purpose the provision of, 'television programmes or electronic programme guides' or both;

- is 'available for reception by members of the public'.[42]

'Television programmes' includes not only conventional television programmes, advertisements, text and still and moving images, but ancillary services (like subtitling, audio-description or interactive programme enhancements) associated with them.[43] Streamed content qualifies as a 'relevant ancillary service'.[44] Some types of service are expressly excluded from the definition of TLCS, including two-way services such as video conferencing, closed user group services, and single premise systems.[45]

'Electronic programme guides' are services that consist of the listing or promotion of programmes and programme services and provide access to them.[46]

---

41   Ofcom has published guidance on the licensing process, the licensing requirements and the conditions that licensees are subject to: see Ofcom, *Television Licensable Content Services: Guidance notes for licence applicants*, 7 May 2013.
42   CA, s 232(1)-(2).
43   CA, s 232(6).
44   CA, s 232(6)
45   CA, s 233.
46   CA, s 232(6).

Example 9.1

A digital channel broadcaster launches a new website to promote a new youth series. The site runs competitions, blogs and forums where viewers can log on and exchange comments and thoughts on the series and engage in live chats with cast members. Sneak preview clips are also available to view by those who join. The site is not providing a 'television licensable content service' and no licence is required.

Example 9.2

The success of the website considered in the previous example proves so great that the broadcaster decides to simultaneously live stream each episode on the site as it goes to air so that users can discuss the show with each other whilst watching. This streaming is a 'television licensable content service' and a licence is required.

If a member of the public is able to receive the service, the service is normally 'available for reception by members of the public' and therefore satisfies the second criterion.[47]

TLCS licences are granted in respect of a particular licensable service, rather than in relation to a particular service provider. A service provider providing multiple separate services will therefore need multiple licences. Generally, the provider of the service, and therefore the person that must be licensed, is the person 'with general control over which programmes and other services and facilities are comprised in the service (whether or not he has control of the content of individual programmes or of the broadcasting or distribution of the service)'.[48] Certain persons, such as local authorities and political bodies, may be excluded from holding a TLCS licence.[49]

A service requires licensing by Ofcom only if the provider falls under UK jurisdiction for the purposes of the AVMS Directive.[50] (See the discussion under the heading 'Definition of ODPS' above.) A service which is licensed (or otherwise appropriately authorised) in one EU member state does not need separate licensing in any other member state.

Conditions of licence

9.15   There is only one form of TLCS licence. Licences address the following matters:

---

47   CA, s 361, as amended. by AVMS Regulations 2009. S 9(a), provides that an OPDS is not to be treated as available for reception by the general public.
48   CA, ss 362(2). See Ofcom, *Guidance regarding the licensing position on the 'provider of a service' and the 'sub-letting' of capacity*, 21 May 2010.
49   Broadcasting Act 1990, s 5(1). Schedule 2, Part II, lists disqualified persons.
50   AVMS Directive, art 2.

Figure 9.2: Outline of TLCS licence conditions	
1.	*Purpose and length of licence*
2.	*Technical standards*
3.	*Fees*
4.	*Programme and advertising standards* The licensee must ensure that all content included in the licensed service complies with all relevant standards codes. Ofcom has contracted-out its advertising standards codes function to the Broadcast Committee of Advertising Practice Limited ('BCAP'). Where services provided over the internet are concerned, the BCAP Television Advertising Standards Code applies.
5.	*Electronic programme guides*
6.	*Listed events* Legislation restricts the acquisition by broadcasters of exclusive rights to the whole or any part of live television coverage of certain sports and other events 'listed' by the Secretary of State. The legislation restricts the acquisition by broadcasters of exclusive rights to the whole or any part of live television coverage of listed events and the broadcasting on an exclusive basis of such coverage without the previous consent of Ofcom.
7.	*Subtitling, signing and audio-description* A television service achieving an average audience share of all UK households of 0.05% or more may be required to provide subtitling, signing and audio description, subject to passing an affordability threshold and not facing technical difficulties that are impracticable to surmount. These obligations would apply from the first anniversary of the launch of the service. Television services aimed exclusively at an overseas audience are exempt from television access service requirements.
8.	*Retention and production of recordings*
9.	*Provision of information to Ofcom*
10.	*Notification of agreement with radio multiplex licensee*
11.	*Fair and effective competition* Ofcom's general policy is to include in Broadcasting Act licences a condition requiring the licensee (a) not to enter into or maintain any arrangements or engage in any practices which are prejudicial to fair and effective competition in the provision of licensed services or connected services, (b) to comply with any code or guidance approved by Ofcom for the purpose of ensuring fair and effective competition in the provision of licensed services or connected services, and (c) to comply with any direction given by Ofcom for that purpose.
12.	*Compliance with ownership restrictions* The licence obliges the licensee to inform Ofcom about changes to the nature, characteristics or control of the licensee body.

13.	*Transferability of the licence* A TLCS licence is transferrable only with the prior written consent of Ofcom.
14.	*Compliance*
15.	*European production quotas* Licensees must meet the requirements for European productions in the AVMS Directive. European productions should account for over 50% of the transmission hours (subject to certain exclusions) and European independent productions must account for at least 10% of transmission hours. Of these, an 'adequate proportion' must be works transmitted within five years of production.
16.	*Government directions and representations*
17.	*Complaints relating to the licensed service*
18.	*Variations to the licence*
19.	*Equal opportunities and training* Any holder of an Ofcom television or radio broadcasting licence who employs more than 20 individuals in connection with the provision of its licensed service and provides a service which is authorised to broadcast for more than 31 days a year is obliged to make and periodically review arrangements for training and retraining of people it employs in connection with the provision of the licensed service or the making of programmes for that service. In making and reviewing those arrangements, any such licensee must comply with any Ofcom guidance.
20.	*Sanctions*
21.	*Revocation and surrender*

Code of practice on electronic programme guides

9.16   The Communications Act requires Ofcom to draw up, and from time to time review and revise, a code giving guidance on the practices to be followed in the provision of electronic programme guides.[51] The Code of Practice on Electronic Programme Guides (undated) sets out these practices. Providers are required, amongst other things, to:

- give appropriate prominence to public service channels;

- provide the features and information needed to enable electronic programme guides to be used by people with disabilities affecting their sight, hearing or both; and

- secure fair and effective competition.

51   CA s 310.

ADVERTISING ON THE INTERNET

9.17   Apart from the specific requirements that apply to OPDS (see **9.8** above),[52] advertising on the internet is largely regulated under a voluntary code published by the Advertising Standards Authority ('ASA'): The UK Code of Non-broadcast Advertising, Sales Promotion and Direct Marketing (twelfth edition, 2010) ('CAP Code'). The CAP Code does not apply to all advertising or marketing material that appears on the internet, but it does apply to:

- emails, text transmissions and other electronic material;

- advertisements in non-broadcast electronic media, such as online advertisements in paid-for space (banners, pop-ups), preferential listings on price-comparison websites, and online sales promotions;

- advertisements and other marketing communications that appear on a company's own website;

- solicitations of donations that are part of an entity's own fund-raising activities.

Example 9.3

An online boutique is running a promotion for its new range of luxury aromatic candles. It puts a big promotional feature on its homepage and also pays for some banner ads on various online newspaper sites. The content of these is subject to the CAP Code. Its prices are also featured on a price-comparison website and the boutique is also subject to the CAP Code in relation to this advertising if the boutique has paid for a preferential listing.

The CAP Code stipulates that marketing communications should be 'legal, decent, honest and truthful'. Marketing communications must reflect the spirit and not merely the letter of the code. Primary responsibility for compliance falls on marketers, but agencies and others involved in preparing or publishing their communications must also abide by the code.

There are specific rules applicable to distance selling. These are designed to complement the Consumer Contract (Information, Cancellation and Additional Charges) Regulations 2013 (discussed in the next section). There are also specific rules applicable to other subjects, including, for example, misleading advertising, political advertisements, and advertising of alcohol and tobacco products.

The ASA cannot impose financial penalties for breach of the CAP Code but, if marketers do not comply with the Code, it may publish a determination to that effect and publish its findings and/or issue alerts to its members and advise them to consult with the ASA before accepting copy from a non-compliant marketer. The ASA may also refer matters to the Competition and Markets Authority, the

---

52   ASA has also published a Help Note on Advertising in video-on-demand services that elaborates on service providers' responsibilities. See ASA, *Advertising in video-on-demand services*, July 2012.

Financial Conduct Authority, or trading standards bodies who can then take appropriate action.

In 2005, the ASA considered a complaint against Orange's 'double talk, double text' airtime promotion which was used across various media including the internet. The ASA found that the advertisements were misleading and in breach of the CAP Code, and Orange agreed to amend the content of the advertisements.

DISTANCE CONTRACTS WITH CONSUMERS

9.18   Businesses that use the internet to sell their goods and services must comply with a variety of laws applicable to consumer contracts, including the Unfair Contract Terms Act 1977 (which deals primarily with exclusion clauses), the Unfair Terms in Consumer Contracts Regulations 1999,[53] and the Consumer Protection from Unfair Trading Regulations.[54] Laws of general application to consumer contracts are not discussed here, but there is one additional measure – the Consumer Contract (Information, Cancellation and Additional Charges) Regulations 2013 (the 'CCR')[55] – that includes provisions applicable to 'distance contracts', such as contracts concluded over the internet or by email (as well as consumer contracts more generally[56]). This section examines those provisions.

Scope

9.19   A 'distance contract' is one 'concluded between a trader and a consumer under an organised distance sales or service-provision scheme without the simultaneous physical presence of the trader and the consumer, with the exclusive use of one or more means of distance communication up to and including the time at which the contract is concluded'. The reference to 'organised sales or service provision schemes' means that contracts for occasional one-off transactions are not 'distance contracts'.

Where a consumer visits a trader's business premises merely for the purpose of gathering information about the goods or services and subsequently negotiates and concludes the contract at a distance, the contract is a 'distance contract'. But a contract negotiated at the trader's business premises and finally concluded by email is not. Nor is a contract initiated by means of distance communication, but finally concluded at the business premises of the trader.[57]

---

53   SI 1999/2083.
54   SI 2008/1277.
55   SI 2013/3134. The CCR came into effect on 14 June 2013. The CCR implement most of the provisions of the EU Consumer Rights Directive 2011/83/EU. The Consumer Protection (Distance Selling) Regulations 2000 apply to distance contracts concluded before 14 June 2013. The application of the latter was described in the third edition of this book, section 9.5.2.
56   The CCR also contain provisions relating to contracts concluded on a trader's premises and contracts concluded off-premises (eg, sales conducted door-to-door).
57   See EU Consumer Rights Directive, recital (20).

For the purposes of the CCR, a 'trader' is 'a person acting for purposes relating to that person's trade, business, craft or profession.' The trader may be acting personally or through another person acting in the trader's name or on the trader's behalf'. Local or public authorities may qualify as 'traders'.[58] A 'consumer' is 'an individual acting for purposes which are wholly or mainly outside that individual's trade, business, craft or profession'.

There are some types of contracts to which the CCR do not generally apply, including contracts relating to gambling; immovable property; accommodation for residential purposes; package travel and financial services.[59] Moreover, not all of the requirements of the CCR necessarily apply even where a contract is in scope. The regulations may only partially apply to sales in certain cases (eg goods or services with fluctuating prices; supply of medicinal or other healthcare product by a prescriber or similar).[60]

Example 9.4

A hotel establishes a website to allow particular types of room to be searched for, reserved and paid for. A credit card must be used to reserve each room, for which a billing address is required. The website does not require the person reserving the room to specify whether it is a corporate or individual booking. To be safe, the hotel will need to assume that every user of the website is a natural person in order to comply with the CCR.

Information requirements

9.20 The CCR distinguish between the following types of contracts:

- sales contracts (ie contracts for the purchase and sale of goods, or both goods and services);

- service contracts (ie contracts, other than sales contract, for the supply of a service);[61]

- contracts for digital content supplied through downloads and streaming.

The CCR specify that, before a consumer is bound by a distance contract, the trader must give or 'make available' to the consumer certain information. The following is the information required.[62] (The list of information required is much more extensive than that required under the Consumer Protection (Distance Selling) Regulations. Key differences between the CCR and the latter are noted.)

---

58 By virtue of the definition of 'business': see CCR r 5.
59 CCR, r 6.
60 CCR, rr 7(1) and 28(1).
61 There are also two types of contracts for telecommunications services to which the CCR do not apply : contracts for the making of a call by means of a pay telephone and to contracts for the use of a telephone, internet or fax service for a single session (for example, a single session in an internet café). See CCR s 6(2).
62 CCR, r 13 and Schedule 2.

	Figure 9.3: Summary of distance contract information requirements
(a)	Main characteristics of the goods, services or digital content.
(b)	Identity of the trader.
(c)	The geographical address at which the trader is established and, where available, the trader's telephone number, fax number and email address. (*The requirement to supply telephone and fax numbers and an email address is one of the requirements introduced in 2013.*)
(d)	Where the trader is acting on behalf of another trader, the geographical address and identity of that other trader. (*New*)
(e)	Geographical address of trader if different from that provided pursuant to paragraph (c) (formerly required only post-contract) and if the trader is acting for another trader the latter's geographical address. (*New*)
(f)	Total price or how it will be calculated. (*New*)
(g)	Additional delivery charges and other costs or how they will be calculated. (*New*)
(h)	Costs per billing period where contract is of indeterminate duration or is a subscription. (*Revised*)
(i)	Communication costs where the cost of using the means of distance communication for the conclusion of the contract is calculated other than at the basic rate.
(j)	Payment delivery and performance arrangements.
(k)	Trader's complaint handling policy. (*New*)
(l)	Information about the right to cancel.
(m)	Consumer's obligation to pay for return of goods. (*Formerly required only post-contract*)
(n)	Consumer must pay for services received if he agrees to their supply during cancellation period. (*New*)
(o)	Whether there is no right to cancel or how it can be lost.
(p)	Reminder of trader's legal duty re supply of goods in conformity with the contract. (*New*)
(q)	Details of after-sales services and guarantees. (*Formerly only required post-contract*)
(r)	Details of applicable codes of conduct. (*New*)
(s)	Contract duration and conditions for terminating. (*Formerly required only post-contract*)
(t)	Minimum duration of the consumer's obligations under the contract, where applicable.
(u)	Details of any consumer deposits and financial guarantees. (*New*)
(v)	Digital content's functionality and technical protection. (*New*)
(w)	Digital content's compatibility. (*New*)
(x)	Complaint and redress mechanisms where applicable. (*New*)

The following additional requirements apply to distance contracts concluded by electronic means. These requirements are also new.

● If the contract places the consumer under an obligation to pay, the trader must make the consumer aware in a clear and prominent manner, and directly before the consumer places the order, of the information listed in paragraphs (a), (f), (g), (h), (s) and (t).

● The trader must ensure that the consumer, when placing the order, explicitly acknowledges that the order implies an obligation to pay.

● If placing an order entails activating a button or a similar function, the trader must ensure that the button or similar function is labelled in an easily legible manner only with the words 'order with obligation to pay' or a corresponding unambiguous formulation indicating that placing the order entails an obligation to pay the trader.[63] Both the European Commission and the UK department for business, Innovation and Skills ('BIS') have provided guidance concerning this requirement. The Commission says that terms such as 'buy now', 'pay now' or 'confirm purchase' would be acceptable but that phrases such as 'register', 'confirm' or 'order now' and unnecessarily long phrases that may effectively conceal the message about the obligation to pay would not be. BIS says that this requirement must be met even if taking payment is to be deferred (eg if preceded by a free trial period).[64]

● The trader must ensure that any trading website through which the contract is concluded indicates clearly and legibly, at the latest at the beginning of the ordering process, whether any delivery restrictions apply and which means of payment are accepted.

One consequence of a failure of a trader to comply with either of the requirements referred to in the second or third bullets is that the consumer is not bound by the contract or order.

Once a distance contract has been concluded, the trader must provide confirmation of the contract in legible form on a 'durable medium'. A durable medium is defined as 'paper or email, or any other medium' that:

● allows information to be addressed personally to the recipient;

● enables the recipient to store the information in a way accessible for future reference for a period that is long enough for the purposes of the information; and

● allows the unchanged reproduction of the information stored.[65]

---

63 CCR, r 14.
64 *DG Justice Guidance Document concerning Directive 2011/83/EU*, June 2014, p. 32; BIS, *Consumer Contracts Information, Cancellation and Additional Changes, Implementing Guidance*, December 2013, section D, item 5.
65 CCR, r 5.

The confirmation must include all the information listed in (a) to (x) of Figure 9.3 unless the trader previously provided that information on a durable medium. This must be done within a 'reasonable time' but in any event no later than the time of delivery of any goods supplied under the contract, and before performance begins of any service supplied under the contract.[66]

Example 9.5

A site's designer ensures that just before someone buys a particular product on his site they are shown a flashy animation summarising the price and delivery details. This cannot be printed. Once the product is ordered, one cannot see the price again. Being ephemeral, the animation does not satisfy the requirement that a trader must provide confirmation of the contract on a 'durable medium.' This must therefore be done separately.

Cancellation

9.21   Subject to certain exceptions mentioned below, a consumer has the right to cancel a distance contract within a period of 14 days[67] without giving any reason. When a contract has been cancelled during the prescribed period, the consumer is entitled to refund of the purchase price subject to adjustments for: the costs of any enhanced delivery method selected by the consumer; the amount by which the value of the goods has diminished as a result of consumer handling of the goods; (generally) the costs of return; and the price of any services provided during the cancellation period before cancellation.[68]

The consumer has no right to cancel a distance contract if the contract is for passenger transport services; or supply of goods or services for which the price is dependent on fluctuations in the financial market which cannot be controlled by the trader and which may occur during the cancellation period (other than water, gas, electricity or public heating); or supply of goods that are made to the consumer's specifications or are clearly personalised; or supply of goods liable to deteriorate or expire rapidly; or supply of alcoholic beverages in certain cases where delivery takes place 30 days after purchase; or for the provision of urgent repairs or maintenance; or supply of a newspaper, periodical or magazine with the exception of subscription contracts. Nor does a consumer have a right to cancel: a contract for the supply of medicines in certain circumstances, a contract concluded at a public auction; or contracts for the supply of accommodation, vehicle rental services, catering or services related to leisure activities, if the contract provides for a specific date or period of performance.[69]

---

66   CCR s 16.
67   CCR s 30. How the cancellation period is calculated is addressed in that section. Delay in providing the information referred to in Figure 9.3 may result in extension of the cancellation period.
68   CCR ss 34–36.
69   CCR ss 27(2) and 28.

Example 9.6

ToughSafe.co.uk runs a website that can be used to store documents and pictures on behalf of individuals. Payment is due in advance. The website and online contract are silent as to whether the hosting can be cancelled after it has commenced. The company cannot prevent a user from lawfully using the site for a few days and then cancelling the contract.

Example 9.7

MugMug.co.uk is a website that sells mugs onto which they will print a photograph supplied by a consumer. Mrs Jones sends a digital photograph of Mr Jones to MugMug. co.uk. Six mugs arrive a week later and Mrs Jones wraps them and gives them to Mr Jones as a present. He hates them. Mr Jones cannot invoke her rights of cancellation; the goods were made to her specification.

A consumer who has a right to cancel may lose it in certain cases (eg in the case of a contract for the supply of sealed audio or video or computer software, if the goods become unsealed after delivery).[70]

Any clear statement by the consumer setting out his decision to cancel is sufficient.[71] The EU Consumer Rights Directive states that a letter, telephone call or returning the goods with a clear statement could meet this requirement.[72]

Special cancellation rules apply in respect of the supply of digital content not on a tangible medium. A trader must not begin the supply of digital content not on a tangible medium before the end of the cancellation period, unless the consumer has consented to this and has acknowledged he will lose his cancellation right and the trader has confirmed this consent and acknowledgement to the consumer.[73] If the consumer has given the consent and acknowledgment referred to, the confirmation must include confirmation of the consent and acknowledgement.[74]

In the event of a dispute, the burden of showing compliance with the preceding requirements is on the trader.[75]

FINANCIAL SERVICES

9.22   Whilst there is no legislation that deals exclusively with the provision of financial services over the internet, a range of more broadly drafted legislation extends to such services and should therefore be considered by anyone looking to promote, provide or, indeed, purchase financial services online. The relevant

---

70   CCR, r 28(3)(b).
71   CCR, r 32(3)(b).
72   Recital (44).
73   CCR, r 37.
74   CCR, r 12(5).
75   CCR, r 17.

legislation serves three broad purposes. First, it is intended to remove restrictions on electronic commerce whilst imposing appropriate safeguards. Second, it imposes requirements and restrictions in regard to how financial services may be promoted. Third, it provides for the provision of pre-contract information and a right to withdraw from a contract in specific circumstances.

Electronic commerce

9.23   As discussed elsewhere, the Electronic Commerce Directive's internal market clause provides for information society services ('ISS') to be subject to the law of the member state in which the service provider is established. In the UK, implementation of the Directive required amendments to the territorial application of the Financial Services and Markets Act 2000, the Financial Services and Markets Act 2000 (Regulated Activities) Order 2001 and the Financial Services and Markets Act 2000 (Financial Promotion) Order 2005 (FPO).[76] The Financial Services Authority (now the Financial Conduct Authority or FCA) also made rules dealing primarily with the provision of information and cancellation rights discussed in conjunction with the FCA's implementation of the Distance Marketing Directive below.

Financial promotions

9.24   A financial promotion is an invitation or inducement to engage in investment activity that is communicated in the course of business. The words 'invitation' and 'inducement' allow for the financial promotions regime to apply to communications to engage in investment activity which might not fall within narrower terms such as 'advertisement'. Whilst the regime applies to financial promotions in all media, certain characteristics of the internet, and more specifically, social media, create increased risks of breaching financial promotion rules.[77] This is due to both the inability to control who can access a financial promotion and the format of certain social media (eg limitations on the number of characters in a post or the length of a video loop) resulting in the increased possibility that risk warnings and other required statements are not included in the promotion.

The FCA defines 'communicate' in the context of financial promotions as 'including causing a communication to be made or directed'. Persons who cause a website or social media communication to be created would be communicators whereas software engineers, website designers or other persons who are involved in the design of a financial promotion on the internet are unlikely to be viewed as communicating the financial promotion so long as their

---

76   See *Implementing the Electronic Commerce Directive, FSA Consultation Paper 129, March 2002 and Implementation of the E-Commerce Directive in Financial Services*, HM Treasury Consultation Document, December 2001.

77   *Social Media and Customer Communications, FCA Finalised Guidance*, March 2015.

activities are so limited. Likewise, internet service providers would most likely be able to avail themselves of exemptions for mere conduits in art 18 or, more probably, art 18A of the FPO. It is worth noting that a person relying on the art 18A exemption must comply with the conditions in arts 12(1), 13(1) and 14(1) of the Electronic Commerce Directive that relate to the liability of intermediary service providers.

Determining whether an invitation to engage in investment activity is made 'in the course of business' and is therefore a 'financial promotion' is often complicated where social media are involved because they may be used in a way that blurs the lines between an employee's personal communications and those made as part of their employment. The test to be considered in these circumstances is whether there is a commercial interest on the part of the communicator.[78] To ensure financial promotion rules are not breached, individuals should take steps to distinguish personal communications from those that may be understood to be made in the course of business.

Further difficulties arise in making financial promotions through media that limit the number of characters the communicator may use (eg Twitter). Limitations such as these make adherence to the FCA's requirement that financial promotions be fair, clear and not misleading difficult since character restrictions may prevent a proper reflection of the risks as well as the benefits of a particular product. Likewise character limitations may prevent compliance with FCA requirements in regard to information on a product's past performance or the requirement to ensure that financial promotions are identified as such. One method firms may employ to comply with FCA requirements within the confines of character limitations is the use of hyperlinks to more comprehensive information.

Distance communications

9.25   Chapter 5 of the Financial Conduct Authority's Conduct of Business Sourcebook (COBS) now contains rules made by the FCA to implement the Electronic Commerce Directive. The rules apply to a firm providing information society services from an establishment in the UK with or for a person in the UK or another EEA state. Specifically, chapter 5.2 of COBS sets out disclosure obligations in regard to the firm and its products or services and requirements relating to the placing and receipt of orders. These rules should be read in conjunction with rules made to implement the Distance Marketing Directive which apply to a firm carrying on distance marketing activity in the same circumstances with or for a person in the UK or another EEA state. Chapter 15 of COBS sets out rules that allow consumers to cancel distance contracts for most types of investment business.

---

78   See *FCA Perimeter Guidance Manual*, chapter 8.22.

ONLINE GAMBLING

9.26   A person who provides facilities for 'gambling' (betting, gaming or participating in a lottery[79]) must hold an operating licence issued by the Gaming Commission under the provisions of the Gambling Act 2005 ('GA'), unless exempted.[80] This requirement extends to provision of facilities offshore which allow persons to participate in gambling by the use of 'remote communications', including the internet, but also telephone, television, radio or any other kind of electronic or other technology for facilitating communication.[81] Until 2014, a remote operating licence[82] was required to provide facilities for remote gambling if, and only if, at least one piece of remote gambling equipment used in the provision of the gambling facilities was located in Great Britain.[83] The consequence was that remote gambling operators who located all of their equipment overseas did not need a remote operating licence regardless of whether they did business with British consumers. In 2014, however, the category of remote gambling operators who need a licence was expanded so that a licence is now required if gambling facilities are *used* in Great Britain even if no equipment[84] is located in Great Britain.[85] If an overseas operator wants to avoid having to obtain a licence, the operator needs to take action to prevent British consumers using its website.

Advertising of offshore gambling is also affected by the recent reforms. Under the arrangements which prevailed before 2014, companies that provided remote gambling services to British citizens from locations outside of Great Britain were permitted to advertise their services in Great Britain without a licence if they were based in the EEA or Gibraltar or had satisfied the Secretary of State that they met certain criteria relating to the regulation of gambling and were placed on a 'white list'.[86] Since 2014, however, all overseas companies wishing to advertise or offer their gambling services in the UK need a licence issued by the Gambling Commission even if they hold a licence in another jurisdiction.

---

79   The terms 'gambling', 'betting', 'gaming' and 'participating in a lottery' are defined in GA, ss 3, 6, 9, 14 and 15.
80   GA, s 33.
81   GA, s 36(3).
82   GA, s 65(2), creates a variety of of licences authorising different forms of gambling activity. 'Remote operating licences' are available for each type of gambling activity listed in section 65(2).
83   GA, s 36(3), as originally enacted in 2005.
84   GA, s 36(4) defines 'remote gambling equipment'.
85   By virtue of the Gambling (Licensing and Advertising) Act 2014, s 1(2), which amended GA, s 36(3).
86   GA, s 331.

Index

[all references are to paragraph number]